BIBLIOGRAPHIA CARTESIANA

ARCHIVES INTERNATIONALES D'HISTOIRE DES IDEES

INTERNATIONAL ARCHIVES OF THE HISTORY OF IDEAS

5

GREGOR SEBBA

BIBLIOGRAPHIA CARTESIANA

GREGOR SEBBA

Graduate Institute of the Liberal Arts,
Emory University

BIBLIOGRAPHIA CARTESIANA

A CRITICAL GUIDE TO THE DESCARTES LITERATURE

1800–1960

THE HAGUE
MARTINUS NIJHOFF
1964

PRINTED IN THE NETHERLANDS

CONTENTS

NOTES TO THE USER

1. To survey the literature in a major area of research, begin with the pertinent section in Part I, then consult the Systematic Index as a guide to the Analytical Index.
2. To locate a given author's work on Descartes, consult Part II under his name; check the Analytical Index under his name for discussions of his contribution.
3. To find the literature on a special topic, consult the Analytical Index, then follow up cross references, and scan the Systematic Index for other pertinent headings.
4. Where the place of publication of a book is not listed, the place is Paris.
5. German *ä, ö, ü* is treated as *ae, oe, ue* in the alphabet. Thus: *Rodriguez, Röd, Rogers,* not: *Röd, Rodriguez, Rogers.*
6. For Descartes literature published since 1960, consult the *Répertoire bibliographique de la philosophie* for titles and reviews, the *Bulletin signalétique* for notices.

PREFACE

This book offers a new type of working tool for Cartesian studies. It presents the literature of the last 160 years in alphabetical order (Part Two), combined with a systematic analytical survey (Part One) and a detailed topical index to the whole (Part Three). This organization makes it possible to turn bibliography from a repository of references into a workshop of research. The systematic survey of Part One and the topical index of Part Three, together, offer a *mise au point* of Descartes studies over their full historical and topical range. The results have often been surprising and illuminating to the author, and if his experience is any guide, the reader, too, will begin to wonder about certain seemingly well-settled points, or marvel at the Protean shapes which our elusive philosopher assumes when mighty commentators force him to reveal his true nature.

A work which has been in the making for fifteen years must show the traces of expansion in scope, and changes in evaluation. *Bibliographia cartesiana* amends my Descartes chapter in *A Critical Bibliography of French Literature, v. 3*, 1961 (see no. 19a), and supersedes an earlier version of Parts One and Two, published in 1959 under the main title *Descartes and his Philosophy, v. 1* (see no. 18a).

Part I (*Introduction to Descartes Studies*) divides the field into eleven broad areas. It offers critical notices and references to the bulk of significant contributions, covering as much as one-fifth of the whole literature. Other useful items which could not be incorporated in Part I for technical or other reasons will be found annotated in Part II; they are of course fully indexed. Each main title in Part I is annotated; in addition I have listed all reviews I could locate, discussions in books and articles as well as book reviews proper; condensed but detailed tables of content indicate the scope of works that cover a great variety of topics. If I could rewrite Part I in the light of the understanding I gained by making the detailed topical index, selection and emphasis as well as my evaluations of some contributions would be different. But the changes would not be decisive. Part I would still include every undoubtedly indispensable work, and most of the works I did select as being exceptionally useful. I would still add important older works of no great current value because they give the necessary historical perspective to the picture of Descartes scholarship. And I would still emphasize contributions neglected because they appeared where the Descartes scholar would hardly look for them, because they were written in a minor language, or because they just had bad luck. Nor would I tone down the language of my notices: I do not think that grey is the only color suitable for painting the Cartesian rainbow. As to my critical evaluations, they are no better than my judgment: caveat emptor. The user will form his own better judgment anyway, and to him the literature will look different, if only because there will be even more of it: "majoremque habemus rerum experientiam," as Descartes said when he was a very young man.

Part II (*Alphabetical Bibliography*) is a comprehensive listing of all the literature on Descartes from 1800 to 1960 which I could locate, including the material contained in Part I. The total is close to 3000. I doubt that anything of major significance has been overlooked, but complete coverage cannot be claimed; besides, the limits of this type of compilation cannot be precisely drawn.

Part III contains the indices that serve as key to the material presented in Part I and II. The *Systematic Index* gives a synopsis of the Analytical Index and draws attention to useful entries that might be overlooked. The *Analytical Index* is quite detailed. Every topic that appears in a title, notice, or table of contents (but not under reviews) has been indexed, with extremely few exceptions (minima non curat praetor). In addition, many books and articles of importance have been indexed from the original, including major works by Alquié, Bouillier, Gilson, Gouhier, Gueroult, Norman Kemp Smith, Thijssen-Schoute and others. The user should not be dismayed if a reference given in the Analytical Index leads him to an entry in Part I or II which does not mention the subject at all; if he will consult the book or article itself, he will find what is promised – unless a typographical error has occurred, in which case I humbly beg his pardon. Needless to say, completeness is impossible in indexing; the user will have to make his own way from the point to which the Analytical Index takes him. He will certainly wish to consult the fundamental works of the literature, whether the Index refers to them or not. This means the ABC of Descartes biography (Adam, Baillet, Cohen), and the Three Cartesian G's (Gilson, Gouhier, Gueroult).

Convenience, not formal consistency, has been the principle adopted in this bibliography. I regret certain minor discrepancies in style and serial numbering;

some material was originally prepared for publications using a different bibliographical style, and new items were added to the very last. The typography has been kept as simple as possible, on the assumption that the user will recognize titles as titles, and foreign words as foreign words, even though they are not typographically distinguished from the rest. And since English is likely to be a foreign language for many – probably for most – users of the work, I have taken the liberty of using philosophical terms freely in their Cartesian form, in French or Latin. Quotations, too, have as a rule been left in their original language.

Moreover, I have used French terms to distinguish their Cartesian from other meanings, and to avoid ambiguity in indexing. Thus, the term *morale* always means the moral philosophy of *Descartes*, as distinct from other philosophers' *ethics*. *Méthode* means the méthode of Descartes which, properly speaking, is more than *method* and *methodology*. *Sagesse* and *générosité* have been left in Descartes' own language, and "*conscience*" (always given between quotation marks) means French "conscience" (awareness, self-awareness, Selbstbewusstsein, autocoscienza), not English "conscience" (a bothersome awareness of right and wrong). *Âme* and *volonté* and *libre-arbitre* stand for *soul*, *will*, *free will*; *pensée* means *pensée*, whether *thought*, *thinking*, *mind*, *understanding*, or that linguistic horror "*thinking-self*" is implied. *Connaissance d'autrui* has not been converted into *The Other Self Problem*; nor did it seem useful to translate *esse & nosse* or *lumen naturale*.

One last word of caution. Condensing means falsifying. Brief notices cast sharp light, and sharp light casts deep shadows that often engulf important areas. In indexing, condensation becomes almost brutal: one word must sum up what a scholar developed, explained, and importantly qualified on perhaps a hundred pages. I hope that no user will treat this bibliography as a source of authoritative information *on* a work, instead of a guide *to* that work. The only claim made for it is that it attempts to be a conscientious if fallible guide; and that it reveals the enormous span, diversity, and depth of Descartes studies in the past 160 years.

Emory University, May 1962 G.S.

FROM THE PREFACE TO

DESCARTES AND HIS PHILOSOPHY (1959)

Johann Nestroy, speaking of the sumptuous private balls of his time, said that he had no trouble understanding people who went to a ball; what he found utterly unexplainable was the existence of people who gave balls. Bibliographies like the present one are in the same category, except that in this case even the existence of people who go to the ball cannot altogether be taken for granted. The very bulk of this bibliography suggests that many writers about Descartes are not readers of what other writers wrote about him. The fact that the Cartesian cogito is (is not) an immediate experience seems to need to be freshly established year after year; there is no end to the flow of irrefutable proofs that Descartes did (did not) commit the Cartesian circle; even the rationalism (antirationalism) of Descartes comes as a surprise to a host of authors who stumble upon it in the course of their original research.

There is a reason for this. When a thinker thinks about Descartes, it is to find out whether Descartes is right or wrong. To this end he must read him and examine his arguments; this is necessary, and sufficient. The greater a philosopher, the less he reads *about* Descartes before writing about him. The greatest and most original among them have as much use for a Descartes bibliography as Descartes himself had for the collected writing of St. Thomas Aquinas. Cartesian method is the enemy of Cartesian bibliography.

However, there are people less interested in finding out whether Descartes was right than in establishing "wie es eigentlich gewesen": the historians of philosophy and of ideas, the biographers, the editors, the exegetes. This bibliography is addressed to them.

The chief limitation of this bibliography is that it does not cover the *literature before 1800*. After considerable efforts I became convinced that only international cooperation among scholars with access to the great European collections can successfully deal with the Cartesian era.

Descartes editions are listed if they are indispensable or exceptionally useful. Even within these limits, only a sample of annotated and commented editions could be included. We still need a good critical list of commentaries and translations of Descartes' works, and a modern bibliography of original editions.

Chapters in *general works* on the history of philosophy, mathematics, science, etc., have been listed only if there was some special reason for it. But *ephemeral literature* has been generously treated regardless of its intrinsic value; someone may look for it some day, trying to trace the changes in Descartes' fortunes, or studying the ever-changing Descartes image and the ways in which Descartes scholarship filters down to popular levels.

The *reliability* of references varies. A large number of items were verified from the originals, and Professor Jules Brody independently verified many hundred of titles and reviews now included in Part I. Where the item was not available, I have followed the best sources I could find. In a few cases, question marks after the title indicate that the title could not be checked. Where a notice had to be written without seeing the contribution, I give my source.

My debt to others is recorded elsewhere. But this is the place to acknowledge my gratitude to the Descartes scholars upon whose work this bibliography rests: Francisque Bouillier, Francesco Olgiati, Jean Boorsch, Henri Gouhier, Ernst Cassirer, Paul Schrecker, Geneviève Rodis-Lewis, Louise C. Thijssen-Schoute, Paul Dibon, and those anonymous workers at Louvain and elsewhere who, over the decades, have raised philosophical bibliography to an enviable degree of perfection.

August 22, 1959 G.S.

ACKNOWLEDGMENTS

For permission to use their Descartes checklists I am indebted to Professor Norman N. Douglas, and to the late A. G. A. Balz who generously placed his collection of some 900 titles at my disposal. To Professor Nathan Edelman I am deeply grateful for his invitation to contribute to the third volume of *A Critical Bibliography of French Literature* and for his superb editorial guidance in this venture; Part I of the present work shows the benefits of our happy collaboration. Professor Jules Brody meticulously verified every reference in the more than 330 items I originally prepared for Professor Edelman's volume; this independent check was most appreciated. To the Syracuse University Press I am grateful for permission to incorporate material that appeared first in the *Critical Bibliography*. Professor Edgar Lehrman directed me to a hitherto overlooked source for Soviet items. My friend and colleague, Professor Thomas R. Hart, and my wife, Helen Sebba, helped me in checking the accuracy of certain foreign language titles and quotations. Needless to say, the responsibility for errors of all kinds remains entirely my own, but this compilation is much the better for their help.

A generous grant-in-aid from the Research Committee at Emory University made the completion of *Bibliographia Cartesiana* possible. I am thankful for this well-timed assistance. From 1947 to 1959 the University of Georgia unfailingly supported my Descartes research; special thanks are due to its excellent staff of librarians. During the same period, grants-in-aid for travel, received from the University Center of Georgia, the Carnegie Foundation, and the Modern Language Association of America, enabled me to use the resources of some twenty great libraries in the Eastern United States and in Europe. I gratefully acknowledge these grants and the library courtesies received on these occasions. To Professors Paul Dibon and Richard H. Popkin I wish to express my appreciation of the honor of being invited to contribute this Descartes bibliography to the *Archives internationals d'histoire des idées*. It is a pleasure to thank the publishers for their cooperation, Mr. G. H. Priem for his service as editor, and the printers for their exceptional care and skill.

PART ONE

INTRODUCTION TO DESCARTES STUDIES

I. BIBLIOGRAPHY AND REFERENCE

1 D'ALVERNY, MARIE-THÉRÈSE: Descartes. Exposition organisée pour le IIIe centenaire du Discours de la méthode. Préface: Julien Cain. "Descartes": Charles Adam (vii-xviii). Texte et notes: Marie-Thérèse d'Alverny. Bibliothèque Nationale, 1937. xviii, 172 p. Frontispiece, 7 pl.

Valuable catalogue of over 800 items of great bibliographical and biographical interest; wide coverage, helpful annotations. Iconography includes a list of portraits of Descartes (68–77), "Le cartésien inconnu" by van Bronckhorst, and Dumesnil's Christina of Sweden surrounded by learned men including Descartes and Mersenne. Reviewed by Paul Mouy in Runiv 46: 1937, 326–331. *Johan Nordström* ("Till Cartesius' iconografi," Lychnos 1957–58, 194–250) ingeniously utilizes the testimony of Erasmus Bartholinus to establish the van Schooten engraving (first distribution dated back to spring 1650) and two portraits at Tours and Amsterdam as the truest likenesses of Descartes, while the famous Hals portrait at the Louvre is "practically a creation of the artist's imagination": Descartes probably never sat for Hals. The richly documented study has some new biographical material, especially on the Abbé Picot and on de Villebressieu. English summary. No comprehensive iconographic study and no complete collection of contemporary portraits of D. exists.

2 BOORSCH, JEAN: État présent des études sur Descartes. Les Belles lettres, 1937. x, 197 p. (Études françaises, v. 39).

Life and work of D. chronologically examined and judiciously summarized. Represents the state of D. studies on the eve of the 1937 tercentenary. An outstandingly precise introduction, particularly to the problems of D.'s biography and the genesis of his works. Well chosen bibliography with helpful hints.

Reviews: C. Ferro in RFNS 42: 1950, 194; H. Gouhier in RIP 1: 1938, 405–07; D. Mornet in RHL 44: 1937, 557–58; A. Schinz in MLN 53: 1938, 610–12; W. McC. Stewart in RR 30; 1939, 80–84 (Descartes and French literature).

3 BRITISH MUSEUM. "René Descartes." In: British Museum. General catalogue of printed books, v. 51, London, 1954, p. 224–57.

Rich list of Descartes editions in many languages and of secondary literature. The Descartes section in the BN catalogue is now badly dated, though important for early editions.

3a CABEEN, D. C. and JULES BRODY (general ed.): A critical bibliography of French literature. v. 3: The seventeenth century, ed. *Nathan Edelman.* Syracuse UP, 1961. xliii, 638 p.

Exceptionally rich, comprehensive, selective, critical guide to 17th-c. literary scholarship, not to original source material. Background material on biography, bibliography, socio-political life, art, science, philosophy, religion, Baroque, Classicism, symbols etc. complements bibliographies of major and minor writers, many of them important to D. studies. Almost uniformly high level of judgment and accuracy. Excellent 80-page index. Indispensable working tool. See also 19a, 397a, 464a.

4 CARLINI, ARMANDO: Il problema di Cartesio. Bari, Laterza, 1948, 194 p. (Bibl. di cultura moderna, v. 452).

"Le interpretazioni di Cartesio" (p. 1–59, reprinted from Gmet 1: 1946, 114–28, 188–203) analyzes views of D.'s contemporaries, and criticist and idealist interpretations from Kant to Husserl. Appendix (p. 175–92) on Laporte, Carabellese, Carbonara. Develops the original but debatable thesis of a four-stage movement in D.'s thought from Regulae through DM to a supposed transcendental spiritualism in MM and to a Timaeus-type cosmogony in PP.

Reviews: P. Decerf in RPhL 37: 1949, 151–53; C. Ferro in RFNS 42: 1950, 199–201; E.G(arin) in GCFI 29: 1950, 522–24; V. Guarella in RSFI 4: 1949, 223–25; G.L.(ewis) in RIP 4: 1950, 321; S. Macaluso in Edu 1: 1950, 250–53; L.P. in Stud 1949, 512; M.M.R. in JP 46: 1949, 721–24, [critical]; G. Santinello in Gmet 4: 1949, 424–28. See also: Gallo Galli, Sul pensiero di A. Carlini (no. 1961).

5 CASSIRER, ERNST: Die Philosophie im XVII. und XVIII. Jahrhundert. Hermann, 1939. 94 p. (Asci, v. 841).

Authoritative survey and critique of main contributions to the 1937–38 Descartes and Malebranche anniversary literature. Cassirer's own viewpoint is applied to problems of Descartes interpretation and to Cartesianism and 18th century French and English philosophy. Handy bibliography of 138 items. No index. See also the complementary article by Colombo (no. 1577).

6 DIBON, PAUL: "Notes bibliographiques sur les cartésiens hollandais." In: Descartes et le cartésianisme hollandais, 1950 (no. 38), p. 261–300.

Outstanding survey and critical discussion of the secondary literature; Bouillier, Bohatec, and of the special studies of Voetius, Regius, Reneri and others. Rich in historical information on Dutch Cartesians.

7 GILSON, ÉTIENNE: Index scolastico-cartésien. Alcan, 1913. 354 p. (Collection historique des grands philosophes). Thèse complémentaire, Paris (1912).

Alphabetical list of D.'s main philosophical terms, each followed by texts from his works and parallel texts from Scholastic literature, in the original Latin or French, showing D.'s indebtedness to the philosophy he repudiated. An indispensable philosophical Descartes dictionary.

8 GIRAUD, JEANNE: Manuel de bibliographie littéraire pour les XVIe, XVIIe, XVIIIe siècles français, 1921–1935. Paris, Vrin, 1939. (Publications de la faculté des lettres de l'Université de Lille, v. 2.)

9 GIRAUD, JEANNE: Manuel de bibliographie littéraire ...., 1936–1945. Nizet, 1956.

Though chiefly devoted to French literature, no. 8 and 9 contain useful bibliographies of D., Malebranche and their contemporaries in philosophy, in chronological order, with occasional references to important reviews.

10 HAGMANN, MORITZ: Descartes in der Auffassung durch die Historiker der Philosophie. Zur Geschichte der neuzeitlichen Philosophiegeschichte. Winterthur, Keller, 1955. viii, 195 p. Dissertation Zürich.

D. judged by Germanic historians of philosophy from Jakob Brucker to Harold Höffding, by Kant and the German Idealists, Schopenhauer, by moderns from Franz Brentano and Kierkegaard to Heidegger and Sartre. Changing D. interpretations linked to changing German views of history of philosophy. Good guide to much material not brought together before. No index.
Review: H.Z. in BP 1956, 1079.

11 LAVELLE, LOUIS: La philosophie française entre les deux guerres. Aubier (Éditions Montaigne), 1942. 279 p. (Les chroniques philosophiques v. 2). Italian translation: no. 2467.

A collection of the noted philosopher's review articles, many from Le Temps, with excellent discussions of main French contributions to D. criticism in the 1930's (p. 15–53, 239–50).
Review: Bianca Magnino in Dcom 5: 1952, 161–62.

12 LEWIS, GENEVIÈVE: "Bilan de cinquante ans d'études cartésiennes." RPFE 141: 1951, 249–67.

Rapidly moving, highly compressed survey of philosophical D. criticism in the first half of century, including ground covered by Boorsch and Olgiati (no. 2, 14). Written with complete technical mastery and fine judgment. Rich bibliographical footnotes, especially for 1937–50. Non-specialists may find the article difficult, despite its almost conversational tone.

13 MORGAN, DOUGLAS N.: Cartesiana: an informal, inconsistent, incomplete and inaccurate list of works by and about René Descartes. September 1955. Northwestern University. 29 pp. (Hectographed.)

Rich bibliographical checklist for students in the author's Descartes course, with witty, shrewd comments.

14 OLGIATI, FRANCESCO: Cartesio. Milan, Vita e pensiero, 1934. xi, 329 p. (UCSC, v. 20).

I. Descartes e la religione [Baillet, recent interpretations, accusation of irreligiosity]. II. Descartes e la scienza [Ch. Adam, Card. Mercier, Gilson; D. and French literature]. III. Descartes e l'idealismo [Hegel, Marburg School, French Neo-idealists, Italian idealism]. IV. Riflessione critiche [Religion in D.'s system and life; physics and metaphysics; the idealistic interpretation]. V. L'anima di Descartes [fenomenismo razionalistico.]

Admirable comprehensive survey and analysis of modern D. criticism with references to some 200 authors. Main interpretations under three headings: religious, scientific, idealistic. A better, more up-to-date classification in *C. Ferro's* excellent article in RFNS 42: 1950, see no. 25. The two concluding sections develop Olgiati's own interpretation (see no. 185). Exposition and critique are lucid, reliable, precise. Unusually full treatment of German and Italian studies. Though inconvenient for quick reference (no bibliographical checklist, organization by topics rather than authors, occasional misspelling of names), the work is an indispensable guide to 19th and early 20th century D. criticism.

Reviews: Barth (O.F.M.) in PJGG 51: 1938, 502; M. Campo in RFNS 26: 1934, 386–401; G. de Giuli in RF 25: 1934, 179–81; A. Lantrùa ("Il ritorno di Cartesio") in Afil 4: 1934, 185–203, and in Conv 6: 1934, 430–443; Ch. Ranwez in RNS 37: 1934, 441–42; H. J. de Vleeschauwer in TP 1: 1939, 870–71. See also reviews of Olgiati, no. 185.

15 REVUE DE SYNTHÈSE, 1937: "La littérature cartésienne au XXe siècle." Rsyn 14/1: 1937, 67–114.

(1) FRANCE by *Gérard Milhaud:* Classified, not error-free; critical introduction.
(2) ITALY by *G. Bontadini:* Outstanding critical bibliography; supplemented in Cartesio (no. 35, 85–104); both reprinted in no. 239, 37–69. See also *E. Chiriotti* in CD 3: 127–33. For the history of Cartesianism in Italy: *Berthé de Besaucèle* (no. 433) and *C. Ottaviano* (no. 461).
(3) GERMANY by *Ernst Bergmann:* Worthless.
(4) POLAND by *N. Lubnicki:* Well-annotated checklist, titles in French. Complete bibliography of Polish D. editions and D. criticism 1717–1947 in *Adam Bar,* Kartezjusz w Polsce, KF 19: 151–60, 1950. Brief discussion of Polish D. literature, in French, by *St. Czajkowski, no. 1678.* See also no. 470;
(5) ENGLISH by *S. V. Keeling:* Insignificant.
(6) HOLLAND by *H. J. Pos and C. A. Steenbergen:* Includes local items of biographical interest. See also *Dibon* (no. 6), *Monchamp* (no. 458), *Thijssen-Schoute* (no. 467).

For CZECHOSLOVAKIA see *J. Tvrdý* in CD 3: 140–45; for JAPAN, *G. Kuwaki* in CD 3: 134–39.

16 ROSENFIELD, LEONORA DAVIDSON COHEN: From beast-machine to man-machine. New York, 1941. [See no. 226.]

"Bibliography" (303–40) on the Cartesian doctrine of the animal soul: French, Latin, English, Italian sources (chiefly material available in the U.S.), modern critical studies in French, English. Preceded by useful biographical notes on 17 lesser Cartesians and anticartesians. See also *author's* bibliography on the beast-machine controversy in England, RLC 17: 1937, 482–87.

17 ROSENFIELD, LEONORA COHEN: "Peripatetic adversaries of cartesianism in 17th century France." RevR 22: 1957, 14–40.

Attempts "to unearth the work of a score of Peripatetics" opposed to Cartesianism (p. 15). Bibliography of 20 Peripatetics, including G. Daniel, J.-B. DuHamel, H. Fabri, P.-D. Huet, La Chaise, Le Valois, and Rapin, with biographical information and summaries of the works listed.

18 SCHRECKER, PAUL: "Bibliographie de Descartes savant." Thalès 3: 1936, 145–54.

Excellent, reliable list of special literature on D.'s contribution to mathematics and science, classified by major fields, from the mid-19th century to the early 1930's. Widest coverage. No annotations.

18a SEBBA, GREGOR: Descartes and his philosophy; a bibliographical guide to the literature, 1800–1958. Vol. 1. Athens, Ga., 1959. xv, xvi, 393 p. (No more published.) Full title: no. 3251a.

Reproduced as manuscript: see Preface to the present book.

Review: C. Wenin in RPhL 57: 1959, 750–51.

19 SEBBA, GREGOR: Nicolas Malebranche, 1638–1715; a preliminary bibliography. Athens, Ga., The University of Georgia, January 1959. 90 p. Mimeographed.

Classified, partly annotated list of Malebranche literature. Includes numerous studies on doctrinal relationships between Descartes and Malebranche and on the development of Cartesianism. *Review:* N. Edelman in MLN 75: 1860, 70-72.

19a SEBBA, GREGOR: "Malebranche." "Descartes." In: A critical bibliography of French literature, v. 3, 1961, 490–503, 504–556; see no. 3a.

Critical notices of essential Malebranche literature; compact introduction to Descartes, absorbed into the present volume.

20 SIRVEN, J.: Bibliographie des Années d'apprentissage de Descartes. Albi, Imprimerie coopérative du Sud-Ouest, 1928. 34 p. (Thèse complémentaire, Paris.) Also in his: Années d'apprentissage de Descartes (no. 100), p. 471–98.

Checklist of sources and secondary literature, dated but still useful for references to sources of Cartesian doctrine and to older literature.

21 VARET, GILBERT: Manuel de bibliographie philosophique. Vol. 1: Les philosophes classiques. PUF, 1956. (Coll. Logos).

"Chrono-bibliography" of Descartes and Cartesianism (353 ff.) with source references in order of first publication. Excellent starting point for a study of ramification of Cartesianism; selected secondary literature, some annotated, with chapter titles of important works. Well worth consulting, despite its confusing organization and misspellings of foreign titles. Valuable references also in *Carlo Cordiè*, Avviamento allo studio della lingua e della letteratura francese (Milano, Marzorati, 1955). For the history of Cartesianism see also *Bouillier* (no. 438), *Thijssen-Schoute* (no. 467) and *Vartanian* (no. 468, 323–32).

22 BANNAN, J. F.: "Contemporary French readings of Descartes." Rmet 13: 1959–60, 412–38.

An analysis of the work of Roger Lefèvre (no. 179a–c) and its relations to Gouhier (no. 96), G. Rodis-Lewis (no. 215c), J. Russier (no. 228), the controversy over the ontological argument (Gouhier-Gueroult, no. 270 and 270a), and Alquié (no. 127). Author sees the prevailing mood of French Descartes interpretation as viewing his philosophy not as a rigid system of clear and distinct ideas but as "dynamic, and maintaining an orientation towards discovery" (437).

23 BALZ, A. G. A.: "Descartes after three centuries." JP 35: 1938, 169–79.

Spirited review of important 1937 contributions, notably by Maritain, Olgiati, Jaspers, Roth; general comment on Descartes criticism.

24 BRÉMOND, ANDRÉ (S.J.): "Quelques essais de 'religion' rationaliste." Aph 8, no. 4: 1931, 60–117.

On the "querelle de l'athéisme" (BSFP 28: 1928, 49–95) and on Brunschvicg's "religion cartésienne de l'Esprit et les reactions qu'elle a provoquées" (60). Also on Alain and Gilson.

25 FERRO, CARMELO: "Intorno ad alcune recenti interpretazioni del pensiero cartesiano." RFNS 42: 1950, 194–221.

Important review article asks why D. interpretations are in plain conflict with each other. Suggested reason: Cartesianism may be a fusion of disparate elements. Classification of more recent interpretations, which are critically discussed. For a less charitable view see *Henri Bouchet*, "Le pseudocartésianisme" (ZPF 4: 1950, 483–97), castigating D. scholarship for arbitrarily inflating some element in D.'s philosophy, usually drawn from DM, to represent the essence of "l'esprit cartésien": mathematicism, rationalism, "clarté," mechanism, cogito, etc.

26 FETSCHER, IRING: "Das französische Descartesbild der Gegenwart." PhRu 3: 1955, 166–98.

Precise, documented critical survey of recent French studies which reveal in D.'s religious metaphysics "eine Tiefe und einen Reichtum ...., von dem sich das herkömmliche Descartesbild nichts träumen lässt." Discusses Gouhier, Laporte, G. Lewis, Gueroult, and Alquié whose interpretation the author prefers as the most dynamic one, though he finds Gouhier's and Gueroult's more faithful.

27 GIORGIANTONIO, MICHELE: "Descartes ed i suoi recenti interpreti, 1937–1950." S 19: 1951, 313–322.

Interpretations (especially of the cogito) by Laporte, Lavelle, Blondel, Chevalier, G. Lewis, Ottaviano.

28 GOUHIER, HENRI: "Notes sur les études cartésiennes." RHPh ns 5: 1937, 199–212.

Stresses the importance of taking D.'s metaphysics into consideration, noting Maritain, Marcel, Heidegger, Brunschvicg, R. Hubert, E. Le Roy, Le Senne. Discusses D.'s "Naissance de la paix," the Huygens-D. correspondence, Gilson, Garin, Espinas, Laberthonnière, Mesnard, Leroy.

29 GUEROULT, MARTIAL: "Descartes au Congrès Descartes." RMM 45: 1938, 105–26.

Outstanding survey, a critical contribution to D. studies in its own right. Supplements Boorsch (no. 2). See no. 36.

30 SEBBA, GREGOR: "Some open questions in Descartes research." MLN 75: 1960, 222–29.

Notes recent literature on questions of D. biography, history of Cartesianism, literary merits of D.'s writing; stresses the need for a new complete Descartes edition.

31 SORIANO, MARC: "Ouvrages récents sur Descartes." Pensée 40: Jan-Feb 1952, 107–14.

Remarkably perceptive Marxist critique of Serrurier, G. Lewis, Alquié, and of Soviet contributions.

32 STEWART, W. F. M.: "A survey of work on 17th century rationalism, 1945–51. Part I: Descartes, Geulincx, Leibniz." PhQ 2: 1952, 359–68.

33 WUNDT, MAX: "Wandlungen des Descartes-Bildes." ZPF 7: 1953, 315–25.

Interesting sketch rapidly surveys D. interpretations from Hegel and Tennemann to Gilson and Espinas. Sees no way of reconciling the conflicting images of D. as physicist-methodologist and as continuator of Scholastic thought except by going back to his unconscious, repressed motivations which broke through in his "Dream."

II. COLLECTANEA

(Full list: no. 501–562 below)

35 [CARTESIO]: Cartesio nel terzo centenario del "Discorso del metodo." Milan, Vita e pensiero, 1937. 807 p. (UCSC Suppl. to RFNS 19, 1937).

Massive international Catholic tribute by 60 D. scholars, medievalists, and historians of philosophy. Contributions, on a high technical level, range from doctrinal exegesis and comparative studies to peripheral topics. The historical approach prevails. The treatment of D. is generally friendly, always respectful, in contr ast to the sharply critical Thomist contributions in E 57: 1937, 369–558.

Reviews: E. Cassirer in no. 5, p. 6–8; C. Fabro in Bolletino filosofico 4: 1938, 189–96; G. Giacon in Greg 18: 1938, 599–603; M. Giorgiantonio in S 6: 1938, 387–91 (with full table of contents); G. Radetti in GCFI 18: 1937, 473–75.

36 CONGRÈS DESCARTES [CD]: Études cartésiennes. Travaux du IXe Congrès international de philosophie (Congrès Descartes), Paris, 1937. Vols. 1–3. 181, 131, 147 p. (Asci, v. 530–32).

Important reference tool. Vols. 1–3 contain abstracts of 66 papers of extraordinary variety on D.'s philosophy, scientific work, life, also on sources, influences, history of Cartesianism. Valuable papers in vols. 4–9 deal with his mathematics, logic, psychology, seen from the viewpoint of contemporary philosophy. *M. Gueroult's* "Descartes au Congrès Descartes" (RMM 45: 1938, 105–26), a searching analysis of the philosophical papers, is eminently helpful in working through CD.

Reviews: E. W. Beth in ANTWP 31: 1937, 30–42; J. Le Blond in Et 232: 1937, 502–09; C. Bouglé in RPar 44: 1937, 368–86; R. M. Bruckberger, R. Jolivet et al. in RThom 44: 1937, 171–93; G. Boas in JP 34: 1937, 561–74; M. de Corte in Flambeau (Brussels) 20: 1937, 443–50; J. Dopp in RNS 40: 1937, 664–71; A. Hayen in NRT 8: 1937, 1116–22; C. Kruse in PhR 47: 1938, 64–70; L. Lavelle in Tatwelt (Berlin) 14: 1938, 74–90 (French tr. in no. 11, p. 239–50); D. S. Robinson in JP 35: 1938, 180–83; H. Robbers in Studiën (s'Hertogenbosch) 49: 1938, 447–61; F. Romero in Sur (Buenos Aires) 7: 1938, 66–73; M. E. dal Verme in RFNS 29: 1937, 422–40.

37 DESCARTES. Par Maxime Leroy, G. Friedmann, J. Luc, Lucie Prenant, P. Labérenne, N. Gutermann et H. Lefèbvre, Gérard Milhaud, et Édouard Beneš. Paris, Rieder, 1937. 147 p. Also in Eur: 15 Jul 1937, 291–430.

Lucie Prenant ingeniously and subtly investigates the meaning of D.'s rationalism; Labérenne sums up the essence of the three Essais of DM; President Beneš of Czechoslovakia discusses D.'s stay in Bohemia, his relation with Komenský (Comenius), his place in Czechoslovak philosophy. Gutermann and Lefèbvre develop the standard Marxist view of D. and the struggle between bourgeoisie and feudalism

Review: Anon. in RMM 45: 1938, suppl. 3, p. 18.

38 DESCARTES ET LE CARTÉSIANISME HOLLANDAIS. ÉTUDES ET DOCUMENTS. PUF – Éditions françaises d'Amsterdam, 1950. 309 p. (Publications de l'Institut Français d'Amsterdam – Maison Descartes.)

Three new D. letters; inedited D. criticism (Delft, 1681) by Du Vaucel, Port-Royal exile. *G. Lewis'* capital study of this document ("Augustinisme et Cartesianisme à Port-Royal") establishes the precise nature and extent of anticartesian feeling among "ces Messieurs," correcting Brunetière's well-known thesis. A related study of D. criticism at the Hotel Liancourt (1669–74) by *J. Orcibal* breaks new ground. *C. L. Thijssen-Schoute's* survey of Dutch Cartesianism abounds with fact. Masterly critique of secondary literature in *Paul Dibon's* "Notes bibliographiques sur les Cartésiens hollandais." The introductory D. appraisals are standard fare.

Reviews: Anon. in BCLF 6: 1951, 770; F. Alquié in RPFE 143: 1953, 281–83; C. Ferro in RFNS 44: 1952, 84–87; H.-D. Gardeil in RSPT 35: 1951, 695–96; R. Hooykaas in AIHS 5: 1952, 123–25; G. Radetti in GCFI 31: 1952, 250–53; M. Soriano in Pensée no. 40: 1952, 110–11; J. N. Wright in PhQ 3: 1953, 82–83.

39 [ESCRITOS]. La Plata. Universidad nacional. Escritos en honor de Descartes en ocasión del tercer centenario del Discurso del método. La Plata, 1938. 335 p.

Twenty-four papers: valid contributions to philosophical and historical D. research, interspersed with some vague effusions. Complements no. 40: same spirit, less vigor.

Review: W. S. Weedon in PPR 1: 1940, 247–50.

40 [HOMENAJE]. Descartes. Homenaje en el tercer centenario del "Discurso del método." Buenos Aires. Universidad nacional, Instituto de filosofía, 1937. 3 vols. 371, 343, 361 p.

The "Descartes years" 1937 and 1950 revealed hitherto unsuspected strength and vigor in Latin-American D. scholarship, reflected in numerous special journal issues and commemorative publications. Among the latter, the Buenos Aires "Homenaje" stand out in freshness, comprehensiveness, orientation toward the present rather than the past. Among its 46 articles are valuable surveys of Descartes' scientific work, noteworthy studies of Cartesian influence upon literary criticism, brief sketches on Cartesian philosophy in Spanish colonial America. Apart from a few weak contributions, the work is well worth consulting.

Reviews: E. Cassirer in no. 5, 8–13; G. Radetti in GCFI 6: 1938, 450–51; Anon. in E 39: 1938, 223–32.

41 [INTERNATIONAL THOMIST CONGRESS, 1936]. Acta Secundi Congressus Thomistici Internationalis, 1936, p. 497–554. Full title: no. 506.

Contributions by J. Beneš, E. de Ivanka, R. Bizzarri, V. de Ruvo, A. Lantrua, J. Sirven, and a study of the Cartesian philosopher and poet Campailla. For reviews see Brie, v. 2, 23464–76.

42 [ROYAUMONT]. Descartes. Cahiers de Royaumont, Philosophie no. II. Paris, Éditions de minuit, 1957. 493 p.

Proceedings of the international colloquium on Descartes' philosophy at Royaumont Abbey in 1955, the most important among recent Descartes collectanea. Galaxy of contributors includes F. Alquié, L. J. Beck, H. Gouhier, M. Gueroult whose "Descartes selon l'ordre des raisons," no. 170, dominates the colloquium, H. Lefèbvre, P. Mesnard, G. Rodis-Lewis, Jean Wahl. Main themes: Cartesian metaphysics, moral philosophy, esthetics; two papers on Descartes' Géométrie; one on Descartes, Galilei and Vico. Outstanding discussions, reproduced verbatim; they are unusually frank, searching, scholarly, and disclose sharply differing viewpoints. The "discussion generale" (443–90) concerning the principles of historical philosophical interpretation brings out the clash between the approaches of Alquié, Gueroult and the Marxists who make an impressive showing throughout the volume, being perceptive, scholarly and remarkably non-doctrinaire. See the discussion by *V. Goldschmidt* in RMM 62: 1957, 67–71 on the Alquié-Gueroult controversy; *A. Robinet,* "Variations sur le nom de Descartes" in Crit 14: 1958, no. 135–36, 774–91; R. Boehm in Eph 11: 1956, 92–93 (an interim report); B. Rochot in Rsyn 79: 1958, 128–29.

III. EDITIONS

BASIC EDITIONS

74 [AT]. Œuvres de Descartes. Publiés par *Charles Adam* et *Paul Tannery*. Cerf, 1897–1913. 13 vols. Reprinted: Vrin, 1957–58.

1–5: Correspondence 1622–50, with index. [Supplements in v. 7, 8, 10, 13.]
6: DM, Dioptrique, Météores, Géométrie [French, Latin].
7: MM [Latin]. Letter to Dinet.
8: PP [Latin]. Polemical writings.
9: MM, PP [both French].
10: Early and undated writings.
11: Le Monde. TP. Scientific writings. Projects.
12: Ch. Adam, Vie et œuvres de D. (no. 121).
13: Supplement: Correspondence, biographical material. Indices.

The Adam-Tannery edition, commonly cited *AT*, is accepted as the definitive text of D.'s writings and supersedes even the original editions. Indispensable introductions; textual and explanatory notes; Tannery's important mathematical annotations. D.'s orthography (discussed in AT I, lvix-cv) is preserved or conjecturally restored. The translations of main works are those authorized by D. himself. The text of the Correspondence is authoritative, but dating and identification of correspondents have been considerably revised (Ch. Adam in RPFE 115: 1933, 373–401; see also no. 79). Edition lacks: most of the correspondence with Huygens (no. 81); Naissance de la paix (no. 78); seven letters (no. 124, v. 2, 169–73; Eur 1937, 406–14; no. 38, p. 71–85, 109–11); "Stammbuchblatt" (K 40: 1935, 264–69). However, the marginal notes, supposedly by D., in a London copy of Galilei's "Systema mundi" are definitely not in his hand (*L. Roth*, "Falsa Cartesiana," RPFE 105: 1928, 149–51) – [A new edition of AT, to include all material now lacking, is being prepared by B. Rochot.]

75 [FOUCHER DE CAREIL]: Œuvres inédites de Descartes. Précédées d'une introduction sur la méthode par Louis Alexandre comte Foucher de Careil. Ladrange et Durand, 1859–60. 2 vols. XVI, cxvii, 158; xii, 238 p.

Leibniz's extracts, now lost, from Descartes' long-lost earliest manuscripts. Modernized Latin spelling faced by Foucher's French translation. The most important discovery are the Cogitationes privatae (Foucher's title) from D.'s earliest philosophical notebook, key to the understanding of his formative period. Charles Adam sharply criticized Foucher's editing of this Leibniz copy, particularly his ignorance of cossic notation. Adam's corrected, annotated text in AT X, 206–256 disregards Foucher's presumably authentic division into "pensées" (which affects the interpretation of certain philosophical items), and "restores" the presumed original spelling, giving a veneer of source authority to his version. Foucher's edition should therefore still be consulted; his 117-page introduction, wholly and unjustly neglected, makes some good psychological points, especially on the Dream of Descartes.

76 [PLÉÏADE]. Œuvres et lettres. Textes présentés par *André Bridoux*. 2nd ed., considerably augmented. Bibliothèque de la Pléïade, v. 4, 1952. 1421 p.

Handiest one-volume desk edition, but vastly inferior to the superb Rousseau edition of the Pléïade. Contains: Regulae; DM; Dioptrics I–VI; Météores VIII;

Géométrie II; MM; Objections and Responses I–VI; PP I, II, end of IV, complete table of contents; TP; Traité de l'homme, not easily available elsewhere; RV; 144 letters by D.; Entretien avec Burman; Baillet on the death of D. Texts in French, modern spelling. Brief introductions. Lacks: Cogitationes privatae, Opuscula 1619–20, Le Monde.

77 [HALDANE-ROSS]: The philosophical works of Descartes. Rendered into English by *Elizabeth S. Haldane* and *G. R. T. Ross*. 2nd ed., corr. Cambridge University Press, 1931. 2 vols. Reprinted: New York, Dover (London, Vision Press), 1955. 2 vols., 452, 380 p. Partly reprinted in: Great Books of the Western World. Chicago, Encyclopedia Britannica, 1952, v. 31, 1–353.

Most comprehensive English version, superseding the earlier standard translations by Veitch (Open Court). All of Regulae, DM, MM, RV, TP, Notae in programma; generous excerpts from PP; v. 2 gives the first complete English translation of the "Objections and Responses" to MM, plus the Letter to Dinet. The translation is philosophically precise rather than fluent or elegant, but the problem of terms like "âme," "mens," "entendement," etc. is not quite solved. The Great Books reprint, widely available, has Regulae, DM, MM with all Objections and Responses, Letter to Dinet, followed by the Smith-Latham version of the Géométrie (no. 88).

Reviews: A. E. Taylor in Mind 22: 1913, 406–08; HJ 1911, 702.

78 [NAISSANCE DE LA PAIX.] *Thibaudet, A.* and *Johan Nordstrøm:* Un ballet de Descartes. RGenève 1: 1920, 163–85.

Text of D.'s long-lost only venture in poetry: "La naissance de la paix. Ballet dansé au Chasteau Royal de Stockholm le jour de la naissance de sa Majesté" (1649), 344 lines. Introduction by Thibaudet (p. 163–72). The timelessness of D.'s rather crude verse, some of it in the spirit of Callot, is attested by *Aragon's* post-1945 free prose version and its translation by *Hans Paeschke:* Die Geburt des Friedens, 1949 (see no. 1072).

79 [AM]. Descartes. Correspondance publiée avec une introduction et des notes par *Charles Adam* et *Gérard Milhaud*. Vol. 1–2: Alcan; vol. 3–8: PUF, 1936–1963.

Indispensable edition (concordance with AT in the last volume) presents all known letters in chronological order, except for new finds in vol. 7. Modernized spelling. Latin and Dutch letters in the original and in French translation, the latter either Clerselier's 1668 translation revised, or new. Dates and identification of recipients are presumably definitive and differ sometimes from AT; in the earlier volumes, changes from AT were not always explicitly indicated; v. 7 brings some new revisions. Essential AT notes are retained, some in expanded form. Vol. 2 has the complete text of D.'s "Introduction à la géométrie" which supersedes the "Calcul de Monsieur Descartes" in AT X, 659–80; also the hitherto unpublished French original of *Florimond Le Beaune's* "Notes brèves" to D.'s Géométrie, which D. himself recommended. An index of names at the end of each volume gives concise biographical sketches of all persons referred to in the letters, thus forming one of the handiest reference tools.

Reviews: P. Brunet in Archeion 18: 1936, 401–403; M.R. in Aph 3: 1937, no. 3, sb p. 45; A. K. Stout in Mind 46: 1937, 530–32 (corrects errors in mathematical formulas of v. 1); L. Millet in Eph 11: 1956, 676 (v. 6); Anon. in BCLF 7: 1952, 108 (v. 5); B. Rochot in RHSA 11: 1958, 179–80.

80 BEECKMAN, ISAAC: Journal tenu par Isaac Beeckman de 1604 à 1634, publié avec une introduction et des notes par *Cornelis de Waard.* 4 vols. La Haye, Nijhoff, 1939–1953.

Beeckman, whom D. called his "awakener," kept a monumental scientific diary of greatest importance to D. studies and early 17th c. history of science. He inserted several D. letters and records of their 1618–19 scientific relationship, first published in AT X. The complete Journal, superably edited by its discoverer, still awaits definitive study to do justice to the remarkable figure of Beeckman and to explore his impact upon young D. Factual biographical introduction, excellent index, terse notes; but the lack of any organization in the sequence of Beeckman's Latin and Dutch entries makes the mastery of this work exceedingly difficult.

81 [HUYGENS]. Correspondence of Descartes and Constantijn Huygens, 1635–1647, ed. from mss. now in the Bibliothèque Nationale, formerly in the possession of the late Harry Wilmot Buxton, by *Leon Roth.* Preface by Charles Adam. Oxford, Clarendon Press, 1926. lxxv, 351 p. 4to.

A capital find of 141 letters enabled L. Roth to publish this masterly definitive edition of the D.-Huygens correspondence, essential to the study of D.'s life and views, and of the genesis of DM. Edition has 58 unpublished letters to Huygens, 4 to other correspondents; correction of texts and dates of letters previously published in AT. Lacks two letters to Huygens, including a note from Stockholm, December 4, 1649 (no. 38, 71–85) rectifying the notion that D. was disappointed by Queen Christina. Important editorial introduction of 78 pages, supplemented by a 1937 paper (CD 2: 101–08) on the value of this edition "for the criticism of the sources of our conceptions of Descartes" (106), showing how Clerselier, the first editor of D.'s correspondence, doctored texts in the interest of orthodoxy and created an image of the "historical" Descartes which influenced interpretation from Baillet to Maritain.
Review: E. Gilson in RPFE 103: 1927. 147–49.

82 [MERSENNE]. Correspondance du P. Marin Mersenne, religieux minime. Éditée et annotée par *Cornélis de Waard.* Vol. 1–7, PUF, Centre national de la recherche scientifique, 1932–1962. (In progress.) [Full title: no. 2713.]

Magnificent edition in very slow progress (v. 1–7 cover the years 1617–1638) adds rich new documentary material and erudite notes by de Waard to Descartes' correspondence with his principal partner. Placing Descartes within P. Mersenne's circle along with Beeckman, Gassendi, Galilei, Peiresc and others, this edition gives a truer picture of D.'s position in his time than emerges from editions of his own correspondence only. Gérard Milhaud and R. Lebègue correct errors in earlier volumes (Thalès 3: 182–96, RHL 44: 1937, 555); see lists of errata in the post-1945 volumes. Robert Lenoble's great Mersenne biography (no. 215) is an indispensable companion to this edition.

Reviews: G. Leger in RSPT 40: 1956, 41; J. Abélé in Aph 20: 1957, 305; J. Gilbert in NRT 79: 1957, 212–13; A. Koyré in RHSA 9: 1956, 364–66 and in AIHS 9: 1956, 257–59; B. Rochot in Rsyn 77: 1956, 108–09 and in DSS no. 31: 1956, 409–10. Other reviews in *no. 3a*, p. 47.

83 [DM]. GILSON, ÉTIENNE. René Descartes: Discours de la méthode; texte et commentaire. 2e éd., corr. Vrin, 1930. 493 p. [See no. 2027.]

Text of the "édition classique" (AT) in original pagination but modern spelling, followed by a monumental 400-page commentary which elucidates the work almost phrase by phrase and discusses every important aspect of D.'s life and work. Excellent analytical index. A. Brémond said without exaggerating that Gilson's commentary, if nothing else were left of D.'s work, would suffice to reconstruct "toute la doctrine vivante avec ses principes profondes, ses incertitudes, ses dépendances, son originalité" (Aph 4, no. 4: 310, 1928). Necessary companion to any study of D.'s life and thought. See Léon Brunschvicg's review article ("Mathématique et métaphysique chez Descartes"), no. 1396, reprinted in no. 159.

OTHER USEFUL EDITIONS

84 [ARNAULD, MORUS]. Correspondance avec Arnauld et Morus. Texte Latin et traduction. Introduction et notes par *Geneviève Lewis*. Vrin, 1953, 187 p. (BTP).

Correspondence with an anonymous opponent ("Hyperaspistes"), with Antoine Arnauld and Henry More, culled from AT, extends the arguments of the "Objections and Responses" to MM. Deals with the nature of the soul, innate ideas in the child, the beast-machine hypothesis, other problems of dualism. Latin text, faced by Clerselier's French translation. Strictly a text edition. English translation of the correspondence with More regarding beast-machine, by *Leonora D. Cohen* [*Rosenfield*], in AnSci 1: 1936, 48–61.

Reviews: J. Dopp in RPhL 52: 1954, 320–21; G. Leger in RSPT 39: 1955, 168–69; P. Hermand in Rthom 54: 1954, 687–92; M. de Mullewie in TP 17: 1955, 547.

86 [BURMAN]. Entretien avec Burman. Manuscrit de Göttingen. Texte présenté, traduit et annoté par *Charles Adam*. Boivin, 1937. xv, 144 p. (Bph).

Precious record, discovered in 1895, of an interview which D. gave in April 1648 to Francis Burman, twenty-year-old Dutch student who asked searching questions about difficult passages in MM and received very frank, good-humored answers. Latin text from AT V, 144–79, faced by Adam's French translation. Authoritative introduction and notes.

Review: Anon. in RMM 4: 1896, sb 2, 2–3.

87 [DIOPTRIQUE]. *Leisegang, Gertrud:* Descartes' Dioptrik. Meisenheim a.G., Westkultur-Verlag Hain, 1954. 168 p. (Monographien zur Naturphilosophie, v. 2).

Text of D.'s Dioptrique with the AT notes, in a none too fluent or precise German translation. Interesting introduction (7–66); elucidates the work in considerable detail, contrasting D.'s "analytical" thought model with Kepler's "more geometrico" approach. D.'s work on lenses is discussed in the light of modern optical theory. Though noting D.'s insistence on the instantaneous transmission of light, author misrepresents him as postulating "very rapid motion."

Reviews: L. G. in Bph 1: 1954, no. 395, p. 49–50; M. H. Pirenne in PhQ 6: 1956, 181–82; M.D.T. in Bijdr 16: 1955, 332; Anna Beckmann in Lychnos 1956, 402–03.

88 [GÉOMÉTRIE]. The Geometry of René Descartes. Tr. from the French and Latin by *David Eugene Smith* and *Marcia L. Latham.* With a facsimile of the first edition, 1637. Chicago, Open Court, 1925. xii, 246 p. Reprinted: New York, Dover, 1954. See also no. 77.

Facsimile of the first edition, faced by a helpfully annotated translation "made to give the meaning of the original in simple English rather than to add to the difficulty of the reader by making it a verbatim reproduction" (Preface). Includes the "Privilège du roi." Helps make this difficult work accessible to non-mathematicians. See also Scott, no. 396.

89 [MM]. Meditationes de prima philosophia. Texte latin et traduction du Duc de Luynes. Introduction et notes par *Geneviève Lewis.* 2nd éd. Vrin, 1946. xiv, (174) p. (BTP). Reprinted 1960.

Handy edition of MM, Descartes' culminating work. Latin text (AT) faced by the French translation of the Duc de Luynes, corrected and approved by D., reproduced from the 1647 edition. Modern spelling. Austere editorial treatment, no commentary.

Review: R. van Court in MSR 1: 1945, 387.

90 LETTRES SUR LA MORALE. Correspondance avec la princesse Élisabeth, Chanut et la reine Christine. Texte revu et présenté par *Jacques Chevalier.* Boivin, 1935. xxviii, 333 p. (Bph). Reprinted 1955.

These letters from D.'s last period form an integral whole, his last statement on ethics. See Chevalier, no. 132, 327–40.

91 [TP]. Les passions de l'âme. Introduction et notes par *Geneviève Rodis-Lewis.* Vrin, 1955. 240 p. (BTP)

Text of TP in modern spelling. The notes utilize the correspondence with Princess Elisabeth. Short glossary of now obsolete terms. Bibliography. Important preface whose "parfaite conduite .... fait de cette nouvelle édition un instrument de travail indispensable" (Leger's review, 37). Another good edition is that of *Pierre Mesnard* (Boivin, 1937; xxix, 167 p.; reprinted 1955, Bph) with an interesting introduction and good annotations (some errors in page references). See the controversy over these editions between Mme Rodis-Lewis and P. Mesnard in Royaumont (no. 42), 209ff.

Reviews: J. Gilbert in NRT 77: 1955, 1112; G. Leger in RSTP 40: 1956, 36–37; C.V. in Bph 2: 1955, no. 752.

92 [REGULAE]. Regulae ad directionem ingenii. Texte de l'édition Adam et Tannery; notice par *H. Gouhier.* 3e éd. Vrin, 1959. 152 p. (BTP)

Latin text only; valuable introduction and list of special studies. For a bilingual edition see: Regulae ad directionem ingenii, texte présenté, revu et traduit par *G. Le Roy* (Boivin, 1933; xxi, 217 p. Bph); the Latin text of this edition is based on Leibniz's copy and the first edition of 1701, with facing French translation. A good French version, fluent and accurate, without the Latin text is: Règles pour la direction de l'esprit, tr. et notes de *J. Sirven* (Vrin, 1959, viii, 192 p. BTP), with explanatory notes and marginal AT pagination. Good companion to the Gouhier edition.

92a [REGIUS]. Lettres à Regius et remarques sur l'explication de l'esprit humain. Texte latin, trad., introd. et notes par *Geneviève Rodis-Lewis.* Vrin, 1959. 216 p. (BTP)

Contains D.'s letters to Regius, 1640–45, his Notae in programma with a French translation from the early editions, D.'s letter to Voetius of May 1643, and selected texts from the Philosophia naturalis of Regius (1654) in which he develops his D. critique. English translation of the Notae in Haldane-Ross, no. 77; Spanish translation of Notae: Notas contra el programa filosófico de Regius, tr., intr., notes by *Elisabeth Goguel de Labrousse,* in: Notas y estudios de filosofía (Tucumán) 1: 1949, 276–92.

92b [LE MONDE]. Il mondo, ovvero Trattato della luce. Torino, P. Boringhieri, 1959. 138 p. (Enciclopedia di autori classici, ed. G. Colli, v. 28).

IV. BIOGRAPHY

ORIGIN AND FORMATIVE YEARS

93 CANTECOR, G.: "L'oisive adolescence de Descartes. Études cartésiennes." RHPh 4: 1930, 1–38, 354–96.

I. Quelques traits significatifs du caractère de Descartes. II. La première démarche de D.: le renoncement à la science; le problème de l'historicité du Discours de la méthode.

Cantecor is the typical debunker of the 1920's: ".... l'office d'un historien n'est pas de préparer le procès de canonisation de son auteur. C'est là d'ailleurs une tâche dont MM Gilson et Gouhier s'acquittent avec toute la piété souhaitable" (7). Denies, against Gilson, the historicity of DM. Calls young Descartes not a systematic searcher for certainty but a capricious amateur who gradually finds his geometry, then generalizes it to a supposedly universal method. "Oisiveté" is fundamental to his nature. This paper and the *author's* earlier "La vocation de Descartes" (RPFE 96: 1923, 372–400), both craftsmanlike, well-documented, malicious, gave impetus to the revaluation of DM. But the decisive step towards a truer Descartes image was taken by Gilson, Blondel, Jaspers, Krüger on philosophical not biographical ground.

94 COUDERC, CAMILLE: "Nouveaux documents sur la situation et la fortune de la famille de René Descartes." Bibliothèque de l'École des Chartes 78: 1918, 269–93. Also: Nogent-le-Rotru, Impr. Daupeley-Gouverneur, 1918. 27 p.

Utilizing records of the 1618 sale of La Chilliolière, patrimonial property of D.'s family, Couderc reconstructs the family assets in D.'s time. The value of D.'s share is found to be extremely modest though sufficient for his equally modest needs. See also no. 99.

95 GALDSTON, IAGO: "Descartes and modern psychiatric thought." Isis 35: 1944, 118–28.

A well-read psychiatrist with broad interests critically scans studies of D.'s childhood and formative period, noting fundamental insecurity and latent homosexuality. Stimulating references to current work on psychology of superior personalities.

96 GOUHIER, HENRI: Les premières pensées de Descartes; contribution à l'histoire de l'anti-renaissance. Vrin, 1958. 167 p. (De Pétrarque à Descartes, v. 2).

I. Un petit registre en parchemin [Item "C" of the Stockholm Inventory]. II. Du Parnasse à l'Olympe. III. 10 et 11 novembre 1619 [The Dream of Descartes]. IV. L'hiver 1619–20. V. Une pensée de jeunesse abandonnée [Olympica]. VI. Polybe le Cosmopolite [Cogitationes privatae]. VII. D. et les Rose-Croix. App.: Le roman rosicrucien.

Modestly offered as material towards a needed "Jeunesse de Descartes," this meticulous study reviews, judges and revises all important earlier studies of D.'s "années d'apprentissage" (1618–20) from Millet (no. 2764) to Sirven (no. 100) and boldly advances beyond them. It finds "le jeune Descartes réagissant violemment contre l'esprit de 'la Renaissance' au moment où il échappe au 'Moyen âge' " (9), a scientistic revolt. This unexpected conclusion is reached by a penetrating, sober scrutiny of sources and imaginative yet never of careless analysis of their content. The book establishes a firm basis for the study of the Opuscula of 1619–20, especially of Olympica, and explodes the legend of D.'s "Rosicrucianism." Hypotheses and conclusions about intricate questions of source criticism are stated with model precision. Not the last but so far the most important word on D.'s formative years and the Cogitationes privatae. Bannan in the review cited below finds Gouhier failing in his attempt "to manage the union of the personal and the historical" (417), but the problem is deeper than the reviewer suggests. On the 17th c. as the Cartesian and the renascent century see *Gouhier*, "Les deux XVIIe siècles" (1948, no. 2090). Note also his studies of the Cartesian problem of a philosophy without rhetorics (no. 2098) and of D.'s rejection of symbolism in his mature philosophy, in contrast to Olympica (no. 2101a), on which see also Rossi, no. 328.

Reviews: G. Micheli in RCSF 14: 1959, 231–33; B. Rochot in Rsyn 79: 1958, 309–20; P. Mesnard in Eph 13: 1958, 191–95; A. Robinet in RIP 12: 1958, 196–201 (notes the emphasis on D.'s Experimenta); M.P. in AUP 28: 1958, 646–47; M. Françon in Renaissance News 13: 1960, 18; W. Doney in Isis 51: 1960, 363–65; J. F. Bannan in Rmet 13: 1959–60, 415–17.

97 MONCHAMP, GEORGES: Notes sur Descartes. Préface de Jacques Laminne. Liège, Société industrielle d'arts et métiers, 1913. xxiv, 125 p.

The two first chapters of a book interrupted by death: I. "Descartes au Collège de La Flèche" (1–62); II. "Chronologie de la vie de Descartes depuis sa sortie du collège jusqu'à son établissement définitif en Hollande, 1614–29" (63–125). Believes that Descartes left La Flèche in 1614. Study of his Jesuit teachers and his friend Chauveau of Melun.

Review: É. Gilson in RNS 21: 1921, 82f.

98 DE ROCHEMONTEIX, CAMILLE (S.J.): Un collège des Jésuites aux XVIIe & XVIIIe siècles: le Collège Henri IV de La Flèche. Le Mans, Leguicheux, 1899. 4 vols.

Minute historical study of the ratio studiorum, daily life of students and teachers, methods of instruction, techniques of silent ubiquitous supervision, holidays and festivities etc. gives an incomparably full and vivid picture of the environment which furnished the setting for D.'s "Dream" of 1619, and the schooling he described and rejected in his DM.

99 ROPARTZ, SIGISMOND: La famille de Descartes en Bretagne, 1586–1762. Rennes, Verdier, 1877. 238 p. (Mémoires de l'Association bretonne, 1876).

Basic documentary study. "Table généalogique et historique." See also: *Xavier d'Haucourt,* "Une dynastie de 'non-originaires' au Parlement de Brétagne: la famille Des-Cartes, 1585–1736" (AnnBr 44: 1937, 408–32; 45: 1938, 3–24); *Alfred Barbier,* "Trois médécins poitevins au XVIe siècle, ou les origines châtelleraudaises de la famille Descartes" (BSAOuest ser. 2, 19: 1897, 51–250; documentation: 80–250; cf. *L. Bossebeuf* in BSATours, 1899–1900). Also *Charles Adam* (no. 121); items 4146–85 and 6213–25 in *Lanson's* Manuel bibliographique (no. 2441); and *Barbier* on the family of D., no. 1142.

100 SIRVEN, J.: Les années d'apprentissage de Descartes (1596–1628). Albi, Impr. coopérative du sud-ouest, 1928; Vrin, 1930. 498 p. (Thèse Paris, 1927).

Milestone in the study of D.'s La Flèche years and earliest writings. This painstaking, most ingenious and subtle reconstruction of the 1619–20 Opuscula must still be reckoned with, despite Gouhier's equally ingenious recent interpretation (no. 96). Asserts that the four rules of method in DM (1637) go back to 1619–20, which would make the Regulae of 1628 a later development. Written without regard for the reader's convenience, the book cries out for subtitles, summaries, subject index. Useful 34-page bibliography lists sources of Cartesian doctrine and some older criticism.

Review: G. Cantecor in RHPh 3: 1929, 234–36.

101 SIX, KARL (S.J.): "Descartes im Jesuitenkolleg von La Flèche. Zur Chronologie im Leben Descartes'." ZKT 38: 1914, 494–508.

Independently of Monchamp, P. Six corrects Baillet by letting D. leave La Flèche in 1614 instead of 1612. Study, based on Jesuit archives, corrects Monchamp and Sirven on minor points and gives valuable details about the Jesuits whom D. knew at La Flèche.

102 ARNOLD, PAUL: "Le 'songe' de Descartes." CDS 39, no. 312: 1952, 274–91. [Reprinted in his: Histoire des Rose-Croix et les origines de la franc-maçonnerie. Mercure de France, 1955, 273–99.] "Descartes et les Rose-Croix." MF 340: 1960, no. 1166, 266–84.

Careful historical study leads the author to deny the existence of a Rosicrucian Brotherhood in D.'s time, hence to absolve him of membership; but Rosicrucian literature existed, and D. was familiar with it. Shows striking similarities between the Dream of D. and the "Noces chymiques de Christian Rosenkrantz" of Johan-Valentin Andreae (1616) and particularly with the "Raptus philosophicus" of "Rhodophilus Staurophorus" published in 1619; D.'s "Dream" of 1619, "absolument dans le goût des rêves-paraboles qui foisonnent alors en Allemagne," thus appears to be "une imagerie forgée par Descartes sur le modèle .... de paraboles connues" (299). Gouhier, though impressed, still asserts there was a dream and tries to ward off the hypothesis of plagiarism or imitation (no. 96, 138–41). See *B. Rochot* in Rsyn 77: 1956, 353–61.

103 FRANZ, MARIE-LOUISE VON: Der Traum des Descartes. In: Zeitlose Dokumente der Seele. Zürich, Rascher, 1952, 49–119. (SJInst, v. 3).

This Jungian interpretation is too unspecific to convince, despite its vast mythological apparatus (14 pages on the "melon" episode alone), but adds rich new association material and a careful reading of the Ausonius poems cited in the "Dream."

Reviews: Bally in RSPPA 13: 1954, 85–86; Herzog-Durok in PsyH 7, no. 8: 1953, 98–101.

104 GEORGES-BERTHIER, AUGUSTE: "Descartes et les Rose-Croix." Rsyn ns 18, no. 1: 1939, 9–30. Notes by Pierre Brunet.

Written in 1914, this study by a gifted young historian killed in the first world war justifies its belated publication by its careful assembly and evaluation of the evidence, though its conclusions are dated. See also the treatment of the question by Ch. Adam (no. 121) and G. Cohen (no. 123, 402–07).

104a LEWIN, BERTRAM D.: Dreams and the uses of regression. New York, International Universities Press, 1958. 64 p. (New York Psychoanalytical Institute, Freud Anniversary Series.)

The Dream of D. might well be the very source of the modern scientific world view which excludes dream from the cognitive process. Rejecting the usual psychoanalytical interpretations, author sees in Dreams I and II merely a struggle to banish actual pain (felt while asleep) into the dream sequence, to guard the sleep. By contrast, in Dream III the dreamer is exactly what the observer is in the Cartesian system – "res cogitans, the pure and irrelevant spectator, the external observer" (18). The "real consequences" of this dreaming were thus what D. claimed – a revelation of the mathematical structure of the world for which separation of mind from matter is the first postulate. Lewin's study utilizes *Paul Federn's* distinction between mental and bodily "Ich-Gefühl" corresponding to Cartesian dualism (see

Federn, no. 1872a: the cogito is mental ego feeling). Lewin adds that my existence in the dream as dreamer has the same validity as my waking existence as a cogitator: *somnio ergo sum.*

105 PERSIGOUT, GABRIEL: "L'illumination de René Descartes rosi-crucien. Contribution à l'étude de l'imagination créatrice." CD 2: 1937, 123–30.

A revelation: The "Dream of Descartes" is the thinly disguised scenario of Rosicrucian initiation, a sort of Cartesian "Zauberflöte." Revelation not accepted by non-Rosicrucians. See Gouhier's discussion of this and other Persigout writings in no. 96, 155–56. Also no. 2938.

106 POULET, GEORGES: "Descartes." In his: Études sur le temps humain. Edinburgh UP. 1949, v. 1, ch. 2, p. 60–88. [Other editions and transl.: no. 2991.]

A brilliant chapter in a brilliant book offers a profound analysis of the Dream, without textual source criticism and without proof other than that of great inner consistency.

107 QUIRING, HEINRICH: "Der Traum des Descartes. Eine Verschlüsselung seiner Kosmologie, seiner Methodik und der Grundlage seiner Philosophie." K 46: 1954–55, 135–56.

The "Dream" is in reality D.'s record in symbolic code of his supposedly heretical discoveries, especially the vortex theory, to escape persecution while safeguarding scientific priority. Impossible hypothesis. *Max Wundt* ("Der Traum des D.", K 46: 1954–55, 367) takes author to task for ignoring French work since Gilson and treating Descartes as a mere theoretical abstraction.

108 SCHÖNBERGER, STEPHAN: "A dream of Descartes; reflections on the unconscious determinants of the sciences." Intern. Jl. of Psychoanalysis 20 : 1939, 43–57.

Disregarding Freud's warning not to read more into the Dream of D. than D. read out of it, author produces an uninhibited coprophilous analysis, misunderstanding even "the unconscious determinants of science." On Sigmund Freud's letter see *no. 124.*

THE DESCARTES LEGEND

109 ANON.: Der klagende Geest van Descartes. s.l. 1685. 4p.

Quarto sheet of doggerel verse (copy in the Cambridge University Library) attacks Dutch anticartesians as violating D.'s "sacred grave" and bones: "Wie wroet aen Cartes heyligh Graf / En knaagt sijn door gebeent, / Wat hert is so versteent / Dat naa den doot nog wraak en straf . . . ." Specimen of hitherto unrecorded, unutilized material reflecting the posthumous rise of popular D. images, especially in Holland. Pamphlet names Spannheim, de Vries, Johannes Nelenus [Neel], "Cocceanen," "Voetianen" etc.

110 MEIJER, W.: "Het leven na den dood van René Descartes." Tijdspiegel (The Hague) 1911/3, 372–84. "Over Descartes' leven na den dood." *Ibid.*, 1916/2, 226–29. "Wat er met het vermeende stoffelijke overschot van Descartes is geschied." *Ibid.*, 74: 1917/2, 135–37.

Descartes' sudden death at only 54, coming after his announcements that a fabulous increase of the human lifespan was now within imminent reach, and the mystery surrounding his Stockholm burial stirred rumors that he had not really died. This underlies *Pierre-Daniel Huet's* notorious "Nouvelles mémoires pour servir à l'histoire du cartésianisme" (1692), *Gervaise de Montpellier's* "Histoire de la conjuration faite à Stockolm contre M. Descartes" (1695), the "Voiage du Monde de Descartes" of the Jesuit *Gabriel Daniel*, and other polemics and satires of the time.

112 MERCIER, LOUIS SÉBASTIEN: Discours, prononcé le 18 Floréal, sur René Descartes. Corps Législatif. Conseil des Cinq-Cents, an IV (1796). 16 p. See: Moniteur Universel, an IV (1796), p. 539, 936–37.

On October 2, 1793, the Convention Nationale ordered the transfer of D.'s remains to the Panthéon. Mercier's vehement attack three years later caused the revocation of the unimplemented decree. Stripped of rhetoric, Mercier's argument echoes encyclopedist criticism: "C'est le cartésianisme qui tua la physique expérimentale, qui fit des pédans d'école au lieu de naturalistes observateurs" (p. 3); regarding "le mécanisme social," "pas une phrase que l'on puisse citer à cet égard: il étoit né pour son monde imaginaire .... Il écrivit sur la morale, sur laquelle il est presque impossible de mal parler" (p. 10). See *H. Gouhier* (RMM 29: 1922, 243–51) on the decrees of 1793 and 1796. On one root of Mercier's antipathy to Descartes see *no. 126*.

113 ANON.: Le Club des Dames, ou Le retour de Descartes. Comédie en une acte, en prose. A Paris, au Bureau de la Bibliothèque des romans, 1784. viii, 40 p.

"J'avois beau crier: Newton est enterré à côté des Rois, and Descartes, son Maître and le vôtre, gît à côté des gueux" (preface). But the Club women root for D. who obligingly descends from heaven for a dénouement. Insipid piece, illustrating the nationalist feeling about Newton and D., and the popular reduction to zero of Cartesianism as in the final Vaudeville: "L'univers est une machine, Où chacun rit à l'unison, Sans m'en vanter, je l'examine, Et crois que chacun a raison," etc. On a 1686 Paris opera performance where the universe is made easy for the ladies, thanks to Descartes, see Spink, no. 466a, p. 202.

114 BOUILLY, JEAN NICOLAS: René Descartes. Trait historique en 2 actes et en prose, par le citoyen Bouilly. Barba, an V. 40 p. [BN].

"Cet ouvrage, d'une morale pure et d'un doux intérêt, obtint un succès assez grand" when performed at Théatre de la République in 1796, after the denial of Panthéon honors to the philosopher. It had been performed at the first D. celebration known (La Haye-Descartes, 9–10 Vendemiaire, An II; cf. no. 124, v. 2, p. 187.) For an account of this weird biographic phantasy see Larousse's Grand Dictionnaire Universel du XIXe s., v. 6, p. 533. Apparently this is Descartes' last personal appearance on stage, though in 1844 he descends to earth once more to berate V. Cousin (Les ombres de Descartes, Kant et Jouffroy à M. Cousin, par un professeur de philosophie [P. H. Mabire?]. Lyon, Pelagaud, 1844. 249 p.)

115 FOREST, LOUIS: Le carnet d'un veilleur de jour. On peut prévoir l'avenir – comment? ou la Descartomancie. Payot, 1918, 255 p.

Collection of wartime articles in Le Matin on how to fight the coal shortage, how to like turnips, solve all war problems etc., in the spirit of "un Descartes créé par le peuple français, imaginé par lui, sorti de sa moëlle" (15), "du M. de la Palisse de la chanson, du Descartes du pauvre" (16). What Friedrich (no. 543) calls "Vulgärkartesianismus," and by no means confined to France.

PERSONAL RELATIONS

116 BEYER, CHARLES JACQUES: "Comment Descartes combattit Gassendi." PMLA 59: 1944, 446–455.

Documented account of the personal relationship between D. and G., "abstraction faite de toute considération doctrinale." Gassendi remains dignified and pleasant while Descartes is almost brutal, even by the standards of the time.

117 GUHRAUER, GOTTSCHALK EDUARD: "Elisabeth, Pfalzgräfin bei Rhein, Äbtissin von Herford." Raumer's Historisches Taschenbuch, 3. Folge 1: 1–150, 2: 417–554, 1850.

Wealth of documents assembled by the noted Leibniz historian covers the life of the Princess. Some additional material in *Max Heinze's* Pfalzgräfin Elisabeth und Descartes (ibid., 6. Folge, 5: 257–304, 1886).

118 HERVEY, HELEN: "Hobbes and Descartes." Osiris 10: 1952, 67–90.

The interesting correspondence between Sir Charles Cavendish and Dr. John Pell (1611–85), both of whom had met D., throws light on the personal relationship between Hobbes and D., especially on the famous dinner meeting between D., Gassendi and Hobbes, probably in 1648. See also *Jean Jacquot*, "Un amateur de science, ami de Hobbes et de Descartes, Sir Charles Cavendish, 1591–1654" (Thalès 6: 1949–50, 81–88).

119 NÉEL, MARGUERITE: Descartes et la princesse Élisabeth. Préface de Jean Laporte. Éditions Elzevir, 1946. 143 p. (Les jeunes études philosophiques, v. 1).

"Charmant et solide essai" finds between D. and Princess "nulle trace d'amour, platonique ou autre, mais beaucoup de preuves .... d'une amitié profonde, confiante et fidèle – mieux encore: de cette tendre dilection qui s'observe entre père et fille, et qui est quelquefois assez douce pour consoler de l'amour ou pour en tenir lieu" (Laporte, p. 9–10). Cantecor reached a similar conclusion on rudely different grounds: D.'s blind admiration of the great which made him find genius, nay, beauty "en ce laideron que fut la princesse Élisabeth" would have made him regard the very idea of considering her a woman as a sacrilege. "Il est vrai qu'il a eu une fille; mais cela ne prouve nullement qu'il ait jamais été amoureux" (no. 93, p. 17).

120 PELSENEER, JEAN: "Gilbert, Bacon, Galilée, Kepler, Harvey et Descartes; leur relations." Isis 17: 1932, 171–208.

Assembles and sifts biographical facts about D.'s relations with each of the others named in the title. Tedious but useful.

BASIC BIOGRAPHIES

121 ADAM, CHARLES: Vie et œuvres de Descartes. Étude historique. Cerf, 1910. xix, 646 p. [= AT XII.]

First modern critical biography, written with incomparable knowledge of texts and sources then available. Corrects errors and misinterpretations of the first biographers, definitively settles numerous details. The analysis of D.'s works and philosophy, leaning on Liard, is dated. Newly found texts and documents, research on the genesis of D.'s works, on D. in Holland, his formative years, etc., invalidate parts of biography without diminishing its stature. Supplementary material in AT XIII and in *Adam's* Descartes, sa vie, son œuvre (revised factual summary of AT XII; Boivin, 1937); Descartes; ses amitiés féminines (Boivin, 1937); "Descartes et ses correspondants anglais" (RLC 17: 1937, 437–60); "Quelques questions à propos de Descartes" (RCC 38: 1937, 577–89; 39: 1–8). See no. 1011–11, 1019–20. All these are important guides to fact, texts, documents.

122 BAILLET, ADRIEN: La vie de Monsieur Des-Cartes. Horthemels, 1691. 2 vols. [6], lxii, 417; 394 p.

Condescendingly treated by certain modern critics, the work remains the fountainhead of D. biography. Preserves much contemporary information and sources since lost. Baillet's fierce asceticism, as well as the then current Jesuit attacks upon Cartesian doctrine, explain the apologetic undertones, but the charge of hagiography sits ill on this "dénicheur des saints" and "hypercriticus." Cartesians and anticartesians alike censured his disclosure of incidents which, in P. Boschet's nice 17th c. phrase, make the hero blush and the reader blench: today this detailed, intimate picture of the man is priceless. Baillet's once internationally popular Abrégé of 1692, reprinted in 1946 and 1950 (see no. 1111), omits the tedious, useless blobs of irrelevant material that swell the original, preserves its spirit and flavor, and occasionally deviates somewhat in pertinent information.

123 COHEN, GUSTAVE: "La philosophie indépendante: Descartes en Hollande." In his: Écrivains français en Hollande dans la première moitié du XVIIe siècle. Champion (La Haye, Nijhoff), 1921, p. 355–689. Thèse Paris, 1920.

Books I and II lovingly describe the life of the French soldiers, poets, scholars and students who went to Holland before D., indirectly clearing up the "puzzle" why the philosopher went there and what made him stay, as Gilson remarks in his important review. Book III follows the life of D. from birth to death, giving broadest space to his years in Holland. Writing with charm, warmth, gift of narrative, but also with the historian's scrupulous attention to detail, Cohen succeeds where Baillet and Adam had failed: in uncovering Dutch documentary material and reaching an intimate understanding of Descartes' Holland. Apart from special points affected by the new Beeckman, Huygens, Mersenne editions, the core of this most readable of D. biographies remains valid. Excellent illustrations and 26-page index of names. Revised, augmented, corrected edition (Rodelin, 1950) was announced but not published.

Reviews: É. Gilson in RMM 28: 1921, 545–56 (reprinted in no. 165, p. 269–80); G. Lanson in RDM Oct. 1, 1921, 575–76; D. Roustan in RFrance 2: 1921, 392–401; R. Waddington in Rcr 88: 1921, 207–09. Other reviews in *no. 3a*, p. 300.

124 LEROY, MAXIME: Descartes, le philosophe au masque. Rieder, 1929. 2 vols. 201, 191 p.

Vol. I: Les années d'apprentissage. Le Discours de la méthode ["La grande peur de D.": the Jesuits]. Vol. II: Le secret de D. [his agnosticism]. Le désenchantement, la mort et la légende. Appendix: Unpublished childhood letter of D.; Les restes de D.; Claude Picot; Les amis de D.

Title from D.'s famous "larvatus prodeo" (AT X, 213). Behind the mask, a sardonic, restlessly intelligent, wise agnostic. The philosopher's boon companions and chance acquaintances are gently transformed into atheists, Rosicrucians etc., as the argument may require. "Très curieux ouvrage et fort utile en ses exaggérations, comme réaction aux fadeurs d'une certaine hagiographie" (Cantecor, no. 93, p. 26, n.) Interesting new biographical material in the appendices, including two pièces de résistance: a letter on D.'s Dream, solicited from *Sigmund Freud* himself (also in his: Gesammelte Werke, London, Imago, v. 14, 1948, 558–60); an unpublished letter from La Flèche "le 12 may" (no year) from one "R. Descartes" to "Mademoiselle ma mère," thanking her for "lescu que non sans nécessité vous mavez envoié." Now tentatively accepted as D.'s only extant childhood letter, to his grandmother (AM, v. 1, 473f.)

Reviews: F. Carassale in GCFI 10: 1929, 506–10; H. Gouhier in RHPh 5: 1937, 212; R. Pintard in Rcr 96: 1929, 416–19; L. Teixeira in no. 345, 187–91 et passim; É. Bréhier in RHPh 3: 1929, 495f.

125 SERRURIER, CORNELIA: Descartes, l'homme et le penseur. Préface de Henri Gouhier. PUF – Éditions françaises d'Amsterdam, 1951. 362 p.

The author's own translation, revised, of her 1930 Dutch-language work (no. 3266) and the only true biography among similar modern shorter works, ".... une aquarelle, pleine de nuances charmantes et d'une réele sensibilité" (M. Soriano, review below), rich in detail (especially on D. in Holland) without being tedious. Good explanation of points at issue between D. and his Dutch adversaries; useful documentation. Complements Cohen (no. 123).

Reviews: C. Ferro in RFNS 44: 1952, 542–43; H.-D. Gardeil in RSPT 35: 1951, 695; Marc Soriano in Pensée no. 40: 1952, 109–10; P.-M. S(chuhl) in RPFE 143: 1953, 280–81; A. Gommers in LR 8: 1954, 84–85.

126 THOMAS, ANTOINE LÉONARD: Éloge de René Descartes. Discours qui a remporté le prix de l'Académie Française en 1765. Regnard, 1765. 126 p. Also in his: Œuvres diverses, Amsterdam, Moutard, 1773. v. 4.

"Du siècle d'Aristote à celui de Descartes j'aperçois un vide de deux mille ans" (Œuvres diverses, 294); no wonder that L. S. Mercier characterized this Éloge as "grand tapage de mots" by "le grand pugilateur en ce genre" (no. 112, p. 16). Yet this set piece superseded Baillet as chief biographical source for nearly a century; Diderot preferred it, along with Marc Aurel and some pages from the "Histoire naturelle," to all of Rousseau (see his: Œuvres complètes, ed. Assézat, v. 3, p. 95; but then he had advised Thomas on this Eloge, see no. 438). V. Cousin placed it at the head of his D. edition of 1824. Competing eulogies were published in 1765 by F. H. Gaillard (who shared the prize), C. H. Couanier Deslandes, Fabre de Charrin, F. De Gourci, Mazarelli, and L. S. Mercier himself who "had not yet learned that the world's greatest charlatans are sometimes its most famous men" (no. 112, p. 3), but missed the prize nonetheless. Comparison of these 1765 products with the 1839 AMP prize essays by Bordas-Desmoulin, Bouillier, Renouvier reveals the impact of 19th century historicism upon D. interpretation.

V. INTRODUCTION TO DESCARTES

127 ALQUIÉ, FERDINAND: Descartes. L'homme et l'œuvre. Hatier-Boivin, 1956. 175 p. (Connaissance des lettres.)

Profound introduction to D.'s metaphysics and epistemology, compressing a wealth of thought into smallest compass. Capsule treatment of his life. Scientific work ignored, except in its philosophical aspects.

Reviews: R. Blanché in RPFE 148: 1958, 381; R. Campbell in RScH 1956, 481–82; L. Millet in Eph 11: 1956, 482–83; X. Tilliette in Et 290: 1956, 300; B. Rochot in Rsyn 78: 1957, 143–57; C. Smith in Phil 33: 1958, 275; J. H. in RHE 53: 1958, 661; J. Kopper in PhLit 10: 1956, 165–68; J. F. Bannan in Rmet 13: 1959–60, 434; H. Bouillard in Et 269: 1951, 417f.

128 ASTER, ERNST VON: Einführung in die Philosophie Descartes'. München, Rösl, 1921. 118 p. (Philosophische Reihe, v. 10.)

Sober, incisive introduction outlines D.'s philosophy in sharp profile. Very good on his philosophy of science. Shortest and best German work of this kind. See also *von Aster's* Geschichte der neueren Erkenntnistheorie von Descartes bis Hegel (Berlin, de Gruyter, 1921), ch. 1 et passim, and C. von Brockdorff, *no. 441.*

129 BARIÈ, GIOVANNI EMMANUELE: Descartes. Milano, Garzanto, 1947. 345 p. (I filosofi, v. 17.)

I. La vita. II. La dottrina: Il pensare come prima verità. L'io pensante e il problema del mondo esteriore. La scienza. La morale. Idealismo e realismo.

Undertakes to show "non il Cartesio 'tradizionale dell'autoscienza', ma l'assertore della 'spiritualità della sostanza' " (Dedication to P. Carabellese). Lively biographical part, followed by five vigorous expository and critical chapters on D.'s metaphysics, science, ethics, ably arguing author's viewpoint against well-considered literature. Complemented by an unusual selection of short, well annotated excerpts from D.'s writings, in Italian translation. Bibliography (335–44).

Reviews: C. Ferro in RFNS 42: 1950, 201–202; M.M.R. in JP 46: 1949, 721–24 (critical).

131 BRUNSCHVICG, LÉON: René Descartes. Rieder, 1937. 97 p., 32 pl. (Maîtres des littératures, v. 22).

"Brunschvicg oppose au cartésianisme de Descartes un cartésianisme vrai," as Alquié (no. 149, p. 350) formulates Brunschvicg's own more circumspect statement of purpose: to lay bare, beneath the deceptive unity of the system, the hidden unity of intuition which revolutionized the science of the time. ".... un petit livre toujours vivant et d'une clarté vraiment cartésienne," as Gueroult says in his discussion of its thesis (RMM 45: 1937, 106–07.) Sections on D.'s life and an impressive set of plates.

Reviews: E. Cassirer in no. 5, 27–29; G. Radetti in GCFI 6: 1938, 258–59; A. Marc in Aph 14: 1938, sb 80–81; A. Rousseaux in FigLit 4 Sept. 1937.

132 CHEVALIER, JACQUES: Descartes. Nouvelle éd. rev. et augm. (first ed.), Plon, 1921. vii, 362 p. (MPF).

Most popular of D. books, reprinted time and again, reproduces a lecture course which drew people "autant que le cinéma" (11). Passionately Gallic, firmly Catholic, Chevalier views D.'s metaphysics as "réalisme de l'idée." Fine critical analyses, blunted by a tendency to rescue D. from the resulting judgment. Very good analytical tables. Editions after 1937 have *Chevalier's* "Sur quelques points de la philosophie de Descartes qu'on peut estimer acquis" (from: *Cartesio*, 221–25). Review: R. Jolivet in RdePh 29: 1922, 95–98.

Louis Dimier's La vie raisonnable de Descartes (1926, no. 1777) is another good introduction; Neothomist viewpoint. See also *André Cresson's* popular biography (no. *1659*) and the pleasant Confessions sans pénitence by *Georges Duhamel* (see note to no. 1808.)

134 DELBOS, VICTOR: "Descartes." In his: Figures et doctrines de philosophes. Plon, 1918, p. 95–141.

"La pensée de Descartes, c'est le type de la pensée classique, aux contours définis, aux lignes nettes, aux directions sûres, sans oscillation et sans fléchissement" (115). These qualities also characterize this masterly lecture which rapidly surveys D.'s life and main doctrines in non-technical language of great precision. See also *Delbos'* La philosophie française (Plon-Nourrit, 1919, 16–48) which reprints a basic paper on the relation of science to philosophy in D. and a short survey of D.'s philosophy. See no. 1708–13.

138 FISCHER, KUNO: Descartes' Leben, Werke und Lehre. Vol. 1 of his: Geschichte der neueren Philosophie. Jubiläumsausgabe (i.e. 4th ed., rev. and augm.), Heidelberg, Winter, 1912. 467 p. Other editions: no. 1894.

Most comprehensive German study, first published in 1852, repeatedly revised, still reprinted. Biographical part obsolete. Reflects Hegel's famous view of Descartes (no. 171a). Vol. 2 (Spinoza's Leben, Werke und Lehre) gives a survey of Cartesianism especially in France and Holland, treating the development of doctrines from the viewpoint of a dialectic unfolding of philosophical history. See Hagmann (no 10), 120–27.

139 GOGUEL [DE LABROUSSE], ELIZABETH: Descartes y su tiempo. La Plata, Yerba buena, 1945. 179 p. (Imagen del tiempo).

Biographical sketch after Ch. Adam and M. Leroy. Some 50 interesting plates with facing explanatory text on the life, works, predecessors and followers of D.

140 HALDANE, ELIZABETH: Descartes, his life and times. London, Murray (New York, Dutton), 1905. xix, 398 p.

Written before AT and Charles Adam's fundamental study, this biography has so far remained the sole English-language life of Descartes. Good journeyman's work, as Harold Laski said.

Review: Charles S. Peirce in The Nation 82: March 22, 1906, 242–43.

142 JANET, PAUL: Descartes, son caractère et son génie. RDM anneé 38, per. 2, 73: 345–69, Jan. 15, 1868. Also in his: Les maîtres de la pensée moderne. Calmann-Lévy, 1883, p. 1–48. Other editions: see no. 2283.

Admirable, finely drawn character sketch of young Descartes, anticipating many research themes of the next sixty years: elevation of DM to the rank of D.'s decisive master piece; the problem of his formative years; the historicity of his autobiographic account in DM; his curiosity, secretiveness, love of travel and spectacles; the apparent contrast between his life and his thought. Spirited defense of Baillet. Rejects French exaggerations and German underrating (H. Ritter's Geschichte der Philosophie, 1829ff.; see no. 3074–75) of Descartes' genius.

144 KOYRÉ, ALEXANDRE: Entretiens sur Descartes. New York-Paris, Brentano, 1944. 113 p. Preface by Robert Tenger.

Substance of three engaging 1938 Cairo lectures (no. 2377): "Le monde incertain," "Le cosmos disparu," "L'univers retrouvé." Opposes Descartes, not to Aristotle and Scholasticism, but to Montaigne; claims that the Cartesian spirit still dominates modern science, although the body of D.'s philosophy and physics is very dead indeed. Good initiation to Descartes when read along with Alquié's no. 127 and Lewis' no. 145.

Reviews: L. Roberts in Isis 37: 1947, 83–84; H. Gouhier in RIP 2: 1939, 405–407; J. Hering in RPPR 19: 1939, 324–25 (of no. 2377).

145 LEWIS, GENEVIÈVE [Mme G. Rodis-Lewis]: René Descartes, Français, philosophe. Tours-Paris, Maison Mame, 1953. 160 p. (Service de la France.)

Brilliant, compact synthesis of D.'s life and work, written with authority, precision, verve. Best introduction for the uninitiated, stimulating to the more advanced.

Reviews: J. Dopp in RPhL 51: 1953, 641; M. Gueroult in RPFE 144: 1954, 439–40; A. Henry in Eph 9: 1954, 377–78; J. Orcibal in DSS no. 23: 1954, 67–68; C.A.V. in RF 47: 1956, 229.

146 LINS, IVAN [i.e., Ivan Monteiro de Barros Lins]: Descartes; época, vida e obra. Preface by Roquette Pinto. Rio de Janeiro, Emiel, 1940. 595 p. Bibliography p. 575–85.

Eight huge, annotated 1937 tercentenary lectures. Popular, vivid, original (partly because of unfamiliarity with major D. literature). One of a "série luminosa de livros admiráveis que vêm consagrado à difusão da cultura no povo brasiliano" (Pinto's Preface, 7). Sees D. as the great precursor of Comte, in the tradition of the first Portuguese translation of DM in the D.-year 1896 [Apostolado positivista do Brazil. Descartes. Discurso sobre o método, tr. Miguel Lemos. Rio de Janeiro, na sede central da igreja positivista do Brazil, Templo de humanidade, Mars 1896, ano CVIII da revolução Franceza e VII da República Brazileira. 12mo. 86 p.]

146a DE SACY, SAMUEL: Descartes par lui-même. Éditions du seuil, 1956. 192 p. (Écrivains de toujours.)

Abundant illustrations and a remarkably good text, most of it by no means "par lui-même," evoke Descartes' time and the intellectual excitement of his extraordinary life. Not a source but a vademecum.

Reviews: L. Millet in Eph 12: 1957, 96; X. Tilliette in Et 292: 1957, 459; B. Rochot in Rsyn 79: 1958, 123–26 (critical, especially of no. 3173a); M. Gueroult in RHLF 59: 1959, 546–47. I. W. Alexander in FS 12: 1958, 156ff.; E. Marcu in RR 49: 1958, 65f.

146b WEIZSÄCKER, CARL FRIEDRICH FREIHERR VON: Descartes und die neuzeitliche Naturwissenschaft. Selbstverlag der Universität Hamburg, 1958. 29 p. (Hamburger Universitätsreden 23.)

In smallest compass, Weizsäcker gives an orderly syllabus of the main points of D.'s thought and scientific contributions, with an original, critical evaluation. D.'s main purpose is firmly viewed as laying the foundations of modern science; D.'s own contributions are judged from the modern viewpoint, with illuminating results. An excellent introduction.

Review: Buchel in Sch 34: 1959, 467.

VI. FUNDAMENTAL INTERPRETATIONS

147 ALAIN [pseud. of Émile Chartier]: "Descartes." In his: Idées; introduction à la philosophie. Hartmann, 1932, 109–99. Reprinted 1947.

"J'ai dit souvent que ce qui nous manque pour comprendre Descartes, c'est l'intelligence" (110). Alain fills this gap with éclat, placing himself, like Descartes, "en dehors de toute discussion, de toute critique" (G. Milhaud's review, 79–80). Contains his "Étude sur Descartes" (1927) and "Sur le Traité des passions" (1928). "Ce petit livre si dense, d'une densité un peu affectée, si original, si riche en suggestions profitables" (A. Brémond, review below, 60), achieves what Alain ascribed to TP: ".... à le lire seulement on prend quelque air et quelque mouvement de cette grande âme" (199). See also no. 1031–35.

Reviews: A. Brémond in Aph 8, no. 4: 1931, 60–68; Gérard Milhaud in Rsyn 14/2: 1937, 78–80.

148 ALAIN [pseud. of Émile Chartier]: "Descartes." In his: Histoire de mes pensées. Gallimard, 1936, 252–57.

Famous description of the Descartes portrait by Frans Hals: "C'est un homme terrible à prendre pour maître. Son œil semble dire: *Encore un qui va se tromper*" (253).

Alain's D. is very much alive, plainly recognizable in that "type de vieux commandant janséniste et polytechnicien, qui savait tout et qui ne croyait rien, hormis l'incroyable .... Ce n'est pas Descartes; rien n'est Descartes; mais enfin c'est le moins étalagiste des hommes que j'ai connus" (253–54). A handful of brilliant pages.

149 ALQUIÉ, FERDINAND: La découverte metaphysique de l'homme chez Descartes. PUF 1950. viii, 384 p. (BPC). Thèse Paris. [Defense, with Gueroult's comment, in RMM 55: 1950, 434–36.] See also no. 1046a–1056.

First great Descartes interpretation since Gilson and Gouhier, rooted in modern philosophical anthropology. A.'s rigorous chronological method, a refusal to interpret later texts in the light of earlier ones, unexpectedly yields "une saisissante vision d'un Descartes découvrant progressivement .... l'Être, et sa situation d'Homme par rapport a l'être" (Sarano's review, 338), passing from "l'espoir mécaniste" through a transcendental distinction between knowledge and being to the "metaphysical discovery of Man" beyond all temptation of ontology. Method and interpretation, irreconcilably at odds with Gueroult's systematic approach (no. 170), are highly original: "On ne peut manquer d'être à la fois séduit et déconcerté par ce genre d'argumentation" (Aimé Patri, review below, 216). Useful chronology of origin and publication of D.'s works in the Appendix.

Review: A. Forest in RQS 52: 1952, 172–77; J. Kopper in PhLit 3: 1951, 130–32; G. Lewis in RPFE 141: 1951, 326–29; A. Patri in RMM 56: 1951, 208–22; R. Prévost in AIHS 4: 1951, 515–18; B. Rochot in RHSA 3: 1950, 277–81; R. Sarano in Eph 6: 1951, 338–42; M. Soriano in Pensée no. 40; 1952, 107–09; A. de Waelhens in RPhL 48: 1950, 576–80; S. Pétrement in JPNP 46: 1953, 247–52; R. Campbell in RScH fasc. 66: 1952, 157–61; I. Fetscher in PhRu 3: 1955, 185–93 (important); L. Oeing-Hanhoff in K 51: 1959–60, 196–217 (critical; see no. 2863b); H. Bouillard in Et 269: 1951, 417f.; H.-D. Gardeil in RSTP 35: 1931, 692f.

150 ASMUS, VALENTIN FERDINANDOVICH: Dekart. Moskva, Gos. izd-vo politicheskoi lit-ry, 1956. 371 p. (In Russian.) See also no. 1091a–c.

Descartes scholarship is more active in the USSR than it was in Czarist Russia (see Index s.v. "Russia"). It has produced substantial critical editions in translation and studies chiefly of his scientific work, but no new translations of important Western D. criticism. Only Kuno Fischer, Fouillée, Krantz are available in Russian, all done before 1910. Asmus' full-length critical work (first printing: 30,000 copies) confirms D.'s reception into the Communist Pantheon as father of French materialism (despite his compromise with Scholasticism) and creator of modern concepts in mathematics and science (forerunner of Pavlov, though his mechanistic materialism, attuned to the rise of the French bourgeoisie, is now superseded by Marxist dialectic materialism.) Philosophical doctrine and Western D. criticism (books only) are treated with considerable acumen, but neither the man nor the spirit of his thinking come alive. Identical approach in the able encyclopedia article by *V. V. Sokolov*, 1952 (see no. 3315, German translation ibid.; also the note to no. 3314), in *Cecile Angrand's* much debated "Les origines françaises du matérialisme" of 1946 (no. 1066), in *Marjorie Barjonet*, "Ce qui mourait et ce qui naissait chez Descartes" (Pensée no. 32: 1950, 21–32). The scriptural text is *Marx*: "Kritische Schlacht gegen den französischen Materialismus" in Marx und Engels, Die heilige Familie, 1845, ch. 4, sec. c. [translations: no. 2663). *F. Alquié* ("Marxisme et cartésianisme," Tmod 1: May 1946, 1378–1400) finds Marxist man dissatisfied and revolutionary because "le fond de sa conscience recèle cet infini, ce pouvoir absolu de dépassement qui, pour Descartes aussi, fonde le cogito" (p. 1398). Alquié counters Angrand's Marxization of Descartes by an equally intrepid Cartesianization of Marx: "La vérité du cogito cartésien est le fond même du Marxisme" (p. 1399). Heidegger might agree, for different reasons.

151 BALZ, A. G. A.: Descartes and the modern mind. New Haven, Yale UP, 1952. xiv, 492 p. Bibliography (486–89).

Claims that D. is "in spirit, in prophetic insight, and in generous ideality the father of the modern mind" (p. viii). A broad, loosely structured exploration of the metaphysics and epistemology of MM, developing the Cartesian image of world, nature, man. Tries to distinguish between "Cartesius," symbolizing "Reason itself," and "René Descartes" as "symbol for every conductor of inquiry" (67), contrasting the systematic aspect with the progressive development of D.'s philosophy. The sum of life-long meditation by an American thinker who found both "Cartesius" and "René Descartes" the more enigmatic the more profoundly he came to understand them.

Reviews: Anon. in RMM 58: 1953, 328–29; L. J. Beck in Nature 171: 1953, 277; E. Denissoff in Thom 16: 1953, 282–88; W. Doney in PhR 62: 1953, 454–57; A. C. Ewing in Mind 63: 1954, 114; A. Gewirth in JRel 33: 1953, 290; W. H. Hay in JP 50: 1953, 563–66 (considers Balz an instrumentalist); T. S. Kuhn in Isis 44: 1953, 285–87; H. D. Spoerl in Pers 34: 1953, 402–03; P. Stubbs in HJ 51: 1952–3, 202–04.

152 BLONDEL, MAURICE: "Le christianisme de Descartes." RMM 4: 551–67, 1896.

"Le christianisme de Descartes, sincère, original, complexe et inconsistant" (567) is diagnosed as an "agnosticisme chrétien" which allows D. to lay down "les conditions d'un positivisme intégral, conséquent, et conscient de ses postulats" (560). Regarding reason and faith, "il n'oppose, il ne sépare, il ne combine pas, il distingue" (563). But a residual of "la foi de tout le monde ...., cette foi banale et commune" (551) perverts D.'s genuine Christianity and reveals its insufficiency. "Le vice profond de son christianisme" is to have suppressed "toute préparation rationnelle de la foi, tout travail de la raison dans la foi, toute intelligence de la foi"(566). Fundamental, deeply penetrating study, unshaken by Gouhier's criticism (no. 168, 187–93, 294–300). *Jacob Epelbaum,* "El agnosticismo de Descartes y su sumisión a lo infinito" (Homenaje, no. 40, v. 2, 311–33) shows that D.'s agnosticism concerning "lo último irracional y no el saber mismo" (321) did not prevent the development of his rationalism and was resolved on the ethical level by "la sumisión a la incomprensibilidad y infalibilidad divinas"; but this participation "en las categorías supremas del Ser" (332) had no Christian character. See also G. Krüger, no. 176 and Blondel on Malebranche's anticartesianism, no. 435b. Also no. 27, and Gouhier's Blondel critique in no. 168, p. 187–93, 294–300.

153 BÖHM, FRANZ: Antikartesianismus: Deutsche Philosophie im Widerstand. Leipzig, Meiner, 1938. vi, 284 p. See also 1266–67.

German "Blut und Boden" contribution to D.'s jubilee; honors him by declaring him the chief philosophical enemy of National Socialist "Weltanschauung." In contrast to dead Cartesian thinking, German thought is "erschliessendes Denken" characterized by depth, dynamism, intensity, "Systemfeindschaft," "Weltweite," mythical roots.

Reviews: E. Cassirer in no. 5, p. 22–26; G. Radetti in GCFI 21: 1940, 117–122, (critical); A. van der Wey in TP 2: 1940, 86–97 (important); RdePh 1941, 80; L. Landgrebe in RomF 55: 1941, 153–54; A. Marc in Aph 14: 1938, suppl. bibl. 80–81.

154 BORKENAU, FRANZ: "Descartes." In his: Der Übergang vom feudalen zum bürgerlichen Weltbild. Studien zur Geschichte der Manufakturperiode. Alcan, 1934 (Schriften des Instituts für Sozialforschung, v. 4), p. 268–383.

Huge study, by a gifted outsider, ignored by D. scholarship. Challenging new interpretation of D. within the movement of ideas from the Renaissance to Pascal, extensively treated in chapters on Molinism, Jansenism, Gassendi, etc. Despite egregious slips in scholarship, reckless conjectures, an unproven and untenable main thesis ("Descartes sucht .... dem aus dem praktischen Verhalten der Manufaktur stammenden Grundsatz der Rechenhaftigkeit metaphysische Bedeutung im Dienste der Apologie der bürgerlichen Gesellschaft zu geben" (371). the book claims serious attention because of the author's uncommon insight, e.g. when noting "die auffallende Tatsache, dass der bedeutendste Begründer des modernen Weltbildes keine Staatstheorie entwickelt hat" (309). Sharp refutation of Borkenau's main thesis in *H. Grossmann*, "Die gesellschaftlichen Grundlagen der mechanistischen Philosophie und die Manufaktur" (ZSoc 4: 1935, 161–64), "critique .... bien plus instructive que ce travail lui-même," as A. Koyré somewhat unjustly remarks (no. 379, vol. 1, 7n).

155 BOWMAN, ARCHIBALD ALLEN: A sacramental universe; being a study in the metaphysics of experience. Vanuxem Lectures, Princeton 1934, edited by J. W. Scott. Princeton, N. J.. Princeton UP, 1939, xviii, 428 p.

Posthumously put together from manuscripts and notes in progress, the book looks forbiddingly difficult; its mystifying title (author's own) refers to the unfinished conclusion which views moral life as process by which man "enters into and enjoys the 'sacrament' of the universe" (Editor, p. vi). However, closer examination shows it to be an extremely rewarding critique of the modern naturalist tendency to pass over the mind-body duality "as if the distinction were wanting in depth and reality" (59). The body of the book is a careful critical examination of philosophy of G. Santayana and A. N. Whitehead, showing that their attempted monism leads to new, irreconcilable dualities: substance and essence in Santayana "becomingness" and permanence in Whitehead, whose system is treated with great penetration and respect. Important complement to Lovejoy's great work on dualism (no. 182). *A. E. Taylor's* review article "Back to Descartes" (Phil 6: 1941, 126–37) is helpful.

Reviews: Ch. Hartshorne in Eth 50: 1940, 364–66; S.P.L. in JP 37: 1940, 19–41; Paul Weiss in PhAb 1: 1939–40, no. 1.

156 BRUNSCHVICG, LÉON: Spinoza et ses contemporains. 3e éd., augm. et revue. Alcan, 1923, p. 239–305.

Great illuminating study of D.'s philosophy as conceptual starting point for Spinoza, Plato towering behind both of them. Rich, subtle analyses of Cartesian epistemology, important as is all of Brunschvicg's work on Descartes.

157 BRUNSCHVICG, LÉON: Le progrès de la conscience dans la philosophie occidentale. Alcan, 1927. Livre 3: "La spiritualité cartésienne." Ch. 3: Descartes."

Only with D. does Montaigne's ideal, "l'humanisme de la sagesse," again take possession of the West. The secret of D.'s revolution is entirely in his "Géométrie" which gave to idealism the tool vainly sought by Plato, the evidence of first verities, the guarantee of the correspondence of universal mathematics with reality (see also no. 358). D. tends towards spiritualist immanence, though with restrictions. Great rationalist interpretation of the history of philosophy; profound analyses of Malebranche, Pascal, Fontenelle, Beyle, etc.

158 BRUNSCHVICG, LÉON: "Descartes." In his: Descartes et Pascal, lecteurs de Montaigne, Neuchâtel, Baconnière, 1942, p. 95–133 (Être et penser, v. 12, reprinted 1945). Also New York, Brentano, 1944, with biographical sketch of Brunschvicg by Robert Tenger.

Descartes opposes Montaigne on every point, though only "après avoir tout accepté de lui" (97). What Montaigne had relegated to nothingness rises again in a "rajeunissement foudroyant": the intimate truth of science, "l'expansion infinie de la raison, la conscience profonde du *moi* impliquant la présence de Dieu" (96). The third act in this intellectual drama is Pascal – "le réalisme va tenter sa revanche sur le spiritualisme" (133). "Émouvant par son intime sérénité" (Cochet, review below, 175), Brunschvicg's last statement on D. may serve as introduction to his earlier work which is ably summarized by Gerard Milhaud in Rsyn 14: 76–78, 1938.

Reviews: Anon. in RPFE 135: 1945, 273–74; G. Bastide in RIP 5: 1951, 78–79; A. M. Boase in FS 2: 1948, 360–61; M.-A. Cochet in RMM 51: 1946, 174–80; A. Guérard in BA 19: 1945, 160–61; R. Lenoir in RTP 35: 1947, 134–36; R. Mehl in RHPR 26: 1946, 315–18; A. Roche in MLJ 28: 1944, 693–94; W. F. M. Stewart in PhQ 2: 365–66, 1952; G. Weill in Renaissance 1: 1943, 445–62; G. Louis in Confluences 15: Dec. 1942, 456–58; R. Lenoir in Rsyn 21: 1947, 114–17; L. Febvre in AESC 6: 1951, 115–17.

159 BRUNSCHVICG, LÉON: "Descartes." In his: Écrits philosophiques, v. 1. PUF, 1951, 11–107. (BPC)

Five studies (1921–37), posthumously reprinted, deal with the position of mathematics and metaphysics in D.'s system, the role of intuition, the relation of D.'s thought to Plato's, D. and Pascal. Two popular commemorative papers in Appendix 305–17. Editor's "Notes bibliographiques" (106–07) usefully refer to parallel sections in B.'s books of which no. 358 offers the clearest statement of his highly original view of D.'s role in the history of ideas.

Reviews: E. Cassirer in no. 5, 43–44; J. Delessalle in MSR 9: 1952, 161–62; M. de Mullewie in TP 15: 1953, 528–29; P. Thévenaz in RTP 3: 1953, 223; P.-M. Schuhl in RPFE 143: 1953, 266–67; A. Stern in Pers 36: 1956, 106–07.

160 CASSIRER, ERNST: Descartes' Kritik der mathematischen und naturwissenschaftlichen Erkenntnis. Dissertation Marburg, 1899. 102 p. Also in his: Leibniz' System in seinen wissenschaftlichen Grundlagen. Marburg, Elwert, 1902, p. 3–102.

Ex ungue leonem: the great historian of philosophical ideas offers as first-fruit a masterly analysis of D.'s criticist epistemology of mathematics of science, his substance concept (substantialization of space, substance and change), his concepts of experience, the infinite, time. Standpoint of the Marburg School.

161 CASSIRER, ERNST: "Descartes." In his: Das Erkenntnisproblem in der Philosophie und Wissenschaft der neueren Zeit. 2. verb. Aufl. Berlin, B. Cassirer, 1911, v. 1, p. 439–505.

Greatest of the author's works on the history of philosophical ideas, the book has a broad D. chapter followed by a discussion of the development of Cartesianism, Pascal to Bayle, unparalleled in its interweaving of related strands of thought without ever blurring the finest doctrinal differences between thinkers. Necessary consequence: Descartes remains the mere locus of a bundle of ideas streaming through him on their turbulent way towards Kant, their appointed goal.

162 CHESTOV, LEON (i.e., Leo Shestov, pseud. of Lev Isakovitch Schwartzmann): "Synov'ia i pasynki vremeni (istoritcheskii zhrebii Spinozy)." Sovremennyia zapiski 25: 1925, 316–42 [signed: Jun. 8, 1922]. French transl. ("Les favoris et les désinherités de l'histoire") and English transl. ("Children and stepchildren of time"): no. 1522.

Strangely beautiful, stirring vision of D. whom "some mighty, insuperable force, which he could not have called by its name and whose name he did not try to discover," Hegel's "Zeitgeist," drove "to banish mystery from our lives at all costs" (English tr., 248). Tremendous view of Spinoza: "he has slain God for history" (273), yet loves Him. Thought speaking the tongue of myth, in the terrifying Old Testament manner.

163 ESPINAS, ALFRED: Descartes et la morale. Études sur l'histoire de la philosophie de l'action. Bossard, 1925. 2 vols. 252, 204 p. Reprinted: Sorlot, 1937.

Vol. 1: La formation du système. Pt. I: Avant le système. 1. Le point de départ de Descartes. Attaques contemporaines contre la religion. Les libertins. 2. Formation des défenseurs de la religion (Descartes à la Flèche). 3. Descartes de 16 à 29 ans (Préoccupations pratiques personelles, le choix d'un état.) 4. Défense des dogmes contre les libertins (Bérulle, Mersenne). *Pt. II: Vers le système.* 1. L'idée initiale de la philosophie de D. (emprunt a Senèque du brutisme; la matière réduite a l'étendue abstraite, parade aux coups du libertinisme.) 3. Pour la morale cartésienne. 4. Platon et Saint-Augustin: emprunts formels. 5. Première rédaction des Méditations (contacts avec les Oratoriens comme théologiens). 6. Rupture avec la théologie (La religion révélée absorbée par la religion naturelle).
Vol. 2: Le système. 1. La morale provisiore. 2. Solution par l'histoire. 3. Exposition dogmatique.

Influential posthumous work. Vol. 1 assembles Espinas' vehemently discussed 1906–07 articles which represent D. as a Catholic apologist, eager to stop Libertinism and to rescue dogma from the fatal encounter with the new science by using the beast-machine concept as "clef de voûte." The analysis of D.'s formative years sees Platonist and Augustinian influences, received through the Oratoire, as decisive. Vol. 2, overshadowed by the first, is a previously unpublished study attempting to distill a definitive "morale" from D.'s later thought, after the removal of the overgrowth of influences. A. Brémond (review below) attacked the author's "érudition incertaine et confuse ou l'arbitraire seul jette des clartés" (288) and his "mauvaise théologie d'universitaire autodidacte, présomptueux et trop pressé" (295). But Gilson, though critical, was impressed and influenced by these "articles si remarquables et d'une analyse si pénétrante" (no. 164, p. 434) which still repay for their wealth of comment on the relationship between D. and earlier thinkers. Besides, Espinas' once discredited main theses have been unexpectedly revived by R. Lefèvre and others.

Reviews: Anon. in RMM 32: suppl. 2, 1–2, 1926; A. Brémond in Aph 4, no. 4, 1926, 288–95; H. Gouhier in no. 168, 20–29 and in RHPh ns 5: 1937, 209–10; F. Olgiati in no. 14, 60–72; R. Tisserand in RHL 33: 1926, 634. See also Blanchet (no. 200) and Teixeira (no. 345). T. de Boer in Neo 14: 1929, 135f.

164 GILSON, ÉTIENNE: La liberté chez Descartes et la théologie. Alcan, 1913. 452 p. (BPC). Thèse Paris: La doctrine cartésienne de la liberté et la théologie, Alcan 1912.

I. La liberté divine: Les textes. Enseignement de La Flèche. L'adversaire de Descartes Les causes finales et l'idée de l'infini. Les sources: Duns Scot et Mersenne. La doctrine cartésienne de la liberté et la théologie de l'Oratoire.
II. La liberté humaine: L'erreur. Rapports entre l'entendement, la volonté et le jugement. La critique de la liberté de l'indifférence. Ses sources. La liberté humaine dans les PP. La liberté de l'indifférence, du De libertate à l'Augustinus (Jansen). Descartes et le Jansénisme naissant. Descartes et les Dogmata theologica du P. Petau.

Though D.'s only weapon against Aristotle was truth, he tried to adapt traditional theology to needs of his science, not to defend the Church, but to protect himself against it by shunning conflict. Although, "historically speaking, this work is now out of date," having been "ably corrected" by Gouhier (Gilson, no. 166, p. xiii and 80, n. 1) it remains a landmark in D. research. For Gilson's defense of his striking theses on divine, human free will, D. and Molinism, early Jansenism, etc. against searching critique of M. de Wulf, L. Levy-Bruhl, V. Delbos, Father Laberthonnière and others, see BSFP 14: 207–58, 1914 (séance du 19 mars 1914). See also no. 248.

Reviews: Anon. in RMM 21, suppl. 3, p. 7, 1913; A. Brémond in Aph 8, no. 4: 1930, 110–17; H. Gouhier in RHPh 5: 1937, 200–01; J. Hoffmans in RNS 21: 1913, 97–102; Gérard Milhaud in Rsyn 14: 1937, 74–76; F. Olgiati in no. 14, 73–75, 175–83. See also Koyré, no. 214.

165 GILSON, ÉTIENNE: Études sur le rôle de la pensée médiévale dans la formation du système cartésien. Deuxième partie des Études de philosophie médiévale, revue et considérablement augmentée (1930). Reprinted: Vrin, 1951. 344 p. (EPM, v. 13).

I. Sources médiévales de quelques doctrines cartésiennes: 1. L'innéisme cartésien et la théologie. 2. D., Harvey et la scolastique. 3. Météores cartésiens et météores scolastiques.
II. Descartes et la métaphysique médiévale. 1. De la critique des formes substantielles au doute méthodique (psychologie de la physique aristotélienne; physique et metaphysique dans le système cartésien; génèse de la Première Méditation). 2. Le cogito et la tradition augustinienne. 3. La preuve de Dieu par la causalité (cause des idées; D. et S. Thomas; psychologie du lecteur scolastique). 4. D. et S. Anselme. 5. Une

nouvelle idée de Dieu. 6. La véracité divine et l'existence du monde extérieur. 7. Anthropologie thomiste et anthropologie cartésienne.
Appendices: 1. Descartes, S. Augustin et Campanella. 2. Descartes en Hollande. 3. La pensée religieuse de D. 4. Spinoza interprète de D.: la preuve cartésienne de l'existence du corps. 5. Critique scholastique du cartésianisme.

Gilson's "Index scolastico-cartésien" (no. 7), his DM commentary (no. 83), and this collection of 15 interrelated studies form the greatest single contribution to the historical understanding of D.'s philosophy, destroying the legend of its invention ab ovo. No comparable work has stood up better, perhaps because Gilson confined himself to laying the foundations instead of erecting a complete structure. Written with precision and graceful ease, the book includes a definitive treatment of D. and Harvey, a comparison of Cartesian and medieval meteorology, and historical explorations of Cartesian key concepts, especially an outstanding study of D.'s critique of substantial forms. Concise "Index des questions traitées." See Garin (no. 209a).

Reviews: A. Brémond in Aph 8, no. 4: 1931, 110–17; R. Dalbiez in RHPh 3: 1929, 464–72; S. V. Keeling in Mind 42: 1933, 75–85; Gérard Milhaud in Rsyn 14: 1937, 74–76.

166 GILSON, ÉTIENNE: "The Cartesian experiment." In his: The unity of philosophical experience. William James lectures 1936–37. New York, Scribner's, 1937, p. 125–220.

Merciless, sometimes sarcastic critique of Descartes "the great dreamer" (148) whose philosophy, "a recklessly conducted experiment to see what becomes of human knowledge when moulded into conformity with the pattern of mathematical evidence" (133), broke down on all fronts: mathematicism, spiritualism, idealism, physics. Astonishing judgment on D. by his greatest historical commentator who as a philosopher found his master in St. Thomas. The book has had no echo whatever in French D. scholarship.

Reviews: J. Dopp in RNS 41: 1938, 476–78; H. Gouhier in VInt June 30, 1938.

167 GILSON, ÉTIENNE: God and Philosophy. New Haven, Yale UP (Oxford UP), 1941. xviii, 147 p. (Powell Lectures in Philosophy at Indiana University, Fifth Series, 1939–40).

Four lectures on the "metaphysical problem of God," continuing the critique of D. (74–108): "Like the innate ideas of Plato, Descartes' innate idea of God was a reminiscence; not, however, the reminiscence of some idea contemplated by the soul in former life, but simply the reminiscence of what he had learned in church when he was a little boy" (82–83); his God "a stillborn God," "an infelicitous hybrid of religious faith and of rational thought" (89). Autobiographical note in the "incomparable little preface" (Veatch, review below, p. 506) explains Gilson's philosophical development and astounding change of attitude towards Descartes.

Reviews: J. Goheen in JP 38: 1941, 712–16; H. Veatch in PPR 1: 1940, 505–10.

168 GOUHIER, HENRI: La pensée religieuse de Descartes. Vrin, 1924. 328 p. (EPM, v. 6). Thèse, École Pratique des Hautes Études, Paris.

I. Les intentions apologétiques de Descartes. II. Les rapports de la raison et de la foi. – Appendix: Le songe de Descartes. La Recherche de la Vérité.

Masterly study of D.'s attitude towards religion in all its aspects, a work of first importance; brings to life the development of his "pensée personnelle," from first conceptions to maturity. Gouhier's Descartes, "incoërciblement fier, cornélien, héroique" (Brémond, Aph 4, no. 4: 298, 1927) takes up God's cause, yet produces a non-religious philosophy. This paradox is ingeniously explored in remarkable analyses of D.'s treatment of Reason vs. Faith, concluding, somewhat surprisingly to more official representatives of the Catholic viewpoint, that "en apportant aux hommes la vraie philosophie, Descartes a donné un allié à la vraie religion" (233). Careful, critical, comprehensive; one of the basic works in the literature. Second edition, considerably augmented and revised, in preparation. See also *Gouhier's* methodological note in Cartesio (no. 35, 414–24) distinguishing three questions in the problem of D.'s religiosity: (a) his sincerity, (b) the Christian elements in his system, (c) Christian vs. Cartesian spirit.

Reviews: A. Brémond in Aph 4, no. 4: 1927, 295–304 (rejects main thesis); A. Forest in Rthom 29 (ns 7): 1924, 596–614; É. Gilson in RMM 32: 1925, 519–37 (reprinted in no. 165, p. 281–98); G. Michaut in RHL 33: 1926, 453; Gérard Milhaud in Rsyn 14: 1937, 73–74; F. Olgiati in no. 14, p. 80–85; L. Teixeira in no. 345, p. 172–87; A. D. Widgery in Mind 34: 1925, 511–13; E. Leroux in Rcr 94: 1927, 463–65.

169 GOUHIER, HENRI: Essais sur Descartes. Vrin, 1937, reprinted 1949. 304 p. (Essais d'art et de philosophie).

I. Comment Descartes est devenu cartésien. II. Un homme content. Le philosophe sans masque. III. L'itinéraire ontologique (le 'je' du cogito). IV. Le malin génie et le bon Dieu. V. L'itinéraire moral. VI. La philosophie de l'homme concret (morale, politique). Appendices: 1. L'historicité du DM. 2. Le songe de Descartes. 3. Le pélérinage de Lorette. 4. 'Larvatus prodeo'. 5. Les diverses formes du doute méthodique.

This small, beautifully written collection of essays may well prove to be the most influential work of the rich 1930's. Its new, enticing D. image and its new view of the architecture of his thought anticipate current French D. scholarship by two decades. From a discussion of D.'s formative years the book rises to magnificent analyses of cogito, Dieu-trompeur, and malin génie in which D.'s movement of thought is intimately, almost lovingly, caught. The book then turns to D.'s "morale" and ends with an anticlimatic, needless defense of his conservative conformism in politics. Gouhier's Descartes is the very opposite of Leroy's: a philosopher without mask, without enigma, without conflict – contented, radiating, just as Frans Hals informally painted him; only the sardonic gleam in the eye (which Alain caught) is missing. Structurally, D.'s metaphysics claims central place. Mathematics and science enter only marginally, while strong emphasis falls on moral philosophy. In unveiling an unsuspected Cartesian political philosophy, Gouhier anticipates not only the findings but the peculiar tone of his latter-day followers; e.g., in D.'s striving to win over the high and mighty, "l'ambition la plus généreuse s'accorde avec le devoir le plus doux" (281). Yet, balance is firmly maintained: this D. remains the irrevocably committed thinker throughout, neither an agnostic nor an apologetic zealot, neither moralizer nor morally obtuse, neither a reckless experimenter nor an archaic fossil. As a living, breathing portrait of Descartes, the book still stands alone.

Reviews: Anon. in RMM 45: 1938, suppl. 3, 17–18; E. Cassirer in no. 5, 51–52; J. Dopp in RNS 39: 1937, 650–56; H.-D. Gardeil in RSPT 34: 1950, 568; G. Mauchaussat in RHPh 6: 1938, 173–81; I. Fetscher in PhRu 3: 1955, 171–76.

170 GUEROULT, MARTIAL: Descartes selon l'ordre des raisons. Aubier, 1953. 2 v. 390, 366 p.

Vol. I: L'âme et Dieu. – 1. Métaphysique cartésienne et ordre des raisons. 2. Le doute; le malin génie. 3–4. Le cogito. 5–6. Deux preuves de Dieu par les effets. 7. Du vrai et du faux. 8. Des essences des corps, de Dieu.
Vol. II: L'âme et le corps (la VIe Méditation). – 9. Existence des choses matérielles. 10. Région de l'entendement: possibilité de l'existence des choses matérielles; théorie générale de la possibilité. 11. Région de l'imagination ; probabilité de l'existence des choses matérielles. 12. Région du sens: certitude de leur existence. 13. Preuve de la distinction réelle de l'âme et du corps. 14. Preuve de l'existence des choses matérielles. 15. Preuve de l'union de l'âme et du corps. 16–18. Du vrai et du faux dans la région du sens. 19–20. Quelques conséquences relatives à la médicine et à la morale.

This most impressive of all systematic Descartes commentaries so far written treats D.'s philosophy rigorously as "profond monument, solide et géométrique, comme une forteresse de Vauban," built by a "penseur de granit" (v. 1, p. 13). The title states its thesis which challenges all previous exegesis: only from an unflinching logical analysis according to the order of arguments ("l'ordre des raisons") does the immense unity and inner coherence of D.'s thought as systematic thought emerge; psychological, historical, chronological "approaches" will not do. See Gueroult's passionate statement cited under no. 193. A contrapuntal "structural analysis" of the nexus rationum clears up apparent contradictions while bringing to light the deeper impasses. The work studies MM as the epitome of D.'s thought, but utilizes all relevant texts. Vol. 2, devoted to the Sixth Meditation, concludes with a 35-page analytical summary of the argument "aussi dense et aussi riche, aussi heureux et aussi beau" as any ever given (Canguilhem's review, 286), and extremely helpful. The tables of content are a veritable outline of Cartesian metaphysics. (Belaval's review below notes inaccuracies in references). The work, which should be consulted on any problem of D.'s metaphysics, has become the center of fundamental controversy over Descartes interpretation. See the Royaumont Colloquium (no. 42), Alquie's review below, V. Goldschmidt's reply in RMM 62: 1957, 67–71, J.-L. Bruch on Gueroult's method applied to Descartes and to Malebranche (RMM 63: 1958, 358–373; see no. 1376a). See also Gueroult's equally monumental work on Malebranche (no. 453b) and the controversy with Gouhier over the ontological argument (no. 270, 270a).

Reviews: Anon. in StU 28: 1954, 433; F. Alquié in RMM 61: 1956, 403–18 (fundamental); Y. Belaval in RMM 60: 1955, 417–45 (critical guide); G. Canguilhem in RPFE 145: 1955, 281–99 (of v. 2); A. Forest in RThom 56: 1956, 549–53; G. Lewis in RPFE 144: 1954, 440–46 (of v.1); G. Rimpot in RScR 29: 1955, 306–09; B. Rochot in RHSA 7: 1954, 182; Kopper, PhLit 9: 1956, 262–70; I. Fetscher in PhRu 3: 1955, 192–98; G. Ducoin in Et, January 1954; A. Robinet, "Variations sur le nom de Descartes," in Crit, August 1958. Also: Nouvelle Gazette (Namur), January 29, 1956; Le Monde, January 7, 1954 (J. Lacroix); Gazette de Lausanne, 1954 (A. Virieux-Reymond); De Tijd (Amsterdam) no. 9, 1955 (B. Delfgaauw); Ami du clergé October 22, 1953; MerF 318: August 1953, 756 (A. Ouy); La Croix, 28 July 1953; Nouvelle critique, Sept.-Oct. 1956, 46ff. (Kleber).

171 HAMELIN, OCTAVE: Le système de Descartes. Alcan, 1911. 2e éd., revue, par L. Robin. Préface par Émile Durckheim. Alcan, 1921. xiv, 400 p. Spanish translation (1949): no. 2177.

Ch. 3–7, Méthode. 6, Déduction, intuition. 8, Doute. 9, Cogito. 10–11, Certitude. 12, Pensée. 13–15, 19, Dieu (preuves, attributs, Dieu et monde.) 16, Existence des choses matérielles. 17–18, Âme – corps. 19, Physique (théorie du mouvement, de la matière.) 22–23, Psychologie (intelligence, passions, volonté.) 24, Esthétique, morale.

Posthumously published course (1903–04). Broke new ground by asserting against Liard the primacy of metaphysics and the systematic unity in D.'s thought. The beautifully reasoned book analyzes the system not from D.'s own but from Hamelin's neo-idealistic standpoint. Important and influential.

Reviews: Anon. in RMM 19: 1911, sb 1, 1–2; É. Callot in no. 447a, 11–45 (on the "system" approach); A. Carlini in no. 4, 53–59 (on neo-idealistic interpretation); J. Guéville in APC ser 4, v. 13, no. 163: 516–23, 1911–12; Régis Jolivet, La notion de substance (Beauchesne, 1929), 114–18; Gérard Milhaud in RSyn 14: 71, 1937; M. Muller in no. 316, 313–52, 157–58; F. Olgiati in no. 185, 215–16.

171a HEGEL, GEORG WILHELM FRIEDRICH: "Descartes." In his: Vorlesungen über die Geschichte der Philosophie, 3. Bd. (Sämtliche Werke, Jubiläumsausgabe, v. 19, 328–67.)

Hegel authoritatively enunciates the fundamental view of Descartes as founding genius and initiator of all modern philosophy, leaving even Bacon outside the pale. "Hier, können wir sagen, sind wir zuhause .... mit ihm hebt die Bildung, das Denken der neueren Zeit an": Descartes tore thinking loose from Scholasticism and "philosophizing theology" and made the inseparable connection of thought and Being the center of philosophy. His two basic and equivalent doctrines, cogito and ontological proof, establish thinking as the pure culmination of inwardness (Innerlichkeit) and thus initiate the rule of "the Protestant principle" of autonomous interiority. All else in D.'s philosophizing is secondary by comparison, including dualism and Cartesian mechanism, which fails to account for the organic, and rather splendidly so: "Es ist aber das Grosse darin, dass das Denken in seinen Bestimmungen fortgeht, und dass es diese Gedankenbestimmungen zu dem Wahrhaften der Natur macht" (362). *Ludwig Feuerbach*, in his Geschichte der neueren Philosophie, 1833 (no. 1889), sees the cogito as "das Wesen des Geistes" and strives for a way out of its pure subjectivity and radical split between subject and object. But he rejects the Hegelian view of D. as the originator of modern philosophy in favor of Bacon. *Johann Eduard Erdmann* (Versuch einer wissenschaftlichen Darstellung der neueren Philosophie, 1834–53; no. 1844a) marks the transition from the Hegelian approach to the new professionalism in the history of philosophy, which will eventually lead to historicism. He fully spells out Hegel's "Protestant principle"; his critical evaluation, chiefly technical, rejects charges of inconsistency against Descartes as failing to understand the fundamental turn which philosophy took with him. See Hagmann's useful monograph (no. 10); on the cogito in German Idealism also F. Medicus (no. 2687).

172 HEIDEGGER, MARTIN: Sein und Zeit. Erste Hälfte. Halle a.S., Niemeyer, 1927, p. 24–26, 89–101. (Jahrbuch für Philosophie und phänomenologische Forschung, v. 8). Reprinted (6th ed.) and English translation: no. 2203.

Heidegger has always considered Descartes a decisive thinker. In Sein und Zeit he makes the first attempt to come to grips with the cogito. Descartes misses "den Seinssinn des *sum*" in the cogito (24) because he transfers medieval ontology upon the res cogitans as an ens creatum. Consequently the decisive relation between time and the cogito does not even become a problem; in this, even Kant dogmatically follows Descartes. Chapter 3 (sec. 19–21) deals with D.'s failure to identify "das innerweltlich Seiende" as "Welt"; the concept of "world" as res extensa "jumps" both "Sein als Zuhandenheit" and "Sein als Substanz." The "phenomenological destruction of the cogito sum" (89), promised for the abandoned sequel to S & Z, is replaced by the lectures on Nihilism (1940, no. 172b), a cogito critique from the viewpoint of "Überwindung der Metaphysik." See Hagmann (no. 10, 157–64), A. de Waelhens in RNS 41: 1938, 574–76; E. Nicol in RMM 61: 1956, 303–27.

172a HEIDEGGER, MARTIN: "Die Zeit des Weltbildes." In his: Holzwege. Frankfurt a.M., Klostermann, 1950, p. 69–104.

This lecture (1943) contains a condensation (91–103) of the extensive analysis offered in no. 172b. It defines D.'s central place in modern metaphysics: "Zur Wissenschaft als Forschung kommt es dann, und nur dann, wenn die Wahrheit zur Gewissheit des Vorstellens sich gewandelt hat .... Die gesamte neuzeitliche Metaphysik, Nietzsche mit eingeschlossen, hält sich in der von Descartes angebahnten Auslegung des Seienden und der Wahrheit" (80). Though German philosophy since Leibniz has essentially transformed D.'s position, it failed to overcome it and thus it indirectly strengthened it; "dagegen hat die blosse Descartes-Scholastik und ihr Rationalismus jede Kraft für die fernere Gestaltung der Neuzeit eingebüsst" (91).

172b HEIDEGGER, MARTIN: "Der europäische Nihilismus." In his: Nietzsche, v. 2. Pfullingen, Neske, 1961, p. 31–256.

The title of this 1940 course marks Heidegger's definitive evaluation of Descartes: in founding modern subjectivism, D. lays the foundations of European Nihilism, in Nietzsche's understanding of the term. Between D. and Nietzsche, modern metaphysics rises and sets; its "Wesensmöglichkeiten" are now exhausted; in Nietzsche, it has been turned upside down ("die Umkehrung,") and a new understanding of Being must be sought. The heart of the argument is an elaborate cogito analysis which considers Protagoras, Descartes, and Nietzsche. Descartes' cogito was the metaphysical foundation for liberating man in this new freedom and self-guaranteed autonomy. With D., "das gesamte Menschentum und seine Geschichte" moves out of Christian speculative truth into the subjective representation (Vorstellung) of "das Seiende," establishing that subject-object relationship without which "die neuzeitliche Herrschaftsstellung des Menschen" would have been impossible (187–88). From Descartes on, "metaphysics is anthropomorphism" (127). Nietzsche could not but misread D.'s cogito as an "ego volo," a declaration of the Will to Power; he did not realize how utterly Cartesian he was in his attack upon Descartes. In Nietzsche, D.'s quest for certain truth as avoidance of error is carried to the ultimate: now truth itself is in essence error, since the Will to Power makes true what it must will to be true, within its own "aggressive" concept of "justice." Written in clear, uncomplicated German and with deliberate repetitions, this large study is easier to grasp than the difficult 1943 summary (no. 172a).

173 HUSSERL, EDMUND: Méditations cartésiennes. Traduit par Gabrielle Peiffer et Emanuel Levinas. Collin, 1931. vii, 136 p. Reprinted: Vrin, 1947 (BTP). – Cartesianische Meditationen und Pariser Vorträge, ed. S. Strasser. The Hague, Nijhoff, 1950. xxxi, 244 p. (Husserliana, v. 1). Italian and English translations: no. 2253.

Husserl develops the core of his own philosophy in a Cartesian "mouvement de la pensée" and in intimate contact with D.'s metaphysics. This second of the three main statements of his phenomenology, originally intended to develop into the "Hauptwerk meines Lebens" (Husserliana, v. 1, p. xxvii) notes his debt to Descartes and defines his point of separation from him. The difficult French version is now superseded by Husserliana, v. 1, which gives the German text of the Paris lectures of 1929, accompanied by Husserl's helpful outline, the original German version of the Méditations cartésiennes in their hitherto unpublished final form, and Roman Ingarden's important critique of the manuscript which influenced Husserl's revision of it. This volume is now the key text for the relation between Husserl and Descartes, but see also no. 174 and no. 2251 (*Husserl's* Formale und transzendentale Logik).

Reviews etc.: no. 174.

174 HUSSERL, EDMUND: Die Krisis der europäischen Wissenschaften und die transzendentale Phänomenologie. Eine Einleitung in die phänomenologische Philosophie. Ed. Walter Biemel. The Hague, Martinus Nijhoff, 1954. xxii, 559 p. (Husserliana, v. 6). First publication, other editions and transl.: no. 2254.
Erste Philosophie (1923/24), ed. Rudolf Böhm. 2 v. The Hague, Nijhoff, 1956, 1959. (Husserliana, v.7, 8.)

According to Böhm, the "Cartesian Meditations" are the "Erste Philosophie" of 1923–24 in the form which Husserl gave it for publication; but "Erste Philosophie" points forward to "Krisis" as well as to the "Cartesian Meditations". It contains important texts on the "Cartesian way to transcendental reduction", on cogito and epoché, and it sharply works out the role of Locke and English empiricism in the Cartesian succession (chief texts noted in *no. 2254a*). *Jean Wahl's* incisive paper "Jugements de Husserl sur Descartes et sur Locke" in the Husserl Colloquium at Royaumont (*no. 3528a*, with discussion) is based on "Erste Philosophie" and on "Die Krisis", which is Husserl's last work and third definitive statement. Here Descartes appears as "der urstiftende Genius der gesamten neuzeitlichen Philosophie" (p. 75). Dualism stems from the acceptance of science as cognitional model (§ 10ff.); Descartes inherits it as an unchallenged presupposition, and it falsifies the cogito (§ 16–21). In the epoché of the radical doubt, the "Galilean certainty of a universal and absolutely pure world of bodies," as well as the distinction between mere sensual experience and pure thought, should have been bracketed out. "Le bon sens" prevented D. from doing so; and the fatal psychological substitution "des eigenen seelischen Ich für das ego" prevents him from seeing "dass das ego, sein durch die Epoché entweltlichtes Ich .... unmöglich in der Welt als Thema auftreten kann, da alles Weltliche eben aus diesen Funktionen seinen Sinn schöpft, also auch das eigene seelische Sein, das Ich im gewöhnlichen Sinne" (p. 81–82). This text marks the exact point of separation between Husserl and Descartes. Valuable auxiliary texts (Beilagen V–X, XVI, p. 392–431, 455–58) greatly expand and elaborate the compressed main text. They include a striking analysis of Meditation I (Beilage VI, p. 402–11).

See *Alexandre Löwit* on epoché and Cartesian doubt in RMM 62: 1957, 399–415 and note to *no. 2564*; *Gaston Berger*, Le cogito dans la philosophie de Husserl, Aubier, 1941, ch. 6, 121–38 (reviewed by E. Bréhier, RPFE 132: 1942, 173–76 and by de Waelhens in RNS 43: 1941–45, 329–32). Also *Pierre Thévenaz*'s brilliant "La question du point de départ radical chez Descartes et chez Husserl" in *no. 3409*, 1952, 9–30, discussed by Gueroult in *no. 170*, v. 2, 318–23.

Also: A.-A. Devaux in Eph 9: 1954, 260–83 (Is phenomenology a Neocartesianism?); M. Farber in PhR 44: 1935, 380–87; P. Filiasi Carcano in RicF 6: 1936, 18–34; J. S. Fulton in PhR 49: 1940, 285–308 ("The Cartesianism of phenomenology"); M. Hagmann in *no. 10*, 142–48; V. J. McGill in JP 48: 1951, 362–68; A. Massolo in GCFI 20: 1939, 434–52; H.-L. Miéville in SPhS 1: 1941, 1–19; F. Olgiati in *no. 14*, 209–12 with additional references; H. J. Pos in ANTWP 31: 1937, 23–38; P. Ricoeur in RPhL 52: 1954, 75–109; Francisco Romero, "Descartes y Husserl," in *no. 39*, 241–62, reviewed by W. S. Weedon in PPR 1: 1940–41, 249–50; S. Vanni-Rovighi in *no. 35*, 767–80 on the cogito in Husserl and Descartes; M. A. Virasoro in *no. 40*, v. 3, 203–42; A. de Waelhens in RNS 41: 1938, 571–89; H. Wagner in PhRu 1: 1953–54, 93ff.

Reviews of no. 173: Anon. in RMM 39: 1932, suppl. 1, 1–2; RMM 57: 1952, 95–96; F. J. Brecht in Univ. 6: 1951, 1021–22; G. Berger in Eph 5: 1950, 265–66; A. Millán-Puelles in RevF 10: 1951, 217–19; J. Paumen in RIP 5: 1951, 400–404; F. I. G. Rawlins in Nature 166: 1950, 919–21; R. Rhees in Mind 60: 1951, 272–74; A. Schutz in PPR 11: 1950–51, 421–23; J. A. Vásquez in NEF 4, no. 13: 1953, 53–58; R. Verneaux in Aph 13, no. 1: 1937, 73–77.

Reviews of no. 174: F. J. Brecht in Univ. 10: 1955, 975; H.-D. Gardeil in RSPT 41: 1957, 196; A. Gurwitsch in PPR 16: 1955–56, 380–99; 17: 1956–57, 370–98; H. Kunz in StP 15: 1955, 238–39; G. Lehmann in Dlit 77: 1956, 10–13; L. Martínez Gómez in PenM 11: 1955, 83–85.

175 JASPERS, KARL: Descartes und die Philosophie. Berlin, de Gruyter, 1937. 104 p. Reprints and French translation: no. 2293.

The German Existentialist undertakes a deeply searching revaluation of the enigmatic person and philosophy of D., a climactic figure who gave fiery impetus to thought, but in the wrong direction. Calls D.'s scientific attitude archaic: Galileo and Leibniz were the true representatives of modern "Wissenschaftsgesinnung." Original, independent, controversial. See E. Cassirer's important critical discussion in no. 5, 18–22, 38–39. *Gertrud Kahl-Furthmann* charges Jaspers with "breaking into Descartes' world" with existentialist categories that fail to accommodate Descartes' thought. The result, she claims, is not damage to Descartes but critical failure on Jaspers' part. (ZPF 14: 1960, 127–38; see no. 2328a).

Reviews: Anon. in RMM 62: 1957, 721; A. G. A. Balz in JP 35: 1938, 171–74; R. Boehm in Eph 11: 1956, 507; J. S. Dickie in PhQ 1: 1951, 274–76; J. Dubois in RSPT 41: 1957, 197f.; Guérin in RHPR 18: 1938, 537–38; G. Galli in no. 209, 330–31; M. Hagmann in no. 10, 172–83; N.B. in RF 30: 1939, 285; M. deMullewie in TP 18: 1956, 500; R. in RMM 46: 1939, 534–35; A. de Waelhens in RNS 41: 1931, 576–88; H. Regnier in Aph 14: 1938, suppl. bibl. 82; B. Groethuysen in NRF 51: 1938, 507–08; Kern in Sch 33: 1958, 457–58.

176 KRÜGER, GERHARD: "Die Herkunft des philosophischen Selbstbewusstseins." Logos T 22: 225–72, 1933. [Reprint: Darmstadt, 1963.]

Outstanding modern German study, hitherto entirely overlooked even by German scholars. Profound assessment of D.'s historical position which underlies the singularity and hidden insecurity of modern metaphysics. D.'s universal doubt "kehrt sich .... im letzten verschwiegenen Grunde gegen den christlichen Glauben" (242); he founds the freedom of philosophizing "aller göttlichen Allmacht *zum Trotz:* hier is keine christliche Innerlichkeit, sondern hier beginnt .... der Aufstand gegen das Christentum, den wir die Aufklärung nennen"(246).Outstanding treatment of D.'s ethics ("générosité," translated as "edler Stolz"), the true meaning of which D. is thought to have concealed. D. does not deny God, he turns away from him: surely he is not a Christian believer, much less a Catholic apologist. His ideal is the strong mind who does not hope for help but helps himself: yet Christianity leaves a residue of doubt in man's own power. The Cartesian problem of autonomous, free philosophizing founded in "Selbstbewusstsein" is still unresolved today. A truer, deeper analysis than Jaspers'. I. Fetscher (PhRu 3: 1935, 170, n. 12) finds Krüger influenced by M. Leroy (no. 124) who sees D.'s metaphysics as a mere screen for his revolutionary and social thought. However, this possible influence does not affect Krüger's argument, as Fetscher admits.

177 LABERTHONNIÈRE, LE P. LUCIEN: Œuvres de Laberthonnière, ed. by Louis Canet. Vol. 1, 2: Études sur Descartes. Vrin, 1935. viii, 468; 360 p. Vol. 3: Études de philosophie cartésienne et premiers écrits philosophiques. Vrin, 1938. X, 590 p.

Vol. I: Introduction (Le dualisme cartésien). I. La méthode. II. La métaphysique. III. La psychologie.
Vol. 2: IV. La morale. V. La religion. – App.: La physique d'Aristote et la physique de Descartes.
Vol. 3: Première Partie: Descartes. I. Le système de D. (1931). II. Deux essais sur la certitude cartésienne. III. Autonomie et héteronomie dans la certitude cartésienne. IV. La théorie de la certitude chez D. et la théorie de la foi chez les scolastiques. V. Naturel et surnaturel chez D. et chez les scolastiques. VI. Sagesse cartésienne et sagesse chrétienne. VII. Critique de l'attitude cartésienne. – Seconde partie: Les cartésiens. I. De Descartes à Spinoza. II. Sagesse cartésienne et sagesse spinoziste. III. Descartes, Malebranche et Leibniz. – Troisième partie: Premiers écrits philosophiques. I. L'esprit cartésien et l'esprit scolastique (1884). V. Cartésianisme.

Posthumous work, written 1905–15, includes Laberthonnière's 1909–11 APC articles. Violently debated interpretation of D. as a practical, utilitarian, reform-minded champion not of religion but of a science designed to conquer the world; Cartesian man is aware of God behind him but he no longer sees God before him. Vols. 1, 2 comprehensively survey D.'s philosophy; v. 3 adds late studies of D., Spinoza, Malebranche and Leibniz, and a youthful essay expressing author's leanings towards a Cartesian independence of reflection and his "horreur du ghetto scolastique," as editor terms it (v. 3, 313). Work condemned (Acta Sedis Apost. 29: 13, 1937) not for preferring D., but for attacking official teachings and ministry. Repetitious writing, eloquent and superficially clear, recalls J. Dedieu's characterization of the celebrated Oratorian's rambling talk: ".... à travers l'emploi des formules hermétiques, un indéfinissable assemblage d'affirmations péremptoires et d'imprécises notions" (RHL 44: 1937, 277).

Reviews: E. Bréhier in RMM 42: 1935, 533–47; C. Bustos ("Un Descartes falsificado") in E 57: 1937, 531–40; H.-D. Gardeil in RSPT 25: 1936, 170–72 and 27: 1938, 635–37; É. Gilson in VInt 34: 1935, 302–05; H. Gouhier in RechPh 5: 1935–36, 525–29 and in RHPh 5: 1937, 209–10; Guérin in RHPR 16: 1936, 83–88; S. V. Keeling in Phil 11: 1936, 336–38; L. Lavelle in no. 11, p. 33–40; F. Olgiati in no. 14, p. 168–70; L. Pelloux in no. 35, p. 685–93; A. Pierini in GCFI 21: 1940, 350–68 (Laberthonnière and his critics); M. R. in Aph 12, no. 3, suppl. bibl.: 45–46, 1947 (on the condemnation of work); J. Segond in Eph 1: 1940, 27–33. See also M. M. d'Hendecourt in RMM 63: 1960, 52–57.

178 LAPORTE, JEAN: Le rationalisme de Descartes (1945). Nouvelle édition revue et augmentée d'un index et d'une table des textes. PUF, 1950. xx, 511 p. (BPC).

Livre I: Nature de la raison. La connaissance: méthode, facultés, objets, origine. Livre II: Valeur de la raison. 1. Certitude et vérité. 2. Limites de la connaissance rationnelle. 3. En deça de la raison: l'union de l'âme et du corps. 4. Au delà de la raison: l'infini.
Livre III: Religion et raison. La religion considerée en elle-même, dans ses rapports avec la physique, avec la morale. Conclusion: Descartes est-il rationaliste?

Laporte defines rationalism as admission of the "réalité spécifique de la raison, sa valeur universelle et sa suffisance" (470). Finds that D. is not rationalist in this particular sense, his philosophy not a system but rather a pluralism, his attitude an authentic "empirisme radical et integral" (477). Meticulous analyses, supported by a stupendous array of texts, take up D.'s views regarding nature, the value of reason, its relation to religion, covering most basic themes of his metaphysics. Cf. the notes to no. 347a (continuity of time?), no 2450 (finality), 2451 (liaison néccssairc), 2454 (méthode), and no. 291 (étendue, liberté). "Volume ottimo per la serietà e scrupulosità dell'intento e delle ricerche. La tesi, in vero, non è molto nuova ...." (A. Carlini in no. 4, p. 175). See also L. Lavelle in no. 11, 17–19, 23–31.

Reviews: Anon. in RMM 51: 1946, 277; A. Carlini in no. 4, 175–80; C. Ferro in RFNS 42: 1950, 207–08; M. de Gandillac in RScH ns 47: 1947, 288–90; M. Giorgiantonio in S 19: 1951, 313–16; A. Koyré in Eur 24: May 1946, 116–24; A. Mercado Vera in Cuad 1: 1948, 88–95; P. Mesnard in Eph 5: 1950, 175–78; C. Ottaviano in S 1947: 223–24; J. F. Thomas in Rsyn (ns 22) no. 1: 1948, 73–85. Critical discussion: I. Fetscher in PhRu 3: 1955, 176–85.

179 LEFEBVRE, HENRI: Descartes. Éditions Hier et Aujourd'hui, 1947. 312 p (Grandes figures.) Polish translation: no. 2484.

Attractive long essay, from the viewpoint of dialectic historical materialism Naturally, DM becomes a manifesto of the rising liberalistic bourgeoisie and its industrial civilization. Ch. 2 ("Les contradictions cartésiennes") is a running polemic against prevalent D. criticism, insisting that Cogitationes privatae and Dream mark the ideological difficulties from which methodical doubt freed Descartes in a process of increasing purification of his thought, though the doubt cannot overcome the consequences of the split between thought and world. This "solitary hero of knowledge" is also "le type éthnographique du sorcier .... maudit et redouté," the outsider who anticipates the solitude of the modern intellectual, the man of transition, complex and troubled (131). The main emphasis, though, falls upon D.'s scientific work and its epistemological underpinnings. Thoughtful, rewarding study, without Borkenau's impetuous, brash freshness (see no. 154).

Reviews: R. Bouvier in Rsyn 63, no. 1: 92–98, 1948; C. Ferro in RFNS 42: 211–15, 1950; R. Taton in AIHS 2: 498–500, 1949; E. Duprat in RPFE 140: 1950, 204–05.

179a LEFÈVRE, ROGER: La vocation de Descartes. PUF 1956. 228 p. (BPC). See notice to no. 179d.

I. La confection du Discours. II. La jeunesse du doute: l'enquête, 1606–1618 (livre de famille, livres d'école, livre du monde). III. La maturité du doute: la méthode, 1619–1620. IV. La fécondité du doute: la doctrine, 1620–1637.

179b LEFÈVRE, ROGER: L'humanisme de Descartes. PUF, 1957. viii, 284 p. (BPC). See notice to no. 179d.

I. La vie morale. 1. Les principes moraux. 2. L'expérience morale. 3. Le progrès moral. 4. L'idéal moral.
II. La vie sociale. 1. Les sources (sentiments; évènements; documents). 2. La doctrine (peuple; prince; philosophe.) 3. La pratique (politique; technique; devenir).
III. La vie religieuse. 1. La situation (libertinage; apologie). 2. L'intention (actes; idées). 3. La prétention (métaphysique; physique).

179c LEFÈVRE, ROGER: Le criticisme de Descartes. PUF 1958. 340 p. (BPC). See notice to no. 179d.

Critique de la pensée sensible. I. L'exploration métaphysique (délivrance de l'âme; renaissance du monde.) II. L'explication physique (Physiologie du sensible: le mouvement. Biologie du sensible: le sentiment. Psychologie du sensible: le jugement).
Critique de la pensée pure. I. Le fondement de la raison, (Le procès des certitudes; les lacunes de la pensée; les sources de l'évidence). II. Le mouvement de la raison: genèse du doute; genèse de la certitude; l'essor de la métaphysique). Conclusion: Le message de Descartes. Appendices.

179d LEFÈVRE, ROGER: La bataille du "cogito". PUF, 1960. 231 p. (BPC)

I. Le cheminement: 1. Existence spirituelle (limitation du doute; délimitation de l'évidence; être et connaître). 2. Essence spirituelle (le sujet pensant). 3. Puissance spirituelle.
II. L'engagement: 1. Bataille de la distinction (distinction essentielle; d. substantielle). 2. Bataille de l'évaluation (le Moi). 3. Bataille de l'explication (aspect intuitif, déductif). Conclusion critique.

"A 40 ans, Descartes imprime, et le doute méthodique paraît" (V 1). This fatuously terse sentence opens an enormous work of 1100 pages in 4 volumes (we cite V, H, C, B), with more to come (Rêveries cartesiennes). With sensitivity, technical virtuosity, clarity, Lefèvre unveils in relentless symmetry and sententiousness his "true Descartes": a religious moralist and Catholic apologist à la Espinas. Lefèvre's discussion of D.'s metaphysics is admirable (see also *his* small La métaphysique de Descartes, PUF, 1959). Descartes moves through four levels of the doubt: empiric, methodic, metaphysic, didactic (i.e., moralist). C and D view him at the fourth and highest of these levels; the analyses of doubt and cogito follow the finest nuances of the masterfully handled texts; the treatment of the Objections and Responses is of exceptional clarity. Penetrating discussion of D.'s theory of sensation in C. For a careful appraisal of V, H. and C see Bannan (no. 22).
Lefèvre's Descartes philosophizes not in a quest for certainty but out of "une sorte de besoin joyeux de plénitude spirituelle" (V 96). Cartesianism is not a philosophical position but "un effort d'amélioration de la nature par la culture [sic], un appel à l'épanouissement de la liberté en verité, une ascension du vouloir .... vers l'univers et vers Dieu. D'un mot, un humanisme" (H viii). The historical setting is enticingly simple: chiefly the Church vs. Atheism, Science vs. the Church. Descartes vanquishes in one blow Atheism and Scholasticism, saving the Church from Science, and Science from the Church. One whole book (H) is given to this "historical" Descartes. In its center is a full-fledged political philosophy woven together from

the ad hoc comments of D., that profoundly unpolitical thinker; the sides of the triptych are a system of ethics and a philosophy of religion, both also by Descartes. The political philosophy is a marvelous web of sophisms designed to refute Machiavelli by deodorizing him. In V and H, the "penseur de granit" looks more like a "penseur de beurre," full of wholesome goodness and yearning for the mould: "Contraint naguère de 'supprimer', pour ne pas heurter l'Église, une physique dont le mérite est de s'ajuster à l'Église; désireux maintenant de l'extraire de l'ombre ou elle s'ensevelit sans cesser de s'enrichir, Descartes entend s'assurer qu'elle ne sera pas refusée par ceux qu'elle prétend servir [the Jesuits?] et cherche a créer le climat qui la rendra désirable" (V 7). Every feature of this "new" Descartes has its paternity (mostly unacknowledged) in Gouhier, Espinas, Cantecor, Gilson, M. Leroy and others. The composite image derives its plausibility from the massive omission (apart from generalities and apologetic claims) of D.'s mathematics and physics; from shifting the whole weight of argument to his moral utterances; and from introducing conjectures as if they were facts. Father Robert Lenoble patiently examined Lefèvre's claim to historicity, saw the rise of "une sorte de scolastique intra-cartésienne" in which masses of detail obscure the great structures, and warned of D. scholarship degenerating into an interminable, barren battle of the texts (his review article below). However, Lefèvre's treatment of D.'s metaphysics is unimpaired (though not unaffected) by his disquieting historical operations.

Reviews: X. Tilliette in Et 292: 1957 (V) and Et 296: 1958, 271 (H); P. Burgelin in RHPR 38: 1958, 202–203 (H); R. Campbell in RScH 91: 1959, 420 (H); D. B. Hawkins in Er 11: 1958, 199–201 (V, H); R. Lenoble in RMM 63: 1958, 349–57 ("La vocation et l'humanisme de D."); A. Montefiore in Phil 35: 1960, 173–74 (H); W. del Negro in PhLit 11: 1958, 59–62 (H); B. Rochot in Rsyn 79: 1958, 129–30 (H); R. Schaerer in RTP 8: 1958, 154–55 (V, H); S. Wermlund in Lychnos 1957–58, 368–69 (H); J. Collins in Cross Currents 9: 1959, 166 (C); E. Denissoff in RPhL 57: 1959, 100–105 (V, C); M. Varin d'Ainvelle in Eph 14: 1959, 100–105 (V, C); J. F. Bannan in Rmet 13: 1959–60, 412–38 (see no. 22); W. Röd (important) in PhLit 14: 1961, 24–26 and AGP 43: 1961, 126–52; R. Schaerer in RTP 11: 1961, 100 (C); J. Colette in RPhL 58: 299–301 (Métaph. de D.); E. F. Kaehlin in PPR 22: 1961, 128–29 (V, B); B. E. Jacob in PPR 18: 1958, 423 (H).

180 [LÉVY-BRUHL, LUCIEN]: "Le 'Descartes' de Lucien Lévy-Bruhl." Par *Étienne Gilson.* RPFE 147: 1957, 432–51.

Lévy-Bruhl's challenging unpublished Descartes course at the Sorbonne left deep traces upon French D. scholarship. Gilson reconstructs the essence of this course from his 1904–06 notes and his recollections. Lévy-Bruhl was first in distinguishing between image, doctrine, and goal of D. The changing D. image since 1650 is traced with emphasis on Voltaire and Cousin (the early naive, the late eclecticist and spiritualist Cousin); Gilson adds valuable comment on the difference between an image and an interpretative argument. After discussing precursors and originality of D., Lévy-Bruhl turned to his most influential proposition, critically discussed by Gilson, that D.'s ultimate goal was not a new metaphysics but a new physics. See also the Descartes chapter in *Lévy-Bruhl's* History of modern philosophy in France, 1899, p. 1–37 (reprints: no. 2523) and his brief note on "The Cartesian spirit and history" in the Cassirer-Festschrift (1935, p. 191–96; see no. 2524).

181 LIARD, LOUIS: Descartes. Baillière, 1882. 230 p. 2nd ed. 1903. 3rd ed. Alcan, 1911 (BPC). 299 p.

A pathbreaking study which turned the traditional viewpoint upside down by taking method and physics to be D.'s all-important concern, while "ce qui s'y trouve inséré de métaphysique peut en être détaché sans blessure" (141). This interpretation profoundly influenced Charles Adam, Lévy-Bruhl, M. Blondel, Laberthonnière and their generation; it is still upheld, with modifications, by Descartes scholars of widely varying observance. The work was at once attacked as "une espèce de coup d'état universitaire. Il consomme l'abandon de la dogmatique cartésienne par la philosophie officielle .... Descartes serait ainsi un précurseur des positivistes" (Mgr. Bourquard in his review below, 187, which represented "une leçon de catéchisme à Descartes, ainsi qu'à l'auteur"; 377). Today it is Descartes who is made to administer this "leçon de catechisme" to those who see in him chiefly the pathbreaker of modern science.

Reviews: L.-C. Bourquard in Bibliogr. catholique 65: 187–95, 372–80, 1882; L. Dauriac in RMM 33: 1926, 417–21; H. Gouhier in no. 168, p. 12–20; O. Hamelin in no. 171, p. 23–29 (attacks Liard's main thesis); P. Janet in no. 142; G. Milhaud in Rsyn 14: 1937, 70–71; F. Olgiati in no. 14, p. 115–19; G. Rebière in RCC 12/1: 97–106, 1903–04; Ch. Renouvier in CrPh 11/1: 81–95, 145–56, 195–204. Mar. 11, Apr. 10, Apr. 29, 1882. See also L. Dauriac's commemorative article in RMM 33: 1926, 417–21.

182 LOVEJOY, ARTHUR ONCKEN: The revolt against dualism. An inquiry concerning the existence of ideas. Chicago, Open Court – New York, Norton, 1930. xii, 325 p. (Paul Carus Foundation Lectures, no. 2).

Brilliant analysis of the 20th c. monistic "revolt" against Descartes, 17th c. philosophy, and their twin dualism, one epistemological (theory of representative perception, the book's main theme), the other psycho-physical. Modern philosophical and physical theories receive penetrating discussion with two important chapters on Bertrand Russell and A. N. Whitehead whose Process and Reality, however, is not considered. *Whitehead* answered Lovejoy in Adventures of Ideas (1933, ch. 11, sec. 23; see 3556): "Throughout the universe there reigns the union of opposites which is the ground of dualism." The author's basic position is epitomized in a "myth" that explains why the Demiurgus created a new kind of animal gifted with knowledge, thus building epistemological dualism into the scheme of things. But *A. E. Murphy* (review below) found "Mr. Lovejoy's Counterrevolution" upholding not two but 18 different dualisms, indicating that the Demiurgus may have done more than he intended.

Reviews: Anon in TLS 29: Oct. 2, 1930, 770; Anon in RMM 38: 1931, 10–11 (suppl.); R. I. Aaron in Mind 40: 1931, 221–30; E. B. McGilvary in PhR 40: 1931, 246–65; A. E. Murphy in IJEth 41: 1931, 265ff., and in JP 28: 1931, 29–42, 57–71; F. A. Wash in *no. 35*, p. 793–801.

183 MARITAIN, JACQUES: Le songe de Descartes, suivi de quelques essais. Corrêa, 1932. xii, 345 p. Engl., Spanish transl.: no. 2636.

1. Le songe de Descartes. 2. Révélation de la Science. 3. Déposition de la Sagesse. 4. Les preuves cartésiennes de Dieu. 5. L'héritage cartésien.

"Descartes a donné à l'anthropothéisme ses lettres de crédit philosophiques. C'est pourquoi nous lui faisons la guerre"; Cartesianism is "le grand péché français" in modern history (286–87), traced from its inception in D.'s "Dream" to its consequences for modern culture, by the Neothomist master of philosophical prose. Maritain asserts that D. was a true believer: "un traître eût été incapable de ravages aussi profonds" (312). Five connected essays, one unpublished; 43 pages of learned, fiery notes for the scholar.

Reviews: A. G. A. Balz in JP 42: 1945, 359–61; R. Bierstedt in SRL 28: Feb. 17, 1945, 34; G. Desgrippes in RdePh 35: 1935, 144–54; L. E. Endres in ModSch 22: May, 1945, 233–34; A.

Grünfeld in ZFSL 58: 1934, 120–21; L. Lavelle in *no. 11*, 41–44; F. Olgiati in *no. 14*, 170–74; A. Patri in Merkur 1: 1947, 615–24; P. A. Reynolds in JRel 25: 1945, 301–02; R. A. Richey in NSch 19: 1945, 178–80.

184 MARITAIN, JACQUES: "Descartes, ou l'incarnation de l'ange." In his: Trois réformateurs: Luther, Descartes, Rousseau. 1925. Nouv. éd. rev. et augm. Plon, 1937, p. 73–128; notes p. 293–306. Italian, English, Spanish, Polish translation: no. 2635.

Descartes' sin is angelism. He made "de la Connaissance et de la Pensée une Perplexité sans remède, un abîme d'inquiétude, parce qu'il a conçu la Pensée humaine sur le type de la Pensée angélique"; "(il) a dévoilé le visage du monstre que l'idéalisme moderne adore sous l'e nom de Pensée" (77–78). Violent, impassioned diatribe, ruthlessly simplifying both Cartesianism and Thomism to destroy the rationalist monster Descartes. But the notes are scholarly as always; hatred dictates some penetrating pages; and the description of St. Thomas' intellectual angels in just five soaring, grammatically fabulous sentences (79–81) is a masterpiece of French prose and the bane of translators. See also Maritain's important technical paper "Le conflit de l'essence et de l'existence dans la philosophie cartésienne" (in no. 40, v. 1, 11–20, and see no. 2645), with M. Gueroult's searching critique of it in RMM 45: 1938 107–10 (illuminating confrontation of Maritain's and Brunschvicg's interpretation.)

Reviews: Anon. in TLS 27: Nov. 8, 1928, 818; A. Brémond in Aph 4, no. 4: 1927, 304–10; A. G. A. Balz in JP 35: 1938, 178–79; M. M. Knappen in SRL 5: 1091, June 8, 1929.

184a MARITAIN, JACQUES et BORIS VYCHESLAVZEFF: Descartes; textes suivis de débats au Studio franco-russe. Cahiers de la quinzaine, 1931. Sér. 21 no. 5. 109 p.

Asked to decide for either Pascal or Descartes, Maritain chooses St. Thomas. He suggests that (pre-Communist) Russian philosophy rejected both theandrism and the anthropotheism of Descartes and the Marxists. To Berdiaeff's amazement and against all Russian tradition, Vycheslavzeff rises to D.'s defense, with interesting comments on the cogito as phenomenological reduction. The critique of Maritain's thesis in the discussion is worth noting; among the participants are L. Gabrilovich, Berdiaeff, Désiré Roustan, O. Lacombe. See also *Maritain's* Réflexions sur l'intelligence et sa vie propre (1924; 3e éd. 1931: no. 2643, 27–142, 288ff.)

185 OLGIATI, FRANCESCO: La filosofia di Descartes. Milano, Vita e pensiero, 1937. xvi, 588 p. (UCSC, science filosofiche, v. 26).
1. A new concept of reality. 2. Metaphysics. 3. Method. 4. Doubt. 5. The cogito. 6. Certainty; the Cartesian circle. 7. Dualism. 8. Immortality 9. Freedom. 10. Perception and qualities. 11. Imagination. 12. Memory. 13. Mathematics. 14. Physics. 15. Space. 16. Time. 17. Mechanism. 18. Determinism. 19. Finality. 20. Religion. 21. Ethics. 22. Law and politics. 23. History. 24. Pedagogy. 25. Esthetics. 26. Philosophy of language.

In his Cartesio (no. 14) Olgiati provided "una specie di 'bilanco filosofico' degli studî principali" of Descartes scholarship, demonstrating their insufficiency (v). Now he makes a comprehensive survey of the fundamental concepts which are "the columns and the constitutive parts of Descartes' palace of ideas" (p. viii). He asserts the primacy of D.'s initial metaphysics which gives unity to his system by establishing a new concept of reality which Olgiati labels "fenomenismo razionalistico." Bariè notes that Olgiati, this clear-sighted critic of the interpretations of others, "non è altrettànto chiaro quando si tratta di esporre la propria" (no. 129, p. 143 n.2). Nonetheless these 26 chapters are invaluable as a complete, comprehensive, reliable mapping of D.'s "palace of ideas" in all its parts, including unfinished ones like law and politics, ethics, history, pedagogy, philosophy of language Olgiati summarized his own interpretation in *his* "Le phénoménisme de Descartes." (CD 1: 105–10, transl. from no. 35, 615–21). See also Bontadini (no. 239) on the "fenomenismo razionalistico" question.

Reviews: G. Bontadini in Rsyn 14: 1937, 92–94 (also no. 239, 42–43); E. Cassirer in no. 5, 29–34; M. Giorgiantonio is S 6: 1938, 389–91; H. Gouhier in RIP 1: 1938–39, 406 and in no. 169, 107–109 (q.v.); A. G. A. Balz in JP 35: 1938, 177–78; G. Martegani in CivC 88, v. 3: 1937, 53–60; G. Radetti in GCFI 5: 1937, 471–73; E. Rochedieu in RTP 26: 1938, 326–27.

186 PÉGUY, CHARLES: Note sur M. Bergson et la philosophie bergsonienne; note conjointe sur Descartes et la philosophie cartésienne. In his: Œuvres complètes, Gallimard, v. 9, 1924, 57–331. [Other ed. and Spanish translation: *no. 2923.*]

Péguy's ultima verba (August 1, 1914) before going to war and death. Brief "Note sur M. Bergson" deals chiefly with Descartes, while the long "Note conjointe sur Descartes" stays with Descartes only long enough to give Péguy's celebrated profile of the philosopher as the "cavalier français qui partit d'un si bon pas" (59). See: *Pierre Mesnard,* "Méditation sur Descartes en la compagnie de Péguy" (Et 230: Feb. 20, 1937, 450–68).

187 PEIRCE, CHARLES SANDERS: "Questions concerning certain faculties claimed for man." "Some consequences of four incapacities.""Grounds of validity of the laws of logic: further consequences of four incapacities." JSPh 2: 1868–69, 103–14, 140–57, 193–208. Also in his Collected papers (no. 2925), v. 5, 1934, 135–222 (§§ 5: 213–5: 357). Other editions: no. 2925.

Famous series on intuitive knowledge, "written in the spirit of opposition to Cartesianism" (Collected Papers, v. 5, p. 126) sums up "The spirit of Cartesianism," (156–58) in four points: universal doubt, individual consciousness as ultimate test of certainty, single thread of inference, the will of God as creator making many created facts inexplicable while Scholasticism "had its mysteries of faith, but undertook to explain all created things" (156). In refutation, Peirce postulates "four incapacities" of mind: it has no power of introspection, of intuition, of thinking without signs, no concept of the absolutely incognizable. These postulates, tested for validity by tracing their consequences, become the foundation of Peirce's own idealist pragmaticism. Most important American contribution to D. debate. See *James Feibleman,* An introduction to Peirce's philosophy, interpreted as a system. New York, Harper, 1946, 69–75 et passim; *C. Eisele-Halpern* on Peirce and 17th century logic of science, no. 1833a.

188 RENOUVIER, CHARLES: Manuel de philosophie moderne. Paulin, 1842, 446 p. Spanish tr. of Book 2: Descartes. Buenos Aires, Espasa Calpe, 1950. 146 p.

Singular attempt to construe all history of philosophy from Plato to Kant as preparation for, appearance of, and deviation from Descartes. Written by France's great neocriticist in his early twenties in an "espèce de fougue philosophique" upon first discovering D. and philosophy (CrPh 6/2 [12]: Nov. 29, 1877, p. 276), the book contains the revised 1839 prize essay on D. which Damiron carefully analyzed, mistaking the tyro author for a foreigner: "Il a plus de variété que de profondeur, plus d'aperçus que d'analyse: il ne démontre et ne preuve pas assez" (no. 451, 1: 146). But Renouvier was first in Cousin's day to restore D.'s mathematics and physics to their rightful place, and the bold, suggestive freshness of his youthful attempt is unimpaired.
See also *Renouvier's* series of papers on Descartes' physics, relating it to Newton, Leibniz, Pascal, Comte, and on interpretations of Liard and T. E. Huxley (CrPh 1874, 1877, 1882; see no. 3044–46); and *his* remarkable series of papers called "Les labyrinthes de la métaphysique" (CrPh 1877–79; no. 3047) on determinism and on the concept of the infinite; particularly "Une évolution personnelle," ibid., on his youthful discovery of Descartes. For his treatment of Malebranche see Sebba, no. 19, p. 74.

189 ROTH, LEON: Descartes' Discourse on Method. Oxford, Clarendon Press, 1937. vi, 142 p.

1. DM and the Cartesian revolution. 2. Literary history of DM. 3. Background of DM (D. and Pascal; the spiritual emergence of D.; the 'vision' of 1619, the 'mission' of 1628; the poetic strain in D. and its repression in Cartesianism). 4. Nature of the method (Bacon's rules, Regulae, 4 rules of DM). 5. Its weakness. 6. Its eclipse (Daniel's Voyage du monde de Descartes; Chr. Huygens; Huet's Censura, etc.). 7. Survival of the method (Locke a Cartesian although rejecting both his metaphysics and physics). 8. Conclusion: The problems of the method (Pascal's criticism of Descartes; the geometric ideal useless, especially in physics, and so recognized by D. himself).

"The Cartesian 'revolution' lay in the attempt to substitute a psysics based on metaphysics for a metaphysics based on physics" (4). This revolution failed: control of nature could not be achieved by the "méthode" as the sole instrument of scientific discovery, as Descartes' mathematicist mind demanded. A remarkable reassessment of the main works gives the "true" date of the Meditations as 1628–29, that of PP as 1629–33. Accordingly, the Discours is not a preliminary manifesto later abandoned, but "the retrospect of a Descartes who has *been through* the stages of Meditations and Principles and now looks back on them" (73), a conglomerate of pieces from different periods, its Pt. VI D.'s confessio fidei. Penetrating pages on Descartes and Bacon, Pascal, Locke. Small, vigorous, original, important study. See *Roth's* summary: "The Discourse on method, 1637–1937" in Mind 46: 1937, 32–43, and his doctrinal critique of DM and méthode in no. 329. Roth's thesis of the non-empirical character of the "méthode" is attacked by *Alan Gewirtz* [Gewirth] in "Experience and the non-mathematical in the Cartesian method" (JHI 2: 1941, 183–210).

Reviews: A. G. A. Balz in JP 35: 1938, 179; H.-D. Gardeil in RSPT 27: 1938, 616–17; S. V. Keeling in Mind 48: 1939, 366–73; G. Radetti in GCFI 6: 1938, 446–50; F. Sisson in MLR 33: 1938, 443–44.

190 RYLE, GILBERT: The concept of mind. London, Hutchinson's University Library, 1949 (New York, Barnes & Noble, 1950), 334 p. Italian transl. by F. Rossi-Landi: Lo spirito come comportamento. Torino, Einaudi, 1955. 372 p.

The editor of *Mind* launches "the most brilliant attack on the mentalism of mind-body dualism in a long time" (Hofstadter, JP 48: 1951, 256). Ryle makes it his "destructive purpose to show that a family of radical category-mistakes is the source of D.'s double-life theory" (18). Calling intelligent conduct "mind," D. treated it as if conduct were in the same logical category as body, not realizing that this "mind" in the body was but a "Ghost in the Machine" (22). "Descartes' myth" (Ch. 1) is by no means the only target of Wittgensteinian expurgation; the "ghost" is chased from every corner of behavior – knowledge, will, emotion, capacities, self-knowledge, sensation, imagination, intellect. In the end, Cartesians receive a backhanded compliment: they were like soldiers who, finding their old stone fortress in collapse, "take up their stand in the most fort-like thing they can see, namely, the shadow of the decrepit fort," thus giving at least "some evidence of teachability" (330). No wonder that the old battle flared up anew; e.g. in the anti-Ryle issue of JP (48: 1951, 257–301): *D. S. Miller* on "Descartes' Myth and Professor Ryle's fallacy" (270–80), *H. R. King, M. Weitz, A. Hofstadter* (Ryle's "present malady": a case of excessive nominalism). The ghost-in-the-machine argument still continues, interlocking with debates on whether machines can think, whether problem of "other minds" (connaissance d'autrui) is a problem or another ghost – 20th century resumptions of 17th century topics. See also *M. Macdonald*, no. 306, *J. Z. Young*, no. 350.

Reviews: Anon. in PhAb 12: 1950, 70; Anon. in Thom 14: 1951, 427–28; R. Caillois in Crit 10, no. 82: 1954, 247–65; J. M. Cameron in DR 68: 1950, 230–32; S. Ceccato in Methodos 3: 1951, 57–59; J. Collins in Thought 26: 1951, 291–94; F. C. Copleston in BJPS 1: 1950–51, 328–32; P. Filiasi Carcano in GCFI 30: 1951, 277–89; W. A. Gerhard in NSch 26: 1952, 125–27; A. M. Goguel in NEF 2: 1951, 79–82; D. W. Gundry in CQR 151: 1950, 107–09; S. Hampshire in Mind 59: 1950, 237–55; A. Leroy in RPFE 141: 1951, 125–26; M. Macdonald in PhR 60: 1951, 80–90; D. M. Mackinnon in PhQ 1: 1951, 248–53; P. H. Nowell-Smith in HJ 48: 1950, 300–02; F. Sibley in Rmet 4: 1950–51, 259–78; T. O. Weldon in Phil 25: 1950, 266.

191 SANTAYANA, GEORGE: Scepticism and animal faith; introduction to a system of philosophy. New York, Scribner's, 1923. xii, 314 p.

Ch. I–VIII develop Santayana's "true" scepticism, opposed to D.'s "histrionic" one, as an ideal attitude, though one impossible to maintain in the face of our compulsory "animal faith" in substance (185–86), which leads to duality between essence and substance and to the failure of this attempt to overcome Cartesian soul-body dualism, as Bowman convincingly showed (no. 155). Harsh critique of the cogito (289–91): D.'s doubt discounted since "his mind was not plastic nor mystical enough to be profoundly sceptical, even histrionically" (289). Awareness of the "inner life of the body was the rock of vulgar belief which Descartes found .... after his not very serious shipwreck .... On this stepping stone to idealism the father of modern philosophy, like another Columbus, set his foot with elegance" (291).

192 SARTRE, JEAN-PAUL: "La liberté cartésienne." In his: Descartes. Paris, Trois collines, 1946, 9–52 (Les classiques de la liberté). Also in his: Situa-

tions, v. 1, 314–35 (Gallimard, 1947). German tr., Preface by Karl Jaspers: no. 3201.

Sartre's controversial contribution to D. criticism sees in D.'s notion of method "une magnifique affirmation humaniste de la liberté créatrice" in fulfillment of man's task: "faire qu'une Vérité existe dans le monde, faire que le monde soit vrai" (24). In the doubt and cogito, Being is bracketed out and man "se surprend comme un pur néant" (36). But Descartes, at the threshold of the existentialist discovery, turned back under the inner pressure of his epoch and gave to God "ce qui nous revient en propre" (51), namely the absolutely free, creative act. D.'s God is therefore the freest of all the Gods which human thought has made, and the only creative God. Existentialism revokes this theologizing compromise: "l'homme est l'être dont l'apparition fait qu'un monde existe" (51). *G. [Rodis-] Lewis* finds Sartre reducing the fruitful part of D.'s theory of freedom to the negativity of doubt "et a l'autonomie de Dieu qu'il interprète comme une sublimation d'une liberté humaine authentique" (RPFE 141: 1951, 265). *Abbé Robert Lenoble* assails Sartre's thesis in a remarkable paper ("Liberté cartésienne ou liberté sartrienne?" in Royaumont, no. 42, 302–24, discussion 325–35). He contrasts Descartes' and Mersenne's God and their notion of freedom. See also the related analysis of Cartesian freedom by Sarano, no. 331.

Reviews: R. Bouvier in Rsyn 63: 1948, 86–90; P. Caes in SynB 7: 1952, 33–42; C. Delasnerie in RInt 3: 1947, 183–84; C. Ferro in RFNS 42: 1950, 216–17; M. Hagmann in no. 10, 164–72; A. Patri in RPFE 80: 1955, 341–48; S. Pétrement in Crit 1: 1946, 612–20; L. Quattrocchi in GCFI 4: 1950, 475–80; H. Riefstahl in PhLit 1: 1950, 62–63; L. Schlötermann in ZPF 3: 1948–49, 448–50; E. Wolff in RPFE 145: 1955, 341–48.

192a SCHELLING, FRIEDRICH WILHELM JOSEPH VON: "Cartesius." In his: Zur Geschichte der neueren Philosophie; Münchener Vorlesungen [Ms. of 1827]. Sämtliche Werke, Stuttgart, Cotta, 1. Abt., v. 10, 4–32. Reprinted: Stuttgart, Kohlhammer, s.a.

Like Hegel, Schelling sees in Descartes the revolutionary originator of modern philosophy; but his view is critical and pessimistic. In his new start, Descartes threw philosophy back into a sort of second childhood and narrowed it down to its one central modern problem, the relation of thought and Being. It widened out again, but its character remained what D. had made it. In his critique of cogito and doubt Schelling dismisses D.'s Dieu-trompeur and malin génie arguments as a mere shying away from the complete Idealism towards which D. was headed; in this context occurs the much-quoted remark that D. was not concerned with understanding things but merely with knowing that they *are* – "the least one can say of them" (SW 10, p. 12). D's most influential doctrine was the ontological argument which, to Schelling, does not prove God's existence but introduces the fundamental concept of his *necessary* existence, which leads to antinomy. Ultimately more influential were Schelling's earlier comments (scattered texts of 1794–1804, conveniently brought together by Hagmann, no. 10, p. 96–101). Here appears the profoundly pessimistic view of Cartesian dualism as both sympton and cause of the radical transformation of Western man's attitude to God, World, Nature, This dualism is a secularized Christian feeling of discord between World and God; it marks the withdrawal of the Numinous from the world (Heidegger's "Fehl Gottes") and the interiorization of the Light. Its consequence is the irremediable split between subject and object upon which the modern view of Nature rests. Metaphysically, the observational empiricism of modern science represents the victory of dualism which alone makes willful mastery over nature possible. In D.'s mechanistic physics, his innermost intention achieved systematic form, while his metaphysics still stopped short of its inevitable consequences. One recognizes the roots of essential elements in Heidegger's view of Descartes as founding father of European Nihilism.

192b SMITH, NORMAN [KEMP]: Studies in the Cartesian philosophy. London, Macmillan, 1902. xiv, 276 p. Reprinted: New York, Russell & Russell, 1962.

Very useful chapters on Cartesian principles in Spinoza, Leibniz, Locke, on Hume's D. critique, and on the transition to Kant who initially accepts a Cartesian mind concept refined in the light of Hume's critique of causality. The first chapters on D.'s method and metaphysics repay reading for their precision and for comparison with author's New Studies of 1952 (no. 193).

Reviewed by Charles S. Peirce in Nation 77: 16 July 1903, 57–58; comparison with New Studies (no. 193) by Leon Roth in Cambridge Jl 7: 1954, 466–75.

193 SMITH, NORMAN KEMP: New studies in the philosophy of Descartes; Descartes as pioneer. London, Macmillan (New York, St. Martin's Press), 1952. xii, 370 p.

1. Biography and summary of D.'s philosophical development. 2. The Method in the Regulae. 3. Applicability of the rules of method. 4. Universal physics (Traité de la lumière). 5. Physiology (Traité de l'homme). 6. The 'embodied self' (Regulae, Traité de l'homme, TP). 7. First thoughts on metaphysics, 1629–30; D.'s restatement of Thomist theology. 8. Relation between his physics and his general philosophy. 9. His later theory of knowledge. 10. His metaphysics. 11. Proofs of God's existence. 12. Substance and causality. 13. Descartes as pioneer.

Great commentary. Not a revision of author's Studies in the Cartesian philosophy (no. 192b) – which were by no means "prentice work" as he now calls them – but a new, comprehensive study of D.'s philosophy excepting ethics. The Descartes of the "New Studies," "un pionnier au goût anglais" as Gueroult rather contemptuously puts it, forces his way into philosophical terram incognitam through a dense forest of difficulties, continually working and reworking the themes of his younger years, handicapped by uncertain terminology, incomplete enumeration of "simple natures," etc. Kemp Smith's radically historical approach, contrary to the conception of Cartesianism as a monolithic system, drew a sharp attack from Gueroult in his anonymous review (RMM 59: 1954, 231–32) for destroying "l'ordre des raisons": .... "au lieu de s'en prendre à Descartes, que ne s'en prend-il à lui-même qui a brisé en mille miettes ce merveilleux ensemble dont Descartes nous dit .... que 'la moindre chose qu'on en ôte ou qu'on y ajoute en entraîne la ruine totale'." The three-cornered conflict between Kemp Smith, Gueroult, Alquié reflects the unhealable cleavages in contemporary Descartes scholarship, stemming from fundamental disagreement on the nature of philosophical interpretation and on the structure of D.'s thought.

Reviews: Anon. [M. Gueroult] in RMM 59: 1954, 231–32; I. W. Alexander in MIR 50: 1955, 80–82; A. G. A. Balz in JP 51: 1954, 192–94; J. D. Bastable in PhS 5: 1955, 150–51; L. J. Beck in HJ 52: 1954, 307–08; E. W. Beth in SynB 9: 411, s.d.; J. Brun in FS 8: 1954, 356–58; J. Collins in Thought 29: 1954, 277–78; E. Denissoff in RphL 53: 1955, 256–59; M. Gueroult in RPFE 145: 1955, 329–39; M. Kneale in Mind 65: 1956, 281–82; T. S. Kuhn in Isis 46: 1955, 377–80; G. Leger in RSPT 39: 1955, 170–71; D. J. McCracken in Phil 30: 1955,

77–78; J. Pariente in RPFE 144: 1954, 446–48; C. A. Viano in RF 47: 1956, 88–93; H. G. Wolz in NSch 32: 1954–55, 77–80; J. N. Wright in PhQ 5: 1955, 365–72; L. Roth (review article) in Cambridge Jl 7: 1954, 466–75. W. Doney on "Descartes' theory of vision" in JP 54: 1957, 775–76 has critical comment on Kemp Smith regarding the Descartes-Berkeley question of priority (see no. 1785).

193a TEMPLE, WILLIAM (Archbishop of York, later of Canterbury): "The Cartesian Faux-Pas." "Mathematics and Logic." In his: Nature, man and God. The Gifford Lectures 1932–33, 1933–34. London, Macmillan, 1934. Lecture III and IV, p. 57–108.

A fighting churchman-scholar adds the Protestant voice to the Catholic lament about "the most disastrous moment in the history of Europe" when René Descartes emerged from the poêle with a cogito whose assurance is purely subjective, a methodical doubt purely artificial, an ontological argument "circular in a vicious manner" (57). Roaming from Aristotle via Bosanquet to Whitehead, from Conservative Party via Machiavelli to "Art for Art's Sake" and points beyond, the great prelate expresses his conviction that every trace of Cartesianism must be removed from modern thought before a sound view of God and Church can be reached. Valuable reference to *Baron von Hügel's* D. critique (78–79). For an urbane reassessment of the Archbishop's "famous indictment" see *R. G. Norburn*, "The Cartesian faux-pas and the malignant demon" (CQR 272: Jan.-Mar. 1946, 127–54), rejecting the charge of impiety against Descartes on interesting Protestant grounds (140–41), but finding him incapable of conquering the "malin génie" of irrationalism, with sad consequences for philosophy. Far briefer, weightier, deeper than Temple is *Karl Barth* (Die kirchliche Dogmatik, v. 1, 1932, p. 401–115; see no. 1149) whose "powerfully realistic outlook in ontology and epistemology" leads him to an equally uncompromising Protestant rejection of Cartesianism in philosophy and theology (*R. E. Cushman*, "Barth's attack upon Cartesianism, and the future in theology." JRel 36: 1956, 207–23).

194 VALÉRY, PAUL: "Fragment d'un Descartes." "Le retour de Hollande: Descartes et Rembrandt." "Une vue de Descartes." "Seconde vue de Descartes." Reprinted in his: Variété, v. 2, 18–38; v. 4, 207–33; v. 5, 209–59. Original publication, reprints, translations: no. 3465–69.

For nearly 20 years Valéry tried to seize the quality of Descartes' "magnifique et mémorable moi" (Variété 5, p. 253.) An interim stage, his opening address before the Congrès Descartes (RMM 1937) was "much elegant phrase-making" (Anon. in Mind 43: 1939, 118.) The final result, "Une vue de Descartes," is a short but astonishingly fruitful essay. On Valéry's affinities with, and aversions to Descartes see *René Fernandat* (no. 1877–1877a) and *G. Vigorelli* in no. 35, 787–91, with further references.

194a WHITEHEAD, ALFRED NORTH: Process and reality; an essay in cosmology. Cambridge UP (New York: Macmillan), 1929. Reprinted: Harper Torchbooks, 1960.

Whitehead develops his "philosophy of organism" in a profound dialogue with the philosophical tradition, chiefly Descartes, Locke and Hume. Descartes is assessed in the light of subsequent development in metaphysics, mathematics, physics. As for all great systematic philosophers, so for Whitehead too Descartes is the philosopher of the cogito who recognized that "those substances which are the subjects enjoying conscious experiences, provide the primary data for philosophy, namely themselves as in the enjoyment of such experience" – "undoubtedly the greatest philosophical discovery since the age of Plato and Aristotle"; but "like Columbus who never visited America, Descartes missed the full sweep of his own discovery" (Pt. II, ch. VII, Sec. I). It is not always easy to recognize Descartes in Whiteheadian garb, but P & R sheds unexpected light on Descartes' thought, e.g. regarding the ontological principle (Whitehead's term, not the ontological argument), D.'s failure to provide for the perception of a particular actual entity and thereby missing a chief point of Whitehead's philosophy of organism. The identity of Cartesian substance and Whiteheadian "actual occasions," the theory of representative ideas, the treatment of dualism are other pertinent issues. See also no. 182 (Lovejoy) and A. G. A. Balz on "Whitehead, Descartes, and the bifurcation of nature" (JP 31: 1934, 281–97) on the dualism problem. Chapter 9 of *Whitehead's* Science and the modern world (1925; see no. 3555a) is devoted to a confrontation of Descartes and James, paradigmatically, and may serve as a non-technical introduction to the difficult Descartes passages in P & R.

VII. THE PHILOSOPHY OF DESCARTES
GENERAL STUDIES AND MONOGRAPHS

195 ARON, ROBERT: Les frontaliers du néant. Éditions de Flore, 1949. 170 p. (Collection Propos). Also: "Descartes y el cartesianismo." Revista de la Universidad de Buenos Aires, v. 5, no. 1: 1949, 98–168.

Boldly speculative fantasy on Genesis, Descartes, and Man: "Descartes, c'est le démiurge prétendant compléter et arrivant à pervertir l'œuvre initiale de Dieu" in a spirit "tout imprégné et tout imbibé de divin" (39). Three chapters on D.'s "night of ecstasy," his Method, its aftermath.

196 ARTIGAS RAMÍREZ, JOSÉ: Descartes y la formación del hombre moderno. Madrid, Consejo superior de investigaciones científicas. Instituto S. José de Calasanz de Pedagogía, 1951. 176 p. See also no. 1087.

Descartes' importance for modern education, the author's theme, cannot be judged from his explicit statements concerning "sagesse" (ch. 1). In the "morale provisoire" (ch. 2) his orientation towards praxis becomes evident; the theme of God is postponed ad Kalendas Graecas, and the "métabasis a lo infinito queda en mera posibilidad y definitivamente desatendida" (156). The core chapter, "Aristas del hombre moderno" (89–150), sees in D.'s metaphysics and "morale provisoire" the root of modern man's operational attitude towards nature and to his "abstención de lo divino." The Cartesian type of modern man is incapable of identifying himself with a community that has a historical social mission; he is "esencialmente profano y morbosamente apegado a lo terreno." The epilogue rapidly surveys the countervailing forces in Spanish education, Thomism and mysticism; these must be called upon for a modern educational ideal of the whole man.

198 BECK, LESLIE J.: The method of Descartes. A study of the "Regulae". Oxford, Clarendon Press (London, Cumberlege), 1952. x, 316 p.

1. Regulae and DM; text, plan of R. 2. The unity of thought and science (perception and imagination). 3. Science and mathematics. 4. Intellectual intuition. 5. Its object (simplicity; simple natures and propositions). 6. The nature of inference (intellectual intuition and deduction; "necessary connections"). 7. Cartesian deduction and the syllogism. 8. Enumeration (memory, complete enumerations). 9. Demonstration. 10. The essentials of method (rules, definition). 11. The rules of analysis and synthesis. 12. The secret of the method. 13. The science of order (mathesis vulgaris, m. universalis). 14. The solution of problems. 15. The method in mathematics (sense and imagination in reasoning; entia jam nota). 16. The method in physics. 17. Theory and practice (mathematics and PP; Dioptrica). 18. The method in philosophy (logic and method; analysis and synthesis; method in MM).

Authoritative, detailed commentary on the Regulae, which are taken, without special proof, to be the main statement of Cartesian method, the Four Rules of DM being a partial reformulation. D.'s méthode is viewed in its own context, not in its connection with D.'s metaphysics. This epistemological orientation, common to modern English D. scholarship, criticized in the Wittgensteinian TLS review below, is not only defensible (see *J. Berthet*, no. 237), but needed to keep the analysis to the technical point. The secondary literature is carefully judged, controversies are firmly dealt with. Wright's review below finds conclusions insufficiently separated from arguments. However, the presentation is always precise and clear. Among the many illuminating pages are those on intellectual intuition (D.'s "intuitus") and on D.'s attitude towards formal logic, with interesting remarks on its relation to later developments (Leibniz, modern symbolic logic.) Index; list of the Regulae texts quoted. See also *Beck's* "L'unité de la pensée et de la méthode" in no. 42, 393–411.

Reviews: Anon. in TLS 52: July 17, 1953; Anon. in S 21: 1953, 118; J. Collins in Thought 29: 1954, 278–79; W. Doney in PhR 63: 1954, 272–73; R. J. Hirst in Mind 64: 1955, 267; G. Leger in RSPT 39: 1954, 172–73; T. S. Kuhn in Isis 46: 1955, 377–80; D. J. McCracken in Phil 29: 29: 1954, 364–65; C. A. Viano in RF 47: 1956, 203–207; J. N. Wright in PhQ 5: 1955, 78–82.

199 BENEŠ, JOSEF: Descartesova metoda ve vědách a ve filosofi. Prague, Nákladem Ceské Akademie věd a Umění, 1936. xiv, 327 p.

Thorough study of D.'s method in the sciences and in philosphy, from the "discovery of method" to the last stage where 'sagesse' becomes the culmination and synthesis of all science. The author stresses the prime methodological and psychological importance of MM as satisfying D.'s need for shoring up his physics. French table of contents. Summary of *Beneš'* viewpoint: "L'importance des Méditations métaphysiques de Descartes au point de vue de sa méthode" (CD 1: 3–9, 1937.) See Gueroult (RMM 45: 1938, 109).

200 BLANCHET, LÉON: Les antécédents historiques du "je pense, donc je suis." Préface par Émile Bréhier. Alcan, 1920. 325 p.

"Le mérite, rare et singulier, du livre," as Bréhier says in his Preface (p. 3) "est d'avoir montré que la portée du cogito dans le système cartésien ne pouvait être entièrement comprise par l'étude de ses antécédents," namely St. Augustine, himself a confluent of older Greek and neoplatonist conceptions, and Campanella. Gilson's important review accepts Blanchet's thesis of a Cartesian transformation of Augustine's "si enim fallor, sum," but rejects his claim of Campanella's influence on D. as manifestly false. Original, exhaustively documented work. See also *Blanchet's* posthumously published "La préparation du cogito cartésien dans la philosophie grecque de l'antiquité" (RMM 40: 1933, 187–230), and *É. Bréhier's* "Une forme archaïque du cogito ergo sum" (RPFE 133: 1943, 143–44) on a passage in Aristotle which by contrast reveals "tout ce qu'il y a d'audace dans la philosophie cartésienne à prendre son appui dans une certitude évanouissante" (144); see the comment by *P. M. Schuhl* in RPFE 138: 1948, 191–94.

Reviews: Anon. in RMM 28: 1921, suppl. 1, 6; H. Gouhier in no. 168, p. 29–35, 290–94; F. Olgiati in no. 14, p. 75–79; É. Gilson in RPFE 91: 1921, 302–10, reprinted in no. 165, 259–68.

200a BOAS, GEORGE: "Homage to Descartes." PPR 11: 1950–51, 149–63.

Since D. recognized three fundamental non-rational ways of understanding, Cartesianism is not pure rationalism. Its core is the concept of perfectly ordered systematic knowledge, still at the root of Western thought but now in need of modification. Delightful commemorative lecture, modern in approach. *Review:* A. in PenM 8: 1952, 260–261.

The chapter "Descartes and the Cartesians" in *Boas'* Dominant themes of modern philosophy (New York, 1957, 90–132; see no. 1264) is a sympathetic though critical discussion of what became fruitful in Descartes and his successors up to Spinoza. The next chapter (133–58) balances the account by following French anticartesianism from Gassendi to Huet. Reviewed by R. H. Popkin in TP, January 15, 1959; J. P. Day in Phil 35: 1960, 175–77.

201 BOUTROUX, ÉMILE: De veritatibus aeternis apud Cartesium. Baillière, 1874. 70 p. Thèse, Paris. French tr. by Georges Canguilhem: Des vérités éternelles chez Descartes. Thèse latine. Préface de Léon Brunschvicg. Alcan, 1927. 146 p. (BPC)

Challenging thesis which tries to establish "que les principes cartésiens constituent tantôt une dualité, tantôt une unité" (137), pivoting about the idea of God as it emerges from D.'s doctrine of eternal verities. This succinct, careful study of the doctrine in relation to other elements of Cartesian philosophy (doubt, cogito, evidence, existence of God and things, dualism, free will, judgment) is still authoritative. For its impact on French scholarship see Brunschvicg's preface to the French translation.

202 CAIRD, EDWARD: "Cartesianism." In his: Essays in literature and philosophy. Glasgow, Maclehose (New York, Macmillan), 1892, v. 2, p. 267–383. Italian transl. by M. C. Bombelli: Il cartesianismo. Firenze, Nuova Italia, 1933. 99 p.

Pellucid critical treatment, in transcendentalist language, of the metaphysics and epistemology of Descartes, Malebranche, Spinoza. Going straight to the core, the essay sheds unexpected light on many a well-worn text, illuminating basic issues and conflicts in D.'s thought. Granted that many pages would read differently if written after Gilson, the essay repays close reading as it stands. See also *Caird's* art. "Cartesianism" in Encyclopedia Britannica, 11th ed., v. 5, 414–26.

203 CANNABRAVA, EURYALO: "René Descartes." In his: Descartes e Bergson. São Paulo, Amigos do livro, 1942, p. 33–99.

Interprets D.'s cogito and Bergson's "durée" as "exemplos incisivos do ato filosófico em sua pureza original e primitiva," rising "como impulsos incoercíveis de um inconsciente rico de imagens e de símbolos, sintetizando tôda uma existência a serviço do ideal especulativo" (32), both losing their authenticity in the laborious rational operation of system-building. Modern analysis, sober despite its colorful language; less than fundamental.

204 CARABELLESE, PANTALEO: Le obbiezioni al cartesianesimo. Messina, D. d'Anna, 1946. 3 vols.: L'idea, xv, 255 p.; La dualità, 220 p.; Il metodo, 243 p. (BCM, V. 9–11). See the notice to no. 204a.

Vol. I: *L'idea.* L'essenza del cartesianesimo nelle Meditazioni. 1. La causazione e l'idea. 2. La causa sui. 3. L'idea dell'infinito. 4. L'argomento ontologico. 5. Il circolo vizioso.
Vol. II: *La dualità.* 6. La dualità della sostanza. 7. La natura del conoscere: intendere o sentire?
Vol. III: *Dal dubbio all'evidenza.* 9. L'errore. 10. L'innatezza. Indici generali: v. 3, 205–11.

204a CARABELLESE, PANTALEO: "La riconquesta del cartesianesimo." In: Augusto Gozzo (ed.), L'attualità dei filosofi classici. Milano, Bocca, 1942, 1–20. Also in his: Da Cartesio a Rosmini, 1946 (see no. 1455).

I. Il cartesianesimo tradizionale: cogitare puro, negatività dell'essere, autocoscienza. II. Il cartesianesimo integrale: l'evidenza come principio della certezza e come regola dell'essere; raggiungimento dell'essere col cogito. III. La scoperta di Cartesio: la spiritualità della sostanza; le incoerenze fondamentali di Cartesio. IV. La riconquesta del cartesianesimo: liberazione dall'autocoscienza – la concezione realistica dell'essere; correzione del circolo vizioso cartesiano.

Carabellese's great work on the Objections and Responses to MM (no. 204), "nato da due corsi di lezioni, 1938–40, già pubblicate in dispense ad uso degli scolari," rigorously analyzes Descartes' Meditations, argument by argument, and offers the fullest systematic study so far of the Objections of Gassendi, Hobbes, Arnauld, etc., and of D.'s Responses, covering all major themes of Descartes' metaphysics. "Lavoro .... di primissimo ordine, meditato seriamente e concretamente construito in ogni sua parte, e col quale dovremo fare i conti nella presentazione del *vero* Cartesio" (Ferro's review, 206). The author's own ontologist philosophy of "ontocoscienzialismo" is applied to Descartes who appears tending towards purest rationalism. The much-discussed analysis of the Cartesian circle (v. 1, 199–248) was first published in 1937 (no. 1454), and reprinted in the author's Da Cartesio a Rosmini, 1946, together with the noteworthy study "La riconquesta dal cartesianesimo" (no. 204a) which sums up Carabellese's own philosophical position as applied to the Descartes problem.

Reviews: P. Filiasi Carcano in GCFI 27: 1948, 178–86; A. Carlini in no. 4, 180–88 and in Gmet 3: 1948, 525–28; C. Ferro in RFNS 42: 1950, 204–06; G. Galli in RRFC 33: 1939, 213–24 and RANL 13: 1937, 471–532 (of C.'s "Circolo vizioso"); N. Petruzzellis in Noesis: July-December 1946, 367–68. On C.'s ontologism see also G. Bontadini in RFNS 1940, no. 5, and G. Fano in GCFI 18 (ns 2–3): 1937, 119–40.

205 CARBONARA, CLETO: Renato Cartesio e la tradizione ontologica. Torino, S.E.I., 1945. 169 p.

Collected studies: the Descartes chapter of his Scienza e filosofia ai principi dell'età moderna: Galilei, Bacone, Cartesio (1935; see no. 1459), "Riflessione e trascendenza in Cartesio" (CD 1: 93–98; also in LogosN 20: 1937, 359–64); his studies of the ontological tradition, with reference to Descartes and Vicenzo Gioberti (GCFI 22: 1941, 48–67 and 24: 1943, 242–72).

Author sees D. driven towards realism by supposedly inevitable exigencies of scientific thought, yet clinging to an idealistic interpretation in purely philosophical matters. Cartesianism is said to derive its power from the Eleatic-Platonic ontological tradition of early medieval philosophy. One of the best Italian studies, by an influential philosopher.

Reviews: G. Bontadini in Rsyn 14: 1937, 95, reprinted in no. 239 [of no. 1459]; A. Carlini in no. 4, 188–90; F. Enriquez in Scientia 1937, 33–35 [of no. 1459]; C. Ferro in RFNS 39: 1949, 58–59, and 42: 1950, 204.

206 COMBÈS, JOSEPH: Le dessein de la sagesse cartésienne. Lyon-Paris, E. Vitte, 1960. 350 p.

This well-documented study exalts D.'s "sagesse" as a triumph over his epistemology, mathematicism, and scientism, thus shifting the emphasis from what has become hard to defend, e.g. his physics, to what is hard to refute. Beginning with a critique of D.'s dialectics and of the cogito, Combès proceeds to analyse D.'s "morale," both the provisional and the supposedly definitive one; his views on the knowledge of man's nature; the supreme good; divine and human freedom; the love of God as "sommet de la Sagesse"; and Cartesian "génerosité." In this perspective, D.'s quest for a mathesis universalis shrivels to "une ascèse, une méthode de purification" (343) as "Sagesse" triumphs over analysis, rises to "l'absolu de l'affirmation" and becomes in an ultimate apotheosis a "pure epistemology" and a "philosophy of pure immanence" (34).

Review: J. Trouillard in RTP 11: 1961, 100.

206a DILTHEY, WILHELM: Weltanschauung und Analyse des Menschen seit der Renaissance und Reformation. Gesammelte Schriften. 3. Aufl., v. 2, Leipzig und Berlin, Teubner, 1923. 528 p.

Influential study. Contains an analysis of D.'s "idealism of freedom" (348–59), a brief comparison of his system with that of Hobbes, Spinoza and Leibniz, and a notable treatment of his theory of passions (479–92) within the context of the changing concept of man.

207 FRANCHI, AUSONIO (pseud. of Cristoforo Bonavino): "Descartes." In his Letture sulla storia della filosofia moderna: Bacone, Descartes, Spinoza, Malebranche. Milano, Ferrari, 1863, v. 1, p. 261–408. Reprinted as: Descartes. Milano, Athena, 1931. 2 vols.

Traces the subjectivism and idealism of modern philosophy back to Descartes. Interesting discussion of the D. criticism of Vico, Gioberti, and lesser Italian opponents of Cartesian psychologism. Original treatment of D.'s controversies: his defenses were a triumph, though his arguments were partly invalid. "Par leur clarté, leur méthode, et par les très intéressantes critiques.... qui pénètrent au vif des apories cartésiennes, ces pages méritaient d'être arrachées à l'oubli" (G. Bontadini in Rsyn 14: 1937). See also Olgiati (no. 14), p. 222–23.

208 DE FINANCE, JOSEPH (S.J.): Cogito cartésien et réflexion thomiste. Aph 16, no. 2. 1946. 185 p.

1. L'intelligence thomiste et son rapport à l'être. 2. La pensée cartésienne et son rapport à soi. 3. Du 'je pense' au 'je suis.' 4. Le statut ontologique de la pensée. La connaissance de l'âme. 5. La garantie de la vérité. Conclusion. Bibliography (180–82).

A commanding study of Thought and Being in Descartes and St. Thomas. The Cartesian cogito is immediate perception, "affirmation du moi substantiel" (ch. 3, 76) while Thomist "réflection" finds Being before finding itself. Ch. 4 seeks the roots of D.'s doctrine of the thinking substance in Francisco Sánchez and the Conimbricenses whom D. studied at La Flèche. The last chapter gives an ontological critique of the cogito: it cannot guarantee absolute certitude; D.'s three attempts to evade the consequences failed. Rich work, going back to primary texts, clarifies D.'s doctrinal relationship to Scholasticism, though some of its theses were challenged. Elaborate table of contents, no index. The bibliography on the cogito lacks essential non-French contributions.

Reviews: A. Forest in RPFE 138: 221–22, 1948; J. D. García Bacca in FyL 15: 337–49, 1948; E. A. M. in Phil 5: 133–34, 1947.

209 GALLI, GALLO: Studi cartesiani. Torino, Chiantore, 1943. xi, 443 p. (Testi e studi do filosofia e pedagogia, v. 1.) Also published without the last chapter as: Il pensiero filosofico di Cartesio (see no. 1959).

1. La dottrina del metodo. 2. Il dubbio e il cogito. 3. Le prove dell'esistenza di Dio. 4. La dimostrazione dell'esistenza del mondo esterno ed il valore pratico delle qualità sensibili. 5. Il problema dell'errore.

This collection of five large studies of the years 1937–39 (see no. 1960–66), a considerable technical contribution, treats Descartes' metaphysics as a concrete, objective, immanentist idealism. The large, almost book-length study of the problem of error is of particular interest. *See A. Pastore,* "Presentazione degli Studi cartesiani di Gallo Galli" in AcTorino v. 79, t. 2, 1943–44.

Reviews: C. Ferro in RFNS 42: 1950, 202–203; E. Oberti in RFNS 37: 1945, 65–66.

209a GARIN, PIERRE: Thèses cartésiennes et thèses thomistes. Desclée de Brouwer, 1931. 178 p. Thèse Grenoble.

A Thomist disciple of Jacques Chevalier meticulously analyzes the doctrine of eternal verities in D. and St. Thomas. Very comprehensive critique of the literature. From this narrow basis he jumps to broad conclusions, contesting Gilson (no. 165): D. knew only the eclectic Jesuit Scholasticism taught at La Flèche, not genuine Thomism, whence his distrust for metaphysics and his leanings towards positive science. But Garin fails, even in Thomist judgment, to give proof of "what is otherwise quite admissible" (E 57: 555, 1937), which does not diminish the value of his analysis of the doctrine of eternal verities.

Reviews: Anon. in E 57: 1937, 555; Anon. in RMM 40: 1933, suppl. 2, p. 9; G. de Giuli in RF 25: 1934, 167; H. Gouhier in RHPh 5: 1937, 200–08 (firm though friendly refutation); F. Olgiati in no. 14, 318–19.

210 GIBSON, A. BOYCE: The philosophy of Descartes. London, Methuen, 1932. xiii, 382 p.

1. D.'s medieval and Renaissance heritage. 2. The Dream: D.'s mission. 3. Cogito. 4. Existence of God. 5–6. Nature and objects of scientific knowledge. 7. Perception. 8. Attributes of God. 9. The vindication of human knowledge. 10. Free will and the moral life.

The only comprehensive British study of D.'s philosophy other than that of N. Kemp Smith, a difficult but rewarding work, attempts to see Descartes' thought as a systematic whole; this, in the author's view, requires separating the philosophical intention from D.'s superficial and misleading statements arising partly from his desire to ease the difficulties of his philosophy, partly from a failure to understand the real drift of his own thinking. This disengagement leads to the central theme: there are two Cartesian methods, one scientific-mathematical, the other metaphysical (see Serrus, no. 231.) "The" Cartesian method of the Regulae and DM is applicable only to the realm of abstraction (mathematics and natural sciences), not to Cartesian metaphysics which Gibson sees as an attempt to prove the inseparable union between the experiencing, experienced real self and a real God. Stout's elaborate critique (below) notes among other essential points Boyce Gisnob's alleged failure to understand D.'s representational theory of ideas and hence his notion of innate ideas. Gibson's contention that the fundamental character of D.'s philosophy does not really require D. to have recourse to the Cartesian circle is challenged by *P. A. Reynolds* in PhR 48: 1939, 423–27. *Boyce Gibson's* general view of Descartes is expressed in the Great Thinkers Lecture no. 6 ("Descartes," Phil. 10: lees in AJPP 11, no. 1, 1933, 72–77.

Reviews: F. Olgiati in no. 14, p. 110–11; A. K. Stout in Mind 42: 1933, 365–74; W. A. Merrylees in AJPP 11, no. 1, 1933, 72–77.

211 HEIMSOETH, HEINZ: Die Methode der Erkenntnis bei Descartes und Leibniz. Giessen, Töpelmann. Pt. I, 1912; Pt. II, 1914. 334 p. (Philosophische Arbeiten). Dissertation Marburg.

Outstanding work from the Marburg neocriticist school. Leonardo da Vinci, Kepler, Galilei, Bacon are stepping stones on the road from empirical science to method, but D. alone found the transition to the epistemological conception of method "als einer umfassenden Charakteristik des Erkennens überhaupt" (26). Part I is a rich, masterly study of D.'s method of clear and distinct knowledge; Part II treats Leibniz' "Methode der formalen Begründung," his epistemology and monadology, with illuminating discussion of his doctrinal relation to Cartesianism. Valuable index that guides quickly to specific Leibniz-Descartes problems and to key doctrines of both thinkers.

Reviews: Anon. in RMM 20: 1912, sb.; N. Hartmann in K 17: 1912, 289–91; H. Heimsoeth in K 17: 1912 (author's abstract); B. Jordan in ZPPK 148: 76; M. Solovine in RPFE 76: 1913, 218.

211a HENRICH, DIETER: Der ontologische Gottesbeweis. Sein Problem und seine Geschichte in der Neuzeit. Tübingen, J. C. B. Mohr, 1960. xii, 275 p. Bibliography: 261–64.

A doctrinal and historical monograph on "ontotheology," tracing the history of the ontological argument from Descartes to the end of German idealism. Author distinguishes between Anselm's and Descartes' argument and finds Anselm's proof by the maximum of essence (ens perfectissimum) wholly ineffective in modern philosophy, while Descartes' proof by the concept of necessary being determined the course of modern metaphysics (cf. also Schelling, no. 192a): this "will always remain one of the most peculiar phenomena in the history of philosophy" (1). With Descartes, the notion of ens necessarium becomes the fundamental problem of metaphysics, leading to a metaphysical climax followed by a deep crisis. The book traces this almost organic growth and decay of "ontotheology" from the establishment of the argument in Descartes, Malebranche, Spinoza, the Cambridge Platonists and Leibniz through the period of criticism (Gassendi and Huet to Hume and Kant); the chapter on Kant's critique of "ontotheology" (137–188) is perhaps the best analytical presentation of this critique and of the Kantian notion of rational theology. The last part treats the unexpected revival of "ontotheology" from Hegel to Chr. H. Weisse, with a melancholy concluding chapter on why the argument is now dead. The careful treatment of many minor yet important contributing thinkers is particularly valuable. *Charles Hartshorne*, in his new Anselm edition (New York, Open Court Philosophical Classics), surveys the formulation of the argument in numerous philosophers, claiming that Anselm remained ineffective because he was quoted but not read. The so-called Cartesian argument by the ens necessarium is the Anselmian argument of the Proslogion, ch. 3. Descartes may have independently invented it, but hardly contributed anything new. See *Hartshorne's* fundamental: The Logic of Perfection (Lasalle, Illinois, Open Court), 1962, ch. 2.

211b JANSEN, BERNHARD (S.J.): "Der Geist des Philosophierens Descartes'". Sch 12: 1937, 161–64, 340–60.

With German directness and cool Thomist precision, the distinguished historian of philosophy and theology goes to what he considers the heart of D.'s philosophizing (his new concept of science). Excellent treatment of the contrast between D.'s method and Aristotelian logic. Required reading for those just talking of "l'esprit cartésien." See also *Jansen's* "Die Methodenlehre des Descartes, ihr Wesen und ihre Bedeutung" in Cartesio (no. 35), 487–512.

212 JOACHIM, HAROLD H.: Descartes' Rules for the direction of the mind. Reconstituted from notes taken by his pupils, ed. by Errol E. Harris. Foreword by Sir David Ross. London, Allen & Unwin (New York, Macmillan), 1957. 124 p.

Joachim's important Oxford course, given in the early 1930's, reconstructed from the editor's and J. Austin's notes, offers a bold, concise analysis and criticism of the Regulae. Third (last) chapter introduces Joachim's idealistic epistemology, his "theory of the concrete". Woozley's markedly unfriendly critique below tries to shake the reconstructed text by pointing to some "staggering" misrepresentations of what D. said (188), but the vigor and originality of these lectures comes through despite rough edges in transcription.

Reviews: Anon. in TLS 56: 1957, Oct. 11, 613; C. L. in Rmet 11: 1957, 347; A. W. Levi in

Ethics 68: 1957–58, 73; L. G. Miller in PhR 67: 1958, 426–27; A. D. Woozley in PhQ 8: 1958, 188–89; A. Wollaston in BJPS 9: 1958–59, 339–40; R. J. C. Burgener in PScience 26: 1959, 272–74; A. M. Ritchie in Phil 34: 1959, 257–59.

212a KASTIL, ALFRED: Studien zur neueren Erkenntnistheorie. Vol. 1: Descartes. Halle a.S., Niemeyer, 1909. xiv, 209 p.

1. Die Grundklassen des Bewustsseins: Descartes, Brentano, voluntaristische Urteilstheorie. 2. Die Ideen: ens objectivum und die Kritik des Caterus, Gassendi, Hobbes. 3. Die eingeborenen Ideen: die idea adventitia; Geulincx, Antoine Arnauld, Sylvain Régis. 4. Die apodiktische Evidenz: apodiktische vs. assertorische Evidenz; Apodiktik und Nativismus; Kritik der Theorie der "klaren und deutlichen" Vorstellungen. – Anhang: 1. Arnauld über das Wesen des Bewusstseins. 2. Nachwirkungen der Lehre von der realitas objectica: Twardowski, Uphues, Meinong.

Epistemological critique of apodeictic evidence in Descartes who did not distinguish between apodeictic and assertory evidence, between the origin of knowledge in concepts and the genesis of these concepts as rooted in perception. His transposition of epistemological apriorism to the genesis of concepts led to the theory of innate ideas which he applied even to the relationship between stimulus and sensation. This forced him to distinguish between causae and occasiones and led to the difficulties inherent in his notion of "clear and distinct" thought. A meticulous, technically clean study, with valuable discussions of Arnauld, Régis, modern voluntaristic interpretations of D.'s epistemology (Kastil uses Broder Christiansen's book as example; see no. 1550). Kastil's own position is indecisive.

213 KEELING, S. V.: Descartes. Oxford UP (London, Benn), 1934. xi,, 282 p. (Leaders of philosophy.)

Examines D.'s philosophy "through conceptions and in language more readily understood today" (p. ix), with some original interpretations. Part Three rapidly surveys the Cartesian school, with interesting comment on changing concepts of causality and substance (to Spinoza and Leibniz). The concluding critical chapter is admittedly sketchy. Reviewed by C. D. Broad in Mind 44: 1935, 70–75. See also *Keeling*'s Descartes: Annual Hertz Lecture on a Master Mind, in Proc. Brit. Acad. 34: 1948, 57–81, cf. note to no. 2347), reviewed by (G. Lewis) in RIP 4: 1950, 320–21.

214 KOYRÉ, ALEXANDRE: Essai sur l'idée de Dieu et les preuves de son existence chez Descartes. Leroux, 1922. xix, 220 p. (Bibliothèque des Hautes Études. Sciences religieuses, v. 33). German edition (with minor revisions): Descartes und die Scholastik. Bonn, F. Cohen, 1923. 244 p.

Introduction: Descartes' insincerity and originality. 1. His notion of God. 2. The sources of the Cartesian system. 3. The proofs of the existence of God. Appendix: The Cartesian theory of innate ideas, St. Thomas, and the illuminism of St. Augustine. Source quotations.

Original, vigorous monograph on D.'s concept and proofs of God, and on the Scholastic roots of his thought. Discounting D.'s ingenuous and strenuous disavowal of his predecessors ("malheureusement, la grandeur intellectuelle et la grandeur personnelle ne vont pas de pair chez D.; en lui, le penseur est plus grand que l'homme [203],) Koyré sees in him not the destroyer of Scholastic philosophy but a successor to genuinely medieval speculation rooted in St. Augustine. Extensive source quotations (341 items, p. 170–244 of the German ed.) include many citations of medieval philosophers, badly marred by printing errors. D.'s views of voluntas humana et divina, of eternal verities, error, lumen naturale etc. are discussed with reference to Bonaventura, St. Thomas, and particularly Duns Scotus. Koyré assumes that D. read Duns in 1626–29 and rates this influence greater than does Gilson. In his proofs of the existence of God, Descartes shows himself a "disciple of Augustine and Plotinus, moving away from the classical Thomistic proofs and going back to the thought of Augustine, Anselm, and Bonaventura" (p. 96 of the German ed.) The Cartesian circle is necessary and legitimate, and indeed inherent in any epistemology; its Cartesian version is held to rest on a doctrine that comes close to a mystical view of God. The roots of D.'s differentiation between the infinite and the indefinite are traced back to Bonaventura; the ontological proof places D. in the context of Neoplatonic-Christian thought. Running critique of Gilson's Liberté (no. 164).

214a LAZZERONI, VIRGILIO [i.e., Virgilio Lazzeroni Albani]: La formazione del pensiero cartesiano e la scolastica. Padova, CEDAM, 1940. 265 p. (Problemi d'oggi).

Scholasticism is still alive in D. who resolves its cardinal problem (God and World) in the spirit of a "scienzato." His concept of truth must appear contradictory to idealist interpreters who fail to see its roots in medieval gnoseology. See *Lazzeroni's* "Il medievalismo di Cartesio" in CD 3: 25–31.

Reviews: G. Ferro in RFNS 42: 1950, 196–97; B. Jansen in Sch 17: 1942, 111–12; G. Soleri in RFNS 35: 1943, 205–10; N. Picard in Ant 18: 1943, 56–57.

215 LENOBLE, ROBERT: Mersenne ou la naissance du mécanisme. Vrin 1943. lxiii, 633 p. (BHP). Thèse Paris.

Masterly monograph built on a magnificent source foundation. The Oratorian historian of science revises the common view of the relationship between Descartes and Mersenne, who was not just a scientific post-office but an influential thinker in his own right; his empirical, pragmatic tendencies were closer to the mainstream of the new mechanistic philosophy of nature than D.'s metaphysical speculation. Mersenne was also a great organizer, subtly and effectively building up a network of scientific intercommunication. Without denying the importance of speculative vision, Father Lenoble gives due credit to "the cautious, non-metaphysical pragmatism of Mersenne and Gassendi" in making acceptable "a world seen descriptively and not causally, a world that could have forces and actions without spirits and magic" (*R. H. Popkin's* Éloge of Lenoble in Isis 51: 1960, 202). Lenoble and de Waard thus remove Mersenne and Beeckman from the oppressive shadow of Descartes which has concealed their true character and stature ever since Baillet. The monograph is indispensable in studying the Mersenne-Descartes correspondence in toto and in its historical context; it elucidates many of the theological, philosophical, mathematical and scientific issues in Descartes.

Reviews: Anon. in RMM 49: 1944, 188–89; H. Gouhier in RPFE 134: 1944, 60–65; G. Sarton in Isis 40: 1946, 270–72. Other reviews in *no. 3a*, p. 470.

215 a LEWIS, GENEVIÈVE [Mme Geneviève Rodis-Lewis]: L'individualité, selon Descartes. PUF 1950. 254 p. (BHP) Thèse Paris.

1. Descartes et la scolastique devant le principe d'individuation: l'enseignement de La Flèche; thomisme et l'individuation par la matière; influences scotistes et

l'individuation par la forme. 2. La différentiation des individus matériels: pluralité des substances corporelles; différentiation physique – figure et mouvement; l'individualité des corps vivants.
3. L'individu humain: L'Eucharistie et le principe de l'individuation; unité de l'individu humain; son unicité; différences individuelles et le nominalisme; les passions. 4. La multiplicité numérique des substances pensantes: âme individuelle posée par le cogito; existence des autres esprits; communication des esprits. 5. Les différents esprits: égalité du bon sens, inégalité des intelligences; défauts, qualités des esprits.
6. Les facteurs subjectifs de la connaisance: sentiment d'évidence, habitude, mémoire, imagination. 7. L'individualité de l'âme séparée du corps: la possibilité de l'immortalité individuelle; mémoire intellectuelle; sentiments intellectuels. Conclusion: L'absence d'individualité des corps; individualité des purs esprits; construction de l'individualité chez l'homme; individu et personne.

The author, schooled by Laporte, pursues the unusual theme of Descartes' difficulties with the principle of individuation to some equally unusual conclusions. In his inability to find individuality in material bodies, Descartes was in premature accord with modern nuclear physics which cannot tell one particle from another either; even modern biology suspects "individuality" of being a bit of psychologising anthromorphism if applied to the beast-machine. This leaves man, for Descartes, as the proper domain of individuality. "L'âme humaine" is indeed an individual substance, "et le degré de développement de sa liberté en assure à la fois l'unité et l'unicité" (231). This root of individuality in freedom is what man has in common with God. Individuality has the moral character of personality; its highest expression is the passion of "générosité." On the subject of the individuality of the immortal soul when divorced from the body Descartes seems less communicative. The fascinating study is at its very best in the pursuit of the rich subthemes listed above.

Reviews: A. Cuvillier in NL, Oct. 26, 1950, p. 7 and in his: Parti pris ...., Colin, 1956, 93–96; H. - D. Gardeil in RSPT 34: 1950, 569–70; G. Lewis in UPA 21: 1951, 625–26 (abstract); P. Mesnard in RPFE 76: 1951, 321–26; M. Nédoncelle in RScR 25: 1951, 206–208; O. Revault d'Allonnes in RScH 64: 1951, 375–77; B. Rochot in RHSc 3: 1950, 277–81; R. N. W. Smith in PhQ 3: 1953, 83–84; I. Fetscher in PhRu 3: 1955, 183 n. 3.

215b LEWIS, GENEVIÈVE: Le problème de l'inconscient et le cartésianisme. PUF 1950. 302 p. (BPC). Thèse complémentaire, Paris.

Introduction. [St. Augustine and Descartes.]
Ch. I: Conscience et l'inconscient. [Cogito. Degrees of consciousness in infantile thought; synesthesis; dreaming; day-dreaming etc. Complete consciousness and the potential unconscious: innate ideas; acquired dispositions. Consciousness the only mark of effective thought, but soul not necessarily a succession of conscious states.]
Ch. II: Degrés de la conscience: les Cartésiens. [Immediate and reflexive consciousness; Régis vs. Huet. Limits of consciousness: Spinoza. Occasionalists and Empiricists. Malebranche: critique of innate ideas. Descartes, Malebranche, Spinoza and the subject-object problem.]
Ch. III. Les profondeurs de l'âme chez les théologiens cartésiens. [Attempted resolution of the theological problem of the unconscious. Poiret: Cartesianism to mysticism; "pensées imperceptibles" and grace (Nicole, Lamy; Arnauld, Huygens). "Intuition divinatrice," "esprit de finesse," the esthetic "je ne sais quoi." Unconscious dispositions: "surface de la pensée et fond du cœur"; actual and habitual grace; revealing behavior; self-love: La Rochefoucauld. Lamy vs. Jansenists; Malebranche;

"pur amour." Cartesianism of Bossuet and Fénelon. Possibility of imperceptible acts. "Direction de conscience" better than introspection. Fénelon vs. Bossuet: reflected action vs. inaccessible "point de l'esprit."]
Conclusion: Leibniz and Cartesianism: "petities perceptions"; defense of innate ideas and permanence of thought against Locke. Cartesianism rejects metaphysical or vitalistic use of the unconscious, recognizes complexity of soul, degrees of consciousness, the subconscious, and still deeper dispositions.

The Doctor subtilis among contemporary French Descartisants examines the problem of admitting the unconscious and the subconscious (not sharply separated here) into a philosophy founded on the evidence of a mind conscious of its operations. The brilliant introduction poses the problem of self-knowledge in St. Augustine and in Descartes who is found to be closer to St. Augustine than to the School. With scrupulous documentation the study reveals Descartes' concerns with subconscious thought, notwithstanding his rigorous insistence on awareness. The two following chapters show how theology forces into the open this problem which D.'s metaphysics had pushed away. The connections between a theory of unconscious and subconscious action and passion with the theory of grace are historically examined. The subtle, original analyses wrung praise even from that grouchy Marxist reviewer, M. Soriano. Searching discussion by E. Bréhier, H. Gouhier and others: Âme et conscience chez Descartes (BSPF 45: 1951, 133–164.)

Reviews: H. - D. Gardeil in RSPT 35: 1951, 693–94; G. Lewis in UPA 21: 1951, 626–27 (abstract); P. Mesnard in RPFE 141: 1951, 321–26; M. Soriano in Pensée no. 40: 1952, 111–13; see also the joint reviews by Cuvillier, Mesnard, Rochot (no. 215a) and I. Fetscher in PhRU 3: 1955, 181 n. 23.

215c [LEWIS] RODIS-LEWIS, GENEVIÈVE: La morale de Descartes. PUF 1957. 132 p. (Initiation philosophique.)

Shortest, and by far the best, introduction to D.'s ethical thought and precepts, very carefully formulated and documented. Recognizing that in D.'s correspondence with Chanut, Elisabeth and Christina "les développements traditionnels .... dominent" (3) and that it is impossible and impermissible to construct on his behalf the ethics he did not live to write, the author stays within the limits of what the texts say rather than what they suggest, and supplies the underlying systematic bond. "La morale qui se dégage ...., met en œuvre à la fois les vérités les plus importantes de la métaphysique, quelques principes de la physique, la déscription des fonctions physiologiques de l'homme et la psychologie des passions" (118), which seems to be the chief distinguishing characteristic of D.'s "morale." The small book discusses D.'s formative years and the morale "par provision"; morale and metaphysics; the union of body and soul, and the mastery of passions; person and community (générosité; prudence de D. et révérence pour les souverains); concluding chapter on the "bien juger et juger le mieux possible" of DM, "a formula which, while holding out the possibility of happiness to man, emphasizes primarily the difficulty of his situation, his distance from the ideal," as Bannan (below, 421) sums up this sane and unexaggerated interpretation.

Reviews: J. F. Bannan in Rmet 13: 1959–60, 420–21; R. Mehl in RHPR 28: 1958, 203–04; B. Rochot in Rsyn 79: 1958, 126–28.

216 LION, FERDINAND: Lebensquellen französischer Metaphysik: Descartes, Rousseau, Bergson. Tr. from the French by Ruth Gillischewski. Ham-

burg, Claassen und Goverts (Zürich, Europa-Verlag), 1949. 128 p. Italian translation: no. 2556.

Bergsonizing, vitalistic interpretation of Cartesianism in three chapters: "Die Lebensquellen des cartesianischen Rationalismus," memory and creation in D., "Die cartesianischen Gewebe." Lively, suggestive, willful; makes Cartesianism a very French, very Latin philosophy where passion is at the core of man, hence of the world. Author does better by Bergson and much, much worse by Rousseau. Still, an effective piece of "Kulturpropaganda."

Reviews: C. Ferro in RFNS 42: 1950, 208–11; Glahn in Sch 26: 1951, 127–28; Grond in PJ 60: 1950, 489.

216a MARCEL, VICTOR: Étendue et conscience. Essai de réfutation du dualisme cartésien. Préface de M. Souriau. Vrin, 1933. viii, 130 p. Thèse complémentaire, Nancy (G. Thomas, 1932).

Sees grave difficulties arising from Descartes' conceiving the "res cogitans" as a substance. Cartesian dualism blocks the road to experimental psychology, tends towards a negation of metaphysics, reduces God from real and objective status to a logical proposition. Marcel's remedy: back to Scholasticism, with modifications. A cogently developed study with concise historical analyses.

Reviews: G. de Giuli in RF 25: 1934, 165–66; R. de Raeymaker in RNS 37: 1934, 252–53.

217 McCRACKEN, DAVID J.: Thinking and valuing; an introduction, partly historical, to the study of the philosophy of value. London, Macmillan, 1950. ix, 238 p.

Applies the thesis that value judgments play an integral part in the intellectual life of man (p. vii) to Descartes, Geulincx, Spinoza. Contrasts the Cartesian spirit with that of the Renaissance philosophers and compares Descartes as critic of the culture of his time with Montaigne, before proceding to an analysis of his ethics and his metaphysical theory of value. Interesting chapters on Arnold Geulincx and his Ethica. Spinoza appears as the ultimate "Cartesian antithesis to the thought of the Renaissance" (196). Boas called the main thesis "Dewey with different emphasis"; the style is slow-moving; but the view of the value principle as binding Cartesian ethics and metaphysics "into a unity of knowledge which is also goodness" (228) is engagingly fresh when encountered in the austere epistemological environment of English Descartes scholarship, however timid and reticent it may look compared to the raptures of the New Quietism across the Channel. "Undoubtedly the most distinguished and rewarding of [recent] English books" on 17th century philosophy (Stewart, review below, 359).

Reviews: L. J. Beck in PhQ 2: 1952, 292; G. B[oas] in JP 48: 1951, 617; J. P. Corbett in Mind 62: 1953, 282–83; R. C. Cross in Phil 27: 1952, 377–78; D. A. Rees in PhQ 1: 1950–51, 454; W. M. Sibley in PhR 61: 1952, 603–605; W. F. M. Stewart in PhQ 2: 1952, 359–61.

218 MATTEI, ANDRÉ: L'homme de Descartes. Aubier, 1940. 262 p. (PhE)

Cartesianism is an all-philosophical attitude of wisdom, "une philosophie de l'amour, une recherche de l'amour par les philtres du doute et du cogito, un amour de l'amour par la mystique de Dieu, une fécondation de l'âme par l'amour de la science" (241). "Descartes joue Dieu et il invente un monde. Or, le monde que

Descartes invente est ce monde même" (234). Brilliant pages on moral, religious aspects of D.'s thought, in poetic language which yet stays this side of bathos and hagiography. But the resemblance between Mattei's theme figure and the sturdy author of René Descartes' works is elusive.

Reviews: J. A. Baisnée in NSch 14: 1940, 420–23; J. G[oheen] in JP 37: 1940, 469; B. Jansen in Sch 17: 1942, 110–11.

219 MERRYLEES, W. A.: Descartes; an examination of some features of his metaphysics and method. Melbourne University Press and Oxford University Press, 1934. xxviii, 330 p.

Sober attempt by a well-trained mind to determine for himself what questions D. raises, and what the true answers are. Topics limited to doubt, cogito, proofs of God, ideas, judgment, method (of Regulae), "simple natures". Cogent discussion, argument by argument, with a useful methodical summary (xi–xxviii). Though critical readers are likely to pepper page margins with questionmarks, this is a good companion for those who, like Descartes, seek to distinguish "le vray d'avec le faux" instead of hunting for the "true" Descartes "dans un tas de si gros volumes, qu'il faudroit plus de temps pour les lire, que nous n'en avons pour demeurer en cette vie," as the true Descartes himself said in his Recherche de la vérité.

Reviews: S. V. Keeling in Phil 11: 1936, 354–56; A. K. Stout in Mind 44: 1935, 367–76.

220 MESNARD, PIERRE: Essai sur la morale de Descartes, Boivin, 1936. 234 p. Thèse supplémentaire, Paris.

I. La conception de la morale. 1. La bona mens; le Dictionnaire et le Corps poétique [the Dream of D.] 2. Première idée de la sagesse. 3. Vers la morale scientifique. 4. Anomalie du DM. 5. Légitimité de la morale provisoire.
II. Les fondements de la morale. 1. Le TP (morale, physique, métaphysique). 2. Actions et passions. 3. L'union de l'âme et du corps. 4. Description et classification des passions.
III. La pratique: 1. Le gouvernement des passions. 2. L'éducation du désir. 3. La générosité cartésienne.
Excursus: Morale et politique; le prétendu machiavélisme de D. Conclusion: La morale cartésienne.

Fundamental. Traces D.'s preoccupation with moral problems from the beginnings in the Cogitationes privatae and the Studium bonae mentis to TP and the "méta-morale" (229) of the late correspondence with Chanut, Elisabeth and Christina. Careful analysis of DM reveals three conceptions: the morale provisoire, a "morale de puissance" connected with the notion of mastery of nature through physics and medicine but actually outside the field of ethics, and the basic elements of a definitive morale, the initial postulate of which is "l'unité réelle du composé humain" (see on this also Segond, no. 230). Thus the problem of dualism and union becomes central to D.'s ethics, which explains the exceptional systematic importance of D.'s treatment of the passions. The moral philosopher must "réaliser l'éducation de cette union, d'une part par l'hygiène du corps, de l'autre par une spiritualisation progressive de l'âme" (Segond's review, 48). "Sagesse", first conceived in the manner of Charron, gradually enters into relationship with other disciplines, to develop a norm of conduct that satisfies both the physicist and the metaphysicist while maintaining the "cohérence interne et l'unité profonde du système" (230). Mesnard, unlike some later commentators, does not try to construe a Cartesian system of ethics but follows the living thought of Descartes which prematurely broke off but had consistently aimed, according to Mesnard, at developing "Sagesse" into an overarching conception which reconciles recognized, legitimate philosophical opposites. The work is essential to the understanding of TP, and helpful in the study of D.'s early thought. See also *Mesnard*'s fine Royaumont paper "L'arbre de la Sagesse" (no. 42, 336–59, with discussion; cf. note to no. 2724) and the controversy between *G. Rodis-Lewis* and Mesnard over her and Gueroult's interpretation of the physiological basis of D.'s theory of passions, following her Royaumont paper "Maîtrise des passions et Sagesse chez Descartes" (ibid., 208–36); also Lefèbvre (no. 295).

Reviews: H. Gouhier in RHPh ns 5: 1937, 211; J. M[aritain] in RCC 37/1: 1936, 767–68 ("Une grande soutenance philosophique"); G. Radetti in GCFI 18: 1937, 292–95; J. Segond in Aph 13, 1937, no. 3 (suppl. bibl.) 47–48; Anon. in RMM 44: 1937, suppl. 1, 123.

221 NATORP, PAUL: Descartes' Erkenntnistheorie. Eine Studie zur Vorgeschichte des Kritizismus. Marburg, Elwert, 1882. viii, 190 p.

Treats D.'s philosophy from the pure epistemological viewpoint as an early idealistic system; elaborates doctrinal affinities with Kant. Valuable chapter on mechanistic philosophies of nature leading to D. and Hobbes. The solidly argued work remains useful for its study of Cartesian key doctrines, though a much deeper understanding of affinities and differences between Descartes and Kant has been achieved since. See also *Natorp*'s "Die Entwickelung Descartes' von den Regeln bis zu den Meditationen" (AGP 10: 10–28, 1897; French translation: no. 2831) and *V. Delbos*' rejection of Natorp's neokantian interpretation: "L'idéalisme et le réalisme dans la philosophie de Descartes" (AnP 22: 39–53, 1911; see the note, no. 1710).

222 OTTAVIANO, CARMELO: L'unità del pensiero cartesiano, e Il cartesianesimo in Italia. Padua, CEDAM, 1943. 221 p. (Problemi d'oggi, ser. 2, v. 3).

The first chapter considers the unity of D.'s philosophy as one of inferential realism ("realismo illazionistico") with the characteristic move from "nosse" to "esse", a middle path between realism and idealism. Ch. 2 takes D.'s "fisica a priori" as focus of unity. The third chapter is a study of Cartesianism in Italy (see no. 461). Intriguing thumbnail characterization of D.'s philosophy: Occasion – collapse of the Aristotelian-Scholastic theory of substantial forms; genetic origin – scepticist; method – idealistic; intention – scientific-mathematical; foundation – metaphysical-religious; conclusion – realist; "visione totale" – unitarian (10–11). Contribution of great independence and originality. See also *no. 27*.

223 REID, THOMAS: Œuvres complètes de Thomas Reid, chef de l'école écossaise, publiées par M. Th. Jouffroy, avec des fragments de M. (Pierre-Paul) Royer-Collard et une introduction de l'éditeur. 6 vols. Santelet (v. 1: Masson), 1828–36.

This translation of the works of Adam Smith's successor, with the influential lectures of Royer-Collard, Dugald Stewart's Life of Reid, and Jouffroy's substantial introduction, was instrumental in shaping dominant French Descartes and Malebranche interpretation from Cousin to Bouillier, Saisset and others. The reaction came in the 1880's with Liard's Descartes and Pillon's Malebranche-Bayle studies in AnP 1895–1904 ("L'évolution de l'idéalisme au XVIIIe siècle"), but Renouvier had already in 1842 torn into the epistemology of the Scottish School in his fierce attempt to establish Descartes as the central modern philosopher and pioneer of science (no. 188, 556–58). For the pertinent texts of Reid, Dugald Stewart and Sir William Hamilton see no. 3038, no. 3350, and no. 2179a. See also Dauriac's essay on Descartes and Reid (no. 249), and Rémusat (no. 224).

224 RÉMUSAT, CHARLES COMTE DE: "Descartes." "De la possibilité d'une conciliation entre Descartes, Reid et Kant." In his: Essais de philosophie. Ladrange, 1842, vol. 1, Ch. 2, 5; p. 94–171, 431–77.

Flowery but clear exposition of Dugald Stewart's view of D. as father of "la philosophie expérimentale de l'esprit humain, de la vraie métaphysique" (169). As to the rest of D.'s work: "Alors commencent les mathématiques et la physique. Nous ne suivons pas Descartes sur ce nouveau terrain" (153); neither did Rémusat's master, V. Cousin. The curious, deplorable essay (ch. 5) on D., Reid and Kant touches a low point in French philosophical D. criticism.

225 RICHTER, LISELOTTE: René Descartes. Dialoge mit deutschen Denkern. Hamburg, Hoffmann und Campe, 1942, 1946. 96 p. (Geistiges Europa).

Purpose: "einen französisch-deutschen Philosophen-Dialog gleichsam aus der Sphäre seliger Geister zu schreiben" (96). The blessed spirits, all German and critical of Descartes – Kant, Goethe, Herder, Hamann, Nietzsche and many others – try to correct D.'s "an sich verständliche Einseitigkeiten" which, "in der Vergröberung durch seine Nachbeter", have become a world power and world menace. Useful for its quotations, though exact references are lacking.

Review: Gerhard Hess in Dlit 63: 1942, 969–71.

225a RIDEAU, ÉMILE (S.J.): "Descartes." In his. Descartes, Pascal, Bergson. Boivin, 1937, p. 11–110.

Sympathetic yet not uncritical appraisal in popular language sufficiently precise to do justice to the "magnifique virilité de Descartes" (105): "cet homme, peu religieux, est un mystique de l'univers" (109). Gingerly treatment of his proofs of existence of God, recognizing D.'s good intentions but doubting their "valeur apostolique": they smack of the sin of excessive intellectualism (37–38).

Review: Anon. in RMM 45, suppl. 3, 24–25.

226 ROSENFIELD, LEONORA DAVIDSON COHEN: From beast-machine to man-machine; animal soul in French letters from Descartes to La Mettrie. Preface by Paul Hazard. New York, Oxford UP, 1941. xxviii, 353 p. Columbia dissertation (OUP 1940).

I. The beast-machine and the Cartesians. D.'s denial of animal soul.
II. Animal soul and anticartesians. 1. Traditionalism [Dualists – Cartesian or anti-

cartesian? Peripatetics and substantial form; Neoplatonists and mystic soul; eclecticism]. 2. Empiricism [Epicureans and flaming soul; freethinkers; the man-machine; sequel]. 3. Poets and the animal soul.
Epilogue. Notes. Appendix. Bibliography.

Erudite, lively historical monograph. The issue in the three-cornered controversy "was less the beast than the system of philosophy" (p. 185) as "Cartesian mechanism [first] defeated [Peripatetic] traditionalism, then, swelled by empiricism, culminated in the man-machine." Part I deals with D.'s doctrine of animal automatism and its subsequent spread in physiology, metaphysics, theology and poetry (Cardinal de Polignac and Louis Racine). Part II introduces the opponents of the doctrine: Peripatetics, Neoplatonists, eclecticists, empiricists (the treatment of La Mettrie has been challenged), and again the poets: La Fontaine, followed by nice pages on Mlle. Cathérine Descartes, Madeleine de Scudéry, Antoinette Deshoulières, and the widely unknown Gilles Morfouace de Beaumont. Exceptionally rich coverage of French and Dutch figures in the controversy, with much biographical and bibliographical information. For related studies by Dix Harwood, George Boas, Hester Hastings see Wade's review below. See also the *author*'s articles on Ignace-Gaston Pardies' "Discours de la connoissance des bestes" of 1696 (PMLA 52: 1937, 763–72); on the 1645–1749 English controversy of the animal machine (Henry More, Sir Kenelm Digby, Antoine Le Grand, John Norris) in RLC 17: 1937, 461–81, bibliography 482–87; and her translation of the Descartes-More correspondence (no. 84). For Holland see *Paul Dibon*, "Le problème de l'âme des bêtes chez Descartes et ses premiers disciples néerlandais" (Sassen Festschrift, no. 1764, 1954, 187–222). *A. G. A. Balz* gives a bold explanation why latter-day Cartesians considered the doctrine crucial ("Whitehead, Descartes and the bifurcation of nature," PhR 31: 1934, 290–92). This and *Balz*'s brilliant study of "Cartesian doctrine and the animal soul; an incident in the formation of the modern philosophical tradition" (in no. 431, 106–57, reprinted from SH 1, v. 3, 1935, 117–77) should not be overlooked. See also Espinas (no. 163), Young (no. 350), Thijssen-Schoute (no. 467).

Reviews: R. Allers in NSch 16: 1942, 184–85; J. Anderson in AJPP 19: 1941, 277–86 (critical); A. G. A. Balz in PhAb 2, no. 5: 1941, 18; F. Baldensperger in MLF 26: 1941, 168–70; J. R. Cantor in PsychB 38: 1941, 772; P. Courtilles in RevR 1941, 80–83; V. Guilleton in AmSocR 7: 1942, 125; H. Hastings in AHR 47: 1942, 842; G. R. Havens in MLN 57: 1942, 681–83; R. Hazelton in JRel 22: 1942, 229; B. M. Laing in Phil 16: 1941, 438–39; H. A. Larrabee in JP 38: 1941, 276–77; H. Kurtz in RR 33: 1942, 84–87; A. Montague in Isis 16: 1942, 153–56; M. Rader in MLQ 2: 1941, 341–43; L. W. Tancock in MLR 37: 1942, 516–17; Ira Wade in FR 16: 1942, 153–56.

227 ROY, JEAN H.: L'imagination selon Descartes. Gallimard, 1944. 203 p. (La jeune philosophie).

Beautiful, sensitive study, dedicated to Sartre whose L'imagination (1936) and L'imaginaire (1940) provide the phenomenological ground upon which it is built. Imagination, cardinal in the Dream of D., is later opposed to understanding, and excluded from the epistemology; yet image and imagery remain a problem. Moreover, analysis of doubt and cogito leads to a difficulty regarding the body as it is experienced in two different ways: dualistically separated from thinking, and in the union of body and mind. While intellectual memory does not concern the body, corporeal memory does; at this point, the problem of the image issues into the problem of reality vs. dream. Ch. 2 establishes that the union cannot be proved by means of the imagination, contrary to some D. interpreters; it also reveals the importance of "l'imagination-passion," which shifts the issue from metaphysics to psychology. The following long chapter on this "imagination-passion" shows dream at the root of Cartesian doubt: Descartes sees in dreaming the rationally uncontrollable workings of the imagination, conceived as a passion. This has profound consequences with regard to the problem of error (ch. 4, L'imagination-passion et la logique): "pour assurer le maximum de securité à l'esprit, D. a soumis le rêve au corps et le corps à un mécanisme rigoureux" (193). Descartes' theory of the image is found to be "une théorie extrèmement poussée du symbole" which permits him "d'échapper a l'hypothèse, d'une espèce qui ne soit ni un corps, ni une pensée, et par conséquent laisse intacte la distinction de l'âme et du corps" (201). This "espèce" is the realm of the Imaginary, particularly the dream: "C'est d'abord le malin génie qu'il faut terrasser, le rêve dont il faut sortir" (203). [This is indeed one of D.'s central problems, which opens the First Meditation and ends the Sixth, leaving a faint question mark after the hesitant solution (see no. 306).] See also *Paul Landormy's* excellent study "La mémoire corporelle et la mémoire intellectuelle dans la philosophie de Descartes" (Bibliothèque du premier Congrès international de philosophie, Colin, 1902, v. 4, p. 259–98).

Reviewed by Kanapa in Pensée no. 5, 1945, 143–35.

228 RUSSIER, JEANNE: Sagesse cartésienne et religion; essai sur la connaissance de l'immortalité de l'âme selon Descartes. PUF, 1958. 156 p. (BPC)

Livre I. *Raison et foi dans la connaissance de l'âme.* 1. Le problème de l'âme au temps de Descartes. 2. Immortalité de nature et immortalité de fait. 3. Doute hyperbolique et certitude vulgaire.
Livre II. *Raison et foi dans les "promesses" de béatitude.* 1. L'état de l'âme après cette vie. 2. Immortalité et individualité.
Conclusion: Sagesse cartésienne et religion. – Bibliographie raisonnée.

The author poses two precise questions: (1) Does Descartes find the assurance of immortality in Reason or in Faith? (2) In what manner is the status of the soul after death knowable for him? The answer to the first question emerges from D.'s dualistic position: the awareness of the res cogitans regarding its separate substantial existence, its indivisibility, and its higher nature allows the affirmation of its essential immortality without taking recourse to Faith. Any assurance of actual immortality after separation from the body however goes beyond Reason and must come from Revelation. Hyperbolic doubt cannot strike at this assurance because this doubt leads to certitude only in questions accessible to Reason; in questions of moral conduct Descartes allows only "certitude vulgaire". Hence (question 2) Faith must serve as the guide to the "promesses de béatitude" after death, since Reason cannot by its own resources ascertain the posthumous status of the soul. The carefully documented study seems to read D.'s texts a bit more closely than they were meant to be read, but the sharp confrontation of Descartes' positions with the Thomistic positions of his time is illuminating.

Reviews: J. F. Bannan in Rmet 13: 1959–60, 423–24; B. Rochot in Rsyn 79: 1958, 123–30; D. d'Orsi in Sophia 28: 1960, 97–98; G. Michaeli in RCSF 14: 1959, 464–65; J. I. in RyF 160: 1959, 269–70; A. Robinet in DSS no. 46–47, 1960, 107; M. Varin d'Ainville in Eph 14: 1959, 100–101.

229 SCHOLZ, HEINRICH, ADOLF KRATZER, and JOSEPH HOFMANN: Descartes. Drei Vorträge. Münster, Aschendorff, 1951. 80 p. (Abhandlun-

gen der Gesellschaft zur Förderung der Westfälischen Landesuniversität, v. 2.)

Three model academic lectures, judging Descartes in the cool, objective, scientific manner. Scholz gives a searching appraisal of D.'s role in transforming the Western mind, classifying his influence under four "necessary and sufficient" axioms of Cartesian doctrine. Kratzer evaluates D.'s physics in precise yet popular fashion. Hofmann assesses his mathematical achievement from the modern viewpoint, against a rich historical background, with a good bibliography of sources.

Review: E. J. Dijksterhuis in AIHS 5: 1952, 123.

230 SEGOND, J.: La sagesse cartésienne et la doctrine de la science. Vrin, 1932. 321 p.

1. Le besoin de certitude. 2. La notion de la sagesse. 3. La lumière naturelle. 4. L'erreur. 5. Le doute et la libération de l'erreur. 6–8. Le cogito. 9. Symbolisme scientifique et l'agnosticisme religieux. 10. L'âme et le corps. 11. La morale et la béatitude.

"Sagesse" is harmonic unity of will and mind; its ultimate stage, a purified rationalistic ethics; its function, the organization of mind for the conquest of science. The main themes of Cartesian metaphysics are subjected to an unusual idealistic interpretation in which the cogito is not a first truth "mais la forme des vérités que développe la science cartésienne" (181), the "morale de puissance" (self-mastery) a morale of free will and condition for mastery of nature through science, D.'s concept of "absolute science" an almost Hegelian panlogism (187) coupled with mild, enlightened, tolerant religious agnosticism. For Segond, morale de puissance is a step from morale provisoire to the ultimate morale de béatitude (sagesse), whereas Mesnard's later book treats it rather as a passing aberration of D.'s (no. 220). Copious text citations, without page references, support Segond's thesis by giving "a violent interpretation to all that D. said to the contrary" (E 57: 1937, 547). What emerges is again the old Cartesian tree of knowledge: metaphysical roots, trunk of physics branching into medicine, mechanics, morals, and no forbidden fruit. More recent interpreters of D.'s ethics love to sit on its highest branch, "le dernier degré de la sagesse," basking in the rays of pure Goodness; no wonder they forget that there is a trunk beneath their lofty seat, holding it up. Segond's idealistic stage illumination, by contrast, bathes the trunk in light; in the green chiaroscuro above it, one dimly discerns "libre-arbitre, amour et contemplation de Dieu, autant de figures encore de cette poursuite [cartésienne] de la vérité idéale" (317). This too is willful, but *Honi soit qui mal y pense.*

Reviews: Anon. in RMM 40: 1933, suppl. bibl. 1, 6–7; G. de Giuli in RF 26: 1935, 359–60; L. Lavelle in no. 11, 45–53; F. Olgiati in no. 14, 219–21.

231 SERRUS, CHARLES: La méthode de Descartes et son application à la métaphysique. Alcan, 1933. 125 p. (BPC). Thèse complémentaire, Paris.

Concise study, "admirably conducted in the very 'modern' manner" (Keeling's review, 339) finds D.'s Method essentially mathematical, and therefore inapplicable to his metaphysics, the principles of which "sont des propositions générales que l'on ne peut utiliser que dans le syllogisme, qui est un raisonnement infécond" (118). They attempt the impossible, i.e. the deductive construction of "une pensée sur les relations que le verbe être insère dans la proposition" (ibid.) D.'s Method,

on the other hand, represents a theory of relations and offers "an imposing theory of analysis and synthesis," vs, the "pauvre théorie aristotélienne" (28). However, prudence and dogmaticism in science prevented. D from recognizing the purely hypothetic and deductive structure of mathematics and the probabilistic nature of physical hypothesis, though both were within his grasp. Seeking to prove the existence of what needed only to be postulated, determined to find truth, certitude, infallible evidence where he needed only observational verification or operational decision, he constructed a metaphysics which, like all metaphysics, is not a rational discipline but one of those wonderful "grandes synthèses" which science, ethics, art, poetry suggest to man: "Il ne faudrait pas les placer avant la science, mais après elle" and "il n'y aurait pas trop lieu de raisonner à leur sujet" (120).
The Method in question is that of the Regulae, as modified by DM. Serrus' brief critical analysis of the methodological difference between Cartesian analysis and synthesis (ch. 1) is remarkable. Ch. 2 judges the significance of the method from the viewpoint of modern logic. Ch. 3 studies the application of the method in MM with regard to nonhypothetical certitude (the cogito), the status of existential and essential statements (the proofs of God) and the "valeur des jugements de perception concernant l'existence sensible" (substance dualism and the union of body and soul). The critique of D.'s application of his Method to metaphysics (ch. 4) show in detail the decisive and fatal role of Scholastic principles deflecting D.'s original metaphysical intuition; see the striking list of such axioms which he, but not his contemporary critics, held to be indisputable, 89–90. D.'s basic mistake, however, was to attempt to present his metaphysics as a science. Father Lenoble calls the small book an "œuvre capital qui .... aide grandement à discerner le philosophe éternel et l'homme des années 1630" (RMM 63: 1958, 351), which is true enough if one adds that for Serrus, Descartes the "philosophe éternel," i.e., the metaphysician, is not the rigorous rational thinker he wanted to be, but a poet – and a very great one indeed.

Reviews: M. Campo in RFNS 26: 1934, 315–20; G. G. in RF 25: 1934, 177–78; S. V. Keeling in Phil 11: 1936, 339–40; M. R. in Aph 13: 1937, no. 3, suppl. bibl. 46–47. See also A. Pastore's critique of Serrus, no. 321a.

231a TEIXEIRA, LIVIO: Ensaio sôbre a moral de Descartes. São Paulo, Boletim da faculdade de filosofia, ciências y letras. 1955. 224 p.

In view of the dominating position of French contributions to the study of D.'s ethics, attention may be drawn to two modern monographs in other languages, Teixeira's substantial Portuguese volume and *Alexandru Tilman-Timon's* short, comprehensive Etica lui Descartes of 1946 (no. 3421), in Rumanian) which ranges from the place of ethics in Cartesianism over the major topics to free will and générosité. Utilized by Gueroult in no. 170.

232 VERNEAUX, ROGER: "La révolution cartésienne." In his: Les sources cartésiennes et kantiennes de l'idéalisme français. Beauchesne, 1936, p. 9–197. (Bibl. des Archives de philosophie.)

"Ce travail n'est pas historique mais doctrinal" (11), a clear, distinct treatment of D.'s supposedly clear, distinct ideas. Finds the Cartesian revolution far less revolutionary than D. did. D.'s philosophy contains the seeds of French idealism, introduces a new spirit of radical criticism, orients philosophy towards the subject by cutting the bond between mind and things. Five valuable chapters on D.'s mathesis universalis, problem of knowledge, cogito, innate ideas, and the "réalisme indirect."

Reviews: M. de Corte in RdePh 37: 1937, 149–56; A. Etcheverry in Aph 14: 1938, no. 1, suppl. bibl.: 37–39; R. Jolivet in RT 43: 1937, 133–37; A. de Waelhens in RNS 40: 1937, 448–53 (important).

233 VERSFELD, MARTHINUS: An essay on the metaphysics of Descartes. London, Methuen, 1940. 192 p.

1–2: Descartes' attitude to metaphysics. 3. Structure of his metaphysics. 4. Circle. 5. Cogito. 6. Self. 7. Definitions of substance. 8. The idea of a thinking substance. 9. First proof of God's existence. 10. The Sixth Meditation.

Earnest, unassuming study in clear English of D.'s problem of bridging the gap between ideas and existence: ".... why a chain of reasoning in our heads, connected by pure logical necessity, should be a true transcription of the real, and why there should be a harmony between the laws of nature and those of the mind" (15). Author takes MM as his chief text, judiciously supplementing it with texts from D.'s other works and from P. S. Régis, J. du Roure, Arnauld. The core chapters patiently explore the Cartesian circle (held to be inevitable in any system), 'cogito', self, substance. Laing's review helps separate D.'s difficulties from author's

Review: B. M. Laing in Phil 16: 1941, 427–29.

VIII. THE PHILOSOPHY OF DESCARTES: SPECIAL TOPICS

235 ABERCROMBIE, NIGEL: "Saint Augustine and the Cartesian metaphysics." In his: Saint Augustine and French classical thought. Oxford, Clarendon Press, 1938, p. 57–90.

Augustinian philosophy was the "safety valve" that allowed D., and particularly Malebranche, to develop systems which would otherwise have discredited their orthodoxy, just as Augustinism "enables orthodoxy to accommodate such thinkers as [Maurice] Blondel today" (10). Although there is a "fundamental affinity" between D. and St. Augustine, the Cartesian cogito is independent of the alleged Augustinian archetype, despite a general "family likeness" (common Platonic tradition). Critical examination of Gilson's position regarding D. and St. Thomas.

Reviews: L. J. Beck in RMM 46: 1939, 350–51; Phil 14: 1939, 480–81.

235a AYER, ALFRED JULES: Language, truth and logic. London, Gollancz, 1936. 2nd ed., rev., 1946. Reprinted: New York, Dover, s.a. See 235b.

235b AYER, ALFRED JULES: "I think, therefore I am." In his: The problem of knowledge. London, Macmillan, 1956, p. 45–54. Reprinted: Penguin Books.

The cogito means, not just "I think," but rather "there is a thought now"; hence the conclusion "I exist" does not follow (no. 235a, 45–46). The "idealistic view that what is immediately given in sense-experience must necessarily be mental" is rejected (ibid., 142) because "the assertion that the mind is a substance, being a metaphysical assertion, cannot follow from anything." These incisive but brief comments of 1936 becomes a full-fledged logical attack on the cogito in Ayer's work twenty years later: the cogito does not prove that Descartes, or anyone, knows anything: "It simply makes the logical point that one sort of statement follows from another" (no. 2356, 47). The cogito is "not meaningless, only peculiar.... and not only peculiar but degenerate," being merely demonstrative: statements like "I exist" have nothing to say "beyond what is implied in the fact that they have a reference" (54). See also Ayer's 1953 Analysis article on the cogito, cited in no. 335. *C. B. Daly* (1961; see no. 1658a) attacks Ayer's view because it denies Descartes the "phenomenological or existential point" which he considered the core of his argument: Cartesianism does not start with "cogito" but with "sum," i.e., existentially. For Daly it is no accident that anticartesian philosophies (including Ayer's) "tend also to be atheistic philosophies" (185), a statement that would have surprised the theologians of Descartes' age.

235c BACHELARD, GASTON: "L'épistémologie non-cartésienne." In his: Le nouvel esprit scientifique. Alcan, 1934, p. 135–179. Italian translation no. 1106.

Modern scientific epistemology "substitue à la clarté en soi [scil. des natures simples] une sorte de clarté opératoire. Loin que ce soit l'être qui illumine la relation, c'est la relation qui illumine l'être" (144). Thesis brilliantly illustrated by comparing D.'s famous meditation on a piece of wax with what a modern physicist does to, and sees in, a drop of wax. The result seems to confirm Jaspers' view of D. the scientist (see no. 175). Reviews: G. Giuli in RF 26: 1935, 362–33; of the Italian transl.: P. Facchi in RCSF 7: 1952, 60–61; D.C. in RSF 4: 1950–51, 107–09; Anon. in CivC 103: 1952, 321–22; V. Melchiorre in RFNS 46: 1954, 87–89.
For the linguistic view of the same example see *J. J. C. Smart*, "Descartes and the wax" in PhQ 1: 1950–51, 50–57: Descartes' question "What, then, was it I knew so distinctly in the piece of wax?" (MM II) "is not a real question because it has no point." See the rejoinders by *P. G. Lucas* and *J. N. Wright* (ibid., 1: 1951, 348–55). Lucas shows that Smart does not give "a true report of what Descartes wrote," as the Latin text proves. Wright offers a very interesting interpretation of Descartes' "Personne n'en doute, personne ne juge autrement" which precedes the question which Smart claims to be senseless.

236 BALTRUŠAITIS, JURGIS: "Descartes: les automates et la doute." In his: Anamorphoses ou perspectives curieuses. Perrin, 1955, p. 33–43. (Jeu savant).

D.'s Cogitationes privatae contain intriguing fragments on automats and mechanical and optical deceptions. His interest in curious and mysterious matters was possibly stimulated by writings of architect Salomon de Caus and mathematician Jean-François Nicéron, also perhaps by Giambattista della Porta's celebrated Magia naturalis. *Geneviève Rodis-Lewis* ("Machineries et perspectives curieuses dans leurs rapports avec le cartésianisme," DSS 6, no. 32: 1956, 461–74) offers a rich critical discussion, judiciously concluding that D., whatever stimulus he may have received from these playful forerunners, yet "met en garde contre le goût de mystère et la curiosité désordonnée" (466). See also Rossi, no. 328.

237 BERTHET, J.: "La méthode de Descartes avant le Discours." RMM 4: 1896, 399–415.

There is no metaphysics in Regulae; their epistemology is independent of DM; they represent a stage of "geometric idealism" between 1619 and the metaphysics of 1628. Their section on imperfect questions, with its theory of sensation, raises the problem of verification where necessity is absent. DM and PP answer the problem: verification decides only between chains of deductive reasoning, an answer which emaciates verification.

238 BOAS, GEORGE: "The role of protophilosophy in intellectual history." JP 45: 1948, 673–84.

Examines the "protophilosophy" (axioms and assertions unproven and not to be proven) underlying D.'s philosophy: basic assumptions, metaphors, syntactical rules of thinking, systematization etc. Develops from DM six such assumptions concerning lumen naturale, pervasive identity of specific forms, uniqueness of the true, similarity of the orders of nature and of logic, substantiality of the subject, similarity of cause and effect.

239 BONTADINI, GUSTAVO: Studi sulla filosofia dell'età cartesiana. Brescia, La Scuola, 1947. 263 p.

Collection of papers, some unpublished, by a judicious Italian Descartes scholar. Reprints his valuable bibliographical studies (see no. 15). The philosophical essays revolve about Olgiati's concept of D.'s "fenomenismo razionalistico." Interesting study of Leibniz' critique of Cartesianism. See no. 1278–86 for other studies in this volume.

Reviews: A. Carlini in Gmet 3: 1948, 528–30, also in no. 4, 190–92; E. Garulli in Humanitas (Brescia) 4: 1949, 947–51.

241 BRÉHIER, ÉMILE: La philosophie et son passé. Alcan, 1940. 146 p. (Nouvelle encycl. philosophique, v. 24.)

Part II includes three important previously published studies, connected by the creation theme: Cartesian matter and creation (RMM 44: 1937, 21–34), showing D.'s resistance towards Henry More's tendency to spiritualize extension, and the "apothéose de l'étendue cartésienne" by Malebranche and Spinoza "qui la fait passer du rang de créature à celui de réalitée incréée" (RMM, p. 21); on the creation of eternal verities (RPFE 123: 1937, 15–29) and its connection with the "malin génie" hypothesis, elucidating a crux in D.'s doctrine of God; Bréhier shows that the doctrine first appears in D.'s correspondence in 1630, is almost forgotten in DM and MM, and revived in response to Gassend's objection; finally a brief paper on continued creation, reprinted from S 5: 1937, 3–10.

Reviews: Anon. in StU 29: 1955, 379–80; E. Cassirer in no. 5, 34–35 and 47–48; P. P. Wiener in PA 1, no. 3: 1940, 12.

242 CANTECOR, G.: "A quelle date Descartes a-t-il écrit la 'Recherche de la vérité'?" RHPh 2: 1928, 254–89.

Attempts to prove that RV may have been written as early as 1619–20, with interesting discussion of D.'s formative years. *Henri Gouhier* (RHPh 3: 1929, 296–320) manfully defends the traditional late date, settling for 1647 on remarkably good grounds. *E. Cassirer* in no. 1486 (Lychnos 1938, RPFE 1939, and no. 243, ch. 2, with critique of Cantecor, Brunetière, Jungmann, Gouhier) calls RV Descartes' last statement, written for Queen Christina, and interrupted by death. Cantecor's thesis is bold, Gouhier's solid, Cassirer's ingenious. All three suffer from the same incurable ill, lack of facts. *K. Jungmann* claimed in 1904 that RV was a first sketch of Le Monde; see the note to no. 2321.

243 CASSIRER, ERNST: Descartes, Lehre, Persönlichkeit, Wirkung. Stockholm, Bermann-Fischer, 1939. 308 p. See also no. 1477–79.

Collection of Cassirer's important contributions to the 1937 anniversary [original publications, French and Swedish editions: no. 1477–79, 1483–86]. Pt. I: D.'s concept of truth; his concept of the unity of the sciences. Pt. II: Important study of D. and Corneille (psychological and moral affinities, notes on tragic art); a study of the genesis of RV (see no. 242); penetrating study of Queen Christina of Sweden from the viewpoint of the history of ideas: universal theism and the problem of natural religion, the Stoicist revival; the significance of the theory of passions; Christina in the light of the heroic ideal of her century. See also *Johan Nordstrøm*, "Cartesius och drottning Christinas omvändelse" (Lychnos 1941, 248–90) on D.'s alleged role in Christina's conversion to Catholicism.

Reviews: E. Bréhier in RPFE 129: 1940, 272–76, and in Theoria 6: 1940, 164–67; H.-D. Gardeil in RSPT 27: 1938, 358; A. Nyman in Theoria 7: 1941, 154–58; R. A. Hofstadter in PA 1, no. 3: 1940, 22–23; H.-J. de Vleeschauwer in Theoria 5: 1939, 86–96; and particularly Konstantin Reichardt on Cassirer's contribution to literary criticism (Descartes, Christina, Corneille; D.'s "influence" on French literature) in: The Philosophy of Ernst Cassirer, 1949 [no. 3037], 663ff., esp. 672–76.

244 CHASTAING, MAXIME: "Descartes, Fauste de Riez et le problème de la connaissance d'autrui." In: Étienne Gilson, philosophe de la chrétienté. Éditions du Cerf, 1949, 187–211. (Rencontres, v. 30.)

".... bien jolie étude" (Bréhier, RPFE 147: 1957, 78) develops the difficulties of the problem seen by St. Augustine, Faustus bishop of Riez (5th c.), and Claudin Mamert. The Cartesian solution: "J'expérience autrui, comme l'union de mon âme et de mon corps" (Bsig 5: 1951, no. 1506). See also *Chastaing's* "L'abbé [G.] de Lanion et le problème cartésien de la connaissance d'autrui" (RPFE 141: 1951, 228–48), on de Lanion's Méditations métaphysiques which he published in 1684 under the pseudonym Guillaume Wander [in Beyle's Recueil de quelques pieces curieuses concernant la philosophie de M. Descartes]; also *Chastaing's* "Le 'Traité' de l'abbé M***.Macy et la 'vieille réponse' cartésienne au problème de la connaissance d'autrui" RPFE 143: 1953, 76–84, on Macy's 'Traité de l'âme des bêtes', 1735, in which Macy opposes David Renaud Boullier's "Essai philosophique sur l'âme des bêtes" of 1728; and *Chastaing's* remarkable monograph L'existence d'autrui (PUF 1951, 355 p. Reviews: no. 1515).

244a DE CORTE, MARCEL: La dialectique poétique de Descartes. Aph 13, no. 2, p. 101–61. 1937.

Noted Thomist draws from D.'s Dream and Cogitationes privatae the unusual thesis that D. considered philosophical cognition as "une activité poétique" which taps the immense capabilities of man's noëtic equipment and store of innate ideas. Regulae I–XI, hypothetically dated back from 1628 to 1619, are said to articulate this epistemology of poetic penetration of reality which Descartes later transformed but never abandoned. *Pierre Mesnard* (Eph 5: 1950, 178–84) rates the study, "malgré toutes ses réticences et ses réserves d'école" (178), the most remarkable and meaningful answer to the enigma of Descartes' "rationalism." For the opposite view regarding poetic cognition see Read, no. 324a. Cf. Balz in JP 35: 1938, 174–76.

245 CUMMING, ROBERT: "Descartes' provisional morality." Rmet 9: 1955–56, 207–35.

Considers, against the common view, D.'s morale provisoire to be neither banal nor unrelated to the rules of method which, in fact, are even implied in it. Original study, critical of Gilson and Lévy-Bruhl; ends on the view of "a relaxed Descartes" (234) who gave most of his time, as he said, "au relasche des sens et au repos de l'esprit" (AT III, 692). No reference to Gouhier who originated this interpretation

246 DĄMBSKA, IZYDORA: "Meditationes Descartes'a na tłe sceptycyzmu frankuskiege XVII wieku." KF 19: 1950, 1–24. French summary 161–62.

Important study. Tries to separate in French scepticism a rationalistic- nominalistic current (Montaigne, La Mothe Le Vayer, Sanchez) and a mystic-fideistic one reaching up from the Greeks through medieval philosophy to Charron, Pascal, Huet. Finds three types of philosophical refutation of scepticism, viz., axiological, logical, and epistemological. The latter type is represented by Mersenne and by D.'s first two Meditations. See also no. 247.

247 DĄMBSKA, IZYDORA: "Sur certains principes méthodologiques dans les Principia philosophiae de Descartes." RMM 62: 1957, 57–66.

Distinguishes between D.'s "official" methodology in the Regulae, DM and MM, according to which scientific hypothesis necessarily flows from the first principles of metaphysics; and a second one, applied in the Dioptrique, Météores, Le Monde, and PP, which allows even false hypotheses to be used, provided their consequences are verified by observation. This second methodology goes beyond Galilei's similar position and anticipates Vaihinger; it brings D. close to the sceptical current of his time. D. is said to have realized the conflict between the apriorism of the first and the instrumentalism of the second methodology. One may ask whether this would not make D. a forerunner of Bridgman's operationalism rather than of Vaihinger's "Als Ob." *J.-P. Weber* (RMM 63: 1958, 246–50; see note to no. 3544a) tries to show that the supposedly methodological differences are merely expository. See no. 3544a

248 DAUDIN, HENRI: La liberté de la volonté. Signification des doctrines classiques. PUF, 1950 (BPC), 77–119.

La notion de la liberté humaine dans la philosophie de Descartes. Les formules de la liberté. Les controverses religieuses sur le libre arbitre à l'époque de Descartes et sa position.

Posthumously published 1939–40 course, carefully edited. Lectures 6–9 place D.'s doctrine of free will in its historical context, stressing its wholly temporal character, and examines the reasons why D. did not extend it to the theological and ethical, field. Sees D.'s decisive advance in having linked freedom to "l'hommme du temps, d'avoir entrepris de prouver que cet homme du temps est capable d'initiative et de création ...." (104). Ninth lecture examines D.'s position to the religious free will controversies of his time, finding affinities with the positions of Guillaume Gibieuf, Jansenius, Arnauld. Running critical commentary to Gilson's La liberté chez Descartes et la théologie (no. 164). Vigorous, faithful to the texts, free of hagiography and apologetics.

Reviews: C. B. in Et 270: 1951, 126–27; V. Niebergall in PhLit 4: 1952, 257–61; A. Stern in Pers 35: 1954, 206–07; R. Tric in JPNP 45: 1952, 234–35.

249 DAURIAC, LIONEL: "Essai sur l'instinct réaliste: Descartes et Thomas Reid." AnP 14: 1903, 85–113.

The realist instinct, "une disposition naturelle et universelle de l'esprit," manifests itself "par une invincible croyance à la réalité des choses" (85). Reid's polemic against D. is misdirected: D. tries to legitimize the realist instinct; Reid himself merely describes it and submits to it. Though the argument is doubtful, the article helps understand the D. image of the Scottish realists, Royer-Collard, and Victor Cousin.

252 DREYFUS, GINETTE: "Discussion sur le 'cogito' et l'axiome 'pour penser il faut être'." RIP 6: 1952, 117–25.

Careful study of conflicting conceptions of the Cartesian cogito proposed by M. Gueroult (a relation innate in our understanding) and H. Gouhier (a necessary articulation between my thought and my existence). Accepts a modified Gueroult view. Mario Levi's review in S 21: 1953, 127 points to *C. Ottaviano*'s resolution of the problem in his theory of synthetic judgments (see no. 2882), not referred to by Dreyfus. For a discussion of the cogito interpretations of Hamelin, Olgiati, Gilson, Gouhier, Jolivet, see: *S. Czajkowski*, "Cogito ergo sum. Kartezjusza i jego nowa koncepcja duszny" (KF 19: 1950, 39–66; French summary, 164–66; see the note to no. 1677).

253 DROETTO, ANTONIO: "Ugone Grozio e l'avversario di Cartesio nella questione delle verità eterne." RIFD 24, ser. 3, no. 1: 1947, 58–80.

Unusual study finds D.'s "adversary" not so much in St. Thomas as in Hugo Grotius who cut the umbilical cord between theology and jurisprudence, formulating "l'ipotesi concessiva della realtá del giusto, independamente dal sapere e dal volere di Dio" (58). This transformation of the metaphysical doctrine of eternal verities in the field of ethics and law, where it had vital practical consequences, is studied by way of contrasting D. and Grotius, Leibniz and Pufendorf, against the background of the Scholastic tradition. See also *Eugenio Colorni*, "Le verità eterne in Descartes e in Leibniz," CD 1: 132–140, noting Grotius' famous affirmation of the validity of natural law "etiamsi daremus, quod sine summo scelere dari nequit, non esse Deum" (137).

256 FERRO, CARMELO: "Cartesio e il problema della metafisica." RFNS 42: 1950, 335–55.

Notable study of D.'s attitude towards metaphysics as shown in his treatment of Being and reality. As against Bacon and Galilei (scientific turn), Descartes' treatment of the problem recalls that of his Scholastic masters; it does not open the road to Kant. Ferro accepts Olgiati's thesis of D.'s "rationalist phaenomenalism" but points to the voluntaristic side of D.'s metaphysics, the physiognomy of which is excellently outlined.

Reviews: C. Dollo in S 20: 1952, 398–99; J. Hellín in PenM 8: 1952, 262; G. Santoro in Sapienza 4: 1951, 544–45.

258 FRANCESCHI, ALFREDO: "El concepto de 'materia sutil' en Descartes." In: Homenaje (no. 40), v. 2, p. 11–41.

Judicious study of the "subtle matter" concept which D. had to develop to save the doctrine of res extensa with its necessary rejection of the notion of the void. *Spinoza's* great commentary to D.'s Principia, the profoundest contribution to its understanding, breaks off exactly at the problem of "subtle matter." Author tests the logical consistency of the concept by a Spinozist 'more geometrico' exegesis; he deals with the charges that it is fictitious, artificial, or barren, and determines its role in the history of physical concepts up to Maxwell, Lord Kelvin and Ernst Mach.

259 FRONDIZI, RISIERI: "Descartes y la substancia pensante." In his: Substancia y función en el problema del yo. Buenos Aires, Losada, 1952, p. 15–30. English transl.: The nature of self; a functional interpretation. New Haven, Yale UP, 1953, Pt. I, Ch. 1, 3–17.

Analyzes in plainest language D.'s transition from "cogito" (as mere awareness) to "res cogitans" (as substance), which, in Frondizi's view, originated the untenable conception of self as a substance. Chapters 2–4 deal with attacks upon this concept from Locke through Berkeley to Hume who reduced the "self" to a mere bundle of perceptions. Having revealed the horns of the Cartesian-Humean dilemma, Frondizi attempts to escape it by basing the "self" on "function" and "Gestalt" (Part Two), but his resolve to be more careful than D. in stepping from one proposition to another seems to come to grief within the first few pages.

Reviews: N. Bosco in F 6: 1955, 530–32; R.T.F. in Pers 36: 1955, 89–90; B. Mayo in Phil 29: 1954, 268–69.

260 GADOFFRE, GILBERT: "Sur la chronologie du 'Discours de la méthode'." RHPh 11: 1943, 45–70. Revised and condensed in Rsyn 63: 1948, 11–27, discussion 28–30.

Following Leon Roth's suggestion, Gadoffre proves the DM to be a conglomerate of texts to which only the boldness of style gives the semblance of coherence and unity of content. Author traces the stages of development from the first conception [a preface to the 'Essais'] to the final stage which incorporated 1627–28 material, with additions and revisions up to the last moment. The consequences of abandoning the illusion of unity are happy ones: "Spéculations sur l'importance de la morale provisoire, acrobaties dialectiques destinées à expliquer la rupture du développement de la logique scientifique ...., conjectures machiavéliques sur la raison d'être du chapitre métaphysique, tout cela cesse tout simplement d'être utile" (Rsyn p. 26; RHPh p. 69). See Láscaris Comneno (no. 292) and R. Jacquin (no. 278). *Elie Denissoff* ("Les étapes de la rédaction du 'Discours de la méthode'," RPhL 54: 1956, 254–82) calls Gadoffre's analysis insufficient but adds little more than detail and background except for a shift of emphasis to D.'s three "Essais." See also Gadoffre's study of the changing fortunes of DM in literary history, no. 404.

260a GALINDO-AGUILAR, E.: "L'homme volant" d'Avicenne et le "cogito" de Descartes." IBLA (Institut des belles lettres arabes) 21: 1958, 279–95.

The basic Avicenna text is Chifa I. 1.6 on the place of man in the Avicennian universe. Compared to the cogito, the purpose of the fiction of the "homme volant" is different, the attitudes are diametrically opposed: pure fiction in Avicenna, real doubt in Descartes. Therefore, the two "allegories" are also radically different. [Bsig 1959, no. 5970.]

262 GIACON, CARLO (S.J.): "Cartesio." In his: La causalità nel razionalismo moderno: Cartesio, Spinoza, Malebranche, Leibniz. Milano, Bocca, 1954, p. 25–78. (Academica. Collezione di corsi universitari, v. l.)

Precise, historically oriented study of the shift, under D.'s influence, from the ontological conception of causality in antiquity to the logical conception in which substance and causality, separated by the ancients, become one, thus elevating causality to the position of the constructive principle of the real world. This, according to Giacon, is the root of the modern confusion regarding the ancient categories of Absolute and Relative, Being and Becoming, Man and God. Giacon finely distinguishes between Descartes' acceptance of the principle of final causes and his rejection of them in science because man cannot perceive and use them. The fact that there is no Hume chapter indicates the orientation of the work. Descartes' and Malebranche's role in preparing the assault on efficient causality remains in the dark, an inevitable consequence of treating the problem within each thinker's own system only. See also J. Wild, no. 348.

Reviews: Anon. in CivC 105, no. 3: 1955, 299; F. Dugnani in Scuola Cattòlica 83: 1955, 325–26; R. Gradi in Sapienza 8: 1955, 512–14; G. Leger in RSPT 40: 1956, 43–44; A. Muñoz Alonso in Crisis 3: 1956, 266–67; P. Montanari in Gmet 10: 1955, 944–46; P.R. in RRFC 49: 1955, 155; F. Selvaggi in Greg 36: 1955, 724; A. Tognolo in StP 2: 1955, 156–58; I. Vecchiotti in RassF 4: 1955, 185–86; F. G. Barberena in EsFil 8: 1959, 286–87; S. Decloux in RPhL 56: 1958, 518.

263 GILEN, LEONHARD (S.J.): "Über die Beziehung Descartes' zur zeitgenössischen Scholastik." Sch 32: 1957, 41–66.

Detailed review of D.'s acquaintance with the work of Suárez, Conimbricenses, Eustachius a Sancto Paulo, perhaps Antonio Rubio and Charles-François Abra de Raconis (not a Jesuit, as Ch. Adam assumes). Results help clarify the controversy between D. and Antoine Arnauld (Fourth Objections and Responses to MM) in which D. displayed his knowledge of Scholasticism in its contemporary rather than Thomistic form. Rich notes refer to some little-known sources and literature. Firmly conducted study which skillfully utilizes historical fact for doctrinal exegesis; the result strengthens Garin's thesis (no. 209a).

264 GIORGIANNI, VIRGILIO: "Intuizioni giuspolitiche di Renato Descartes." S 17: 1949, 334–50.

Sum and substance of what can be reasonably said about D.'s social attitude and his influence on development of legal thought. See also *author's* note on "Ripercussioni filosofico-giuridiche dello studio delle passioni in Cartesio" (S 17: 1949, 254–58) with assembly of texts, and *G. Gonella's* "Cartesio giurista" (RIFD 18: 1938, 440–45) who rightly concludes that "Cartesio giurista è un Cartesio che interessa più la biografia che la storia del pensiero" (445). See also Droetto, no. 253, and Tabbah, no. 466d.

265 GOGUEL DE LABROUSSE, ELISABETH: "Descartes y la pedagogía." In: Actas del primer congreso nacional de filosofía. Mendoza, 1949, v. 3, p. 1816–25.

D. sharply criticizes the education he received, but proposes no pedagogy of his own; he is authoritarian about the education of children, autodidactic about that of adults. Similarly *Celia Ortiz de Montoya* ("Descartes en la historia de la educación y de la cultura," no. 40, vol. 2, 209–33): "La Pedagogía cartesiana no es Pedagogía de infantes" (225). *Saúl A. Taborda's* interesting study "Descartes y el ideal pedagógico francés" (no. 39: 301–20), however, tries to pin the 1789 educational ideal of "ciudadano idóneo y nacionalista" (307) to the Cartesian spirit, its after-effects still visible in Émile Durckheim's philosophy of education and in the attempted reform of French secondary education in the 1920's. *Hugo Calzetti's* "La influencia del pensamiento cartesiano en el hacer pedagógico moderno" (no. 40, 2: 235–60) accuses D. of having upset the equilibrium of educational values to establish "el dominio de los Robots" (258) – "planes, programas, horarios, minuciosa enumeración de asuntos, distribución de los mismos a lo largo del curso escolar, exámenes, escalafones, reglamentos" and particularly "los *tests*," a French invention "llevado a su máximo perfeccionamiento por los investigadores yanquis" (260), unsuspecting executors of D.'s will. See E. Cassirer's discussion in no. 5, p. 9–10, and Olgiati's excellent chapter on D. and pedagogy in no. 185.

266 GOLDSCHMIDT, VICTOR: "Le paradigme platonicien et les Regulae de Descartes." RPFE 141: 1951, 199–210.

Fascinating study by a Plato scholar of the "démarche du raisonnement par paradigme" as reflected in D.'s earliest, fragmentary attempt at a systematic treatment of epistemology. See also Gouhier's work on the genesis of MM and the role of Socratic inquiry in the Regulae, no. 269.

267 GOUHIER, HENRI: "La crise de la théologie au temps de Descartes." RTPL ser. 3, v. 4: 1954, 19–54.

The subtilities and "barbarism" of Scholastic speculative theology, falling into decay when the new sciences were destroying the old physics, led to the 17th c. crisis in theology. Two ways out were tried: "positive" (scriptural, traditional, historical) theology and the "mystical theology" of F. de Sales, the Oratoire, Saint-Cyran, with its "dialogue sans paroles" and union with God (37), paying little attention to science. D.'s relations with Bérulle, de Condren, Gibieuf are seen as part of this crisis, in the context of which "certains propos de Descartes perdent leur audace avec leur originalité" (49), e.g., his snide remarks about theologians and angels. His own simplified theology was neither positive nor mystical but in line with St. Thomas' idea of speculative theology, "except that he wanted to replace the old handmaid by a new one." Complements no. 168.

Reviews: Julien-Eymard Chesneau in DSS 4, no. 28: 1955, 295–96; A. Lantrùa in S 23: 1955, 129–30.

268 GOUHIER, HENRI: "Doute méthodique ou négation méthodique?" Eph 9: 1945, 135–62.

Great study, linked in theme and style to Gouhier's Essais (no. 169). Shows that the methodical doubt is carried to methodical negation to defeat it (cf. Popkin, no. 322a.)

Whence does D. derive the certainty that clear, distinct ideas never deceive us when he remembers having been so deceived? The answer leads to a suggestive psychological analysis of childhood as D. saw it. See also *Hans Pollnow* who traces D's "psychologie infantile," from embryo to adulthood (no. 2981).

Review: Julien-Eymard Chesneau in DDS 4, no. 28: 1955, 295.

268a GOUHIER, H.: "Le refus du symbolisme dans l'humanisme cartésien." Afil 1958, no. 2–3 (Umanesimo e simbolismo), 65–74.

Defining symbolism as affirmation that the world is a language with a rhetoric in which metaphor is a means not only of expressing but of understanding reality, Gouhier opens up a wide, as yet unexplored perspective on the 17th century in one paragraph (p. 66) on the opposition between the two traditional symbolisms (Christian theology, magical cosmology) and the scientific concept of nature. Young Descartes (1619–21) saw symbolism as a language of man, not of things, as Gouhier notes with regard to Olympica: once in the possession of his metaphysics and physics, D. rejected all symbolism. "Signal" now replaces "sign;" and his images and metaphors are now mere analogies. The rich paper concludes with a most fruitful comparison: Bérulle's depreciation of childhood leads him to a theological symbolism, while Descartes finds in the psychology of the child the root of symbolistic thought, i.e., of error. See also no. 268 and 2098.

Review by Julien-Aymard d'Angers in DSS no. 44, 1959, 258–59.

269 GOUHIER, HENRI: "Pour une histoire des 'Méditations métaphysiques'." RScH ns 61: 1951, 5–29.

Indispensable historical study, boldly speculative on a foundation of minutely examined fact. Descartes' 1628 project on "Divinité" becomes the Latin ms. of 1629, the content and changes of which are imaginatively reconstructed. It dealt with the connaissance de Dieu et de soi-même; surprisingly, the cogito appears linked not to methodical doubt but to the impression which "la docte ignorance socratique" made on young D. (11). It contained neither the ontological proof nor the creation of eternal verities; these highly controversial doctrines were not inserted in the 1639 manuscript, the genesis of which is linked to that of DM and Essais. The study bears on the controversy over the chronological vs. the systematic interpretation of D.'s philosophy.

270 GOUHIER, HENRI: "La preuve ontologique de Descartes." RIP 8: 1954, 295–303. See 270a.

270a GUEROULT, MARTIAL: Nouvelles réflexions sur la preuve ontologique de Descartes. Vrin, 1955. 117 p. (Coll. Problèmes et controverses.)

A controversy about the status of the ontological proof of the Fifth Meditation. Gouhier (no. 270) argues against Gueroult (no. 170) that the proof is wholly independent and does not require, to be valid, the prior "proof a posteriori" of God's existence in the Third Meditation. Gueroult's answer rests on a set of interlocking distinctions. The order of nature derives its evidence from the cogito, the order of metaphysics from the guarantee of God. This metaphysical order must be shored up against the destructive malin génie argument, "la grande doute philosophique par laquelle je frappe d'interdit les évidences mêmes"; the natural order is helpless against the malin génie, though it resists the Dieu-trompeur doubt, "ce petit doute naturel" which merely attacks the memory of such evidence. The proof a posteriori of MM III is metaphysically valid; the ontological proof a priori holds only on the lower plane of nature: though psychologically convincing and a guide to right action, it is metaphysically useless until fitted into the "ordre des raisons." Thus the dependence of the ontological proof upon the proof a posteriori flows from the "general dependence of the order of fact upon the order of ultimate justifications" (Bannan's review, 430; critique of Lefèvre's attempt in no. 179c to improve upon Gueroult, ibid., p. 431). Gouhier's paper at Royaumont (no. 42, 72–87; discussion 88–107) on the "ordre des raisons" and Gueroult's paper on "vérité de la science et vérité de la chose" in the proofs of God (ibid., 108–140 with discussion of Kant's critique of the argument) continue the controversy, revived in 1960 by *Jacques Brunschwicg* who invoked against Gueroult the lesser distinction between "ordo" as structural order and as ratio demonstrandi or, in Cartesian terms, analytic vs. synthetic method (RPFE 150: 1960, 251–65), and was sharply refuted by *B. Rochot* in RPFE 1951: 1961, 125–30. See also *W. Röd* in AGP 43: 1961, 128–52 (no. 3107b, *q.v.*), and Lavelle's discussion of cogito and ontological proof in no. 293.

Reviewed by J. F. Bannan in Rmet 13: 1959–60, 429–31; Julien-Eymard Chesneau in DSS no. 28: 1955, 296–97; L. Cognet in DSS no. 32: 1956, 568–70; J. École in Eph 10: 1955, 744; J. Kopper in PhLit 9: 1956, 262–70; G. Leger in RSPT 40: 1956, 38–39; J. M. in Bphil 2: 1955, 517, p. 235–36; B. Rochot in Rsyn 77: 1956, 79–87; Kern in Sch 33: 1958, 458.

272 GUEROULT, MARTIAL: "Le cogito et l'ordre des axiomes métaphysiques dans les Principia philosophiae cartesianae de Spinoza." Aph 23: 1960, 171–85.

Spinoza's rigorous formulation of D.'s axiomatics is not a mere reordering and logical sharpening of the Cartesian argument, but a transformation. The cogito ergo sum, for example, becomes an ego sum cogitans. The cogito no longer emerges from doubt: only if I know that I am, can I doubt, and therefore think. The order of demonstration of the underlying axioms, which is "l'ordre naturel de leur dépendance" (174) differs in both thinkers. Spinoza ends where D. begins, with the universal formulation of the principle of causality. Spinoza's reversal of the cogito formula indicates a realistic reversal of D.'s idealistic movement from awareness to existential affirmation. In showing the danger of using Spinoza's commentary to elucidate Descartes, Gueroult contradicts *Gilson* who, in a remarkable study of the Cartesian proof of the existence of material things, (no. 2036, reprinted in no. 165), calls for greater use of Spinoza's Principia on the grounds that D. is the one great modern philosopher who found an interpreter of equal rank among his successors. See also 258.

273 HANNEQUIN, ARTHUR: Études d'histoire des sciences et d'histoire de philosophie. Alcan, 1908. V. 1, 209–31, 233–64.

Reprints two important articles: "La méthode de Descartes" (RMM 14: 1906, 755–74); and a defense of D.'s ontological proof (RMM 4: 1896, 433–58) against Leibniz' critique, hinging on the possibility of contradiction in a perfect being. Hannequin, accepting the synthetic character of D.'s philosophy, finds D.'s ontological proof logically rigorous.

274 DE LA HARPE, JEAN: "De l'évidence cartésienne au probabilisme de Cournot: évidence, certitude et probabilité." RTP 1938, 31–49. Abstract in CD 7: 115–21 (1937).

In D., certainty is a terminus a quo; Cournot, completely reversing the problem› makes it the terminus ad quem, "limite extrème de l'effort rationel," or the limiting value of probability; this profoundly modifies modern rationalism. Brief, incisive treatment of Cournot's D. criticism. See also *author's* De l'ordre et du hasard: le réalisme critique d'Antoine-Augustin Cournot. Vrin, 1936, 377 p. (see no. 2184).

Reviews: H. Walgrave in TP 1: 1939, 655–56. Of De l'ordre et du hasard: R. Aron in ZSoz 6: 1937, 419–20; H. R. Miéville in RTP ns 25: 1937, 211–226.

276 HEINTEL, ERICH: "Tierseele und Organismusproblem im cartesianischen System." WZPP 3: 1950, 73–120.

D.'s theory of the automatism of brutes reflects the typical confusion between the thought models of common sense, philosophy, and exact science. D. denies interiority in animals (methodological exactitude); considers the res cogitans incorporeal (equivocation between 'ego sum' and 'sum'); attempts to limit the consequences of the automatism doctrine by stressing the 'non sicut nos' (failure to solve the awareness problem on a plane common to animal and man). His inability to differentiate between "automatism" in organism and in mechanical artifact is rooted in his conception of "Natur ohne Innerlichkeit" (78). Diffuse, meandering article, probing the methodological foundations of D.'s anthropology and concept of Being.

277 IRIARTE AGIRREZABAL, JOAQUIN: Kartesischer oder Sanchezischer Zweifel? Ein kritischer und philosophischer Vergleich zwischen dem kartesischen Discours de la méthode und dem sanchezischen Quod nihil scitur. Bottrop i.W., Postberg, 1935. 146 p. Dissertation Bonn.

Francisco Sanchez' Quod nihil scitur (1581) proposes universal doubt as the foundation of certitude. Analyzing this work and its critics (including Leibniz), the author finds an indubitable resemblance between Sanchez' and D.'s universal doubt (e.g. parallel passages on "les mauvaises doctrines," p. 126–27). D. might have known 'Quod nihil scitur' through the study of Sanchez' medical works, published 1635. See also *author's* "Francisco Sánchez, el autor de Quod nihil scitur, a la luz de muy recientes estudios" (RyF 110: 1936, 23–42, 157–81) and *Ciribini Spruzzola's* "Francisco Sánchez alla luce delle ultime ricerche," RFNS 28: 1936, 372–91.

Reviews: Anon. in RMM 45, suppl. 1. 1938, 12; M. Rast in Sch 11: 1936, 430.

278 JACQUIN, R.: "Le titre du 'Discours de la méthode' est-il emprunté?" RScR 26: 1952, 142–45.

In 1558 Giacomo Aconzio published an Opusculum de metodo, hoc est de recta investigandarum tradendarumque artium ac scientiarum ratione, a treatise on logic having no metaphysical significance. Author modestly notes the resemblance between the DM and Opusculum titles; *E. Denissoff* (RPhL 54: 1956, 271) jumps to the conclusion that D. used the Aconzio title: "nul doute est permis." *H. de Vleeschauwer*, editor of Jacobus Acontius' Tractaat de metodo (Antwerp 1932, see 3500) carefully compares it with DM; sees no influence.

279 JANSEN, F.: "Les systèmes eucharistiques cartésiens," s.v. "Eucharistiques (accidents), 5." In: Dictionnaire de théologie catholique, v. 52, 1913, col. 1427–52.

Very useful article, with bibliography, on the Cartesian theories of transsubstantiation which, in 1663, caused the condemnation of D.'s works, donec corrigantur.

281 JOLIVET, RÉGIS (S.J.): "L'intuition intellectuelle et le problème de la métaphysique selon Descartes." Aph 11, no. 2: 1934, 1–111.

The concept of "intellectual intuition," broadly developed (3–64), takes different forms in St. Thomas, Descartes, Kant, Bergson. In Thomism it bears upon external bodies, postulating abstractions; in Cartesianism upon innate simple ideas, ruling out abstraction. Bergson's concept of intuition is "foncièrement anti-cartésien"(88). Interesting distinction between intellectual intuition in D.'s Regulae (road to Idealism) and in his cogito (its consequences have hitherto made him pass for the father of metaphysical realism).

Review: J. Jacques in RNS 38: 1935, 253–55.

282 JOLIVET, RÉGIS (S.J.): La notion de substance. Essai historique et critique sur le développement des doctrines d'Aristote à nos jours. Beauchesne, 1929. 339 p. (Bibliothèque des Archives de philosophie.)

Assesses the role of the Cartesian revolution in the development of the substance concept as it defines substance by a principal attribute from which all else derives. In this transformation, Thomistic accident becomes a modification or determination of substance.

283 JULIEN-EYMARD D'ANGERS, O.F.M. CAP. [i.e. Julien-Eymard Chesneau]: "Sénèque, Épictète et le stoïcisme dans l'œuvre de René Descartes." RTPL ser 3, v. 4: 1954, 169–96.

After surveying the literature on stoicism in Descartes, author claims that D.'s 'refutation' and 'utilization' of stoicism were both undertaken from a purely rational viewpoint, giving new orientation to moral philosophy; while "les humanistes chrétiens" refute and utilize stoicism from the theological standpoint (195). Excellent study of the subject, rich in precise comparisons and tabular schemes illustrating stoic concepts in D. and other thinkers.

286 KAHL-FURTHMANN, GERTRUD: "Descartes' Betonung seiner Unabhängigkeit von der Tradition und Leibnizens Kritik." ZPF 4: 1950, 377–84.

Leibniz sharply criticized D.'s "chef de secte" attitude (contemptuous, ostentatious show of ignorance of his predecessors) though the evidence points to his familiarity with their work, a criticism echoed by some good modern scholars. Author carefully examines this charge in respect to Scholastic philosophy. Unexpected result: Leibniz had a poor, second-hand knowledge of it, while D. had studied it thoroughly at La Flèche but thought little of it. His show of independence was justified in view of his genuinely novel style of philosophizing: going to problems, not authorities.

288 KATKOV, GEORG: "Descartes und Brentano. Eine erkenntnistheoretische Gegenüberstellung." In: Emge (no. 523), 116–51. 1937.

Interesting study of Franz Brentano whose Jesuit education, comparable to D.'s, enabled him to see the Scholastic side in Descartes before Gilson did. Evidence of analogy between Brentano's and D.'s philosophical doctrine in their common errors as well as in their common achievements. Katkov claims that it was Thomas Reid's analysis of the Cartesian concept of evidence that led Brentano to anticipate phenomenology and to foresee its dangers. One of two substantial contributions to the 1937 German memorial volume, the other being *W. Burkamp's* "Das denkende Ich bei Descartes" (3–26), reviewed by E. Cassirer (no. 5, p. 26); summarized in no. 1413.

290 LAING, B. M.: "Descartes on material things." Phil 16: 1941, 389–411.

Since in D.'s doctrine matter is defined as res extensa, the existence of individual bodies (hence proof of such existence) appears impossible, there being but one "body". See also Whitehead, no. 194a.

291 LAPORTE, JEAN: Études d'histoire de la philosophie française au XVIIe siècle. Préface par André Bridoux. Note par Janine Pignet. Vrin, 1951. 269 p. (BHP).

Posthumously published collection of important studies, including "La connaissance de l'étendue chez Descartes" (11–36) and "La liberté selon Descartes" (37–87; RMM 44: 1937, 101–64). Laporte argues against Gilson and others that Descartes' preoccupation with physics did not prevent him from developing an genuine, original, defensible doctrine of freedom. The paper on extension raises once more the question posed by Gassendi and Malebranche: How is the idea of extension possible on Cartesian principles? Both themes, freedom and extension, are carried forward to Malebranche in two parallel papers (153–248; see Lavelle in no. 11, p. 17–19 and 23–31; Cassirer in no. 5, p. 35).

291a LAPORTE, JEAN: "La finalité chez Descartes." RHPh 2: 1928, 366–96. Reprinted in no. 178, 2nd ed., Livre III, ch. 2, sec. 1.

Carefully noting the difference between Descartes' terminology and ours, Laporte deviates from Gilson and other commentators by having Descartes distinguish external causality (final causes) from internal finality which he calls "nature." The search for the former is useless precisely because the latter, as the divine design and government of the world, transcends the analytical power of reason: "Voilà la conception cartésienne. N'est-ce pas exactement la conception chrétienne?" (no. 178, p. 361).

292 LÁSCARIS COMNENO, CONSTANTINO: "Análisis del Discurso del método." RevF 14: 1955, 293–351. Abstract: see no. 2460.

"El simple hecho de la importancia que se ha dado al Discurso es ya una deformación del pensamiento cartesiano" (294). This boldly conceived paper recognizes DM as a composite of parts lacking unity, and analyzes the importance and genesis of the principal ones. The reconstruction and separation of the material that went into DM is achieved by chronology, contents analysis, and a unique statistical study of its formal elements. Last section on repercussions of DM in D.'s later work The author, evidently uneaware of Gadoffre's work (no. 260), reaches similar result by more comprehensive, bolder methods. The careful study is important despite the evident lack of access to critical literature.

293 LAVELLE, LOUIS: Introduction à l'ontologie. PUF, 1947. 136 p.

Lavelle's profound, concise, much-discussed ontology touches importantly upon Cartesian studies (sec. 17, 21–23) concerning D.'s ontological argument. "C'est dans l'argument ontologique que l'on saisit le mieux l'identité de l'être avec la puissance infinie de l'affirmation" (21). Infinitude beyond finitude of the pensée is interpreted as infinitude of an act "qui s'engendre éternellement et sans lequel sa pensée ne pourrait pas s'exercer, c'est-à-dire se donner l'être à elle-même" (22). The cogito is therefore doubly subordinated to the ontological argument: logically, since the infinite is the very condition of the finite; metaphysically, because the cogito merely expresses the limitation of the power of pensée to give itself being. See also no. 11.

Reviews: G. Berger in Eph 4: 1949, 98–99; L. B. Geiger in RSPT 35: 1951, 100; M. Mindán in RevF 8: 1949, 688–89; H. Riefstahl in ZPF 4: 1950, 292–94; M. F. Sciacca in Gmet 4: 1949, 407–11; F. de Raedemaeker in KCTS 1: 1947, 215–16; M. Giorgiantonio in S 19: 1951, 317–18.

295 LEFEBVRE, HENRI: "De la morale provisoire à la générosité." In: Royaumont (no. 42), 237–55; discussion 256–72.

Das Unvermeidliche, hier ist's getan: under the spell of historical materialism, D. at long last reveals "quelque chose qui l'apparente au Docteur Faustus"; exorcized by Gueroult's mighty word, the poodle of a malin génie turns into the Devil himself; and D.'s hypothetical argument was a veritable "Nuit de Walpurgis spéculative" (239). No wonder the discussion happily dwells on Faust-Descartes, Hamlet, Goethe, Christopher Marlowe ("C'est le Faust pré-rationaliste," 258), before returning to 'générosité' with illuminating comments on Corneille and Lanson's "très vieil article" (no. 413), Mesnard's thesis of the exceptional position of D.'s "morale provisoire," and the role of egotistic "prudence" in making "les grandes âmes" socially conscious and "généreux". The last word is the Devil's: "l'égoisme est spécifiquement celui de la bourgeoisie" (272).

298 LEROY, MAXIME: Descartes social. Avec un portrait inédit de Descartes, dessiné par Jean Lievens aux environs de 1643. Vrin, 1931. xxxix, 73 p.

Discovers in D. "un très grand homme social" whose "premières paroles de l'optimisme moderne" inspired the most diverse tendencies of thought, "même la dernière, la sociale et la socialiste" (73). Amiably rambling essay, full of suggestive, often misleading comments. "Avant-propos" recalls less discussed D. interpretations, including A. Comte's. A charming Preface tells the story of the Lievens portrait which shows an uncommonly humble Descartes ("C'est un paysan!" as Lévy-Bruhl exclaimed, p. ix). See also *Leroy's* "Descartes précurseur du social moderne" with discussion (Rsyn 63: 1948, 59–67) and *his* "L'humain Descartes" (Eur 44, no 175: July 15, 1937, 289–96), showing D. as controversialist and pamphleteer; also Prévost no. 324.

299 LEVI, ADOLFO: "La filosofia razionalistica dal Descares al Leibniz." In. his: Il pensiero di Francesco Bacone considerato in relazione con le

filosofie della natura, del Rinascimento e col razionalismo cartesiano. Torino, Paravia, 1925, 89–144.

Stresses the common elements (rationalistic traits in Bacon's empiricism, the position of experience in D.) rather than the differences between rationalist and empiricist currents in pre-Kantian philosophy. See also *Levi's* critical study of a favorite Italian theme: "Il problema dell'errore nella filosofia di Descartes" (LogosN 11, no. 2: 1928, 93–108), concluding that D. failed to reconcile the existence of error with Theism, and finding the root of his error concept in a Baconian belief in the lumen naturale.

Reviews: Anon. in RMM 33, suppl. 4: 1926, 9–10; G. Bontadini in Rsyn 14: 1937, 96 (also in no. 239, 44–45).

302 LEWIS, GENEVIÈVE: "Augustinisme et cartésianisme." In: Augustinus magister; Congrès international Augustinien, Études Augustiniennes, 1954, v. 2, 1087–1104.

Indispensable mise au point of a historical relationship. Rich references to the texts, but only key French criticism is considered. Campanella and Mersenne receive their just place. Sresses the originality of D.'s possible use of the Augustinian 'si fallor': "seul il en a compris la force spécifique, parce que seul il en a fait un principe" (1103). Notes that "c'est à travers Descartes qu'on revenait à saint Augustin" during the dominance of Cartesianism, systematizing Augustinian thought "dans le plus pur style cartésien." The seemingly insuperable Cartesian obstacles to understanding, namely "les thèses anticartésiens de saint Augustin" with regard to matter, accident, animal soul (1104) were not overcome until Malebranche produced a Christian alliance between the Cartesian and the Augustinian spirit. See also Abercrombie (no. 235) and Scholz (no. 334).

304 LÖWITH, KARL: "Descartes' vernünftiger Zweifel und Kierkegaards Leidenschaft der Verzweiflung." CD, v. 1, p. 74–79 (1937).

Kierkegaard's "Ärgernis an Descartes' vernünftigem Zweifel" is symptomatic of Germany's passionate revolt against rationalism from Luther to Nietzsche. Kierkegaard pushes D.'s methodical doubt to extreme existential doubt in order to arrive at certainty of faith; for Hegel, the Cartesian dualism between "true" and "apparent" world is dead; Nietzsche's "new enlightenment" starts out with "Ironie gegen Descartes" but fails to bridge the gap between Self and World. See no. 2355a (*Kierkegaard's* Johannes Climacus).

306 MACDONALD, MARGARET: "Sleeping and waking." Mind 62: 1953, 202–15.

"N'avés vous jamais ouy ce mot d'estonnement dedans les comedies: 'Veille-je, ou si je dors?' " asks Eudoxe in D.'s RV (AT X, 511), but the Sixth Meditation leaves the problem of a reality criterion half-suspended. Miss M., editor of Analysis (Oxford), attacks D.'s problem by Oxford "analysis". The word "dream" cannot be used like other words with which it has been confused, and D.'s "lament" is needless (215). Similarly *L.E. Thomas*, "Waking and dreaming" (Analysis 13: 1953, 121–37): D.'s methodological doubt is inappropriate to the "self-authenticating" experiences of waking and dreaming (127). The Macdonald article drew a spate of critical comment: *M. J. Baker* in Mind 63: 1954, 539-43 argued that her paper left the Cartesian argument intact: sleeping and waking cannot in *fact* be infallibly distinguished from each other, and the problem is not just verbal. *R. M. Yost, Jr.* and *D. Kalisch* try "to play the same language game" as Miss Macdonald (PhQ 5: 1955, 109–24) to prove that her criteria for separating sleeping, consciousness, and dreaming do not hold and do not disprove D.'s scepticism of the senses. Also *W. von Leyden*, "Descartes and Hobbes on waking and dreaming" (RIP 1956, 95–101) and above all *Norman Malcolm* in PhR 65: 1956, 14–37 who resumed the linguistic attack and whose book Dreaming (London, 1959; see no. 2623a) became the focus of a new controversy (Ayer and others), by now far removed from its Cartesian starting point. See *Yost*, no. 3596.

307 MACMURRAY, JOHN: "The rejection of dualism." In his: The self as agent. The Gifford lectures 1953. London, Faber & Faber, 1957, ch. 3, 62–83.

Macmurray radically rejects the notion of self as an isolated individual; the self is a person whose personal existence is constituted in its relations to other persons. Hence M.'s utter rejection of the Kantian dualism between theoretical and practical reason, and of the asserted primacy of theoretical reason. The disastrous Kantian dualism stems from the Cartesian mind-matter dualism as the dichotomy between "thinking" and "acting." The primacy of theoretical reason is an inevitable consequence of the cogito fallacy: the cogito does not infer existence from thought, it merely identifies both. Only the *activity* of the self as it thinks constitutes existence; thinking as such is nonaction; therefore: Cogito ergo non sum (81).

Reviewed: by A. R. C. Duncan in Phil 36: 1961, 233–34.

310. MARTIN, W. A. P.: "The Cartesian philosophy before Descartes." Jl of the Peking Oriental Society 2: 1888, 121–41. Also: Peking, Pei T'ang Press, 1888. 21 p.

An Old China hand compares D.'s cosmology with that of the Chinese classical philosophers and uncovers some interesting but faint parallels. *Ralph Tyler Flewelling's* "Chinese influences in late Cartesianism" (CD 3: 37–42) deals with the Chinese impact upon such "late Cartesians" as Pierre Bayle, Leibniz, Adam Smith ("nature religion" and "nature economics"). See also *Prabhu Dutt Shastri*, "Descartes' method in the light of Hindu metaphysics" (CD 3: 99–104) and *Jean Grenier*, "Du 'cogito' au 'credo' " (CD 3:94–98), via the âtman-brahma distinction.

311 MEIER, MATTHIAS: Descartes und die Renaissance. Münster i.W. (München, Haber), 1914. x, 68 p.

Substantial, condensed study of Renaissance influences upon D. finds "dass Descartes' Lehren weder dem Renaissance-Platonismus noch dem Renaissance-Stoicismus gesondert entstammen, dass ihre Wurzeln vielmehr in beiden Bewegungen zu suchen sind, die sich .... aufs mannigfaltigste durchkreuzen. Auch Descartes kann sich der Atmosphäre nicht entziehen, in welcher er atmet" (64). Good survey of Gilson's precursors (Freudenthal, von Hertling, Picavet), but it neglects French D. literature.

311a MERLEAU-PONTY, MAURICE: "Le cogito." In his: Phénoménologie de la perception. Gallimard, 1945, 423–68.

Descartes' cogito is untenable: consciousness is no more beyond the reach of doubt than that which is perceived. There is a "cogito véritable" in which my own being is constituted as a being in contact with the world (my "être-au-monde"). This "cogito véritable," however, is no more indubitable than the Cartesian one. Only a "conscience engagée" can overcome doubt and establish the certainty of existence: "The only indubitable consciousness is committed consciousness," as *Herbert Spiegelberg* puts it in his critical analysis of this unusual repudiation of Descartes (a post-Husserlian phenomenologist attempting to give a noncartesian turn to phenomenology). See Spiegelberg, "The new cogito," in no. 3333a v. 2, 549–52. Merleau-Ponty's discussion of the mind-body dualism in *his:* La structure du comportement, ch. 4: "Les relations de l'âme et du corps et le problème de la conscience perceptive" (1942 and 1949; see no. 2709) is critical of Descartes' realism.

312 MERCIER, DÉSIRÉ-JOSEPH (CARDINAL): "Pourquoi le doute méthodique ne peut être universel." RNS 4: 1897, 182–98.

" .... dès là que le doute devenait universel, il ne pouvait plus demeurer méthodique, mais dégénérait fatalement en doute réel" (198). Penetrating logical analysis by the great Neoscholastic. Similarly *Régis Jolivet*, "Le doute méthodique de Descartes" (RdePh 29: 1922, 139–58): to save the methodical doubt, we must conceive it as limited.

313 MESNARD, PIERRE: "L'esprit cartésien est-il compatible avec le sens de l'histoire?" In: L'homme et l'histoire. Sociéte Strasbourgeoise de philosophie. Actes du VIe Congres des SPLF. Paris, PUF 1952, 273–80.

Rich paper, condensed almost to obscurity, traces the successive deformation of D.'s doctrine of history. Bossuet's Christian view represents "l'élargissement de la conception cartésienne par un esprit directement au contact de la réalité historique' (276). Malebranche embraces one of the two possible heresies regarding D.'s doctrine, i.e., depreciation of all historical reality even on the level of action. Fontenelle commits the other: rational history subjected to deduction is no more than "l'occasion d'un spectacle divertissant" – the rising 18th c. has already lost the anthropological meaning of D.'s teaching (280).

314 MILLER, LEONARD G.: "Descartes, mathematics, and God." PhR 66: 1957, 451–65.

Perplexities arise when D. applies the contrasting doctrines of simple natures and lumen naturale to proving the necessary truth of mathematical reasoning. The explanation is sought in conflicting patterns of thought in D., and ultimately traced back to his tendency towards irrationalism while tenaciously adhering to rationalism.

315 MOREAU, JOSEPH: "La réalité de l'étendue chez Descartes." Eph 5: 1950, 185–200.

"En ramenant à l'étendue la substance des corps, Descartes fondait l'intelligibilité du monde physique; il répondait en langue réaliste, au voeu même de l'idéalisme: assurer la portée et la valeur de la connaissance" (200). Difficult study of a difficult subject (identification of extension and space with the substance of bodies, Henry More's objection regarding empty space). For a paralel study of Malebranche see *Moreau's* "Le réalisme de Malebranche et la fonction de l'idée" (RMM 51: 1946, 97–14).

316 MULLER, MAURICE: De Descartes à Marcel Proust. Essais sur la théorie des essences, le positivisme et les méthodes dialectique et réflexive. Neuchâtel, Baconnière, 1943 and 1947. 161 p. (Être et pensée, v. 2).

The thoughtful first essay traces "l'essence relationelle" (the problem of philosophical abstraction) from Descartes through its transformation in Leibniz, Kant, Condillac to modern mathematics. The second essay "(L'essence émotive") distinguishes in Proust's work "ce qu'il y a d'analyse psychologique, de ce qu'il y a de recherche presque cartésienne d'un absolu dans le moi" (55), reflecting two characteristic streams in French literature and philosophy, one stemming from Racine and the "moralistes," the other from D.'s "reflexive analysis." Original study, with Descartes, Comte, Hamelin, and Proust as cornerstones. Choice quotations from a wide range of thinkers.

Review: I. W. Alexander in FS 1: 1947, 66–68.

317 NASON, JOHN W.: "Leibniz's attack on the Cartesian doctrine of extension." JHI 7: 1946, 447–83.

Good exposition of Leibniz' metaphysical objections to D.'s doctrine of extension. Takes up his six arguments: from Transsubstantiation, from the inadequacy of concepts in the explanation of phenomena, from individuality, from the principle of plenitude ,from complexity and relativity, and from the status of extended objects. See also *Emile Baas*, "La critique leibnizienne de la physique de Descartes" with *M. Gueroult's* "Observations sur ce memoire" (BFL Strasbourg, v. 11, Nov. 1932); *Geneviève Lewis*, "La critique leibnizienne du dualisme cartésien" (RPFE 136: 1946, 473–85), and, for Leibniz' role as D. critic in French intellectual life, *W. H. Barber*, Leibniz in France from Arnauld to Voltaire: a study in French reactions to Leibnizianism, 1670–1760. Oxford, Clarendon Press, 1955 (no. 1138).

318 NELSON, ROBERT J.: "Descartes and Pascal, a study of likenesses." PMLA 69: 1954, 542–65.

Opposing the common view that "Descartes pays lip service to Religion which Pascal pays to Reason" (542), author studies affinities between these thinkers regarding the three Pascalian orders (cœur, esprit, chair), with highly suggestive parallel passages. Finds a corresponding third term in D.'s dualism for which D. makes "an obvious allowance" (545); and the God of Descartes is by no means the "Dieu de la chiquenaude" which Pascal took him to be. Interesting reappraisal.

319 DEL NOCE, AUGUSTO: "La crisi del molinismo in Descartes." In: Metafisica ed esperienza religiosa, Afil 1956, 39–77.

Remarkable study, difficult and digressive, views D.'s philosophy as the second form of Counterreformation philosophy (Spanish Scholasticism being the first), as the meeting ground of Molinism and "preilluminismo", and as the precursor of modern laicism. D.'s solution of the Faith-Reason problem may be related to the Thomistic one, as Gouhier suggests, but its spirit is no longer that of authentic Thomism, being more in line with the Molinist view of the state of pure nature. D.'s deep religious ambiguity reflects the opposition of his antinaturalism to Molinist naturalism, though the could well believe himself loyal to the Molinist Catholicism from which he started out. Interesting sidelights on Jansenism and Pascal. The study is part of the progressive revaluation of 17th-century French philosophy under the impact of the organized Italian post-1945 studies of Renaissance and post-Renaissance humanism; note also Gouhier's comment on the "Anti-Renaissance" concept in no. 96, p. 9.

320 DEL NOCE, AUGUSTO: "Spiritualità cartesiana e machiavellismo." In: Enrico Castelli (ed.), Umanesimo e scienza politica. Roma, Firenze, 1949, 105–27. [Full title: no. 2847.]

Perceptive, documented doctrinal study. Starts from the view that D.'s religious agnosticism is founded on the idea of absolute transcendence of the infinite; for Descartes, "ogni ordine politico è storico e soltanto dalla storia trae la sua ragion d'essere e non da una necessità religiosa o razionale" (123). D. therefore admits a pluralism of social orders, but does not develop a criterion for selecting the best. (Essential literature cited on p. 120, n. 35.) *Del Noce's* "Cartesio e la politica" (RF 41: 1950, 3–30, reviewed by I. González in PenM 8: 1952, 263), finds that D.'s metaphysical starting point seems to imply absolutism as political order, though it cannot be reconciled with his philosophy as an integral structure. For a broad historical as well as doctrinal treatment see *Pierre Mesnard's* excursus on "Le prétendu machiavélisme de Descartes" in no. 220, p. 190–212. See also *H. Gouhier*, no. 169; *R. Lefèvre*, no. 179b; *V. Giorgianni*, no. 264; and *Umberto Padovani*, "Cartesio e Machiavelli; osservazione sui rapporti tra politica e morale" (Cartesio, no. 35, 623–34).

321 OEDINGEN, KARLO: "Der genius malignus et summe potens et callidus bei Descartes." K 50: 1958–59, 178–187.

Malin génie and Dieu-trompeur express Cartesian doubt at its most radical and do not succumb to Descartes' logical operations. He gains the security of certainty by his never seriously doubted belief in the lumen naturale, not by rationally defeating fundamental doubt. Radical doubt would have to attack the proposition that our principles of cognition yield absolute insights; but Descartes' "proof" of the identity of human and divine cognition makes the tacit assumption that God is knowable, and this assumption is precisely what should but can not be proved.

321a PASTORE, ANNIBALE: "Novità sulla logica di Descartes." Afil 4: 1934, 337–49. "Approfondimento del pensiero di Descartes." F 1: 1950, 229–37.

Against Serrus (no. 231) who claimed that D. missed the hypothetic-deductive character of modern mathematics and considered syllogistic logic utterly barren, Pastore finds D. using the hypothetic-deductive method in mathematics (solving a problem by considering it solved, as in the example of the anaclastic). The Cartesian equation is an analytical machine or experiment. Similarly, the syllogism is for D. an Euclidean analogy. Using his own "logica del potenziamento", Pastore explains the character of D.'s analytic geometry as a logical transform of one system into another. Pastore thus anticipates the view of Vuillemin (no. 398) of D.'s geometry as a theory of proportions. Extending his analysis to D.'s metaphysics (F 1950) he finds in the "ergo" of cogito ergo sum the dualism of "intuitus" and "deductio". Like Vuillemin, he sees D.'s metaphysics as a metamathematical transformation of the mathesis universalis, but deviates in his final conclusion: "Tutto induce a credere che anche per Descartes esista un punto di reciproca impertinenza, in cui la ragione e la fede cessano d'essere affermate contradittoriamente. Il cartesianesimo ha la missione di significare al mondo la rivelazione di questo mistero" (F 1: 1550, 235). Descartes' metaphysics thus expresses operative dualities between the deductive and the intuitive, the logical and the mystical, the real and the ideal. Pastore's use of the term "mystical" is odd since he finds that "Il Dio di Descartes è il Dio della testa non del cuore, dell'Intelligenza non dell'Amore." Referring to Le Senne's "I suffer, hence I am" which "accetta il dolore sofferto come fonte di moralità," Pastore adds: "Questo pensiero è ignoto a Descartes" (F 1950, p. 237, n. 15).

322 POPKIN, RICHARD H.: "Charron and Descartes: the fruits of systematic doubt." JP 51: 1954, 831–37.

Excellent differentiation between D.'s use of doubt to produce certainty (discovery of truth is not miraculous), and Charron's use of it to avoid heresy (leap into Revelation). "But D.'s contemporaries saw that he had either taken the Sceptics too seriously, or not seriously enough" (837) – forgetting that D. had not genuinely met the sceptic challenge for good reason: "The Conquest of Everest was never really attempted, because he was already on top." See also Dąmbska (no. 246 and 247) and especially Julien-Eymard (no. 283).

322a POPKIN, RICHARD H.: "Descartes: conqueror of scepticism." "Descartes: sceptique malgré lui." In his: The history of scepticism from Erasmus to Descartes, ch. 9, 10. Assen, van Gorkum, 1960, p. 174–216.

Monographic study of the Pyrrhonist phase initiated by the Renaissance rediscovery of Sextus Empiricus and ending, according to Popkin, with Descartes' Pyrrhic victory over scepticism which set the stage for the next phase (Pascal to Kierkegaard). Only by the "super-Pyrrhonism" of the First Meditation, i.e. by carrying methodical doubt to methodical negation (Gouhier's thesis, no. 268), did D. conquer scepticism. But this "super-Pyrrhonism" made the sceptics turn from their old enemies to D. as their new target: in the second half of the 17th c., scepticism "changed from being anti-Scholastic and anti-Platonic, to being anti-Cartesian" (xiii). Ch. 10 impressively shows D.'s dilemma: either the malin génie and Dieu-trompeur arguments are accepted at full weight, then a Pyrrhonistic crisis ensues; or the emphasis falls on the cogito assertion, then the position becomes dogmatic and fails to refute scepticism. This dilemma is fully exploited by D.'s century, from his contemporaries Pierre Petit, Bourdin, Voetius, Schoock, and above all Gassendi, to Huet and Gabriel Daniel. Ch. 3–8 contain valuable studies of the scepticism of Montaigne, Gassendi, Garrasse, Chanet, Mersenne, Herbert of Cherbury and others. The historical thesis is boldly novel and carefully documented.

Reviews: Donald M. Frame in RR 52: 1961, 226–28; Neal W. Gilbert in Renaissance News 14: 1961, 176–78.

323 PRENANT, LUCIE: "Rôle et limite de la psychologie dans la méthode et la philosophie de Descartes." Royaumont (no. 42), 413–37.

The term "psychologie .... n'est pas un terme cartésien" (430); the author uses it confusingly to denote the originality of a philosophy "où les valeurs de la vérité .... se présentent comme des certitudes personelles, qui ont l'assurance intime de leur droit à l'universalité." A study of D.'s Method and metaphysics, perceptively original and "nuancée" as all of author's work on D.

324 PRÉVOST, RENÉ: "L'humanisme économique de Descartes." RHES 29: 1951, 130–46.

Criticizes Jacques Maritain, Maxime Leroy, Henri Lefebvre for failing to recognize D.'s true position regarding labor: antiquity despised technology, Marxism stressed social change, but only D. showed the liberating promise. See the comment by *E. Dolléans*, "La technique soumise à la générosité" (ibid., 125–30). All these "pros" and "cons" are doubly anachronistic: they falsify Descartes' 17th century thought and falsify 20th century socio-economics as well, being unable to break away from the dated 19th century image of the "modern" world they are supposedly discussing.

324a READ, SIR HERBERT: "Descartes." In his: The sense of glory; essays in criticism. Cambridge University Press, 1929, ch. 3, p. 57–77.

Revision of a TLS article. Discusses the Descartes views of J. Maritain and A. N. Whitehead, against the background furnished by Baillet. "Intuition," a cognitive "process of poetry," provides "the sense of integral unity with which .... no philosophy .... is ever possible" (77) – and "Descartes' method or system of reasoning is non-poetic in a very profound sense" (72). Sir Herbert, himself more poet than philosopher, fails to draw the conclusion he implies.

325 ROCHOT, BERNARD: "La vie, le caractère et la formation intellectuelle." "Le philosophe." In: Pierre Gassendi, 1592–1656. A. Michel, 1955, 9–58, 71–115. (Centre international de synthèse.)

Revaluation of the D.-Gassendi relationship, stressing the importance of Gassendi's largely ignored Instances written in rejoinder to D.'s Responses to his objections. Despite philosophical opposition, D. should have been Gassendi's ally, not his enemy. Good comment on the misunderstanding that separated them (106–07). See also *René Pintard*, "Descartes et Gassendi" (CD 2: 115–22) on the metaphysical as well as the physical and logical antagonism between the two.

Reviews: J. Abelé in Et 288: 1956, 292–93; N.B. in RF 47: 1956, 101–02; G. Gilbert in NRT 78: 1956, 95–96; J. L. in RIP 9: 1955, 444–45; R. Lenoble in RHSA 9: 1956, 183–85; G. Leger in RSPT 40: 1956, 39–41; M. Millet in Eph 11: 1956, 114–15; C. de Waard in AIHS 8: 1956, 383–85; F. Russo in RQS 17: 1956, 127–28.

326 ROCHOT, BERNARD: "Gassendi et la 'Logique' de Descartes." RPFE 145: 1945, 300–08.

Translates Gassendi's fragment on the Logic of D. in Gassendi's Syntagma philosophicum, noting that D.'s contemporaries were disappointed in the Discours de la méthode, being more interested in his logic and methodology than in his metaphysics. This supports Gadoffre (no. 404). See also *Rochot's* "Gassendi et le Syntagma philosophicum" (Rsyn 67: 1950, 67–79) on G.'s non-metaphysical concept of science, failing to understand the mathematicism of the new science. Good study by *Rochot* of "Les vérités éternelles dans la querelle entre Descartes et Gassendi" (RPFE 141: 1951, 280–98) claims that both, despite Gassendi's misunderstanding D.'s position, had an equal share in the origin of rationalism.

326a RÖD, WOLFGANG: "Zum Problem des premier principe in Descartes' Metaphysik." K 51: 1959–60, 176–95.

Distinguishes a first fact (cogito), a supreme axiom (If I think, I am), and a first principle (cogito ergo sum); this first principle again includes "the first self-supporting certainty" as well as its logical explication: the formula of the cogito is *already* explication. The well-conceived paper ends with a noteworthy comment on the implicit conflict in D. between metaphysical foundation and mathematicism.

327 ROME, BEATRICE K.: "Created truth and 'causa sui' in Descartes." PPR 17: 1956, 66–78.

The doctrines of created essences and of God's incomprehensible freedom enabled D. to abandon final causes. But to guarantee certainty in science, he needed a Deity more perfect than a mere creative force, yet one still indifferent: hence the causa sui concept to guarantee God's immutability; but this wreaks havoc with indifferent creation, free will, and the veracity of God. Conclusion: D.'s doctrine of created truth needs justification of God's existence far more than it needs God to justify created truths. Sharp logical analysis in the contemporary English-American style.

328 ROSSI, PAOLO: "La memoria artificiale come sezione della logica: Ramo, Bacone, Cartesio." RCSF 15: 1960, 22–62.

Part of a remarkable, erudite study of the problem of artificial memory and mnemotechnics in the literature of magic ["Studi sul Lullismo e sull'arte della memoria nel Rinascimento," in RCSF 13: 1958, 149–91, 243–79; 14: 1959, 29–60], this fascinating article shows that Descartes, though rejecting Lullism from the very first, was thoroughly aware of the late 16th and early 17th century literature on these subjects. Many of the most characteristical Cartesian notions occur in it; the Royal physician and astrologer Lazare Meyssonnier has a "méthode de conduire la raison," a "logique naturelle pour resoudre toutes sortes de questions," the universal science, the catena scientiarum (1639); Jean Belot (1603) has "tourbillons de la matière"; there are remarkable similarities regarding the catena scientiarum between Descartes and "il medico e mago Jean d'Aubry" (47–48). D.'s arguments against Lullism ("ars combinatoria" and "ars memorativa") are in "singular agreement" with those of Bacon; yet the method of the Regulae shows that, at least before 1628, Descartes made considerable use of images and symbols in the theory of the thought process, notwithstanding his later rejection of all symbolism [section on "Aids to memory and the doctrine of enumeration in the Regulae," 55–61, with comments on intuitus, deduction, logical enumeration, etc.]. Of particular interest are Rossi's comments on the Cogitationes privatae and Olympica: striking formulae like "larvatus prodeo" or "Una est in rebus activa vis" were commonplaces in the hermeneutic literature before and in D.'s times. This hardly weakens Gouhier's interpretation in no. 96, to which Rossi refers, though it affects some of Gouhier's reconstructions of their probable sources. On Lull's Ars inveniendi veritatem see no. 3000a; on his influence upon D. see José Bertran Guëll, no. 1217.

329 ROTH, LEON: Spinoza, Descartes and Maimonides. Oxford, Clarendon Press, 1924. 148 p. See also his: "Spinoza and Cartesianism," Mind 32: 1923, 12–37, 160–78 (no. 3139).

Spinoza's Ethics is "one continued and conscious protest against the scepticism o. Descartes" (Mind 1923, p. 13), a scepticism implicit in the methode of DM itself; Df fails to explain the connection of one clear and distinct idea with another; the introduction of a voluntaristic God as creator of eternal verities, after a passing appeal to Revelation, marks the collapse of the méthode, makes knowledge impossible, and renders proof meaningless. This is what Spinoza found inacceptable. The anticartesian weapons he needed he found in Maimonides' Guide for the Perplexed. This thesis is developed using "toutes les resources d'une imagination historique inépuisable et dont la hardiesse n'est certainement pas toujours consciente d'elle-même" (review below). Roth's Mind article outlines with precision his doctrinal critique of the méthode, then shows the "precise opposition" of Spinoza's logic to that of D., using Ludwig Meyer's Preface to the Ethics as a starting point. In Roth's monograph on DM (no. 189) the critique of D.'s methode is carried into the genesis of D.'s thought, and completed by an analysis of the failure of the méthode to serve the needs of physics, a systematic failure which inevitably turns into an historical one.

Review: Anon. in RMM 31: 1924, suppl. bibl. 4, 13–14.

331 SARANO, R.: "De la liberté chez Descartes, plus particulièrement de la liberté humaine." Eph 5: 1950, 202–22.

An uncommonly clear exposition of the difficulties in D.'s theory of free will, which stem from two conflicting views of freedom (power of indetermination vs. absolute determination by the True and the Good); it concludes with a critique of three Cartesian ways of understanding freedom.

Review: Corrado Dollo in S 19: 1951, 135–36. See also *Segond's* note on divine and humane freedom ("Prélude cartésien à l'existentialisme," *ibid.*, 223–32), and Sartre, no. 192.

333 SCHOLZ, HEINRICH: "Über das cogito, ergo sum." K 36: 1931, 126–47.

Capital study of the question whether the cogito can be syllogistically proved. If not syllogistically interpreted, it must be transformed into "dubito ergo sum," as D. himself suggests; in this form it is the fundamental proposition of Cartesian metaphysics. D.'s claim that the cogito is unprovable is shown to be false; it can be transformed into a proposition provable by Aristotelian logic. The article comments on the cogito interpretations of Spinoza, Kant, Heidegger, Hegel, Schopenhauer, and others. See no. 334.

334 SCHOLZ, HEINRICH: "Augustinus und Descartes." BDtPh 5: 1931–32, 405–23.

Keen analytical comparison of Descartes' cogito and St. Augustine's "si fallor." Finds an overwhelming metaphysical similarity. Differences arise regarding "die Unantastbarkeit" of mathematics (411): for St. Augustine it is an axiom, for D. a "probandum." The fateful impact of Cartesianism is explained by D.'s "Auslieferung der Evidenzkontrolle an die Mathematiker," purpose and consequence of the Cartesian key formula "dubito, ergo sum" (see no. 333).

335 SCHRECKER, PAUL: "La méthode cartésienne et la logique." RPFE 123: 1937, 336–37.

Remarkable study, discussed by E. Cassirer (no. 5, 44–46), of D.'s rejection of logical formalism, and its present-day acceptance. Modern logic admits an infinity of equivalent, closed isomorphic systems, but cannot determine which of them can grasp reality; it therefore still faces the problem which D. solved by taking the necessarily metalogical step towards a material truth criterion. The paper carefully determines the role of the cogito regarding both material and formal certainty, but does not concern itself with new methodologies, some of them related to formal logic, which treat the "reality" problem as illusoty or attack it by rather uncartesian means. See, as an example, *A. J. Ayer's* "Cogito ergo sum" (Analysis 14: 27–31, Dec. 1953, reviewed by A. Gianquinto in RassF 3: 1954, 199–200). *J. A. Passmore's* "Descartes, the British empiricists, and formal logic" (PhR 62: 1953, 545–53) points out that D.'s rather than Bacon's rejection of formal logic in favor of an "ars inveniendi," adopted by Locke, remained dominant until J. S. Mill attempted, and failed, to to formalize what, according to D., could not be formalized. Hence (?) Bertrand Russell's return to formalism. See also Serrus, no. 231.

338 SIX, KARL (S.J.): "Die 'Objectiones septimae' zu Descartes' 'Meditationes.' Zur Charakteristik der Beziehungen zwischen Descartes und den Jesuiten." ZKT 38: 1914, 161–182.

Studiously objective study of D.'s attitude towards the Jesuits as evidenced in his correspondence regarding Bourdin, whose threat to denounce D. in Rome caused D.'s sharp reaction. Bourdin did not have many Jesuits on his side: author considers it not impossible that a formal order was issued to Bourdin to refrain from any polemic with D. with whom the Order wanted to maintain good relations for reasons of prudence. After the Bourdin affair, these relations rapidly improved: "Man hat sich gegenseitig die Bitterkeiten vergessen und ist gut Freund geworden" (182) – for a while, anyway. Utilizes the Jesuit archives in Rome.

340 STOUT, A. K.: "Descartes' proof of the existence of matter." Mind 41: 1932, 191–207.

Taking issue with Gilson's DM commentary, author uses D.'s proof of the existence of matter in the Sixth Meditation to show the part which "the impulse to believe 'the teachings of nature' plays in Descartes' proof" (191). These "teachings" are the experience of the link between bodily affectations and the sensation of pain etc., of mind-body unity (Ryle's "ghost-in-the-machine"), of body being distinct from other bodies. The interesting question why D. believed these "teachings of nature" to be error-free is somewhat doubtfully answered by reference to "the biological utility of the more specific instinctive beliefs" (197).

342 STRUVE, WOLFGANG: "Das 'ergo' in Descartes' 'ego cogito, ergo sum' und 'sum, ergo Deus est'." Lexis 2: 1950–51, 239–61.

Laborious, clumsy analysis which yet offers a happy little discovery: D.'s conception of intellectus as intuitus reflects the ancient primacy of the eye over the other senses, hence makes for a philosophy that sees, oversees, and dominates, not for one that listens and obeys ("Wir sprechen vom 'herrischen Auge' und 'demütigen Ohr'; das Umgekehrte ist nicht möglich," 262). From Heidegger's school.

344 TEICHER, JACOB: "Spunti cartesiani nella filosofia arabo-giudaica." GCFI 16: 1935, 101–30, 235–49.

Seeks, and finds, antecedents of the methodical doubt and cogito in al-Ghazzālī, Averroës, Maimonides: " .... la parentela spirituale profonda che lege Cartesio con i pensatori arabo-ebrei si basa in fondo sull' indirizzo spirituale commune di concepire Dio come la realità suprema razionale accessibile alla mente umana e di sviluppare questa idea di Dio con il procedimento mentale intuitivo unicamente adeguato a questa realità" (247). Useful references. See also *Ch. Saumagne's* "Notes sur l'Iman Abou-Hamed al-Ghazali et le doute méthodique de Descartes" (Con 2: July 1921, 541–49). On Maimonides see Roth (no. 329).

345 TEIXEIRA, LIVIO: "A religião de Descartes; notas à margem de alguns livros." Revista de história (São Paulo), 6 (v. 10): 1955, 171–208.

Critical review of the French literature of the 1920's and 1930's on D.'s religiosity, emphasizing Espinas, Gouhier, Maxime Leroy. Conclusions: Descartes was not intentionally a Catholic apologist (against Espinas), but he was not insincere either (against Leroy); he accepted revealed theology sincerely but also for convenience; this admission was coupled with indifference towards Christian religious experience, which explains his tolerance for, and liking of, non-Catholic company; yet, there is a note of (admittedly rationalist) mysticism underneath. A pretty example of synthetic judgment a posteriori, leaving the author and D. with one leg each dangling on either side of the religious fence.

346 VERNEAUX, ROGER: "La sincérité critique chez Descartes." Aph 13, no. 2, 1937: 15–100.

D. saw well enough that his new concept of science required a critique of knowledge "remaniant à la fois .... le monde et l'esprit. Mais cette même idée qui soulève le problème critique interdit de le poser avec une sincérité complète. La question posée est étroite, la phénoménologie reste courte, et la méthode imprécise" (100). Distinguishes critical sincerity (doubting the evidence) from moral, artistic, psychological, intellectual sincerity. Good pages on Cartesian and Socratic irony (Kant continues Descartes as Descartes continues Socrates, 64–77).

Review: A. G. A. Balz in JP 35: 1938, 176–77. See also Verneaux, no. 232.

347 DE WAELHENS, ALPHONSE: "Descartes et la pensée phénoménologique." RNS 41: 1938, 571–89.

"On the radical opposition between the spirit of 17th c. rationalism and that of recent existential philosophies" (Anon. in Mind 48: 1939, 239), with extensive discussion of Heidegger's and Jasper's hostility towards Descartes. Brief section on Husserl.

347a WAHL, JEAN: Du rôle de l'idée de l'instant dans la philosophie de Descartes. Alcan, 1920. 48 p. Thèse Paris. Reprinted: Vrin, 1953 (BHP).

Magnificent study, justly dedicated to Bergson, of D.'s conception of time, motion, causality: "voir les choses dans l'instant" (44), "simultanéité nécessaire par laquelle s'exprime l'unité de l'action physique, l'unité du moi, l'unité de Dieu" (45), apprehending the discontinuous instant and continuing creation in one intuition. This view of time is traced through (or rather built up from) its expressions in D.'s dominant doctrines of metaphysics and physics. See also *J. Vigier*, "Les idées de temps, de durée et d'éternité dans Descartes" (RPFE 89: 1920, 196–233, 321–48); *Geneviève Lewis*' comments on Wahl and Vigier in RIP 4: 1950, 190–93 ("L'âme et la durée d'après une controverse cartésienne"); and *Laporte* (no. 178) whose view of Cartesian time as continuous is refuted by Gueroult, no. 170, v. I.

Reviews: E. Gilson in RPFE 94: 1922, 350–51; R. Ceñal in PenM 9: 1953, 527–28.

347b WEIN, HERMANN: "Von Descartes zur heutigen Anthropologie." ZPF 2: 1947–48, 296–314.

Important, profoundly serious reading of DM I–III from the viewpoint of post-war existential philosophizing. D.'s morale provisoire is an admission that Cartesian doubt cannot encompass (as the cogito cannot solve) the whole of the problem of human existence; "der Übergang von der Unruhe eines philosophierenden Menschen zur absolutistischen Substanzenmetaphysik eines Welt-Systems ist die negative Seite dessen, was uns der cartesische Zweifelsversuch vormachen kann" (302). But D. was not just "l'homme de lettres dans son cabinet"; his morale provisoire with its "il suffit de bien juger pour bien faire" indicates that his philosophizing should have led "zu einer dialektischen Feststellung über den Menschen" (302) rather than to his two-substance dualism. *Wein's* "Der wahre cartesische Dualismus" (ibid., 10: 1956, 3–28) consequently finds the true Cartesian dualism in the contrast between D.'s search for absolute truth and his advocacy of a morale provisoire. One of the best recent German contributions.

348 WILD, JOHN: "The Cartesian deformation of the structure of change and its influence on modern thought." PhR 50: 1941, 36–59.

D.'s account of change as efficient causation is irreconcilable with Aristotle's. Prevailing modern thought looks upon change as Descartes did. Even Hume's critique of D. stays within the Cartesian framework. A problem article, profound in its confrontation of Aristotle and D., disquieting in its vista of modern thought developments.

349 WOLFSON, H. A.: "Causality and freedom in Descartes, Leibniz, and Hume." In: Freedom and experience. Essays presented to Horace M. Kallen. Ed. by Sidney Hook and Milton R. Konvitz. Cornell UP, 1947, 97–114.

Distinguishes two basic Western theories of freedom: the Philonic (God endows man's will with His own miraculous power to act freely and indeterminedly) and the Epicurean (undetermined freedom of human will in a world without causality). D. is in Philo's tradition, but "while lavishing upon man the miraculous power of the free will, he begrudges God, in this old world of ours, a few reported miracles; and, in his own imaginary world, he denies Him outright the power of miracle-working." (103). Leibniz too departs from Philo's theory, while Hume "starts with a denial of causality but denies causeless free will" (114).

350 YOUNG, JOHN Z.: Doubt and certainty in science; a biologist's reflections on the brain. The B.B.C. Reith Lectures 1950. Oxford, Clarendon Press, 1951. viii, 167 p.

The road from beast-machine to man-machine does not end in man becoming machine but in "the machine's becoming a man, i.e., in the establishment of biology and other sciences of man as needing no foundation either in physics or in theology," as A. M. Ritchie rightly notes (Mind 64: 1955, 563). The proposition is borne out in Young's lecture series, popular by Third Programme standards, on current biological knowledge of the brain and on "the human calculating machine" (Lecture 3), showing the road from the beginnings in Descartes to the era of cybernetics and electronic "brains." Author draws oddly groping but far-reaching conclusions concerning the Cartesian problem of doubt and certainty in science, calling for a new epistemology based on the biologists' recognition that truth can no longer be defined "as that which can be observed and verified by anyone"; and that individual observers "are not the basic units of life" (154). The noted biologist's epistemological qualms are one aspect of the machine-man challenging the cogito; for the leap from the mathematical theory of automatism to mastery of the human world, paralleling D.'s leap from Method to "mastery and possession of nature," see *Norbert Wiener's* Cybernetics, or control and communication in the animal and the machine (New York: Wiley, 1948, 194 p.). On the question whether machines "think": *W. R. Ashby*, "Can a mechanical chessplayer outplay its designer?" (BJPS 3: 1952–53, 44–57) with comments by *J B. S. Haldane* (189–91) and *B. M. Adkins* ("The dictum of Descartes," 259–60). The issue merges in part with the "ghost-in-the-machine" issue; see no. 190; *Pinsky's* facetious question "Do machines think about machines thinking?" (Mind 60: 1951, 397f., a jeu d'esprit on D., Spinoza and the therapeutic positivists) was unexpectedly answered in a New Yorker cartoon by Richter (November 1, 1958): Mathematician, reading the tape coming from a giant computer, to another mathematician: "I'll be damned. It says, *cogito ergo sum*."

IX. MATHEMATICS AND SCIENCES

351 BELOT, ÉMILE: Essai de cosmogonie tourbillonnaire: L'origine dualiste des mondes. Gauthier-Villars, 1911. xi, 280 p. See also no. 1189–90.

Develops a cosmology from the principle of "dualisme tourbillonnaire," declaring that nothing in modern science contradicts D.'s vortex hypothesis. Belot's novel "dualism" hypothesis rigorously deduces the formation of a planetary system from the deformation of a very rapidly turning tube-vortex of gaseous matter under the impact of collision with a slow-moving body. See Busco's chapter on Belot's theory in no. 359, and Parenty, no. 392.

352 BLOCH, ERNST: "Die chemischen Theorien bei Descartes und den Cartesianern." Isis 1: 1913–14, 590–636.

Documented study balances the detrimental influence upon chemistry of D. and his followers against their "epochal" contribution to the radical weeding out of all animistic, teleological and mystical explanations. Rich material on John Mayow (1645–79), English Cartesian chemist, whom the author considers the greatest predecessor of Lavoisier, and on other Cartesian chemists less helpful to the new science. See also Thijssen-Schoute (no. 467), 258–60.

353 BOUTROUX, PIERRE: L'imagination et les mathématiques selon Descartes. Alcan, 1900. 45 p. From: UPL 10: 1, 1900, 1–47.

Original, stirring interpretation of D.'s concept of mathesis universalis as a science of pure, naked quantities without any concrete reality, hence independent of imagination in D.'s sense. Descartes recognized this conception to be practically unattainable; his algebraic geometry was merely the most useful and convenient compromise he could find. The thesis rests on distinctions between "imagination" acting in time and "understanding" outside time; memory and perception; deductive reasoning and immediate cognition. Important appendix on D.'s and Vieta's analysis "au point du vue du rôle de l'imagination" (37–41); also on D.'s Regulae (42–45), to the understanding of which this study makes a profound contribution. See also J. Klein, no. 378; Boutroux, no. 355; Brunschvicg, no. 358.

354 BOUTROUX, PIERRE: "L'histoire des principes de la dynamique avant Newton." RMM 28: 1921, 657–88.

Traces the development of dynamics from Aristotelian physics to Roberval and Newton, defining D.'s place with precision.

355 BOUTROUX, PIERRE: "Sur la signification de la Géométrie de Descartes." RMM 22: 1914, 814–27.

The fortunes of algebra, stepchild of mathematics, changed suddenly when D.'s Géométrie broke the tradition by shifting interest from formal proof to certainty and problem-solving. Fermat, independent inventor of analytical geometry, failed to recognize it as an autonomous development, while D. saw the consequences, if too sanguinely. Even his errors were fruitful: his treatment of the tangent problem emphasized the limits as well as the success of his approach which, in fact, contained the seeds of the whole modern development of analysis. *Julian Lowell Coolidge* ("The origin of analytical geometry," Osiris 1: 1936, 231–50; also: A history of the geometrical method, Oxford, Clarendon Press, 1940, 122–29) traces analytical geometry from the Greek study of loci by means of their equations to Fermat and D., confirming in more pedestrian fashion Boutroux' and Brunschvicg's assessment. See also *H. L. de Vries*, "De 'Géométrie' van Descartes en de 'Isagoge' van Fermat" (NTW 4: 1916–17, 145–68); *A. Boyce Gibson's* "La 'Géométrie' de Descartes au point de vue de sa méthode" (RMM 4: 1896, 386–98), using the Regulae to explain the general method of the Géométrie; and *M. Hyppolite*, "Du sens de la 'Géométrie' de Descartes dans son œuvre" (in Royaumont, no. 42, 166–86, with discussion).

Review: M. D. Crane in PhR 1916, 630–31.

355a BOYER, CARL B.: History of analytic geometry. New York, Scripta mathematica at Yeshiva University. 1956. ix, 291 p. (Scripta mathematica studies no. 6–7).

This monograph treats analytical geometry from its Greek roots to the later part of the 19th c. only. In this vast perspective the priority between Descartes and Fermat is less important than the question of how much they contributed to analytic geometry as a whole. René Taton's review (Isis 50: 1959, 489–92) sums up the best answer: "They discovered the two aspects of the fundamental principle of analytic geometry, but they did not make the subject what it is today."

356 BOYER, CARL B.: The rainbow: from myth to mathematics. New York-London, Thomas Yoseloff, 1959. 376 p.

Voltaire had charged D. with the unacknowledged use of Marco Antonio de Domini's work on the rainbow. *Paul Mouy* (CD v. 2, 47–53) finds D.'s real yet equally unacknowledged source to be Francesco Maurolyco of Messina, though the mathematization of the problem is Descartes' own undisputed and brilliant achievement. Boyer's well-illustrated, agreeably written and carefully documented book is the definitive history, from Aristotle to our day. Here and in his papers (no. 1335a,b) Boyer explains the fundamental contribution of medieval European and Arab physicists to the observation and measurement of the rainbow, with a fine chapter on D.'s most important predecessor, Dietrich (Theodoric) von Freiberg. Ch. 8 (The Cartesian theory and its reception, 200–232) shows Descartes the research man solving the problem by a combination of brilliant insight and indefatigable calculations, then proudly assuming that his solution is the final word, and "in his arbitrary impatience" missing the crowning glory that was his for the asking: having explained the secondary rainbow, he could easily have predicted the phenomenon of the tertiary one, and completed the theory. Good brief statement on Snell's law and D.'s law of sines (182–94); tables comparing D.'s tables of angles with those of predecessors. Though D. rightly considered his explanation of the rainbow a triumph of his method, this pièce de résistance had a curiously cold reception, described in the remainder of the chapter. The book contributes to the understanding of D.'s character and manner of procedure as a scientist. See also *Isnardi* (no. 376, 122–26) who refutes Poggendorf's notorious charges of plagiarism against D., and Mouy's treatment of the problem in no. 391.

357 BRUNET, PIERRE: L'introduction des théories de Newton en France au XVIIIe siècle. Tome 1: Avant 1738. Blanchard, 1931. vii, 355 p. (No more published.)

Very detailed account of the struggle of the Cartesians against the Newtonians, 1700–1738, assessing the role of many little-known as well as of the major figures among both. Period divided into three parts: initial Newtonian influences and Cartesian resistance, 1700–20 (1–78); "Les préliminaires du débat, 1720–28" (p. 79–152); "L'effort des grands cartésiens, 1728–38" (153–202). Inestimable source of information. Bibliography. See also *Léon Bloch's* La physique de Newton (Alcan, 1908, 642 p., BPC), especially Ch. 9 on Newton's metaphysical ideas, and E. A. Burtt's broad treatment of the philosophical background, no. 444.

Reviews: Ch. Ranwez in RNS 38: 1935, 394; T. E. Jessup in Mind 41: 1932, 259–60.

358 BRUNSCHVICG, LÉON: "La géométrie analytique." "La philosophie mathématique des cartésiens." In his: Les étapes de la philosophie mathématique [1912], 3rd ed., PUF, 1947. Ch. 7, 8, p. 98–151.

Great idealistic history of mathematical thought. Sees in D. a decisive turn in the conception and philosophy of mathematics, though Brunschvicg recognizes that this science would not be perceptibly different today had D.'s Géométrie remained unwritten. The heart of his singular interpretation of D.'s analytical geometry is on p. 120–21. The contrast between Regulae and Géométrie is ingeniously analyzed. The chapter on Cartesian mathematics notes the Géométrie commentaries of Florimond de Beaune and Erasmus Bartholinus, and gives a trenchant analysis of mathematics in Malebranche's and Spinoza's philosophy. The discussion is in non-mathematical language.

Reviews: A. Darbon in RPFE 75: 1913, 297–305; B. E. B. Jourdain in Mind 22: 1913, 567–74 (sharply critical); Gérard Milhaud in Rsyn 14: 1937, 77–78.

359 BUSCO, PIERRE: Les cosmogonies modernes et la théorie de la connaissance. Alcan, 1924, 436 p.

Sir Edmund Whittaker in his History of the theories of ether and electricity, 2nd ed. (no. 3558) wonders what the fate of Newtonianism would have been if the spiral nebulae had been discovered before the overthrow of D.'s theory of vortices (v. 1, p. 9, n. 2). Busco's detailed history of cosmologies from Descartes and Malebranche through Newton and Laplace to the early century up to Belot's vortex theory provides some sort of answer. Ch. 13 on the relationship between cosmogony and epistemology expresses the scientist's disdain at "l'incohérence et l'inanité .... de la métaphysique, qui n'a ni méthode, ni affirmations propres," praising the modern abandonment of the "faux idéal de rationalité, de simplicité, ainsi que la recherche des origines absolus" (432), i.e. the anticartesian turn in the scientific spirit; at the same time the book demonstrates the persistence of Descartes' vortex concept in modern cosmology, despite its collapse when Newton's celestial mechanics appeared. Ch. 12 has an interesting discussion of the concept of chaos and the theory of actual causes.

360 CANGUILHEM, GEORGES: "La théorie cartésienne du mouvement involontaire." In his: La formation du concept de réflexe au XVIIe et XVIIIe siècles. PUF, 1955, 27–57. (BPC).

Though D. is commonly considered the anticipator if not the creator of the modern concept of reflex, Canguilhem's meticulous, absorbing study gives not without regrets Thomas Willis' "De motu musculari" of 1670 credit for its first authentic formulation (169–72). The chapter on D. is a first-rate contribution to the understanding of his physiology and the philosophical spirit behind it. Ch. 1 outlines the state of the problem before Descartes. Valuable bibliography. No index.

Reviews: Anon. in RMM 62: 1957, 99–101; P. Delaunay in AIHS 9: 1956, 161–63; A. B. Dobservage in PPR 18: 1958, 568–69; G. Leger in RSTP 40: 1956, 529–30; F. Russo in Et 287: 1955, 268; R. Ruyer in Eph 10: 1955, 712–20.

361 CARTERON, HENRI: "L'idée de la force mécanique dans le système de Descartes." RPFE 94: 1922, 243–77, 483–511.

Penetrating analysis of D.'s difficulty in making the transition from mathematics to physics, from statics to dynamics. D.'s mechanics is compared to that of his contemporary adversaries, with precise assessment of the relationship. See M. Gueroult (no. 373a).

363 DIJKSTERHUIS, EDUARD JAN: Val en worp; een bijdrage tot de geschiedenis der mechanica van Aristoteles tot Newton. Groningen, Noordhoff, 1924. 466 p.

Detailed history of theories of free fall and throw, with chapters on Isaac Beeckman [also in: NAW ser. 2, v. 14, 186–208, 1924] who found the law of free fall before Galileo but never published it, and on D. (342–57) who made an odd but revealing error in his own account of the law. See Koyré, no. 379.

365 DREYFUS-LE FOYER, H.: "Les conceptions médicales de Descartes." RMM 44: 1937, 237–86.

Capital study treats a wealth of fact with deep understanding of its philosophical and biographical implications. Explains why D., so preoccupied with longevity, neglected therapeutics in favor of anatomy, physiology, embryonics; his treatment of Hippocratic theory of humors; the gap between his physiology and moral philosophy; Princess Elisabeth's influence upon his medical interest, etc. Finds D.'s neglect of therapeutics normal for his time, points to anticipations of modern discoveries (notably his treatment of fever and infections), sees him develop towards a vitalistic type of "animisme partiel et indirect," tending to define (in van Helmont's manner) "toute une série d'entités morbides par l'isolement anarchique d'une idée" (275). Excellent on TP and the dualism problem. *Guillaume Scipion Bertrand de Saint-Germain's* Descartes considéré comme physiologiste et comme médecin (Masson, 1889, xi, 532 p.), out of V. Cousin's school, is an unproblematic account of D.'s physiology and gerontology, listing anticipatory achievements (importance of elementary cells in the formation of higher beings, the role of gastric juices in digestion, of capillary vessels in nutrition, etc.) See also two Paris thèses: *Robert Charles Gontran Martin,* Descartes médecin (Legrand, 1924, 72 p.); *Auguste Tellier,* Descartes et la médecine, ou les relations de Descartes avec les médecins de son temps; suivi d'un exposé des idées médicales de Descartes (Vigne, 1928, 72 p.).

366 DREYFUS, GINETTE: "Physique et géométrie chez Descartes et chez Malebranche." In: Royaumont (no. 42), 187–207.

Courageous attack upon the view, firmly held by L. Brunschvicg and followed by the majority of interpreters, that Malebranche's concept of physics as an essentially empirical science is sharply opposed to D.'s reduction of physics to geometry. A close, well documented analysis shows M. admitting, on principle, three possible geometries and physics, and adopting the one which accords best with observation. Fundamentally, M.'s concept is identical with Descartes'; but in his philosophy this concept leads to insoluble metaphysical blocks. Interesting discussion (200–03).

367 DUGAS, RENÉ: "La pensée mécanique de Descartes." In his: La mécanique au XVIIe siècle: des antécédents scolastiques à la pensée classique. Paris, Dunod (Neuchâtel, Éd. du Griffon) 1954, ch. 7, p. 117–202. [English transl.: no. 1804a.]

After his Histoire de la mécanique (Neuchâtel, 1950), Dugas offers in this last work a huge, well organized history of 17th c. mechanics which gives central place to Galilei, Descartes, Pascal, Newton, Leibniz without neglecting important lesser figures, e.g., Beeckman whose extraordinary anticipatory mind shines forth from Dugas' list of his findings. The value of the work lies in what is also its weakness: it is not analytical like Mouy's, but offers generous excerpts from the texts, with sparse yet precise comments. Good picture of the nexus between great and lesser physicists of the century, and of the struggle between Cartesians and Newtonians. The role of metaphysics in 17th c. physics is not a topic here. Critical review by C. Truesdall in Isis 47: 1956, 449–52.
In "Sur le cartesianisme de Huygens," RHSA 7: 1954, 22–33, *Dugas* finds that young Christian Huygens "s'est libéré, après mûre réflexion, de l'obédience cartésienne" (24) but returned to D.'s "relativité généralisée" under the impact of Newton's Principia, refusing to accept Newton's absolutes; in cosmology, he preferred D.'s world as the more intelligible one. See also *Dugas,* "De Descartes à Newton par l'école anglaise," 1952 (no. 1805) on Hobbes, Henry More, Robert Boyle and J. Barrow, pointing out that in England too D.'s physics fared better than his metaphysics. *Paul Mouy's* chapter on Huygens in no. 390, 180–217, a thorough analysis of Cartesian element in Huygens' works, presents Huygens not without some hesitation as being in the strict Cartesian tradition, a view now modified by Dugas.

368 DUHEM, PIERRE: Les origines de la statique. V. 1, Hermann, 1905, p. 327–52.

Masterly, authoritative treatment of D.'s statics, from the factual historical viewpoint, yields a harsh judgment: "En la statique de Descartes, il n'est aucune vérité que les hommes n'aient connue avant Descartes"; echoing J. C. Poggendorf, Duhem finds that D., "aveuglé par son prodigieux orgueil, ... ne voit qu'erreurs dans les œuvres de ses prédécesseurs et de ses contemporains" (352). See also Ch. 13 on Roberval and Mersenne, and V. 2, ch. 17 on Mersenne, Pascal, Honoré Fabri and the Cartesian physicists. *François Mentré*, in an open letter to Duhem ("un plaidoyer d'exégèse en faveur de Descartes") respectfully reminds the great historian of the relationship between metaphysics and physics which must be considered when judging D. the philosopher (RdePh 5: 1904/2, 217–25).

369 DUHEM, PIERRE: "Bernardino Baldi, Roberval et Descartes." Bulletin Italien 6: 1906, 25–53. Also in his: Études sur Léonard de Vinci, ceux qu'il a lus et ceux qui l'ont lu. V. 1, Hermann, 1906 (reprinted: de Nobele, 1955), 127–56.

Traces the problem of centers of oscillation (the pendulum problem) from Leonardo da Vinci to its ultimate solution by Christiaan Huygens, "un des plus re marquables exemples de la continuité suivant laquelle s'enchaînent les découvertes scientifiques" (Études, p. 156), D. being just a link in this chain. D. and Roberval were both partly right, partly wrong in their heated controversy, their contributions finding a joint place in the final solution. *Pierre Costabel's* "La controverse Descartes-Roberval au sujet du centre d'oscillation" (RScH no. 61: 1951, 74–86) minutely studies the texts and Lagrange's criticism of D.'s solution; he finds D.'s methodological approach intellectually superior, though Roberval was technically better. Cf. also *Costabel*. "La démonstration cartésienne relative au centre d'équilibre de la balance" (AIHS 9: 1956, 133–46). On the Roberval-D. controversy over the tangent problem see *Léon Auger's* "La polémique entre Descartes et Gilles Personne de Roberval" (Thalès 6: 1949–50, 59–67).

370 FERRIER, RAOUL: De Descartes à Ampère, ou Progrès vers l'unité rationelle. Basel, Verlag für Recht und Gesellschaft, 1949. xv, 294 p. 2nd ed.: Ulman, 1953, 95 p. (only the revised Ch. 2).

The book, laden with forbidding mathematical and physical apparatus, distinguishes two basic attitudes in physics. One, Cartesian in spirit, is exemplified by Faraday, Lorentz and Einstein, the other by Ampère (the author's hero), Helmholtz and Poincaré. The two currents meet in Maxwell to yield a theoretical physics rich in results but heterogeneous in foundation. Admiral Ferrier attempts an Ampérian reconciliation in the unifying spirit of Cartesian method, but without the infertility of Cartesian systematization. Nonphysicists will find his "Aperçus nouveaux sur la cosmologie cartésienne" (Rsyn 63: 1948, 31–52) and the interesting discussion (53–58) a good, accessible summary of his theses, leaving the distinct impression that D.'s concepts of extension, space and number evaporate when translated from classical 17th century metaphysical language into that of modern mathematics and physics. Ferrier's placing D. in relation to modern physics is similar to R. Ingarden's, despite his different approach (see no. 375).

Reviews: Anon. in S 19: 1951, 406; E.B. in RPFE 141: 1951, 329–30; E. Biser in PhS 17: 1950, 282–83; L. Bouckaert in RPhL 48: 1950, 310; C. Ferro in RFNS 44: 1952, 543–44; M. L.

Guérard des Lauriers in RSPT 35: 1951, 431–32, and 37: 1953, 487–88; A. Reymond in RFNS 41: 1949, 395; V. Somenzi in Methodos 3: 1951, 69.

371 FLECKENSTEIN, JOACHIM OTTO: "Cartesische Erkenntnistheorie und mathematische Physik des 17. Jahrhunderts." Gesnerus 7: 1950, 120–39.

D.'s Géométrie is the work of an analytical mind, his physics that of a geometer who only formally surpassed Greek physics. Cartesian method is essentially a mapping of different concepts upon each other, limited to relations among extended things and excluding the time parameter: "Ihm ist 'mouvement' ein 'état', nicht eine zeitliche Zustandsänderung" (128). This is exemplified by a brief, nice discussion of the law of free fall (Galileo, D. and Beeckman who read D.'s false solution in Galileo's spirit and ascribed to D. the correct quadratic law). Original commemorative lecture, with comment on D., Kepler and Newton. Similarly *S. Gagnebin's* "La réforme cartésienne et son fondement géométrique" (ibid., 105–20), with an important extension: D.'s physics, in which the instant only is real (as Jean Wahl has shown), is not predictive like modern physics; its procedure is "construire les appareils comme le géomètre construit des figures" (117), a judgment which falls or stands with the author's assertion that "la géométrie de Descartes est déjà une physique" (116).

372 FLECKENSTEIN, JOACHIM OTTO: "Pierre Varignon (1654–1722) und die mathematischen Wissenschaften im Zeitalter des Cartesianismus." AIHS 2, no. 5: 1948, 76–138.

Very detailed study of Varignon, late Cartesian mathematician, in his double role as physicist and geometer; case study of the transition from Cartesianism to the new world of Leibniz and Newton, showing Varignon moving easily from statics and kinetics to dynamics, but having trouble understanding the spirit of the infinitesimal calculus, despite the Marquis de l'Hôpital's and Bernoulli's help. Author considers Varignon "das mathematische Optimum, welches der Spätcartesianismus in Frankreich hervorgebracht hat" (82).

373 GEORGES-BERTHIER, AUGUSTE: "Le mécanisme cartésien et la physiologie au XVIIe siècle." Isis 2: 1914, 37–89; 3: 1920, 21–58.

Posthumously published study covers D.'s physiology in detail, assessing its contemporary position and subsequent influence. The author's judgment was mature despite his years, his erudition comprehensive, his documentation extremely rich; the study is still almost indispensable for reference to problems, sources, literature. The quite negative assessment of the scientific importance of D.'s physiology may be compared to Mesnard's judgment of its philosophical character (no. 386).

373a GUEROULT, MARTIAL: "Métaphysique et physique de la force chez Descartes et chez Malebranche. RMM 59: 1954, 1–37, 113–34.

Metaphysically, D. identifies the concept of force with the continuous creative action of God. But basing his laws of motion upon the distinction between force at rest and force of motion, he asserts that both are secondary causes and modes of substance, both effects of divine force, both positive entities; whence his difficulty in establishing valid metaphysical and physical differences between them, and in moving from statics to dynamics. Absorbing but difficult study, carried forward to Malebranche and Leibniz: To escape Descartes' dilemma, Malebranche imagines that God created the world at rest, then added a different reality (viz., motion) by "chiquenaude." M.'s view of rest as simple privation of motion leads him into gravest difficulties regarding the laws of impact. By his theory, a small body should have greater force in motion than a large one. However, he contents himself with the distinction between dead force of inertia and live force of motion, without entering the field of physics, while Leibniz, to save phenomena, goes on to define mass as "vis primitiva et derivativa patiendi." The article rejects the common view concerning M.'s treatment of Descartes' concept of force at rest. On Leibniz and the concept of (mechanical) work see *Gueroult*, Dynamique et métaphysique Leibniziennes (Les Belles lettres, 1934 and PFL Strasbourg, v. 68; on Leibniz and Descartes: ch. 6). See also Carteron (no. 361).

Reviews: G. Leger in RSPT 38: 1954, 813; A. M. dell'Oro in S 23: 1955, 246; Anon. in Bsig 10: 1956, no. 11611–12.

374 HOFFMANN, ABRAHAM: "Die Lehre von der Bildung des Universums bei Descartes und ihre geschichtliche Bedeutung." AGP 17: 1904, 237–71, 371–412. Dissertation Berlin. Partly printed: Berlin, 1903, 37 p.

First part deals with D.'s predecessors and his philosophy of nature, second part with his cosmogony and its influence. Still useful.

375 INGARDEN, ROMAN S.: "Descartes a fizyka nowozytna." KF 19: 1950, 71–150. French summary 167–69.

Spirited defense of D.'s physics against Ernst Mach and J. C. Poggendorf; re-appraises it in the light of 20th-century physics. D. laid the ground for Newton whose refutation of Descartes regarding Kepler's laws is held to be in triple error. Credits D. with the "philosophy of inertia," notion of ether, paternity to modern field theories etc., riding roughshod over Galileo, Huygens, Snell. Even D.'s assertion of the constant total quantity of movement is rescued as the prototype of modern thermodynamic concepts. D.'s metaphysical speculations have nothing to do with his science; they merely serve to reconcile his sceptical leanings with his realism. Author ranges Descartes with Maxwell, Lorentz, Einstein as "maximalist" (complete, deterministic, causal, deductive program), against the "minimalists" Newton, Mach, Ostwald, Born and the quantum theorists. Very rich article, quite Cartesian in its treatment of physicists other than the master himself.

376 ISNARDI, TEÓFILO: "La física de Descartes." In: Homenaje (no. 40), v. 1, 75–139.

Comprehensive expository and critical survey of D.'s physics, with texts and illustrations, judges it to be largely a "roman de la nature," result of D.'s attempt to combine philosophy of science and concrete research, to the detriment of experimentalism. On this and related studies see E. Cassirer in no. 5, 10–13.

377 JAMMER, MAX: Das Problem des Raumes. Die Entwicklung der Raumtheorien. Vorwort von Albert Einstein. Darmstadt, Wissenschaftliche

Buchgesellschaft, 1960. xiii, 220 p. Translation by Paul Wilpert, augmented, of: Concepts of space. Harvard UP, 1954. See no. 377a.

377a JAMMER, MAX: Concepts of force. A study in the foundations of dynamics. Harvard UP, 1957. viii, 269 p.

Two model studies, written with clarity, precision, economy, wide source knowledge, of ideas (space, force) in physics, not philosophy. Thus D. does not appear at all in the history of space concepts (no. 377); regarding force (a concept he rejected), his mechanics plays a small part, but his influence reaches to the early 19th c. (Maine de Biran). Both books anticipate and confirm Koyré (no. 379a). Lucid explanation of D.'s vortex theory of gravity and of Huygens' consequent work on centrifugal forces in no. 377a, elaborated in no. 377 with regard to D., Leibniz, Huygens. Henry More's theologization of space (no. 377) is treated in the context of Jewish-Christian space theologies, while the chapter on the overthrow of Aristotelian space begins with Jewish-Arabic-Scholastic thought and ends with Gassendi and Campanella, omitting D. altogether. Both books are eminently helpful in historically placing D.'s physics; no. 377a clearly sets forth the development of the concepts of force, work, impetus, etc.

378 KLEIN, JAKOB: "Vieta's Formelsprache und die Umwandlung des Anzahl-Begriffs." "Der Begriff der *Zahl* bei Stevin, Descartes und Wallis." In his: "Die griechische Logistik und die Entstehung der Algebra." Quellen und Studien zur Geschichte der Mathematik, Abt. B, 3: 1934–36, 152–94, 195–235.

Booklength article of stupendous erudition treats with great clarity the Greek heritage in the genesis of modern algebra. Vast scholarly apparatus, relegated to footnotes, some of them little monographs: on D.'s "imagination", Greek φαντασία and Stoic "imaginatio" (212–14); on the sources of D.'s figurative symbolism (217–20). The Vieta chapter shows this conservative French mathematician reaching notions which will look revolutionary in D.: "nullum non problema solvere"; the problema problematum (mathematics as ars inveniendi); mathesis universalis, which becomes D.'s starting point. Regarding D.'s relationship to Vieta, Klein finds D. raising Vieta's ars analytica to the status of a symbolic science. Lively picture of Stevin who figures in D.'s decision to serve under Maurice of Nassau in 1618; Stevin's number concept is judged deeper, far less traditional than D.'s. The relatively brief but important section on D. sees his great achievement, never again lost, in identifying general symbolic mathesis with extension, thus creating the foundations of classical physics (Euclidean space) on which Newton was to build. Klein's analysis of "imaginatio" in D.'s Regulae as guaranteeing that the mathesis universalis will grasp the structure of the real world (Klein considers this to be D.'s scientia mirabilis) is superb. On D.'s indebtedness to the Greeks see *André Robert*, "Descartes et l'analyse des anciens" (Aph 13, no. 2: 1937, 221–45) and Milhaud, no. 388.

379 KOYRÉ, ALEXANDRE: Études galiléennes. 3 vols. Hermann, 1939. Histoire de la pensée, Asci, no. 852–854.

Vol. 1: À l'aube de la science classique (Aristote. Discussions médiévales: Bonamico. Physique de l'impetus: Benedetti; Galilei.) Vol. 2: La loi de la chute des corps:

Descartes et Galilée. Vol. 3: Galilée et la loi d'inertie. Appendix: L'élimination de la pesanteur: Galiléens (Cavalieri, Torricelli, Gassendi); Descartes (Monde. Principes).

Outstanding study. The first volume sketches the genesis of modern physics from Aristotle to the medieval study of impetus and on to Galileo. Vol. 2, enlarged from RPFE 123: 1937, 149–204, skillfully elucidates technical issues to bare the contrast between Galileo and Descartes. Best account of the curious Beeckman-D. discussions or free fall (25–40): Beeckman fully understood the physical problem but could not mathematize it; D. combines "une suprême élégance mathématique avec la plus irrémédiable confusion physique" (36). The long note on p. 26–27 serves as a warning not to take any Beeckman appraisal as final until a complete study of B.'s Journal is available. Vol. 3 has an excellent chapter on D.'s treatment of inertia in Le Monde and PP (158–81), confirming Koyré's assessment of the different scientific temperaments of D. and Galileo. D. errs, if fruitfully, by unconsciously sliding "du temps à l'espace, du physique au géométrique" (v. 2, 43): his physics is "géométrisation à outrance," "élimination du temps," in short, "une revanche de Platon" (v. 2, 53f.) which failed as Plato's physics had failed. Ultimately, D. aimed at a concrete physics, while Galileo treated physics as an abstract Archimedean science; this D. could not accept. See *E. Cassirer's* valuable discussion of this and other 1937 Galileo-D. studies in no. 5, 38–42. See also *Carmelo Ferro's* "Galilei e Cartesio" in: Nel terzo centenario della morte di Galileo Galilei, Milan, 1942, 327–50 (UCSC, v. 20).

Review: R. Chastel in Pensée no. 6: 1946, 143–46.

379a KOYRÉ, ALEXANDRE: From the closed world to the infinite universe. Baltimore, Johns Hopkins UP (Oxford UP), 1957. [Full title and reprint: no. 2380.]

This history of the "destruction of the cosmos and the geometrization of space" (Preface) could have been called the history of the theologization of space up to the point where "the mighty, energetic God of Newton," the Divine Artifex, becomes Laplace's "hypothesis we no longer make." Ch. 4 contrasts Galileo and Descartes. The latter's distinction between the infinite and the indefinite is patiently explained as to relevance and consequences, but the heart of these Hideyo Moguchi Lectures is in the following chapters: Henry More's critique of the Cartesian identification of matter and extension; his eventual assertion of an indeterminately vast but finite world, merged in an infinite space; "absolute space, absolute time and their relations to God" (Malebranche, Newton and Bentley); the divinization of space (Joseph Raphson); and three fine chapters on Newton, Berkeley, Leibniz ("The work-day God and the God of the Sabbath"), with a brief "Abgesang" on God's departure from the new physical cosmology, leaving His ontological attributes behind and taking all the rest with Him. A rare combination of scientific, philosophical and theological analysis applied to the 17th-c. scientific revolution, and the perfect complement to Burtt, no. 444.

Reviews: Lynn Thorndyke in AHR 63: 1958, 370–71; Yvon Belaval in AIHS 10: 1957, 250–52; Marie Boas in Isis 49: 1958, 363–66; Th. S. Kuhn in Science 127: 1958, 641; Serge Moscovici in RHSci 11: 1958, 356–58.

380 LASSWITZ, KURD: Geschichte der Atomistik vom Mittelalter bis Newton. 2. Band: Höhepunkt und Verfall der Korpuskulartheorie des 17. Jahrhunderts. Hamburg & Leipzig, Voss, 1890, 55–126. Reprinted 1962.

Lasswitz, an early German pioneer of space opera, gives a thorough, detailed study of the genesis, character, and transformation of Cartesian corpuscular physics under the impact of dynamics. Dated in its details, unconcerned with underlying metaphysics, often crude in judgment, but useful as a factual historical introduction. See also *Lasswitz*, "Zur Genesis der cartesischen Corpuscularphysik" (VWPh 10: 1886, 166–89).

381 LENOBLE, ROBERT: "La psychologie cartésienne." RIP 4: 1950, 160–89.

Lively, unusually well-written study tries to "éclairer l'œuvre par l'homme" (171), linking Cartesian psychology to the "psychology de Descartes," i.e., his personality traits, particularly his supposedly perfect equilibrium. Impressive, surprising list of D.'s achievements that anticipate moderne findings, such as the theory of reflexes (but see Canguilhem, no. 360), the association of ideas, the impact of prenatal and early childhood experiences. Though D.'s conceptual apparatus was archaic, his ideas were new. Very good treatment of dualism as foundation of Cartesian psychology, linking it with his physics, metaphysics, moral philosophy.

382 LORIA, GINO: Storia delle matematiche dell'alba della civiltà al secolo XIX. 2. ed. riv. e aggiornata. Milano, Hoepli, 1950, 974 p.

Great, authoritative history of mathematics, assessing the Descartes-Fermat priority question in Ch. 24, esp. 455–73; cf. *Loria*, "Da Descartes e Fermat a Monge e Lagrange. Contributo alla storia della geometria analitica" (AcLincei, Mem., classe di sc. fisiche, ser. 5a, 14: 1923, 777–845). Essential.

383 LUCAS DE PESLOÜAN, C.: "La théorie d'Einstein, système cartésien." RdePh 29: 1922, 225–58.

When Einstein rose to glory, a French attempt to Cartesianize him was called for. Author prepares the ground by finding it impossible to link Einstein with Newton, then discovers Einstein's Cartesianism, consisting in (1) his belief in invariant laws of nature, (2) his "recherche de la géométrie de l'univers." What is more, both stimulated speculation yet discouraged it by their greatness! Thirty years later, *F. Le Lionnais* ("Descartes et Einstein," RHSA 5: 1952, 139–54) makes a point-by-point inventory of similarities and differences, including their common concern over discord and war. But it still remains true that Newton's system is a special case of Einstein's, while D.'s is not.

385 MERCIER, DÉSIRÉ-JOSEPH (CARDINAL): Les origines de la psychologie contemporaine. 2nd ed. Louvain, Institut supérieur de philosophie; Alcan, 1908. xvi, 493 p.

Lays the foundations of a Neothomist psychology by analyzing and rejecting D.'s dualistic psychology as combining excessive spiritualism with mechanistic physiology, both in its original form (Ch. 1) and its historical transformations (Ch. 2) which lead to Spinozism, ontologism, idealism on the one hand, to Comtean positivism on the other. Mercier's critique culminates in a confrontation of D.'s dualistic psychology with Thomist anthropology (Ch. 4). Ch. 1, 2 were first published as: "La psychologie de Descartes et l'anthropologie scolastique" (RNS 1896–98; see 2704).

386 MESNARD, PIERRE: "L'esprit de la physiologie cartésienne." Aph 13, no. 2: 1937, 181–220.

D.'s radical departure, "l'explication génétique de l'homme" (197), is contrasted with the "lamentable" state of biology at the beginning of the 17th c. Corrects erroneous views of the Descartes-Harvey relationship: Descartes was instrumental in winning acceptance for Harvey's chief discovery. The animal-machine doctrine is held to follow necessarily from D.'s animal spirits hypothesis; D. answered criticism by merely refining it. D.'s cardinal achievement: giving autonomy and unity to physiology, his main defect: too rigorous exclusion of final causes from biology, though his late moral philosophy reopens a place for them. Original study, to be taken cum grano salis: the same story reads differently when the hero is Science, not Descartes, as Georges-Berthier has shown (no. 373).

387 METZGER, HÉLÈNE: Les doctrines chimiques en France, du début du XVIIe siècle. Vol. 1, PUF, 1923, 496 p.

Notes the influence of atomism, mechanism and of D.'s concepts of matter and creation upon medicine and chemistry. By reducing matter to space, the Cartesians deprive particles, capable of transmutation, of their individuality, as exemplified in the work of Daniel Duncan (1682), the author's one and only example of a Cartesian chemist. The theory of Nicolas Leméry is characterized as superficially classical and Cartesian. Written with much detail and from the sources, but naive and narrow compared to Bloch (no. 352). See also Thijssen-Schoute, no. 467.

388 MILHAUD, GASTON: Descartes savant. Alcan, 1921. 249 p .(BPC).

Intr.: Sincérité de D. 1. Premiers essais scientifiques. 2. Crise mystique [Dream.] 3. Hiver 1619–20. 4. La date du 11 novembre, 1620. 5. Travaux d'optique, 1620–29. 6. Problème de Pappus et géométrie analytique (1631). Géométrie (1637). 7. D.et Fermat: tangentes. D. et l'analyse infinitésimale. 8. Notion de travail. 9. D. expérimentateur. 10. D. et Bacon. 11. Double aspect de l'œuvre scientifique de D.

Posthumously collected 1916–19 articles [titles and dates of first publication: no. 2742–54] on D.'s mathematics, optics and mechanics, flanked by biographical studies and general assessments. Milhaud's work remains basic; only the Introduction and Ch. 2 (D.'s "sincerity" and his Dream) are now out of date. Milhaud writes with precision and authority, explaining technical points in generally understandable language. Chapter 1, 3, 4 translate the scientific part of D.'s Cogitationes privatae and other early writings into modern terms, elucidating the growth of his scientific interests. Among the studies of D.'s mathematics, "Descartes et l'analyse infinitésimale" (162–75) is particularly valuable, analyzing three instances where his "génie naturel" found solutions to problems "qui ne semblent solubles qu'avec l'algorithme du calcul différentiel" not available to him (174–75). Good studies of "Descartes expérimentateur" and "Descartes et Bacon" (Ch. 9, 10). In a brilliant page, D. is evaluated as original but not revolutionary in science, not the creator of modern but the conserver of ancient mathematics, his PP "le dernier des magnifiques romans" in the style of Artistotle, Plato, Lucretius (246). *H. J. E. Beth* ("Descartes als mathematicus," ANTWP 42: 1950, 134–44) exemplifies D.'s mathematical method by his procedure in solving Pappus' problem, supplementing Milhaud's Ch. 6. See Gérard Milhaud in Rsyn 14: 1937, 80–81.

390 MOUY, PAUL: Le développement de la physique cartésienne, 1646–1712. Vrin, 1934. x, 343 p. (BHP)

Introd.: L'héritage scientifique des cartésiens. Ch. I: Les professeurs cartésiens [Utrecht: Henri Le Roy (Regius). Autres "Cartesii Sequaces" en pays flamand et allemand. Cartésiens français: Conférences cartésiennes, Cordemoy, la Forge, Rohault, Claude Gadrois, Pierre-Sylvain Régis. Le triomphe de la physique cartésienne. Fontenelle.] Ch. II: La physique mathématique cartésienne de Huygens. Ch. III: Les physiques anticartésiennes de Leibniz et de Newton. Ch. IV: La physique de Malebranche. Ch. V: Conclusions.

The standard work on Cartesian physics after Descartes. An excellent historical survey of D.'s work and heritage in physics (1–71) introduces a large chapter on D.'s disciples, especially Rohault and Régis (not one "expérimentateur" among them). Huygens' mathematical physics is characterized as Cartesian, without disguising the points of basic difference. Ch. 5 is the best analysis available of Malebranche's physics. Disappointing philosophical evaluation of the findings in the "Conclusions."

Reviews: Jean Abelé in Aph 11, no. 3, suppl. bibl.: 1934–35, 90–91; Anon. in RMM 42: April 1935, sb p. 4–5; G. de Giuli in RF 26: 1935, 361–62; S. V. Keeling in Phil 11: 1936, 340; Gérard Milhaud in Rsyn 14: 1937, 81–82; G. Radetti in GCFI 5: 1937, 179–83; A. Vartanian in no. 397a, p. 472.

392 PARENTY, HENRI: Les tourbillons de Descartes et la science moderne. Champion, 1903. viii, 220 p. (Mémoires, Acad. de Clermont-Ferrand, ser. 2, v. 16).

Genial forages in late 19th-c. physics by a scientist with patent limitations. Ch. 3 ("Évolution cartésienne des sciences au XIXe siècle") indiscriminately discusses the "tourbillons" of Cauchy, Helmholtz, Thompson, Maxwell, the Hertzian waves, "les tourbillons sonores," spiral stress lines, and any other example of spirality, turbulence or vortical motion that comes to mind.

393 POGGENDORF, JOHANN CHRISTIAN: "Descartes." In his: Geschichte der Physik. Leipzig, Barth, 1879, p. 305–18.

Aggressively anticartesian assessment of D.'s net contributions to physics as mostly a host of errors, plus false claims of priority. Curious for its obvious lack of knowledge about D., in contrast to German physicists and historians of physics of a later generation. See R. Ingarden and T. Isnardi (no. 375, 376).

394 ROJAS, NERIO: "Descartes y Claudio Bernard." In: Homenaje, no. 40, v. 3, p. 97–104.

Interesting comparison of D.'s methodological approach to physiology with that of Claude Bernard, one of the great 19th century founders of experimental physiology. Discussed by E. Cassirer, no. 5, p. 12.

396 SCOTT, JOSEPH F.: The scientific work of René Descartes (1596–1650). Foreword by H. W. Turnbull. London, Taylor & Francis, 1952. vii, 211 p.

A patient, clear, trustworthy explanation in modern notation and terms of what D. actually says in his Dioptrique, Météores, Géométrie (analyzed in four excellent chapters, 84–166), and in the PP sections on physics. Excludes biology, physiology, medicine, psychology. The historical development before D. is well handled, but the assessment of D.'s "originality" suffers from lack of acquaintance with modern special studies and approaches. Useful but not error-free biographical notes on 41 contemporaries and predecessors. Best companion-guide of its kind.

Reviews: E. J. Finan in CHR 40: 1954, 369–70; R. Hooykaas in AIHS 6: 1953, 493–95; J. Jacquot in RHSA 8: 1955, 181–82; T. S. Kuhn in Isis 44: 1953, 285–87; L. Roth in Nature 171: 1953, 1083–84; E. T. Whittaker in Endeavour 12: 1953, 53–54.

397 TANNERY, PAUL: Mémoires scientifiques publiés par J. L. Heiberg et H. G. Zeuthen. Vol. 6, edited by Gino Loria. Gauthier-Villars, 1926. 608 p.

Contains most of author's Descartes studies in connection with his work as mathematical editor of AT, the completion of which he did not live to see. Tannery remains the foremost authority on textual criticism and historical elucidation of D.'s mathematics. Vol. 6 includes his rich study of the D. correspondence in the Fonds Libri, from the viewpoint of the history of mathematics (149–268); his historical study of the inverse tangent problem (457–77); and other papers related to D. and the preparation of AT. Some other D. papers are scattered in v. 13–18. For an assessment of Tannery's achievement see *Pierre Duhem's* obituary article in RdePh 6: 1905, 215–30.

397a VARTANIAN, ARAM: "Scientific literature. Medicine." In: A critical bibliography of French Literature, v. 3 (see no. 3a), 462–76.

Complements the present section. Critical notices of important works on scientific organization and general scientific development in the 17th c., studies of scientists important to D. studies. Includes several works listed above. In the same volume: "General philosophical background" by *Charles J. Beyer*. See also no. 18, and no. 464a.

398 VUILLEMIN, JULES: Mathématiques et métaphysique chez Descartes. PUF 1960. 188 p. (Collection Epiméthée).

I. *Courbes et opérations non reçues dans la Géométrie.* 1. Deux courbes transcendantes; exemples d'application: Courbe logarithmique; psycho-physique, psychophysiologie de D. et lois de la sensation. Spirale logarithmique: nombre d'or, phyllotaxie. 2. Substitutes cartésiens du calcul infinitésimal: méthodes des tangentes dans la *Géométrie*, méthode extragéométrique; quadrature chez D.
II. *Géométrie et métaphysique.* 3. Classification des courbes: constructions méchaniques; classification cartésienne; consequences sur la physique mathématique; caractère "critique" du système de D. 4. Théorie des proportions: problème de Pappus; géométrie comme théorie des proportions; analogies métaphysiques. 5. Équations algébriques: théorie cartésienne; la 4° règle du DM, réflexion de la méthode.

D. excluded transcendental curves from his Géométrie, but his correspondence deals with the logarithmic curve and the logarithmic spiral. Vuillemin's study of them is fundamental; it investigates D.'s mathematical method as model for his metaphysics, his metaphysics as obstacle to his mathematics and science. Beast-machine doctrine and geometrization of space, both metaphysical, prevented D. from applying his transcendental curves to psychophysical and other problems (human sensation he considered non-measurable), although the logarithmic curve was to serve the study of sensation from Bouguer (1792) to Fechner, while the logarithmic spiral became the organic growth model of phyllotaxy. D. clung to the Greek notion of geometry as theory of proportions; hence the curious emptiness of his (only metaphysically mathematized) physics. His brilliant substitutions for the infinitesimal calculus were blocked by his metaphysically motivated insistence upon precision. Thus, transcendental curves – which were to open new realms in mathematics – fell outside the curve classification of the Géométrie. Mathematical method as mathesis universalis determines and limits D.'s metaphysics; his concept of mathematics requires only order, not measurability; hence mathematization is not necessarily quantification. A fine discussion of D.'s number concept shows the effect of his self-imposed mathematical limitations upon his metaphysics, with a section on Cartesian and Kantian critique of reason (Fichte resumes the broken continuity of Cartesian criticist philosophy). The study confirms the iron consistency in D.'s thought (no change in premises as D. moves from one field to another); it suggests that D.'s metaphysics and epistemology cannot be analyzed without his mathesis which is indeed universal as the matrix and model of all his thought. The small book, which can be mastered by non-mathematicians, is the best critical analysis of D.'s mature mathematical concepts; note however, P. Boutroux's different conception of D.'s mathesis universalis (no. 353), viewing the Géométrie in the light of the early Regulae. See also Vuillemin on Cartesian evidence, no. 3512, and on methodology of mathematics in D. and Leibniz, no. 3512b.

Reviews: J. Dopp in RPhL 58: 1960, 301–2; G. Pflug in AGP 43: 1961, 202–205 (important survey of V.'s work on D. since 1951.)

399 DE WAARD, CORNELIUS: "Le manuscrit perdu de Snellius sur la réfraction." Janus 39: 1935, 51–73.

Leibniz and Huygens charged that D. had found the law of refraction, his great claim in optics, in a ms. of Willibroord Snell or Snel (died 1626). In 1896, *J. D. Korteweg* ("Descartes et les manuscrits de Snellius d'après quelques documents nouveaux," RMM 4: 1896, 489–501) acknowledged D.'s originality and suggested independent discovery, but had to admit difficulties not to be solved without new documents. Four decades later, C. de Waard, a great finder of mss., identifies a ms., hitherto ascribed to Johann Gerhard Voss's son Dionysius, as Snell's lost work which scholars from Golius to Huygens had seen. Gives the annotated text of the ms., but does not settle the question of D.'s independence from Snell. Good treatment of the controversy in *G. Leisegang* (no. 87, p. 54–61) with discussion of Leibniz, Huygens, Ernst Mach, and modern historians of optics, elucidating the difference between Snell's and D.'s formulation of the law.

400 DE WAARD, CORNELIUS: "Les objections de P. Petit contre le 'Discours' et les 'Essais' de Descartes." RMM 32: 1925, 53–89.

Another find of de Waard's: Pierre Petit's objections to D.'s Dioptrique, resulting from experiments he made at Mersenne's suggestion. D. abusively refused to answer: "il faut laisser abboyer les petitz chiens sans prendre la peyne de leur resister" (AT II, 533). On the merits of the case and on the eventual reconciliation between D. and the "petit chien" see the note in AM (no. 79), 2: 380–82.

401 WHITTAKER, SIR EDMUND [TAYLOR]: The modern approach to Descartes' problem: the relation of the mathematical and physical

sciences to philosophy. Herbert Spencer Lecture, Oxford. London, Nelson, 1948. 30 p.

D.'s problem: to find a general philosophy or universal science as rigorous and convincing as mathematics. The distinguished historian of science rapidly surveys Descartes' mathematico-physical discoveries and the changes they forced upon philosophy, to find that D. failed because he wanted philosophy to precede, not follow, the sciences; he fails equally himself, proposing a Neocartesianism without Cartesian dualism and without Cartesian (or, for that matter, any other) method.

Reviews: M. T. Antonelli in Gmet 6: 1951, 198–99; G. E. in CleR 31: 1949, 205–10; E. M. in JP 47: 1950, 109–10.

402 WRIGHT, GEORG HENRIK VON: "Descartes och den vetenskapliga idéutvecklingen." Aj 16: 1950, 103–71.

1. Aristotelian vs. Cartesian science. 2. Science and method [La Flèche; the Essais]. 3. Metaphysics and science [PP, TP, Puy de Dôme, free fall, force, cosmology, vortices.] 4. Nature and man [Harvey, physiology, reflex action, pineal gland.]

Excellent short survey views D.'s scientific contributions in their epistemological context, finds Dioptrique and Météores to be his outstanding achievement in physics. Thoughtful comment on causal research vs. D.'s "thought experiment."

X. ESTHETICS AND LITERARY INFLUENCE

402a BECKETT, SAMUEL: Whoroscope. Paris, The Hours Press, 1930.

Exemplifies the reaction to D. of the "literature of the absurd." D.'s first published poem presents D. "meditating on time, hens' eggs, and evanescence" (M. Esslin, The Theatre of the Absurd, New York, 1961, p. 3). Another Beckett theme is Geulincx and the breakdown of the soul-body link; see *R. Cohen* in CompLit 12: 1960, 93–94 and *Hugh Kenner*, "The Cartesian Centaur" (Perspective 9: 1959, 132–41, and in *his* Samuel Beckett, New York, Grove Press, 1961.)

403 EDELMAN, NATHAN: "The mixed metaphor in Descartes." RR 41: 1950, 167–78.

Noting two persistent metaphors in D. (the philosopher-architect: certainty; the philosopher-traveler: method), the author perceives uneasiness beneath them. Digging deeper, he unexpectedly strikes gold in the barren wastes of the Jesuit Pierre Bourdin's Seventh Objections – a long, heavy, ironical play on these very metaphors suggesting D.'s impatience, uncertainty, anxiety. D.'s equally heavy ironical Responses to Bourdin are a refutation close to "rire jaune". *Th. Spoerri's* brilliant paper, brilliantly discussed, on "La puissance métaphorique de Descartes" (in: Royaumont, no. 42, 273–301) contrasts D.'s style of "construction cohérente" with Pascal's "espace constellé", penetrates deeply into the character of metaphor in D., but misses its "mixed" character which Edelman uncovered, though noting the Bourdin-D. exchange. *Hartwig Tornau's* Syntaktische und stilistische Studien über Descartes (Diss. Leipzig, Hoffmann, 1900, 94 p.) has a classified lists of D.'s metaphors (73–91); its discussion of D.'s French usage is based on V. Cousin's now obsolete uncritical edition.

404 GADOFFRE, GILBERT: "Le 'Discours de la méthode' et l'histoire littéraire." FS 2: 1948, 301–14.

Completes the dethronement of DM. "Pour l'homme du Discours de la méthode, Montaigne est un point de départ" (305), while Guez de Balzac gave D. the style and "la forme même de l'essai" (310). Ironically, PP and TP did what DM was supposed to do: attract "le lecteur honnête homme," who preferred these more substantial later works. The role of DM after D.'s death was more than modest: "Résignons-nous à abandonner la légende du Discours de la méthode, Évangile de la Littérature classique," (314), for not until the 19th c. did the work attain this stature. Though none of author's theses is novel, he stands alone in drawing their combined consequences.

405 GADOFFRE, GILBERT: "Corneille et Descartes." In: Traditions de notre culture. Éditions du Cerf, 1941, 76–91. (Rencontres, v. 2).

Greatly exaggerating the importance of D.'s brief military service in 1618–19, author collects passages in which Corneille seems to underline, not without malice, "certains aspects héroiques et militaires du Discours" (84), ridiculing D. as "miles gloriosus élegant" (86); in support, author cites a famous yet unexploited epigram by Constantijn Huygens.

406 GARAI, PIERRE: "Le cartésianisme et le classicisme anglais." RLC 31: 1957, 373–87.

In the Cartesian "spirit" Garai finds the explanation of the long rule of classical esthetics in England, against the native grain of English literature. Between 1637 and 1700, Cartesianism was acclaimed at first, curiously enough because of its mystic, poetic appeal; then subtly revised, openly attacked, and in the end, completely rejected. By then, it had already done its work, helping to substitute the new esthetics of order accepted by the philosophers and scholars for the élan lyrique of the poets. See *Garai's* unpublished 1954 Columbia dissertation: The shield of order; a study of the influence of Cartesianism on English literary doctrine, 1668–1774 (Ann Arbor Microfilms; Diss. Abstr. 14/12: 1954, 2335–36). See also Nicolson (no. 460) on D.'s influence upon the changing English prose style.

407 HÉBERT, RODOLPHE-LOUIS: "An episode in Molière's Amphitryon and Cartesian epistemology." MLN 70: 1955, 416–22.

A comic scene (Act 1, 2, in which Sosie tries to prove that he exists) leads author to conclude that M., "more logical than Descartes," was spoofing Descartes' "abuse of speculation" in the cogito.

408 HENSCH, THOMAS: Über den Stil in Descartes' Discours de la méthode. Zürich, Schwarzenbach, 1949. 90 p. Dissertation Zürich.

Tries to evaluate D.'s style in the light of language psychology, studying D.'s syntax in connection with his images, particularly metaphors expressing solidity, lucidity, "Geradlinigkeit." The last section assembles some recent critical judgments; *Paul Claudel's* (in his: Contracts et circonstances, Gallimard, 11th ed., 1938, 149–53) is the most interesting, holding style and argument of the Discours to be equally inferior. Author's judgment is brash, but he poses some suggestive questions.

409 HERFORD, C. H.: "Shakespeare and Descartes; a chapter in the intellectual history of Europe." HJ 24: 1925, 88–100.

The Cartesian insistence on clarity and distinctness, and on the singleness of truth hurt English as well as French literature, particularly the treatment of dramatic character. But the rationalistic Cartesian "denudation of nature" (88) soon gave way to a truly English notion of Nature's richness, embodied in Shakespeare, carrying over into German Romanticism. The article provides the English background to Baader's anticartesian opposition of "Natur" vs. "Geist" (see Steinbüchel, no. 466b). See also Robertson no. 420, and Nicolson, no. 460, and the literature cited there.

410 HUMBERT, PIERRE: "Descartes et le style scientifique français." Eph 5: 1950, 169–73.

Punctures the claim of D.'s originality in using French in scientific writing; points to a small but remarkable body of pre-1637 scientific manuscripts in French, especially Mydorge's and Gassendi's whose scientific French is by no means inferior to D.'s. But then, D. had the courage they lacked: he *published* in French.

411 KRANTZ, ÉMILE: Étude sur l'esthétique de Descartes, étudiée dans les rapports de la doctrine cartésienne avec la littérature classique française au XVIIe siècle. Baillière. 1882. iv, 376 p. Thèse Paris.

Despite Brunetière's and Lanson's annihilating attacks, the book has retained its subterranean influence to this day, with its "brilliant paradox that this great thinker, who never wrote a line on aesthetics, was virtually the creator of France's aesthetic canon" (J. G. Robertson, no. 420, p. 6), its claim that D. did have an aesthetics after all, its fertile lines of inquiry. Though Krantz failed through exaggeration, he was original and perceptive even when wrong. His book is better than its awful reputation, and still more useful than some recent studies which are its equal in imprudence and confusion. On the Krantzian "tourbillon" in the critical tea pot see Olgiati's informative treatment of the controversy over D.'s literary influence, from Nisard (who started it) and Sainte-Beuve through Brunetière and Lanson to the eloquent silences of Vial and Denise (no. 14, 184–95). *N. Abercrombie* (MLR 31: 1936, 358–76) gives a summary and critique: "all the constructive principles of 17th c. criticism were already guiding the minds of Malherbe and his contemporaries when Descartes began to write" (376). In particular, Abercrombie finds no sign of D.'s influence upon Boileau. See also Brunetière no. 442; F. Bouillier in RPFE 14: 1882, 556–62; Lanson, no. 412; R. Weibel Richard, no. 429; and H. von Stein, no. 424.

412 LANSON, GUSTAVE: "L'influence de la philosophie cartésienne sur la littérature française." RMM 4: 1896, 517–50. Also in his: Études d'histoire littéraire. Champion, 1929, 58–96.

Classical article which long dominated French literary criticism, though D. scholars paid no attention to it. Lanson takes his Descartes image from Liard. Carefully determining the meaning of "influence," he finds between the "esprit" of D. and that of his contemporaries in literature "d'étroits rapports, mais sans influence possible" (519). Only after D.'s death did his influence begin (Pascal, Bossuet, Boileau, La Bruyère), but merely in the form of reinforcing independently developing thought:

"Je n'apperçois dans la doctrine de Descartes aucune possibilité d'une esthétique. Le beau se confond dans le vrai" (534). Finds only two instances of direct influence: Bossuet, and Montesquieu's Esprit des lois. E. Cassirer (no. 5, p. 10) cites *René Bray*, La formation de la doctrine classique en France, Paris, 1927, as confirming Lanson "on all essential points"; but later studies reveal D.'s indirect influence upon French classicism, and reappraise the notion of "influence" both conceptually and in its historical application to the case in question. See also Lee (no. 415) and Michéa (no. 417).

413 LANSON, GUSTAVE: "Le héros cornélien et le 'généreux' selon Descartes." RHL 1: 1894, 397–411. Also in his: Hommes et livres, Lecène et Oudin, 1895, 113–33.

Another influential article which made the treatment of Descartes' TP mandatory in French literature courses on Corneille and became the father and ancestor of a host of studies on D.'s concept of "générosité." See the discussion in Hensch, no. 408, 78–81; also Cassirer (no. 243 and Reichardt's and Hofstadter's reviews); Serrurier, no. 423; against Lanson's thesis: R. Champigny, no. 1509b, and H. Gillot, no. 2024a.

414 LAPP, JOHN C.: "The 'Traité des passions' and Racine." MLQ 3: 1942, 611–19.

Adds to Lanson by trying to show that Racine's concept of passions, too, was kin to D.'s. See also *William McC. Stewart*, "Racine et Descartes" (RCC 39, ser. 2: 1938, 385–94, 499–511) on new evidence of on Racine's contact with D.'s philosophy. See also Lion, no. 2556a.

415 LEE, RENSSELAER W.: "Ut pictura poesis: the humanistic theory of painting." Art Bulletin 22: 1940, 197–269.

Considerable study includes an important assessment of D.'s influence upon French 17th century art (221–25, 266–67). Suggests a connection between Poussin and Descartes and points out that through Le Brun the central concept of D.'s physics as well as his rationalist method became the basis of the "esthetic legislation" of the Academy as it bodily applied D.'s physiology of passions, animal spirits and all, "to specify the minute changes in facial expression by which each passion manifests itself" (221). *Geneviève Lewis* ("Descartes et Poussin," DSS 23: 1954, 521–49) admits that in the absence of tangible fact about the Poussin-D. relationship any "confrontation ne saurait .... être que dérivée," but finds a common contemporary ideal in "certaines analogies entre les deux hommes, et quelque formules curieusement accordées" (521), engagingly widening her meager theme into an early 17th century background study, rich in nuances. See also Raquel Sajón's notable study (no. 422) and *François Bénoit*, "Le cartésianisme et l'art français" (RHPh ns 5: 1937, 189–98).

417 MICHÉA, R.: "Les variations de la raison au XVIIe siècle. Essai sur la valeur du langage employé en histoire litteraire." RPFE 126: 1938, 183–201.

Temperamental attack on Lanson's thesis (no. 412): "Tant s'en faut que le cartésianisme soit pour rien dans l'art classique, que bientôt il va le détruire. La querelle des anciens et des modernes est la revanche de l'esprit cartésien sur le goût antique, de l'analyse sur la poésie, de l'idée sur la forme , de la science sur l'art" (188–89). The only trouble with this is that the "querelle" opened long before the time of Descartes. Author finds D.'s "bon sens" very similar to Pascal's "cœur."

418 PIRRO, ANDRÉ: Descartes et la musique. Fischbacher, 1907. vii, 127 p.

Pleasantly old-fashioned, learned monograph, based on D.'s Compendium musicae of 1618 and his correspondence. Accords D. a merely honorable, rather than an outstanding place in the history of music, in contrast to Hugo Riemann and the conductor-scholar Hermann Scherchen (no. 3218). Pirro's chief concern is musicology, but there are interesting sidelights: "Descartes et la danse" (85–89); in music, too, D. serves "la cause qu'il se refuse à reconnaître juste, et facilite la réforme qu'il n'accepte point" (19), regarding the equal-temperament scale). See also *Jan Branberger*, René Descartes, filosof hudby: příspěvek k dějinám hudebni estetiky (Praha, Urbánek, 1933, 74p. Prague dissertation, 1909), and L. Prenant (no. 419).

419 PRENANT, LUCIE: "Esthétique et sagesse cartésiennes." RHPh ns. 10: 1942, 3–13, 99–114.

Superior investigation. Opens with the best discussion so far of esthetics in D.'s Compendium musicae, comparing it with Regulae: from the outset D. recognizes esthetic pleasure to be subjective; in 1630 he abandons the notion of a necessary correspondence between specific consonances and passions (same point in no. 421). For him, no objective esthetic judgment is possible, only a psychological analysis – and life is too short to indulge in that. Metaphysics is essential to "sagesse," as are technology and the passions which contribute to moral control; music, merely being personal delectation, "prend sa place dans la vie du philosophe; non dans son œuvre" (114). *O. Revault d'Allonnes* (L'esthétique de Descartes," RScH 1: 1951, 50–55) follows one of Krantz's leads, finds D. in his "situation de chef de file" defining "l'art idéal" or "l'art cartésien" (50) in his letters to Guez de Balzac, from which the author manages to extract a whole Cartesian classification of literary art forms. See also *Victor Basch* who asks: "Y-a-t-il une esthétique cartésienne?" (CD 2:67–76) and answers yes.

420 ROBERTSON, JOHN GEORGE: Studies in the genesis of romantic theory in the eighteenth century. Cambridge UP, 1923.

This distinguished work on Italian literary criticism is above all a study of Gian Vincenzo Gravina and Lodovico Muratori. Tries to show "that the conception of 'creative imagination,' with the help of which Europe emancipated herself from the pincers of pseudoclassicism, was virtually born in Italy" (p. vi). Adopting the viewpoint of Krantz, author finds Cartesianism a factor on either side in the quarrel of the ancients and moderns, more clearly so in Italy than in France. Gravina and Muratori both "set out to discover the irrefutable 'cogito ergo sum' of poetry" (92); Muratori's concept of verisimilitude is linked to the Cartesian revolution in criticism. But these démarches degenerated into a placid acceptance of dogmas, equally placidly abandoned when they led to impasses. Cartesianism, an initial stimulus, thus failed to become a formative element. Good chapter on Vico and his anticartesianism; interesting discussion of the indebtedness of French criticism to Italy.

Review: G. Maugin, RLC 5: 1925, 522–29. See also Toffanin (no. 3436) on Descartes and Aristotelian classicism, and Cottugno (no. 1648) on Caloprese.

421 ROLAND-MANUEL: "Descartes et le problème de l'expression musicale." In: Royaumont (no. 42), 438–42.

Interesting note, supplementing Prenant (no. 419), on D.'s denial that musical expression evokes specific emotional reactions, on his distinction between "le pur délectable et l'agréable proprement dit" (440), and on his anticipation of the Pavlovian conditioned reflex in explaining individual reaction to musical expression.

422 SAJÓN, RAQUEL: "El amor y la expresión en Descartes y en algunas teorías estéticas del siglo XVII." In: Homenaje, no. 40, v. 2, 261–87.

Workmanlike study of the concept of amour in Chapelain, Descartes, Pascal, with a notable section on Henri Testelin's theory of "l'expression générale et particulière," which applies D.'s theory of passions to visual art (282–85). Denies the originality of D.'s concept of amour and links the theory of expression of Testelin and French 17th century painters to Italian renaissance art, D.'s TP merely providing "una exposición más completa y acabada de lo subjectivo en lo objectivo" (287). See also Lee, no. 415.

423 SERRURIER, C.: "Saint-François de Sales, Descartes, Corneille." Neo 3: 1918, 89–99.

Points to St. François de Sales' Traité de l'amour de Dieu of 1616 as underlying both the drama of Corneille and the TP of Descartes, thus explaining (if the explanation holds) the correspondence between their strictly contemporary concepts of passions.

424 STEIN, KARL HEINRICH VON: "Ueber den Zusammenhang Boileau's mit Descartes." ZPPK 86: 1885, 199–275.

Rich study. Anticipates many later results while avoiding traps into which Krantz and others stepped. Undertaken at Wilhelm Dilthey's suggestion, it corroborates his view that D.'s influence upon Boileau was indirect. Makes the nice point that D.'s own doctrine was the more effective upon Boileau since it was not itself an object of controversy, as distinct from Cartesian "Partei-Doktrin." Finds the mediary between D. and Boileau in Arnauld and Port-Royal. The length of the article is accounted for by extensive, well-documented, dry but useful digressions on Cartesian doctrines and development of French criticism from Ronsard to de la Mesnardière, Boileau and his contemporaries.

425 STEWART, WILLIAM McC.: "Descartes and poetry." RR 29: 1938, 212–42.

Discusses D.'s genuine if infertile love of poetry. Reprints a sonnet by an unidentified student at La Flèche which some conjecture to be by Descartes, and discusses D.'s ballet for Queen Christina, the sole surviving print of which is assumed to be a specimen of the program distributed to the audience at the time.

426 DE VIGNY, ALFRED: "Le compas ou la prière de Descartes." Journal d'un poête (1829). In his: Œuvres complètes. Pléïade, 1948, v. 1, p. 901–02.

Vigny read and re-read Descartes; result: "poême à faire." A girl plays with a compass. D. warns her: ".... 'L'une de ces branches est appuyée au centre, mais elle le perce et le détruit, tandis que l'autre trace un cercle mystérieux. Moi, j'ai servi de centre à ce poignard savant. Il m'a trué.' – Et il regarda la mer et les vertes îles de Stockholm." Poem fortunately remained unmade, But *Bernhard Bergonzoni* did make and publish his Poems 1948–1954, under the title: Descartes and the animals (no. 1209).

427 VIGORELLI, GIANCARLO: "Circonstanze cartesiane della letteratura francese contemporanea." In: Cartesio (no. 35), 781–91.

A suggestive article, with out-of-the-way references, discusses particularly André Gide and Valéry.

429 WEIBEL RICHARD, ROBERTO: "Notas sobre el clasicismo francés y el pensamiento cartesiano." In: Homenaje (no. 40), v. 3, 261–93.

Important, original attack upon the problem. Author judiciously appraises Krantz ("perfectamente plausible en su intención primera," though he understood neither D. nor Classicism), Brunetière and Lanson (who formulated the problem in the very terms he exposed as false in Krantz). Rejecting the view that Cartesianism influenced the pseudo-classicism of 1680–1750, author makes the important distinction between D.'s proper thought and a later "racionalismo trunco y vulgarizado," better called pseudocartesianism (288). Positively, he suggests a bold new approach. Casting out the old prop of Cartesianism as order, clarity, mathematicism, and recognizing D. as the founder of the belief in the creative power of thought and the cognitive power of poetry (M. de Corte's view, no. 244a), he interprets Classicism as a perennial attitude in art and finds "la verdadera estética cartesiana" alive in modern "classicists" concerned with poetic creativity, from Baudelaire to Valéry and Gide. Written from thorough knowledge of the critical and philosophical literature.

429a WILLEY, BASIL: The seventeenth century background; studies in the thought of the age in relation to poetry and religion. London, Chatto & Windus, 1934. Reprinted: New York, Doubleday Anchor, 1953.

The interest in Willey's Descartes chapter lies in its estimate of the effect of the "Cartesian spirit" upon poetry: it sharpened the distinction between prose and poetry, and lowered the status of poetry. The intervening Cartesian spirit explains the onset of the "dissociation of sensibility" (T. S. Eliot's term) after Donne. Tempting comparison between Descartes' and Wordsworth's views of the experience of childhood. Good chapters on the rational theology of the Cambridge Platonists, especially John Smith, and a useful chapter on Joseph Glanvill.

XI. AFTER DESCARTES

430 ANDRADE, ANTÓNIO DE: Descartes em Portugal nos séculos XVII e XVIII. Bro 51: 1950, 432–51.

Traces D.'s none too conspicuous role in Portugal from the arrival in 1641 of D.'s best student, Jean Gillot, and of the Jesuit J. P. Ciermans (Cosmander) to about 1775. Rich references. See also *Domingos Mauricio Gomes dos Santos*, "Para a história do cartesianismo entre os Jesuítas do século XVIII" (RPFil 1: 1945, 27–44, which utilizes philosophy courses dictated by Jesuits around 1740, based on P. António Vieira and others; same author's "A primeira alusão a Descartes em Portugal" (Bro 25: 1937, 177–87; *Augusto da Silva Carvalho*, "O cartesianismo e a medicina em Portugal" (AcLisboa 2:

1939, 71–107, showing that no Cartesian influence was felt in Portugal until the middle of the 18th c., and then but briefly. *Joaquim de Carvalho's* "Descartes e a cultura filosófica portuguêsa" (*ibid.*, 39–69) deals with D.'s use of Fonseca and the Commentarii Conimbricenses.

431 BALZ, A. G. A.: Cartesian studies. New York, Columbia UP, 1951. vi, 328 p.

Eleven large-scale papers [see no. 1118–30] published between 1930 and 1947, here reprinted with minor changes, form an indispensable scholarly work on important Cartesians (G. de Cordemoy, Clerselier, J. Rohault, L. de la Chambre, L. de la Forge, Johann Clauberg, Samuel Sorbière) and on the development of Cartesian doctrine: the critique of substantial forms, the animal soul problem, occasionalism and psychophysical parallelism, the Spinoza critique of Giacinto Sigismondo Gerdil and François Lamy. The important chapter "Man, Thomistic and Cartesian" (from RevR 11: 1947, 339–80) claims that D. and St. Thomas both conceived man dualistically, which John A. Mourant sharply denies (JP 54: 1957, 373–83; rejoinder by Balz, p. 383–90.)

Reviews: G. Boas in AIHS 5: 1952, 383; G. Caló in Scientia 87: 1952, 288; J. P. Corbett in Mind 62: 1953, 282; W. Doney in PhR 62: 1953, 457–58; A. Gewirth in JRel 33: 1953, 290; H. A. Larrabee in JP 49: 1952, 54–56; G. Leger in RSTP 37: 1953, 454–55; B. Moellenhauser in Pers 34: 1955, 58; P. Stubbs in HJ 50: 1952, 413–14; C. L. Thijssen-Schoute in ANTWP 45: 1952–53, 78–79; J. N. Wright in PhQ 3: 1953, 273.

431a BAUDIN, ÉMILE: Études historiques et critiques sur la philosophie de Pascal. Vol. 1: Sa philosophie critique. Pascal et Descartes. Neuchâtel, Baconnière, 1946. iv, 345 p. (Être et pensée, v. 16.)

Important work. Main theme: Jansenism ruined Pascal. The relationship between Pascal and Descartes is sharply worked out, noting the differences in attitude, tone and range of interest as well as in doctrine. Baudin finds no real "borrowings" from Descartes in Pascal, whose anticartesianism is evident not only in many of his conclusions but also in the fact that their common Augustinian heritage developed into "deux Augustinismes" which are poles apart from each other.

Reviews: Anon. in RMM 54: 1949, 105–06; A. Béguin in Crit 4: 1948, 1067–79; P. Braido in Salesianum 10: 1948, 687–90; C. Calvetti in RFNS 40: 1949, 247–51; E. B[réhier] in RPFE 141: 1951, 331–32; J. Perdomo in RevF 8: 1949, 693–99; H.-D. Gardeil in RSPT 31: 1947, 415–20; J. Rohmer in RScR 22: 1948, 57–73, 260–72; 23: 1949, 53–63; B. Romeyer in Aph 18: 1949, 128–31.

432 BELAVAL, YVON: Leibniz critique de Descartes. Gallimard, 1960. 560 p. (Bibl. des idées).

Capital work, rich in well-documented detail. Deals with the relationship between the two philosophers within the dual framework of both systems, with emphasis on D.'s separation of philosophy and science from theology, Leibniz's defense of their traditional alliance. Part I (L'esprit de la méthode) brilliantly contrasts the two thinkers: intuitionism vs. formalism, revolution vs. tradition. Part II (Le modèle mathématique) offers a penetrating, fruitful contrast of Leibniz and Descartes ("Archimède contre Apollonius.") The last part is a searching study of similarities and differences between "the two last great physicist-philosophers" regarding the principles of physics which both, each in his way, conceive in pre-Newtonian fashion, i.e., metaphysically.

Review: M. Deguy in NRF 8, no. 96, Dec. 1, 1960, 1094–1101.

432a BENSE, MAX: Descartes und die Folgen. Ein aktueller Traktat. 2. Auflage. Krefeld, Agis-Verlag, 1955. 64 p. (Augenblick, Supplementbd no. 2.) See no. 1200 for 3rd ed.

A post-war German seeks a European intellectual reorientation founded on an existential rationalism which he sees embodied in the thought of Descartes. How is humanistic man to survive in an age of technology, under the pressures of "ideologies" (Communism) on one side, of eschatology (Christianity) on the other? Descartes offers a solution: renouncing the urge towards unattainable perfection, acknowledging the hard facts of philosophical anthropology, and accepting the limitations which Descartes had the courage to see. Only the Cartesian "reduced man" (der reduzierte Mensch) can preserve freedom and human dignity. Interesting discussions of Simone Weil, Bertolt Brecht and others. But see also P. Engelhardt, no. 1840.

433 BERTHÉ DE BESAUCÈLE, LOUIS: Les cartésiens d'Italie; recherches sur l'influence de la philosophie de Descartes dans l'évolution de la pensée italienne aux XVIIe et XVIIIe siècles. Picard, 1920. xxiv, 377 p. Thèse d'Aix-Marseille.

Worst-printed item in the literature, swarming with errors (by retribution, author's name is usually misspelled "Besancèle"). Naive in judgment, summaries and quotations without adequate references, yet indispensable, since author has actually read his recondite material and reports honestly and fully. Deals with Cartesians, anticartesians, eclectics at Naples, Pisa, Padua and other centers. Ch. 4 on Malebranche's influence upon P. Giovenale, B. Trevisan, F. M. Zannotti, G. S. Gerdil and others. Two chapters on Cartesian influence on art and poetry, with special reference to Antonio Conti. The bibliography, like the rest, is useful and sloppy. See also Ottaviano (no. 461); *E. Garin*, "Cartesio e l'Italia" (GCFI 29: 1950, 385–405, with section on Vico). On Malebranche's influence in Italy see *Karl Werner*, "Die cartesisch-malebranchische Philosophie in Italien" (AcWien, Philos.-histor. Klasse, Sitzungsber. 102: 1883, 75–141, 679–794 on Fardella and Gerdil); *A. Banfi*, "Malebranche et l'Italie" (RPFE 125: 1938, 253–74); Balz (no. 431).

434 BEYER, CHARLES J.: "Du cartésianisme à la philosophie des lumières." RR 34: 1943, 18–39.

Critique of the concepts of "esprit cartésien" and "Cartesian heritage"; clears up the fog created by the great debate on D.'s "influence" (see Lanson, no. 412). Deplores the common tendency to label any brand of rationalism "Cartesian" and exposes the decisive difference between D.'s and Voltaire's philosophizing. "Attempts to show that the Cartesian triumph after 1660 was not that of Descartes' metaphysical rationalism, but that of a positivistic mechanism, which Descartes had opposed, and which was to merge with epicurean and 'libertin' thought later in the century" (author's notice in no. 3a). In the quarrel of the Ancients and the Moderns "c'est le 'dynamisme' militant de la pensée épicurienne, positiviste et scientifique, qui l'a emporté" (33).

435 BEYER, CHARLES J.: "Montesquieu et l'esprit cartésien." In: Actes du Congrès Montesquieu, Bordeaux, 23–26 mai 1955, 159–73.

The Cartesian "spirit" influenced Montesquieu in the form of logical criticism (Fontenelle) and rational metaphysics (Malebranche), as evidenced in his concept of natural mechanical order vs. spiritual order of ideal justice, and in his striving for general, invariable laws characterized by "rapport de convenance." See also Buss, no. 445.

435a BIZER, ERNST: "Die reformierte Orthodoxie und der Cartesianismus." ZTK 55: 1958, 306–372.

Thorough, liberally documented study of the controversy between Voetius and Cocceius, with ample citations from hard-to-find sources. The charge against "Cartesianism" was "concealed atheism," implied in Cartesian doubt and hermeneutics. The paper deals with the controversies aroused by Ludwig Meyer, Ludwig v. Wolzogen, Christoph Wittich, and Samuel Maresius (Desmarets). The orthodox foes of "theological Cartesianism," Peter van Mastricht and Melchior Leydekker, receive special consideration. Supplements Bohatec and Dibon (no. 436; no. 38; no. 1763–65). See also *Hirsch* (note to no. 2228a) on the general impact of Cartesianism upon Protestant theology.

435b BLONDEL, MAURICE: "L'anticartésianisme de Malebranche." RMM 23: 1916, 1–26.

Incomparable study which penetrates to the "personne profonde du philosophe .... sa volonté et sa vie" to uncover a radical opposition between Malebranche and Descartes, despite tributes and borrowings. Descartes seeks knowledge of God so that he may master nature; to Malebranche, life, science, philosophy are so many "échelons de notre réintégration en Dieu" (3). Shows the anticartesian character of M.'s "idole de la Sagesse et de la Simplicité, de ce monstre de l'égoisme divin, de cette liberté serve d'une sorte d'esthétique emprisonnante" (10), of his theory of ideas, intelligible extension, notion of the soul. Yet, thinking himself a Cartesian, M. influenced the fate of Cartesianism more deeply than had he stood outside. Blondel's thesis is disputed by *Fagnola* (Archivio della cultura Ital. 1942: 163–76): Malebranche is the most typical of all Cartesians; his theory of ideas has "cartesianizzato Cartesio" (176). *A. Del Noce's* digressive but important "Nota sull'anticartesianismo di Malebranche (RFNS 26: 1934, 53–73), with rich critical literature references, finds in the end that Malebranche, in linking "il Dio filosofico" and "il Dio religioso" within a Cartesian universe, profoundly transformed Cartesianism. For a fundamental treatment on broadest philosophical basis see *H. Gouhier*, La philosophie de Malebranche et son expérience religieuse (1926, 1948; see no. 2079), a monumental work written with deep understanding of Malebranche's religiosity and carefully reconstructing the Descartes image of Malebranche; also *Gouhier's* La vocation de Malebranche (1924; see no. 2078) which examines the question why M. did not read Descartes before 1664 and how D.'s Traité de l'homme, of all things, could have had such a decisive impact upon the future metaphysician. See also *Gueroult*, no. 453c, 7–26 and ch. 1–3; also *Gilson*, no. 453a, and *Gueroult*, no. 373a.

Reviews: A. del Noce in: Malebranche nel terzo centenario della nascità, UCSC 1938 [RFNS 30: 1938, suppl.], 227–28; G. Truc in RHLF 23: 1916, 517–20.

436 BOHATEC, JOSEF: Die cartesianische Scholastik in der Philosophie und reformierten Dogmatik des 17. Jahrhunderts. 1. Teil: Entstehung, Eigenart, Geschichte und philosophische Ausprägung der cartesianischen Scholastik. Leipzig, Deichert, 1912. 158 p. (No more published.)

Great study, "presque inconnue en France" (Dibon, no. 6, 272), shows that Cartesian theologians in Holland did not wish to break away from orthodoxy but created an authentic Cartesian Scholasticism, a theologia novantiqua, trying to prove that Cartesianism and traditional philosophy are not incompatible. This thesis is developed with great doctrinal acumen and complete mastery of the historical sources. Ch. 2 surveys the development of Cartesian philosophy and theology at Dutch, German, Swiss universities, with brief sections on England and France. Ch. 3 (Die cartesianische Scholastik in der Philosophie) is the only study so far of the philosophia novantiqua in regard to logic, epistemology, metaphysics, philosophy of nature. The appendix reproduces university documents including opinions of Dutch schools on D.'s doctrine (1651).

Review: P. Dibon in no. 6, 272–76. See also Bizer, no. 435a.

437 BORDAS-DEMOULIN, JEAN BAPTISTE: Le cartésianisme, ou La véritable rénovation des sciences .... suivi de la théorie de la substance et de celle de l'infini. Précédé d'un discours .... par F. Huet. J. Hetzel, 1853. 2 vols. cliii, 318; 520 p. 2nd ed.: Gauthier-Villars, 1874.

The most original of the prize entries in the 1839 ASMP contest; "plein d'éclairs" but fragmentary and poorly organized (P. Janet in no. 142, p. 7). Part I discusses four Cartesian "tendencies" regarding ideas and substances as evidenced in doctrinal development from Descartes to Locke; Cartesian dualism; and the theological themes of original sin, grace, love of God. Part Two (physics, mathematics) leads into the author's own theory of substance and his metaphysics of the infinitesimal calculus. See Damiron's thorough critique in no. 451, 1: 61–79; G. L. in Revue catholique 2: 1845 (16p.); Hermann Lotze in Gött 1846, no. 89–91, 881–93 (also in his: Kleine Schriften. Leipzig, Hirzel, 1891, 1: 388–97).

438 BOUILLIER, FRANCISQUE: Histoire de la philosophie cartésienne. 3rd ed. Delagrave, 1868. 2 vols. viii, 620; 658 p. [Earlier editions: no. 1304]

Grown from a prize-winning entry in the 1839 ASMP contest to full stature 30 years later, the work has weathered its first century well, still the only comprehensive account of Cartesianism as the 19th century understood it. Covers France thoroughly, Holland and Italy reasonably well, Switzerland, Germany, England sketchily. Lotze (review below) noted Bouillier's French bias and disregard of all foreign-language sources; philosophically "il n'est pas le plus profond, le plus fort" despite his "bon sens" and "bon langage" (Damiron, below, 59); "mais c'est surtout le détail des faits qu'il a étudié avec une exactitude et une précision supérieures" (Janet's review, p. 7), rich in capsule summaries of minor works and leads to major and lesser themes. His Malebranche (20 out of the 32 chapters in v.2) remains the most comprehensive survey of Malebranche's relations with his contemporaries and his influence upon successors. No longer indispensible, but still discussed and very useful, though the lack of indexes is deplorable.

Reviews: E. Blampignon in Corr 85: 25 Nov. 1871, 709–22; Ph. Damiron in no. 451, 1: 41–84 (of the original prize essay); Adolphe Franck in his: Moralistes et philosophes, Didier, 1872, 157–227; P. Janet in no. 142, 7–8; Hermann Lotze in Gött 1854, no. 170–72: 1695–1710, reprinted in his: Kleine Schriften, Leipzig, 1885, 1: 257–67. See also V. Delbos' obituary article (AMP 10 Nov. 1902) on Bouillier in his: Études de philosophie ancienne et philosophie moderne (2nd ed., Vrin, 1954), 541–59.

440 BRATTLE, WILLIAM: Compendium logicae secundum principia D. Renati Cartesii plerumque efformatum, et catechisticè propositum. Bostoni, in Nov-Anglia, denuò impressum à Johanne Draper, 1758. 60 p.

First formal appearance of Cartesianism in North America. The principles are those of the Logic of Port-Royal.

441 BROCKDORFF, BARON CAY VON: Descartes und die Fortbildung der kartesianischen Lehre. München, Reinhardt, 1923. 227 p. (Geschichte der Philosophie in Einzeldarstellungen, Abt. IV/I, v. 16–17.)

Clear, well organized exposition and urbane appraisal of D.'s "theoretical" and "practical" philosophies, followed by a compact survey of later developments of Cartesianism (mainly Arnauld, Geulincx, Malebranche). Chapter on "Die Gesinnung des kartesianischen Kreises." Competent, unprejudiced, popular in the best sense.

441a BRUCKER, JAKOB: "De Renato Cartesio." In his: Historia critica philosophiae. Lipsiae, Breitkopf, 1743 (Weidemann & Reich, 1764), v. 4, pt. 2, p. 200–334.

Beginning of a historical appraisal at the close of the Cartesian era. D. as "philosophiae reformator" ranks with Bruno, Giordano, Bacon, Campanella, Hobbes, followed by Leibniz and Thomasius. Abundant references to opponents, successors, early 18th c. controversies. See Hagmann, no. 10, 57–60.

442 BRUNETIÈRE, FERDINAND: "Jansénistes et cartésiens." In his: Études critiques sur l'histoire de la littérature française, sér. 4, Hachette, 1898, 111–78. "Descartes et la littérature classique." Ibid., sér. 3, 1–28. "Jansénistes et cartésiens." In his: Histoire de la littérature française classique, 1515–1830. Vol. 2, Delagrave 1912, Ch. 13, 273–85, 318–37.

Despite Brunetière's great name and influence, his contribution to Cartesian studies is weak and now of little interest except in regard to the controversy over Descartes' direct influence upon French literature (see Lanson, no. 412). *F. Bouillier* sharply attacked Brunetière on historical grounds: "Deux nouveaux historiens de Descartes" (RPFE 37: 1894/I, 287–97), the other "new historian" being A. Fouillée who discovered Schopenhauer in D. and defended his discovery against Bouillier (ibid., 535–46). Best summary of Brunetière's "filippica" in Olgiati, no. 14, 188ff.

443 BRUNO, ANTONIO: Cartesio e l'illuminismo. Bari, Laterza, 1949. 55 p.

Attempts to link Descartes and the Enlightenment through precise references to Cartesian doctrine, stressing the autonomy of reason, mathematicism (dubiously equated with "esprit de géométrie"), dualism, etc. But the connection, pushed into the field of classical esthetics, natural law, and natural religion, becomes rather weak. Stimulating but unconvincing. Bibliography (several names misspelled).

444 BURTT, EDWIN ARTHUR: "Descartes." In his: The metaphysical foundations of modern physical science. A historical and critical essay.

New York, Harcourt, Brace, 1925. 2nd ed., revised: London, Routledge and Kegan Paul, 1932 (reprinted 1950), p. 96–116. (ILPP). Reprinted: New York, Doubleday-Anchor, 1954.

Now a classic in its own right, the book treats pre-Newtonian metaphysics as the key to the understanding of the upheaval in modern physical speculation and as the source of dogma, uncritically taken over along with genuine advances. The eloquent ch. 4 shows Descartes "on the verge of most far-reaching discoveries" (100) which he never made, yet causing "an incalculable change in the viewpoint of the world held by intelligent opinion in Europe" (116). Excellent discussion of Hobbes' and Henry More's reaction to Cartesianism (ch. 5). List of useful secondary literature to 1920. See also Koyré, no. 379a.

Reviews: Anon. in TLS 24: June 4, 1925, 376; H. W. Carr in Nature 116: 1925, 235–36; T. Costello in JP 23: 1926, 47–50: Bertrand Russell in Dial 79: Sept. 1925, 255–58 and in Nation & Athenaeum 37: June 1925, 326.

445 BUSS, E.: "Montesquieu und Cartesius." Philosophische Monatshefte 4: Wintersemester 1869–70, no. 1, 1–38.

Robust paper, seeing D. as the creator of the exalted deism at the roots of the French social revolution. Distinguishes the Cartesianism of the Lettres persanes from the subsequent Malebranchean impact upon Montesquieu.

446 BUSSON, HENRI: "Descartes." In his: La pensée française de Charron à Pascal. Vrin, 1933, ch. 9, 429–45.

D.'s religious preoccupations were basically the same as those of his contemporaries, chiefly an apologetic urge. Before 1660 Cartesianism played a very small part in French religious life; afterwards "l'esprit cartésien" destroyed the very sentiment which Descartes had displayed. Important background study, very rich in references (bibliography 615–42). See no. 447.

Reviews: Anon. in BSHP 83: 1934, 152–53; J. Dedieu in RHEF 20: 1934, 115–22; F. Schalk in Dlit 55: 1934, 928–35; H. M. Féret in RSPT 23: 1934, 499–501; P. Groult in RHE 30: 1934, 168–73; H. Hauser in RHist 176: Jul.- Aug. 1935, 47–49; F. Mentré in RdePh ns 4: 1933, 219–33; Anon. in RMM 41, April 1934, suppl., 12–13; A. Barthélémy in MerF 245: July 1, 1933, 186.

447 BUSSON, HENRI: La religion des classiques (1660–1685). PUF, 1948. 476 p.

Justly famous work, written in glittering language and with great learning, as indispensable as no. 446; background study bringing to life the intellectual atmosphere and thoroughly displaying the overt concerns of the period, but disappointing in its assessment of Descartes and Cartesianism, and impermissibly insufficient in its treatment of Malebranche (see Sebba, no. 19.)

Reviews: R. Bray in RHL 51: 1951, 96–98; H. Gouhier in RHR 138: 1950, 232–35; H. Peyre in RR 40: 1949, 130–32; S. de Sacy in MerF 305: March 1, 1949, 547–50; R. Derathé in RPFE 141: 1951, 604–06.

447a CALLOT, ÉMILE: Problèmes du cartésianisme: Descartes, Malebranche, Spinoza. Annecy, Gardet, 1956. 280 p.

Interesting group of essays on the proper order of exposition of a philosophical system, on the various forms of Cartesian intuition, on the meaning of the cogito and on its relation to Descartes' proofs of the existence of God (11–177). Also a comparison between Malebranche's proof of God by excellence and D.'s ontological proof (181–89).

Reviews: S. Colnort-Bodet in Eph ns 12: 1957, 78; D. J. McCracken in PhQ 7: 1957, 379–80; S. Sarti in Gmet 13: 1958, 121–25.

448 CARBIA, RÓMULO D.: "Descartes en la cultura colonial de América." In: Homenaje (no. 40), v. 3, 35–40.

Despite the "oscurantismo español," D.'s writings, though condemned, were known and studied in the Latin American colonies at least since the end of the 18th century. *Enrique Martínez Paz,* "La influencia de Descartes en el pensamiento filosófico de la Colonia" (*ibid.*, 3: 15–33) supports this revision of the accepted view with details about philosophical instruction at the Universidad de Córdoba (Argentina) since 1750. However, interest in D. seems to have been weak, and neither paper explains the formidable rise of D. scholarship in modern Latin America, as contrasted to the comparative lack of specific interest in North America.

449 CEÑAL, RAMON (S.J.): "Cartesianismo en España. Notas para su historia (1650–1750)." FyL Oviedo 6: 1945, 3–95.

Amply documented study notes "el carácter secundario, epigónico, de la escuela cartesiana" in Spain (11). Discusses first contacts (Juan Caramuel, Luis Rodríguez de Pedroso and others), the Sevilla school (Diego Mateo de Zapata); Emmanuel Maignan and his followers and opponents in Sevilla and Valencia; Peripatetics, Eclectics, and Feijóo. Though the author's sympathies are not with D., he remains scrupulously factual. See also *Ceñal's* "La filosofía de Emmanuel Maignan" (RevF 13, no. 48: 1954, 15–68, with detailed account of points of disagreement between Maignan and D. despite their common opposition to Aristotelian physics) and his "La vida, las obras y la influencia de Emmanuel Maignan" (Revista de estudios políticos no. 46: 1952, 111–149). For the background see *Eloy Bullón y Fernández,* De los orígines de la filosofía moderna: los precursores españoles de Bacon y Descartes (Salamanca, Calatrava, 1905, 250 p.) on Luis Vives, Gómez Pereira, Francisco Vallés, Sebastián Fox Morcillo and others. On Feijóo see *G. Delpy,* Feijóo et l'esprit européen (Hachette, 1936, Ch. 3, especially p. 81–89) and *Charles Neff Staubach,* "Feijóo on Cartesianism; a chapter on French influence in Spain" (Michigan Academy of science 24, no. 4: 1938 79–87; Michigan thesis abstract) and his "Feijóo and Malebranche" (HR 1941, 287–96)

Reviews: R. Ceñal in Educ 1: 1950, 149–50; M. Lizzio in S 24: 1956, 428; G. B. Martínez in RevF 5: 1946, 509–11.

450 COUSIN, VICTOR: Fragments philosophiques pour servir à l'histoire de la philosophie. 5th edition. Didier, 1866, v. 3, 4: La philosophie moderne. [First edition: no. 1653.]

Cousin launched the modern French D. revival with his enthusiastic but hasty edition of the philosopher's works which served for nearly 80 years, and with his equally enthusiastic Cours de l'histoire de la philosophie (Pichon et Didiers, 1829) presenting D. as "le fondateur de l'école idéaliste moderne" (v. 1, 458). His eclecticism and spiritualist D. interpretation dominated French D. scholarship for decades; but his enduring contribution are the small Fragments de philosophie cartésienne of 1845 which grew to two substantial volumes in the fifth edition of

1866, a collection of hitherto unpublished material of exceptional interest, presented with a rich historical commentary. Vol. 3 contains, among others, correspondence concerning Baillet's Descartes biography; the minutes of a Cartesian meeting in Paris, end of the 17th c.; a commentary by the Cardinal de Retz on a D. paper by Dom Robert Desgabets; a study of Roberval; and "De la persécution du cartésianisme" (297–332), still the best account of the gradual subjugation under steady Jesuit pressure of French orders and congregations teaching D.'s philosophy. Vols. 3 and 4 contain invaluable Malebranche material (see Sebba, no. 19, 30–31).

451 DAMIRON, JEAN PHILIBERT: Essai sur l'histoire de la philosophie en France au XVIIe siècle. Hachette, 1846. 2 vols. lxxiv, 521; 840 p. Partly in: AMPM 4: 165–243, 1844.

Vol. 1: Descartes (85–312); Hobbes, Gassendi, Bacon, Vol. 2: Rohault, de la Forge, Régis, Antoine Le Grand, Andreae, de la Chambre, Clauberg, Geulincx (1–176); Spinoza (177–351); Malebranche (352–596); Lami, Boursier, Bossuet, Fénélon.

The introduction is Damiron's official report on the 1839 prize contest of the Académie des sciences morales et politiques, with trenchant, extensive reviews and critiques of Bouillier, Renouvier, Bordas-Demoulin and a survey of the history of Cartesianism. The body of the work expands this sketch by a detailed, careful if uninspired treatment of D.'s philosophy and of Cartesianism from Rohault and Régis to Boursier, Bossuet and Fénélon. Less historical and searching than Balz (no. 431), more analytical and critical than Bouillier (no. 438), v. 2 remains one of the few comprehensive histories of French Cartesianism.

451a DELBOS, VICTOR: "La controverse d'Arnauld et de Malebranche sur la nature et l'origine des idées." APC année 84, v. 16, May 1913. Reprinted in his: Étude de la philosophie de Malebranche, 1924.

Arnauld seems to have lacked understanding for the problems raised by the development of Cartesianism and the new science, while Malebranche more rigorously than any rationalist before Kant asked under what conditions knowledge can be "objective." Arnauld's strong interpretation of Cartesianism pointed directly towards criticist idealism, but failed to grasp the epistemological problem which M. methodically formulated, giving one of the boldest and most profound solutions in modern philosophy.

452 DIBON, PAUL: La philosophie néerlandaise au siècle d'or. Vol. 1: L'enseignement philosophique dans les universités à l'époque précartésienne, 1575–1650. Amsterdam, Elsevier, 1954. x, 274 p. (Publications de l'Institut français d'Amsterdam, Maison Descartes.) Proefschrift Leiden.

First of three volumes in progress, this very learned book gives a detailed "administrative and pedagogical inventory" of philosophical propaedeutics at the Dutch universities in D.'s lifetime: curricula, course content, analysis of textbooks, modus docendi, relation to other disciplines. Pioneering utilization of academic "disputationes" and "theses," a hitherto neglected primary source, here helpfully discussed and classified (34–49). Under Cartesian impact, the tendency towards compromise (philosophia novantiqua) gains among adherents of D., while opponents are driven back to medieval Scholasticism. Important material on Martin Schoock, Henri Reneri, Adrian Heereboord rectifies onesided views of their philosophical position. The second volume (Aristotélisme et Cartésianisme) will fully develop the important philosophia novantiqua theme, while v. 3 (Méthode cartésienne et théologie) promises to revise and complete J. Bohatec's pioneering work. See also the Leiden thesis of *Sybrand H. M. Galama,* Het wijsgerig onderwijs aan de Hogeschool te Franeker, 1585–1811 (Franeker, Wever, 1954. 358 p).

Reviews: G. N. Clark in EHR 70: 1955, 665; E. C(oreth) in ZKT 77: 1955, 232–33; J. Gilbert in NRT 77: 1955, 883–85; N. Gonzáles Caminero in PenM 12: 1956, 92–93; M. de Grève in BHR 18: 1956, 156–58; J. Lecler in Et 285: 1955, 267; J. H. Nota in Streven 8: 1955, 485; C. L. Thijssen-Schoute in ANTWP 47: 1954–55, 213–14; C. Láscaris Comneno in RevF 15: 1956, 144; Sven Wermlund in Lychnos 1956, 336–37.

452a EMERY, ABBÉ JACQUES ANDRÉ: Pensées de Descartes sur la religion et la morale. Le Clère, 1811. ccviii, 397 p. Reprinted in: J. P. Migne, Démonstrations évangéliques, v. 2, 1843; also Tours, Mame, 1870, 1879 (Les apologistes du Christianisme au XVIIe siècle).

Emery's "Discours préliminaire" (i–clviii) and "Vie religieuse de Descartes" (clix–ccviii, after Baillet) were first during the reign of V. Cousin and his school to recall attention to Descartes as a moralist and Catholic. The 400 pages of "Pensées" are extracts from MM and the correspondence; first publication of D.'s second and fourth letter to P. Mesland on Transsubstantiation, which Clerselier reported suppressed by the Archbishop of Paris in 1671 and 1672 on behalf of the King "pour empêcher le trouble que cela pourroit causer à l'état" (no. 79, v. 6, p. 362). See also Gouhier, no. 168, 3–4.

453 FRIEDRICH, HUGO: Descartes und der französische Geist. Leipzig, Meiner, 1937. 78 p. (Wissenschaft und Zeitgeist).

The distinguished German Romanist discounts any direct influence of Descartes beyond the time of Voltaire, but sees Descartes' "spirit" remain alive in the French moralistes and even in Diderot and Rousseau. "Der französische Geist" is Montaigne's cosmopolitan Renaissance humanism, transformed into a Nationalgeist with loss of its cosmopolitan basis, and definitely shaped by Descartes. From Victor Cousin onwards, the "Cartesian spirit" becomes the "myth of Descartes" and the foundation of French self-interpretation as the spirit of order, clarity etc. come to be taken as innate French characteristics. This myth then degenerates into a "Vulgärkartesianismus." Suggestive discussions of symbolism and of Valéry's "poetry of dreams" constructed by the waking, working mind. The limitations of the "French mind" are traced by means of considering the Descartes criticism of Vico, Hegel, Schelling, and by contrasting it with Goethe's organic "Weltbild," i.e. by oversimplification with built-in bias. An obligatory bow to race and genius reflects "Hitler und der deutsche Geist" at the time of writing. Varet erroneously cites a first edition 1913.

Reviews: G. Radetti in GCFI 6: 1938, 445–46; Anon. in RMM 45: 1938, p. 19; E. Duprat in Revue germanique 29: 1938, p. 92; A. Marc in Aph 14: 1938, sb 80–81.

453a GILSON, ÉTIENNE: "Malebranche." In his: God and Philosophy [*no. 167*], 1941, 88–98.

"In his effort to re-Christianize the natural theology of Descartes, Malebranche has Cartesianized the Christian God" (p. 88, n. 12). Malebranche, asking why God created this world among all possible worlds, answers naturally: "because God is supremely intelligent, he could not fail to do what Descartes would have done, had Descartes been God" (96). Evidently, Gilson has no use for this Christian philosopher's God. See also *Gilson's* The unity of philosophical experience [no. *166*, 1937, 193ff.] on the concept of causality from Descartes via Malebranche, John Norris, Locke to Hume who drew the ultimate conclusion from Descartes' impasse.

453b GRIMM, EDUARD: "Malebranches Erkenntnistheorie und deren Verhältniss zur Erkenntnisstheorie des Descartes." ZPPK 70: 1877, 15–55.

Malebranche's concept of clear and distinct cognition as cognition of all possible modifications of a thing leads to difficulties regarding infinite extension, and to contradictions regarding inner awareness. Malebranche, unlike Geulincx, was an independent critic of Descartes' metaphysics. A stimulating analysis.

453c GUEROULT, MARTIAL: Malebranche. Vol. 1: La vision en Dieu. Aubier, 1955, 327 p.

Vol. 1 offers a monumental confrontation of the philosophies of Descartes and Malebranche. Their proofs of God are held to be in patent opposition to each other. In the thought of Malebranche the doctrine of the "vision des choses en Dieu" gradually rises to dominance over the Cartesian cogito, as Malebranche moves from his early Cartesian premises towards the "anéantissement de la véritable philosophie des idées claires et distinctes au profit d'une vaste intuition mystique" (327).

Reviews: of v. 1: E. Barbotin in RScR 31: 1957, 102–03; F. Brunner in StP 16: 1956, 235–36 and in RTP 6: 1956, 29–35; A. Henry in Eph 11: 1956, 502–03 and in RScR, January 1957; J. L. Bruch in RMM 63: 1958, 358–73 ("La méthode de M. Gueroult et son application à la philosophie de Malebranche"); P. Blanchard in Bull. des facultés de Lyon, no. 21, 1956; B. Delfgaauw in De Tijd (Amsterdam), June 30, 1956; Anon. in La Croix, February 14, 1956; J. Bruch in Nouvelle Gazette de Bruxelles, January 29, 1956 and in La revue de Caire, May 1956, 415–17; A. Virieux-Reymond in Gazette de Lausanne, 1956; also MerF February 1, 1956.

454 HAZARD, PAUL: La crise de la conscience européenne, 1680–1715. Boivin, 1935. x, 474 p. [English transl.: The European mind. Yale UP, 1953.]. La pensée européenne au XVIIIe siècle, de Montesquieu à Lessing. Boivin, 1946. 3 vols.

Brilliant works that overflow with main and glancing references to major and minor philosophers, scientists, theologians, writers, travelers etc. Sparkling character sketch of D.: "Quelle aventure!" – to be so Catholic, yet give to Reason "une telle place qu'elle semble absorber tout, même Dieu!" (La crise, p. 140). The three-volume sequel [La pensée] illuminates the 18th c. decline and disappearance of Cartesian influence as other streams swell or enter: Descartes "a foudroyé les saints de l'École, et maintenant il est abattu" – which is the signal for the Jesuits to change over to his side, with reservations (v. 2, p. 33). The "Notes et références" are a bibliographical treasure for the browser.

455 HUBERT, RENÉ: "Descartes et l'Encyclopédie." Rsyn 14: April 1937, 29–50.

Though the philosophes followed Bacon rather than D. in their general notion of a system of sciences, they deviated from him in their emphasis upon order and the logical interrelation of the forms of knowledge. This implicit influence of D. made them sacrifice historicism; yet they conceived the interrelationship of all knowledge more like disciples of Locke and Condillac than of Descartes. See also Mougin, no. 459, and Vartanian, no. 468.

455a LACHIÈZE-REY, PIERRE: Les origines cartésiennes du Dieu de Spinoza. Alcan, 1932. Reprinted: Vrin, 1950. xii, 288 p. (BHP). Thèse complémentaire, Paris.

Excellent monograph. Spinoza's conception of universe held to be original and independent of Cartesianism, though D. gave him the theory of substances and attributes, his tool for making this universe intelligible. Claims a double filiation, direct and indirect, between D.'s and Spinoza's proofs of the existence of God, but carefully points out "identités de formules qui ne correspondent pas à une identité de pensée" (261). The magnificently organized subject index is a compendium of doctrines and problems, the index of "noms et textes" a guide to the literature. See also the *author's* important chapter on "Cogito kantien et cogito cartésien" in his thèse (L'idéalisme kantien [Alcan, 1931], Vrin, 1950, 5–59), an equally careful study of a thorny subject.

Reviews: Anon. in BCLF 6: 1951, 449–50; Anon. in RMM 40, suppl. 1: 1933, 5–6; G. deGiuli in RF 25: 1934, 167–68.

456 LAIRD, JOHN: "L'influence de Descartes sur la philosophie anglaise du XVIIe siècle." RPFE 123: 1937, 226–56. Transl. by L. L. Herbert.

Studies D.'s influence upon the clergy, the Cambridge Platonists, and the English scientists of the century, with particular stress upon Hobbes, Henry More, Cudworth, Locke and Newton. *Charlotte S. Ware's* valuable study "The influence of Descartes on John Locke" (RIP 4: 1950, 210–39) gives the results of an examination of the Locke papers in the Bodleian Library for references to Descartes and the Cartesians, noting the chief doctrinal points of agreement and contrast. See also *Leon Roth's* "Note on the relationship between Descartes and Locke" in Mind 44: 1935, 414–16, and *Charlotte Johnston*, "Locke's 'Examination' of Malebranche and Norris" (JHI 19: 1958, 550–58); for the Locke controversy over Malebranche see Sebba, no. 19, nos. 113–18.

457 LANSON, GUSTAVE: "Origines et premierès manifestations de l'esprit philosophique dans la littérature française de 1675 à 1748." RCC 16/1–2: 1907–08. "Formation et développement de l'esprit philosophique au XVIIIe siècle." RCC 17/1–2: 1908–09.

Lanson's course gives a rich, detailed account of the interrelationship between philosophy, theology and literature in the rise of French 18th century thought, stressing the continuity rather than the break between the 17th and the 18th century, cautiously leaning towards Brunetière's views. The present value of the course lies in its vast scope and in the concise, masterly treatment of the material.

457a LEMAIRE, PAUL: Le cartésianisme chez les Bénédictins. Dom Robert Desgabets: son système, son influence et son école, d'après plusieurs manuscrits et des documents rares. Alcan, 1901. 424 p. Thèse Grenoble.

Comprehensive study of an original, impulsive philosopher, follower of Malebranche, member of the circle of Cardinal de Retz. See also *Cousin's* Fragments philosophiques (no. 450) and *Geneviève Lewis*' "L'âme et la durée d'après une controverse cartésienne" in RIP 4: 1950, 190–209 [Desgabets, Cardinal de Retz and Malebranche on the question: is divine action instantaneous or continuous?]

457b LE MOINE, AUGUSTIN: Des vérités éternelles selon Malebranche. Vrin (Marseille, Ged), 1936. 292 p. Thèse-lettres, Aix-Marseille.

Descartes' doctrine of eternal verities rests on divine freedom and points to the natural sciences; Malebranche's doctrine flows from divine essence and serves a theocentric, anticartesian philosophy. Competent academic exercise, hewing close to received opinion.

Reviews: Anon. in RMM 1936, July suppl., 3–4; H.-D. Gardeil in RSPT 25: 1936, 731.

457c MARSAK, LEONARD M.: "Cartesianism in Fontenelle and French science, 1686–1752." Isis 50: 1959, 51–60.

Denies that Fontenelle is a Cartesian: he accepted only D.'s cosmology, for reasons which were a challenge to Descartes. Moreover, he attacked the Malebranchists and wanted science freed from dependence on God as explanation. Though admitting that science needs mathematics, he rejected mathematicism and admired empirical observation. His chief claim to Cartesianism was that he dared to challenge vested authority, which is not much of a claim to the title.

458 MONCHAMP, ABBÉ GEORGES: Histoire du cartésianisme en Belgique. Bruxelles, Hayez, 1886. 643 p. (AcBelg, Mémoires couronnées. Collection in-8°, v. 39).

1. Philosophy in Belgium before Descartes. 2. Cartesianism in Belgium, 1628–1637. 3–5. Descartes' controversies with Froidmont, Ciermans, Plempius. 6. Influence of Jansen's Augustinus, 1640. 7. Descartes and van Gutschoven and Caterus, 1639–1641. 8–9. Struggle over Cartesianism in and outside Louvain. 10. Descartes and the Belgians. 11. Biographia posthuma, 1650–52. 12. Geulincx. 13–20. The struggles over Cartesianism at Louvain; its condemnation in 1662 (Ch. 14: attitude of the Louvain Jesuits before the condemnation). 21–24. Cartesianism and anticartesianism in Belgium and Louvain, 1664–91. 26. Defections and persecutions, 1675–1694. 27–28. Cartesianism in the monastic and secular clergy, 18th century. – Pièces justificatives.

Monumental documentary study, agreeably written, deals in great detail with D.'s personal relations with Belgian theologians and philosophers and records his views of "Belgian" doctrines from Nicolaus Cusanus to Jansenius. The next 18 chapters give an unparalleled chronological survey of Cartesians and anticartesians in Belgium and of the struggle against Cartesianism at Louvain, leading to its condemnation under heavy pressure in 1662. Generous quotations and summaries, accurate biographical information, extensive table of names make the work indispensable for the study of D.'s life and of Cartesianism. Since Louvain's library has been twice destroyed, Monchamp now remains our only source for the unique material he drew from it. See also *Monchamp's* very interesting study "Le Flamand et Descartes, d'après des documents nouveaux" (1889; see no. 2779a) on D. and the Flemish language; also on D. at La Flèche, no. 97.

459 MOUGIN, HENRI: "L'esprit encyclopédique et la tradition philosophique française." Pensée no. 5: 1945, 8–18; no. 6: 1946, 24–38; no. 7: 1946, 65–74.

Harsh attack upon the modern idealistic "falsification" of Descartes whose metaphysics were merely a mask. In true fact he was an "encyclopedist" embracing all knowledge of man, acknowledging the primacy of experience, recognizing the failure of his mathematicism. His three great paradoxes (independence of thought from extension, of mathematics from physical experience, of philosophy from science) resolve themselves when the primacy of experience and science, and the existence of mens corporea, is acknowledged. The Cartesians started this deliberate systematic falsification by spiritualizing true Cartesianism. D.'s real heir was "le cartésianisme encyclopédiste et matérialiste du XVIIIe siècle" (p. 17), as Hegel already recognized in his appraisal of Diderot and the French Revolution. One of the most intelligent pieces of French Marxist historical acrobatics.

460 NICOLSON, MARJORIE: "The early stages of Cartesianism in England." SP 26: 1929, 356–74.

Pleads for greater attention to Descartes' influence upon the changing English prose style. Notes the role of Cartesianism in the quarrel of Moderns and Ancients, the effect of D.'s concept of the "indefinite" upon English notions of infinity, and the gradual psychologizing transformation of Descartes' "thinking-self." See also *Sterling P. Lamprecht's* survey of "The role of Descartes in seventeenth-century England" (SHI v. 3, 178–240; 1935) and *Paul Russell Anderson's* brief paper on "Descartes' influence in 17th century England" (CD 3: 113–21; see particularly no. 1063). Among older works, the Edinburgh thesis of *William Cunningham*, Archdeacon of Ely, may be used with caution (The influence of Descartes on metaphysical speculation in England. London, Macmillan, 1876. xlviii, 188p.). Also *Georges Lyon's* once hotly debated L'idéalisme en Angleterre au XVIIIe siècle (Alcan, 1888. 483 p.), despite its untenable thesis that English idealistic philosophy if rooted in D. and especially in Malebranche. For background and bibliography see *Georges Ascoli*, La Grande-Bretagne devant l'opinion française au XVIIIe siècle (Gamber, 1930; see no. 1089). Also Garai, no. 406, and Herford, no. 409.

461 OTTAVIANO, CARMELO: "Il cartesianesimo in Italia." In his: L'unità .... (no. 222). Ch. 3, 127–221.

Galileo's analytical-experimental method overthrew Aristotelian physics in Italy; congenial Gassendist atomism completed the work. Descartes' influence was effective in Italy only within the Galilean-Gassendist current in physics, "e fu sempre influsso transitorio e fugace" (137). "Se Galilei ha un continuatore, è non certo Cartesio, ma Locke" who, "incredibile dictu," merely revives Aristotelian empiricism purged of substantial forms (138–39). The author's verve is surpassed only by his volcanic erudition which erupts in lavalike footnotes that all but bury the text, indispensable critical references to sources and literature. Ottaviano heavily utilizes that "inesauribile repertorio di notizie aneddotiche" (184), *Gabriel Maugain's* Étude sur l'évolution intellectuelle de l'Italie de 1657 a 1750 environ

(Hachette, 1909) which excellently describes the conflict between Cartesianism and the scientific movement culminating in Gassendi. On the Vico-Descartes relationship, neither Maugin nor Ottaviano is satisfactory; see in addition *Giuseppe Scerbo*, G. B. Vico e il cartesianismo a Napoli (Roma, Signorelli, 1933); *F. Tocco's* terse, still useful "Descartes jugé par Vico" (RMM 4: 1896, 568–72); *Jean Lameere*, "Giambattista Vivo, critique italien de Descartes" (CD 1: 31–37); *Eugène Bouvy's* Paris thèse: De Vico, Cartesii adversario (1889, 67p.); *Giovanni Vidari*, "L'educazione cartesiana in Italia e le idee pedagogiche di G. B. Vico" (AcTorino, Atti 61: 1926, 585–602). *Walter Witzenmann*, "Giambattista Vico und René Descartes; die geschichtliche Kritik des cartesischen Realismus" in Emge (no. 50), 97–115, gives a summary of Vico's anticartesian theses and claims that they furnished two capital concepts to Italian Fascism (creation of true society by an élite, and myth of society) as well as the notion of social atomism as an inevitable consequence of Descartes' philosophy; and especially *Giovanni Gentile*, Studi vichiani (2nd ed., Firenze, 1927, 3–18) and *Robertson* (no. 420). M. Giorgiantonio discusses Ottaviano in S 19: 1951, 321. Cf. also Berthé de Besaucèle (no. 433) and the literature cited there.

462 PILLON, FRANÇOIS: "L'évolution de l'idéalisme au XVIIIe siècle." AnPh 6–15: 1895–1903. [See no. 2958.]

Twelve lengthy articles expound the view that the true history of idealism begins with Malebranche's profoundly Catholic philosophy (first two articles) and with Bayle, "le sceptique d'esprit ouvert, subtil et pénétrant" (4: 1893, 110) to whom the bulk of the work is devoted. Pillon marks the revolt against the epistemological interpretations (especially of Malebranche) of Thomas Reid and of V. Cousin, Royer-Collard and the "spiritualistes universitaires." Note especially the studies of Bayle's critique of Cartesian spiritualism and theism (11: 1900, 65–131, 12: 1901, 85–154) and of the metaphysical attributes of God (last three articles).

463 PROST, JOSEPH: Essai sur l'atomisme et l'occasionalisme dans la philosophie cartésienne. Paulin, 1907. 275 p. Thèse Lyon.

1. Théorie de la matière chez Descartes; ses rapports avec l'atomisme. 2. Les causes occasionnelles chez Descartes. 3–7. Cordemoy et Louis de la Forge. 8. Les critiques de l'occasionalisme de Cordemoy: Desgabets etc. 9. L'occasionalisme de Malebranche. 10. L'occasionalisme en dehors de Malebranche en France. Les critiques de Cordemoy et de la Forge. 11. Leibniz.

Asserting that the res extensa is continuous, while admitting multiple individual substances, D. invited an atomistic interpretation; his failure to provide any transition from divine to human and natural causality laid the ground for occasionalism. The body of the work is devoted to a detailed, still useful study of Géraud de Cordemoy and Louis de la Forge, with an informed but inadequate chapter on Malebranche. See *A. G. A. Balz*' important "Louis de la Forge and the critique of substantial forms" in no. 431, 80–105, reprinted from PhR 41: 1932, 551–76, and Laing, no. 290.

464 PROST, JOSEPH: La philosophie à l'Académie protestante de Saumur, 1606–1685. Paulin, 1907. 180 p.

Chapter 4 (69–101) on Cartesianism at Saumur (Jean-Robert Chouet); Ch. 5 on the ecleticism of de Villemandy (102–29). Appendix: unpublished documents, bibliography.

464a ROSENFIELD, LEONORA COHEN: "Aristotelian and Scholastic tradition." In: A Critical bibliography of French literature, v. 3 (see no. 3a), 486–90.

Supplements the present section, with references to trends and to many contemporary figures. Useful complementary material also in *Richard H. Popkin's* "Libertinage," *ibid.*, 478–86. See also *Rosenfield*, "Peripatetic adversaries of Cartesianism in 17th-c. France," no. 17.

465 SAVESON, J. E.: "Descartes' influence on John Smith, Cambridge Platonist." JHI 20: 1959, 258–62. "Differing reactions to Descartes among the Cambridge Platonists." JHI 21: 1960, 560–67.

Within the Neoplatonism of the Cambridge School, the theology of John Smith differs sharply from that of Cudworth and Henry More, partly because of their different attitudes towards Cartesianism: Smith accepts dualism uncritically and "seems scarcely aware of the full significance of the mechanical philosophy" which Cudworth and More oppose in the name of a Neoplatonic "cosmology" (JHI 1960, 567). Smith's view of Descartes is considered similar to that of the Oratoire. His Select Discourses of 1660 show his debt to Descartes in the beast-machine theory, physiology of passions, and the body-soul dualism. See also Willey, no. 429a, and Tulloch, no. 3450a, on John Smith and the Cambridge Platonists. *Ernst Cassirer*, Die Platonische Renaissance in England und die Schule von Cambridge, 1932 (see no. 1482, also English transl.) is fundamental; Ch. 4 on the philosophy of nature in the Cambridge School deals more specifically with the Cartesianism issue.

465a SAXL, FRITZ: "Veritas filia temporis." In: Philosophy and History. Essays presented to Ernst Cassirer, ed. R. Klibansky and H. J. Paton. Oxford, Clarendon, 1936, 197ff.

In tracing the iconographic theme of "Time revealing Truth" from Pietro Aretino to Bacon, Saxl comes up with an odd note on "Descartes and Newton" (218–22). In 1707, Bernard Picart engraves a frontispiece showing Time dispelling the clouds that veil Truth whose light illuminates Descartes, while the Ancients are still in half-darkness. An English version of Picart's engraving slavishly imitates both picture and text, except that Descartes is replaced by Newton; and since the word "Tourbillons," inscribed on the scroll D. holds in his hands, would have been inappropriate, the anonymous master, not knowing what to replace it with, left the scroll – empty. "These documents together raise up a monument to the inherent constancy of symbols which human genius and human folly are alike slow to modify"; the English parodist thus "created unintentionally a symbol of D.'s defeat through Newton" (221).

466 SORTAIS, GASTON (S.J.): Le cartésianisme chez les Jésuites français au XVIIe et au XVIIIe siècle. Aph 6, no. 3, 1929. 109 p.

The last work of the erudite Jesuit, barely completed while his powers were failing. Basically a rich, useful collection of material on the Jesuit attitude towards D.'s scientific work, on his relations with P. Vatier and P. Mesland, and on P. André and other Jesuit followers of Malebranche, with a concluding chapter on Jesuit adversaries of Cartesianism. There is no penetrating historical analysis or evaluation, but the raw stuff is there, less comprehensive but better documented and easier to use than in Bouillier (no. 438). *Sortais'* "Descartes et la Compagnie de Jésus; ménaces et avances, 1640–46" (E 57: 1937, 441–68), also posthumous, gives a detailed account of D.'s attempts to stay on the right side of La Compagnie and to win Jesuit approbation for MM. Finds Jesuit opposition confined to D.'s metaphysics (and vindicated by history), while the scientific aspect of Cartesianism appealled to many Jesuits, whose persistent "attitude bienveillante" (468) is heavily underscored. See also *Emmy Allard's* Die Angriffe gegen Descartes und Malebranche im Journal de Trévoux, 1701–1715, Halle, Niemeyer 1914, 58p. (APGE, v. 43), noted in Cabeen 4, nr. 2826; also Six, (no. 101 and especially no. 338).

466a SPINK, J. S.: French free-thought from Gassendi to Voltaire. University of London, Athlone Press, 1960. ix, 345 p.

Important background study of libertinism, scepticism, and the "roughly parallel but sometimes divergent .... paths" of French naturalism and rationalism, in two parts: Gassendi and the Libertins; Descartes and the Rationalists. Part I gives a richly documented introduction to free-thought and Epicureanism in D.'s own time. Good chapter on Maignan between Aristotle and Epicurus. Part II opens with D.'s "nature without consciousness," followed by a valuable chapter on the fortunes of D. in the schools, among natural scientists, physiologists and students of medicine. Chapters on the beast-machine controversy (Bossuet, Jesuits, Bayle, Leibniz), on Spinozism: "Monopsychism and the reaction to Spinoza," "Le grand tout" (noting Cartesians misrepresentations of Spinoza), on clandestine erudition and sociology, on Voltaire vs. Pascal. Thorough mastery of sources, with ample quotations; includes much new or scattered material; index with long list of anonymous manuscript works. Interesting chronological list of authors (1643 to 1719) whose books refer to D. on the title page: 50 for, 60 against, with place of publication.

466b STEINBÜCHEL, THEODOR: "Franz von Baaders Descartes-Kritik im Rahmen ihrer Zeit und in ihrer grundsätzlichen Bedeutung." WW 10: 1943, 41–60, 103–26; 11: 1944, 24–42.

Thorough study of the D. criticism of Baader, the key figure in the German Romantic Catholic revival at beginning of the 19th century. Baader claimed for his purpose in life putting an end to Cartesianism in philosophy, upholding the mysticism of Jacob Boehme against Descartes' rationalism. Baader's work became influential again a century later in Othmar Spann and in German Catholic thought. Steinbüchel carefully traces the positions of the rationalist Georg Hermes (1775–1831) who defended D. against Baader, of the anticartesians Anton Günther (1783–1863) and Martin Deutinger, the sharpest thinker in the group who considered the defeat of Cartesianism a prerequisite for establishing a personal philosophy compatible with Christian faith. *Deutinger's* Denklehre of 1844 (no. 1754, § 31, 49–51; cf. no. 1755) criticizes the cogito because it disregards the difference between being and existence, confounds absolute content and absolute form, and makes knowledge absolute. Thus logic came to incorporate metaphysics and thereby "engulfed thought altogether; and since thought is being, it engulfed the latter too" (51). The last part of Steinbüchel's article systematically presents Baader's critique under three headings: Catholic Romantic restauration vs. Cartesian revolution; "Ich-Verbundenheit" vs. "Ich-Einsamkeit" (the cogito); "Geist" vs. "Natur" ("die Entgeistigung des Menschen"). The article is a mine of factual information on major and minor figures in this D. controversy, but for a masterly exposition of its place in development of German Catholic thought one must turn to *Alois Dempf's* "Erneuerung und Umbildung des Cartesianismus in der christlichen Philosophie des 19. Jahrhunderts" (in: Cartesio, no. 35, 285–92) where the emphasis properly falls on Anton Günther and Martin Deutinger. Baader's texts on D. are conveniently collected in *E. Susini*, Franz von Baader et le romantisme mystique, Vrin, 1942, v. 3, 185–94.

466c STROH, ALFRED H.: "The Cartesian controversy at Upsala, 1663–1689, its connections with Swedenborg's nebular hypothesis." In: Bericht über den III. Internationalen Kongress für Philosophie zu Heidelberg, 1908, 248–55.

The Cartesian controversy, unconnected with D.'s stay in Sweden, had considerable influence upon Swedish intellectual life, leading to much wider freedom of thought In 1710 a scientific society was founded in Upsala; Swedenborg was a prominent founding member. His astronomical studies (1716 ff.) led him to a cosmology between D.'s vortex theory and the Kant-Laplace hypothesis. Whether Kant had access to his work is unknown.

466d TABBAH, BICHARE (i.e., BISHĀRA TABBĀKH): "Le cartésianisme et l'École du droit de la nature des gens." In his: Du heurt à l'harmonie des droits. Desclée de Brouwers, 1936, 67–102. Thèse Paris. [Full title: no. 3383.]

From a Descartes interpretation taken second-hand from Maritain, the author concludes that the aprioristic method of Pufendorf and his followers derives from Descartes (law is deduced, more geometrico, from clear and distinct ideas). Superficial and shallow. *Alessandro Levi* ("L'influence de l'esprit cartésien dans le droit, ses avantages et ses limites," CD 3: 49–54) does better in just six pages, stressing Cartesian individualism rather than Cartesian apriorism and noting the role of innate ideas (see Droetto, no. 253) as pointing to Domat, Montesquieu, and even to the Code Napoléon.

467 THIJSSEN-SCHOUTE, C. LOUISE: Nederlands cartesianisme. Amsterdam, N.V. Noord-Hollandsche Uitgevers, 1954. 744 p. (Verhandelingen der K. Nederlandse Akademie van Wetenschappen, Afd. Letterkunde, ns v. 60).

Enormous work of superior erudition, independent in judgment, sometimes polemical, worked up from primary sources while critically considering the secondary literature. It covers all conceivable aspects of its subject in 399 independent sections which follow each other in only roughly chronological order. The study extends from D.'s relations to Dutch and some non-Dutch contemporaries to the remotest ramifications of Cartesianism in Dutch philosophy, science and theology, taking into its fold French, Italian, English, German, Swedish figures of major and minor Cartesian importance. Sidelights fall upon D.'s influence on French literature, on voyages imaginaires, Dutch influences upon Gassendi, to mention but a few of the uncounted bonus items that unexpectedly turn up. The work demands utmost patience and perseverance on the reader's part, but should be consulted on any historical question regarding Cartesianism and its literature. A French summary, translated by Paul Dibon, barely manages to cover the main findings and is as unorganized as the rest; but the index of some 1400 names and the list of 399 section titles (also in French) will serve as a guide in the absence of an alphabetical subject matter index.

Reviews: P. Dibon in ANTWP 47: 1954–55, 163–65 and in Het Spinozahuis 58: 1956, 35–37 (Jaarverslag 1954–55); E. Dijksterhuis in RHSA 7: 1954, 382; J. Dopp in RPhL 53: 1955, 101–02; R. Hooykaas in AIHS 8: 1955, 76–77; M.v.R. in NAK 41: 1955, 61–62.

468 VARTANIAN, ARAM: Diderot and Descartes. A study of scientific naturalism in enlightenment. Princeton UP, 1953. 336 p. (History of ideas series, v. 6). [Italian transl.: no. 3473.] Columbia dissertation.

1. An aspect of the Cartesian heritage. 2. From Descartes' Le Monde to the worlds of Diderot and materialistic science. 3. Scientific method from Descartes to the Philosophes. 4. From the Cartesian mechanistic biology to the man-machine and evolutionary materialism.

Traces the uninterrupted, often subterranean current of ideas flowing from Descartes to La Mettrie and Diderot, vindicating the view, developing since the 1930's, that D.'s physics, biology and methodology, not his rejected metaphysics, influenced the philosophes' thought more than did English sensationalism. Their tactical, propagandistic denial of kinship with D. is treated with great skill and penetration. Chapter 1–3 link the heritage of D., especially the beast-machine concept and its implied radical materialism, with the philosophes' materialism and quest for scientific method. Here Vartanian sheds fresh light upon the influential nonmetaphysical aspects of D.'s metaphysical doctrines. Chapter 4, more controversial, finds Cartesian mechanistic biology at the root of the man-machine concept and of evolutionary materialism. The concluding ch. 5 revaluates Diderot, showing the profound dissimilarity between the views of man of Descartes and Diderot, Locke and Helvetius. Rich quotations from minor and major works. Basically an 18th century historical study, the book reveals the sharp contrast between the turbulent flow of the philosophes' not always disinterested ideas and the architectonic thought of Gueroult's "penseur de granit," shedding light on the manner in which a monolithic philosophy fertilizes thinking even in its historical decay. See also R. Hubert and H. Mougin, no. 455 and 459.

Reviews: Anon. in TLS 52: 496, July 31, 1956; P. H. Beik in AHR 59: 1953, 97–98; S. Dresden in Museum (Leiden) 60: 1955, 177–78; C. C. Gillispie in Isis 44: 1953, 389–91; G. Leger in RSPT 40: 1956, 685; G. May in MLN 69: 1954, 376–79; R. Nicolaus in MLR 49: 1954, 514–15; R. Peach in SAQ 52: 1953, 619–20; A. M. Ritchie in Mind 64: 1955, 563–65 (critical); L. C. Rosenfield in JP 53: 1956, 556–64; H. D. Spoerl in Pers 35: 1954, 173–74; H. Dieckmann in MP 53: 1955, 61–66; P. Rossi in RF 48: 1956, 444–48; G. Crocker in MLQ 15: 1954, 381–86.

469 TROSTLER, JOSEPH TURÓCZI: "Les cartésiens hongrois." Revue des études hongroises 12: 1934, 100–25.

A good survey of the rather meager subject. See also *Joseph Halasy-Nagy's* short, uncritical but informative "Le cartésianisme en Hongrie" (CD 3: 122–26); also his: "A Cartesianismus és a magyar szellemiség" (Pannonia 1937, no. 7–10, 220–30).

470 WASIK, W.: "Kartezjusz w Polsce." Prz 40: 1937, 199–240, 414–463.

Detailed study of D.'s influence upon Polish thought, summarized by *Ludwik Chmaj*, "Le cartésianisme en Pologne au XVIIe et au XVIIIe siècle" 1937 (see no. 1544). See also the references to Bar, Lubnicki and Czajkowski in no. 15.

XII. COLLECTANEA, COMMEMORATIONS, EXHIBITIONS: CHECKLIST

1596–1896: BIRTH OF DESCARTES

501 [*Prague*]. Jednota československých matematikú a fysikú v Praze: Slavnost pořadaná na pamět 300-letých zenin R. Descartesa v Praze dne 6. Prosince 1896. Náklada Jednoty ceských matematikú, 1897. 36 p. See 3371.

502 *Revue de métaphysique et de morale*. RMM 4: 1896, 386–567.

Milestone in modern Descartes studies, with influential articles by É. Boutroux, G. Lanson, M. Blondel, V. Brochard, A. Boyce Gibson, and others.

503 [*Russia*]. VFP 1896, no. 4. See nos. 2131a, 2567, 3456. Also Ljubimov, no. 2561a.

504 [*Tours*]. Troisième centenaire de Descartes. Tours, L. Péricat, 1897. 110 p. Reprinted from: Société archéologique de Touraine 11: 1897, 1er trimestre, 1–110.

General and biographical articles. Bossebeuf on the iconography of Descartes. Celebration at Tours, 1896. Documents.

1629–1929: DESCARTES ENROLLS AT FRANEKER UNIVERSITY

505 [*Franeker*]. Catalogus van de tentoonstelling van handschriften, gravures en werken van R.D. en werken over dezen Franschen geleerden te Franeker. 26 April 1929. 7 p. (Typescript. Utrecht Univ. Bibl.) "Geschilderd portret van R.D., waarschijnlijk van onbekende meester, door het Friesch Museum Leeuwarden, afkomstig van Jr. R. C. V. Cammingha" (p. 1).

1637–1937: DISCOURS DE LA MÉTHODE

506 *Acta Secundi Congressus Thomistici Internationalis* (1936). Torino, Marietti, 1937. 585 p. (Acta Pontificae Academ. Rom. S. Thomae Aquinatis et Religionis Catholicae, ns 3: 1937). See no. 41.

507 *Algemeen Nederlands Tijdschrift voor wijsbegeerte en psychologie* 31: 1937, 1–56.

508 [*Albania*]. Perpjekja Squiptare 2: 1937. [Brief articles on Descartes.]

508a *Archiv für Rechts- und Sozialphilosophie.* See 523.

509 *Archives de philosophie. Autour du Discours de la méthode.* Aph 13, no. 2, 1937. 245 p.

Studies by Chevalier, R. Verneaux, M. de Corte, J. M. Le Blond, P. Mesnard and A. Robert.

510 [*Argentina*]. See 512, 524.

511 *Bibliothèque Nationale. Descartes.* Exposition organisée pour le IIIe centenaire du Discours de la méthode. Préface: Julien Cain. ["Descartes" (vii–xviii) by Charles Adam. Text and notes by Marie-Thérèse d'Alverny.] Paris, Bibliothèque Nationale, 1937. xviii, 172 p. Frontispiece, 7 pl. See no. 1.

512 *Buenos Aires* [HOMENAJE]. *Descartes.* Homenaje en el tercer centenario del Discurso del método. Buenos Aires. Universidad Nacional. Instituto de filosofía, 1937. 3 vols. 371, 343, 361 p. See no. 40.

513 *Bulletin de l'Alliance française en Hollande.* BAFH 15, no. 3: September 1937. [Short commemorative talks and articles.]

514 [CARTESIO]. *Cartesio nel terzo centenario del Discorso del metodo.* Ed. and Preface by A. Gemelli. Milano, Vita e pensiero, 1937. 807 p. (UCSC Supplement to RFNS 19: 1937). See no. 35.

515 *Causeries* à propos du troisième centenaire du Discours de la méthode, par G. Beaulavon, É. Bréhier, L. Brunschvicg, L. Flavien, A. Lalande, M. Leroy, D. Parodi, D. Roustan. Paris, Delagrave, 1938. 58 p. (Reprinted from: L'enseignement public, November 1937, February 1938.)

Some of France's outstanding Descartes scholars discuss aspects of Descartes' work for young people.

Reviews: J. Rimaud in Et 240: 1939, 278; H. J. de Vleeschauwer in TP 1: 1939, 870.

516 [*Cercle Descartes*]. *Descartes.* Cahiers du Cercle Descartes, paraissant tous les trois mois, no. 6, automne 1937 (Paris, M. Maupoint, 1938). 44 p. 16mo. [Two articles, by H. Daudin and H. Wallon.]

517 [*Cercle philosophique Lorrain*]. Tricentenaire de la parution du Discours de la méthode, célébré à Metz le 25 avril par le Cercle philosophique Lorrain. Metz, P. Frentz, 1937. 27 p.

518 [*Châtellerault*]. *Descartes.* Tricentenaire du Discours de la méthode. 1637–1937. Châtellerault, impr. H. Videau. 1937. 24 p. 4to. Reprinted from: Le glaneur châtelleraudais 4: May 1937.

"Articles consacrés aux origines de Descartes, à ses pérégrinations posthumes, aux fêtes de mai 1937 à Châtellerault, et la société cartésienne de cette ville" [BP]. See nos. 1699, 2566, 2876–78, 3072. Also "Descartes à Châtellerault," NL, 27 May 1937, on the celebrations.

519 [*Congrès Descartes*]. Travaux du IXe Congrès international de philosophie (Congrès Descartes). Paris. Hermann, 1937, v. 1–3: Études cartésiennes. 181, 131, 147 p. (Asci, v. 530–32). See no. 36.

520 "*René Descartes: a symposium.*" St. Bonaventura scientific studies, June 1937, 3–10. [A. Jerome Miller et al. Insignificant.]

521 *Descartes*, par M. Leroy, G. Friedmann, J. Luc, Lucie Prenant, P. Labérenne, N. Gutermann et H. Lefebvre, G. Milhaud, Édouard Benes. Paris, Rieder, (1937). 147 p. [Same as: *Hommages à René Descartes.* Eur 15 July 1937, 291–430.] See no. 37.

522 *Descartes et le cartésianisme hollandais*, par E. J. Dijksterhuis, Cornelia Serrurier, Paul Dibon, Hendrik J. Pos, Jean Orcibal, C. -LouiseThijssen-Schoute, Geneviève Lewis. Études et documents. Paris, PUF-Éditions françaises d'Amsterdam, 1950 (c. 1951). 309 p. (Publications de l'Institut français d'Amsterdam – Maison Descartes). See no. 38.

523 [EMGE]. *Dem Gedächtnis an René Descartes* .... Erinnerungsgabe der Internationalen Vereinigung für Rechts- und Sozialphilosophie, hg. von C. A. Emge. Archiv für Rechts- und Sozialphilosophie 30, no. 4: 1937. 204 p.

Germany's chief collective 1937 contribution; not impressive, except for Burkamp on D.'s theory of knowledge, Witzenmann on Vico's anticartesianism, and Katkov's study of Descartes and Brentano.

Review: Anon. in RMM 45: 1938, suppl. 3, 19–20.

524 [ESCRITOS]. *Escritos en honor de Descartes* en ocasión del tercer centenario del Discurso del método. La Plata, Universidad nacional, 1908. 337 p. See no. 39.

525 *L'esprit cartésien.* Entretien. Le 16 janvier 1937, à la suite d'un exposé de M. Bréhier. Union pour la vérité (Paris). Bulletin 44, no. 7–8: 1937. [Contributors: Émile Bréhier, J. Maritain, Léon Robin.]

526 *Estudios. Homenaje a Renato Descartes.* E 37: 1937, 369–558.

Remarkable Neothomist contribution. Includes Sortais on D. and the Jesuits, Derisi on S. Thomas and Descartes, and Busto's critique of Laberthonnière. Short, annotated bibliography.

527 [*"Europe."*] *Hommages à René Descartes.* Eur July 15, 1937, 291–430. [Also separately: *Descartes,* par M. Leroy, G. Friedmann, et al. Paris, Rieder, 1937.] See no. 37 and 521.

528 [*La Haye*]. *Ville de La Haye-Descartes, 31 Octobre 1937.* Fête commémorative du troisième centenaire du Discours de la méthode .... Exposition Descartes. Portraits et documents, manuscrits et livres rares. n.d. (1937). 8vo. 20 p.

Illustrations, including portraits of Descartes.

529 [HOMENAJE]. See Buenos Aires, no. 512.

530 *Nouvelles litteraires.* "Hommages à Descartes." NL July 1937, p. 1–3.

531 [*Poitiers*]. Hommage à Descartes, 1637–1937, à l'occasion du IXe Congrès international de philosophie (Congrès Descartes). Poitiers, 1937. 8vo. 72 p. [Reprint, with separate pagination, of the Descartes issue of the Revue générale du Centre-Ouest de France, no. 44, August 1937].

Articles by L. Beauduc, J. Moreau, P. Mesnard, H. Lesage, A. Forest, J. Pucelle.

532 [*Poland.*] Prz 45: 1937, 120–140. Also separately: Zeszyt Kartezjański. Wydany w trzechsetną rocznicę Rozprawy o metodzie. Warszawa, 1937. See no. 1544, 1673, 1680, 1935, 470 = 3539, 3540, 3602.

533 *Revue de métaphysique et de morale.* RMM 44: 1937, 1–352. Also as: *Études sur Descartes.* Paris, Colin, 1937. 352 p.

Outstanding collection of studies by L. Brunschvicg, H. Gouhier, G. Loria, S. V. Keeling, E. Signoret, F. Enriques.

534 *Revue de synthèse.* "1637–1937." Rsyn 14: April-October 1937, 1–114.

E. Cassirer, R. Hubert, P. Ducasse, and an international Descartes-bibliography (no. 15).

535 *Revue d'histoire de la philosophie.* RHPh ns 5: no. 18, 15 April 1937.

Radio talks on Descartes, some of them models of popular scholarship.

536 *Revue philosophique. Descartes à l'occasion du troisième centenaire du Discours de la méthode*. RPFE année 62, v. 123: 1937. 372 p.

Essential contributions by Brunschvicg, Laporte and others.

537 [*Santa Fé, Argentina*]. *Descartes*. Homenaje en el tercer centenario del Discurso del método .... Santa Fé, R. Argentina. Universidad nacional del Litoral. 1937. 46 p.

University catalogue, containing a commemorative article on DM by Josef Babini.

538 [*Tours*]. *René Descartes .... et le siècle de Louis XIV en Touraine*. Grande semaine de Tours, 8–17 mai 1937. Exposition rétrospective. Tours, Impr. Arrault, 1937. 39 p.

Lists 199 Descartes items, including 63 portraits, medals and statues.

539 [*USSR*]. Pod znamenem Marksizma, nr. 7, 8, 1937. [DM, methodology, physiology, cosmology, D. and Enlightenment, esthetics.] See no. 1091c, 1426b,c, 1941a, 1950a, 2770a, 3296.

540 [*USSR*]. Front nauki i tekhniki, nr. 1, 5, 6, 7, 1937. See no. 1426d,e, 2283a, 2337a.

1596–1946: BIRTH OF DESCARTES

541 *Atomes*. "Le 350e anniversaire de la naissance de Descartes." Atomes (Paris) 4: 1946, 25.

Comments by Jacques Hadamard, Langevin, and Grasse on Descartes as mathematician, physicist and biologist. (BAn 1947, no. 6909).

1650–1950: DEATH OF DESCARTES

542 *Algemeen Nederlands Tijdschrift*. Descartes-nummer ter herdenking van Descartes' sterfdag op 11 Februari 1950. ANTWP 42: 1950, 113–59.

Contributions by H. J. Pos, H. Robbers, H. J. E. Beth, P. Dibon, C. L. Thijssen-Schoute.

543 [*Berlin*]. *Gedenkfeier* anlässlich des dreihundertjährigen Todestages des Philosophen René Descartes, veranstaltet von der Freien Universität Berlin am 11. Februar 1950. 32 p.

Memorial address by Hans Leisegang.

544 [*Chile*]. *Homenaje a Descartes*. Santiago de Chile, Sociedad chilena de filosofía, y Universidad de Chile, 1950. p. 397–567. Reprinted from a special issue of the Revista de filosofía (Chile), 1: 1950, no. 4.

545 [*Cuba*]. Universidad de Oriente. Departamento de extension y relaciones culturales. Conmemoracion del III centenario de Renato Descartes. Discursos. Santiago de Cuba, 1950. 68 p. (General commemorative lectures).

546 [*Cuba*]. See 555.

547 *Études philosophiques*. Eph ns 5: 1950, 151–243.

Julien Benda, G. Berger, G. Devivaise, P. Humbert, P. Mesnard, J. Moreau, R. Sarano, J. Segond.

548 *Endeavour*. "Descartes, 1596–1650." Endeavour 9, no. 35: 1950.

549 *Glanes*. Glanes (Cahiers de l'amité franco-néerlandaise, Amsterdam), April 1950. [Brief articles on D. and Holland].

550 *Kwartalnik filosoficzny*. KF 19: 1950, 1–169.

Polish studies, with French summaries, by I. Dąmbska, S. Luszczewska-Romahnova, St. Czajkowski, W. Ślebodziński, R. Ingarden; A. Bar's bibliography of D. in Poland.

551 *Pensamiento*. PenM 6: 1950, no. 23.

552 *Pensée*. Pensée ns, no. 32, September-October 1950.

Descartes from the viewpoint of historical materialism: Barjonnet, Wallon, Marx himself.

553 [*Poitiers*]. Les journées universitaires poitevines. Hommage à Descartes, 26 avril–1 mai 1950. Poitiers, G. Basile, 1950. 8vo. 71 p. ill. [Commemorative addresses by H. Pos, H. Gouhier et al.]

554 *Psyché*. PsyP no. 40, February 1950, 98–160. [Articles by M. Choisy, G. Cohen, et al.]

555 *Revista cubana de filosofía* 1/6: January-December 1950. [No more published?] Short articles on Descartes by Latin American scholars.

556 *Revue des sciences humaines.* Numero consacré à Descartes, avec la collaboration de H. Gouhier, G. Lewis, J. Vuillemin, O. Revault d'Allones, P. Golliet, P. Costabel, F. Alquié. RScH ns no. 61: January-March 1951, 1–88.

557 *Revue internationale de philosophie.* Descartes à l'occasion du tricentenaire de sa mort. RIP 4: 1950, 121–247.

Important studies by H. Gouhier, F. Alquié, R. Lenoble, G. Lewis, Ch. S. Ware.

558 *Revue philosophique.* Commémoration centenaire de la mort de Descartes. RPFE année 76, v. 141: 1951, no. 4–6.

559 *Société française de philosophie.* Hommage solennel rendu à la mémoire de René Descartes à l'occasion du IIIe centenaire de sa mort. Allocutions de Raymond Bayer, André Bridoux, Gustave Cohen, Martial Gueroult, Georges Davy, Jean Cabannès, W. van Boetzelaer, Yvon Delbos. BSFP 44, no. 1, 1950, 1–42. Also: Colin, 1950. 42 p.

560 [*USSR*]. Akad. Nauk SSSR. Commemorative session, May 1950. See no. 3403.

OTHER COLLECTANEA

561 *Revue de synthèse.* "Les journées cartesiennes du Centre de Synthèse." "Pages cartésiennes." Rsyn 63 (ns 22): January-June 1948, 1–98.

Articles by Gadoffre, Ferrier, M. Leroy. Review articles by Thomas and Bouvier.

562 [*ROYAUMONT*]. Descartes. Cahiers de Royaumont, Philosophie no. II. Éditions de minuit, 1957. 493 p. See no. 42.

PART TWO

ALPHABETICAL BIBLIOGRAPHY

1800–1960

A

1001 *Abbagnano, Nicola:* "Descartes." In his: Storia della filosofia. Torino, UTET, 1946–50, v.2, pt.1, 166–89. 2nd ed., rev., 1949–50.

Existentialist interpretation. See C. Ferro in RFNS 52: 1950, 217–19.

1001a *Abele, J.:* "Descartes, précurseur de la cinématique relativiste." RGS 64: 1957, 356–75.

On D.'s three material qualities (shape, rest, motion) and his inertia formulation; Einstein following in the same spirit of geometrization.

1002 *Abercrombie, Nigel:* "Saint Augustine and the Cartesian metaphysics." In his: Saint Augustine and French classical thought. Oxford, Clarendon Press, 1938, 57–90. See 235.

1003 —: "Cartesianism and classicism." MLR 31: 1936, 358–76. See 411.

1003a *Abranches, Cassiano:* "Acerca de Descartes." RevPF sb 1: 1952, 198–201.

1004 *Ackermann, A.* (Abbé): "La physique de Descartes et la philosophie moderne." APC Feb. 1897, 605ff. June 1898, 299–319. ()

1004a —: "La liberté dans la croyance chez Descartes." APC Febr. 1893.

1005 *Acta* Secundi Congressus Thomistici Internationalis [1936]. Torino, Marietti, 1937. 585 p. See 41 and 506.

1005a *Actes* du Symposium international des sciences physicales et mathématiques dans la première moitié du XVIIe siècle, Pisa, 16–18 juin 1958. Paris, Hermann, 1960. (Travaux de l'Académie internationale d'histoire des sciences.

Valuable background studies. See 1833a and 2831a.

1006 *Adam, Charles [Ernest]* et P. Tannery (editors): Œuvres de Descartes [AT]. 13 vols. Paris, Cerf, 1896–1913. Reprinted: Vrin, 1957–58. See 74.

1007 —: Vie et œuvres de Descartes; étude historique. Supplément à l'édition de Descartes publiée sous les auspices du Ministère de l'Instruction Publique. Paris, Cerf, 1910. xix, 646 p. [= AT XII]. Reprinted: Vrin, 1958. See 121.

1008 — et Gérard Milhaud (editors): Descartes. Correspondance [AM] publiée avec une introduction et des notes par Charles Adam et Gérard Milhaud. v. 1, 2: Paris, Alcan, 1936, 1939. v. 3–6: Paris, PUF, 1941, 1947, 1951, 1956. v. 7 [1646–1647]: PUF, 1960. See 79.

1009 — (editor): Descartes. Entretiens avec Burman. Paris Boivin, 1937. xv, 144 p. See 86.

1010 —: Descartes, sa vie, son œuvre. Paris, Boivin, 1937. 180 p. See 121.

1011 —: Descartes, ses amitiés féminines. Paris, Boivin, 1937. 164 p. See 121.

1012 — [Adam, Carolus E.]: De methodo apud Cartesium, Spinozam et Leibnitium .Paris, Hachette, 1885. 115 p. Thèse Paris.

1013 —: "Pascal et Descartes. Les expériences du vide (1646–1651.)" RPFE 24: 1887/2, 612–24; 25: 1888/1, 65–90.

1014 —: "Notes sur les Regulae ad directionem ingenii de Descartes." RPFE 40: 1895/2, 288–93. Reprinted in AT X.

1015 —: "Correspondance de Descartes. Autographes et manuscrits." RMM 4: 1896, 573–83. Reprinted in the Introduction to AT I.

1016 —: "Le père Mersenne et ses correspondants en France." Bulletin historique et philosophique, 1896.

1017 —: "Correspondance de Descartes. Nouveau classement." RPFE 115: 1933, 373–401.

Important revision of the AT classification and dating of Descartes' correspondence. See 74, 79.

1018 —: "Descartes." In: Bibliothèque Nationale, Descartes [no. 1, no. 511], vii–xviii.

1019 —: "Descartes et sa correspondance féminine." RIE 57: 1937, 5–16.

1020 —: "Descartes et ses correspondants anglais." RLC 17: 1937, 437–60. See 121.

Sir Kenelm Digby, Hobbes, John Pell, Samson Johnson, Cherbury, Thomas White, Charles and William Cavendish, Henry More.

1021 —: "Descartes: ses trois notions fondamentales." RPFE 123: 1937, 1–14.

"Ce sont, pour l'âme seule, celle de la pensée (connaissance de l'âme et de Dieu); pour le corps seul, celle de l'étendue; et pour l'âme et le corps ensemble, celle de leur union."

1022 —: "Quelques questions à propos de Descartes." RCC 38: 1937, 577–89; 39: 1938, 1–8. See 121.

Descartes in Bohemia (Komenský, Battle of the White Mountain); at the siege of La Rochelle; his views on longevity; biographical documents. Section on longevity also in: Progrès médical, 1937, p. 1267.

1023 *Adams, E. M.:* "Cartesianism in ethics." PPR 16: 1955–56, 353–66.

Critique of R. M. Hare (The language of morals, Oxford, 1952) who defines Cartesianism in ethics as deduction of particular duties from some self-evident first principle, with or without factual premises.

1024 *Adamson, Robert K.:* "Descartes and intellectualism." In his: The development of modern philosophy, ed. W. R. Sorley. Edinburgh, Blackwood, 1903, v. 1, p. 7–42.

1025 *Adkins, B. M.:* "The dictum of Descartes." BJPS 3: 1952–53, 259–60. [A reply to W. R. Ashby, no. 1090.] See 350.

1026 *Adler, Adam:* "Die philosophische Anthropologie des Descartes." PJ 59: 1949, 169–80.

Agirrezabal: see Iriarte Agirrezabal, J.

1027 *Agoglia, R.* and *F. Moffey:* "Itinerario de la verdad en Descartes." RF Chile 1950, 536–40.

1027a *Aiton, E. J.:* "Descartes' theory of the tides." AnSci 11: 1955, 337–48.

Within the 100 years following D.'s theory of the tides (PP), only the Cartesian de Catelet (1677) advanced a critique of it. Varenius (1650), Rohault (1671) and A. Cavalleri (1740) merely took it over, ignoring the advances made by Henry Philips and Joseph Childrey. [Bsig 1958, 8143.]

1027b —: "Newton and the Cartesians." School Science Rev 40: 1959, 406–13.
Notwithstanding Newton's destruction of the vortex theory, the Cartesian system was not entirely discarded until the mid-18th century.

1027c —: "The Cartesian theories of the planetary motions. I." AnSci 13: 1957 (1959), 249ff.

1028 *Aja, Pedro Vicente:* "Cuatro visiones de la libertad moral." RcubF 1/6: 1950, 62–65.

1029 *Alain* [i.e. Émile Chartier]: "Descartes." In his: Idées. Introduction à la philosophie. Paris, Hartmann, 1932, 109–99. Reprinted 1947. See 147.

1030 —: Histoire de mes pensées. 2nd ed. Paris, Gallimard, 1936, 252–57. (Les idées). See 148.

1031 — (ed.): René Descartes. Discours de la méthode, précédé d'une étude d'Alain. Paris, Les arts et le livre, 1927. 227 p. (L'Intelligence, v. 8). See 147.

1032 —: René Descartes. Traité des passions. Étude d'Alain. Paris, Jonquières, 1928. 333 p. (L'intelligence, v. 10). See 147.

1033 —: Étude sur Descartes. Paris, Hartmann, 1928. 107 p. See 147.

1034 —: Abrégés pour les aveugles. Portraits et doctrines de philosophes anciens et modernes. Paris, Hartmann, 1943. 179 p.

1035 —: Humanités. Paris, Méridien, 1946. 286 p. (Collection Parentés, 12/18).
Contains an unpublished essay on Descartes [Rsyn 68: 1948, p. 192].

1036 *Alberti, José L.:* "La cultura cartesiana desde un punto de vista psicológico." Homenaje 2: 1937, 289–301.

1037 *Alcorta, José Ignacio:* "Aspecto esencial y existencial del cogito cartesiano." RevF 10: 1951, 433–63.

1038 *Aldrich, Virgil C.:* "Descartes' method of doubt. An interpretation and appreciation." Pscience 4: 1937, 395–411, 521–45. [Commemorative lecture.]

1039 *Alejandro, José María:* "Reflexiones sobre la duda cartesiana." CyF 6: 1950, 7–48.

1040 *Alexandre, Michel* (editor): Descartes. Lettres. Textes choisies par Michel Alexandre. Paris, PUF, 1955. viii, 226 p. (Les grands textes).

Excellent selection from D.'s vast correspondence, with biographical index of correspondents and detailed "table analytique."

Reviews: F. Alquié in Eph 10: 1955, 294–95; M. Dambuyant in Pensée no. 67: 1956, 151; G. Leger in RSPT 40: 1956, 35–36; J. C. Piguet in RTP 6: 1956, 145.

1041 *Allard, Emmy:* Die Angriffe gegen Descartes und Malebranche im Journal de Trévoux, 1701–1715. Halle, Niemeyer, 1914. viii, 58 p. (EAPG, v. 43). See 466.

1042 *Allendes, Eulogio:* "Descartes." In his: Los genios de la ciencia. Santiago de Chile, Los Debates, 1889, 244–61.

1043 *Allers, Rudolf:* "Bemerkungen zur Anthropologie und Willenslehre des Descartes." Cartesio 1–12. 1937.

Relates Descartes' voluntarism to Augustinian Scholasticism and to Occamism.

1044 *Almeida, D. de:* "Una faceta poco explorada: Descartes en su Compendium Musicae." E 57: 1937, 451–47.

Sees in Descartes' treatment of the technical structure of music an aid to the understanding of his philosophical and mathematical manner of thinking.

1045 *Alquié, Ferdinand:* La découverte métaphyqisue de l'homme chez Descartes. Paris, PUF, 1950. viii, 384 p. See 149.

1046 —: Descartes, l'homme et l'œuvre. Paris, Hatier-Boivin, 1956. 175 p. See 127.

1046a —: La nostalgie de l'être. Paris, PUF, 1950. 159 p.

Alquié develops his own metaphysical position in a dialogue with the philosophical tradition and especially with Descartes.

1047 —: Notes sur la première partie des Principes de la Philosophie de Descartes. Carcassonne, Editions Chantiers, 1933. 58 p.

A guide through the argument of PP I.

1048 —: "Marxisme ou cartésianisme?" Tmod 1: May 1946, 1378–1400. See 150.

1049 —: "Descartes et l'immédiat." RMM 55: 1950, 37–75.

Descartes cannot in any sense be called an existentialist. Refusing to give unique ontological immediacy to experience, he places the immediate in the factual rather than the epistemological order, retaining the dialectic relationship between the being of the self and Being. Cf. C. Dollo in S 19: 1951, 126.

1050 —: "Descartes et l'ontologie négative." RIP 4: 1950, 153–59.

1051 —: "La démarche métaphysique de Descartes." RScH ns no. 61: 1951, 87–88.

1051a —: "L'ordre cartésien." RPFE 141: 1951, 161–67.

Distinguishes in Descartes' logic the systematic and genetic orders (ordre du système, ordre du temps) which find their unity in man. Cartesian order is therefore not a uniquely logical system (against Gueroult). See 1056.

1052 —: "L'actualité de Descartes." CDS 40: 1953, no. 320, 143–50.

1053 —: Science et métaphysique chez Descartes. Centre de documentation universitaire. 1955. 136 p. (Les cours de Sorbonne). Mimeographed.

1054 —: "Descartes, 1596–1650." In: Les philosophes célèbres, ed. M. Merleau-Ponty. Paris, Mazenod, 1956, 146–53. (Gallérie des hommes célèbres, v. 10).

Portrait of Descartes by J. B. Weenix, accompanied by a brief, appreciative introduction.

1055 —: "Notes sur l'interpretation de Descartes par l'ordre des raisons" [by M. Gueroult]. RMM 61: 1956, 403–18. See 170.

".... pour ce qui est du sens de la philosophie de Descartes, M. Gueroult et moi en avons déjà si souvent, mais si vainement, discuté qu'on peut tenir pour établi que nul de nous deux ne convaincra jamais l'autre" (463). See 1051a.

1056 —: "Expérience ontologique et déduction systématique dans la constitution de la métaphysique de Descartes." Royaumont, 10–31; discussion 32–57; on the "cogito," 58–71. 1957.

For Descartes, scientific and metaphysical ideas are not of the same order. His main problem: "comment mettre d'accord la religion et la science" (27). His two "démarches intellectuelles," creation of eternal verities and cogito, rest on the same unique experience of the insufficiency of all finite essence, of the contingency "de tout nécessaire d'ordre scientifique," of the "déréalisation [de l'objet] par l'être" (31). The discussion is largely an intellectual duel between Alquié and Gueroult. See 1051a.

1056a —: "Conscience et signes dans la philosophie moderne et le cartésianisme." In: Polarité du symbole. Bruges, Desclée de Brouwer, 1960.

Alvarez, A. Gonzáles: see Gonzáles Alvarez.

1057 *Alvarez Turienzo, Saturnino:* "Naturaleza: la omisión cartesiana." Ciudad de Dios (El Escorial) 163, no. 1: 1951, 5–58.

1058 *d'Alverny, Thérèse:* Descartes. Exposition organisée pour le IIIe centenaire du Discours de la méthode. Paris, BN, 1937. xiii. 172 p. See 1 and 511.

1059 *Âme* et conscience chez Descartes. BSPF 45: 1951, 133–64. (Discussion of the theses of G. Lewis). See 215b.

1060 *Amerio, Romano:* "Arbitrarismo divino, libertà umana e implicanze teologiche nella dottrina di Cartesio." Cartesio, 13–39. 1937.

Descartes' voluntarism logically leads to a negative theology and to a concept of freedom as arbitrarism. On D.'s concept of eternal verities and Molinist viewpoints in his letters to Princess Elisabeth.

1061 *Anderson, F. A.:* "Locke and the polemic against Cartesian philosophy: causality and cognition." Proceedings of the Seventh Intern. Cong. of Philosophy. Oxford, 1930, 457–60.

1062 *Anderson, John:* "The cogito of Descartes." AJPP 14: 1936, 48–68.

1063 *Anderson, Paul Russell:* Science in defense of liberal religion. A study of Henry More's attempt to link seventeenth century religion with science. New York, Putnam, 1933. Columbia dissertation. 232 p.

1064 —: "Descartes' influence in 17th century England." CD 3: 113–21. 1937. See 460.

1065 *Andrade, António A. de:* "Descartes em Portugal nos s. XVII e XVIII." Bro 51: 1950, 432–51. See 430.

1065a *André, Désiré:* Sur les écrits scientifiques de Montesquieu. Paris, J. Gervais, 1880. BN in-8°, pièce. [On Montesquieu's Cartesianism.]

Angers: see Julien-Aymard d'Angers.

1066 *Angrand, Cécile:* Cours de philosophie: Les origines françaises du matérialisme. Paris, Editions sociales, 1946, 3–18. (CUN). See 150.

1067 *Angyal, Andreas:* "Zur Literaturgeschichte des deutschen Cartesianismus. Germanisch-Romanische Monatsschrift 29: 1943, 69–72. [A book review.]

1067a *Anokhin, Pëtr Kuz'mič:* Ot Dekarta do Pavlova. Moskva, Medgiz, 1945. 190 p.

From D. to Pavlov. [In Russian.]

1068 *Anquin, Nimio de:* "Incongruencias cartesianas y posibilidades idealísticas en la noción de substancia." Homenaje 3: 295–332. 1937.

Idealistic Descartes interpretation (though radically opposed to Hamelin's) reveals D.'s difficulties in reconciling substance with relativity of change, as exemplified by his treatment of mechanics.

1069 *Antonelli, Maria Teresa:* "Riflessioni in margine a Cartesio." Humanitas (Brescia) 1949, 1033–42.

1070 —: "Unità intenzionale e dualismo metodologico nella filosofia de Descartes." Gmet 12: 1957, 341–66.

Metaphysical dualism in Descartes results from a wavering between "science" and "sagesse." His central truth problem implies both a moralism and perfect theoricity. Though his intention is unity, he is methodologically led into the insurmountable difficulties of mediating between deduction and induction. Cf. Bsig 1959, 11687.

1071 *Arago, François:* "Descartes." In his: Œuvres complètes, ed. J.-A. Barral. Paris, Gide & Baudry (Leipzig, Weigel), v. 3, 1855, 297–309.

Defends D. against accusations of plagiarism (law of refraction and explanation of the rainbow).

1072 *Aragon, Louis:* René Descartes. La Naissance de la paix. Ballet dansé au château royal de Stockholm .... 1649. Prose d'Aragon. Paris, La Bibliothèque Française. 4°. s.d. 37 p. (Limited edition). Tr.: Die Geburt des Friedens. Prosa von Louis Aragon .... übertragen von Hans Paeschke. Neuwied a.Rhein, Lancelot Verlag, 1949. 38 p. See 78.

The ballet was first translated into German by Johann Freinsheimius at the court of Christina of Sweden: Des Friedens Geburtstag. (s. l.), H. Keysern, s.d. [d'Alverny, no. 1, p. 85].

1073 *Arana, Martha V.:* "La correspondencia de Descartes." Homenaje 2: 303–10. 1937.

Characteristic passages assembled under six headings.

1074 *Ardley, Gavin:* "The Cartesian projection." PhS 7: 1957, 83–100.

Descartes projects a universe of anonymous entities; his system is therefore neither metaphysical nor ontological but projective in the sense of Oresme amd Buridan, though it goes beyond them in its mathematicism. [Bsig 1959, 167.]

1075 *Arès, R. (S.J.):* "Le catholicisme de René Descartes." Canada Français 1937, 803–21, 936–58.

Sharply apologetic polemic against Ch. Adam's scepticism concerning D.'s religiosity. Superficial survey of pertinent incidents in his life leads author to conclude that D. was faithful to the Church, notwithstanding its subsequent condemnation of his work.

1076 *d'Argenson:* 'Note sur la famille Descartes et l'origine de son nom." MSA Touraine 4: 1847, 87. ()

1077 *Arias, Alejandro C.:* "Descartes." In his: Estudios literarios y filosóficos. Montevideo, C. García, 1941, 204–32. (Biblioteca Rodó, v. 74–75).

Arigós de Montoya: see Ortiz de Montoya.

1078 *Armitage, Angus:* "René Descartes, 1596–1650, and the early Royal Society." Notes and Records of the Royal Society of London 8: 1950, 1–19.

1079 *Arnellos, J.:* Βάκων, Καρτέσιος, Σπινόζας. 'Αθήναις, 1957. 80 p.

1080 *Arnold, G. L.:* "The New Commonwealth." Twentieth Century 151, no. 899: Jan. 1952, 55–71.

Discussion of Gordon Walker, A restatement of liberty (on the "Cartesian" view of society.) See Walker, no. 3529.

1081 *Arnold, Matthew:* "The God of metaphysics." In his: God and the Bible. New York, Macmillan, 1875, 58–110.

In answer to Huxley's "extrachristian" Descartes, Arnold's address to "plain, simple people" (p. 63) takes the high road from Cartesian mechanism via necessary truth, cogito, and the etymology of "is" and "being" to the God of Metaphysics, leaving Descartes behind in the end.

1082 *Arnold, Paul:* "Le 'songe' de Descartes." CDS 39, no. 312: 274–91, 1952. See 102.

1082a —: Histoire des Rose-Croix et les origines de la franc-maçonnerie. Paris, Mercure de France, 1955, Appendix, 273–99 (same as 1082).

1082b —: "Descartes et les Rose-Croix." MF 340: 1960, no. 1166, 266–84. See 102.

1083 *Arnoux, Alexandre:* "La revanche des mathématiques." La Revue: Hommes et mondes 1954, 353–67.

1084 *Aron, Robert:* Les frontaliers du néant. Paris, Éditions de Flore, 1949. 170 p. See 195.

1085 —: "Descartes y el cartesianismo." Revista de la Universidad de Buenos Aires, v. 5, no. 1: 1949, 98–168. See 195.

1086 *Artigas Ramírez, José:* Descartes y la formación del hombre moderno. Madrid, 1951. 176 p. See 196.

1087 —: "Raíz cartesiana del hombre actual." RevF 11: 1952, 37–42.

1088 *Arvesen, Ole Peder:* "Descartes og hans geometri." Det Kongelige norske videnskaber selskab, Tronheim. Forhandlinger 10: 1938, 37–52.

1089 *Ascoli, Georges:* La Grande-Bretagne devant l'opinion française au XVIIIe siecle. Paris, Gamber, 1930, v. 2. See 460.

1090 *Ashby, W. R.:* "Can a mechanical chess-player outplay its designer?" BJPS 3: 1952–53, 44–57. See 350.

1091 *Asmus, Valentin Ferdinandovitch:* Dekart. Moskwa, 1956. 371 p. See 150.

1091a —: Art. "Dekart" in: F. V. Konstantinov (ed.), Filosofskaja enciclopedija, v. 1, 477–50. Gos. Naučnoe izd-vo, Moskwa, 1960. (Institut filosofii Akad. Nauk SSSR.)

Lists Russian translations of D.'s works and all pertinent passages in Marx and Engels.

1091b —: "Dialektika v sisteme Dekarta: doklad." Vestnik Kommun. Akad. no. 25, 1928, 116–182.

Dialectics in D.'s system, [In Russian.]

1091c —: "Kosmogonija i kosmologija Dekarta." Pod znamenem marksizma, no. 8, 1937.

D.'s cosmogony and cosmology. [In Russian.]

1092 *Aspelin, Gunnar:* "Descartes' genombrottsskrift." Vetenskaps societaten i Lund. Årsbok 1936, 1–12.

1093 *Aster, Ernst von:* Einführung in die Philosophie Descartes's. München, Rösl, 1921. 118 p. See 128.

1094 —: Geschichte der neueren Erkenntnistheorie von Descartes bis Hegel. Berlin, 1921. See 128.

1095 *Astie, Adrien:* "La naissance de René Descartes." SLSA Saumurois 26/85: 1938, 3–13. (BP 1938, pt. 1).

1096 *Astrada, Carlos:* "La dualidad del concepto de verdad en Descartes." Homenaje 1: 195–201. 1937.

1097 *Aubry, Jean-Baptiste:* Mélanges de philosophie catholique: Le cartésianisme, le rationalisme et la scolastique. Pt. 2 of his: Œuvres complètes, publiés par son frère. Paris, V. Retaux, 1895. 305 p.

Contains: La doute méthodique – Descartes père du naturalisme (ch. 9, 196–224); Descartes et l'induction (ch. 10, 225–50); Le 17e siècle cartésien: l'école cartésienne et le progrès de la science (ch. 11, 251–64).

1098 *Auger, Léon:* "La polémique entre Descartes et .... Roberval." Thalès 6: 1949–50, 59–67. See 369.

1098a *Autour* du Discours de la méthode. Aph 1937. See 509.

1099 *Avellaneda, Justo:* "Papel sobre la física de Descartes. Manuscrito Peruano del siglo XVIII." Boletín bibliográfico (Lima, Univ. de San Marcos) 18: 1948, 210–16.

1100 *Avord, René:* "A propos de la morale cartésienne." France libre Oct. 1941, 492–501.

1101 *Ayer, Alfred Jules:* Language, truth and logic. London, Gollancz, 1936. 2nd ed., rev., c. 1946. Reprinted: New York, Dover. See 235a.

1101a —: The problem of knowledge. London, Macmillan, 1956, 45–54. See 235b.

1101b —: "Cogito ergo sum." Analysis, December 1953, 27–31. See 235 a–b, also 335.

B

1102 *Baas, Émile:* "La critique leibnizienne de la physique de Descartes." BFL Strasbourg, 1942. See: M. Gueroult, "Observations sur ce mémoire," and no. 373.

1103 *Babini, José:* "La matemática en Descartes y el mundo exterior." Escritos, 11–19. 1937.

Review by W. S. Weedon in PPR 1: 1940, 248: Descartes' mathematics are less closely linked to his metaphysics than Babini would have it.

1104 —: "El Discurso del Método." Universidad Nacional del Litoral (Santa Fé) 1: 1937, no. 3, 81–94. See 537.

Bacca: see García Bacca.

1105 *Bach, Hubert zum:* "Über die Angeborenheit der Gottesidee nach Cartesius." PJGG 31: 1918, 239–60.

1106 *Bachelard, Gaston:* Le nouvel esprit scientifique. Paris, Alcan, 1934. 179 p. Italian transl. by Fortuna Albérgamo: Il nuovo spirito scientifico. Introd. by Francesco Albérgamo. Bari, Laterza, 1951. 224 p. (Filosofi della scienza, v. 2). See 235c.

1107 —: "Un livre d'un nommé R. Descartes." Archeion 19: 1937, 161–71.

Astrological work (Les véritables connaissances des influences célestes et sublunaires, Paris, 1667) by one R. Descartes; no connection with the philosopher.

1108 *Bad, H.:* "Snellius .... non Cartesius." Ruch filozoficzny (Lwów) 12: 1930–31, 208.

1109 *Bäumker, Clemens:* "Neue Beiträge zur Lebens- und Entwicklungsgeschichte des R. Descartes." PJ 22: 1909, 144–58, 345.

Review of AT X (Descartes' earliest works and letters).

1110 *Baillet, Adrien:* La vie de Monsieur Des-Cartes. Paris, 1691. See 122.

1111 —: Vie de Monsieur Descartes (reprint of the abridged version of 1692). Paris, 1946. See 122.

Bain, A.: see Hodgson, S.H., and A. Bain.

1112 *Baker, M. J.:* "Sleeping and waking." Mind 63: 1954, 539–43. See 306.

1112a *Baladi, Naguib:* Descartes. Cairo, Al-Ma'arif, 1959. 222 p. (Génies de la pensée occidentale, v. 4.)

Introduction for the Middle-Eastern reader. A. Hayen notes the discussion of D.'s formative years and of the influence of the Exercitia of St. Ignatius of Loyola (RPhL 59: 1961, 133–36).

1113 *Baldensperger, Ferdinand:* "Intellectuels français hors de France. I: De Descartes à Voltaire." RCC 35, v. 1: 1934, 316–24, 421–34.

1114 *Ballard, Edward G.:* "Descartes' revision of the Cartesian dualism." PhQ 7: 1957, 249–59.

Distinguishing different meanings of ego, doubt, cogito, author finds that the fertility and generality of Descartes' ideas outran his efforts to systematize them. From A. G. A. Balz' school.

1114a —: "On Kant's refutation of metaphysics." NSch 32: 1958, 235–52.

Discusses among other themes the ontological argument in St. Anselm's and D.'s formulation, with Kant's critique.

1115 *Baltrušaitis, Jurgis:* Anamorphoses ou perspectives curieuses. Paris, Perrin, 1955. See 236.

1116 *Balz, A. G. A.* [Albert George Adam]: Cartesian studies. New York, Columbia UP, 1951. vi, 328 p. See 431.

1117 —: Descartes and the modern mind. New Haven, Yale UP, 1952. xiv, 492 p. See 151.

1118 —: "Dualism in Cartesian psychology and epistemology." In: SHI v. 2, 1925, 83–157.

1119 —: "Louis de la Chambre, 1595–1669." PhR 39: 1930, 375–97. Reprinted: no. 1116, ch. 3.

1120 —: "Samuel Sorbière, 1615–1670." PhR 39: 1930, 573–86. Reprinted: no. 1116, ch. 4.

1121 —: "Géraud de Cordemoy, 1600–1684." PhR 40: 1931, 221–45. Reprinted: no. 1116, ch. 1.

1122 —: "Louis de la Forge and the critique of substantial forms." PhR 41: 1932, 551–76. Reprinted: no. 1116, ch. 5. See also 463.

1123 —: "Clauberg and the development of occasionalism." PhR 42: 1933, 553–72; 43: 1934, 48–64. Reprinted: no. 1116, ch. 7.

1124 —: "Whitehead, Descartes, and the bifurcation of nature." PhR 31: 1934, 281–97. See 226.

1125 —: "Cartesian doctrine and the animal soul: an incident in the formation of the modern philosophical tradition." SHI, v. 3, 1935, 117–77. Reprinted: no. 1116, ch. 6. See 226.

1126 —: "Some historical steps towards parallelism." PhR 44: 1935. Reprinted: no. 1116, ch. 8.

1127 —: "Cartesian refutations of Spinoza" [Gerdil and Lamy]. PhR 46: 1937, 461–84. Reprinted: no. 1116, ch. 9.

1128 —: "Descartes after three centuries." JP 35: 1938, 169–79. See 23.

1129 —: "Matter and scientific efficiency: I. St. Thomas and the divinity of matter. II. St. Thomas, Descartes and Whitehead." JP 41: 1944, 645–64, 673–85. Reprinted: no. 1116, ch. 10.

1130 —: "Man, Thomistic and Cartesian." RevR 11: 1947, 339–80. Reprinted: no. 1116, ch. 11.

Denies that St. Thomas and Descartes can be sharply opposed to each other in their anthropology. Both conceived man dualistically, and both opposed organic monism. See 431 and Mourant (No. 801) with B.'s refutation, no. 1132.

1131 —: "Concerning the ontological argument." Rmet 7: 1953, 207–24.

Attempts to rehabilitate the argument, by the Third Meditation.

1132 —: "Concerning the Thomistic and Cartesian dualisms." JP 44: 1957, 383–90.

Rejoinder to Mourant's criticism. See 431.

1133 *Baltzer, R.:* "Zur Geschichte des Euler'schen Satzes von den Polyedern und der regulären Sternpolyeder." Ac Berlin, Monatsberichte 1861, 1043–46. [Schrecker]

1134 *Banfi, A.:* "Malebranche et l'Italie." RPFE 125: 1938, 253–74. See 433.

1135 —: "Galilée, Descartes et Vico." Transl. by A. Orsini. Royaumont, 376–92. 1957.

Summary exposition of the "processus corrélatif de développement .... des différentes orientations du savoir – philosophique, scientifique et historique" (376) represented by these three thinkers. No discussion of the Descartes-Vico relationship.

1135a *Bannan, J. F.:* "Contemporary French readings of Descartes." Rmet 13: 1959–60, 412–38. See 22.

1136 *Banovič, Aleksandar:* "Dekartov značaj za pedagogiku. Povodom tristagodišnjice od njegove smrti." Savremena škola (Beograd) 5, no. 1–2: 1950, 27–38.

Descartes as a pedagogue, on the tercentenary of his death. [In Serbian].

1137 *Bar, Adam:* "Kartezjusz w Polsce." KF 19: 1950, 151–60. See 15.

Bibliography of Polish Descartes studies and translations, 1717–1947. Cartesian manuscripts (17th and 18th c.) in Polish libraries.

1138 *Barber, W. H.:* Leibniz in France from Arnauld to Voltaire; a study in French reactions to Leibnizianism, 1670–1760. London, Oxford, Clarendon Press (Cumberledge), 1955, xi, 276 p. See 317.

First part discusses French reactions to Leibniz as critic of Descartes and Voltaire.

1139 *Barberena, F. G.:* "Dos actitudes ante el realismo: Descartes y Santo Tomás." Estudios filosóficos 6: 1957, 187–201.

1140 *Barbier, Alfred:* Trois médecins poitevins au XVIe siècle, ou les origines châtelleraudaises de la famille Descartes. Poitiers, E. Marche, 1897. 201 p. Reprinted from: BSA Ouest, ser. 2, 19: 1897, 51–250 (documentation: 180 250). See 99.

1141 —: Sur le lieu ou est né Descartes (31 mars 1596). Poitiers, Blais & Roy, 1898. 30 p. Reprinted from: BSA Ouest ser. 2, v. 20: 1897, 774–803.

1142 —: René Descartes, sa famille, son lieu de naissance; documents et communications nouveaux. Poitiers, Blais & Roy, 1901. 73 p. Reprinted from: BSA Ouest ser. 3, 8: 1901, 550–76, 618–54. "Suite à celles qui ont paru dans les Mémoires de la Société de l'Ouest, t. 19, sér. 2, 51–250; t. 20, ser. 2, 774–803, 1896–97."

1143 *Bariè, Giovanni Emmanuele:* Descartes. Milano, Garzanto, 1947. 345 p. See 129.

1144 —: "Du cogito cartésien au moi transcendental." RPFE 141: 1951, 211–27.

Tries to eliminate the circle as follows: "Ego cogito et cogito me – ergo sum res cogitans et cogitata – ergo sum." On Descartes, Kant, Hegel.

1145 *Barja, César:* "Descartes .... a distancia." Revista iberoamericana (Mexico) 2: April 1940, 103–20.

1146 *Barjonet, Marjorie:* "Ce qui mourait et ce qui naissait chez Descartes." Pensée ns no. 32: Sept.-Oct. 1950, 21–32. See 150.

1147 *Bark, Friedrich:* Descartes' Lehre von den Leidenschaften, ihre Darstellung nebst einer kritischen Untersuchung der Frage: in welchem Zusammenhange steht jene mit seinen Lehren in der Metaphysik? Rostock, C. Boldtsche, 1892. 66 p. Dissertation Rostock.

1147a *Barry, Robert M.:* "[É. Gilson's] History of Christian philosophy in the Middle Ages." JHI 20: 1959, 105–10.

Questions Gilson's view of medieval philosophy as showing marks of working back to the Middle Ages from Descartes. The real link between medieval and Cartesian thought is extraphilosophical: Descartes' "deep sense of interiority" – he uses the word "je" 583 times in DM – links him to the mystics, as do other parallels, e.g., rigorous control of self which leads to mystical asceticism as well as to scientific objectivity.

1147b *Barrio Gutiérrez, J.:* "Dos pruebas matemáticas para demonstrar la existencia de Dios." RevF 19: 1960, 21–35.

Under the influence of Cartesian method and mathematical progress in the 17th c., mathematical proofs of God's existence flourish. Gives two examples, including Pardies' using asymptotic areas to reinforce Thomistic proof, a metaphysically improper usage.

1148 *Barth, Heinrich:* Descartes' Begründung der Erkenntnis. Bern, Drechsel, 1913. 89 p. Dissertation Bern.

Claims that the foundation of human knowledge in Descartes is not the cogito but the concept of God, disregards D.'s development from the Regulae to MM. The thesis is rejected in M. Solovine's review in RPFE 76: 1913, 220–31. Other reviews in PhdG 5: 1913, 1225.

1149 *Barth, Karl:* Die kirchliche Dogmatik. München, Chr. Kaiser, 1932, v. 1: 401–15. English transl. by G. T. Thomson: The doctrine of the word of God. New York, Scribner, 1936, 1: 222ff., 244ff. See 193a and 1667.

1150 *Barthel, Alexander:* Descartes' Leben und Metaphysik auf Grund der Quellen. Erlangen, Junge & John, 1885. 156 p. Dissertation Erlangen.

1151 *Bartók, Györgi:* "Descartes sorsa Magyarországon." Szellem és Élet (Szeged) 2: 1938, no. 3–4, 69–73.

Descartes' destinies in Hungary. [In Magyar.]

1152 *Barzilay, Jacob:* "René Descartes u' michnate." Hapoël Hatzaïr (Israel), 8, no. 44: 1938, 19–20.

Descartes and his theory. [In Hebrew].

1153 *Barzin, M.:* "Le cogito cartésien." AcBelg (lettres), Bulletin 40: 528–35, 1954.

1154 *Basch, Victor:* "Y-a-t-il une esthétique cartésienne?" CD 2: 67–76. 1937. See 419.

1155 *Bastide, Georges:* "Léon Brunschvicg, lecteur de Descartes et de Pascal." RIP 5: 1951, 78–99.

Review of Brunschvicg, no. 158 and 1390.

1155a —: "Le 'malin génie' et la condition humaine." RMM 63: 1958, 233–45.

The malin génie discloses the rift between a luminous "pensée .... dans l'ordre désincarné des essences, et l'épaisseur concrète d'une action qui reste irrationelle en son fond" (236). The hypothesis thus creates "des intervalles éthiques, dans les diverses dimensions de la philosophie" (243). One more step, and Descartes shades off into Teilhard de Chardin.

1156 *Baudin, Émile:* Études historiques et critiques sur la philosophie de Pascal. Vol. 1: Sa philosophie critique. Pascal et Descartes. Neuchâtel, Baconnière, 1946. iv, 345 p. (Être et pensée, v. 16). See 431a and 1437.

1157 *Baudoin, Abbé E.:* "Histoire de la philosophie." RScR 3: 1923, 349–57.

Descartes and Pascal represent two forms of Augustinism, reunited in Malebranche. Descartes' Augustinism, however, does not start out from revelation, reason being insufficient. [Gerard Milhaud in no. 15, p. 75.]

1158 *Baudoin, Paul:* Les ovales de Descartes et le limaçon de Pascal. Paris, Vuibert, 1938. 144 p. ill. (Mathématique élémentaire).

Review: G.P. in RGSPA 50: 1939, 299–300.

1159 *Baudry, J.:* "Notes en marge du Discours de la méthode." Rhéb 46: Aug. 1937.

1160 *Bauer, Wilhelm:* "Die Bedeutung des Gottesbegriffes bei Descartes." AGP 27 (ns 20): 1914, 89–118.

1161 *Baumann, Julius* [i.e. Johann Julius]: Doctrina cartesiana de vero et falso explicata et examinata. Berlin, Schade, 1863. iv, 94 p. Dissertation Berlin.

1162 —: Die Lehre von Raum, Zeit und Mathematik in der neueren Philosophie. Vol. 1. Berlin, Reimer, 1868, 68–156.

Baumann's treatment of Descartes is criticized and rectified by Natorp (see 221, 147–63).

1163 —: "Dürfen die Regeln für die Leitung des Geistes als gültige Quelle bei der Darstellung cartesianischer Philosophie und Methode gebraucht werden?" ZPPK ns 53: 1868, 189–205.

Regards Regulae as an early stage in D.'s thought, superseded by his published work and therefore invalid in interpretating it.

1164 *Bayer, Raymond:* "Descartes et la pensée contemporaine." BSFP 44, no. 1: 1950, 1–4.

1165 *Bayet, Albert:* "Le tricentenaire du Discours de la méthode." Cahiers rationalistes 59: 1937, 127–50. [Brie 11936]

1166 —: "Le rationalisme métaphysique." Cahiers rationalistes no. 68: 1938, 158–175.

1167 *Bayon, H. P.:* "René Descartes. 1596–1650. A short notice on his part in the history of medicine." Proceedings of the Royal Society of Medicine 43: 1950, 783–85.

1168 *Bazy, Jean-Pierre-Antoine:* Thesis philosophica de Fr. Bacone et Renato Cartesio. Universitas regia, facultas litterarum in Academia Parisiensis. Paris, Veuve Thouau, 1833. 34 p. Thèse Paris.

1169 *Beauduc, L.:* "L'idée de méthode chez Descartes." RCO no. 44, 1937, 641–49. Also in no. 531, p. 3–9.

1170 *Beaulavon, Georges:* "La philosophie de J.-J. Rousseau et l'esprit cartésien." RMM 44: 1937, 325–52.

Slightly adapted version of B.'s introduction to his 1937 edition of Rousseau's La profession de foi, arguing against P. Masson's view of the role of reason in this work. B.'s attempt to inject "l'esprit cartésien" into the discussion is necessarily perfunctory, since he rightly recognizes the thought of D. and Rousseau to be incommensurable.

1171 —: See 515 (Causeries .... 1938).

1172 *Beaussire, E.:* "Étude sur deux étudiants de l'Université de Poitiers: Bacon et Descartes." Mémoires lues à la Sorbonne, 1868, Histoire, 435–52.

1173 *Beccari, Arturo:* "Dell'interpretazione di Cartesio." S 1:1933, 447–53. [Against Guido de Giuli's Cartesio. See 2049].

1174 *Beck, L. J.:* [i.e. Leslie J. Beck]: The method of Descartes, Oxford, Clarendon Press, 1952. x, 316 p. See 198.

1175 —: "Cogitatio in Descartes." Cartesio, 41–52. 1937.

Cogitatio and extensio are both naturae particulares to D., who fails to specify: he "never seems to do more than 'describe' Cogitatio and the best one could say of his description is that it is unsatisfactory" (52).

1176 —: "L'unité de la pensée et de la méthode." Royaumont, 393–411. 1957. See 198.

1177 *Beck, Robert N:* Attacks on the cartesian cogito. Dissertation, Boston University. 1950. Unpublished.

1178 —: "Descartes' cogito reexamined." PPR 14: 1953–54, 212–20.

The cogito is an immediate inference; for Descartes, intuition and deduction are not opposites. Most critics of the cogito misunderstand him – the validity of his formulation of the cogito is incontestable. Brief comment on the cogito critiques of Kant, Huxley, Veitch, Koyré.

1179 *Becker, Oskar:* "Descartes und seine Zeit." In his: "Mathematische Existenz." Jahrbuch für philosophische und phänomenologische Forschung, v. 8, Halle, 1927, 705–14.

1180 —: "Husserl und Descartes." Emge 152–57. 1937.

A summary of Husserl's Cartesian Meditations, pt. 1.

1181 *Beckers, Humbert:* Dissertatio de Cartesii Tractatu de methodo rationem recte utendi et veritatem in scientiis investigandi. Monachii, 1831. [Harvard. Not in BM, BN, Deutscher Gesamtkatalog.]

1181a *Beckett, Samuel:* Whorosope. Paris, The Hours Press, 1930. See 402a.

1182 *Beckmann, Karl:* "Der Wille bei Descartes." AGPs 14: 1909, 43–101.

1183 *Béclère, A.:* "Descartes et la médecine." Bulletin de l'Académie de médecine 118: 1937, 322–37; Extract: "Descartes consultant" in Progrès médical 1937, p. 1781.

1184 *Bedel, M.:* "Descartes, noble homme poitevin." NL, 24 July 1937.

1185 *Beeckman, Isaac:* Journal tenu par I. Beeckman. Ed. Cornelius de Waard. La Haye, Nijhoff, 1939–53. 4 vols. See 80.

1186 *Behn, Irene:* Der Philosoph und die Königin. Renatus Descartes und Christina Wasa. Briefwechsel und Begegnung. Freiburg-München, Alber, 1957. 118 p.

1187 *Belaval, Yvon:* "Descartes selon l'ordre des raisons" (by M. Gueroult). RMM 60: 1955, 417–45. See 170.

1187a —: Leibniz critique de Descartes. Paris, Gallimard, 1960. 560 p. (Bibl. des idées.) See 432.

1188 *Belot, Émile:* L'origine dualiste des mondes: essai de cosmogonie tourbillonnaire. Paris, Gauthier-Villars, 1911. xi, 280 p. See 351.

1189 —: Exposition synthétique de l'origine dualiste des mondes. Cosmogonie tourbillonnaire. Paris, PUF, 1922. 31 p. (Union astronomique internationale. Congrès de Rome, Mai 1922).

1190 —: "Revision du procès fait par Newton à la theorie des tourbillons de Descartes." La Nature, 1 February, 1929.

1191 *Beltrán, Juan Ramón:* "Descartes en la historia de la medicina." Homenaje 3: 89–96. 1937.

1192 *Benda, Julien:* "Descartes devant la pensée contemporaine." Eph ns 5: 1950, 151–55.

Contemporary French philosophy is faithful to Descartes in spirit but not in the letter, influenced less by Cartesian intellectualism than by German insistence on the troubled areas of the soul, from Schelling to Nietzsche and Heidegger. The same holds of French literature and science. See Dollo in S 19: 1951, 137.

1193 *Beneš, Édouard:* "René Descartes et la Bohème." Eur 44, no. 175: 15 July 1937, 415–30. Also in 37.

Descartes in Bohemia (1620–21); Comenius; Cartesianism and philosophical thought in Czechoslovakia (T. G. Masaryk and others). Sympathetic commemorative article by the President of Czechoslovakia, once a student in Paris.

1194 *Beneš, Jaroslav:* "Quomodo Cartesius problema criticum posuerit et solverit." DTP 40: 1937, 472–87. Also in: no. 41, 502–07.

1195 *Beneš, Josef:* Descartesova metoda ve vědách a ve filosofii. Praha, 1936. xiv, 327 p. See 199.

1196 —: "L'importance des Méditations métaphysiques de Descartes au point de vue de sa méthode." CD 1: 3–9. 1937.

See 199 and M. Gueroult in RMM 45: 1938, 109.

1197 *Beneš, Václav Edvard:* Four notes concerning Cartesian metaphysics. (Unpublished.) "Submitted for the Bechtel Prize 1950." Harvard.

1198 *Bénézé, G.:* "Le Congrès Descartes." RMM 45: 1938, 127–43.

Discusses only the non-cartesian papers.

1199 *Bénoit, François:* "Le cartésianisme et l'art français." RHPh 5: 1937, 189–98. See 415.

1200 *Bense, Max:* Descartes und die Folgen. Ein aktueller Traktat. 2nd ed. Krefeld, Agis Verlag, 1955. 64 p. (Augenblick, Supplementband no. 2.) 3rd ed.: Descartes und die Folgen, II. Ein Geräusch in der Strasse. Anhang: Descartes und die Folgen, I. 104 p. See 432a.

1201 *Bergara, Ulises L.:* "La cosmogonía de Descartes." Homenaje 1:341–51. 1937.

1202 *Berger, Alfred A. M. J. Baron von:* "Hielt Descartes die Thiere für bewusstlos?" AcWien, Philos.-hist. Klasse. Sitzungsber. v. 126, Abh. 4. 1892. 18 p.

Spirited apology of Descartes by a humanist-philosopher-jurist-huntsman: Descartes' doctrine of the automatism of brutes is not as unnatural as would appear; he denied animal reason, not animal consciousness. See 276 (Heintel).

1203 *Berger, Gaston:* Le cogito dans la philosophie de Husserl. Paris, Aubier, 1941. See 173.

1204 —: "Pour un retour à Descartes." Eph ns 5: 1950, 156–64.

Modern epistemology is estranged from Cartesianism. A return to Descartes would help achieve a "practical philosophy." See C. Dollo in S 19: 1951, 137–38.

1205 *Berger, Herman:* "Het scepticisme van Socrates en Descartes." ANTWP 45: 1953, 243–49.

1206 *Bergmann, Artur:* Zur Grundlegung des Erkenntnisproblems in der neueren Philosophie. Die Bedeutung der Zweiweltenlehre des Descartes für das Transzendenzproblem der Erkenntnis. Berlin, Juncker & Dünnhaupt, 1937. 110 p. (Neue deutsche Forschungen, Abt. Philosophie, v. 22). Dissertation Berlin.

Against the idealistic interpretation of Cartesian dualism. Traces the subject-object problem from Descartes, Geulincx and Malebranche to Kant. From Nikolai Hartmann's school.

1207 *Bergmann, Ernst:* "Les principaux ouvrages sur Descartes .... en Allemagne." Rsyn 1937. See 15.

All copied from Überweg.

1208 —: "Die Einflüsse der cartesischen Philosophie in Deutschland." CD 3: 105–12. 1937.

From Leibniz to Kant, the German Idealists, and the Neokantians only.

1209 *Bergonzoni, Bernhard:* Descartes and the animals. Poems 1948–1954. London, Platform, 1954. 50 p. See 426.

1210 *Bernhart, Joseph:* "Das Tier bei Descartes und Augustinus." Cartesio, 53–67. 1937.

Engaging sketch. The beast-machine theme merges into a discussion of the animal-man problem within the philosophical anthropology of the two thinkers.

1211 *Berr, Henri:* "1637–1937." Rsyn 14: 1937, 5–6.

1212 —: "L'homme Descartes." Rsyn 63/1: 1948, 5–10.

1213 *Berthé de Besaucèle, Louis:* Les cartésiens d'Italie .... Paris, Picard, 1920. xxiv, 379 p. See 433.

1214 *Berthet, J.:* "La méthode de Descartes avant le Discours." RMM 4: 1896, 399–415. See 237.

1215 *Bertini:* "Schiarimento alla filosofia cartesiana." AcTorino. Memorie, ser. 2, v. 18. [Berthé de Besaucèle]

1216 *Bertolino, Vittorio:* "Attendendo il III centenario del Discorso sul metodo." Afil 6: 1936.

1217 *Bertran Güell, José:* Origens de l'idealisme filosófie modern. Influéncies Lulianes en el sistemo de Descartes. (Preface by A. Thierry). Barcelona, Galve, 1930. 125 p. See 328.

Ch. 1: The combinatory system of Raymond Lull. Ch. 2: Descartes. Ch. 3: The origin of the Cartesian system.

1218 *Bertrand, Joseph:* "Une amie de Descartes: Elisabeth, princesse de Bohème." RDM année 60, pér. 3, v. 102: 1 Nov. 1890, 93–122.

1219 —: "Un ennemi de Descartes: Gisbert Voet." RDM année 61, pér. 3, v. 103: 1 Jan. 1891, 45–67.

Attempts a rehabilitation of Voëtius: Descartes abused the privileges of genius in this controversy.

1220 *Bertrand, René:* Sagesse et chimère. Préface de Jean Cocteau. Paris, Grasset, 1953. 336 p.

Descartes the heretic locked Western thought in a vicious circle from which only Christian Wisdom promises liberation [Bphil 1: 1954, no. 158].

1221 *Bertrand de Saint-Germain, Guillaume Scipion:* Descartes considéré comme physiologiste et comme médecin. Paris, Masson, 1889. xi, 532 p. See 365.

Besaucèle: see Berthé de Besaucèle.

1222 *Bessel-Hagen, E.* "Die Geometrie des Descartes." Semester-Berichte, Mathematisches Seminar, Münster, 14: 1939, 39–70.

Review: J. E. Hoffmann in Jahrb. ü.d. Fortschritte der Mathematik 1941, 13.

1223 *Betancur, C.:* "Descartes." UC Bolivariana (Medellin) 1: 1937, 313–47.

1224 *Beth, E. W.:* "D.'s idee eener mathesis universalis en haar betekenis voor de natuurphilosophie." ANTWP (Suppl.: Annalen der critische philosophie) 31: 1937, 41–50.

Descartes' concept of mathesis universalis and its importance for the philosophy of nature.

1225 —: "Wiskunde, logica en natuurphilosophie op het Congrès Descartes. ANTWP 31: 1937, 130–42.

1226 —: "Le savoir déductif dans la pensée de Descartes." Royaumont, 141–53; discussion, 154–65. 1957.

Makes a sharp distinction between intuitionism and traditional logical formalism. Descartes had already certain notions anticipating modern symbolic logic, but his aversion against traditional syllogistics prevented him from conceiving a universal logic. Gueroult and others (discussion, p. 161) object to the suggested link between Cartesian and Kantian deduction.

1226a —: "Cogito ergo sum: raisonnement ou intuition?" Dialectica 12: 1958, 223–35.

The cogito, being intuitive, is not circular; neither is it plausible. Intuitive proof tends either to be recast in purely logical form, or to be abandoned (e.g. the ontological argument.) Intuitive proof need not be rejected, so long as it is regarded as "acquired evidence" (Paul Bernays) rather than as grounded in "innate ideas."

1227 *Beth, H. J. E.:* "Descartes als mathematicus." ANTWP 42: 1950, 134–44. See 388.

Descartes' method exemplified by his treatment and solution of Pappus' problem.

1228 *Beyer, Charles Jacques:* "Du cartésianisme à la philosophie des lumières". RR 34: 1943, 18–39. See 434.

1229 —: "Comment Descartes combattit Gassendi." PMLA 59: 1944, 446–55. See 116.

1230 —: "Montesquieu et l'esprit cartésien." Congrès Montesquieu, 1955, 159–73. See 435.

1231 "*Bibliografía* sumaria de los estudios cartesianos (1925–1936)." E 37: 1937, 548–56.

Essential literature, with brief Neothomist comment.

1232 *Bierendempfel, Georg:* Descartes als Gegner des Sensualismus und Materialismus. Wolfenbüttel, J. Zwissler, 1884. 77 p. Dissertation Jena.

1233 *Bierens de Haan, David:* "J. J. Stampioen de Jonge en Jacob a Waessenaer." In his: Bouwstoffen voor de geschiedenis der wis- en natuurkundige wetenschappen in de Nederlanden. Amsterdam, J. Miller, 1887, 69–119. Also in: Verslagen en mededeelingen der k.Akad. van wetenschappen, Afd. Natuurkunde, ser. 3, pt. 3.

Document study of the Stampioen-Waessenaer affair.

1234 *Bierens de Haan, Johannes Diderik:* "Cartesius." In his: Hoofdfiguren der geschiedenis van het wijsgeerig denken (tijdperk van Cartesius tot Kant.) Haarlem, F. Bohn, 1921, 1–20. 3rd ed. 1943. (Volksuniversiteitsbibliotheek, v. 9).

1235 —: "Descartes." TW 23: October 1929, 214–26.

Address on the anniversary of D.'s matriculation at Franeker University in 1629.

1236 *Bièvre, C. de:* Descartes et Pascal. Examen critique de leur œuvre scientifique. Brasschatt-Anvers, Impr. de Bièvre, 1956. 69 p. ill.

1237 *Bilharz, Alfons:* Descartes, Hume, Kant. Eine kritische Studie zur Geschichte der Philosophie. Wiesbaden, J. F. Bergmann, 1910. 78 p.

Kant destroyed the rationalist (Cartesian) error of placing thinking before being (hysteron-proteron), but his epistemology failed to go beyond "Vernunft" towards ontogenesis.

Review: M. Schlick in VWPh v. 35, no. 2; PhdG 2: 1910, no. 565.

1238 *Billia, Michelangelo:* "Per l'io di Cartesio e di tutti." RF 3: 1911, 428–32.

Defense of the Cartesian self against the Louvain Neoscholastics. "Étrange par sa forme, mais assez intéressant par son contenu" (Bontadini).

1239 *Binder, F. und G. Jöchner:* "Descartes." Historisch-politische Blätter für das katholische Deutschland (München) 124: 1899, 29–35.

1240 *Binet, Pierre:* "La morale de Descartes. 1. Les premiers essais et les solutions provisoires. 2. Les bases et les fins de la morale. 3. La morale particulière; la sanction. Conclusion." APC: Feb. 1898, 543ff., April 1898, 57–75, May 1898, 191–213.

Important series of articles (H. Gouhier).

1241 *Biot et Feuillet:* Art. "Descartes." In (Michaud's) Biographie universelle, nouvelle éd., v. 10: 1870, 477–83.

1241a *Bizer, Ernst:* "Die reformierte Orthodoxie und der Cartesianismus." ZThK 55: 1958, 306–72. See 435a.

1242 *Bizzarri, Romualdo:* "Il problema gnoseologico in Cartesio." Acta Secundi Congressus Thom. Intern. (see 41), 508–41. 1937.

1243 *Blake, Ralph M.:* "The role of experience in Descartes theory of method." PhR 38: 1929, 125–43, 201–18.

Induction and *deduction* used as synonyms for *inference* by Descartes.

1244 —: "Note on the use of the term 'idée' prior to Descartes." PhR 48: 1939, 532–35.

A certain R. de l'Encre used "idée" for "pensée" 50 years before Descartes.

1245 *Blanchet, Léon:* Les antecédents historiques du "je pense, donc je suis." Paris, Alcan, 1920. 325 p. See 200.

1246 —: "La préparation du cogito cartésien dans la philosophie grecque de l'antiquité." RMM 40: 1933, 187–230. See 200.

1247 *Bloch, A.:* "Descartes et Pascal." VP, 10 January 1922.

1248 *Bloch, Ernst:* "Die chemischen Theorien bei Descartes und den Cartesianern." Isis 1: 1913–14, 590–636. See 352.

1249 *Bloch, Léon:* La physique de Newton. Paris, Alcan, 1908. 642 p. See 357.

1250 *Blond, Jean M. Le.:* "Cartesian method and classical logic." ModSch 15: 1937, 4–6.

Cartesian and Aristotlelic conceptions of science.

1251 —: "De naturis simplicibus apud Cartesium." Acta secundi congressus thom. intern. (see 41), 535–542. 1937.

1252 —: "Les natures simples chez Descartes." Aph 13: 1937, no. 2, 163–80.

Consequences and obscurities of the concept. D.'s methodical mathematicism profoundly modifies logic, and since it leaves aside quantification, it results in a "transformation profonde de la notion même de définition" (p. 170). Agrees with Maritain: Descartes is a "métaphysicien infidèle à la métaphysique" (p. 179).

1253 *Blondel, Maurice:* "Le christianisme de Descartes." RMM 4: 1896, 551–69. See 152.

1254 —: "L'anticartésianisme de Malebranche." RMM 23: 1916, 1–26. See 435b.

1255 —: Une énigme historique: le vinculum substantiale d'après Leibniz et l'ébauche d'un réalisme supérieur. Paris, 1930. xxiv, 145 p.

1256 —: La pensée. Vol. 1, Paris, Alcan, 1934. 216ff. [Critique of the cogito. See M. Giorgianni in S 19: 1951, 316–17.]

1257 —: "La clef de voûte du système cartésien." Cartesio, 69–77. 1937.

The ontological proof, central point of Descartes' system, is not a logical artifice, hence free of the objections to the Anselmian proof. God's omnipotence and immutability holds D.'s metaphysical and scientific edifice together.

Review: M. Giorgiantonio in S 6: 1938, 388–89.

1258 *Blumenfeld, Walter:* "El concepto de origen en la metafísica y en la ciencia." Escritos, 21–47. 1937.

Translated from the German: "Der Begriff des Ursprungs in Metaphysik und Wissenschaft." Philosophia (Belgrade) 3: 1938, 220–51. Not on Descartes.

1259 *Boas, B.:* Über die Bedeutung der inneren Wahrnehmung für die Erkenntnis der Seele bei Descartes, Malebranche und Spinoza. München, Kastner & Callwey, 1924. 64 p. Dissertation München.

1260 *Boas, George:* The happy beast in French thought of the seventeenth century. Baltimore, John Hopkins Press (Oxford UP), 1933. vii, 159 p. (Contributions to the history of primitivism).

Descartes (p. 82–91), Chanet, de la Chambre, etc.

1261 —: "The Ninth International Congress of Philosophy." JP 34: 1937, 561–74.

1262 —: "The role of protophilosophy in intellectual history." JP 45: 1948, 673–84. See 238.

1263 —: "Homage to Descartes." PPR 11: 1950–51, 149–63. See 200a.

Abstract in: Proceedings of the Tenth International Congress of Philosophy (1948).

1264 —: Dominant themes of modern philosophy. New York, Ronald Press, 1957. See 200a.

1265 *Bobba, Romualdo:* Saggio intorno ad alcuni filosofi italiani meno noti prima e dopo la pretesa riforma cartesiana. Benevento, 1860. Also Torino, Loescher, 1868. x, 420 p.

1265a *Bobrov, Je. A.:* "Filosofskie ĕtjudy: I. Dekart." Varšavskija univ. Izvestija. Warsaw, 1911, no. 3, p. 1ff.

1265b *Bobrovnikov:* "Metodologija Dekarta." In: Istoriko-filosofskij sbornik, s predisloviem A. Deborina. Moskva, Komm. Akad., 1925.

1266 *Böhm, Franz:* Anticartesianismus: Deutsche Philosophie im Widerstand. Leipzig, F. Meiner, 1938. vi, 284 p. ("Das Buch erscheint im Descartes-Jahr 1937." Preface.) See 153.

1267 —: "Ewiger Cartesianismus?" Volk im Werden (Frankfurt) 5: 1937, 555–62.

1268 *Boehm, Rudolf:* "Le colloque international sur la philosophie de Descartes à Royaumont." Eph 11: 1956, 92–93. See 42.

1269 *Boer, Julius de:* Descartes (Cartesius). Baarn, Hollandia, 1911. (Grote denkers, ser. 3, no. 2).

1270 *Boetzelaer, W. van:* (Descartes et l'Hollande). BSPF 44/1: 1950, 35–37.

1271 *Bohatec, Josef:* Die cartesianische Scholastik in der Philosophie und reformierten Dogmatik des 17. Jahrhunderts. v. 1. Leipzig, Deichert, 1912. 158 p. See 436.

1272 *Boisdé, Raymond:* Découverte de l'Amérique. Descartes et les États Unis. Paris, Michel, 1949. 78 p. (Collection Descartes. Pour la vérité.)

A French engineer's American travelogue. Descartes serves merely as a jumping-off platform for a discussion of American "méchanisme."

1273 *Bonald, Louis Gabriel Ambroise vicomte de:* Recherches sur les premiers objets des connaissances morales. Paris, Le Clère, 1818. 2 vols. Also in his: Œuvres, 3e éd., Le Clère, 1838, v. 8, 9. – See Ventura d Raulica, no. 3481.

1274 —: "Descartes défendu contre la nouvelle école philosophique." Corr 1853. [Varet]

1275 —: "Du monde indéfini de Descartes." Corr 25 mai 1854. [Schrecker]

1276 —: "Figure du monde: Descartes à l'index." Corr 1854. [Varet]

Bonavino, Cristoforo: see Franchi, Ausonio.

1277 *Bontadini, Gustavo:* Studi sulla filosofia dell'età cartesiana. Brescia, La scuola, 1947. 263 p. See 239.

1278 —: "Les ouvrages italiens sur Descartes ...." Rsyn 14: 1937, 87–97, and in his: Studi (see 1277), 37–45. See 15.

1279 —: "Annotazioni ad alcuni scritti italiani su Cartesio." Cartesio, 85–104. 1937. Also in 1277, 47–69. See 15.

1280 —: "Introduzione al Discorso sul metodo." In his: Studi (see 1277), 9–27. Reprinted from: Cartesio. Il Discorso sul metodo. Introduzione e commentario di G. Bontadini. Brescia, La Scuola, 1938. xxxviii, 115 p. (Collezione Il pensiero.)

Good summary statement of Bontadini's position regarding the phaenomenalism (fenomenismo) of Descartes.

1281 —: "Note cartesiane." (1937). In his: Studi (see 1277), 29–35.

(1) "Il cogito ergo sum: interpretazione dell'ergo." (2) "Il dualismo cartesiano: sua dipendenza dal dualismo gnoseologico." (3) "L'innatismo e la metafisica."

1282 —: "Il fenomenismo razionalistico da Cartesio a Malebranche." In: Malebranche nel terzo centenario della nascità. Milano, Vita e pensiero, 1938 (UCSC; Suppl. speciale, RFNS 30: 1938), 249–77. Also in Bontadini's Studi (see 1277), 71–105.

Olgiati's concept of "fenomenismo razionalistico" elaborated in a Malebranche study which draws all relevant parallels with Descartes.

Review: F. Parlatore in GCFI 1940, 127ff. Bontadini's rejoinder in his: Studi 247–51. See also Sebba, no. 19, p. 44.

1283 —: "A proposito dei concetti di 'realismo' e di 'fenomenismo'." RFNS 32: 1940, 353–66.

1284 —: "L'essenza dell'idealismo come essenza della filosofia moderna. I. Il fenomenismo cartesiano. II. Dualismo gnoseologico e monismo metafisico in Spinoza." RFNS 32: 1940, 548–70; 33: 1942, 158–65. Also in his: Studi (see 1277), 107–37.

The second article discusses the Descartes-Spinoza relationship, the ontological proof, and the cogito.

1285 —: "La critica leibniziana del cartesianismo." (1947). In his: Studi (see 1277), 205–18.

1286 —: "Polemiche sulla interpretazione della filosofia moderna." In his: Studi (see 1277), 219–58.

1. "Polemica con F. Olgiati," 1940, bearing on Descartes criticism. 2. "Repliche a vari autori" (G. Brasca, C. Ferro, C. Giacon, G. di Napoli, G. Soleri and others) on the divergence between Olgiati's and Bontadini's concept of "fenomenismo."

1287 *Boorsch, Jean:* État présent des études sur Descartes. Paris, Les belles lettres, 1937. x, 197 p. Bibliography, 185–96. See 2.

1288 *Boos, R.:* "Descartes in der Geschichte des Lichtes." Goetheanum 10: 1931, 187ff.

From Rudolf Steiner's anthroposophic school.

1289 *Bordas-Demoulin, Jean Baptiste:* Le cartésianisme, ou la véritable rénovation des sciences .... Suivi de la théorie de la substance et de celle de l'infini. Précédé d'un discours sur la réformation de la philosophie au XIXe siècle pour servir d'introduction générale, par F. Huet. 2 vols. Paris, Hetzel, 1843. 320, 475 p. Nouvelle édition, Paris, Gautheir-Villars, 1784. See 437.

1290 *Borelli, P.:* Contributi alla storia della filosofia. Alessandria, tip. L. Viscardi, 1937. 141 p.

Contains a study of Descartes' Traité des passions. [Giraud.]

1291 *Borkenau, Franz:* Der Übergang vom feudalen zum bürgerlichen Weltbild. Studien zur Geschichte der Philosophie der Manufakturperiode. Paris, Alcan, 1934. xx, 559 p. See 154.

1292 *Borne, Étienne:* "Essai sur le dualisme de la doctrine de l'action dans la philosophie cartésienne." Cartesio, 105–27. 1937.

Logic of action vs. logic of thought, provisional vs. definitive morale, générosité vs. sagesse, Cartesianism vs. Christianity.

1293 —: "Du style de la pensée cartésienne." VInt 53: 1937, 408–23.

1294 *Bosmans, H.:* "A propos de la correspondance de Descartes avec Constantijn Huygens. L'auteur principal de l'Onwissen wiskonstenaer J. J. Stampioenius ontdeckt door Jacobus a Waessenaer." RQS ser. 4, 11: 1927, 113–41.

Detailed study of the Stampioen-Waessenaer quarrel. See Thijssen-Schoute, Nederlands Cartesianisme (1954), 74–79 for discussion and rich references to sources.

1295 *Bosseboeuf, Abbé Louis:* "Descartes et son œuvre." BSA Touraine 11: 1897, 1er trim. 47–63.

1296 —: "L'iconographie de Descartes." BSA Touraine 11: 1897, 1er trim., 68–82.

1297 —: "Discours pour la clôture du centenaire de Descartes." BSA Touraine 11: 1897, 1er trim., 83–97.

1298 —: "Les ancêtres de R. Descartes." BSA Touraine 12: 1900, 2e trim., 50–68, 248–64. See 99.

1299 *Botero, F. H.:* "Renato Descartes y su influjo en la filosofía." Revista Javeriana (Bogotá) 8: 1937, 270–76.

1300 *Bouasse, Henri Pierre Maxime:* De la méthode dans les sciences (physique générale). Alcan, 1909.

1301 *Bouché, Abbé Ch.:* Descartes. Reims, 1858. 34 p. [BN]

1302 *Bouchet, Henri:* "Le pseudocartésianisme." ZPF 4: 1950, 483–97. See 25.

1303 *Bouglé, C.:* "Sous le signe de Descartes." [Congrès Descartes.] RPar année 44, 4: 1937, 368–86.

1304 *Bouillier, Francisque* [i.e. Francisque Cyrille]: Histoire de la philosophie cartésienne. 3rd edition. Paris, Delagrave, 1868. 2 vols. viii, 620; 658 p. First edition: Histoire et critique de la révolution cartésienne. Lyon, L. Boitel, 1842. vii, 448 p. Second edition: Paris, Durand, 1854. 2 vols. See 438.

1305 —: Du principe vital et de l'âme pensante, ou examen des diverses doctrines médicales et psychologiques sur les rapports de l'âme et de la vie. Paris, 1862. 431 p.

From Hippocrates to the mid-19th century. On Descartes: Ch. 11, 167–79.

1306 —: "Deux nouveaux historiens de Descartes" (i.e. F. Brunetière and A. Fouillée). RPFE 37: 1894, 287–97. See 442 and Fouillée's rejoinder, RPFE 37: 1894, 535–46.

1307 *Bouilly, Jean-Nicolas:* René Descartes; trait historique en 2 actes et en prose .... Paris, Barba, an IV (1796). [BN] See 114.

1308 *Boulay de la Meurthe, comte Alfred* (ed.): "Translation des restes de Descartes à l'abbaye de Saint-Germain-des-Près. Documents." BSA Touraine 13: 1901, 55–80. Also: Tours, impr. de P. Bousrez, 1901, 28 p.

1309 *Bouligand, G.:* "Les prolongements de la pensée de Descartes en géométrie moderne." Journées universitaires poitevines, April-May 1950, 67–70 (see 553.)

"L'étude de l'outillage qu'utilisent les géomètres non-euclidiens ne fait que confirmer la portée de l'arithmétisation cartésienne de la géométrie" [BAn 1952, 7720].

1310 *Bouquet, H.:* "De Descartes à nous." Temps, 28 March 1937.

Various theories about the pineal gland.

1311 *Bourdeau, J.:* La philosophie affective. Nouveaux courants et nouveaux problèmes dans la philosophie contemporaine. Descartes et Schopenhauer, W. James et Bergson, Ribot, Fouillée, Tolstoi et Leopardi. Alcan 1912. 181 p. BPC.

Philosophy of sentiment against philosophy of mind: Pascal vs. Descartes, Rousseau vs. the Encyclopedists, etc.

Review: Th. Ribot in RPFE 74: 1912/2, 391–92, PhdG 4: 1912 no. 877.

1312 *Bourdon, B.-B.:* De qualitatibus sensibilibus apud Cartesium. Paris, Alcan. 1892. 52 p. Thèse Paris.

1313 *Bourdon, B.:* "La théorie des sensations chez Descartes." JPNP 36: 1939, 321–43.

1314 *Bourquard, L.-C.* (Msgr.): "Descartes. Critique de l'ouvrage de M. L. Liard." Bibliographie catholique 65: 1882, 187–95, 372–80. Also Bray & Retaux, 1882. 22 pp. See 181.

1315 *Boutroux, Émile:* De veritatibus aeternis apud Cartesium. Parisiis, Baillière 1874. 70 p. Thèse Paris. French transl. by G. Canguilhem: Des vérités éternelles chez Descartes; thèse latine. Préface de Léon Brunschvicg. Paris, Alcan, 1927. 146 p. See 201.

1316 —: Études d'histoire de philosophie (1897). Paris, Alcan, 1908. Engl. transl. by Fred Rothwell: Historical studies in philosophy. London. Macmillan, 1912. ("Descartes". 234–54).

Review: L. J. Russell in Mind 22: 1913, 138–40.

1317 —: La philosophie allemande au XVIIIe siècle. Les prédécesseurs de Leibniz: Bacon, Descartes, Hobbes, Spinoza, Malebranche, Locke, et la philosophie de Leibniz. Paris, Vrin, 1929. 243 p. BHP.

1318 —: "Valeur de la métaphysique cartésienne." "La morale provisoire." APC 118 (ns 20), June 1889, 278–88. (Two lectures).

1319 —: "Du rapport de la morale à la science dans la philosophie de Descartes." RMM 4: 1896, 502–11. Also in his: Études (1316), 299–316.

D.'s morale changed from early Stoic morale provisoire to rationalist anthropology (self-perfection of reason through use of the natural mechanism).

1320 —: "Descartes and Cartesianism." In: Cambridge Modern History, v. 4 (1906), ch. 27, 776–99.

1321 *Boutroux, Pierre [Léon]*: L'imagination et les mathématiques selon Descartes. Paris, Alcan, 1900. 45 p. See 353.

1322 —: Les principes de l'analyse mathématique; exposé historique et critique. Hermann, 1914. Vol. 1, passim. See 398.

1323 —: "L'algèbre cartésienne." In his: L'idéal scientifique des mathematiques dans l'antiquité et les temps modernes. (Alcan, 1920). Nouvelle ed. PUF, 1955, 92–110.

Descartes' mathesis universalis was to be "une explication mécanique de l'univers: mais ce n'était point une algèbre" (p. 101). His mathematical activity remained episodic. His break with the tradition of the Greek "virtuoses de la démonstration" marks the difference between him and Fermat. Brilliant assessment of the Cartesian method in mathematics: "c'est l'usine succédant au métier" (p. 110).

1324 —: "Sur la signification de la Géometrie de Descartes." RMM 22: 1914, 814–27. See 355.

1325 —: "L'histoire des principes de dynamique avant Newton." RMM 28: 1921, 657–88. See 354.

1326 *Boutry, Georges-Albert*: "Pascaliens et cartésiens: deux aspects de la théorie physique." LTP 2: 1946, 36–48.

Descartes and Pascal at opposite ends in their methodical treatment of physics and metaphysics.

1327 *Bouttier, Louis*: "Descartes y la ciencia positiva." Homenaje 3: 1937, 349–58.

1328 *Bouvier, Robert*: "Descartes s'est-il contredit?" Rsyn 63: 1948,, 86–98.

On Sartre, Lefebvre, Mury.

1329 *Bouvy, Eugène:* De Vico, Cartesii adversario. Thèse Paris. 1889. 67 p. See 461.

1330 *Bouwsma, O. K.:* "Descartes' scepticism of the senses." Mind 54: 1945, 312–23.

"Wittgenstein goes to work on Descartes with wit and charm" (Morgan.)

1331 —: "Descartes' evil genius." PhR 58: 1949, 141–51. Abstract in: Proceedings, Tenth Intern. Congr. of Philos., Amsterdam, 1949, v. 2, 1122–24.

Another "exercise in language," exorcizing the poor "malin génie" by finding his deception indistinguishable from non-deception, except in name.

1332 *Bowman, Archibald Allen:* A sacramental universe. Being s study in the metaphysics of experience. Princeton UP (Oxford UP), 1939. xxviii, 428 p. See 155.

1333 *Boy* [i.e.T. Zeleński]: Descartes. In his: Mózg i pleć. Warszawa, 1926, 223–52.

Boyce Gibson: see Gibson, A. Boyce.

1334 *Boyer, Carl B.:* History of analytic geometry. New York, Scripta Mathematica at Yeshiva University, 1956. ix, 291 p. (Scripta Mathematica Studies, no. 6, 7.) See 355a.

1334a —: "Analytic geometry: the discovery of Fermat and Descartes." The Mathematics Teacher 37: 1944, 99–105.

1334b —: "Descartes and the geometrization of algebra." Amer. Mathem. Monthly 66: 1959, 390–93. See 355a.

1335 —: The rainbow. From myth to mathematics. New York-London, Thomas Yoseloff, 1959. See 356.

1335a —: "Descartes and the radius of the rainbow." Isis 43: 1952, 95–98. See 356.

1335b —: "The theory of the rainbow: medieval triumph and failure." Isis 49: 1958, 378–90. See 356.

1336 *Boyer, Charles (S.J.):* "Le cogito dans Saint Augustin." Cartesio, 79–83, 1937, and CD 1: 89–92, 1937.

Cartesian cogito lacks the immediate link between the act of understanding and its ontological conditions: St. Augustine's leaves man his proper reality, shows him oriented towards his Creator.

Review: M. Giorgiantonio in S 6: 1938, 389.

1337 —: L'idée de vérité dans la philosophie de S. Augustin. Paris, Beauchaisne, 1920. 272 p. Thèse Paris. 2nd ed., rev., 1940, 310 p. (Bibl. des Arch. de Ph.)

Ch. 1 on doubt and cogito in St. Augustine and Descartes.

1338 *Braccialini, Salvadore:* "Cartesio e Leibniz. Quantità di moto e forze vive." Politecnico, Jan. 1929. Also: Milano, Vallardi, 1929. ()

1339 *Bradish, Norman C.:* "John Sergeant, a forgotten critic of Descartes and Locke." Monist 39: 1929, 571–628.

Text of Sergeant's "Non ultra: or a Letter to a Learned Cartesian: Settling the Rule of Truth, and First Principles, Upon their Deepest Grounds .... London, printed for A. Roper, 1698," p. 593–628, with an account of Sergeant and his polemics, including his attacks on Descartes and Anthony Le Grand in 1696 and 1698.

1340 *Bradlaugh, Charles, et al.:* Biographies of ancient and modern celebrated freethinkers, reprinted from an English work entitled "Half-hours with the freethinkers" by "Iconoclast," (Anthony) Collins and (John) Watts. New York, P. Eckler (Boston, Mendum), 1871. 344 p.

1341 *Bradshaw, Marion John:* "Descartes: the great dualist." In his: Philosophical foundations of faith. A contribution towards a philosophy of religion (Hazen Lectures). New York, Columbia UP, 1941, 21–62.

1342 *Braham, Ernest Goodall:* The problem of the self and immortality; an estimate and criticism of the subject from Descartes to Kant. London, Epworth Press, 1925. xii, 208 p.

1343 *Branberger, Jan:* René Descartes, filosof hudby .... V Praze, Urbánek, 1933. 74 p. See 418.

1344 *Brasca, Giancarlo:* "Intorno a due diverse concezioni della filosofia moderna." RFNS 35: 1943, 220–40. See 1277.

1345 *Brattle, William:* Compendium logicae secundum principia Renati Cartesii .... Bostoni, J. Draper, 1758. 60 p. See 440.

1346 *Braure, M.:* "Descartes et les sciences de l'homme: érudition, histoire et politique." RHPh ns 5: 1937, 181–88.

1347 *Bray, René:* La formation de la doctrine classique en France. Paris, 1927. See 412.

1348 *Breen, J. C.:* "De woning van Descartes op de Westermarkt (te Amsterdam)." De Amsterdammer (Weekly), October 9, 1920.

See also Pos-Steenberghen (Rsyn 1937, p. 112–13, items 11 a, b, c) on Descartes in Amsterdam.

1349 *Bréhier, Émilie:* Histoire de la philosophie moderne: Descartes. Notes prises .... au cours professé .... par É. Bréhier. Fasc. 1, 2, 3. Paris, R. Gouillon, 1929. 61 p. (See 1350).

1350 —: Histoire de la philosophie, v. 2: La philosophie moderne. Fasc. 1: Le dix-septième siècle. Paris, Alcan, 1929. Reprinted: PUF, 1950. Bibliography.

Ch. 3: "Descartes et le cartésianisme," 46–128.

1351 —: La philosophie et son passé. Paris, Alcan (PUF), 1940. (Nouvelle encyclopédie philosophique, v. 24). See 241.

1352 —: "Descartes d'après le P. Laberthonnière." RMM 42: 1935, 533–47. See 177.

1352a —: "Matière cartésienne et création." RMM 44: 1937, 21–34. See 241.

1353 —: "La création des vérités éternelles dans le système de Descartes." RPFE 123: 1937, 15–29; and in his: La philosophie et son passé. See 241.

1354 —: "La création continue chez Descartes." S 5: 1937, 3–10; and in his: La philosophie et son passé. See 241.

1355 —: See 525 (L'esprit cartésien, 1937).

1356 —: "Les lectures malebranchistes de Rousseau." RIP 1: 1938, 98–120.

Adds to the evidence of influence upon Rousseau through Malebranche and Bernard Lamy, indirect sources of some of his knowledge of Descartes.

1357 —: See 515 (Causeries).

1358 —: "La langue française et la philosophie." In: L'homme. Métaphysique et conscience de soi. Neuchâtel, Baconnière, August 1947, 9–15 (Être et penser, v. 27).

Descartes and Voltaire.

1359 —: "Une forme archaïque du cogito ergo sum." RPFE 67: 1942–43, 143–44. See 200.

1360 *Brémond, André (S.J.):* "Quelques essais de 'religion' rationaliste." Aph 8, no. 4: 1931, 60–117. See 24.

1361 *Brentano, Franz:* "Über das cartesianische 'clare et distincte percipere'." In his: Psychologie vom empirischen Standpunkt, v. 3: Vom sinnlichen und noetischen Bewusstsein. (Ed. Oskar Kraus). Leipzig, Meiner, 1928. (First volume: 1874).

1362 *Bretall, Robert W.:* "Descartes – rationalist and mystic." Christendom (Chicago) 3: 1938, 240–48.

1363 *Brett, George Sidney:* "Descartes." In: Brett's history of psychology (1921). 2nd edition, abridged by R. S. Peters. London, Allen & Unwin, 1953, 359–66. (Muirhead's library of philosophy and psychology.)

English standard history of psychology. Finds no unity in D.'s psychological doctrines; in his view of man he "belongs to the last phase of the medieval tradition" (367). Editor's extensive note (345–48) lists the Cartesian heritage as "dualism, atomism, 'psychologism', introspectionism, intellectualism, mechanical physiology"; D.'s revolt against Aristotle may have done more harm than good to psychology.

1364 *Bridoux, André* (editor): Descartes. Œuvres et lettres. Bibl. de la Pléïade. 1952. See 76.

1365 —: "La générosité chez Descartes." BSPF 44/1: 1950, 5–9.

1366 *British Museum:* General catalogue of printed books, v. 51. London, 1954. "Descartes," 224–57. See 3.

1367 *Broad, C. D.:* "The new philosophy: Bruno to Descartes." Cambridge Historical Journal 8: 1944–45, 36–54.

"Elementary review of Scholasticism, Galileo, Descartes" (Morgan.)

1368 *Brochard, Victor:* De l'erreur. Paris, Beyer-Levrault, 1879. 211 p. 2e éd. Alcan, 1897.

Ch. 2, 3 on Descartes and Spinoza.

1369 —: Études de philosophie ancienne et de philosophie moderne. Recueillies et précédées d'une introduction par Victor Delbos. Paris, Alcan, 1912. Reprinted: Vrin, 1954. xxviii, 562 p. (BHP)

Contains nos. 1370 and 1371, and an obituary appreciation of F. Bouillier (p. 541–59).

Reviews: APC 14: 1911/2, 445ff.; G. Huit in RdePh 20: 1913, 639ff; L. Robin in RPFE 74: 1912, 172–79.

1370 —: "Descartes stoïcien. Contribution à l'histoire de la philosophie cartésienne." RPFE 1: 1880, 548–52, and in his: Études (see 1369), 320–27.

Brief but important summary of what Descartes owes to the Stoics.

1371 —: "Le Traité des passions de Descartes et l'Éthique de Spinoza." RMM 4: 1896, 512–16, and in his: Études (see 1369), 327–31.)

Descartes' TP contains the seminal idea of Spinoza's Ethics which, without it, might not have come into existence.

1372 *Brock, Erich:* "Die Maximen des Descartes." Hochland (München) 35, no. 1: 1937–38, 113–20.

1373 *Brockdorff, Cay* [i.e. Ludwig Georg Conrad] *Baron von:* Descartes und die Fortbildung der kartesianischen Lehre. Munchen, Reinhardt, 1923. 227 p. See 441.

1374 —: "Descartes et les lumières françaises." RMM 44: 1937, 305–24.

Rich study in the history of ideas, from Condillac and d'Alembert to Rousseau, Condorcet and early 19th century probabilism. More valuable for the material and its handling than for the conclusions.

1375 *Brown, Harcourt:* "The utilitarian motive in the age of Descartes." AnSci 1: 182–92.

1376 *Brown, Sarah:* "The fundamental postulates of the Cartesian systems." CD 1: 10–16. 1937.

A logical inquiry into "Cartesian systems."

1376a *Bruch, Jean-Louis:* "La méthode de M. Gueroult et son application à la philosophie de Malebranche." RMM 63: 1958, 358–73.

Gueroult's method of structural analysis perfectly fits the case of Descartes; tested in the application to Malebranche, it shows its limitations as well as its strength. See 170.

1377 *Brucker, Jacob:* Historia critica philosophiae. Lipsiae, 1743, 1764. See 441a.

1377a *Brüning, Walter:* "Möglichkeiten und Grenzen des methodischen Zweifels bei Descartes." ZPF 14: 1960, 536–52.

Questions the radicality of D.'s doubt: it is merely an attempt at doubting (Zweifelsversuch). The existential assertion is not the only indubitable result of the cogito, since the existence of some object distinct from the self emerges as equally indubitable. "Utmost certainty" can be obtained only through a step-by-step critico-phenomenological analysis, not from D.'s deductive-constructive method; and "absolute certainty" is unattainable altogether, as D.'s own "Zweifelsversuch" demonstrates.

1378 *Brugmans, Henri L.:* Le séjour de Christian Huygens à Paris et ses relations avec les milieux scientifiques français. Suivi de son journal de voyage à Paris et Londres. P. André, 1935. 200 p. Thèse Paris.

1379 —: "Descartes et les pasteurs de Hollande." RLC 17: 1937, 498–521.

Brief, well-documented introduction to Descartes and his influence in Holland; many source references.

1380 *Brunet, Pierre:* L'introduction des théories de Newton en France au XVIIIe siècle. v. 1: Avant 1738. Paris, Blanchard, 1931. viii, 366 p. See 357.

1381 *Brunetière, Ferdinand:* "Jansénistes et cartésiens." In his: Études critiques sur l'histoire de la littérature française, sér. 4. Paris, Hachette, 1899, 111–78. See 442.

1382 —: "Descartes et la littérature classique." *Ibid.*, sér. 3, 1–28. See 442.

1383 —: "Jansénistes et cartésiens." In his: Histoire de la littérature française classique, 1515–1830. Vol. 2, Delagrave 1912, ch. 13. See 442.

1384 *Brunner, A.:* "Descartes und sein Erbe." Stimmen der Zeit 132: 1937, 273–83.

1385 *Bruno, Antonio:* Cartesio e l'Illuminismo. Bari, Laterza, 1949. 56 p. See 443.

1386 —: "Il limiti del razionalismo cartesiano nel problema morale." Siculorum Gymnasium (Catania) 10: 1957, 57–81.

1387 *Brunschvicg, Léon:* Écrits philosophiques. V. 1. Paris, PUF, 1941, 11–107. See 159.

1388 —: Spinoza et ses contemporains. 3e éd. Paris, Alcan, 1923, 239–305. Reprinted 1951. See 156.

1389 —: Descartes. Paris, Rieder, 1937. 97 p., 32 pl. (Maîtres des littératures). See 131.

1390 —: "Descartes." In his: Descartes et Pascal, lecteurs de Montaigne. Neuchâtel, Baconnière, 1942, p. 95–133 (Être et penser, v. 12, reprinted

1945). Also New York, Brentano, 1944, with biographical sketch of Brunschvicg by Robert Tenger. See 158.

1391 —: "La révolution cartésienne et la notion spinoziste de la substance." RMM 12: 1904, 755–98. Also in his: Spinoza et ses contemporains (see 156), ch. 9.

1392 —: Les étapes de la philosophie mathématique. Paris, 1912. See 358.

1393 —: "Descartes et Pascal." In: Nature et liberté (Paris, Flammarion, 1921), pt. 1, 13–35. Also in his: Écrits (see 159), 92–106, bibliographical references p. 106.

Probing their "opposition intégrale," Brunschvicg finds that "Pascal croit à la science autant que Descartes croit à la religion"; but their systems clasj, as they try to meet problems as pressing and harsh today as they were in their time.

1394 —: L'expérience humaine et la causalité physique. Alcan, 1922. xvi, 625 p. BPC.

1395 —: "Descartes." In: La tradition philosophique et la pensée moderne française. Paris, Alcan, 1922, 48–58.

1396 —: "Mathématique et métaphysique chez Descartes." RMM 34: 1927, 277–324. Also in his: Écrits (see 159), 11–54; bibliographical references p. 106.

Broad discussion of Gilson's Commentary to DM (see 83) serves as basis for developing Brunschvicg's own interpretation of Descartes' Method in mathematics and metaphysics.

1397 —: Le progrès de la conscience dans la philosophie occidentale. Paris, Alcan, 1927, 139–61. 2nd ed., PUF 1953. See 157.

1398 —: "Platon et Descartes." TW 1929, 113–26. Also in his: Écrits (see 159), 81–91; bibliographical references p. 107.

Without any direct filiation, Plato and Descartes represent, in turn, the "dialectical hope" of mathematical idealism, and its triumphant realization.

1399 —: De la connaissance de soi. Alcan, 1931. xi, 196 p. [1929–30 Sorbonne lectures, not directly concerned with Descartes].

1400 —: Les âges de l'intelligence. Paris, Alcan, 1934. (Nouvelle encyclopédie française).

On Descartes see p. 69–71, 87–99.

1401 —: "La pensée intuitive chez Descartes et chez les cartésiens" RMM 44: 1937, 1–20. Also in his: Écrits (see 159), 55–72; bibliographical references p. 106–07.

On "intuition" in Descartes, Malebranche, Spinoza.

1402 —: "Note sur l'epistémologie cartésienne." RPFE 123: 1937, 30–38. Also in his: Écrits (see 159), 73–80; bibliographical references p. 107.

Cartesian epistemology vs. Cartesian mechanism; Descartes' method is reductive rather than inductive (Bachelard's formula). Stresses Descartes' awareness of the unlimited fecundity of the double process of analytical decomposition and intellectual reconstruction. Contrasts the intuitive unity of system as D. should have seen it with the dismaying "dimorphism" of the philosophy he actually developped.

1403 —: "La méthode cartésienne. Discours prononcé à Amsterdam, le 8 mai 1937." ANTWP, 31: 1937, 1–7. Also in his: Écrits (see 159), 305–12.

1404 —: "Le troisième centenaire du Discours de la méthode." Philosophia (Belgrade) 2: 1937, 245–51. Also in his: Écrits (see 159), 313–17.

1405 —: "Le IXe Congrès international de philosophie." RMM 45: 1938, 1–7. (Presidential address).

1406 —: See 515 (Causeries).

1406a *Brunschwicg, Jacques:* 'La preuve ontologique interprétée par M. Gueroult." RPFE 150: 1960, 251–65. See 270, 270a, 3104c.

1407 *Bruyne, Edgar de:* "De la réflexion intellectuelle à la conscience morale." Cartesio 249–57. 1937.

Independent meditation on the cogito as "le sentiment vital le plus profondément et le plus parfaitement mien" (p. 252), "le plaisir étrange et métaphysique d'être soi, même vis-à-vis du vrai" (p. 253).

1408 —: "In het teken van Descartes?" In: Gedenkboek uitgegeven naar aanleiding van het tienjarig bestaan van de philosophische Bibliotheek, 1927–1937. Antwerpen, Brussel, Standaard-Boekhandel, 1937, 27–39.

1409 *Budde, Enno:* Die Beweise für das Dasein Gottes von Anselm von Canterbury bis zu René Descartes. Erlangen, E. T. Jacob, 1898. 45 p. Diss. Erlangen.

1410 *Buddeberg, Karl Theodor:* "Descartes und der politische Absolutismus. Die politischen Konsequenzen des theoretischen Nominalismu s.' Emge, 77–96. 1937.

The absolute monarch is the Cartesian God transposed into the world of politics.

Buenos Aires. Universidad Nacional. Homenaje (1937). See 40.

1411 *Bullón y Fernández, Eloy:* De los orígines de la filosofía moderna .... Salamanca, Calatrava, 1905. See 449.

1412 *Bunge, Mario:* "Do computers think?" BJPS 7: 1956–57, 139–48, 212–19. Attack on cybernetics. See R. O. Kapp, T. R. Miles, T. S. Szasz (No. 3380).

1413 *Burkamp, Wilhelm:* "Das denkende Ich bei Descartes." Emge, 3–26, 1937. See 288.

Shows the importance of D's thinking-self concept for a theory of knowledge which, like Kant's and Fichte's, is opposed to the Aristotle-to-Husserl standpoint which admits absolute evidence. But Descartes, unlike the German Idealists, rejects a transcendental self.

1414 *Burke, Henry R.:* "Substance and accident in the philosophy of Descartes." NSch 10: 1936, 338–382.

1414a *Burkhill, T. A.:* "L'attitude subjectiviste et ses dangers, de Descartes à Bergson." RPFE 149: 1959, 325–37.

Critique of subjectivist tendencies in Locke, Berkeley, Kant, Bergson. Descartes' methodological separation of self and nature resulted in an isolation of ideas from nature and in the idealistic subjugation of nature. His insistence on clear and distinct ideas produced a misinterpretation of the status and function of conscious perception. Experience is not composed of an infinity of discrete elements but of an a priori causal continuity of events, a continuity which is no more subjective than the events themselves.

1415 *Burnego, G.:* "Il metodo cartesiano nell'insegnamento medio." Bolletino di matematica 23: 1927, 29–40. [Schrecker]

1416 *Burns, C. Delisle:* "Leibniz and Descartes." Monist 26: 1916, 524–33.

Claims that Leibniz depended on Descartes for his conceptions of method, his psychology, and for Cartesian mechanism in science.

1417 *Burtt, Edwin Arthur:* "Descartes". In his: The metaphysical foundations of modern physical science. A historical and critical essay. New York,

Harcourt, Brace, 1925. 2nd. ed., revised: London, Routledge and Kegan Paul, 1932 (reprinted 1950), p. 96–116. (ILPP). Reprinted: New York, Doubleday-Anchor, 1954.

1418 *Bury, John Bagnell:* "Cartesianism." Ch. 3 of his: The idea of progress. London, Macmillan, 1920. Also: New York, Macmillan, 1932, p. 64–77.

Though Cartesianism developed no concept of progress as such, it opened the road to it by declaring the independence of man and causing the old theories of degeneration to be abandoned. Chief emphasis on Malebranche and Leibniz.

1419 *Busco, Pierre:* Les cosmogonies modernes et la théorie de la connaissance. Paris, Alcan, 1924. 436 p. See 359.

1420 *Bush, Wendell T.:* "A factor in the genesis of idealism." In: Essays philosophical and psychological in honor of William James. New York, Longmans Green, 1908. [Balz]

1421 *Busnelli, Giovanni (S.J.):* "Il metodo cartesiano e il metodo aristotelico." Cartesio 139–173. 1937.

1422 *Buss, E.:* "Montesquieu und Cartesius." Philosophische Monatshefte 4, no. 1: 1869–70, 1–38. See 445.

1423 *Busson, Henri:* La pensée religieuse française de Charron à Pascal. Paris, Vrin, 1933. Bibliography 615–42. See 446.

1424 —: La religion des classiques (1660–85). Paris, PUF, 1948. 476 p. Bibliography 427–62. See 447.

1425 *Busto, Jorge del:* "Descartes y la escolastica." RUC Perú 13: 1945, 41–54.

1426 *Bustos, C.:* "Un Descartes falsificado. Estudio critico sobre los Études sur Descartes de Laberthonnière." E 57: 1937, 531–40. See 177.

1426a *Bykhovski, Bernard Emanulovič:* "Dekart i religija." Pod znamenem Marksizma, no. 7, 1937.

D. and religion. [In Russian.]

1426b —: "Metafizika Dekarta." *Ibid.*, nr. 8, 1937. [In Russian.]

1426c —: "Filosofskie osnovy fiziki Dekarta." Front nauki i tekhniki, no. 5, 1937.

The philosophical foundation of D.'s physics. [In Russian.]

1426d —: "Metodologija Dekarta (K 300-letiju Rassuždenija o metode.)" *Ibid.*, nr. 7, 1937.

D.'s methodology. On the tercentenary of DM. [In Russian.]

C

1427 *Caballeria, J. M. (S.J.):* "Lo mesurable como objeto de la física." Cartesio, 185–89. 1937.

Cartesian quantification of reality makes the quantifiable the sole object of physics, as it still is for Einstein and Heisenberg.

1428 *Cabanès, Auguste:* "Descartes." In his: Médecins amateurs. Paris, Michel, 1932. 382 p.

1429 *Cabannes, Jean:* Allocution. BSPF 44/1: 1950, 27–34. [Descartes and experimental science.]

429a *Cabeen, D. C.* (general editor): A critical bibliography of French literature, Vol. 3: The seventeenth century, ed. Nathan Edelman. Syracuse UP, 1960. See 3a.

1430 *Caes, P.:* "De Descartes à Sartre." SynB 7: 1952, no. 78, 33–42. (Review of Sartre, see 192).

1430a *Cahiers du Cercle Descartes.* Paris, Maupoint, 1937 (published 1938). 16mo. 44 p. See 516.

1431 *Caillat, Jules:* "La méthode scientifique de Pascal." RHL 30: 1923, 129–62, 273–99.

Comparison between Pascal's and Descartes' scientific method.

1432 *Caird, Edward:* "Cartesianism." In his: Essays on literature and philosophy. Glasgow, Maclehose (New York, Macmillan), 1892, v. 2, 267–383. Italian transl. by M. C. Bombelli: Il cartesianismo. Firenze, Nuova Italia, 1933. See 202.

1433 —: Art. "Cartesianism." Encycl. Britannica, 11th ed. See 202.

1434 *Cairola, Giovanni:* Scritti. Torino, Taylor, 1954. 303 p.

Contains historical studies of Descartes (Bph 2, no. 2).

1435 *Cajori, Florian:* "Ce que Newton doit à Descartes. " L'enseignement mathématique 25: 1926, no. 1–3, 7–11.

1436 *Callot, Émile:* Problèmes du cartésianisme. Descartes, Malebranche, Spinoza. Annecy, Gardet, 1956. 280 p. ("Descartes," 11–177). See 447a.

1436a —: "La position capitale de Montaigne, Descartes and Pascal." In his: Questions de doctrine et d'histoire de la philosophie. Vol. 1: Questions générales d'histoire. Annecy, Gardet, 1959. 254 p.

See also Vol. 2 (Questions spéciales) on the notion of space from Descartes to Kant.

1437 *Calvetti, C.:* "In margine ad un'opera su Pascal e Descartes." RFNS 40: 1949, 247–51. [É. Baudin's Études historiques, no. 1156].

1438 *Calzetti, Hugo:* "La influencia del pensamiento cartesiano en el hacer pedagógico moderno." Homenaje 2: 235–60. 1937. See 265.

1438a *Camón Aznar, José:* "Descartes entre el trentino y el barroco." Revista de ideas estéticas 15: 1957, 109–19.

With Descartes, philosophy begins to discard problems concerning the things themselves, in favor of the instrument of knowledge of things. The artist, instead of presenting objects in their concrete value, tries to reproduce the relationship between forms, utilizing light, atmosphere, and above all movement. [Bsig 1958, no. 9201.]

1439 [*Campailla.*] "Tommaso Campailla, filosofo cartesiano." In: Acta Secundi Congr. Thom. Intern., 543–54 (Acta Pontificae Academiae Romanae ns 3: 1938). See 41.

T. Campailla, 1668–1740, author of the Cartesian poem "Adamo, ovvero il mondo creato" (Catania 1709) and of scientific writings on physics (against Newton), on animal motion, etc.

1440 *Campo, Mariano:* "La filosofia di Descartes ed il suo significato. A proposito del volume di Olgiati" (see 14). RFNS 26: 1934, 386–401.

1441 *Canguilhem, Georges:* "Descartes et la technique." CD 2: 77–85. 1937.

Thoughtful reassessment of Descartes' thoughts about the relation of theory and technology (knowledge convertible into technological action, but with significant restrictions). Penetrating closing remarks on the reason why Descartes does not have "une théorie de la création, c'est-à-dire au fond une esthétique" (p. 85).

1442 —: La formation du concept de réflexe au XVIIe et XVIIIe siècles." Paris, PUF, 1955, 27–57. See 360.

1443 —: "Organisme et modèles mécaniques: Réflexions sur la biologie cartésienne. I. De l'union de l'âme et du corps, et du sentiment, dans la philosophie de Descartes, selon M. Gueroult" (see 170). RPFE 80: 1955, 281–99. (Pt. II, "L'organisme et ses modèles" promised but not published).

Discussing Gueroult's v. 2 (on the Sixth Meditation), Canguilhem analyzes the problem of the conditions of biological individuation in Cartesian man and in the animal as developed in Gueroult's analysis. See 170.

1444 *Cannabrava, Euryalo:* Descartes e Bergson. São Paulo, Amigos do livro, 1942, 33–99. See 203.

1445 *Cantecor, G.:* "La vocation Descartes." RPFE 96: 1923, 372–400. See 93.

1446 —: "A quelle date Descartes a-t-il écrit la Recherche de la vérité?" RHPh 2: 1928, 254–89. See 242.

1447 —: "L'oisive adolescence de Descartes. Études cartésiennes." RHPh 4: 1930, 1–38, 354–96. See 93.

1448 *Cantor, Moritz:* "Descartes und Fermat." In his: Vorlesungen über Geschichte der Mathematik. Leibniz, Teubner, 1892, v. 2, 851–76.

1449 *Capello, Francisco:* "Reflexiones sobre Descartes." Homenaje 2: 67–78. 1937.

Today philosophy tends to speak in analogies and metaphors, another proof that the world is coming to an end: "uno de los signos que da el Apocalipsis es que habrá hombres que echen humo de la boca, y no es probable que aluda a los cigarrillos" (78). As to Descartes, he is farther from our philosophy and "menos renacentista" than Aristotle himself.

1450 *Capone-Braga, Gaetano:* "Il valore del cogito." Afil 5: 1935, 13–20.

If the cogito can serve as starting point of philosophical inquiry, it cannot be the origin from which all the rest of the Cartesian system can be deduced: "Descartes, comme S. Augustin, le dépasse en se fondant sur l'idée de Dieu" (Bontadini, Rsyn 1937, p. 95.)

1451 —: La filosofia francese e italiana del settecento. 2nd ed. Padova, CEDAM. Vol. 1, 1941, 322 p. Vol. 2, 1942, 307 p.

1452 *Carabellese, Pantaleo:* Le obbiezioni al cartesianesimo. Messina, d'Anna, 1946. 3 vols. BCM. See 204.

1453 —: Da Cartesio a Rosmini. Fondazione storica dell'ontologismo critico. Firenze, Sansoni, 1946. 308 p. See 204.

1454 —: "Il circolo vizioso di Cartesio." AcLincei, scienze morali. Rendiconti ser. 6, 13: 1937, 471–532. Also in his: Da Cartesio a Rosmini. See 204a.

1455 —: "La riconquesta del cartesianismo." In: Augusto Guzzo (ed.), L'attualità dei filosofi classici. Milano, Bocca, 1942, 1–20. Also in his: Da Cartesio a Rosmini. See 204a.

1456 —: L'idealismo italiano. (1938). 2nd ed., rev. and augm. Roma, Edizione italiane, 1946.
Section on Descartes and Vico (2nd edition only).

1457 *Carbia, Rómulo D.:* "Descartes en la cultura colonial de America." Homenaje 3: 35–40. 1937. See 448.

1458 *Carbonara, Cleto:* Renato Cartesio e la tradizione ontologica. Torino, Società editrice internazionale (SEI), 1945. 169 p. See 205.

1459 —: Scienza e filosofia ai principi dell'età moderna: Galilei, Bacone, Cartesio. Napoli, Perella, 1935, 117–260. (Biblioteca di filosofia, ed. A. Aliotta). Also in his: Renato Cartesio (see 205).

1460 —: "Riflessione e trascendenza in Cartesio." CD 1: 93–98. 1937. Also in his: Renato Cartesio (see 205.)

1461 *Carlini, Armando:* Il problema di Cartesio. Bari, Laterza, 1948. 194 p. BCM, v. 452. See 4.

1462 —: "Le interpretazioni di Cartesio." Gmet 1: 1946, 114–28, 188–203. Also in his: Il problema (see 4), 1–59.

1463 —: "Il metodo cartesiano nelle Regulae e nel Discorso." Gmet 1: 1946, 375–93. Also in his: Il problema (see 4), 64–98.

1464 *Carr, Herbert Wildon:* Descartes and the rise of modern philosophy. A lecture .... Liverpool, C. Tinling, (1923). 20 p. [BM]

1465 —: "The scientific concept of reality. I. Copernicus and Descartes. II. Leibniz and Newton." Pers 16: 1935, 146–56, 241–48.

1466 *Carrau, Ludovico:* Exposition critique de la théorie des passions dans Descartes, Malebranche et Spinoza. Strasbourg, Silbermann, 1870. 300 p. Thèse Paris.

1467 *Carré, J.-R.:* "Le bon sens d'un gentilhomme poitevin, René Descartes." Univ. de Poitiers, Faculté des lettres. Mélanges .... publiés à l'occasion du centenaire de sa restauration, 1946, 37–56. (Publications de l'Université de Poitiers, v. 10).

1468 *Carruccio, Ettore:* "La matematica nel pensiero di Cartesio." Rivista di matematica della U. di Parma, 1951, no. 2, 133–152.

1469 *Cartan, Élie:* "Le rôle de la géometrie analytique dans l'évolution de la géometrie." CD 6: 147–53. 1937.

1470 *Carteron, Henri:* "L'idée de la force mécanique dans le système de Descartes." RPFE 94: 1922, 243–77, 483–511. See 361.

1470a *CARTESIO* nel terzo centenario .... 1937. See 35.

Carvalho, Augusto: see Silva Carvalho.

1471 *Carvalho, Joaquim de:* "Descartes e a cultura filosófica portuguêsa." AcLisboa, Mémorias .... Classe de ciências 2: 1939, 39–69. See 430.

Carvalho, Ramos de: see Ramos de Carvalho.

1472 *Casanova.* Mémoires du Vénitien J. Casanova de Seingalt. Paris, Tournachon-Molin, 1825. 1: xxii.

"Je sais que j'existe, et j'en suis sûr par ce que j'ai senti. Je sais aussi que je n'existerai plus quand je cesserai de sentir .... Avant (l'âge de huit ans) je n'avais pas vécu en prenant *vivere* dans le sens de *cogitare* (penser); j'avais végété." (Casanova's Preface).

1472a *Casares, Jorge A.:* "Actualidad y vigencia del cogito cartesiano." Universidad (Argentina) 1954, no. 28, 187–235.

Critical discussion of the cogito analyses of Kant, Husserl, Heidegger.

1473 *Caso, A.:* "Don Juan Benito Díaz de Gamarra, un filósofo mexicano discípulo de Descartes." Revista de lit. mexicana 1: 1940. [Baldensperger]

1474 *Casotti, Mario:* "La pedagogia di Cartesio nella sua formazione." Cartesio 185–89. 1937.

1475 *Cassirer, Ernst:* Descartes' Kritik der mathematischen und naturwissenschaftlichen Erkenntnis. Dissertation Marburg. 1899. 102 p. Also in his: Leibniz's System in seinen wissenschaftlichen Grundlagen. Marburg, Elwert, 1902, 3–102. See 160.

1476 —: Das Erkenntnisproblem in der Philosophie und Wissenschaft der neueren Zeit. Vol. 1, 1906. 2 verb. Aufl., Berlin, B. Cassirer, 1911. See 161.

1477 —: Descartes: Lehre, Persönlichkeit, Wirkung. Stockholm, Bermann-Fischer, 1939. 308 p. See 243.

Pt. I. 1. Descartes' Wahrheitsbegriff. 2. Die Idee der 'Einheit der Wissenschaft' in der Philosophie Descartes.' – Pt. II. 1. Descartes und Corneille. 2. Descartes' Recherche de la vérité. 3. Descartes und die Königin von Schweden.

1478 —: Descartes, Corneille, Christine de Suède. Traduit par Madeleine Francès et Paul Schrecker. Paris, Vrin, 1942. 125 p. (Études de psychologie et de philosophie, ed. P. Guillaume, v. 5). Also in his: Descartes: Lehre (see 243).

1. Descartes et Corneille (3–37). 2. Descartes et la reine Christine de Suède (39–121).

1479 —: Drottning Christina och Descartes. Ett bidrag till 1600-talets idéhistoria. Stockholm, Bonniers, 1940. 140 p. (Forskninger och föreläsinger vid Göteborgs Högskola). Also in his: Descartes (1477) and in his: Descartes, Corneille (1478.)

Lectures delivered in October 1938: "Das Verhältnis von Descartes und .... Christina als geistesgeschichtliches Problem"; universal theism and the problem of natural religion in the 17th century; the renaissance of stoicism in 17th century ethics; the theory of passions in the history of ideas; Christina and the heroic ideal of the 17th century.

1480 —: Die Philosophie im 17. und 18. Jahrhundert. Paris, Hermann, 1939. 94 p. (Asci, v. 841). See 5.

1481 —: Individuum und Kosmos in der Philosophie der Renaissance. Berlin-Leipzig, Teubner, 1927. (Studien der Bibliothek Warburg, v. 10). Ch. 4: Das Subjekt-Objekt-Problem in der Philosophie der Renaissance.

1482 —: Die platonische Renaissance in England und die Schule von Cambridge. Leipzig-Berlin, Teubner. 1932. (Studien der Bibliothek Warburg,

v. 24.) – English tr. by James P. Pettegrove: The Platonic Renaissance in England. Edinburgh, Nelson (Univ. of Texas Press) 1953 (published 1954). vii, 207 p. See 465.

1483 —: "Descartes' Wahrheitsbegriff. Betrachtungen zur 300-Jahresfeier des Discours de la méthode. Zum Problem der Wahrheit als lumen naturale." Theoria 3: 1937, 161–87. Also in his: Descartes (1477.)

1484 —: "Descartes et l'idée de l'unité de la science." Rsyn 14: 1937, 7–28. Also in his: Descartes (1477).

The unity of the thinking self assures the unity of science; the individual sciences are not parts adding up to science as a whole; the genesis of numbers is Descartes' prototype for his notion of their enchainment.

1485 —: "Über die Bedeutung und Abfassungszeit von Descartes' Recherche de la vérité par la lumière naturelle." Theoria 4: 1938, 193–294. Also in his: Descartes (1477.) See 242.

1486 —: "Descartes' Dialog Recherche de la vérité .... und seine Stellung im Ganzen der cartesischen Philosophie. Ein Interpretationsversuch." Lärdomshistoriska Samfundets Arsbok. Lychnos 1938, 139–79. – French transl. by Paul Schrecker: "La place de la Recherche de la vérité dans l'œuvre de Descartes." RPFE 127: 1939, 261–300. Also in his: Descartes (1477.)

1487 *Castellani, Leonardo (S.J.):* Notas sobre la psicología cartesiana." Escritos 49–59. 1937.

Comparison with modern psychology would indicate that Descartes did not have a psychology proper.

Review: W. S. Weedon in PPR 1: 1940, 248.

1488 —: "San Augustín y Descartes." Homenaje 3: 117–59. 1937.

1489 *Castiella, Leopoldo Garcés:* "Las ideas políticas en Descartes." Homenaje 3: 73–88. 1937.

1490 *Castro, Anna de:* Il Discorso sul metodo di Cartesio e il De intellectus emendatione di Spinoza. Portici, Bellavista, 1938. 69 p.

1491 *Castro Turbiano, Máximo:* "Presencia de Descartes en la filosofia contemporánea." RcubF 1: 1950, 33–41.

1492 "*Catalogue* de la collection de portraits, bustes, miniatures et médaillons de la bibliothèque de Genève. Index des noms cités." Genava 16: 1938, 177–80.

Index to Genava 10–14: 1932–36, "à consulter pour l'iconographique de Descartes" (Giraud.)

1492a *Causeries* à propos du troisième centenaire du Discours de la méthode. Delagrave, 1938. See 515.

1493 *Cavazzana, J. E.:* "Génesis y principios de la moral cartesiana." RUC Perú 5: 1937, 483–504.

1494 *Celier, Paul:* "Sur deux U contestables. En marge de l'histoire du cartésianisme." RHPh ns 7: 1939, 283–90.

"Poure": "pure" and "pauvre".

1495 *Celle, H. de la:* "Descartes et le problème de la connaissance." Cth, 25 March 1934.

1496 *Celli, L.:* "La dottrina delle idee innate secondo Descartes, Locke e Leibniz." La filosofia delle scuole italiane 12: 1875, 89–128, 359–89; 13: 1876, 55–84.

Rich in references and comparative doctrinal analyses.

1497 *Ceñal, Ramón (S.J.):* "Cartesianismo en España. Notas para su historia (1650–1750)." FyL (Revista de la U. de Oviedo), 6: 1945, 3–95. See 449.

1498 —: "Cogito cartesiano y ontología fundamental." RevF 9: 1950, 5–23.

1499 —: "La vida, las obras y la influencia de Emmanuel Maignan." Revista de estudios políticos no. 46: 1952, 111–149. See 449.

1500 —: "La filosofía de Emmanuel Maignan." RevF 13, no. 48: 1954, 15–68. See 449.

1501 [*Cendres.*] "A propos des cendres de Descartes." Chronique des lettres françaises 1928, 159–60.

1502 *Čepublič, Drago:* Descartesova kriza. Zagreb, 1937. 39 p. [The crisis of Descartes.]

1502a *Cercle Descartes.* 1937. See 516.

1502b *Cercle philosophique Lorrain.* Tricentenaire .... 1937. See 517.

1503 *Ceriani, Grazioso:* "La riduzione cartesiana al 'primo filosofico' come nuova 'creazione nel reale.' " Cartesio, 191–220. 1937.

Neothomist study of Descartes' "fenomenismo," viewed as merely "una situazione storica, non .... un noema che s'afferma e sta" (220). Problem placed in its historical context (Scotism, Cusanus, etc.)

1504 *Ceyssens, Lucien (O.F.M.):* "François de Saint-Augustin de Macedo. Son attitude au début du Jansénisme." Archivum Franciscanum Historicum (Quaracchi) 49: 241–54, 1956. See also Sousa-Ribeiro (3329).

1505 *Chuigne, Édouard, et Charles Sédail:* De l'influence de Bacon et de Descartes sur la marche de l'esprit humain. Bordeaux, impr. de C. Gounouilhou, 1865. 83. p.

1506 *Chaix-Ruy, Jules:* "Il 'buono senso' di Descartes e il 'senso commune' di Vico." Humanitas 5: 1950, 571–88.

1506a —: "Note sur le doute hyperbolique de Descartes." Aph 22: 1959, 432–40.

Underneath hyperbolic doubt lies a particular time concept. Only a permanent intuition founded in Being can destroy the effects of this doubt: the cogito, in which the fundamental relationship between eternity and time is attained. The affirmation of a perfect, hence truthful God elevates the self from thought founded in being to the Being which founds it. The undeceiving God destroys the hypothesis of hyperbolic doubt. [Bsig 1960, no. 16354.]

1507 *Challaye, Félicien:* "Descartes et le rationalisme au XVIIIe siècle." In his: Petite histoire des grands philosophes. 4e éd., rév. et corr., Paris, PUF, 1948, 114–30.

1508 *Chalmers, G. K.:* "The lodestone and the understanding of matter in 17th century England." Philosophy of Science (London) 4: 1937, 75–95.

1509 *Chamberlain, Houston Stewart:* Immanuel Kant. München, Bruckmann, 1905. Engl. transl. by Lord Redesdale: Immanuel Kant. A study and comparison with Goethe, Leonardo, Bruno, Plato and Descartes. London, Lane, 1914.

Ch. 3: "Descartes (Verstand und Sinnlichkeit)," with exposition of his analytical geometry (p. 173–275; Engl. tr., p. 195–307). Influential work of popular "Weltanschauung" in the old Imperial days of Germany, struggling hard to fit Descartes into it but not getting far beyond the expository.

1509a *Champigny, Robert:* "The theatrical aspect of the cogito." Rmet 12: 1959, 370–77.

The self posited by D. was not a quality of experience but a belief, a "persona" or theatrical mask. This belief is normal in a dramatic situation; the suggestiveness of MM is "due to dramatic technique" (376). "Persona" and "dramatic technique" are epistemological forms of D.'s "larvatus prodeo." MM, not concerned with selfness, is dramatic (Ego appears on the philosophical stage); theatrical (a second Ego judges, destroys the first one, then allows it to reappear). Methodic doubt misses the existential quality of selfness which cannot be detached from experience.

1509b —: "Corneille et le Traité des passions." FR 26: 1952–53, 112–20.

Corneille's "reasoning fanatics" are surely not examples of Cartesian passion· Against Lanson, no. 413.

1510 *Charpentier, Thomas Victor:* Essai sur la méthode de Descartes. Delagrave, 1869. 210 p. Thèse Paris.

Good piece of work, still occasionally cited.

Charrin: see Fabre de Charrin.

Chartier, Émile: see Alain.

1511 *Chastaing, Maxime:* "Descartes, introduction à la vie personnelle." Esprit (Paris) 5/58: June 1937, 531–47.

Descartes' personal road as a road for others; to lead men to "sagesse", Descartes uses his Method as a "truc".

1512 —: "Descartes, Fauste de Riez et le problème de la connaissance d'autrui." In: Étienne Gilson, philosophe de la chrétienté. Paris, Éditions du Cerf. 1949, 187–211 (i.e.: Rencontres 30: 1949, 187–211). See 244.

1513 —: "L'abbé de Lanion et le problème cartésien de la connaissance d'autrui." RPFE 141: 1951, 228–48. See 244.

1514 —: "Le 'Traité' de l'abbé Macy et la 'vieille réponse' cartésienne au problème de la connaissance d'autrui." RPFE 143: 1953, 76–84. See 244.

1515 —: L'existence d'autrui. Paris, PUF, 1951. 355 p. See 244.

Reviews: R. Blanché in JPNP 44: 1951, 580–82; J. I. in RyF 144: 1951, 418–19; G. Ballanti in RFNS 45: 1953, 78–79; A. Hayen in NRT 74: 1952, 1105–1106; A. Voelke in RTP 3: 1953, 152–

54; L. B. Geiger in RSPT 38: 1954, 300–301; J. Kemp in PQ 5: 1955, 183–184; H. Riefstahl in PhLit 7: 1954–55, 170–171; J. Taminiaux in RPL 52: 1954, 462–468; P. Ricœur in Esprit (Paris) 22: 1954, no. 211, 289–297; I. M. Crombie in Mind 66: 1957, 116.

1516 *Chatelain, Urbanus Victor:* Quas ob causas docti inter nostros viri e Gallia, regente Ludovico XIV, 1643–1715, vel ad tempus vel in perpetuum egressi essent. Paris, Pedone, 1904. 209 p. Bibliogr. Thèse, Paris.

Descartes' reasons for his self-chosen "exile" in Holland.

1517 *Chattelun, L.:* "Lois de Descartes, principe de Fermat, théorème de Malus.' Revue de mathématiques spéciales 42–43: 1931, 193–95. [Schrecker].

1518 *Chauvin, abbé A. et G. Le Bidois:* La littérature française par les critiques contemporains. Du moyen-âge au XVIIe siècle. Paris, 1922.

Reprints Paul Janet's "Descartes, son caractère" (323–31), and A. Chauvin's "Descartes, son influence littérare" (331–33, a discussion of A. Fouillée's Descartes.)

1519 *Chazottes, J.:* "Sur une prétendue faute de raisonnement que Descartes aurait commise." AGP 17 (ns 10): 1904, 171–75.

Descartes' erroneous interpretation of the law of free fall. See Paul Tannery's refutation of Cazottes' error concerning Descartes' error, *ibid.*, 334–40.

1520 *Chénier, Marie-Joseph Blaise:* Rapport fait à la Convention Nationale .... suivi du décret rendu à la séance du 2 octobre 1793. Paris, Impr. Nationale, 1793. 6 p.

Transfer of Descartes' remains to the Pantheon.

1521 —: Rapport fait par M.-J. Chénier, sur la translation des cendres de René Descartes au Panthéon, séance du 18 floréal, l'an IV de la République (i.e. 6 mai 1796). Corps législatif. Conseil des cinq-cents. Paris, Floréal, an IV (1796). 6 p.

On Chénier see also Fr. Picavet, Les Idéologues (1891), 408–11.

1522 *Chestov, Léon* (i.e. Leo Shestov, pseud. of Lev Isakovitch Schwartzmann): "Synov'ia i pasynki vremeni (istoričeskii žrebii Spinozy)." Sovremennyia zapiski 25: 1925, 316–42 (signed: Jun. 8, 1922). French translation by J. Exempliarski: "Les favoris et les désinhérités de l'histoire: Descartes et Spinoza." MerF 164: 1923, 640 74. English transl. by Camilla Coventry and C. A. Macartney: "Children and stepchildren of time," in: Leo Chestov, In Job's balances: on the sources of eternal truths. London, Dent, 1932, 247–73. See 162.

1523 *Chevalier, Jacques:* Descartes. Paris, Plon, 1921. vii, 362 p. See 132.

1524 — (editor): Descartes. Lettres sur la morale. Paris, Boivin, 1935. xxviii, 333 p. Bph. See 90.

1525 —: "Le tempérament spirituel de la France dans la philosophie de Descartes." Rbleue 1921, 733–35.

1526 —: "Le Discours de la méthode." Aph 13: no. 2, 1937, 1–13.

God the Father and Creator is the center of DM "et non pas comme pour Pascal, le Fils, l'Homme-Dieu, Jésus-Christ" (p. 10). Careful consideration of Descartes' "Cogitationes privatae".

1527 —: "Sur quelques points de la philosophie de Descartes qu'on peut estimer acquis." Cartesio 221–25. 1937. Also in no. 132.

Despite all the critical razzmatazz, 8 points are assured: the sincerity of the man, the unity of his doctrine, God as its true center, D.'s striving for sagesse and beatitude (not mastery of nature), etc.

1528 —: "L'unité de la philosophie de Descartes." CD 1: 17–22. 1937.

From the standpoint of D.'s "intuition originelle", his goal of establishing the unity of knowing has been achieved.

1529 —: "La philosophie de Descartes à Bergson et à Maurice Blondel. Esquisse des tendances philosophiques actuelles en France." Rbleue 75: 1937, 131–33.

1530 —: "Descartes et le monde moderne." NL 24 July 1937.

1531 —: "Essai sur la personnalité de Descartes." Huy (Belgique), Orientations, 1938. iv, 23 p. Reprinted from: Orientations religieuses, intellectuelles et littéraires (La Sarte-Huy) 11: 1938, 255–73.

1532 —: "Kartezjusz," transl. by W. Jakubowski. Przegląd Współczesny 17: 1938, no. 12, 1–19.

1533 —: "La spiritualité de Descartes." DSS 1953, no. 19, 155–72. Engl. transl.: "The spirituality of Descartes." Dublin Review 114: 1950, 36–50.

Calls for rectification of the excessively rationalistic interpretations of Laporte and others: Descartes' rationalism places God, not man in the center of things. He seeks mastery of himself, not of nature.

1534 *Chevallier, Abbé C.:* "Note sur l'origine tourangelle de Descartes. (Pièces justificatives, 1956 – an XI.)" BSA Touraine, 1871–73. [Lanson, no. 4154]

1535 *Chialvo, Guido:* Sull'intendimento umano: Cartesio, Locke, Leibniz, Kant. Saggio critico-filosofico. Roma, Lux, 1902. 100 p.

1536 *Chiocchetti, Emilio:* "Per studiare Cartesio." RFN 4: 1912, 411–15.

On the "neuralgies" of his system (Bontadini I.)

1537 —: "Meditando su Cartesio." S 5: 1937, 375–83.

1538 *Chiriboga, Julio C.:* "Cogito ergo sum." Letras (Lima, Peru), 1937/1, 51–63.

1539 *Chiriotti, Edilio:* "Stato actuale degli studi cartesiani in Italia." CD 3: 127–33. 1937. See 15.

1540 *Chmaj, Ludwik:* Rozwój filozoficzny Kartezjusza. Kraków, Polska Akademja Umiejętności, 1930. 203 p.

Comprehensive Polish study of Descartes' philosophical development to 1637. Tries to uncover by "historical method" the persistent oscillations in Descartes' thought, with polemics against interpreters who stress the unity of the Cartesian system. Author's ambitious aim of giving a definitive monograph is only partly achieved (Lubnicki's review; see 15, p. 106).

1541 —: "Wolzogen przeciw Descartesowi." Archiwum Komisji do badania historii filozofii w Polsce (Kraków) 1917/1, 81–132.

"Ludwig Wolzogen against Descartes: the connection between Polish Arianism and Western philosophical thought."

1542 —: "Zagadnienie 'trzech faz' w rozwoju filozoficznym Kartezjusza." Prz 30: 1927, 149–63.

The problem of the "three phases" in Descartes' philosophy. See also Chmaj's "Le problème du développement philosophique de Descartes" (IIe Congrès polonais de philosophie, tenu à Varsovie 1927. Rapports et comptes-rendus, Varsovie, 1930, 40–41); and his "L'évolution philosophique de Descartes jusqu'à l'année 1637" (Bull. international de l'Académie des sciences et des lettres, Cracovie, 1929, no. 1–3).

1543 "Kartezjusz i jego filozofia w świetle ostatnich badań." KF 6: 1928, 69–96, 242–72, 275–97, 419–42.

Critical discussion of recent studies of Descartes' philosophy.

1544 —: "Le cartésianisme en Pologne au XVIIe et au XVIIIe siècle." Bull. internat. de l'Académie polonaise des sciences et des lettres, classe de philosophie, 1937 (7–10), 87–91. Transl. from the Comptes-rendus of the Academy, 1937, 241–45. See 470.

1545 —: "Pojęcie przyczynowości w filozofii Kartezjusza." Prz 45: 1937, 120–32.

The concept of causality in Descartes unites the certitude of inner experience with the stability of the physical order.

1546 *Choisy, Maryse:* "L'angoisse cartésienne." PsyP 3, no. 21–22: July-Aug. 1948, 738–51.

For three centuries, Cartesianism furnished blinkers "contre l'angoisse .... Le cartésianisme est la philosophie du refoulement," Descartes "l'homme qui ne fait pas scandale," the scandal being the abrupt passing from the psychological to the thought level (p. 150).

1547 —: "Le héros, surmoi français. Enquête sur Descartes, Pasteur, Jeanne d'Arc." PsyP no. 40, 5 February 1950, 98–134.

Psychoanalysis and questionnaire survey (see "Deux enquêtes de l'I.F.U.P.", *ibid.*, 134–49) combine to produce the desired result, expressed in the title.

1548 *Chollet, A.:* Art. "Descartes." "Doute." In: Dictionnaire de théologie catholique 4, pt. 1: 1920, col. 555–65, 1811ff. Bibliogr.

1549 *Chollet, Louis:* "À Descartes" [a poem]. BSA Touraine 11: 1897, 1er trim., 64–67.

1550 *Christiansen, Broder:* Das Urteil bei Descartes. Ein Beitrag zur Vorgeschichte der Erkenntnistheorie. Hanau, Clauss & Feddersen; also Freiburg i.B., Lehmann, 1902. 107 p. Dissertation Freiburg i.B.

Valuable analyses, precise and well documented. Critical use of the literature. Considers psychological elements of propositions; the truth criterion; the problem of transcendence; existential propositions. Its voluntaristic interpretation of judgment in D. is criticized by Kastil, no. 212a.

1551 *Christiansen, S. A.:* "Oversigt over inholdet af Descartes geometri, grundlaget for den analytisk geometri." Norsk Matematisk Tidschrift 1933, 64ff.

[Survey of Descartes' Geometrie, basis of analytical geometry.]

1552 *Cincinato, D.:* "Pericolosi sviluppi del cogito." Città di vita 1949, 543–46.

1553 *Cidade, Hernani António:* Lições sôbre a cultura e a literatura portuguesas. Coimbra, Coimbra editora. 2 vols. 1933, 1939 (cover: 1940).

Descartes' influence in Portugal.

1554 *Claros, R. F.:* "La teoría cartesiana de las verdades eternas." La Universidad (San Salvador) 1938, no. 2, 137–57.

1555 *Claudel, E.:* Discours de la Méthode de Descartes au XIXe siècle, suivi d'une application didactique, ou Traité des fonctions arithmétiques. Paris, V. Delmont, 1856. 182 p.

Confused and generally trivial remarks on the four rules of method, introducing a long didactic exposition of algebraic functions.

1556 *Claudel, Paul:* Contacts et circonstances. Paris, Gallimard, 1938. Also NL, 24 July 1937 ("Descartes vu par Paul Claudel.") See 408.

1557 *Clavery, Edouard:* Descartes et la diplomatie. A propos du IIIe centenaire du Discours .... Caen, impr. de Caron, 1937. 4 p. (From: Génie français, March 1937). On y a joint un article de l'auteur: "Comment l'initiative de Descartes en 1637 a aidé à l'adoption de la langue française comme langue diplomatique." (BN 87 *E. Pièce. 681)

1558 *Cléments (abbé):* "Le cartésianisme à Vendôme. Le P. Nicolas-Joseph Poisson, supérieur du collège de l'Oratoire." BSA du Vendômois, 1898–99. [Lanson 6223].

1559 *Clère, Jules:* Histoire de l'école de La Flèche, depuis sa fondation par Henri IV, jusqu'à sa réorganisation en Prytanée impérial militaire. La Flèche, Jourdain, 1853.

1560 *Le Club des Dames,* ou Le retour de Descartes. Comédie en une acte, en prose. À Paris, au Bureau de la Bibliothèque des romans, 1784. viii, 40 p. See 113.

1561 *Cobianchi, Lodovico:* Di Descartes, e della evoluzione filosofica operatasi nell'epoca del Risorgimento. Bologna, G. Monti, 1875. 28 p.

A school lecture. No new material.

1562 *Cochet, Marie-Anne:* "Les conditions de la liberté dans le système cartésien." CD 1: 147–51. 1937.

These conditions rest on the relation of infinite freedom to finite understanding. A dialectic rhythm "se scande entre le déterminisme de l'action et la liberté de la pensée."

1563 —: Le Congrès Descartes. Réflexions sur quelques-unes des orientations qui s'y sont manifestées: XIIIe, XXe, XXIe. Bruges, Impr.St.Cathérine, 1938. 141 p.

Sumptuous limited edition (100 copies) of reflections stimulated by some of the papers at the Congress.

1564 *Cochin, Denys:* Descartes. Paris, Alcan, 1913. 283 p. (Les grands philosophes.)

Académicien Cochin's biography of Descartes "n'apporte à l'historien contemporain rien que de déceptions". (Anon. in RMM 22: 1914, suppl. 1). All of Kant's "relativism" is already in Descartes' doubt "et dans les supercheries du démon malin" (author's notice, PhdG 5: 1913, no. 535).

1565 *Cohen, Gustave:* Écrivains français en Hollande dans la première moitié du XVIIe siècle. Paris, Champion (The Hague, Nijhoff), 1921, 355–689. Thèse Paris. See 123.

1566 —: "Le dernier projet littéraire de Maurice Barrès: Descartes et la princesse Elisabeth." Figaro, 10 December 1927.

1567 —: "Descartes en Constantijn Huygens (naar aanleiding van eenige onlangs ontdekte documenten). Haagsch Maandblad 1928/10, 148–61.

1568 — et G. Lucas de Pesloüan: Le dernier projet littéraire de Maurice Barrès. Paris, Les amis d'Édouard, 143. 1929. 85 p. 16mo.

1569 —: "Descartes in Franeker 1629 - 26 April 1929." Haagsch Maandblad 1929/1, 624–32.

1570 —: "La maison Descartes à Amsterdam." NL, 4 November 1933.

1571 —: "Descartes en Hollande." NL, 24 July 1937.

1572 —: "Descartes en Hollande." BSFP 44/1: 1950, 9–13.

1573 —: "Descartes et les Rose-croix." PsyP no. 40: Feb. 5, 1950, 165–77.

1574 —: "Note additionnelle." PsyP no. 40: Feb. 5, 1950, p. 471.

On Descartes' "scientia mirabilis". Quotes the Introitus to the Easter Mass, from Psalm 138: ".... posuisti super me manum tuam, alleluia; *mirabilis* facta est *scientia* tua, alleluia."

Cohen, Leonora Davidson: see Rosenfield, Leonora Cohen.

1575 *Cohn, Julius:* Die Dialektik der Gewissheit in Descartes' Entwurf der sapientia universalis. Hamburg, Proctor, 1933. 57 p. Dissertation Hamburg.

1576 *Colins, J. G. E. A. H. de:* Science sociale. 3 vols. Paris, Didot, 1857 (1858).

Vol. 1 has an "Examen des philosophies de Descartes, Bacon, Comte," etc., with discussion of the beast-machine problem (Descartes, Bayle, Pardies). Antimaterialistic.

1577 *Colombo, Carlo:* "Pubblicazioni in occasione del centenario cartesiano." RFNS 30: 1930, 62–85. See 25.

1578 *Colorni, Eugenio:* "Le verità eterne in Descartes e in Leibniz." CD 1: 132–40. 1937. See 253.

1579 *Comarnesco, Petru:* "Les normes et la vie sociale chez Descartes." CD 2: 86–94. 1937.

Descartes' ideal society should be "dirigée par une aristocratie intellectuelle, créée sur des bases démocratiques," perhaps headed by "un roi-philosophe, législateur unique et prévoyant." Cartesian man a synthesis "de la sagesse antique, de l'artisan moderne et de l'homme créateur" (p. 86).

1580 —: "The social and ethical conceptions of Descartes." Ethics 52: 1942, 493–503.

1581 *Combès, Joseph:* Le dessein de la sagesse cartésienne. Lyon-Paris, E. Vitte, 1960. 350 p. See 206.

1582 *Commémoration centenaire* de la mort de Descartes. RPFE 141: 1951, no. 4–6. See 558.

Comneno: see Láscaris Comneno.

1634 *Congrès Descartes. Travaux.* (1937). See 36 and 519.

1635 *Conmemoración* del III centenario de Renato Descartes. Discursos. Santiago de Cuba, 1950. See 545.

1636 *Coolidge, Julian Lowell:* "The origin of analytical geometry." Osiris 1: 1936, 231–50. See 355.

1637 —: A history of geometrical method. Oxford, Clarendon Press, 1940. See 355.

1638 *Corsano, Antonio:* "Misticismo e voluntarismo nelle cartesiane Regulae ad directionem ingenii." GCFI 11: 1930, 337–62.

"Most important technical contribution published in Italy, 1900–37," with much reference to "l'immense bibliographie existant sur ce philosophe .... Cet essai mérite d'être signalé d'une façon toute particulière" (Bontadini).

1639 *Corte, Marcel de:* "La dialectique poétique de Descartes." Aph 13, no. 2: 1937, 101–61. See 244a.

1640 —: "Malebranche ou le cartésien endurci." Revue catholique des idées et des faits 18: 1938, 8–10.

Through Malebranche, Cartesianism became the foundation of the antichristian rationalism of the Enlightenment. Hostile profile of Malebranche, by a Thomist. See Sebba, no. 19, p. 51.

1641 —: "Le Congrès Descartes." Le Flambeau (Bruxelles) 20: 1937, 443–50.

1642 *Cosenza, Paolo:* "Il linguaggio della percezione sensibile ed il problema metafisico per Descartes." Actes du IIe Congrès international de l'Union internationale de philosophie des sciences (1954), v. 4, 109–16 (Zürich 1955).

1643 *Costa, Filippo:* "Une 'lecture' de Descartes du point de vue phénoménologique." RMM 59: 1954, 135–56.

This "phenomenological reading" of Descartes' metaphysics centers upon the distinction between "esse formale" and "esse objectivum." In the Regulae, thinking is measuring and proportioning; in DM, metaphysical problems (doubt) open; in MM Descartes finds the transition from "esse" to "nosse."

1644 *Costabel, Pierre:* "La controverse Descartes-Roberval au sujet du centre d'oscillation." RScH no. 61: 1951, 74–86. See 369.

1645 —: "La démonstration cartésienne relative au centre d'équilibre de la balance." AIHS 9: 1956, 133–46. See 369.

1645a —: "Contribution à l'étude des lois du choc: Mariotte et Malebranche, ou deux manières de corriger Descartes." IXe Congrès International d'histoire des sciences, Barcelona-Madrid, 1959. Communication.

1646 *Costantini, Giuseppe M.:* "Sulle prove cartesiane dell'esistenza di Dio." RCSF 8: 1953, 607–09.

The order of proofs is exacter in PP than in DM or MM.

1647 *Cottier, Athanas:* Der Gottesbeweis in der modernen Aufklärungsphilosophie. Descartes, Spinoza, Leibniz, Wolff, Kant. Bern, Lüthy, 1940. 176 p. Dissertation Freiburg (Schweiz).

1648 *Cotugno, R.:* Gregorio Caloprese. Trani, 1910.

Caloprese, teacher of Gravina and "gran filosofo renatisto" to whom Vico attributed the diffusion of Cartesianism in Naples (Robertson; see 420, p. 25, note 2).

1649 *Couanier Deslandes, Claude Henri:* Éloge de Descartes. Discours qui a obtenu l'accessit, au jugement de l'Académie Françoise, en 1765. Paris, Regnard, 1765. 130 p. See 126.

1650 *Couderc, Camille.* "Nouveaux documents sur la situation et la fortune de la famille de René Descartes." Bibliothèque de l'École des Chartes 78: 1918, 269–93. Also: Nogent-le-Rotru, Impr. Daupely-Gouverneur, 1918. 27 p. 8vo. See 94.

1651 *Coussin, Pierre:* "Carnéade et Descartes." CD 3: 9–16. 1937.

The epoché of Carneades and his error theory compared with Cartesian doubt: their character similar, but Carneades derives high probability, not certainty from the epoché.

1652 *Courtney, William Leonard:* "Mask of Descartes." In his: Studies at leisure. London, Chapman & Hall, 1892, 69–81.

1653 *Cousin, Victor:* Fragments de philosophie cartésienne. Paris, Charpentier, 1845. xii, 470 p. (Nouvelle édition, 1856). Later incorporated, with additions, in his: Fragments philosophiques pour servir à l'histoire de la philosophie. 5e édition, Paris, Didier, 1866, v. 3, 4 (Philosophie moderne, I, II). See 450.

1654 —: Cours de philosophie. Introduction à l'histoire de la philosophie. Paris, Pichon & Didier, 1828. (3e leçon, 29 avril 1828).

1655 —: "Über Descartes und sein Verhältnis zur Philosophie in Frankreich." In: Religion und Philosophie in Frankreich, eine Folge von Abhandlungen, übers. u.hg. von F. W. Carové, v. 2, Göttingen, 1827, 1–10.

Translated from the prospectus of Cousin's edition of Descartes' works (1824). Interesting from the viewpoint of the diffusion of Cousin's Descartes revival.

1656 *Covotti, A.:* Spinoza. La trasformazione della dottrina di Cartesio: il puro naturalismo. Napoli, SIEM, 1935. 30 p.

1657 *Crahay, Franz:* "L'argument ontologique chez Descartes et Leibniz et la critique kantienne." RPhL 47: 1949, 458–68.

Review: A.B. in P 7: 1950, 112–13.

1658 *Cramer, Jan Anthony:* Abraham Heidanus en zijn cartesianisme. Dissertation Utrecht, J. van Druten, 1889. 208 p.

Heidanus, an unquestionably orthodox theologian and one of Descartes' most faithful followers, the first Cartesian at Leiden.

Reviewed by Dibon (see 6), p. 267–72.

1659 *Cresson, André.* Descartes: sa vie, son œuvre, avec un exposé de sa philosophie. (1942). 3rd ed., PUF, 1950. 148 p. (Philosophes).

Readable, conscientious if unexciting introduction, by a professional philosophical biographer.

1660 —: "Descartes." In his: Les courants de la pensée philosophique française. Paris, Colin, 1927, v. 1, 35–69.

1661 *Crombie, A. C.:* "Galileo, Descartes and metaphysics." The Month (London) 191: 1951, 354–63.

1661a —: "Descartes on method and physiology." Cambridge Jl 5: 1951, 178–86.

1661b —: "Descartes." Scientific American 201: 1959, 160–173.

1661c *Cronin, T. J. (S.J.):* "Eternal truth in the thought of Descartes and of his adversary." JHI 21: 1960, 553–59.

Descartes cited and opposed the view that the eternal verities do not depend on their being known by God. Author shows that the adversary referred to is Suárez (Disput. metaph.). Good critical survey of literature on eternal truth in D.

1662 *Cuccaro, Jacinto J.:* "Descartes y Vico." Homenaje 2: 149–71. 1937.

First part deals with Algazali (following Teicher, see 344), second part with Vico (cogito and gnoseology).

1663 *Cultrera, Salvatore (S.J.):* "A proposito del cogito, ergo sum." S 6: 1938,290–94.

Confronts Thomist and Cartesian cogito, suggests as acceptable: "aliquid cogitans sum." Neothomist viewpoint.

1664 *Cumming, Robert:* "Descartes' provisional morality." Rmet 9: 1955–56, 207–35. See 245.

1665 *Cunningham, William* (Archdeacon of Ely): The influence of Descartes on metaphysical speculation in England. A degree thesis (Edinburgh). London, Macmillan, 1876. xlviii, 188 p. See 460.

1666 *Curtis, R.*: "An extension of Descartes' rules of signs." Mathematische Annalen 73: 1913, 424–35.

1667 *Cushman, Robert E.*: "Barth's attack upon Cartesianism and the future in theology." JRel 36: 1956, 207–23. See 193a.

1668 *Cuvillier, Armand*: Partis pris sur l'art, la philosophie, l'histoire. Paris Colin, 1956. 532 p.

Reprint of scattered pieces in Rsyn and NL, including reviews of G. Lewis and F. Alquié, and two Malebranche papers.

Reviews: G. Besse in Pensée no. 73: 1957, 111–17; A. W(ylleman) in RPhL 55: 1957, 137.

1669 —: "Descartes et l'esprit cartésien." Rsyn 67: 1950, 81–99; discussion 100–13. Also in his: Parti pris, 97–119.

Cartesian synthesis remained incomplete, as Gassendi noted; it unduly neglected experimental science; later remedied by Malebranche.

1670 —: "L'invention humaine: Progrès de la connaissance et pressentiment de son pouvoir (Bacon, Descartes, l'Encyclopédie)." Rsyn 74: 1953, 5–23. Also in his: Parti pris, no. 1668, 68–85.

1671 *Cysarz, Herbert*: Welträtsel im Wort. Vaduz, Liechtenstein-Vlg., 1948.

Chapter on "Barocke Philosophie – ein Weg zu Descartes?" (p. 92–124) is an attractively written attempt, by the Viennese critic of Baroque Literature, to understand Descartes through the "Baroque spirit," without the heavy spade work such an attempt requires. The "universe as a clockwork" idea alone is hardly enough.

1672 *Czajkowski, Stanislaw*: "Intuicja twórcza w filozofii Kartezjusza i znaczenia pojęcia Boga w jego teorii poznania." Prz 38: 1930, 41–64. (Dissertation).

"Creative intuition in Descartes' philosophy and the significance of the idea of God in his epistemology": the unity of creative intuition guarantees the perfect unity of the system. With the Dream of 1619 Descartes "est en pleine possession de la vision créatrice de son système"; the detailed working-out occupied his life. Bergsonizing analysis, an "objective and impartial historical study" (Lubnicki's review, see 15, 106–07). See also de Corte, no. 244a.

1673 —: "Dowód ontologiczny Kartezjusza i jego nowa idea Boga." Prz 45: 1937, 133–51.

Descartes' ontological proof and his new concept of God.

1674 —: "Dowódy istnienia Boga z Jego skutków u Kartezjusza." KF 1936: 292–316.

On Descartes' proofs of the existence of God by the effects.

1675 —: "Descartes i Spinoza." Myśl narodowa (Warszawa) 1938/19.

1676 —: "Mickiewicz i Descartes. Nacjonalizm i filozofia." Myśl narodowa (Warszawa) 1938/45.

1677 —: "Cogito ergo sum Kartezjusza i jego nowa concepcja duszy." KF 19: 1950, 39–65. French summary, 164–66.

Surveying idealist, phenomenalist, realist cogito interpretations, author finds that they can be viewed as successive stages in the development of Descartes' spiritualist idealism. Regarding "intuitus", Bergson's "attention à la vie" has its parallel in Descartes. As to will, voluntarism imposes itself upon rationalism in D.'s system. See also 252.

1678 —: "Descartes et la Pologne." Académie polonaise des sciences et des lettres. Centre polonais de recherches scientifiques de Paris. Bulletin, June 1950, no. 6, 2–8.

1679 —: "Essai sur les fondements de la philosophie de Descartes." Collectanea Theologica (Poland) 24: 1953, no. 1–4, 30–56.

Attempts to find the root of the system and to determine its historical moment. [BAn 1955, 7578].

1680 *Czeżowski, Tadeusz:* "Metodologiczne postulaty Descartesa." Prz 45: 1937, 111–19.

Descartes' methodological postulates.

1681 *D., A. H.* (Montevideo): "De Descartes à James." RPFE 76: 1913, 202–03.

Brief note calling attention to Descartes' anticipating William James on several points.

1682 *Dagens, J.:* "La sagesse, suivant Descartes et suivant Pascal." Studia catholica 1: 1924–25, 225–40.

The experimental spirit of Pascal versus Descartes' extreme confidence in human reason (Pos-Steenberger, Rsyn 1937, p. 113).

d'Alverny: see Alverny.

d'Argenson: see Argenson.

1683 *Dahlström, Axel:* "Filosofen Descartes' sista öden." In: Eros och Eris. Kulturessäer tillägnade Rolf Lagerborg. Stockholm, Natur och Kultur, 1944, 60–75. [Descartes' last destinies.]

1684 *Dainville, François de (S.J.):* La naissance de l'humanisme moderne; les Jésuites et l'éducation de la société française. Vol. 1, Beauchesne, 1940. XX, 393 p. Bibliogr. 373–83.

Deals with the principles of Jesuit education, the ratio studiorum which governed La Flèche, etc.

1685 *Dalbiez, R.* "Les sources scolastiques de la théorie cartésienne de l'être objectif. A propos du 'Descartes' de M. Gilson." RHPh 3: 464–72, 1929.

Finds in Cajetan and Duns Scotus "plus qu'une ébauche de la théorie de l'être objectif" (p. 467, against Gilson who in his Commentary to DM, no. 83, 318–23, stresses the originality of D.'s conception.)

1685a *Daly, C. B.:* "Metaphysics and the limits of language." In Ian Ramsey (ed.), Prospects for metaphysics; essays of metaphysical exploration. London, Allen & Unwin, 1961, 181–185. See 235b.

Dal Verme: see Verme.

1686 *Dąmbska, Izydora:* "Meditationes Descartes' a na tle sceptycyzmu frankuskiege XVII wieku." KF 19: 1950, 1–24. See 246.

1687 —: "Sur certains principes méthodologiques dans les Principia philosophiae de Descartes." RMM 62: 1957, 57–66. See 247.

1688 *Damiron, Jean Philibert:* Essai sur l'histoire de la philosophie en France au XVIIe siècle. Paris, Hachette, 1846. 2 vols. See 451.

1689 *Damjanovič, Milan:* "Beleske o Dekartu." Polet (Beograd) 6: June 1950, 43–45.

Remarks on Descartes on the tercentenary of his death.

1689a *Damodos, Vikentios:* Σύνοψις Ἠθικῆς Φιλοσοφίας. Reprinted: Athens, 1940. Also in: E. P. Papanoutsos, Νεοελλενικὴ Φιλοσοφία (Α'). Ἀθήναις, Ἀετος Α.Ε. 1953.

Damodos (1679–1752), a Ionian islander who studied at Padua, philosophized "still on traditional (i.e. Aristotelian) lines," but "a section on the passions of the soul is obviously Cartesian in inspiration" (G. P. Henderson in PhQ 5: 1955, p. 159).

1690 *Daniel, Gabriel (S.J.):* Voiage du monde de Descartes 1690. See 110.

1691 *Dankmeijer, Johann:* De biologische studies van R. Descartes. Voordracht gehouden van 26 November 1951 te Leeuwarden. Leiden, Universitaire Pers, 1951. 23 p. (Leidse voordrachten, v. 9). Summary: "Les travaux biologiques de R. Descartes (1596–1650)." AIHS 4: 1951, 675–80.

1692 *Daubrée, Auguste:* "Descartes, l'un des créateurs de la cosmologie et de la géologie." Jl. des savants, March-April, 1880. 27 p.

1693 *Daudin, Henri:* La liberté de la volonté. Signification des doctrines classiques. Paris, PUF, 1950. 250 p. BPC. See 248.

1694 —: "Le rationalisme de Descartes." In: Cahiers du Cercle Descartes (see 516), 6: 1937, 5–33.

1695 *Daujat, J.:* "Un curieux adversaire de Descartes: Mallemans de Messanges." Thalès 4: 1937–39 (published 1940), 184–85.

1696 *Dauriac, Lionel:* "Essai sur l'instinct réaliste: Descartes et Thomas Reid." AnP 14: 1903, 85–113. See 249.

1697 *Davis, W. G.:* see Hodgson, S. H. et al.

1698 *Davy, Georges:* Allocution. BSPF 44/1: 1950, 21–25.

1699 *Day, A.:* "Les propriétés de la famille Descartes." (With illustrations). Le glaneur châtelleraudais 4, no. 14: May 1937. (See 518.)

1700 *Debricon, L.:* (ed.) Descartes. Choix des textes. Michaud, 1909. (Grands philosophes). Spanish tr. by Anselmo Gonzales: Descartes. Selección de textos, con estudio de sistema filosófico y notas biográficas y bibliográficas. Michaud, 1910. 223 p.

Introduction (7–52) argues that Descartes' science cannot be separated from his philosophy.

1701 *Debrou, Dr.:* "Le cartésianisme de la marquise de Sévigné et de son entourage." SAg Orléans. Mémoires 26: 1886, 1–36.

No new sources.

de Bruyne: see Bruyne. *de Carvalho, J.:* see Carvalho. *de Carvalho, R.:* see Ramos de C. *de Charrin:* see Fabre de Ch. *de Corte:* see Corte. *de Coya:* see García Tuduri de C. *de Dainville:* see Dainville. *De Feo:* see Feo. *de Fériet:* see Kampé de F. *de Finance:* see Finance.

1701a *Defrennes, P.:* "Chefs de file: Descartes, Franklin, Auguste Comte, Péguy.' Et, 20 July 1931, 169–88.

de Gallagher: see Parks de G. *de Giuli:* see Giuli. *de Groot:* see Groot. *de Haan:* see Bierens de Haan.

1702 *Dehove, Henri:* "L'évidence et la véracité divine chez Descartes." RdePh 27: 1920, 244–62.

1703 —: "Le libre arbitre chez Descartes." RdePh 31: 1924, 261–88.

1704 —: "L'union de l'âme et du corps chez Descartes." RdePh 32: 1925, 389–409.

1705 —: "Note sur la preuve ontologique de Descartes." FC Lille. Mémoires et travaux 32: 1927, 159–67. (Mélanges de philologie et d'histoire publ. à l'occasion du cinquantenaire de la Faculté des lettres de l'Université catholique de Lille.)

de la Harpe: see Harpe. *de la Meurthe:* see Boulay de la M. *de Lanesseau:* see Lanesseau.

1705a *De Lara Minguez, D.:* "Descartes el reformador." RcubF 1/6: 1950, 55–61.

de Launay: see Launay.

1706 *Delasnerie, C.:* "Descartes." Rint 3/13: Feb. 1947, 183–84.

1707 *Delavaud, L.:* [Note in:] Corr 10 October 1913.

About an attempt by Dr. Paul Richer to authenticate the skull in the Musée de l'homme (Paris), supposedly that of Descartes, by comparing its measurements with those of a drawing of Descartes' skull based on the portrait by Frans Hals. Richer found a close correspondence in these measurements. See 3068.

1708 *Delbos, Victor:* Figures et doctrines de philosophes. Paris, Plon, 1918, 95–141. See 134.

1709 —: La philosophie française. Paris, Plon-Nourrit, 1919, 16–48. See 134.

"Le rapport de la science à la philosophie dans Descartes." 16–30. "La philosophie de Descartes." 31–48. "Malebranche" (Ch. 3, 91–132).

1710 —: "L'idéalisme et le réalisme dans la philosophie de Descartes". AnP 22: 1911, 39–53.

For Descartes, Reason does not establish the a priori conditions of objective cognition, but presupposes Being. Descartes' gnoseology is a far cry from Berkeley's "esse est percipi," Kant's "gesetzgebende Vernunft," or Fichte's creative activity. Critique of Natorp's idealistic interpretation (see 221). See also 14 (Olgiati, Cartesio, p. 268).

1711 —: "Le cogito de Descartes et la philosophie de Locke." AnP 24: 1913, 1–14.

1712 —: "Descartes et la pensée classique." Revue des Français 31 mai 1914. Also in his: Figures (see 134).

1713 —: "Descartes." In: Estudio (Barcelona) 30: 1920, 234–51, 422–39.

1713a —: "La controverse d'Arnauld et de Malebranche sur la nature et l'origine des idées." APC année 84, v. 16, May 1913. Reprinted in his: Étude de la philosophie de Malebranche, 1924. See 451a.

1714 *Delbos, Yvon:* Allocution. BSPF 44/1: 1950, 39–42.

del Busto: see Busto. *dell'Oro:* see Maros dell'Oro. *Del Noce:* see Noce.

1715 *Delpy, G.:* Feijóo et l'esprit européen. Paris, Hachette, 1936, 81–89. See 449.

1716 *Delvaille, Jules:* Essai sur l'histoire de l'idée du progrès jusqu'à la fin du XVIIIe siècle. Alcan, 1910. xii, 761 p. Thèse Paris.

See Ch. 3 (177–89) on "une philosophie nouvelle: Descartes," Ch. 5 (203–10) on the querelle des anciens et des modernes.

1717 *Delvolvé, Jean:* "La fécondité du dualisme cartésien." CD 1: 23–30. 1937.

1718 *Dempf, Alois:* "Erneuerung und Umbildung des Cartesianismus in der christlichen Philosophie des 19. Jh." Cartesio 285–92. 1937. See 466b.

1719 *Denis-Boulet, N.-M.:* "La pensée religieuse de Descartes." RU 1 April 1925.

Review of Gouhier's no. 168.

1720 *Denissoff, Élie:* "The nature of mathematical knowledge according to René Descartes." Proceedings of the American Catholic Philosophical Association 26: 1952, 179–84. In French: "La nature de la connaissance mathématique selon Descartes." Actes du XIe Congrès international de philosophie, v. 13, 13–17, 1953.

Distinguishes mathematics as study of numerical relations and geometric properties (rudimentary physics) from mathematical physics which deals with all other relations between bodies. Useful collection of texts on D.'s concept of mathematics.

1721 —: "Les étapes de la redaction du Discours de la methode." RPhL 54: 1956, 254–82. See 260 and 278.

1721a —: "L'énigme de la science cartésienne. La physique de Descartes est-elle positive ou déductive? Essai d'interprétation de deux extraits du Discours de la Méthode." RPhL 59: 1961, 31–75.

The passages discussed are AT VI, 1–2 (DM on "le bon sens") and 63–65 (DM, Part VI). Author believes that his elaborate analysis "a porté .... le coup de grâce à l'image établi d'un Descartes fondant sa physique dans l'abstrait." On the contrary, D. in the name of "le bon sens" calls for freedom of research, for the experimental and mathematical method, and for a new, non-Aristotelian dynamics.

de Pesloüan: see Lucas de P.

1722 *Derisi, Octavio Nicolas:* "Reflexiones sobre el cogito cartesiano." Cartesio 293–97. 1937.

Critique of universal doubt and cogito. Descartes' "sad bequest" to modern philosophy is the insoluble contradiction: "a proceder como idealista con las fórmulas conceptuales de una inteligencia esencialmente realista" (p. 297).

1723 —: "El espíritu de dos filosofías. Realismo metafísico e realismo racionalista. S. Tomás de Aquino y Renato Descartes." E 57: 1937, 469–54.

Sharply formulated, lucid confrontation of the Thomistic and Cartesian attitude to Being. Sees D.'s insistence on independence of intelligence with respect to Being, "con intenciones de divinarse," as basic cause of unending contradictions and eventual historical collapse of Cartesianism.

1724 —: "El racionalismo, raíz del sistema cartesiano." PenM 6/22: 1950, 131–45.

1725 *Derriey, M.:* "Descartes et la psycho-physiologie de la glande pinéale." France médicale 59: 1913, 309ff.

De Ruvo: see Ruvo. *de Sacy:* see Sacy. *de Saint-Germain:* see Bertrand de Saint-Germain.

1726 *Desanti, Jean:* "Tricentenaire de Descartes. Descartes et les petit-bourgeois." Nouvelle critique 2, no. 17: 1950, 67–74.

Descartes and Bacon were philosophers of action. Modern interpretations beginning with Husserl see them as philosophers of resignation concerned with introspection, rather than with nature and its mastery.

1727 *Descartes, René* (author): [AT]. Œuvres de Descartes. Publiés par Charles Adam et Paul Tannery. 1897–1913. 13 vols. See 74.

1728 —: Œuvres inédites de Descartes .... par Louis Alexandre comte Foucher de Careil. 2 vols. 1859–60. See 75.

1729 —: Œuvres et lettres. Textes présentés par André Bridoux. Bibl. de la Pléiade, v. 4. 2nd ed., 1952. See 76.

1730 —: The philosophical works of Descartes. Rendered into English by E. S. Haldane and G. R. T. Ross. 2nd ed. 1931. See 77.

1731 —: [AM]. Correspondance. Publiée par Ch. Adam et G. Milhaud. 1936ff. See 79.

1732 —: Correspondence of Descartes and Constantijn Huygens, 1635–47, edited by Leon Roth. 1926. See 81.

1733 —: Correspondance avec Arnauld et Morus, ed. Geneviève Lewis. 1953. See 84.

1734 —: Descartes. Lettres. Textes choisies par Michel Alexandre. PUF, 1955. viii, 226 p. (Les grands textes.)

Excellent selection from D.'s vast correspondence, with biographical index of correspondents and detailed "table analytique."

Reviews: F. Alquié in Eph 10: 294–95; M. Dambuyant in Pensée no. 67: 151, 1956; G. Leger in RSPT 40: 1956, 35–36; J. C. Piguet in RTP 6: 1956, 145.

1735 —: [Dioptrique]. G. Leisegang, Descartes' Dioptrik. 1943. See 87 and 2494.

1736 —: Discours de la méthode. Texte et commentaire par Étienne Gilson. 2nd ed. 1925. See 83.

1737 —: Discurso sôbre o método, tr. Miguel Lemos. Apostolado positivista do Brazil. 1896. See 146.

1737a —: Rassuždenie o metode, o priloženijami: Dioptrika, Meteory, Geometrija. Red., perevod, stat'i i kommentarii G. G. Sljusareva i A. P. Juškeviča. Leningrad, Akad. Nauk SSSR, 1953. 650 pp. [DM, Dioptr., Météores, Géometrie. Ed., transl., notes, commentary by G. G. Sljusarev and A. P. Juškevič. In Russian.]

1738 —: Entretien avec Burman. Manuscrit de Göttingen. Ed. Charles Adam. 1937. See 86.

1739 —: [Géométrie]. The geometry of René Descartes. Translated by D. E. Smith and M. L. Latham. 1925. See 88.

1739a —: Kosmogonija. Perevod, predislovie i vstupitel'naja stat'ja S. F. Vasil'eva. Baku, Azerb. gos. naučno-issledovatel'skogo institut, 1932. 152 p. [Cosmogony, tr. with foreword and introd. by S. F. Vasilieff. In Russian.]

1740 —: Lettres à Regius et remarques sur l'explication de l'esprit humain, ed. Geneviève Rodis-Lewis. 1949. See 92a.

1740a —: Lettres sur la morale. Correspondance avec la princesse Élisabeth, Chanut et la reine Christine, ed. J. Chevalier. 1935. See 90.

1740b —: Il mondo, ovvero Trattato della luce. Torino, Boringhieri, 1959. 138 p. See 92b.

1740c —: Meditationes de prima philosophia, ed. Geneviève Lewis. 1946. See 89.

1741 —: La naissance de la paix. See 78. See also 1072, 2890.

1742 —: Notas contra el programa filosófico de Regius, ed. Elisabeth Goguel de Labrousse. 1949. See 92a.

1743 —: Les passions de l'âme, ed. Geneviève Lewis. 1955. See 91.

1744 —: Les passions de l'âme, ed. P. Mesnard. 1937. See 91.

1745 —: Règles pour la direction de l'esprit, ed. J. Sirven. 1945. See 92.

1746 —: Regulae ad directionem ingenii, ed. G. Le Roy. 1933. See 92.

1747 —: Regulae ad directionem ingenii, ed. H. Gouhier. 2nd ed., 1946. See 92.

1747a *Descartes à l'occasion du tricentenaire de sa mort.* RIP 1950. See 557.

1747b *Descartes à l'occasion du troisième centenaire ....* RPFE 132: 1937. See 536.

1747c *Descartes.* 31 Octobre 1937. Ville de la Haye. See 528.

1747d *Descartes. Cahiers de Royaumont*, 1957. See 42.

1747e *Descartes. Cahiers du Cercle Descartes.* 1937. See 516.

1747f *Descartes. Exposition* (Bibl. Nationale, 1937). See 1.

1747g *Descartes. Homenaje.* Buenos Aires, 1937. See 40.

1747h *Descartes. Homenaje.* Sante Fé. 1937. See 537.

1748 *Descartes à Châtellerault.* NL, 27 May 1937. [Celebrations.]

1748a *Descartes et le cartésianisme hollandais* 1950. See 38.

1748b *René Descartes et le siècle de Louis XIV en Touraine.* Tours, 1937. See 538.

1749 "*Descartes*, o la aventura del angelismo (1650–1950)." Sapientia (Buenos Aires) 5: 1950, 163–67.

1750 "*Descartes-i, dhene.*" [Descartes et nous.] Perpj 2: 1937, 137–40, 200–03. [In Albanian.]

1750a *Descartes*, par M. Leroy et al. 1937. See 37.

1751 "*Descartes*" *(pseudonym):* Politik und Strategie (Ich verurteilte nicht, ich kritisiere nur). Buenos Aires, Amt für internationale argentinische Veröffentlichungen. 1951, 265 p. 1952, 255 p. [Not in the book trade].

1752 *Deschamps, G.:* "La fête de Descartes à Franeker-en-Friese." Revue de l'Alliance française, July 1929.

1753 *Desgrippes, G.:* "Le songe de Descartes." RdePh 35: 1935, 144–54. [Review of no. 183.]

Deslandes: see Couanier Deslandes. *De Urmeneta:* see Urmeneta.

1754 *Deutinger, Martin:* Die Denklehre. Regensburg, G. A. Manz, 1884. (His: Grundlinien einer positiven Philosophie als vorläufiger Versuch einer Zurückführung aller Theile der Philosophie auf christliche Principien, Dritter Teil.) See 466b.

1755 —: "Cartesius." In his: Das Princip der neueren Philosophie und die christliche Wissenschaft. Regensburg, G. A. Manz, 1852, ch. 4, 62–69. See 466b.

1756 *Devaux, André-A.:* "La phénoménologie de Husserl est-elle un 'néocartésianisme'?" Rph 9: 1954, 260–83. See 174.

Alleged relationship between the two philosophers: Although there probably is no historical "progress" in philosophy, "en revanche, il y a des 'gestes' philosophiques constamment à retrouver et à reprendre" (282). What unites D. and H. is the conviction of the seriousness of philosophical responsibility, rather than community of doctrine. References to important earlier studies.

1757 —: "Histoire de la philosophie moderne." In: Raymond Bayer (ed.), Philosophie. Chronique des années de guerre, 1939–1945. Paris, Hermann (Asci 1088, v. 1), 54–57. Continued in: Chronique des années d'après-guerre, 1946–48, v. 12, 1950 (Asci 1104), 54–62.

Brief critical appraisals of important contributions to Cartesian studies.

1758 *Devaux, Philippe:* "Descartes philosophe." Combat (Bruxelles) 11: 1937, 4. [Brie 11487]

1759 *Deventer, Ch. M. van:* "Spinoza's leer 'De natura corporum' beschouwd in betrekking tot Descartes' Mechanica." TW 15: 1921, 265–93.

1760 *Devivaise, C.:* "Descartes et la mort." Eph ns 5: 1950, 165–68.

His regimen for longevity. How he faced death.

1761 *Dibon, Paul:* La philosophie néerlandaise au siècle d'or. Vol. 1: L'enseignement philosophique dans les universités à l'époque précartésienne, 1575–1650. Amsterdam, Elsevier, 1954. x, 274 p. (Publications de l'Institut français d'Amsterdam, Maison Descartes). Proefschrift Leiden. See 452.

1762 —: "Notes bibliographiques sur le cartésianisme hollandais." In: Descartes et le cartésianisme hollandais, 1950, 261–300. See 6 and 38.

1763 —: "Descartes et ses premiers disciples hollandais." ANTWP 42: 1950, 144–52. Also in De Gids 113: 1950, 98–108.

1764 —: "Le problème de l'âme des bêtes chez Descartes et ses premiers disciples néerlandais" (in: Mens en dier; een bundel angeboden aan F. L. R. Sassen. Antwerp-Amsterdam, N.V. Standaard, 1954, 187–222). See 226.

1765 —: Sur l'histoire de la philosophie cartésienne. Openbare les gegeven bij de aanvaarding van het ambt van privaat-docent aan de Rijks-universiteit te Leiden op 17 Mei 1955. Groningen-Djakarta, J. B. Wolters, 1955. 20 p.

Inaugural lecture on 20th century French Descartes criticism; Hamelin, Laporte, Gueroult.

1766 *Dickstein, S.:* "Czy Karteziusz był plagiatorem?" Wszechświat (Warszawa) 1883, no. 28. [Bar]

The distinguished Polish mathematician discusses the question whether Descartes was a plagiarist.

1767 *Dijksterhuis, Eduard Jan:* Val en worp; een bijdrage tot de geschiedenis der mechanica van Aristoteles tot Newton. Groningen, Noordhoff, 1924. 466 p. See 363.

1768 —: "Het aandeel van Isaak Beeckman in de ontwikkeling der valwetten." NAW ser. 2, 14: 1924, 186–208.

Beeckman's share in the development of the laws of free fall, anticipating Galilei. See 363.

1769 —: Descartes als wiskundige. Groningen, 1932. 22 p.

1770 —: "De proefstukken der cartesiaansche methode." De Gids 101/2: 1937, 285–300.

Météores. Dioptrique etc. as examples of Cartesian method in action.

1771 —: "Simon Stevin." In: Twee Nederlandsche figuren uit de zestiende en zeventiende eeuw. The Hague, Nijhoff, 1941.

1772 —: "Descartes, Pascal en de proef op de Puy-de-Dôme." Euclides 25: 1950, 265–270.

Brief historical exposition of the D.-Pascal controversy in its scientific and personal aspects.

1773 —: "Bij een bibliofiele uitgave van het Discours de la méthode." De Gids 113/2: Feb. 1950, 90–94.

On a luxury edition of the work, edited by G. de Roos (Édition La Rose, 1948).

1774 —: "La méthode et les essais de Descartes." In: Descartes et le cartésianisme hollandais (see 38), 1950, 21–44.

1775 *Dilthey, Wilhelm:* Weltanschauung und Analyse des Menschen seit der Renaissance und Reformation. Gesammelte Schriften, 3. Aufl., v. 2. Leipzig und Berlin, Teubner, 1923. See 206a.

1776 *Dimier, Louis:* Descartes. Paris, Nouvelle libraire nationale, 1918. 310 p.

Solid, factual popular introduction to Descartes' philosophy. Neothomist viewpoint. See 132.

1777 —: La vie raisonnable de Descartes. Paris, Plon, 1926. 281 p. (Le roman des grandes existences, v. 5). See 132.

Competent popular biography. Catholic viewpoint.

1778 *Dingle, H.:* "René Descartes. 1596–1650." Nature 165: 1950, 213–14.

1779 *Dixit, Shriniwas:* "Descartes' dogmatism." PhQ (Amalner) 22: 1949–50, 175–78.

1780 *Dolléans, E.:* "À propos de Descartes: la technique soumise à la générosité." RHES 29: 1951, 125–30. See 324.

1781 *Domela Nieuwenhuis, Ferdinand Jacob:* Commentatio de Renati Cartesii commercio cum philosophis Belgicis .... Lovanii, 1827. 115 p. See also 458.

1782 *Donder, Théophile de:* "Quelques réflexions sur le Discours de la méthode." RUB 43: 1937–38, 142–54.

1783 — et J. Pelseneer: "La vitesse de propagation de la lumière selon Descartes." AcBelg Bulletin de la classe des sciences 23: 1937, 689–92.

1784 *Doney, Willis:* "The Cartesian circle." JHI 16: 1955, 324–38.

Descartes vindicated: There is no circle.

1785 —: "Descartes' theory of vision." JP 54: 1957, 775–76.

Abstract of a paper taking issue with Th. Reid and N. Kemp Smith over D.'s theory of the perception of material objects.

1786 *Doniselli, Casimiro:* Sulle funzioni della coclea: La spirale di Cartesio e la coclea organo aritmetico. Bologna, Gamberini & Parmeggiani, 1911. 5 p.

1787 *Dorner, Otto:* Die Rolle der Erfahrung in Descartes' Naturauffassung. Programm Altessen, 1913.

1788 *Doumic, René:* "Les fêtes de Descartes à Amsterdam." RDM 1 novembre 1920 (Per. 6, v. 60), 151–56.

Celebrations held on October 16, 1919 in Amsterdam.

1789 *Dräseke, Johannes:* "In welchem Verhältnis steht Spinozas Lehre von Leib und Seele zu der seiner Vorgänger?" AGP 29 (ns 22): 1916, 144–68.

1790 —: "Zu René Descartes' cogito ergo sum." AGP 32 (ns 25): 1919–20, 45–55. [Descartes, St. Anselm, St. Augustine].

1791 *Dreyfus, Ginette:* "Discussion sur le 'cogito' et l'axiome 'pour penser il faut être' ". RIP 6: 1952, 117–25. See 252.

1792 —: "Physique et géométrie chez Descartes et chez Malebranche." Royaumont 187–99; discussion, 200–207. 1957. See 366.

1793 *Dreyfus-Le Foyer, H.:* "Les conceptions médicales de Descartes." RMM 44: 1937, 237–86. See 365.

1794 *Droetto, Antonio:* "Ugone Grozio e l'avversario di Cartesio nella questione delle verità eterne." RIFD 24, ser. 3, no. 1: 1947, 58–80. See 253.

1795 *Dubarle, D. (O.P.):* "L'esprit de la physique cartésienne." RSPT 26: 1937, 213–43.

The unity of philosophical intent and scientific execution in Descartes' physics, and the viability of his findings.

1796 —: "Remarques sur les règles du choc." Cartesio 325–34. 1937.

Interesting attempt to determine with precision how D. arrived at his laws of collision, and to interpret the difficulties of doing so.

1797 —: "Témoignages actuels sur Descartes." VInt 53: 1937, 433–48.

1798 —: "Recherche socratique, recherche cartésienne et pensée chrétienne". RSPT 27: 369–85, 556–76, 1938.

Somewhat weak analysis of Socratic and Cartesian inquiry as the two main departures in Western philosophizing which cannot leave Christian philosophy indifferent. Redeeming closing pages on the Catholic position which seeks to transcend rationalism by separating wisdom and intelligence; P. Dubarle earnestly recognizes the urgency and the difficulty of reconciling them again.

1799 *Duboux, Émile:* Étude sur la physiologie de Descartes. Paris, Parent, 1871. 71 p. (Paris, École de médecine, Collection de thèses, an 1871, v. 4).

1800 *Ducassé, Pierre:* "Méthode positive et méthode cartésienne." Rsyn 14: 1937, 51–66. Also in: CD 3: 81–87 and in: Scientia 62: 1937, 1–6.

Attempts to minimize the contradictions between Descartes and Comte: "Réveil nécessaire de l'esprit positif, synthétique et cartésien, dans l'expérience scientifique contemporaine."

1801 *Dufrenoy, M.-L.:* "Où Gassendi l'emporte sur Descartes: L'Histoire véritable de Montesquieu." Revue trimestr. canadienne 36: 1950–51, 403–08.

Descartes figures only in the title of this note on a recently edited work of Montesquieu, said to show Gassendi's influence.

1802 *Dugas, L.:* "Une amitié intellectuelle: Descartes et la Princesse Elisabeth". Rennes, Oberthur, 1891. 42 p. [BN]

Elisabeth chose William Penn as her last "directeur spirituel."

1803 *Dugas, L.:* Penseurs libres et liberté de pensée: Montaigne, Descartes, St. Mill, E. Gosse. Dissolution de la foi. Protestantisme et libre pensée. Alcan, 1914. vi, 187 p.

1804 *Dugas, L.:* "Descartes humaniste." Rbleue 1934, 233–34.

1804a *Dugas, René:* La mécanique au XVIIe siècle: des antécédents scolastiques à la pensée classique. Préface de Louis de Broglie. Paris, Dunod (Neuchâtel: Éditions du Griffon), 1954. 624 p. (Bibl. scientifique t. 26, Philosophie et histoire). English tr. by J. R. Maddox: History of mechanics. London, Routledge, 1957. 671 p. See 367.

1805 —: "De Descartes à Newton par l'école anglaise." Université de Paris. Les conférences du Palais de la Découverte, ser. D, no. 16 (6 décembre 1952). Alençon, 1953. 20 p. 16mo. See 367.

1806 —: "Sur le cartésianisme de Huygens." RHSA 7: 1954, 22–33. See 367.

1807 —: "Huygens devant le système du monde, entre Descartes et Newton". Comptes rendus de l'Académie des Sciences 237: 1953, no. 23, 1477–78.

1808 *Duhamel, Georges:* Les confessions sans pénitence. Suivi de trois autres entretiens: Rousseau, Montesquieu, Descartes, Pascal. Plon, 1941. 249 p. (L'abeille, v. 1). See 132.

Romanticized, lively sketch of "Le maître à penser" (p. 95–138), by an avowed "agnostique respectueux et attentif" (p. 113). D. the physicist "s'est condamné .... au pensum métaphysique" (p. 125), though the essence of Cartesianism lies in the Method which is "un instrument de science, et ce n'est donc pas un évangile de sagesse" (p. 135). Pleasant way to meet D.

1808a *Duhamel, J. M. C.:* Mémoire sur la methode des maxima et des minima de Fermat et sur les méthodes des tangentes de Fermat et de Descartes. Mém. de l'ac. des Sciences de l'Inst. Impérial de France 32:1864, 269 ff. [See Vuillemin, no. 398].

1809 *Duhem, Pierre:* Les origines de la statique. Vol. 1. Paris, Hermann, 1905, 327–52. See 368.

1810 —: "De l'accéleration produite par une force constante. Notes pour servir à l'histoire de la dynamique." Congr. int. de philosophie, Genève, 1904. Rapports et comptes-rendus, Genève 1905, 859–915.

1811 —: "Bernardino Baldi, Roberval et Descartes." Bulletin Italien 6: 25–53, 1906. Also in his: Études sur Léonard de Vinci, ceux qu'il a lus et ceux qui l'ont lu. V. 1, Hermann, 1906 (reprinted: de Nobele, 1955), p. 127–56. See 369.

1812 —: "Paul Tannery." RdePh année 5, v. 6: 1905, 215–30. See 397.

1813 *Duinkeerden, Anton van:* "Descartes." De Gemeenschap 5: 1929, 363–74.

"Critique religieuse d'inspiration catholique" (Pos-Steenbergen.)

1814 *Duker, Arnold Cornelius:* Disquisitio historico-theologica de pugna Voetium inter et Cartesium. School-gezag en Eigen-onderzoek. Historisch-critische studie van den strijd tusschen Voetius en Descartes. Leiden, D. Noordhoven van Goor, 1861. vii, 350 p. Dissertation Leiden.

Definitive study of the controversy between Voetius and Descartes from the viewpoint of authority of the School vs. personal inquiry. "La dissertation du jeune théologien reste d'une lecture captivante" (Dibon's review, see 6, 278–80).

1815 —: Gijsbertus Voetius. 4 pts. Leiden, Brill, 1897, 1910, 1914, 1915.

1815a *Dulauney, Paul:* "L'évolution philosophique et médicale du biomécanisme: De Descartes à Boerhaave, de Leibniz à Cabanis." Progrès médical 1927, 1289–93, 1337–42, 1347–52, 1369–84.

1816 *Dumitriu, Anton:* "Misticismul lui Descartes." Revista de filosofie (Bucureşti) 23: 1938, 148–60. [BP 1938/1]

1817 *Dumont:* "L'Oratoire et le cartésianisme en Anjou." AcAngers 15: 1864, 1–206.

1818 *Dunan, Charles:* "Descartes et sa méthode." APC 81: 1910, 377–97.

General critique of Descartes' philosophy as mechanistic. [PhdG 2: 1910, no. 566]

1819 —: Les deux idéalismes. Alcan, 1911, 203 p.

"Tout l'effort de la philosophie moderne a échoué parce qu'à la suite de Descartes on a appliqué à la philosophie une méthode qui ne convient qu'à la science" – speculation operating 'more geometrico' on ideas unrelated to experience and not even remotely resembling a metaphysics (p. 83, and see PhdG 3: 1911).

Reviews: Garrigou-Lagrange in Rthom 20, 233; Anon. in RMM 19, suppl. 1; F. Blanché in RSPT 61, 97; A. Penjon in RPFE 72: 1911/2, 186–95.

1820 *Dupont, Paul:* Descartes, théoricien, géant et solitaire. Histoire du chercheur a travers les âges. Avant-propos par Christian Dietrich. Paris, Clé d'or, 1951. iv, 212 p.

Highly original Descartes appraisal by an Ingénieur général de l'air, who not unexpectedly leaves behind "l'énorme bagage littéraire" of epistemology, metaphysics, ethics etc., to show the "pouvoir magnétique" ("métapsychique") of Descartes the scientist as "théoréticien, expérimentateur, réalisateur." Succint survey of Descartes' scientific work, item by item. Traces the eclipse of this scientific "génie sans équipe," the 19th century scientific renaissance, and the 20th century "apothéose" of his ideas.

Reviews: Anon. in BCLF 6: 1951, 770–71; Gommes in Les lettres Romanes 1954, 84; B. Rochot in RHSA 5: 1952, 274–75.

1821 *DuPont-Bertris:* "Descartes." In his: Éloges et caractères des philosophes les plus célèbres depuis la naissance de Jésus-Christ jusqu'à présent. Paris, H.-S.-.P. Gissey, 1726, 288–326. [BN]

1822 *Dupréel, Émile:* "La place du moment cartésien dans l'histoire de la pensée morale." CD 2: 95–100. 1937. Also in his: Essais pluralistes. Paris, PUF 1949, ch. 13, 318–23 (Univ. libre de Bruxelles, Travaux de la faculté de philosophie et des lettres).

Cartesianism an end product of the classical belief in the uniqueness of values. The modern mind breaks away from it to move towards pluralism.

1823 *Durdík, Josef:* O významu filosofie Descartesovy .... v Praze, Otto, 1897. 16 p. (Sbírska přednášek a rozprav, ed. J. Goll, ser. 4, no. 7).

Commemorative address and congratulatory telegrams on the occasion of the 1896 Prague D. celebration.

1824 *Dryoff, A.:* "Drei philosophische Jubiläen: Descartes, Wolff, Bolzano." Jahrbuch der Görres-Gesellschaft 1937, 77–87.

E

1824a *E. G.:* "Le polemiche cartesiane ai tempi di Vico." GCFI 38: 1959, 286–88.

On the complex position of the "moderns" and the controversies in Toscana, Naples (Tommaso Cornelio) and Padua (Elia Astorini).

1824b —: "La diffusione del cartesianismo fra i medici." GCFI 38: 1959, 427–28. (On the German Johann Jakob Waldschmidt.)

1824c *Eastwood, Dorothy Margaret:* The revival of Pascal. A study of his relation to modern French thought. Oxford, Clarendon Press, 1936. (Oxford studies in modern languages and literature).

Important study of Maurice Blondel, Father Laberthonnière, Pierre Duhem and many other modern French philosophers and historians of philosophy and science, who played a notable role in the shaping of the modern Pascal and Descartes images.

Review: J. Dedieu in RHL 44: 1937, 275–78.

1824d *Ebbinghaus, Julius:* "Der Gebrauch des Prinzipes 'cogito ergo sum' in der Descartes' schen Philosophie." CD 1: 99–104. 1937.

Finds no circularity in Descartes' argument.

1825 *Eberhardt, Karl Friedrich:* Die Kosmogonie des Descartes im Zusammenhang der Geschichte und Philosophie. Berlin, Trenkel, 1908. 98 p. Diss. Berlin.

Descartes' cosmogony ("Eine notwendige Tat"), its predecessors and its influence to the time of Kant. Author's notice in PhdG 1: 1908–09, n. 610. [Rsyn 1937 lists author erroneously as "Berhardt."]

1826 *Echarri, J.:* "Descartes y Malebranche en las concepciones espacio-temporales de Balmes." PenM 3: 1947, 185–240.

1827 —: "Un influjo español desconocido en la formación del sistema cartesiano; dos textos paralelos de Toledo y Descartes sobre el espacio." PenM 6: 1950, 291–232.

Francesco de Toledo and late Scholasticism in general influenced Descartes through his study at La Flèche. See also 263 (Gilen).

1828 *Echeverria, J. R.:* "En torno al cogito y la noción de existencia." RF Chile 1: 1950, 491–507.

Discusses Husserl, Maine de Biran, Dilthey, Scheler and the reality problem: doubt and solipsism.

1829 *Edelman, Nathan:* "The mixed metaphor in Descartes." RR 41: 1950, 167–78. See 403.

1830 *Ehrlich, Richard:* Die Neubildung der metaphysischen Grundbegriffe durch Descartes und die Motive, die ihn dazu antrieben. Lenzen a. Elbe, 1903. 87 p. Dissertation Erlangen.

1831 *Ehrmann, P.:* L'indépendence de l'esprit et de la matière. Pourquoi avons-nous oublié la démonstration qu'en donne Descartes? Vrin 1946. 28 p. Also in: Revue de théologie et d'action évangélique d'Aix-en-Provence, July 1946.

Descartes' proofs of dualism are reassuringly perennial; they guarantee that Western philosophizing will retain its spirituality and independence.

1831a —: "Utilisation pratique d'une préface méconnue." Presse médicale 66: 1958, 949–50. Also MF 334: 1958, 349–52. "Histoire d'une préface méconnue en France et inédite en Hollande." Philosophia reformata 25: 1960, 36–45.

The French Preface to the 1647 edition of MM ("Le Libraire au Lecteur") was approved by Descartes and is therefore authoritative; however, ever since V. Cousin's D. edition it has customarily been replaced by the Latin Preface of 1641. Interesting sidelights on D. editions.

1832 *Eibl, Hans:* "Descartes und der scholastische Gedanke." CD 3: 17–24. 1937.

Nicely balanced, firm appraisal of common points of departure and basic differences.

1833 *Eicke, Werner A.:* "Due interpretazioni di Cartesio." RFNS 31: 1939, 425–27.

1833a *Eisele-Halpern, C.:* "Some remarks on the logic of science of the 17th century as interpreted by Charles Peirce." In: Actes du symposium intern. des sciences phys. et math. dans la première moitié du XVIIe siècle (see no. 1005a).

1834 *Ellend, Josef:* (Descartes' system of the universe). Athenaeum no. 21: 1912, 111–118. In Hungarian. [Not traceable]

1835 *Elvenich, Peter Josef:* Doe Beweise für das Dasein Gottes nach Cartesius. Zur Jubel-Feier der Rheinischen Friedrich-Wilhelms-Universität. Breslau, 1868. 4to.

1836 *Emery, Abbé Jacques André:* Pensées de Descartes sur la religion et la morale. Le Clère, 1811. ccviii, 397 p. Reprinted in: J. P. Migne, Démonstrations évangéliques, v. 2, 1843; also Tours, Mame, 1870, 1879 (Les apologistes du Christianisme au XVIIe siècle). See 452a.

1837 *Emge, C. A.:* "Dem Gedächtnis an Descartes." Emge 1–2. 1938. See 523.

1838 — (editor): Dem Gedächtnis an René Descartes (1937). See 523.

1838a *Emmet, Dorothy:* "Descartes on body and mind: After 300 years." Cambridge Jl 4: 1950, 67–82.

1839 *Enes, J.:* "Influências mecanísticas no pensamento filosófico do Padre António Cordeiro." RPFil 11: 1955, 554–60.

Cordeiro as example of the development of Scholastic philosophy towards mechanism in D.'s time. Cordeiro claims that material form is something new, produced by efficient causes not as "ens quod" but as "ens quo." [Bsig 10: 1955, 11608.]

1840 *Engelhardt, P.:* "Das heimatlose Ich: Descartes und wir." Neue Ordnung 11: 1957, 241–43.

1841 *Enriques, Federigo:* "Descartes et Galilée." RMM 44: 1937, 221–35.

1842 *Epelbaum, Jacob:* "El agnosticismo de Descartes y su sumisión a lo infinito." Homenaje, 2: 311–33. 1937. See 152.

1843 *Erdmann, Benno:* "Zur Methode der Geschichte der Philosophie mit spezieller Rücksicht auf die Metaphysik des Cartesius." In: Eduard Zeller Festschrift, Berlin, G. Reimer, 1894, p. 32–39.

Introduction to a paper which was apparently not completed.

1844 —: "Descartes und seine Schule. Literaturbericht." AGP 7: 1893–4, 521–534.

Critical discussion of E. Goldbeck, L. Fischer, H. Kolligs, Twardowski, H. Müller on Clauberg, Novaro on Malebranche.

1844a *Erdmann, Johann Eduard:* Von Cartesius bis Kant. Vol. 1: Einleitung. Cartesius. In his: Versuch einer wissenschaftlichen Darstellung der Geschichte der neuern Philosophie [1834ff.] Faksimile-Neudruck, Stuttgart 1932, 1.-2. Abteilung, Bd. 1. See 171a.

1845 *Eringa, S.:* "Descartes et Pascal." Stemmen der Tijds 15: 1926/1, 217–46.

"Étude d'inspiration calviniste," emphasizing Pascal's religious thought (Pos-Steenberghen, Rsyn 1937.)

1846 *Ernst, Christian:* "Hielt Descartes die Tiere für bewusstlos?" AGPs 11: 1908, 433ff.

1847 *Ernst, W.:* Descartes, sein Leben und Denken. Skizze. Leipa. Boehm, 1869. [Balz]

1847a *Escritos* en honor de Descartes (La Plata, 1938). See 39.

1848 *Espinas, Alfred* (A. V. Espinas): Descartes et la morale. 2 vols. Paris, Bossard, 1925. 252, 204 p. Reprinted: Paris, Sorlot, 1937. See 163.

1849 —: "Pour l'histoire du cartésianisme." RMM 14: 1906, 265–93. Reprinted in his: Descartes (see 163).

1850 —: "Le point de départ de Descartes." Rbleue March 3, March 10, 1906: 257–61, 293–98. Reprinted in his: Descartes. (see 163).

1851 —: "L'idée initiale de la philosophie de Descartes." RMM 15: 1907, 253–78. Reprinted in his: Descartes (see 163).

1852 —: "Descartes de seize à vingt-neuf ans." Rbleue March 23, March 30: 1907, 353–56, 389–92. Also in AMP 68: 1907. Reprinted in his: Descartes (see 163).

1852a *L'esprit cartésien.* Entretien. 1937. See 525.

1853 *Estiu, E.:* "La fundamentación del mecanismo en la física de Descartes." Universidad (Santa Fé) 13: 1942, 31–53.

1853a *Études cartésiennes* (Congrès Descartes, 1937). See 36.

1853b *Études sur Descartes* (RMM 1937.) See 533.

1854 "*Extraits* des manuscrits de M. Phélippes Beaulieux sur la famille Descartes." BSA Touraine 1871–73, 1897–98. [Lanson 4153]

F

1855 *F., J. B.:* "Los grandes pedagogos: Renato Descartes." El monitor de la educación común (Buenos Aires) 59: June 1940, no. 805.

1856 *Fabre de Charrin:* Éloge de René Descartes proposé par l'Académie Francaise. Paris, S. Jorry, 1765. 69 p. See 126.

1857 *Fabri, E.:* "Lo studio delle passioni in Cartesio, Malebranche e Spinoza." Cfil 5: 1911, 133–65.

1858 *Fabro, C.:* "Cartesianismo e neoscolastica." Bolletino filosofico (Roma) 4: 1938, 189–96.

Discussion of CARTESIO, see 35.

1859 *Faggi, Adolfo:* "Cartesio e le passioni dell'anima." Rendiconti del R. Istituto Lombardo di scienze e lettere, ser. 2, 42: 1909, 509–27. Reprinted in author's: Studi filosofici e letterari, R. Università di Torino, 1938, 12–18.

Careful determination of what Descartes means by emotions and passions.

1860 —: "Cartesio e Newton." AcTorino. Atti 58: 1923, 323–37.

1861 — e Gino Loria: Art. "Descartes" in: Enciclopedia Italiana 12: 661–65.

1861a *Fagnola, Franco:* "Dell'anticartesianismo di Malebranche." Archivio della cultura Italiana (ASFI) 1942: 163–76. See 435b.

1862 *Faguet, Émile:* "Descartes." In his: Dix-septième siècle; études littéraires. Éd. revue et augm. Paris, Société fr. d'imprimerie 1903, 1–71. Also in RCC 12: 1903–04, v. 1, 19–22, 162–71, 241–51, 289–305.

Descartes is a Christian in his metaphysics, a semi-stoic in his ethics. Castigates the 19th century Descartes revival as falsifying him through overemphasizing the cogito.

1863 "*La famille Descartes à Sucé.*" BSA Nantes 12: 1873, 168–72.

1864 "*La famille Descartes en Bretagne.*" BSA Bretagne 1876. [Lanson 4155]

1865 *Farez, P.:* "Descartes et la préexcellence de la médicine." Jdeb, 12 October 1924.

1866 *Farges, Albert (Msgr.):* La philosophie de Descartes. La bonne presse, (1917). 32 p. (Apologétique contemporaine).

Thomist of purest observance treats Cartesianism as rationalist virus infection. D. may have been a Christian and a philosopher, but was not a Christian philosopher, whatever his intentions.

1866a —: La crise de la certitude. Paris, Berche, 1908.

On Cartesian doubt.

1867 *Faust, A.:* Descartes und Augustin zur Unterscheidung von theoretischer und religiöser "Gewissheit." München, 1924. 39 p. Dissertation Heidelberg.

1868 *Favaro, A.:* "Adversaria Galileiana. Ser. 3: 19. Nuovi supplementi al Carteggio Galileano." AcPadova, Atti e mem., ns 34: 1917–18, 25–43.

On Descartes, Mersenne, Nicéron. See also ser. 4. [Cordiè]

1869 *Favières, A.:* "Descartes et la morale." RHPh ns 5: 1937, 172–80.

1870 *Faye, H.:* Descartes, l'homme et le penseur. Discours. Tours, impr. de Deslis frères. 1897. Reprinted from BSA Touraine 11: 1897, ler trimestre, 19–46.

1871 *Faye, Hervé Auguste:* Sur l'origine du monde. Théories cosmogoniques des anciens et des modernes. 2e éd. Gauthier-Villars, 1885. xi, 309 p.

1872 *Fearing, F.:* "Descartes. A study in the history of reflex action." Psychological Review (Lancaster) 36: 1929, 375–88.

1872a *Federn, Paul:* "Some variations in ego feeling." International Journal of Psycho-Analysis 7: 1926, 434ff. See 104a.

1873 *Feibleman, James:* An introduction to Peirce's philosophy. 1946. See 187.

1874 *Felsch, Carl:* Der Kausalitätsbegriff bei Descartes. Langensalza, 1891 (Berlin, 1892.) 59 p. Dissertation Bern. Also: Zeitschrift für exakte Philosophie 18: 1891.

1875 *Feo, I. de:* Introduzione critica al Discorso sul metodo. Napoli, Pironti, 1936. 22 p.

1876 *Féret, P.:* "L'aristotélisme et le cartésianisme dans l'Université [de Paris] au XVIIe siècle." APC April 1903. ()

Fériet: see Kampé de Fériet.

1877 *Fernandat, René:* "Descartes et P. Valéry." In his: Autour de Paul Valéry: Lignes d'horizon. 2e éd., considérablement augmentée, précédée d'une lettre-préface de M. Paul Valéry. Paris, Arthaud, c. 1944. Ch. 6, 111–124. See 194.

1877a —: "Les thèmes valéryens. I: Paul Valéry et Descartes." Christus 40: 1938, 25–33. See 1877.

1878 *Fernández Alonzo, Aniceto (O.P.):* "El concepto antiguo y tradicional de filosofía." Cartesio, 353–74. 1937.

Definitions of philosophy from Plato to Balmes.

1879 *Ferretti, Gino:* "Descartes et le problème: Le monde n'est-il un rêve?" CD 1: 61–68. 1937.

The "Dream of Descartes" is linked to his antithesis of imaginary dream world vs. intellectual reality, to his formulation of doubt, and to his attitude towards imagination.

1880 *Ferrier, Raoul:* De Descartes à Ampère, ou Progrès vers l'unité rationnelle. Basel, Verlag für Recht und Gesellschaft, 1949. xv, 294 p. See 370.

1881 —: De Descartes à Ampère .... (see 1880). Seconde éd. Deuxième partie: L'ampérien dans la théorie corpusculaire .... Paris, Ulman, 1953. 95 p. [Revision of ch. 5.] See 370.

1882 —: Progrès vers l'unité rationnelle; réflexions proposées d'après les œuvres de Descartes et d'Ampère. Ch. 6: La cosmologie méthodique. Ulman, 1954, 265–306. [Revision of Ch. 6 of his: De Descartes à Ampère, see 370.

1882a —: "Aperçus nouveaux sur la cosmologie cartésienne." Rsyn 63: 1948, 31–52. Discussion, 53–58. See 370.

1883 *Ferro, Carmelo:* "Il problema del fenomenismo razionalistico." RFNS 32: 1940, 150–72.

1884 —: "A proposito di due diverse concezioni del fenomenismo." RFNS 33: 1941, 71–83.

1885 —: "Galilei e Cartesio." In: Nel terzo centenario della morte di Galileo Galilei. Milano, Vita e pensiero, 1942 (UCSC v. 20), 327–50.

1886 —: "Cartesio e il problema della metafisica." RFNS 42: 1950, 335–55. See 256.

1887 —: "Intorno ad alcune recenti interpretazioni del pensiero cartesiano." RFNS 42: 1950, 194–221. See 14 and 25.

1888 *Fetscher, Iring:* "Das französische Descartesbild der Gegenwart," PhRu 3: 1955, 166–98. See 26.

1889 *Feuerbach, Ludwig:* "Descartes." Ch. 5 in his: Geschichte der neueren Philosophie von Bacon von Verulam bis Benedikt Spinoza (1833). Also in his: Sämtliche Werke, ed. Bolin und Jodl, v. 3, Stuttgart 1906, 180–246. See 171a.

Feuillet: See Biot et Feuillet.

1890 *Feuling, Daniel (O.S.B.):* "Descartes' Persönlichkeit im Spiegel des Discours de la méthode." Cartesio 375–91. 1937.

Routine piece, except for an interesting appraisal of D.'s personality from the style of DM (381–3).

1891 *Filiasi Carcano, P.:* "Da Cartesio a Husserl." Ricerche filosofiche (Messina) 6: 1936, 18–34.

1892 *Filipovič, Vladimir:* "René Descartes. Povodom 300 godišnjice smrti.' Vjesnik (Zagreb) 10: April 1950, p. 2. [Anniversary of D.'s death.]

1893 *Finance, Joseph de:* Cogito cartésien et réflexion thomiste. Aph 16, no. 2: 1946, 1–189. See 208.

1893a —: "Position anselmienne et démarche cartésienne." In: Spicilegium Beccense I: Congrès international du IXe centenaire de l'arrivée d'Anselme au Bec. Paris, Vrin, 1959, 259–72.

A comparison of the two ontological proofs shows a wholly different philosophical spirit despite obvious technical similarities.

1894 *Fischer, Kuno:* Descartes' Leben, Werke und Lehre. (1852). 4. neubearbeitete Auflage. Heidelberg, Winter, 1897. (Vol. 1 of his: Geschichte der neueren Philosophie. Jubiläumsausgabe.) Descartes and his school. Transl. from the third German edition by J. P. Gordy, edited by Noah Porter. New York, Scribner, 1887. xvi, 589 p. (Fischer's History of philosophy). Russian tr. 1906. See 138, 150.

1895 —: Spinozas Leben, Werke und Lehre. 1912. See 138.

1896 *Fischer, Ludwig:* Cogito ergo sum. Wiesbaden, Bergmann, 1890. 58 p. Dissertation Leipzig.

Author's remarks about the antecedents of the cogito "achieve a broader basis only by virtue of the fact that he does not stick to his subject" (Erdmann, see 1844.)

1896a *Fitzgerald, Desmond J.:* "Descartes, defender of the faith." Thought 34: 1959, 384–404.

Descartes the architect building a church to the greater glory of God, always refraining from endangering faith, shoring it up by his metaphysics.

1897 *Flam, Leo:* Plato – Descartes – Kant. Antwerpen, Uitgeverij "Ontwikkeling," 1952. xviii, 357 p.

1898 *Flavien, L.:* "Le troisième centenaire du Discours de la méthode." Enseignement publique Dec. 1937, 332–46; Feb. 1938, 109–19; March 1938, 221–28. See 592.

1899 *Fleckenstein, Joachim Otto:* "Pierre Varignon (1654–1722) und die mathematischen Wissenschaften im Zeitalter des Cartesianismus." AIHS 5: 1948, 76–138. See 372.

1900 —: "Cartesianische Erkenntnistheorie und mathematische Physik des 17. Jh." Gesnerus 7: 1950, 120–39. See 371.

1901 —: "Descartes und die exakten Wissenschaften des Barock." Forschungen und Fortschritte 30: 1956, 116–21.

The Cartesian model is too simple for the modern scientist: physics cannot be mapped onto mathematics as geometry can be mapped onto algebra. D.'s metaphysical geometricism of extension plunges into depths not needed to constitute science even in his own time. Sharp attack on Jaspers. No evaluation of the Baroque aspect of Descartes.

1902 *Flewelling, Ralph Tyler:* "Chinese influences in late Cartesian thought." CD 3: 37–42. 1937. See 310.

1903 *Flex, Werner:* Über den baconischen und den cartesischen Zweifel. Heidelberg, Hörning, 1903. 69 p. Dissertation Heidelberg.

1904 *Flórez, G.:* "El problema del conocimiento según Descartes." RUC Perú 5: 1937, 340–58.

1905 *Flori, Miguel (S.J.):* "Descartes y Balmes." Cartesio 335–52. 1937.

Jaime Balmes' "excessive eulogies" addressed to Descartes should not conceal the profound philosophical differences between them. Balmes did not see D. as a rationalist but as a kindred Catholic apologist. Good brief comparison of their thought.

1906 *Flourens, Pierre:* Fontenelle, ou De la philosophie moderne relativement aux sciences physiques. (s. l.) [1847.] 242 p.

1907 *Focht, Ivo:* "O historijskom značenju Descartesovog učenja o metodu." Studentski list (Zagreb) 6, no. 9: April 1950, 4–5.

The historical significance of D.'s doctrine of method.

1908 *Fog, Bruun Juul:* Cartesius, den nyere philosophies fader. Kjoebenhavn, F. H. Eibe, 1856. 141 p. Dissertation.

Cartesianism moving towards Spinozism.

1909 *Foncin, P.:* "A propos d'un autographe de Descartes et d'un document inédit sur le cogito ergo sum." MSAS Carcassonne, 1884, 367ff. [Alquié in no. 149; Lanson in no. 4167 gives the publication date as 1879.]

A copy of PP and Specimina, 1644 edition, at Carcassonne, dedicated to Ogier by "Des Cartis" (sic), has a ms. note of Ogier saying that the cogito is taken from Eusebius.

1910 *Fonsegrive:* "Les prétendues contradictions de Descartes." RPFE 15: 1883, 510–32, 643–57.

Cogito and cartesian circle: Kant, Maine de Biran, Liard.

1911 *Font Puig, Pedro:* "Significación de Descartes como promotor de la ciencia físico-matemática y del espíritu crítico en filosofía." RevF 9: 1950, 643–68.

Review: J. Díez-Alegría in PenM 8: 1952, 263.

1912 *Forest, Aimé:* "Descartes et la tradition médiévale." RCO 11: 1937, 687–700. Also: Hommage à Descartes. Poitiers, 1937 (see 531), 47–60.

Review: S. in Bulletin thomiste 5: 1937–38, 152.

1913 —: "Réflexions sur la morale cartésienne." RSPT 26: 1937, 43–57.

On the difference between Cartesian and Thomist ethics.

1914 *Forest, Ceslas:* "Le cartésianisme et l'orientation de la science moderne." Rdom November 1937. Also Paris-Liège, La pensée catholique, 1938. 19 p.

1915 *Forest, Louis:* Le carnet d'un veilleur de jour. On peut prévoir l'avenir – comment? ou la Descartomancie. Payot, 1918, 255 p. See 115.

1916 *Foster, (Sir) Michael:* Lectures on the history of physiology during the 16th, 17th and 18th centuries. The Lane Lectures, 1900. Cambridge Natural Science Manuals, Biological Series, 1901. 310 p. Republished: Cambridge UP, 1924, 306 p.

Rich, vigorous but sparsely documented work. Very brief treatment of Descartes himself, enlivened by quoting the characteristic judgment of his contribution to physiology by Nicolaus Stensen (1638–1686).

1917 *Foucher de Careil, Louis Alexandre comte de* (editor): Œuvres inédites de Descartes. Précéedés d'une introduction sur la méthode par Louis Alexandre comte Foucher de Careil. Ladrange et Durand, 1859–60. 2 vols. XVI, cxvii, 158; xii, 238 p. See 75.

1918 —: "De la persécution du cartésianisme en Hollande, d'après des nouveaux documents (Mémoire de Descartes à M. de la Thuillerie contre Gisbert Voetius d'Utrecht, 1644). AMPS 62: 1862, 217ff.

1919 —: Leibniz, Descartes et Spinoza. Avec un rapport par Victor Cousin. Paris, Ladrange, 1862. 292 p.

Cousin's report deals with Foucher de Careil's "Réfutation de Spinoza par Leibniz."

1920 —: Descartes et la princesse palatine, ou De l'influence du cartésianisme sur les femmes au XVIIIe siècle. Paris, Durand, 1862. 131 p. Reprinted from AMPS 62: 1862, 401–56; 63: 1863, 57–97.

1921 —: "Histoire d'une âme sincère. Descartes et la Princesse Elisabeth. (Lettres, 1646–1650)." AMPS 107: 1877, 672ff.

1922 —: Descartes, la princesse Elisabeth et la reine Christine, d'après des lettres inédites. Paris-Amsterdam, Baillière, 1879. 220 p. Nouvelle éd.: Alcan, 1909, vi, 219 p. Also AMPS 107: 1879, 789ff.

Introduction (7–45) and correspondence.

1923 *Fouillée, Alfred:* Descartes. Paris, Hachette, 1893. 207 p. (Les grands écrivains français.) Russian tr.: Dekart, Moskva, 1895. Spanish tr. by Alberto A. Graziano: Descartes. Buenos Aires, Ed. Americalee, 1944.

Rapidly moving, lively introduction to Descartes, popular without being fuzzy, with an unconcealed "parti pris" for Descartes and some sideswipes at Pascal. Kant was the "grand continuateur et renovateur du cartésianisme au XIXe siècle," and Schopenhauer recognized the cogito as equivalent with his "Welt als meine Vorstellung" (p. 198).

Reviews: Bouillier in RPFE 37: 1894, 287–97; Joseph Bertrans in Journal des savants July-August 1893; C. Adam in RPFE 36: 1893, 436–38; A. Chauvin in no. 1518, 331–33.

1924 —: "Descartes et les doctrines contemporaines." RPFE 37: 1894, 534–46.

Fouillée's reply to Bouillier's sharp critique (ibid., 287–97) of his book, regarding the affinity of Cartesian and modern philosophy, esp. Schopenhauer.

1925 —: "L'influence et l'avenir des idées cartésiennes." RDM 15 January 1893, 359–90.

Fouquer de Jonquières, Ernest: see Jonquières, Ernest.

1926 *Fraga, Gustavo de:* "Fenomelologia e cartesianismo." Filosofia (Lisboa) 4: 1957, no. 14, 89–97.

1927 *Franceschi, Alfredo:* "El concepto de materia sutil en Descartes." Homenaje, 2: 11–41. 1937. See 258.

1928 *Franchi, Ausonio* (pseud. of Cristoforo Bonavino): "Descartes." In his: Letture sulla storia della filosofia moderna: Bacone, Descartes, Spinoza, Malebranche. Milano, Ferrari, 1863, v.1, p. 261–408. Reprinted: Descartes. Milano, Athena, 1931. 2 vols. See 207.

1929 *Franck, Adolphe:* Moralistes et philosophes. Didier, 1872, 157–227.

Discussion of Descartes and Cartesianism, following and critically appraising Bouillier's Histoire du cartésianisme.

1930 *François, Enriques:* "Descartes y los antiguos." Homenaje 2: 129–74. 1937. "L'honnête homme" and the classicist milieu of the 17th c.

1930a *Franeker.* Descartes exhibition 1929. See 505.

1931 *Frankel, Charles:* The faith of reason: the idea of progress in the French Enlightenment. New York, Kings Crown Press, 1948. x, 165 p. Columbia dissertation. Ch. 2 on the "philosophes" and Descartes.

1932 *Frankl, Victor:* "La posición de Descartes en la evolución espiritual del Occidente." Univ. nacional de Colombia 15: 1950, 227–42.

1933 *Franken, J.:* "Descartes en de Utrechtsche Universiteit." Handelingen van het zeventiende Nederlandsche Philologen-Congres (Groningen) 1937, 136–37.

1934 *Franz, Marie-Louise von:* Der Traum des Descartes. In: Zeitlose Dokumente der Seele. Zürich, Rascher, 1952 (Studien aus dem C.-G. Jung-Institut, v. 3), p. 49–119. See 103.

1935 *Frauenglass, Edward:* "Descartes i filozofia XVIII-go wieku." Prz 40/2: 1937, 185–198.

18th century philosophy is linked to Descartes by the tendency to subordinate knowledge to practical ends, and by its interest in medicine, technology, man and his needs, (BP 1937/2.)

1935a *Frédérix, Pierre:* Monsieur René Descartes en son temps. Paris, Gallimard, 1959, 344 p. (Leurs figures.)

Well-written, briskly debunking piece of popularisation which could have been very good if the author had made at least his basic facts complete and right.

1936 *Freud, Sigmund:* "Brief an Maxime Leroy über den Traum des Descartes." In his: Gesammelte Werke, London, Imago, v. 14, 1948, 558–60. Also in his: Gesammelte Schriften, Vienna, Intern. psychoanalytischer Verlag, v. 12, 1934; and in M. Leroy (see 124).

1937 *Freudenthal, Jakob:* "Spinoza und die Scholastik." In: Philosophische Aufsätze Eduard Zeller zu seinem 50. Doktorjubiläum gewidmet. Leipzig, 1887, 83–138.

Commonly cited as starting point of the reappraisal of Descartes' relationship to Scholasticism, but see 214 (Koyré, German ed., 6–7.) See also Lewkowitz, 2544.

1938 *Friedmann, Georges:* 'Un prince des temps modernes." Eur 44, no. 175: 15 July 1937, 297–311, also in: Descartes (see 37).

Descartes as a rallying point when man "seems to be possessed by a kind of rage against himself."

1939 *Friedrich, Hugo:* Descartes und der französische Geist. Leipzig, Meiner, 1937. 78 p. (Wissenschaft und Zeitgeist, v. 6). See 453.

1940 *Fries, August de:* Die Substanzenlehre J. Locke's mit Beziehung auf die cartesianische Philosophie kritisch entwickelt und untersucht. Bremen, Hauschild 1879. 77 p. Dissertation Jena.

1941 *Frischeisen-Köhler, Max:* "Descartes." In: Grosse Denker, ed. Ernst von Aster. v. 1. Leipzig, Quelle und Meyer, 1911, 347 83. 2nd ed. 1913. Also Spanish: "Descartes." In: Descartes, Spinoza, Leibnitz. Collección Los grandes pensadores. Revista de Occidente.

1941a *Frolov, Iu.:* "Fiziologičeskoe učenie Dekarta i teorija uslovnykh refleksov Pavlova." Pod znamenem Marksizma, no. 8, 1937.

The physiological doctrine of D. and Pavlov's theory of the conditioned reflex. [In Russian.]

1942 *Frondizi, Risieri:* Descartes y la substancia pensante. In his: Substancia y función en el problema del yo. Buenos Aires, Losada, 1952, p. 15–30. English transl: The nature of the self; a functional interpretation. New Haven, Yale UP 1953, Pt. I, Ch. 1, 3–17. See 259.

1943 —: "Influencia de Descartes sobre el idealismo de Berkeley." Homenaje 1: 329–40. 1937.

Chiefly on Malebranche's influence upon Berkeley, with scattered comment and references regarding the title theme.

1944 —: "Descartes y la filosofía inglesa del siglo XVII." Escritos 61–74. 1937.

Tries to reveal a latent Cartesianism in English philosophy in the second half of the century, carrying into the beginning of the 18th c., the formative period of Berkeley.

1945 *Fueter, E.:* "Descartes und die Entstehung der modernen exakten Schweizer Naturwissenschaft." Verhandlungen der Schweizer naturforschenden Gesellschaft, 1935. ()

1946 *Fulton, James Stewart:* "The Cartesianism of phenomenology." PhR 49: 1940, 285–308. See 173.

1947 *Furlani, G.:* "Avicenna e il cogito ergo sum di Cartesio." Islamica, v. 3, fasc. 1. ()

1948 *Furschtschick, Mejer:* Die Ethik in Descartes' System der Philosophie. Bern, P. Haupt, 1920. ii, 72 p. Dissertation Bern.

G

1949 *Gabaude, Jean-Marc:* La liberté chez Descartes, Spinoza, Leibniz et Kant. Thèse-lettres, Toulouse. 30 Oct. 1951. (Unpublished).

1950 *Gabriel, Leo:* "Der Denker zwischen den Zeiten." Die Warte (Blätter für Forschung, Kunst und Wissenschaft) March 18, 1950, no. 12. p. 1.

"Mit Descartes begann das Sterben Gottes, aber gleichzeitig das Sterben des Menschen."

1950a *Gachev, D.:* "Dekart i estetika." Pod znamenem Marksizma, no. 8, 1937.

Descartes and esthetics. [In Russian.]

1951 *Gadoffre, Gilbert* (ed.): Descartes. Discours de la méthode. Manchester UP 1941. xliii, 94 p.

Useful for Gadoffre's 44-page introduction, stressing the "trompe l'oeil" character of D.'s clarity, and the notes (75–94), especially on the chronology of DM.

1952 —: "Corneille et Descartes." In: Traditions de notre culture. Éditions du Cerf, 1941, p. 76–91. (Collection Rencontres, v. 2). See 405.

1953 —: "Sur la chronologie du 'Discours de la méthode' ". RHPh 11: 1943, 45–70. Revised, condensed in Rsyn 63: 1948, 11–27, discussion 28–30. See 260.

1954 —: "Le Discours de la méthode et l'histoire littéraire." FS 2: 301–14, 1948. See 404.

1955 *Gagnebin, S.:* "La réforme cartésienne et son fondement géométrique." Gesnerus 7: 1950, 105–20. See 371.

1956 *Gaillard, Gabriel Henri* (1726–1806): Éloge de René Descartes. Discours qui a remporté le prix de l'Académie Française en 1765. Paris, Regnard, 1765. See 126.

1957 *Galama, Sybrand H.M.:* Het wijsgerig onderwijs aan de Hogeschool te Franeker, 1585–1811. Franeker, T. Wever, 1943. 358 p. Thesis Leiden. See 452.

1958 *Galdstone, Iago:* "Descartes and modern psychiatric thought." Isis 35: 1944, 118–28. See 95.

Gallagher, Mercedes Parks de: see Parks de Gallagher.

1958a *Galindo-Aguilar, E.:* " 'L'homme volant' d'Avicenne et le cogito de Descartes." IBLA (Institut des belles lettres arabes) 21: 1958, 279–95. See 260a.

1959 *Galli, Gallo:* Il pensiero filosofico di Cartesio. Torino, Chiantore, 1943. xii, 334 p.

Identical with Galli's Studi (no. 1960), except that the last chapter (Il problema dell'errore) is lacking.

1960 —: Studi cartesiani. Torino, Chiantore, 1943. xi, 443 p. (Testi e studi di filosofia e pedagogia, v.l). See 209.

1961 —: Sul pensiero di A. Carlini ed altri studi. Torino, Gheroni, 1950. 335 p. See 4 and 1967a.

".... scritto equilibrato e profondo" [M. Schiavone in RFNS 43: 1951, 464–67]; N. Jimenez in RevF 13: 1954, 344–34; V. Stella in Gmet 14: 1959, 109–12.

1962 —: La dottrina cartesiana del metodo. Roma, Albrighi Segati, 1937. 73 p. Also in no. 1960, p. 1–64. See 209.

1963 —: Il dubbio e il cogito di Cartesio. AnCagl 7, no. 2: 1937. 59 p. Also in no. 1960, p. 67–114. See 209.

1964 —: "Il problema dell'errore in Cartesio." Cagliari 1938–39. Also Portici, Bellavista, 1939. 114 p. Also in his: Studi (see 1960), p. 335–444. See 209.

1965 —: "Le prove dell'esistenza di Dio in Cartesio." Cagliari 7: 1938, 150 p. Also in no. 1960, p. 117–244.

1966 —: "Dalla filosofia di Cartesio alla filosofia della concretezza." RRFC 31: 1939, 213–24.

Review article on Carbonara's "Circolo vizioso." See 205.

1967 —: "La dimostrazione dell'esistenza del mondo esterno e il valore pratico delle qualità sensibili." Cagliari 9/4: 1939. 108 p. Also in no. 1960, 47–331.

1967a —: "Il problema di Cartesio." In his: no. 1961, p. 119–35, and in his: Filosofi d'oggi ed altri scritti. Torino, Gheroni, 1958, 241–57.

D.'s chief concern was philosophical, not scientific, least of all ethical (in ethics and politics, "non fu un eroe, Cartesio": his strength lay elsewhere.) His meditative inclination explains the "larvatus prodeo" as well as the "bene vixit qui bene latuit." Commemorative 1950 lecture.

1968 *Gallois, P.:* "Descartes et sa méthode." La nouvelle revue 59 (ser. 4, v. 150), July-Aug. 1937: 265–72; v. 151: Aug.-Sept. 1937, 40–52.

Pt. 2 criticizes Descartes' method in science for ignoring the principle of empirical verification.

1969 —: "La méthode de Descartes et la médicine." Hippocrate (Paris) 6, no. 2: 1938, 65–77.

1970 *Gandev, Hristo:* "Quelques textes de l'Institution de la religion chrestienne sur les passions de l'âme." Studia histor.-philologica Serdiciana (Sofia) 1: 1938, 225–30.

On Calvin's Institutions and Descartes' Traité des passions.

1971 *Gandillot, Maurice:* Essai sur la gamme. Gauthier-Villars, 1907. xvi, 575 p. See also his: "Le débat sur la gamme. Les conceptions de Pythagore et de Descartes." RGSPA 1907.

Review: W. Mercadier in RGSPA 18: June 1907, 509–12.

1972 *Ganguli, Sanjiban:* Descartes. An outline of his philosophy. Bombay, Seymour Hale, 1900. x, 58 p.

1973 *Ganovsky, S. Tz.:* Is filosofiata ña vasrajdañeto. René Descartes. Sofia, Kameñ del, 1938, 108 p. (Bibl. Navuka i vaspitanie). [In Bulgarian].

Descartes and the renaissance of philosophy. The problem of method in the 17th century. Descartes' method, metaphysics, physics, physiology, psychology. Descartes and religion. Descartes and literature; his place in modern science. [BP 38/2.]

1974 *Garai, Pierre:* "Le cartésianisme et le classicisme anglais." RLC 31: 1957, 373–87. See 406.

1975 —: The shield of order. A study of the influence of Cartesianism on English literary doctrine, 1668–1774 (Ann Arbor Microfilms; cf. Diss. Abstr. 14/12: 1954, 2335–36). Bibliography (p. 245–58). Columbia dissertation, unpublished. See 406.

1976 *Garaudy, Roger:* "Descartes le constructeur." Les lettres françaises 6: 1946, no. 2.

Garcès Castiella: see Castiella.

1977 *García Bacca, Juan David:* Siete modelos de filosofar. Caracas, Universidad Central, Facultad de filos. y letras, 1950. 168 p. "Descartes, modelo del método inmanente de filosofar," 65–89.

The other "models" are Plato, Aristotle, St. Thomas, Kant, Husserl and Heidegger. *Reviews:* L. van Hecht in RPhL 50: 1952, 350–51; J. Barrio in RevF 12: 1953, 310–33.

1978 —: "La determinación del ser central en la ontología fundamental, según Descartes." RFChile 1: 1950, 509–22.

Man does not need God to reinforce the certitude of his existence: from Aristotle through Descartes to Heidegger. [BAn 1953, no. 78.]

1979 *García Lopez, Jesús:* "La primera prueba cartesiana de la existencia de Dios." P 7: 1950, 73–103.

1980 —: "El conocimiento natural de Dios. Un estudio a través Descartes y S. Tomás." Anales de la Universidad de Murcia 13, no. 1. 1955. 255 p. [?]

1981 *García-Miralles, M.:* "La opinión de Balmes-Descartes sobre un viejo problema cosmológico." RevF 5: 1946, 151–60.

Existence of more than one independent world. Distance and contiguity in Balmes and Descartes (his concept of space.)

1982 *García Tuduri de Coya, Mercedes:* "El cartesianismo y la crisis." RcubF 1/6: 1950, 23–24.

1983 —: "Descartes y el pensar." RcubF 1/6: 1950, 31–32.

1984 *Garin, E.:* "Cartesio e l'Italia." GCFI 29: 1950, 385–405. See 433.

1985 *Garin, Pierre:* Thèses cartésiennes et thèses thomistes. Paris, Desclée de Brouwer, 1931. 178 p. Thèse Grenoble. See 209a.

1986 *Garrigós, Antonio:* "René Descartes, padre del intelectualismo científico moderno y poderoso afirmador de la personalidad humana." Revista de correos y telégrafos 4: 1940, no. 39. [Brie 11713]

1987 *Garrigou-Lagrange, Réginald (O.P).:* "La critique thomiste du cogito cartésien." Cartesio, 393–400. Spanish tr.: "La crítica tomista del cogito cartesiano." Frumentum (Mexico) 2: 1950, 273–83.

Late and Neo-Thomist critiques of the cogito from Goudin (1724) to Gredt (1922), with author's own objections against transition from thought to existence.

1987a *Garulli, E.:* Saggi su Spinoza, con traduzione dei Cogitata Metaphysica. Urbino, Publ. dell'Università, 1958.

Examines, among other themes, the divergence between Descartes and Spinoza. [Bsig 1960, 16357]

1988 *Gaultier, Jules de:* "Le problème de Descartes." Revue des idées 2: 1905, 89–107.

The "mask" of Descartes, Mona Lisa of philosophy.

1989 *Gazzaniga, P.:* "Il Cartesio giudicato dal Gioberti." Rassegna di scienze moderne, Dec. 1940. [Baldensperger]

1989a *Dem Gedächtnis an René Descartes.* Erinnerungsgabe, ed. C. A. Emge. 1937. See 523.

1989b *Gedenkfeier,* veranstaltet von der Freien Universität Berlin. 1950. See 543.

1990 *Geer, P. van:* "Naar aanleiding van een vergeten standbeeld: Descartes in den tuin van de H.B.S. te s'Gravenhage." Het Vaderland, February 9, 1910 (evening).

On the "forgotten" Descartes monument in The Hague. See also Rsyn 1937, p. 112 (nos. 2, 4, 5, 6) on the action taken.

1991 *Der klagende Geest van Descartes.* 1685. See 109.

1992 *Gehlen, Arnold:* "Descartes im Urteil Schellings." CD 3: 70–74, 1937.

Useful for the Schelling references.

1993 —: "Die Bedeutung Descartes' für eine Geschichte des Bewusstseins." Emge 37–47.

On "logocratic idealism" which makes, not Being, but concepts "den Gegenstand des Bewusstseins." Sees in Descartes' Dream an attack of acute tuberculosis releasing a crisis of liberation from Jesuitism. Repeats Schelling's Descartes criticism. Cartesianism a philosophy destructive to family, government, fatherland.

Review: Anon. in RMM 45: 1938, suppl. 3, 19–20.

1994 *Geil, Georg:* Über die Abhängigkeit Locke's von Descartes. Strassburg, Heitz, 1887. 98 p. Dissertation Strassburg.

Lumen naturale in Descartes and Locke (who is not an opponent). Hobbes' relationship to Locke regarding knowledge of nature.

1994a *Genève.* See: Catalogue de la collection de portraits, Bibliothèque de Genève, 1938 (see 1492.)

1995 *Gent, Werner:* Philosophie des Raumes und der Zeit. Historische, kritische und analytische Untersuchungen. Die Geschichte der Begriffe des Raumes und der Zeit von Aristoteles bis zum vorkritischen Kant (1768). Bonn, K. Cohn, 1926. 273 p.

1996 *Genta, Jordán B.:* "Sentido y crisis del cartesianismo." Escritos 75–87. 1937.

".... Descartes es idealmente posterior a Aristóteles. El pensamiento moderno nace y se sostiene en la negación de la Metafísica, hasta anularse finalmente en la afirmación de su propria negación" (p. 75). Descartes "el momento crítico" in Western conscience.

1997 *Gentile, Giovanni:* Studi vichiani. (2nd ed., revised and augm.) Firenze. Le Monnier, 1927, p. 38ff, 58ff. See 461.

1997a —: "Cartesio e Vico." AcLincei, Classe di scienze morali, Rendiconti ser. 6, v. 15: 1938, 603–04.

1998 *George, A.:* "L'actualité scientifique de Descartes." VInt 53: 1937, 423–33.

1999 *Georges-Berthier, Auguste:* "Le mécanisme cartésien et la physiologie au XVIIe siècle." Isis 2: 1914, 37–89; 3: 1920, 21–58. See 373.

2000 —: "Descartes et les Rose-Croix." Rsyn ns 18, no. 1: 1939, 9–30. Notes by Pierre Brunet. See 104.

2001 *Georgoulis, K. D.*: "Ἡ πνευματικῆ ἐξέλιζη τοῦ Καρτεσίου." Νέα Ἑστία 24/47/551: 15 June 1950, 774–80. [The spiritual evolution of Descartes.]

2002 *Gérard-Varet, Louis-A.*: De possibili apud Cartesium. Divione, Barbier-Marilier, 1898. 73 p. Thèse Paris.

2003 *Gerini, C. B.*: "I seguaci di Cartesio in Italia sul finire del secolo XVII ed il principio del XVIII." In: Il nuovo Risorgimento, 1899, 426ff. ()

2004 *Gerlache, Baron P. de*: "À l'Académie Française: Descartes contre Pascal." Rgén 15 December 1933.

2004a [*Gervaise de Montpellier*:] Histoire de la conjuration faite à Stockolm contre Mr. Descartes. 1695. [Published anonymously.] Also in: Gabriel Daniel, Voiage autour du monde de Descartes. 2nd ed., Amsterdam, Pierre Mortier, 1700, 219–47. Summary in: Cassirer, no. 243, 150–52. See 110.

2005 *Gewirtz, Alan* [Alan Gewirth]: "The Cartesian circle." PhR 50: 1941, 368–95.

First of three Cartesian studies by the Marsilius of Padua scholar and editor. Distinguishes (a) methodology from metaphysical argument, (b) analytical from synthetic demonstration. Conclusion: no circularity.

2006 —: "Experience and the non-mathematical in the Cartesian method." JHI 2: 1941, 183–210. See 189.

2007 —: "Clearness and distinctness in Descartes." Phil 18: 1943, 17–36.

Examines Descartes' definitions of 'clare et distincte' without finding conclusive criteria for determining what is so perceived; hence D.'s difficulties in distinguishing between ideas and acts of perception.

2008 *Geymonat, Ludovico*: "Aspetti moderni della metodologia di Cartesio." RF 42: 1951, 134–53.

Tries to find traits of Cartesian metaphysics that are still alive and useful today. See: Ezio Mascia, "Strumentalismo vecchio e nuovo," RF 43: 1952, 194–200.

2009 *Geyser, Joseph*: "Zu Descartes' Grundlegung des Realismus durch das Dasein der menschlichen Seele." Cartesio 401–16. 1937.

Thoughtful analysis of the "ego" in the "cogito." Descartes does not clearly answer the question: "Wie können wesensverschiedene Bewusstseinsregungen eine substanziale Daseinseinheit, die Seele, bilden?" (416).

2010 —: "Die erkenntnistheoretische Grundlage des Wissens bei Descartes." PJ 13: 1900, 109–22, 259–76.

Valuable study of Descartes' epistemology.

2011 *Giacomin, Vittorio:* Il pensiero filosofico di Cartesio. Milano, La Prora, 1933. 179 p.

"Penetrating, though with an alarming lack of cohesion" (Bontadini I.) See also the detailed discussion of this book which, with the work of de Giuli and Ruggiero, marks the Italian Descartes revival of the 1930's, in Bontadini II (Cartesio, 87–92; his: Studi, 48–55).

2012 *Giacon, Carlo (S.J.):* "Cartesio." In his: La causalità nel razionalismo moderno: Cartesio, Spinoza, Malebranche, Leibniz. Milano, Bocca, 1954, p. 25–78. (Academica. Collezione di corsi universitari, v. 1). See 262.

2013 —: "La filosofia contemporanea in un congresso internazionale" [Congrès Descartes.] CivC 88: 1937, 326–36.

2014 —: "Le pubblicazione dell'Università Cattolica del S. Cuore per celebrare il centenario cartesiano." Greg 18: 1937, 599–603.

2015 —: "Fenomenismo, realismo e idealismo." RFNS 33: 1941, 168–194. See 1277 (Bontadini, Studi, p. 242–46.)

2016 *Giannattasio, Nicola:* "Per il centenario del Discours de la méthode di Descartes." La scuola cattolica (Venegono) 66: 1938, 616–23.

2017 *Gibson, Alexander Boyce:* The philosophy of Descartes. London, Methuen, 1932. xiii, 382 p. See 210.

2018 —: "Descartes." Phil 10: 1935, 428–40. (Great Thinkers, VI). See 210.

2019 —: "La Géométrie de Descartes au point de vue de sa méthode." RMM 4: 1896, 386–98. See 355.

2020 —: "The Regulae of Descartes." Mind ns 7: 1898, 145–58, 332–63.

2021 —: "The eternal verities and the will of God in the philosophy of Descartes." Proc. Aristotelian Society ns 30: 1929–30, 31–54.

2022 *Gibson, James:* Locke's theory of knowledge and its historical relation. Cambridge UP, 1917. xiv, 338 p.

Locke and Descartes (ch. 9).

2023 *Gilen, Leonhard (S.J.):* "Kleutgen und die Erkenntnistheorie Descartes'." Sch 30: 1955, 50–72.

2024 —: "Über die Beziehung Descartes' zur zeitgenössischen Scholastik." Sch 32: 1957, 41–66. See 263.

2024a *Gillot, H.:* "Les origines de l'héroisme cornélien." RCC 23, sér. 2: 1921–22, 628–37.

Influences up on Corneille's ideal hero include TP. See 413.

2025 *Gilson, Étienne:* Index scolastico-cartésien. Paris, Alcan, 1913. ix, 354 p. Thèse Paris (1912). See 7.

2026 —: La liberté chez Descartes et la théologie. Paris, Alcan, 1913. 452 p. (BPC). Thèse Paris (Title of thesis print: "La doctrine cartésienne de la liberté et la théologie.") See 164.

2027 —: Descartes. Discours de la méthode; texte et commentaire. Paris, Vrin, 1925. 2e éd., revue, 1930; reprinted 1939ff. 494 p. See 83.

2028 —: Études sur le rôle de la pensée médiévale dans la formation du système cartésien. Deuxième partie des Études de philosophie médiévale (1921), revue et considérablement augmentée. 2e éd. Paris, Vrin, 1930. 336 p. EPM, v. 13. Reprinted: Paris, Vrin, 1951. 344 p. See 165.

2029 —: "The Cartesian experiment." In his: The unity of philosophical experience. William James lectures 1936–37. New York, Scribner's, 1937, 125–220. Reprinted 1948, 1950. See 166.

2030 —: God and Philosophy. New Haven, Yale UP (Oxford UP), 1941. xviii, 147 p. (Powell Lectures in Philosophy at Indiana University, Fifth series, 1939–40.) Reprinted 1940, 1944, 1946, 1949, 1951. Yale Paperbound, 1960. See 167.

2031 —: "La doctrine cartésienne de la liberté et la théologie." Discussion by M. de Wulf, L. Lévy-Bruhl, V. Delbos, L. Laberthonnière, Parodi, R. Berthelet; reply by Gilson. BSFP 14: 1914, 207–58. See 164.

2032 —: "L'innéisme cartésien et la théologie." RMM 22: 1914, 500–16. Also in no. 165 (2028).

2033 —: "Météores cartésiens et météores scolastiques." RNS 22: 1920, 358–84: 23: 1921, 73–84. Also in no. 165 (2028).

2034 —: "Descartes et Harvey." RPFE 90: 1920, 432–58; 91: 1921, 108–39. Also in no. 165 (2028).

2035 —: "Descartes en Hollande." RMM 28: 1921, 545–56. [Discusses G.Cohen, Écrivains.] Also in no. 165 (2028).

2036 —: "Spinoza interprète de Descartes: La preuve cartésienne de l'existence des corps." Chronicon Spinoz. 3: 1923, 681–87. Also in no. 2028. See 272.

2036a —: "Descartes et la pensée religieuse de son temps." Annuaire de l'École pratique des Hautes-Études, section des sciences relig., 1923–24, 56–57. [A course report.]

2037 —: Descartes et la métaphysique scolastique. Positions des six leçons professées à l'Université libre de Bruxelles. Bruxelles, M. Weissenbruch, 1924. 35 p. Also in: RUB no. 29, 1923–24, 105–39 and in no. 165 (2028).

2038 —: "Projet d'un commentaire historique du Discours de la méthode." BSFP 24: December 1924, 135–38, 150. See 83.

2039 —: "La pensée religieuse de Descartes." RMM 32: 1925, 519–37. (Review of Gouhier, no. 2073). Also in no. 165 (2028).

2040 —: "Recherches sur la formation du système cartésien. I. La critique des formes substantielles." RHPh 1929, 113–64. Also in no. 165 (2028).

2041 —: "Le réalisme méthodique." In: Philosophia perennis; Abhandlungen .... hg. von F. J. von Rintelen. Regensburg, J. Habel, 1930. (Festgabe Josef Geyser.) Vol. 2, 743–55.

Announces Gilson's break with D.: "cogito ergo res sunt" is the Cartesian ruin of Scholastic realism. *Gabriel Picard's* Le problème critique fondamental (Beauchesne, 1930) is cited as cartesianizing Scholasticism.

2042 —: "Le Traité des passions de Descartes inspira-t-il la Phèdre de Racine?" ML 15 April 1939.

2042a —: "Au pays de Descartes." Le Monde 21 July 1950, p. 1.

2043 —: "Le Descartes de Lévy-Bruhl." RPFE 147: 1957, 432–51. See 180.

2043a *Gioberti, Vicenzo:* Introduzione allo studio della filosofia. Capolago, 1845. v. 1.

2044 *Giorgianni, Virgilio:* "Intuizioni giuspolitiche di Renato Descartes." S 17: 1949, 334–50. See 264.

2045 —: "Ripercussioni filosofico-giuridiche dello studio delle passioni in Descartes." S 17: 1949, 254–58. See 264.

2046 *Giorgiantonio, Michele:* "Hume e Descartes." S 5: 1937, 30–40. [French summary].

2047 —: "Descartes e i suoi recenti interpreti." S 19: 1951, 313–22. See 27.

2047a *Giraud, Jeanne:* Manuel de bibliographie littéraire pour les XVIe, XVIIe, XVIIIe siècles français, 1921–1935. Paris, Vrin, 1939. (Publications de la faculté des lettres de l'Université de Lille, v. 2.) *Idem*, 1936–45. Nizet, 1956. See 8 and 9.

Gironella: see Roig Gironella.

2048 *Giuli, Guido de:* "La teoria cartesiana dell'errore". GCFI 7: 1927, 107–15.

2049 —: Cartesio. Firenze, Le Monnier, 1933. 269 p. (Studi filosofici, ns 8).

First Italian monograph of Descartes' philosophy, idealistically interpreted. See Bontadini in Cartesio, 93–97 (also in his: Studi, p. 55–61). Critique by A. Beccari in S 1: 1933, 447–53.

2050 —: "Galilée et Descartes." Scientia 49: 1931, suppl. 85–96. [Schrecker].

2051 —: "Edizioni e studi cartesiani." RF 25: 1934, 165–69.

2052 —: "Rassegna cartesiana." RF 26: 1935, 258–64.

Marcel, Garin, Lachièze-Rey, Gouhier, Campo, Lantrúa, Olgiati, Segond, Mouy, Bachelard.

2053 *Giunchi, Olinda:* L'individualismo nel Cartesio e nel Rousseau. Novara, Gaddi, 1918. 176 p.

2053a *Le glaneur châtelleraudais*, 1937. See 518.

2054 *Gliozzi, Mario:* "La fisica di Descartes." Humanitas 6: 1951, 613–30.

2055 *Glockner, Hermann:* "René Descartes." ZdtK 5: 1939, 271–87.

2056 *Glogau, Gustav:* "Darlegung und Kritik des Grundgedankens der kartesischen Metaphysik." ZPPK 73: 1878, 209–63.

2057 *Goethe, J. W. von:* Zur Farbenlehre. Historischer Teil. 5. Abt.: 17. Jahrhundert. (Sophien-Ausgabe, 2. Abt. v. 3, 276–80).

Remarkable sketch of Descartes, anticipating Péguy: "Das Leben dieses feinsinnigen Mannes wie auch seine Lehre wird kaum begreiflich, wenn man sich ihn nicht immer zugleich als französischen Edelmann denkt."

2058 *Goguel de Labrousse, Elisabeth:* Descartes y su tiempo. By Elisabeth Goguel. La Plata, Yerba buena, 1945. 129 p. (Imagen del tiempo). See 139.

2059 —: "Descartes y la pedagogía." Actas del primer congreso nacional de filosofía (Mendoza, Argentina), 1949, 3: 1816–25. Se 265.

2060 —: "La evidencia en la etica cartesiana." RF Chile 1: 1950, 540–44.

2061 *Goldbeck, Ernst:* Descartes' mathematisches Wissenschaftsideal. Halle a.S., 1892. 44 p. Dissertation Berlin. Reprinted in his: Der Mensch und sein Weltbild, Leipzig, 1925, 296ff.

Review: B. Erdmann in AGP 7: 1893–94, 512–22.

2062 *Goldschmidt, Victor:* "Le paradigme platonicien et les Regulae de Descartes." RPFE 141: 1951, 199–210. See 266.

2063 —: "À propos du 'Descartes par l'ordre des raisons' " (by M. Gueroult). RMM 62: 1957, 67–71. See 170.

2064 *Golliet, P.:* "Le problème de la méthode chez Descartes." RScH no. 61; 1951, 56–73.

Genesis of D.'s development of his method in "moments décisifs qui ont été ceux de la maturation et de l'explosion d'une découverte" (p. 67).

Gomes dos Santos: see Mauríco Gomes dos Santos.

2065 *Gómez, L. M.:* "La luz natural, superviviente de la duda cartesiana." PenM 6: 1950, 147–71.

2066 *Gondin, William Richard:* Prefaces to inquiry. A study in the origin and relevance of modern themes of knowledge. New York, Kings Crown Press, 1941. x, 220 p. Columbia dissertation.

2067 *Gonella, G.:* "Cartesio giurista." RIFD 18: 1938, 440–45. See 264.

2068 *González Alvarez, A.:* "El dudo inicial de la filosofía cartesiana." Anales de la Universidad de Murcia 1948–49, no. 2–3, 117–48.

2069 —: "La primera prueba cartesiana de la existencia de Dios." P 7: 1950, 73–103.

Thomist critique.

2070 *González Ríos, Francisco:* Descartes. Su mundo moral y religioso. Universidad de Buenos Aires, Facultad de filos. y letras, 1950. 50 p. Instituto de filosofía, ser. Ensayos, v. 3.

Valuable commemorative lecture on the problem of freedom and reason.

Reviews: N. Laffranque in RPFE 143: 1953, 283–84; L. Rebecchi in DTP 55: 1952, 269; L. Washington in RbrasF 1: 1951, 366.

2071 *González, Victoria:* "El argumento ontológico en Descartes." RcubF 1/6: 1950, 42–45.

2072 *Gordon, Abraham:* Spinozas Psychologie der Affekte mit Rücksicht auf Descartes. Breslau, H. Sulzbach, 1874. 89 p. Dissertation Leipzig.

2073 *Gouhier, Henri:* La pensée religieuse de Descartes. Paris, Vrin, 1924. 328 p. (EPM v. 6). Thèse, École Pratique des Hautes Études, Paris. See 168.

2074 —: Essais sur Descartes. Paris, Vrin, 1937 (reprinted 1949). 304 p. (Essais d'art et de philosophie.) See 169.

2075 — (editor): Descartes. Regulae ad directionem ingenii. Paris, Boivin. 1946. See 92.

2076 —: Les premières pensées de Descartes; contribution à l'histoire de l'anti-renaissance. Vrin, 1958. 167 p. (De Pétrarque à Descartes, v. 2). See 96.

2077 —: "Descartes à la Convention et aux Cinq-cents." RMM 29: 1922, 243–51. See 112.

2078 —: La vocation de Malebranche. Paris, Vrin, 1926. 172 p. (BHP). See 435b.

2079 —: La philosophie de Malebranche et son expérience religieuse. Paris, Vrin, 1926. 431 p. 2nd ed. augm. Vrin, 1948. 440 p. (BHP). See 435b.

2080 —: "Sur la date de la Recherche de la vérité de Descartes." RHPh 3: 1929, 296–320. See 242.

2081 —: "L'itinéraire ontologique de D." RFNS 26: 1934, 259–76. Reprinted in no. 169 (2074), Ch. 3; concluding section expanded into Ch. 4.

2082 —: "Le Congrès Descartes." VInt 52: 1937, 431–34.

2083 —: "Descartes et la religion. Note méthodologique." Cartesio, 417–24. 1937. See 168.

2084 —: "Descartes et la vie morale." RMM 44: 1937, 165–97. Reprinted in no. 169 (2074), Ch. 5; conclusion expanded into Ch. 6.

2085 —: "L'esprit de la métaphysique cartésienne." RHPh 5: 1937, 137–44. [Radio talk.]

2086 —: "Le grand trompeur et la signification de la métaphysique cartésienne." CD 1: 69–73. 1937.

Summarizes Gouhier's argument.

2087 —: "Le malin génie dans l'itinéraire cartésien." RdePh 37 (ns 6): 1937, 1–21. Reprinted in no. 169 (2074), Ch. 4.

2088 —: "Notes sur les études cartésiennes." RHPh ns 5: 1937, 199–212. See 28.

2089 —: "L'homme cartésien." Ren no. 2: 1941, 119–130.

2090 —: "Les deux XVIIe siècles." Congr. intern. de filosofía. Barcelona, 1948. Actas III, 171–81. See 96.

2091 —: "La connaissance de Dieu selon Descartes." Gmet 5: 1950, 483–502.

2092 —: "Les exigences de l'existence dans la métaphysique de Descartes." RIP 4: 1950, 123–52.

Profound study of Cartesian doubt, circle, cogito. Concludes that "aucun existant n'échappe au contrôle du doute méthodique" any more than any axiom, notion or verity other than "les principes inscrits dans l'existence même" (i.e. propositions about Nothingness.)

2093 —: "Pour une histoire des Méditations Métaphysiques." RScH no. 61: 1951, 5–29. See 269.

2094 —: "Le nouvel humanisme selon Descartes et la politique." In: Cristianesimo e ragione di stato nell'arte e nella filosofia dell umanesimo e del rinascimento (Atti del II Congr. intern. di studi umanistici). Roma-Milano, Bocca, 1953, 77–86.

2095 —: "La crise de la théologie au temps de Descartes." RTPL 4: 1954, 19–54. See 267.

2096 —: "Doute méthodique ou négation méthodique?" Eph 9: 1954, 135–62. See 268.

2097 —: "La preuve ontologique de Descartes." RIP 8: 1954, 295–303. See 270.

2098 —: "La résistance au vrai et le problème cartésien d'une philosophie sans rhétorique." In: Retorica e Barocco. Atti del III Congr. intern. di studi umanistici, ed. Enrico Costello. Roma, Bocca, 1955, 85–97. (Centro internazionale di studi umanistici.) See 268a.

2099 —: "Descartes a-t-il rêvé?" RIP 10: 1956, 203–08. Reprinted in no. 96 (2076), Ch. 2.

2100 —: "La véracité divine dans la Méditation IV." Eph 1956, 296–310.

2101 —: "L'ordre des raisons selon Descartes." Royaumont, 72–87; discussion 88–107. 1957. See 42.

Continuation of the controversy with Gueroult over the ontological argument (see 270). Gueroult opens the discussion with a defense of his interpretation "selon l'ordre des raisons."

2101a —: "Le refus du symbolisme dans l'humanisme cartésien." Afil 1958, no. 2–3 (Umanesimo e simbolismo), 65–74. See 268a.

2102 *Gouilhou, Étienne:* "Descartes en Hollande et en Suède." BAFH 15/3: Sept. 1937, 2–5. [A radio talk.J]

2103 *Gouiran, Emilio* (Émile): "Interpretación existencial de la inducción en el pensamiento cartesiano. El problema de la existencia de Dios." Homenaje 2: 199–207. 1937.

Concludes that in Descartes intuition and induction are the same, signifying the totality of thought in different degree but without contradiction: induction of the imperfect, the created, resolves itself in the intuition of the perfect, the uncreated. See 2104.

2104 —: "Interpretation existentielle du doute cartésien." CD 1: 80–88. 1937.

2105 —: Interpretación existencial de la duda cartesiana. Córdoba (Argentina), Universidad, 1937. 21 p.

2106 —: "El pensamiento religioso de Descartes." Escritos 89–94. 1937.

2107 —: "Sobre Descartes." Sur (Buenos Aires) 7, no. 41: 1937, 71–74.

2108 —: "La filosofía de Descartes. Problemas fundamentales." Revista de la Universidad Nacional de Córdoba (Argentina) 26: 1939, 435–65.

2109 *Gourci, François Antoine Étienne de:* Éloge de René Descartes. Paris, Regnard, 1765. 48 p. See 126.

2110 *Grabmann, Martin:* "Die Philosophie des Cartesius und die Eucharistielehre des Emmanuel Maignan O. Minim." Cartesio 425–36. 1937.

Valuable study by the eminent Munich medievalist, with an unpublished "Judicium theologicum de philosophia Maignani coordinata per Johannem Saguens," partly reprinted and critically appraised.

2111 *Grammatico, Alberto (O.C.D.):* "Un cenaculo cartesiano a Padova alla fine del settecento." Cartesio 437–43. 1937.

P. Agostino Molin (O.C.), i.e. Giacomo de Violis (died 1840), his teacher P. Filiberto Perricone (O.D.), and other eminent clerics at Padua formed a philosophical circle devoutly critical of Scholasticism, though the epithet "Cartesian" seems misplaced. Author cites unpublished mss.

2112 *Grand, Adolphe:* Rappel au bon sens, ou du danger de l'analyse et des fictions. Jouve, 1934. 42 p. [BN 8°. R. Pièce 19680]

2113 *Grandmaison, Louis de:* "Nouvelles recherches sur l'origine et le lieu de naissance de Descartes." Bibl. de l'École des Chartes 60: 1899, 423–46.

2114 —: "Le lieu de naissance de Descartes." Illustration (Paris) 197: 1937, August 21, 531–32.

Reply to J. Rondeau, no. 3121.

2115 *Grappe, André:* "Les rapports de la pensée et de la vie chez Descartes." In: La vie, la pensée. Actes du VII Cong. des sociétés de philos. de langue française. Grenoble 1954. PUF, 1954. ()

2116 *Grappe, G.:* "Un amour de Descartes." Gaulois, 24 December 1921.

2117 *Gratien-Annoult:* "Polémique de Descartes et de Fermat dans les années 1637 et 1638." AcToulouse, Mémoires, 1870, 384–401. [Schrecker]

2118 *Grau, A.:* "Enemics de la intel'ligència." Criterion (Barcelona) 10: 1934, 218–21.

Descartes, Luther, Rousseau, Renan.

2119 *Grau, Patricio J.:* "Algunas aclaraciones sobre el método cartesiano." Escritos 95–122. 1937.

2120 —: "El problema de Descartes y la experiencia." Homenaje 1: 203–42. 1937.

Descartes' methodological problem: "a encontrar un órgano racional que le permitiese llegar a conocer plenamente lo natural" (209). Detailed analysis of experience in the Regulae.

2121 *Gregory, Joshua C.:* "Cudworth and Descartes." Phil 8: 1933, 454–67.

2121a *Gregory, T.:* "La polemica antimetafisica di Gassendi." RCSF 14: 1959, 131–61, 243–82.

On Gassendi's Syntagma philosophicum: impossibility of metaphysics as a science; his controversies with Fludd, Cherbury, and particularly Descartes over this proposition.

2122 *Grenier, Jean:* "Du cogito au credo." CD 3: 94–98. 1937. See 310.

2123 *Griffith, Gwilym O.:* "Descartes." In his: Makers of modern thought. London, Lutterworth Press, 1948, ch. 3, p. 34–54.

2124 *Grimm, Eduard:* Die Lehre von den angeborenen Ideen. Jena, Mauke (H. Dufft), 1873. x, 77 p. Dissertation Jena.

2124a —: "Malebranches Erkenntnistheorie und deren Verhältniss zur Erkenntnistheorie des Descartes." ZPPK 70: 1877, 15–55. See 453b.

2125 *Griselle, Eugène:* "Descartes et Malaval." Et 96: Aug. 5, 1903, 402–14.

Malaval (Malleval), born 1627, blinded at age 9.

2126 *Groeger, E. M. R.:* Expositio, ideam substantiae in recentiori philosophia propius accessisse ad ideam subjecti. Vratislavae, Leopold Freund, [1850]. 26 p. [NN]

2127 *Grössel, Paul:* Die Gottesbeweise Descartes'. Weiden i.Th. 1912. 50 p. Dissertation Leipzig.

2128 *Gronau, Gotthelf:* Die Naturlehre Geulincx' und ihr Zusammenhang mit der Naturlehre Descartes'. Wolfenbüttel, 1911. 48 p. Dissertation Jena.

2129 *Groot, J. V. de:* "René Descartes en zijn wijsbegeerte van den mensch." In: Denkers over ziel en leven. Amsterdam, 1917, 80–165.

"Belle étude compréhensive qui envisage la pensée de Descartes dans ses rapports avec la Scolastique" [Pos-Steenbergen.]

2130 *Grooten, J. E. C.:* Art. "R. Descartes." In: Katholieke Encyclopaedie voor opvoeding en onderwijs. Antwerpen-s'Gravenhage, 1951, 1: 454.

2131 *Grossmann, H.:* "Die gesellschaftlichen Grundlagen der mechanistischen Philosophie und die Manufaktur." Zeitschrift für Sozialforschung 4: 1935, 161–64. See 154.

2131a *Grot, N. Ja.:* "O žizni i ličnosti Dekarta." VFP 1896, 645–59.

D.'s life and personality. [In Russian.]

2132 *Grotowski, Marian:* "Descartes i Newton." Wiedza i życie (Poland) 15: 1946, 289–94.

2133 *Grubbe, Samuel:* Bernhard Stabeck et Nicolaus Beckmann. De philosophia Cartesii observationes. Upsala, Edmann, 1807. ii, 16 p. [Harvard]

2134 *Grundy, J.:* "Descartes and atomism." Nature (London) 173: 1953, 89.

2135 *Gruzenberg, S.:* "Bogoponimanie Dekarta." VFP 1913, 283–96.

D.'s concept of God. [In Russian.]

2135a —: "Ispověd' Fausta XVII-go veka." Vestnik znanija (St. Petersburg), 1912, 307–19.

The creed of a 17th c. Faust. [In Russian.]

2135b —: "Problema svobodi voli v filosofii Dekarta." VFP 1914, 363–83.

The problem of free will in D.'s philosophy. [In Russian.]

2136 *Gruyer, Louis-Auguste:* Méthode de Descartes, rassemblée et mise en ordre par L. A. Gruyer. Préface, contenant le résumé et l'analyse de cet œuvre. Lugan, 1829. 116 p. Another edition: Bruxelles, Méline, Cans & Cie, 1838. xxv, 108 p. See also his: Essais philosophiques. Nouvelle éd. contenant toutes ses publications antérieures, révues, corrigées, augmentées. Ladrange, 1855. 4 vols.

2137 *Guandique, Salvador:* "Renacimiento cartesiano." Letras de México v. 3, no. 19. [Brie 11924]

Güel, José Bertran: see Bertran Güell.

2138 *Güell, Oscar N.:* "Algunas consideraciones en torno al pensamiento cartesiano." Ortodoxia 1947, no. 16–17, 217–32. [Rep. 1949, no. 3522]

2139 *Guérard, G.:* "Descartes anatomiste." La semaine dentaire 9, no. 39: 25 Sept. 1927, 902–05.

2139a *Guerlac, Henry:* "Newton's changing reputation in the eighteenth century." In: Raymond O. Rickwood (ed.), Carl Becker's Heavenly City revisited. Ithaca, N.Y., Cornell UP, 1958, 3–26.

Leading the demolition experts in levelling Becker's Heavenly City, Guerlac stresses the persistence of Cartesianism in the course of the 18th century as against the fluctuation in the fortunes of Newtonism. Good bibliographical notes.

2139b —: "Three eighteenth-century social philosophers: scientific influences on their thought." Daedalus, Winter 1958, 8–24.

From Descartes, there derived crude materialism, and "a Neo-Epicurean revival" in thinkers of the second half of the century.

2140 *Gueroult, Martial:* Descartes selon l'ordre des raisons. Paris, Aubier, 1953. 2 vols. I. L'âme et Dieu (La VIe Méditation). 390 p. II. L'âme et le corps. 366 p. See 170.

2141 —: Nouvelles réflexions sur la preuve ontologique de Descartes. Paris, Vrin, 1955. 117 p. (Problèmes et controverses.) See 270a.

2142 —: Malebranche. Paris, Aubier, 1955–59. 3 vols. Vol. 1: La vision en Dieu. 1955. 327 p. Vol. 2, 3: Les cinq abîmes de la Providence. Part 1 (i.e., vol. 2): L'ordre et l'occasionalisme. 1958. 283 p. Part 2 (i.e., vol. 3): La nature et la grâce. 1959. 120 p. See 453c.

2143 —: "Observations sur ce mémoire" (i.e., Émile Baas: La critique leibnizienne de la physique de Descartes, no. 1102). BFL Strasbourg, v. 11, November 1932. See 317.

2144 —: "L'économie et les fins essentielles de la doctrine cartésienne." BFL Strasbourg, 1933. ()

2145 —: Dynamique et métaphysique leibniziennes. Paris, Les belles lettres, 1934, 240 p. Publications de la faculté des lettres de Strasbourg, v. 68. See 373a.

2146 —: "L'Ars combinatoria et les méthodes de Leibniz et de Descartes." BFL Strasbourg 1935. ()

2147 —: "Sur deux abbés cartésiens que l'on peut confondre" (Abbé de Catelan, Abbé de Conti). "Note complementaire: Sur trois abbés cartésiens ...." (Abbé Catelet.) BFL Strasbourg 14: 1935–36, 93–97, 276–77.

2148 —: "Le cogito et la notion: pour penser, il faut être." CD 1: 53–60. 1937. Also in no. 170 & 2140, v. 2, Appendix.

2149 —: "Descartes au Congrès Descartes." RMM 45: 1938, 105–26. See 29.

2150 —: Étendue et psychologie chez Malebranche. Les belles lettres, 1939. 115 p. (Publications de la Faculté des lettres de l'Université de Strasbourg, v. 91). See Sebba, no. 19, p. 59.

2151 —: Psychologie cartésienne et psychologie malebranchiste. BFL Strasbourg 19: 1940–41. See 2150.

2152 —: "Descartes père de la philosophie moderne." BSFP 44, no. 1: 1950, 15–20.

2153 —: "Métaphysique et physique de la force chez Descartes et chez Malebranche. I. Descartes. II. Malebranche." RMM 59: 1954, 1–37, 113–34. See 373a.

2154 —: "Études cartésiennes. Un Descartes au goût anglais: Descartes pionnier." (Review of N. Kemp Smith). RPFE 59: 1954, 231–32. See 193.

2155 —: "La vérité de la science et la vérité de la chose dans les preuves de l'existence de Dieu." Royaumont, 108–20; discussion 121–40. 1957.

On the systematic relationship of the two proofs, a posteriori and a priori, in Descartes, refuting Kant's criticism, with considerable discussion. See 270a.

2156 —: Berkeley: Quatre études sur la perception et sur Dieu. Paris, Aubier, 1956. 189 p. (Philosophie de l'esprit).

Monographic treatment of the problem of the relation between Malebranche's and Berkeley's theories of perception, ideas, God, and the order of nature, with references to Descartes and Cartesian thought in general. See Sebba, no. 19, p. 60.

2157 —: "Le cogito et l'ordre des axiomes métaphysiques dans les Principia philosophiae cartesianae de Spinoza." Aph 23: 1960, 171–85. See 272.

2158 *Guerrero, Luis Juan:* "La generosidad en la filosofía cartesiana." Homenaje 3: 41–72. 1937.

Parallel between générosité in D.'s ethics and the cogito in his epistemology: as the self in the cogito grasps the certainty criterion, so it may freely recognize its own intrinsic value and become capable of ordering all other values. This recognition is the basis of générosité which recognizes man's autonomy and God's independent free will, and becomes the basis of practical knowledge in its entire latitude.

Review: Cassirer, no. 5, 50–51.

2159 *Guéville, J.:* "L'idealisme cartésien d'après M. Hamelin." APC 12, no. 63: 1911–12, 516–23.

2160 *Guhrauer, Gottschalk Eduard:* De J. Jungio commentatio. Adjecta est Jungii epistola de Cartesii philosophia. Dissertation Breslau, 1846. 38 p. [BM].

2161 —: J. Jungius und sein Zeitalter. Nebst Goethe's Fragmenten über Jungius. Stuttgart & Tübingen, 1850. [BM]

Rich material, including unpublished Jungius fragments, etc.

2162 —: "Elisabeth, Pfalzgräfin bei Rhein, Äbtissin von Herford." Raumer's historisches Taschenbuch, ser. 3, 1850, 1: 1–150, 2: 417–554. See 117.

2163 *Gurwitsch, Aron:* "The last work of Edmund Husserl" (i.e. his: Krise der europ. Wissenschaften). PPR 16: 1955–56, 380–99; 17: 1956–57, 370–98. See 174.

2164 *Gutermann, N., et Henri Lefebvre:* "Le problème de la conscience." Eur 15: 15 July 1937, 384–405 (see 37 and 527). Also as introduction to: Lenin. Cahiers sur la dialectique. Gallimard.

On differing notions of "conscience" in Descartes, Hegel, Nietzsche, Marx and Lenin. Defense of materialism against Hegelianism. "Conscience dans le sense plûtot existentiel" (BP 1937/2).

2165 *Guttman, Jacobus:* De Cartesii Spinozaeque philosophiis, et quae inter eas intercedat, ratione. Vratislavae, F. W. Jungfer, 1868. 58 p. Diss. Breslau.

2166 *Gutzeit, Berthold:* Descartes' angeborene Ideen verglichen mit Kants Anschauungs- und Denkformen a priori. Bromberg, Programm des Städtischen Realgymnasiums, 1883. 29 p. [Col.]

2167 *Guyénot, Émile:* L'évolution de la pensée scientifique. Les sciences de la vie au XVIIe et XVIIIe siècles. L'idée de l'évolution. Michel, 1941. xxi, 462 p. (Collection L'évolution de l'humanité, v. 68).

2168 *Guzzo, Augusto Barone Francesco:* "Il concetto d'anima da Cartesio a Hegel." In: L'anima, ed. Michele Federico Sciacca. Brescia, Morcelliana, 1954, 171–233.

H

Haan: see Bierens de Haan.

2169 *Hadamard, Jacques:* See 541 (Atomes, 1946).

2170 *Hagmann, Moritz:* Descartes in der Auffassung durch die Historiker der Philosophie. Winterthur, P. G. Keller, 1955. viii, 195 p. Dissertation Zürich. See 10.

2171 *Halasy-Nagy, Joseph:* "Le cartésianisme en Hongrie." CD 3: 122–26. 1937. See 469.

2172 —: "A Cartesianismuz és a magyar szellemiség." Pannonia (Budapest) 1937/7–10, 222–30. See 469. [Cartesianism and the spirit of Hungary].

2173 *Haldane, Elizabeth:* Descartes, his life and times. London, John Murray (New York, Dutton), 1905. xviii, 398 p. See 140.

2174 — and G. R. T. Ross (translators): The philosophical works of Descartes, 1931. See 77.

2175 *Haldane, J. B. S.:* Reply to W. R. Ashby, "Can a mechanical chessplayer outplay its designer?" BJPS 3: 44–57, 1952–53. See 350.

2176 *Hallays, A.:* "Descartes et le Conseil général de la Seine." Jdeb, 18 December 1927.

2177 *Hamelin, Octave:* Le système de Descartes. Paris, Alcan, 1911. 2e éd. revue, ed. L. Robin. Préface d'Émile Durckheim. Alcan, 1921. xiv, 400 p. Transl. by Amalia Haydée Raggio: El sistema de Descartes. Buenos Aires, Losada, 1949, 398 p. See 171.

2178 —: "Sur une des origines du Spinozisme." AnPh 11: 1901, 15–28.

2179 —: "L'union de l'âme et du corps d'après Descartes." AnPh 15: 1904, 39–50.

2179a *Hamilton, Sir William:* Lectures on metaphysics and logic, v. 1. Edinburgh and London, Blackwood, 1859–60. See also 3038.

2180 *Hann, Franz Gustav:* Die Ethik Spinozas und die Philosophie Descartes'. Innsbruck, Wagner, 1875. 124 p.

2181 *Hannequin, Arthur:* Études d'histoire des sciences et d'histoire de philosophie. Paris, Alcan, 1908. [Vol. 1 reprints 2182, 2183. See 273.]

2182 —: "La preuve ontologique de D. défendue contre Leibnitz." RMM 4: 1896, 433–58. Also in 273 (2181), v. 1: 233–64.

2183 —: "Fragments posthumes: La méthode de Descartes." RMM 14: 1906, 755–74. Also in 273 (2181), v. 1: 209–31.

2183a *Hare, R. M.:* The language of morals. Oxford UP, 1952. See 1023.

2184 *Harpe, Jean de la:* De l'ordre et du hasard. Le réalisme critique d'Antoine-Augustin Cournot. Préface d'Arnold Reymond. Paris, Vrin, 1936. xx, 377 p. (Mémoires de l'Université de Neuchâtel, v. 9). See 274.

2185 —: "De l'évidence cartésienne au probabilisme de Cournot." CD 7: 115–21. 1937. See 274.

2186 —: "De l'évidence cartésienne au probabilisme de Cournot: évidence, certitude et probabilité." RTP 1938, 31–49. See 274.

2187 *Harris, Errol E.:* Nature, mind and modern science. London and New York, 1954. 455 p. (Muirhead's Library of Philosophy). "The Cartesian dichotomy" (pt. 3, ch. 6, sec. 2, p. 120ff.)

Attempts a critique and refutation of neopositivism based on a survey of what may be accepted as definitive gain from past philosophizing. The contradiction that material objects have a causal relationship to mind though mind and matter are totally different and separate is avoided by Descartes "only at some considerable cost; but Locke embraces it without the slightest qualm."

2188 *Harris, Marjorie S.:* "Romero on Cartesian reason." JP 50: 1953, 242–49.

Francisco Romero criticizes Cartesian reason as immanent and leading to a concept of matter that excludes becoming. Descartes insists on clarity as if reason were omnipotent. See 3119a.

2188a —: Francisco Romero on problems of philosophy. New York, Philosophical Library, 1960. ix, 115 p.

Ch. 2 on Romero and Cartesian reason, incorporating no. 2188.

2189 *Hartill, Isaac:* "Descartes." Philosopher (London) 14: 1936, 98–100.

2190 *Hartland-Swann, John:* "Descartes' simple natures". Phil 22: 1947, 139–42.

The "simple natures" of Regula XII become the innate ideas of Descartes' later works.

2191 *Hartmann, Nikolai:* See: Springmeyer on res simplices (no. 3338), quoting Hartmann's Ontologie, v. 3 and his: Aufbau der realen Welt, Einleitung; ch. 1; ch. 16.

Hartmann seems to assume that Descartes can simply deduce "das 'concretum' .... aus den vorerkannten und vorgegebenen Prinzipien," which reduces his Descartes critique to a rejection of "aprioristic-deductive ontology."

2192 *Hastings, Hester:* Man and beast in French thought of the eighteenth century. Baltimore, Johns Hopkins Press, 1936. 297 p. (Johns Hopkins dissertation). See 226.

2194 *d'Haucourt, Xavier:* "Une dynastie de 'non-originaires' au Parlement de Bretagne: la famille Des-Cartes, 1585–1736." AnnBr 44: 1937, 408–32; 45: 1938, 3–24. See 99.

2195 *Hauter, Ch.:* "Descartes et la spiritualité moderne." RHPR 17: 1937, 474–502.

2196 *Hayen, André (S.J.):* "La présence à soi de la pensée chez Descartes et saint Thomas d'Aquin." CD 8: 144–52. 1937.

2197 —: "La signification métaphysique du cercle cartésien." Cartesio 445–55. 1937.

Rejecting the usual form of the circularity claim, author sees in the "circle" "non pas certes l'élaboration .... rigoureuse d'une philosophie transcendentale de l'esprit," but an anticipation of it.

2198 —: "Réflexions d'un clerc sur un congrès de philosophie" [Congrès Descartes.] NRT 8: 1937, 1116–22.

2199 *Hazard, Paul:* La crise de la conscience européenne, 1680–1715. Boivin, 1935. 3 vols. English transl.: The European mind: the critical years. 1680–1715. New Haven, Yale UP, 1953. See 454.

2200 —: La pensée européenne au XVIIIe siècle, de Montesquieu a Lessing. Boivin, 1946. 3 vols. v, 375 p.; 301 p.; (Notes et références) 156 p. See 454.

2200a —: "Les rationaux, 1670–1700." RLC 12: 1932, 677–711. Incorporated, with revisions, in his: La crise (see 2199), Pt. 2, Ch. 1.

2201 *Hébert, Rodolphe-Louis:* "An episode in Molière's Amphitryon and Cartesian epistemology." MLN 70: 1955, 416–22. See 407.

2202 *Hegel, Georg Wilhelm Friedrich:* "René Descartes." In his: Vorlesungen über die Geschichte der Philosophie, v. 3, 2. Abschn., ch. 1. (Werke, Jubiläumsausgabe, v. 19, 331–67). See 171a.

2203 *Heidegger, Martin:* Sein und Zeit. Erste Hälfte. Halle a.S., Niemayer, 1927, 19–27, 89–90. (Jahrbuch für Philosophie und phänomenologische Forschung, v. 8). Reprinted (6th ed.): Tübingen, Neomarius Verlag, 1949. English tr. by J. Macquarrie and E. Robinson: Being and time. London, Student Christian Movement Press, 1962. See 172.

2204 —: Holzwege. Frankfurt a.M., Klostermann, 1950, 69–104. See 172a.

2204a —: Nietzsche. 2 v. Pfullingen, Neske, 1961. See 172b.

2205 *Heidenfeld, Albrecht Friedrich Theodor:* Darstellung der von Cartesius, Spinoza und Leibniz gegebenen Beweise für das Dasein Gottes. 1. Theil. Breslau, Lindner, 1855. 34 p. [No Part 2 located]. [NN]

2206 *Heimsoeth, Heinz:* Die Methode der Erkenntnis bei Descartes und Leibniz. Giessen, Töpelmann. Pt. I, 1912; Pt. II, 1914. 334 p. (Philosophische Arbeiten, ed. Cohen und Natorp, v. 6, no. 1). Dissertation Marburg. See 211.

2207 —: "Sur quelques rapports des Règles de Descartes avec les Méditations". RMM 21: 1913, 526–36.

2208 *Heinrich, Wł:* "O przedmiotowości u Kartezjusza i u sofistów." Sprawozdania z Czynności i Posiedzeń Polskiej Akademii Umiejętności, Kraków, 1920, no. 1. [Bar]

Objectivity in Descartes and in the Stoics.

2209 *Heintel, Erich:* "Tierseele und Organismusproblem im cartesianischen System." WZPP 3: 1950, 73–120. See 276.

2210 *Heinze, Max:* Die Sittenlehre des Descartes. Leipzig, Hinrich, 1872. 28 p. (Habilitationsvortrag).

"Antrittsvorlesung" (Leipzig) gives the prevalent view of the time: Descartes' "morale provisoire" is scientifically worthless though humanly respectable, while the "Lettres sur la morale" are refurbished Stoicism, or what Descartes took Stoicism to be, since he knew the Stoics only at second-hand.

2211 —: "Pfalzgräfin Elisabeth und Descartes." Historisches Taschenbuch, ser. 6, 5: 1886, 257–304. See 117.

2212 *Heller, Ernst:* "Bemerkungën zur Lehre von der distinctio rationis." Cartesio 803–07. 1937.

On the distinctio rationis between substance and its attributes.

2213 *Hennion, Horace:* "Sur un portrait de René Descartes perdu et retrouvé." BSA Touraine 27: 1938, no. 1–2, 87–93. Portrait.

Portrait, not at the Tours or BN exhibitions of 1937, in the Musée des Beaux-arts de Tours, the original of the drawing by Jacquet which Ch. Adam had made for AT, later "lost." Also on the Tours portrait of Descartes as a young man.

2213a *Henrich, Dieter:* Der ontologische Gottesbeweis. Sein Problem und seine Geschichte in der Neuzeit. Tübingen, Mohr, 1960. See 211a.

2214 *Henriot, E.:* "Descartes, Galilée et le Discours de la méthode." Temps, 2 December 1924.

2215 —: "Des lettres inédites de Descartes." Temps, 9 February 1926. [L. Roth, Correspondence of D. and Huygens.]

2216 —: "Les Lettres morales de Descartes." Temps, 9 April 1935.

2217 —: "Descartes, sa fille et l'automate." Temps, 23 November 1937.

2218 *Hensch, Thomas:* Über den Stil in Descartes' Discours de la méthode. Zürich, Schwarzenbach, 1949. 90 p. Dissertation Zürich. See 408.

2219 *Herford, C. H.:* "Shakespeare and Descartes; a chapter in the intellectual history of Europe." HJ 24: 88–100, 1925. See 409.

2220 *Heriberto, Hno:* "Descartes ante la razón y la fe." La Universidad (San Salvador) 1938, no. 2, 65–88.

2221 *Hertling, Georg Freiherr von:* "Descartes' Beziehungen zur Scholastik." Kgl. Bayerische Akad. d. Wissenschaften in München. Sitzungsber. d. philos.-histor. Klasse, 1897, pt. 2, 339–81; pt. 1, 3–36. Also in his: Historische Beiträge zur Philosophie. München (s.d.) 181–242.

Helped initiate the revaluation of D.'s relationship to Scholasticism.

2222 *Hervey, Helen:* "Hobbes and Descartes in the light of some unpublished letters of the correspondence between Sir Charles Cavendish and Dr. John Pell." Osiris 10: 1952, 67–90. See 118.

2223 *Herzfeld, F.:* Der Begriff der erkenntnistheoretischen Evidenz im Anschluss an Descartes. Dissertation Erlangen, 1922.

2224 *Hess, Mary Witcomb* (Mrs. John Ambrose Hess): "A note on the individualism of Descartes." JP 35: 1938, 183–88.

2225 —: "Descartes and Richard Crashaw." Commonweal 42: August 24, 1945, 455–57.

2226 *Heussler, H:* "Descartes." In his: Der Rationalismus des 17. Jahrhunderts in seinen Beziehungen zur Entwicklungslehre. Berlin, 1885, 28–65.

2227 *Heyde, Johannes Erich:* "Die Bedeutung der cartesischen Lehre vom Verhältnis zwischen Leib und Seele für die Philosophie der Gegenwart." Emge 48–76. 1937.

Critique of modern refutations of Descartes' dualism, including that of Ludwig Klages. No proper analysis.

2228 *Himstedt, A.:* "Die Secanten und Tangenten des Folium Cartesii." Archiv für Mathematik und Physik 15: 1896, 129–45.

2228a *Hirsch, Emanuel:* Geschichte der neueren evangelischen Theologie im Zusammenhang mit den allgemeinen Bewegungen des europäischen Denkens. Vol. 1. Gütersloh, C. Bertelsmann, 1949, ch. 8, p. 158–74; ch. 9, 175–203.

A simplified, yet useful view of the effects upon Protestant theology of the changing philosophical climate of the 17th and 18th century. The very emphasis (Malebranche and Spinoza rather than Descartes; Derham, Wittich, the Cambridge Platonists, Poiret, etc.) is revealing. See 435a.

2229 *Hock, Karl Freiherr von:* Descartes und seine Gegner. Ein Beitrag zur Charakteristik der wissenschaftlichen Bestrebungen unserer Zeit. Wien, Beck, 1835. 114 p.

Catholic apologist, argues Descartes' Catholic orthodoxy. Varet (p. 393) characterizes von Hock as "pro-Günther."

2230 *Hodgson, Shadworth H., A. Main, A. Bain, and W. G. Davis:* Discussion of Descartes' cogito. Mind 1: 1876, 568–70; 2: 1877, 126–30, 259–64, 412–13.

2231 *Hoenen, Pierre (S.J.):* "Descartes en zijn Discours de la méthode, 1637–1937." Studiën 128: 1937, 9–25, 91–101.

2232 —: "Le cogito ergo sum comme intuition et comme mouvement de la pensée." Cartesio 457–71. 1937.

2232a —: La théorie du jugement d'après saint Thomas d'Aquin. Roma, Pontif. Univers. Gregoriana, 1953. x, 384p. Engl. tr.: Reality and judgment according to St. Thomas. Chicago, Regnery, 1952.

Contains a discussion of the cogito and related problems in St. Thomas, with reference to Descartes.

2233 *Hoffmann, Abraham:* René Descartes. Stuttgart, Fromann, 1905. 194 p. 2nd ed., rev., 1923. (Fromanns Klassiker der Philosophie).

Descartes viewed in Kantian retrospect. Written before AT.

2234 —: "Die Lehre von der Bildung des Universums bei Descartes und ihre geschichtliche Bedeutung." AGP 17: 237–71, 371–412, 1904. Dissertation Berlin. Partly printed: Berlin, 1903, 37 p. See 374.

2235 *Hofmann, Joseph Ehrenfried:* "Descartes und die Mathematik." In: H. Scholz, A. Kratzer und J. Hoffmann, Descartes. Drei Vorträge. 1951, 48–73; bibliography, 75–80. See 229.

2236 *Hofstadter, Albert:* "Professor Ryle's category-mistake." JP 48: 1951, 256–70. See 190.

2237 *Hofsten, Nils von:* Franskt inflytande pa svensk biologisk forskning före Linné. Med särskild hänsyn till cartesianismens genombrott i Sverige. Leipzig, Harrassowitz, 1944. 38 p. (Uppsala Universitets Arsskrift 1944, v. 1).

French influence upon Swedish biological research before Linné, with notes on the development of Cartesianism in Sweden.

2238 *Holzer, Hermann:* Mathematik und Philosophie bei Descartes und Leibniz. Dissertation Wien, 1941. 132 p. [Unpublished]

2238a *HOMENAJE.* Descartes. Buenos Aires, 1937. 3 vols. See 40.

2238b *Homenaje a Descartes* (Chile, 1950). See 544.

2238c *Homenaje a Renato Descartes.* E 37: 1937, 369–558. See 526.

2239 "*El homenaje a Descartes de la Universidad de Buenos Aires.*" E 59: 1938, 223–32.

2239a *Hommage à Descartes.* Poitiers, 1950. See 553.

2239b *Hommage à Descartes.* Poitiers 1937. See 531.

2239c *Hommage solennel.* BSFP 1950. See 559.

2239d *Hommages à Descartes.* NL 24 July 1937, 1–3.

2239e *Hommages à René Descartes.* Eur 15 July 1937. See 527.

2240 *Hoppe, Marie Louise:* Die Abhängigkeit der Wirbeltheorie des Descartes von William Gilberts Lehre vom Magnetismus. Halle a.S., Kaemmerer, 1913. 61 p. Dissertation Halle.

2241 *Hornstein, Herbert:* "Das Problem des Kritischen, mit besonderer Rücksicht auf Descartes und Kant." WZPP 6: 1957, 67–125.

The "critical problem" ("Philosophie als Denken des Denkens") developed by analysis of Descartes (77–102) and Kant. Cartesian certitude, method, lumen naturale, universal science, "Systemlogik." Rather far from the texts and vaguely general, the study manages to show old results in a somewhat different light.

2242 *Horton, Lydiard H.:* "What is known about brain patterns." Bio-Psychology (Philadelphia) no. 2: 1925–26 i–xxiv, 1–33.

"Bio-psychology, Bulletin of the Cartesian Research Society of Philadelphia."

2243 *Hotho, Heinrich Gustav:* De philosophia cartesiana. Berlin, 1826.

2244 *Houssay, Bernardo A.:* "La fisiología y la medicina de Descartes." Homenaje 1: 33–55. 1937. [Expository article with good photographic illustrations].

2245 *Huber, J. N.:* Die cartesischen Beweise vom Dasein Gottes. Augsburg, Himmer, 1854. 55 p.

2246 *Hubert, René:* "La théorie cartésienne de l'énumération." RMM 23: 1916, 489–516.

Within Cartesian method, enumeration represents the concern with the concrete as it guarantees that a scientific system exactly reproduces the reality of things. Good study of Regulae.

2247 —: "Descartes et l'Encyclopédie." Rsyn 14: April 1937, 29–50. See 455.

2248 —: "Le cartésianisme et le mouvement des idées philosophiques au XVIIIe siècle." RHPh ns 5: 1937, 121–36. ("Causerie au radio.)"

2249 *Huet, Pierre-Daniel:* Nouvelles mémoires pour servir à l'histoire du cartésianisme. 1692. See 110 and Urbain, Vertés, no. 3457 and 3490.

2250 *Humbert, Pierre:* "Descartes et le style scientifique français." Eph ns 5: 1950, 169–73. See 410.

2251 *Husserl, Edmund:* Formale und transzendentale Logik. Jahrbuch für phänomenologische Forschung 10: 1929, Ergänzungsband; especially § 100–102, p. 225ff. See 173.

2252 —: Méditations cartésiennes. Introduction à la phénoménologie. Tr. Gabrielle Peiffer et Emmanuel Levinas. Paris, Colin, 1931. vii, 136 p. (Bibl. de la Soc. française de philosophie, v. 5). Reprinted: Vrin, 1947 (BTP.) See 173.

2253 —: Cartesianische Meditationen und Pariser Vorträge, ed. S. Strasser. The Hague, Nijhoff, 1950. xxxi, 244 p. (Husserliana, v. 1.) Italian tr.: Meditazioni cartesiane e i Discorsi Parigini. Tr., intr. Filippo Costa. Milano, Bompiani, 1960. xiv, 216 p. (Idee nuove, v. 31.) English tr. by Dorion Cairns: Cartesian meditations. The Hague, Nijhoff, 1960, xii, 157 p. See 173.

2254 —: Die Krisis der europäischen Wissenschaften und die transzendentale Phänomenologie. Eine Einleitung in die phänomenologische Philosophie. Ed. Walter Biemel. Husserliana, v. 6. The Hague, Nijhoff, 1954. xxii, 559 p. (Husserliana v. 6). First published in Philosophia (Belgrade) 1: 1936, 77–176 (incomplete); the same (in French translation) in Eph 4: 1949, 229–302. See 174.

2254a —: Erste Philosophie (1923/24), ed. Rudolf Böhm. 2 v. Haag, Nijhoff, 1956. (Husserliana v. 7, 8.) See 174.

Vol. 1: Kritische Ideengeschichte. 9.–11. Vorlesung [Descartes bis Locke] 58–77. Beilage X: Descartes und die Skepsis, XI [Evidenz und cogito], XII [Modern egology from D. to Hume], XIII [The importance of Descartes, Locke, Leibniz, Brentano for the development of phenomenology] 330–50. *Vol. 2: Theorie der phänomenologischen Reduktion.* III. 3–46. Der cartesianische und der Weg des Psychologen zur transzendentaleh Reduktion 126–31. Supplementary texts on the "cartesian way of 'Ideen'": 259–301. Also: Beilagen XVIIff. on cogito-epoché.

2254b *Husserl.* Cahiers de Royaumont. Philosophie no. 3. Paris, Éditions de Minuit, 1959. 438 p. See 173 and 3528a.

2255 *Huxley, Thomas Henry:* "On Descartes' Discourse touching the method of using one's reason rightly and of seeking scientific truth" (1870). In his: Lay Sermons, Addresses, and Reviews. London, 1870, 351–78 (New York, Appleton, 1872, 320–44). French transl. by J. Sarazini: Th. H. Huxley, Les sciences naturelles et les problèmes qu'ils font surgir. Lay sermons. 1877. German tr. by Fritz Schultze: Th. H. Huxley, Reden und Aufsätze naturwissenschaftlichen .... Inhalts. Berlin, Grieben, 1877. Also in his: Methods and results. Essays. London (New York: Appleton), 1894, 166–98 (Collected essays, v. 1).

Of the two paths opened up by DM, "the one leads, by way of Berkeley and Hume, to Kant and Idealism; while the other leads, by way of De La Mettrie to Priestley, to modern physiology and Materialism" (p. 338). Interesting excursus into "this Extra-christian world" (p. 342) in which the scientist Huxley happily follows both of Descartes' paths at once, and with much spirit.

Review: Ch. Renouvier in CrPh 12: 1877–78, 209–19.

2256 —: "On the hypothesis that animals are automata, and its history." (1874). In his: Methods and results, 1894, 199–250. (Collected essays, v. 1).

Descartes anticipated Davis Hartley's fundamental conceptions about the physiology of the nervous system; but Huxley shrinks from the bête-machine doctrine; "considering the terrible practical consequences to domestic animals which might ensue from any error on our part, it is as well to err on the right side, if we err at all" (p. 237), a very English reaction.

2257 *Huygens, Constantijn:* Correspondence of Descartes and C. Huygens, ed. Leon Roth. Oxford UP, 1936. See 81.

2258 *Hyppolite, M.:* "Du sens de la Géométrie de Descartes dans son œuvre." Royaumont 166–75; discussion, 176–86. 1957. See 355.

2259 *Ibarra, J. T.:* "Nociones de psicología empírica en la filosofía de Descartes". RUC Perú 5: 1937, 509–39.

2260 *Iberico, Mariano:* "Breves reflexiones sobre el racionalismo de Descartes." Escritos 123–26, 1937.

2261 —: "Concepto y sentido de la claridad en la filosofía del siglo XVII. Descartes, Spinoza, Leibniz." Actas del primer Congreso nacional de filosofía, Mendoza (Argentina) 1949, v. 3, 1963–67. [See BAn 1952, 6933].

2262 *Ingarden, Roman S.:* "Descartes a fizyka nowożytna." KF 19: 1950, 71–150. See 375.

2263 *Inglesis, A. A.:* Ὁ Καρτέσιος καὶ ἡ ἑλληνικὴ φιλοσοφία. Νέα Ἑστία 24/48/554: 1 August 1950, 1015–20.

2264 *Iriarte Agirrezabal, Joaquin:* Kartesischer oder Sanchezischer Zweifel? Ein kritischer und philosophischer Vergleich zwischen dem kartesischen Discours de la méthode und dem sanchezischen 'Quod nihil scitur.' Bottrop i.W., Postberg, 1935. 146 p. Dissertation Bonn. See 277.

2265 —: "Francisco Sánchez el autor de Quod nihil scitur, a la luz de muy recientes estudios." RyF 110: 1936, 23–42, 157–81. See 277.

2266 —: "La filosofía 'geométrica' en Descartes, Spinoza y Leibniz." Greg 19: 1938, 481–97.

"La realidad universal no se deja aprehender en solas dós líneas rígidas, ni en solo centro monístico, ni en meras tensiones dinámicas." [BP 1938/2.]

2267 *Irons, David:* "Descartes and modern theories of emotion." PhR 4: 1895, 291–302.

Descartes' TP can stand comparison with late 19th c. theories; even his contradictions help refute William James.

Review: Anon. in RMM 4: 1896, supplement 1, p. 7.

2268 *Isnardi, Teófilo:* "La física de Descartes." Homenaje 1: 75–139. 1937. See 376.

2268a *Itard, Jean:* "La géometrie de Descartes." Université de Paris, 1956. 14p. (Les conférences du Palais de la Découverte, sér. D, no. 39.)

2269 *Iturrioz, J.:* "Leibniz en la bifurcación cartesiana." PenM 6: 1950, 207–22.

2270 *Ivaldi, Gaetano:* Il platonismo di Plotino, Sant'Agostino, Cartesio, Leibniz. Napoli, 1922. 21 p. (From: La luce del pensiero 15, no. 7, July 1922).

Deals only with Descartes and Leibniz.

2271 *Ivánka, Endre von* [Andreas de Ivánka]: "Die Stellung des Cartesianismus in der Geschichte der Philosophie." Cartesio 473–85. 1937.

Rejects the view of Descartes as father of "modern philosophy." Descartes is to Kant as Plato is to Aristotle. His merit lies not in his system but in his method which alone has remained effective.

2272 —: "Cartesianismus, Aristotelismus et Platonismus." In: Acta II Cong. Thom. Int. (see 41), 497–501. 1937.

2273 —: "Augustinus oder Cartesius?" Gloria Dei (Wien) 2: 1947, 19–23.

2274 *Iverach, J.:* Descartes, Spinoza and the new philosophy. Edinburgh, Clark (New York, Scribner), 1904. xii, 245 p. (The world's epoch makers, v. 19).

2275 *Jackson, Reginald:* "The doctrine of substance in Descartes and Spinoza." AJPP 4: 1926, 205–11.

2276 *Jacob, S. M.:* Notes on Descartes' Règles pour la direction de l'esprit. London, The Author (also: International Book Club), 1948. 35 p.

Comforting conclusion: "The lasting good done by Descartes the mathematician will far exceed any harm done by Descartes the philosopher" (p. 35).

2277 *Jacobi, Carl Gustav Jacob:* Über Descartes' Leben und seine Methode die Vernunft richtig zu leiten. Vorlesung gehalten den 3ten Juni 1846. Berlin, W. Adolf, 1846. 26 p. (Also in his: Gesammelte Werke).

2278 *Jacquin, R.:* "Le titre du Discours de la méthode est-il emprunté?" RScR 26: 1952, 142–45. See 278.

2279 *Jacquot, Jean:* "Un amateur de science, ami de Hobbes et de Descartes, Sir Charles Cavendish, 1591–1654." Thalès 6: 1949–50, 81–88. See 118.

2280 *Jahnke:* Über den ontologischen Beweis vom Dasein Gottes mit besonderem Bezug auf Anselm und Descartes. Stralsund, 1875.

2281 *Jakob, Christofredo:* "Descartes en la biología." Homenaje 1: 57–66. 1937. 9 pl.

Interesting confrontation of Descartes' biology with modern findings; D.'s illustrations and modern photographs.

2282 —: "La psicología de Descartes a través de tres siglos." Anales del Instituto de psicología (Buenos Aires) 2: 1938, 297–328.

2282a *Jammer, Max:* Concepts of space. Harvard UP, 1954. 2nd ed., augm., transl. by Paul Wilpert: Das Problem des Raumes. Die Entwicklung der Raumtheorien. Vorwort von Albert Einstein. Darmstadt, Wissenschaftliche Buchgesellschaft, 1960. xiii, 220 p. See 377.

2282b —: Concepts of force. A study in the foundations of dynamics. Harvard UP, 1957. viii, 269 p. See 377a.

2283 *Janet, Paul:* Descartes, son caractère et son génie. RDM année 38, pér 2, 73: 345–69, Jan. 15, 1868. Also in his: Les maîtres de la pensée moderne. Paris. Calmann-Lévy, 1883, p. 1–48 (2nd ed. 1888, p. 1–66) and in: Chauvin & Bidois (see 1518), 1922, 324–31. See 142.

2283a *Janovskaja, S.:* " 'Geometrija' Dekarta: K 300-letiju so vremeni vykhoda v svet." Front nauki i tekhniki, no. 6, 1937.

On D.'s Géometrie. Tercentenary paper. [In Russian.]

2284 *Jansen, Bernhard* (S.J.): "Descartes, der Vater der heutigen Philosophie." Stimmen der Zeit 113: 1927, 368–79.

2285 —: "Der Geist des Philosophierens Descartes'. " Sch 12: 1937, 161–74, 340–60. See 211b.

2286 —: "Die Methodenlehre des Descartes, ihr Wesen und ihre Bedeutung." Cartesio 487–512, 1937. See 211b.

2287 —: "Die Pflege der Philosophie im Jesuitenorden während des 17.–18. Jahrhunderts." PJGG 51: 1938, 172–215, 345–66, 435–56. Also: Fulda, Parzeller, 1938. 96 p.

Extremely detailed international survey by countries. "Der philosophische Jesuitenstil" of the time: a healthy, critical, conservative eclecticism, far from rigid Scholasticism. Notes its lack of constructive contributions, its quickness in introducing new thought. Valuable background material.

2288 *Jansen, F.:* "Les systèmes eucharistiques cartésiens." Dict. de théol. cath. v. 52 (1913), col. 1427–52, s.v. "Eucharistiques (accidents) 5." Bibliography. See 279.

2289 *Jansen, W.:* "Descartes." In his: Geschiedenis der wijsbegeerte, v. 2. Zutphen 1921, 355–403.

2290 *Jarry-Guérolt, Robert:* Les rapports limites de l'ordre et du libre-arbitre dans l'évolution des sociétés humaines. Vol. 1: Figuration cartésienne du fait social. Paris, Hermann, 1936. 68 p. (Asci, v. 430).

2291 *Jascalevich, Alejandro A.:* Three conceptions of mind, their bearing on the denaturalization of the mind in history. New York, Columbia UP. 1926. ix, 107 p. Columbia dissertation. Spanish: Interpretes del alma: Aristoteles, San Augustín, Descartes y Locke. Buenos Aires, J. Samet, 1931. 123 p.

Very poor treatment of Aristotle, but "what he says about Descartes seems to me much better and often, indeed, very good" (J. Laird's review in Mind 26: 1937, p. 244).

2292 *Jaśniewicz, Otto:* Der Gottesbegriff und die Erkennbarkeit Gottes, von Anselm von Canterbury bis zu René Descartes. Erlangen, E. T. Jacob, 1906. viii, 57 p. Dissertation Erlangen.

2293 *Jaspers, Karl:* Descartes und die Philosophie. Berlin, Walter de Gruyter, 1937. 104 p. Reprinted 1949, 1956. French transl. by Hanns Pollnow: "La pensée de Descartes et la philosophie." RPFE 123: 1937, 39–148, and separately: Descartes et la philosophie. Paris, Alcan (PUF), 1938. 112 p. BPC. See 175.

2294 —: Preface to: Descartes. Discours de la méthode, ed. K. Fischer. Mainz, Universum-Verlag, 1948. ()

Jastrebov: see Yastreboff.

2295 *Jeannel, Charles-Julien:* Descartes et la princesse Palatine. Paris, Douniol, 1869. 25 p. (Reprinted from: Le Correspondant).

2296 *Jefferson, Geoffrey:* "René Descartes on the localization of the soul." Irish Journal of Medical Science, September 1949, no. 285, 691–706.

Cheerfully digressive, informative account of early views on the location of the soul. Anatomists had long before D. accepted the pineal gland as gate-keeper regulating the flow of animal spirits; but "so much did Descartes improve on the beliefs on his forerunners and contemporaries, that he eventually undid the pineal gland. His one mistake was to be too lucid and too exact" (703).

2297 *Jeffreys, Harold:* Cartesian tensors. Cambridge UP. 1931. vi, 92 p.

A mathematical monograph.

2298 *Jezierski, F.:* "Nieznane dotąd uwagi Leibnitza nad zasadami Descartesa." Przeglad naukowy (Warszawa) 1844/3, 293–310.

On a hitherto unknown Descartes comment by Leibniz.

2299 *Joachim, Harold H.:* Descartes' 'Rules for the direction of the mind.' Reconstituted from notes taken by his pupils, ed. by Errol E. Harris. Foreword by Sir David Ross. London, Allen & Unwin (New York, Macmillan), 1957. 124 p. See 212.

Jöchner, G.: see Binder, F. et al.

2300 *Jörges, Rudolf:* Die Lehre von den Empfindungen bei Descartes. Düsseldorf, L. Schwann, 1901. 68 p. Dissertation Bonn.

2301 *Johnston, Charlotte:* "Locke's 'Examination' of Malebranche and Norris." JHI 19: 1958, 550–58. See 456.

2302 *Jolivet, Régis:* "Le doute méthodique de Descartes." RdePh 29: 1922, 139–58. See 312.

2303 —: "L'anticartésianisme de Pascal." Aph 1, no. 3: 1923, 54–67.

Pascal's Jansenism the hidden source of his conflict with Descartes.

2304 —: La notion de substance. Essai historique et critique sur le développement des doctrines d'Aristote à nos jours. Paris, Beauchesne, 1929. 339 p. (Bibliothèque des Archives de philosophie). See 282.

2305 —: "L'intuition intellectuelle et le problème de la métaphysique selon Descartes." Aph 11, no. 2: 1934, 1–111. See 281.

2306 —: "Trois critiques de l'humanité cartésienne: Proudhon, Cournot, Nietzsche." Rthom 41 (ns 19): 1936, 164–93.

Three pessimists against that optimism of technological progress and mastery of nature which the author labels "Cartesian."

2307 —: "Les conflits du cartésianisme." Cartesio 513–25. 1937.

In the Cartesian system, "la plupart des oppositions de doctrines restent à l'état brut, sans principe supérieur de conciliation ou de synthèse" (p. 515): idealism and realism, absolute rationalism and radical empiricism, ambiguity in the Method and in the cogito – no wonder that the Cartesian system as such had but one adherent, namely Descartes himself.

2308 —: "Le troisième centenaire du Discours de la méthode." Christus 16: 1937, 113–19.

2309 —: "Science et sagesse chez Descartes." Educ 1: 1950, 193–95.

2310 *Jolly, Jules:* Histoire du mouvement intellectuel au XVIe siècle et pendant la première partie du XVIIe. 2 vols. Paris, Amyot, 1860.

2311 *Jonquières, Ernest de* [i.e. Ernest Fouquer de Jonquières]: "Étude sur les équations algébraiques numériques dans leur relation avec la régle des signes de Descartes." Atti dell' Acad. Pontifica de' Nuovi Lincei 38: 1885. 22 p. [Schrecker]

2312 —: Écrit posthume de Descartes De solidorum elementis. Texte latin (original et revu) suivi d'une traduction française avec notes. Mémoire présenté à l'Académie des sciences. Paris, 1890. 55 p. 4to. Reprinted in: Zeitschrift für Geschichte der Mathematik ns 4: 1890.

See AT X, 257–63 on the curious history of the repeated "discoveries" and translations of this work. See also Prouhet, no. 3005.

2313 —: "Descartes et son œuvre posthume De solidorum elementis." Comptes-rendus des séances de l'Académie des sciences 110: 1890, 261ff., 315ff., 677ff. (See AT X, 259–60).

2314 *Jordan, Leo:* "Descartes' philosophischer Dilettantismus." In: Festgabe zum 60. Geburtstage Karl Vosslers. München, Hueber, 1932, p. 149–59. (Münchner romanistische Arbeiten, v.1).

Discusses Descartes' "Begriffssprache."

2315 *Jordan, Pascual:* Physik im Vordringen. Braunschweig, Vieweg, 1949. viii, 112 p. (Die Wissenschaft, v. 99). [BN]

2316 *Jorge Casares, A.:* "Actualidad y vigencia del cogito cartesiano." Universidad (Argentina) no. 28, July 1954, 187–225.

Despite all antecedents, the cogito is new: it envisages the passage from thought to being not as a deduction but as an instantaneous vision; this truth beyond history is still useful (BAn 1955, 3772.)

2317 *Joulia, P.:* "Descartes au Collège de La Flèche, 1606–1614." SLSA du Saumurois 26/85: 1938, 14–31.

2317a —: "Descartes et la sagesse mésoccidentale." F 10: 1959, 772–93.

"Mésoccidental" refers to the countries of D.'s life and travel. Standard popular lecture.

2317b *Les journées universitaires poitevines.* Hommage à Descartes, 1950. See 553.

2318 *Jüngst, Walter:* Das Verhältnis von Philosophie und Theologie bei den Cartesianern Malebranche, Poiret und Spinoza. Eine philosophiegeschichtliche Untersuchung. Leipzig, Quelle & Meyer, 1912. 94 p. (APGF, v. 22). [Enlarged from author's Erlangen dissertation: Das Problem von Glauben und Wissen bei Malebranche und Poiret 1912. 64 p.]

Sees in Malebranche, the supposed mystic, a pure rationalist. The true antirationalistic mystic among the Cartesians is Poiret who recognizes the mystical element in D.'s doctrine of the creation of eternal verities.

2319 *Julien-Eymard d'Angers (O.F.M. cap.):* "Sénèque, Épictète et le stoïcisme dans l'œuvre de René Descartes." RTPL ser. 3, v. 4: 1954, 169–96. See 283.

2320 *Jung, Gertrud:* "Das Methodenproblem bei Vives." CD 5: 134–39, 1937.

2321 *Jungmann, K.* " 'Le Monde' de Descartes." In: Congrès international de philosophie, 2 sess, 1904. Rapports et comptes rendus. Genève, 1905, p. 247–51.

Considers RV a first sketch of Le Monde; what is now known as Le Monde and Traité de l'homme is the intended substitute for the work abandoned in 1633. RV corresponds exactly to what is known of the 1629 project of Le Monde, except for its rounding out the facts into an artistic picture.

2322 *Jungmann, Carl:* René Descartes. Eine Einführung in seine Werke. Leipzig, F. Eckardt, 1908. viii, 234 p.

Shows how D. used the factual knowledge of his time to achieve a unified framework for mastering science, thereby setting "unveräusserliche Normen des menschlichen Geisteslebens." Solid, faithful but too schematic in assigning a specific preoccupation to each period of D.'s life (method-mathematics-epistemology-science).

Reviews: Anon. in RMM 17: 1909, 10–11; D. N. Dolson in JP 6: 1909, 556–57; Kersten in RNS 16: 1909, 147–48; J. Koch in PJ 22: 1909, 201–03.

2323 —: Die Weltentstehungslehre des Descartes. Bern, Scheitlin, 1907. 51 p. (Berner Studien z. Philosophie u.ihrer Geschichte, v. 54).

2324 *Jungmann, C.* "Descartes und die Jesuiten." AGP 39 (ns 32): 1929, 38–53, 263–73.

Title misleading. Useful article examines D.'s physical theory of transsubstantiation, which the Jesuits opposed.

2325 *Jury, Paul:* "Descartes psychanalyste." PsyP no. 40: Feb .5, 1950, 150–64.

Surprise. Descartes was no psychoanalyst.

K

2326 *K., R.:* "Descartes au Panthéon." Temps, 24 February 1935.

2327 *Kahl, Wilhelm:* Die Lehre vom Primat des Willens bei Augustinus, Duns Scotus und Descartes. Strassburg, Trübner, 1886. ix, 126 p. Dissertation Strassburg.

Useful doctrinal comparisons.

2328 *Kahl-Furthmann, G.:* "Descartes' Betonung seiner Unabhängigkeit von der Tradition und Leibnizens Kritik." ZPF 4: 1950, 377–84. See 286.

2328a —: "Philosophische Interpretation. Ein Wort zur dritten Auflage zu Karl Jaspers' Schrift 'Descartes und die Philosophie' ". ZPF 14: 1960, 127–38. See 175.

Kalisch, Donald: see Yost & Kalisch.

2329 *Kahn, Lina:* Metaphysics of the supernatural as illustrated by Descartes. New York, Columbia UP, 1918. vii, 66 p. (Archives of philosophy no. 9, January 1918.)

The conflict between science and theology induced Descartes to disguise his scientific ideas "in a theological garb".

Kalish, Donald: see: R. M. Yost, Jr. and D. Kalish.

2330 *Kampé de Fériet, J.:* "Ce que la mathématique doit à Descartes." RHPh ns 5: 1937, 161–71.

2330a *Kamlah, Wilhelm:* "Der Anfang der Vernunft bei Descartes – autobiographisch und historisch." AGP 43: 1961, 70–84.

2331 *Kantonen, T. A.:* "The influence of Descartes on Berkeley." PhR 43: 1934, 483–500.

2332 *Kapp, Reginald O.:* "Living and lifeless machines." BJPS 5: 1954–55, 91–103.

Kapp, a "latter-day Cartesian" (Walker, ibid. 6: 1955–56, 285) turns the usual cartesian and anticartesian arguments upside down; still, "certain hard facts tell against the hypothesis that living organisms are 100% automatic." See the comments by Miles and Szasz, no. 2739 and 3380.

2333 *Karam:* "Descartes." Al Moktataf (Kairo), Oct. 1937, 273–80; Nov. 1937, 419–28. In Arabic. (BP 1937/2).

2334 *Karpinski, L. C.:* "Is there progress in mathematical discovery, and did the Greeks have analytical geometry?" Isis 27/73: 1937, 46–52.

2335 —: "Descartes and the modern world; his contribution to mathematics." Science 89: February 1939, 150–52.

2336 *Kastil, Alfred:* Studien zur neueren Erkenntnistheorie. Vol. 1: Descartes. Halle a.S., Niemeyer, 1909. xiv, 209 p. See 212a.

2337 *Katkov, Georg:* "Descartes und Brentano. Eine erkenntnistheoretische Gegenüberstellung." Emge (see 523), 116–51. 1937. See 288.

2337a *Kazarin, A.:* "Rene Dekart, Pravila dlja rukovodstva uma." Front nauki i tekhniki, no. 1, 1937.

On D.'s Regulae. [In Russian.]

2337b *Katsoff, Louis O.:* "Cogito ergo sum." RMM 63: 1958, 251–62.

Formal logical analysis confirms that "sum" does not refer to an undefined existential quantifier, that "ergo" is non-inferential, that the argument is neither a material implication nor a nominal definition but "un énoncé de la structure .... du moi et du genre de réalité que constitute le moi" (260). D.'s method of argument consists in stating a doubt such that doubting the statement of doubt will confirm it. Some strange consequences concerning the existence of material objects and regarding freedom are suggested.

2338 *Kayserling, Arthur:* Die Idee der Kausalität in den Lehren der Occasionalisten. Ein Beitrag zur Geschichte des Cartesianismus. Heidelberg, Weiss, 1896. viii, 72 p.

2339 *Keeler, Leo William (S.J.):* The problem of error from Plato to Kant. A historical and critical study. Roma, Pontifica Universitas Gregoriana, 1934. xiii, 281 p. (Analecta Gregoriana, v. 6).

Review: L. Noël in RNS 38: 1935, 329–33.

2340 *Keeling, S. V.* [i.e. Stanley Victor Keeling]: Descartes. Oxford UP (London, Benn), 1934. xi, 282 p. (Leaders of philosophy). See 213.

2341 —: "Cartesian mechanism." Phil 9: 1934, 51–66.

2342 —: "Philosophy in France. Recent interpretations of Cartesianism." Phil 11: 1936, 336–40.

2343 —: "Livres et articles publiés en langue anglaise sur Descartes et le cartésianisme depuis 1900." Rsyn 14: 1937, 109–11.

2344 —: "En quoi consiste l'idéalisme cartésien?" CD 2: 3–8. 1937.

Cartesianism is neither realism nor idealism; it went too far towards representationa idealism (simple natures), not far enough towards absolute idealism.

2345 —: "Le réalisme de Descartes et le rôle des natures simples." (Tr. Y. Feldman). RMM 44: 1937, 63–99.

The synthesis of realism and conceptionalism in Descartes' theory of knowledge is at the root of the increasing abstractness of physics.

2346 —: "Leon Roth: Descartes' Discourse on Method." Mind 48: 1939, 366–73. [A critical review.]

2347 —: "Descartes. Annual Lecture on a Master Mind. Henriette Hertz Trust of the British Academy." Proceedings of the British Academy of Science 34: 1948, 57–81. Also separately: London, 1948. 24 p. See 213.

Answering contemporary philosophical aspirations, Descartes instituted new methods which adequated reason to reality, and opened the road to a solid movement of scientific investigation. [BAn 1952, 6934.]

2348 —: Art. "Cartesians." Encyclopedia Britannica, 14th edition.

2349 *Kehr, Marguerite Witmer:* "The doctrine of the self in St. Augustine and in Descartes." PhR 25: 1916, 587–615.

2349a *Kennington, Richard:* "Descartes' 'Olympica.' " Social Research 28: 1961, 171–204.

Baillet's text is carefully examined from the viewpoint of testing the currently prevalent belief that Olympica proves that D. did not consider reason the sole authority. Kennington sees no rational theology in the Dreams but a pagan or Stoic quest for tranquility. The detailed study of the three dreams in their dramatic articulation (pagan ascent followed by descent from the peak) clarifies several issues of detail and reveals striking parallels between the Dream and the Pythagorean Idyllia of Ausonius, though author does not document his claim that D. had read the whole sequence of them.

Kemp Smith: see Smith, Norman Kemp.

2350 *Kerékjarto, B. de:* "La méthode de Descartes et la géométrie moderne." CD 6: 166–73. 1937.

On axiomatic systems.

2351 *Kerstiens, B.:* "Untersuchungen zur Seelenlehre des Descartes." AGPs 16: 1910, 237–78. Also Leipzig, Engelmann, 1909. 42 p. Dissertation Münster.

2352 *Keussen, Rudolf:* Bewusstsein und Erkenntnis bei Descartes. Halle a.S., Niemeyer, 1906. ix, 95 p. (EAGP v. 22). Dissertation Bonn.

Competent study of cogito, psycho-physical conditions of cognition, psychological determinations of consciousness in Descartes, utilizing his "Notae in programma quoddam." Diagrammatic comparison of Descartes' classification of "Bewusstseinsvorgänge" in Regulae, MM, PP, and Programma (85–90).

2353 *Keyser, Cassius Jackson:* Portraits of famous philosophers who were also mathematicians. New York, Pictorial mathematics, 1939. Folio.

Portfolio containing a conventional posthumous engraving of Descartes at his working table, brief biographical comment.

2354 —: "Symposium on the life and writings of R. Descartes, celebrating the tercentenary of his Géométrie." Scientific Monthly 44: 1937, 477–80.

2355 —: "El tricentenario de D." Ultra (Havana, Cuba) July 1937, 42–43.

2355a *Kierkegaard, Søren:* Johannes Climacus, or De omnibus dubitandum. (About 1842–43.) Unfinished manuscript. See 304.

For a brief summary of the turn which Kierkegaard gave to Cartesian universal doubt see: Walter Lowrie, Kierkegaard (Oxford UP, 1938), 268.

2356 *Kirchmann, Julius Hermann von:* Erläuterungen zu B. von Spinozas Bearbeitung der Prinzipien der Philosophie des R. Descartes. Berlin, L. Heimann, 1863 (reprinted 1871). 112 p. (Philosophische Bibliothek, v. 42).

The commentaries of this enthusiastic amateur who founded the "Philosophische Bibliothek," a jurist with vast but unscholarly philosophical reading, laid a broad foundation of popular interest in Germany. Arthur Buchenau's meticulous translations now take the place of von Kirchmann's unusable editions.

2357 *Kirwan, C. de:* "Un disciple de Descartes original et peu connu" (Dom Robert Desgabets). Bulletin de l'Académie delphinale, 1904. [Lanson 6225].

2358 —: La méthode cartésienne rectifiée et simplifiée. Arras, Sueur-Charruey, 1905. 16 p. (Reprinted from: La science catholique, Lille, July 1905).

2359 *Kjaer, Nils:* "Descartes." In his: Bøger og billeder. Kritiske forsøg. Kristiania, Feilberg & Landmark, 1898, ch. 3. [LC]

2360 *Klattenhoff, Friedrich:* Die Gotteslehre des Malebranche in ihrem Verhältnis zur Gotteslehre des Descartes. Dissertation Leipzig. 1894. 126 p.

2361 *Klein, Jacob.* "Vieta's Formelsprache und die Umwandlung des Anzahl-Begriffs." "Der Begriff der *Zahl* bei Stevin, Descartes und Wallis." In his: "Die griechische Logistik und die Entstehung der Algebra." Quellen und Studien zur Geschichte der Mathematik, Abt. B, 3: 152–94, 195–235, 1934–36. See 378.

2362 *Klobasa, L.:* "O zasadniczej myśli transcendentalnego idealizmu Kanta, z uwzględnieniem poznania zasady Kartezjusza i Fichtego." Studium z historii teorii poznania. Kraków, 1881. [Bar]

Kant's transcendental idealism, in relation to the epistemological principles of Descartes and Fichte.

2363 *Klöpel, Bernhard:* Das lumen naturale bei Descartes. Dissertation Leipzig. 1896. 49 p.

2364 *Knoodt, P.:* De Cartesii sententia: cogito ergo sum. Breslau, 1845.

2365 *Koch, Anton:* Die Psychologie Descartes' systematisch und historisch-kritisch bearbeitet. München, Chr. Kaiser, 1881. viii, 316 p. Dissertation Marburg.

Voluminous but diffuse and of little value.

2366 *König, Edmund:* "Descartes." In his: Die Entwickelung des Causalproblems von Cartesius bis Kant. Studien zur Orientierung über die Aufgabe der Metaphysik und Erkenntnislehre. (2 vols.) Vol. 1, Leipzig, Otto Wigand, 1880, 39–66.

2367 —: Das Problem des Zusammenhanges von Leib und Seele und seine Bearbeitung in der Cartesischen Schule. Programm Sonderhausen, 1895 and 1897.

2368 *Kohler, Sylvester:* Jansenismus und Cartesianismus. Eine Studie zur Geschichte der Philosophie und zur Kirchengeschichte. Düsseldorf, Schaub, 1905. 51 p. Dissertation (Bonn?).

2369 *Kolligs, Hans:* Des Cartesius Ansicht über den Ursprung unserer Vorstellungen, mit besonderer Berücksichtigung der eingeborenen Vorstellungen. Jahrbuch des Königl. Gymnasiums zu Vinzburg, 91–92 (Programm 458, 1892). 19 p.

See Bruno Erdmann's review in AGP 7: 1893–94, 521–22.

2369a *Kondo, Yoitsu:* Dekaruto no Shirenzo. Tokyo, Iwanami Sholen, 1959. 368 p.

Descartes' view of the physical world. [In Japanese.] Descartes' cosmogony and genetics gave him an evolutionary though mechanistic outlook on the physical world which, when linked to his metaphysics, produced his chief difficulties, viz. regarding the theory of matter, the union problem, the Cartesian circle. Author asserts against Laporte and others that Descartes never doubted this evolutionary view. [Author's notice in Bph 7: 1960, 264.]

2370 *Koningk, C. de:* "Sedeo, ergo sum: Considerations on the touchstone of certitude." LTP 6: 1950, 343–48.

Descartes should not have downgraded the "tangible" qualities as secondary ones (importance of senses other than sight).

2371 *Korteweg, Diderik Johannes:* "Notes sur Constantijn Huygens considéré comme amateur des sciences exactes, et sur ses relations avec Descartes." Archives néerlandaises, v. 22, 1888. 45 p.

2372 —: "Descartes et Snellius, d'après quelques documents nouveaux." RMM 4: 1896, 489–501. See 399.

2373 —: "Descartes et le journal de Beeckman." Archives néerlandaises ser. 2, v. 3: 1906, suppl. p. VI–XX.

2374 *Kowalewski, Arnold:* "Eine Descartes-Reliquie in Königsberg." K 40: 1935, 264–69.

Entry in the "Stammbuch" of Christian Otter, b. 1598, who studied fortifications in Holland and was present at the siege of Breda. "Domino Ottero solertissimo et studiosissimo/cultori matheseos, memoria et benevolentia/ergo scripsit./Renatus Des Cartes/". If this reading of Kowalewski's is correct, this would be one instance of Descartes' spelling his name "Des Cartes."

2375 *Koyré, Alexandre:* Essai sur l'idée de Dieu et les preuves de son existence chez Descartes. Paris, Leroux, 1922. xix, 220 p. (Bibliothèque des Hautes Études. Sciences religieuses, v. 33). German edition (with minor revisions): Descartes und die Scholastik. Bonn, F. Cohen, 1923. 244 p. See 214.

2376 —: Études galiléennes. 3 vols. Paris, Hermann, 1939. (Histoire de la pensée). Asci, no. 852–854. See 379.

2377 —: Trois leçons sur Descartes, publiées par la Faculté des lettres de l'Université égyptienne. Texte français et traduction arabe. Le Caire, Imprimerie Nationale, 1937. 56 p., 49 p. Reprinted in his: Entretiens sur Descartes (see 144 and 2378).

2378 —: Entretiens sur Descartes. New York and Paris, Brentano, 1944. 113 p. (Préface de Robert Tenger). See 144.

2379 —: Descartes after three hundred years. University of Buffalo studies v. 19, no. 1 (Monographs in philosophy 2), 1951. 37 p. Also published as introduction to: Descartes, Philosophical writings .... by E. Anscombe and P. T. Geach. Edinburgh, Nelson, 1954, vii–xliv.

2380 —: From the closed world to the infinite universe. Baltimore, Johns Hopkins UP (London, Oxford UP) 1957. x, 304. (Publications of the Institute for the history of medicine, Johns Hopkins University. Third series: The Hideyo Moguchi Lectures, v. 7). Reprinted: Harper Torchbooks 1958. See 379a.

2380a —: "Galilée et Descartes." CD 2: 41–46. 1937.

The historical picture of their relationship, created by Descartes himself, is false. Both are Platonists, mathematical apriorists, believers in innate ideas.

2381 —: "La loi de la chute des corps. Galilée et Descartes." RPFE 123: 1937, 149–204. Reprinted in no. 379 (2376).

2382 —: "Descartes et le Discours de la méthode." Revue des conférences françaises en Orient (Cairo) 2: 1938, 235–42.

2383 —: "Galileo and the scientific revolution of the seventeenth century." PhR 52: 1942, 333–48.

2384 —: "Le rationalisme de Descartes, d'après M. Laporte." Eur 24: 1946, 116–24.

2385 *Kramer, Paul Matthias:* "Descartes und das Brechungsgesetz des Lichtes." Abhandlungen zur Geschichte der Mathematik. Leipzig, Teubner, 1882, no. 4, 233–78 (Zeitschrift für Mathematik und Physik 27: 1882, Supplement).

2386 *Krantz, Émile:* Étude sur l'esthétique de Descartes, étudiée dans les rapports de la doctrine cartésienne avec la littérature classique française au XVIIIe siècle. Paris, Baillière, 1882. iv, 376 p. Thèse Paris. Russian trans.: Opyt filosofii literatury: Dekart i Francuskij klasicizm. St. Petersburg, 1902. See 411, 150.

2387 *Krassmöller, Wilhelm:* Darstellung und Kritik der Lehre des Descartes über die Bildung des Universums. Rostock, Hinsdorff, 1903. 78 p. Dissertation Rostock.

2388 *Kratzer, Adolf:* "Descartes als Physiker." In: H. Scholz, A. Kratzer und J. Hofmann: Descartes. Drei Vorträge. 1951, 38–47. See 229.

2389 *Krebs, Albert:* Geschichte der Beweise für das Dasein Gottes, von Cartesius bis Kant. Wiesbaden, 1876. 21 p. Dissertation. [BM]

2389a *Kretschmar, Johann:* "Zu Descartes' Briefen." AGP 7: 1893–94, 516–17.
A note on the dating of Descartes' letters to Elisabeth.

2390 *Krishnaswami Ayyangar, A. A.:* "René Descartes." Mathem. Student (Madras) 8: 1940, 101–08.

2391 *Kronenberg, M.:* "Descartes und Faust." Morgen (Berlin) 1908, no. 27. [Überweg]

2392 *Krüger, Gerhard:* "Die Herkunft des philosophischen Selbstbewusstseins." LogosT 22: 1933, 255–72. See 176.

2393 —: "Descartes-Bibliographie." Emge 203–04. 1937. [Unimportant].

2394 *Kubitz, O. A.:* "Scepticism and intuition in the philosophy of Descartes." PhR 48: 1939, 472–91.

2395 *Kuçi, Ali:* "Racionalizmi i Descartes-it." Perpjeka Shqiptare 2: 1937, 184–86. [In Albanian.]

2396 *Kühn, F. R.:* Descartes' Verhältnis zur Mathematik und Physik, zugleich eine Einführung in die Philosophie für Mathematiker und Physiker. München, Rösl, 1923. (Philosophische Reihe, v. 77).

Elementary, reliable first introduction to Descartes' thought, method and scientific work.

2397 *Küppers, Ferdinand:* Descartes' Lehre von der Trennbarkeit und Untrennbarkeit der Ideen. Dissertation Bonn, 1922.

2398 *Kuiper, Vincent M.* (O.P.): "Le réalisme de Descartes." Cartesio 527–45. 1937.

Descartes prepared the way for idealism, not positively but through weaknesses of his realism which this article explores.

2399 *Kupka, Paul:* "Die Willenstheorie des Descartes." AGP 10: 1897, 29–39.

2399a *Kusnetsov, B. G.:* ["Descartes and contemporary physics." In Russian.] In: Iztorii frantzuskoi nauki. Sbornik Statei: Moskva, Akadem. Nauk SSSR. 1960. [Isis 52: 1961, p. 452.]

2400 *Kuwaki, Genyoku:* "L'état actuel des études cartésiennes au Japon." CD 3: 134–39. 1937. See 15.

2401 *Kuypers, H.:* "Descartes en het moderne denken." De Gids 113/2, Feb. 1950, 81–89.

2402 *Kvačala, Jan:* "Komenský a Des Cartes." Praha, Narodni Museum Časopis 68: 1894, 50–68.

L

2403 *L., G.:* "Le cartésianisme ou la véritable renovation des sciences." Revue catholique 2: 1845. 16 p.

Discusses Bordas-Demoulin's book of the same title.

2404 *Labérenne, Paul:* "Les trois premiers 'Essais' de la méthode." Eur 15: 15 July 1937, 364–83. See 37.

Descartes is closer to a Marxist scientist than the modern defenders of "la science pour la science," if the accent falls on the Essais rather than on DM, as it should.

2405 —: "Un savant discuté: René Descartes." Commune (Paris) 1937, 1354–61.

Excerpt from a book on Descartes planned (but not executed) in collaboration with Lucie Prenant.

2406 *Laberthonnière, Le P. Lucien:* Études sur Descartes. 2 vols. (Œuvres de Laberthonnière, ed. Louis Canet, v. 1, 2). Paris, Vrin, 1935. viii, 468 p.; 360 p. See 177.

2406a —: Études de philosophie cartésienne et premiers écrits philosophiques. (Œuvres de Laberthonnière, ed. Louis Canet, v. 3). Paris, Vrin, 1938, x, 590 p. See 177.

2407 —: "Le dualisme cartésien." APC 80: 1909, 35–92. Also in no. 177 (2406), v. 1, p. 5–73.

2408 —: "La théorie de la foi chez Descartes." APC 12: 1911, 382–403. Also in no. 177 (2406), v. 2, p. 213–37.

2409 —: "La religion de Descartes." APC 12: August 1911, 510–23, 619–40. Also in no. 177 (2406), v. 2, p. 238–86.

2410 —: "Le prétendu rationalisme de Descartes au point de vue religieux." APC 12: September 1911. Also in no. 177 (2406), v. 2, p. 254–63.

2411 *Labordère, Marcel:* Une profession de foi cartésienne. Paris, Colin, 1919. 143 p.

Introduction (1–45) and selected texts.

Labrousse, Elisabeth: see Goguel de Labrousse.

2412 *Lachièze-Rey, Pierre:* L'idealisme kantien. Paris, Alcan, 1931. Thèse Paris. Reprinted: Paris, Vrin, 1950 (BHP). "Cogito kantien et cogito cartésien," p. 5–59. See 455a.

2413 —: Les origines cartésiennes du Dieu de Spinoza. Paris, Alcan, 1932. Reprinted: Vrin, 1950. xii, 288 p. (BHP). Thèse complémentaire, Paris. See 455a.

2414 —: "Réflexions sur le cercle cartésien." RPFE 123: 1937, 205–24.

2415 *Lacombe, Olivier:* Descartes. (Turkish transl. by Mehmet Karasan.) Ankara, 1943. 124 p. (Dil ve tarih-cografya Fakültesi felsefe enstitütü, v. 6. Felsefe tarihi, ser. 1.)

2416 *Lacoste, Paul:* "Le sens commun chez Descartes." Rdom 52: 1946, 147–58.

2417 *Lacroix, Jean:* "La signification du doute cartésien." Cartesio 547–54.

"Le doute, héroisme du vouloir" – "La dialectique du doute" – "La spiritualité de l'esprit": angelism in Descartes is but a tendency. Having separated "le parti-pris d'évidence et le parti-pris de spiritualité," Descartes died before he could reunite them again in a great final reconstruction of his philosophy.

2418 —: "Sodobni pomen Descartesa." Misel in delo (Ljubliana) 3: 1937, 164–67. [In Slovene.]

"Descartes' present importance." [In Slovene.]

2418a *Ladière, J.:* "Philosophy and science." PhSt Dec. 1958, 3–23.

Starting from Descartes and Husserl, author examines the distinction between philosophy and science. Both symbolize, not logos, but sagesse. [Bsig 1960, no. 329].

2419 *Lafleur, Lawrence J.:* "Descartes, father of modern meteorology." Bulletin of the American meteorological society 31: 1950, 138–40.

2420 —: "A footnote on Descartes and Hume." JP 40: 1952, 780–83.

On Descartes' concept of lumière naturelle (against H. J. McLendon's "Has Russell answered Hume?")

2421 —: "Descartes and scientific presuppositions." Pers 35: 1954, 25–31.

2422 *Lagerlöf, Bengt Christian:* Jemförelse imellan Cartesii medfödda ideer och Kants rena förstandsbegrepp. Dissertation Upsala, 1857.

Compares Descartes' "innate ideas" with Kant's concept of pure reason.

La Harpe: see Harpe, J. de la.

2423 *Laing, B. M.:* "Descartes on material things." Phil 16: 389–411, 1941. See 290.

2424 *Laird, John:* "L'influence de Descartes sur la philosophie anglaise du XVIIe siècle." RPFE 123: 1937, 226–56. See 456.

2425 *Lalande, André:* "Sur quelques textes de Bacon et Descartes." RMM 19: 296–311, 1911.

Surprising "similarities" of doctrine suggested by the notorious method of parallel quotations, but the assembly of texts is useful independently of conclusions.

Review: Roland-Gosselin in RSPT 5: 1911, 778.

2426 *Lalande, A.:* See 515 (Causeries .... 1938).

2427 *Lalo, Ch.:* "La discipline cartésienne commande-t-elle une esthétique?" NL, 24 July 1937.

2428 *Lameere, Jean:* "Giambattista Vico, critique italien de Descartes." CD 1: 31–37. 1937. See 461.

2429 *Lamprecht, Sterling P.:* "The role of Descartes in 17th century England." SHI 3: 178–240. 1935. See 460.

2430 *Landgrebe, Ludwig:* "Descartes." In: Gottfried Wilhelm Leibniz. Vorträge.. aus Anlass seines 300. Geburtstages .... Hamburg, Hansischer Gildenverlag, 1946, 213–30.

Substantial lecture on Descartes and Leibniz.

2431 *Landormy, Paul:* Descartes. Paris, Delaplane, 1902. 5th ed. 1917. 143 p. – Spanish tr. by R. G. Trevino: Descartes, su vida, su obra, su pensamiento. México, Editorial América, 1940. 158 p. (Biblioteca filos., v. 1).

Nice introduction, worth the honor of translation.

2432 —: "La mémoire corporelle et la mémoire intellectuelle dans la philosophie de Descartes." In: Bibliothèque du Premier congrès international de philosophie (1900), Paris, Colin, 1902, v.4, 259–98. See 227.

2433 *Lanesseau, J.-J. de:* "Descartes et le transformisme." Revue anthropologique (Paris) 22: 1912, 177–99. [Schrecker]

2434 *Lange, Friedrich Albert:* Geschichte des Materialismus und Kritik seiner Bedeutung in der Gegenwart. 1865. Engl. tr. by Ernest Chester: The history of materialism (3 vols., 1877–92). 3rd ed., with introd. by Bertrand Russell, London, 1945 (reprinted 1950), ILPP.

Considers Descartes the true father of materialism, as La Mettrie had asserted, though the idealistic side of his dualism must be taken seriously. See Book I, Pt. 2, Ch. 3.

2435 *Lange, L.:* "Descartes und sein Gegner Henry More." In his: Die geschichtliche Entwickelung des Bewegungsbegriffes und ihr voraussichtliches Endergebnis. Leipzig, 1886, 33–47.

2436 *Langer, R. E.:* "René Descartes." American Mathematical Monthly 44: 1937, 495–512.

2437 *Lanson, Gustave:* "Le héros cornélien et le généreux selon Descartes." RHL 1: 1894, 397–411. Also in his: Hommes et livres; études morales et littéraires. Paris, Lecène et Oudin, 1895, 113–33. See 413.

2438 —: "L'influence de la philosophie cartésienne sur la littérature française." RMM 4: 1896, 517–50. Also in his: Études d'histoire littéraire. Paris, Champion, 1929, 58–96. See 412.

2439 —: "La prose de Descartes." Annales politiques et littéraires, June 1905. Also in his: L'art de la prose, 1909.

2440 —: "Origines et premières manifestations de l'esprit philosophique dans la littérature française de 1675 à 1748." RCC 1907–09. See 457.

2441 —: Manuel bibliographique de la littérature française moderne. 4 vols. Paris, Hachette, 1909–14.

2442 *Lantrùa, A.:* "Aspetti nuovi di antichi volti: il 'Cartesio' dell' Olgiati" (see 14). Conv 6: 1934, 430–43.

2443 —: "Il ritorno di Cartesio." Afil 4: 1934, 185–203. [Discussion of Olgiati's Cartesio (see 14)].

2444 —: "Sulla legittimità del dubbio come posizione gnoseologica iniziale." Cartesio 555–65. 1937.

Denies that Descartes' position regarding doubt is legitimate. "Inevitabilmente si è recondotti all'idea di essere ed al principio di contradizzione," the sole primary data in the order of knowing (p. 565).

2445 —: "Sul preteso idealismo del Cartesio." In Acta Secundi Cong. Thom. Intern. (see 41), 523–28. 1937.

In the system of Descartes the characteristic of idealism (resolution of the object in the subject) is lacking.

2446 —: "Sul circolo vizioso nella dimostrazione cartesiana di Dio." Acta Secundi Cong. Thom. Intern. (see 41), 529–34. 1937.

The deduction of God's existence based on the concept of clear and distinct ideas is critically examined.

2447 *Lantsheere, Léon Marie Joseph Antoine de:* Introduction à la philosophie moderne, suivie d'un fragment de leçon sur Descartes. Univ. de Louvain, Annales de l'Institut supérieur de philosophie 2: 1913, 238ff.

2448 *Laporte, Jean:* Le rationalisme de Descartes. Paris, PUF, 1945. 487 p. 2nd ed., revised and augmented, Paris, PUF, 1950, xx, 511 p. See 178.

2449 —: Études d'histoire de la philosophie française au XVIIe siècle. Préface par André Bridoux. Note par Janine Pignet. Paris, Vrin, 1951. BHP. See 291.

2450 —: "La finalité chez Descartes." RHPh 2: 1928, 366–96. Incorporated in his: Le rationalisme, no. 178 (2448).

2451 —: "L'idée de 'liaison nécessaire' chez Descartes." CD 2: 9–14. 1937.

The concept, in Descartes, refers to the contrast between distinction in thought and real distinction, revealed in its purity not in the notion of cause but in that of substance.

2452 —: "La connaissance de l'étendue chez Descartes." RPFE 123: 1937, 257–89. Also in his: Études, no. 291, 11–36.

2453 —: "La liberté selon Descartes." RMM 44: 1937, 101–64. Also in his: Études, no. 291 (2449), 37–87.

2454 —: "Le sens de la méthode cartésienne." Études de métaphysique et de morale [i.e. RMM] 49: 1944, 193–237. Incorporated in the first chapter of his: Le rationalisme, no. 178 (2448).

Descartes' Method is only outwardly mathematical. Its meaning is experience and freedom.

2455 —: "Le dualisme de l'être et du connaître chez Descartes." RPFE 135: 1945, 97–117. Incorporated in his: Le rationalisme, no. 178 (2448).

2456 *Lapp, John C.:* "The Traité des passions and Racine." MLQ 3: 1942, 611–19. See 414.

2457 *Lapradette, A. de:* "Descartes en Hollande." Vie des peuples (Paris) 2: 1920, 271–90.

2458 *Larroque, Gaston:* "Descartes et la sociologie." RdePh 17: 1910/2, 599–607.

The Method of Descartes: "Méthode de la Table Rase, méthode anarchique!" (p. 606).

2459 *Láscaris Comneno, Constantino:* "Análisis del Discurso del método." RevF 14: 1955, 293–351. See 292.

2460 —: "Las etapas de la redacción del Discurso del método." Revista de filosofía de la Universidad de Costa Rica 1: 1957, no. 2, 149–51.

2461 *Lasserre, Pierre:* "Christianisme et cartésianisme." MerF 1 November 1927, 513–35.

The Cartesian aftermath: Malebranche, Fénelon, Bossuet. Stresses the capital importance of Bossuet's insistence, against Descartes, upon the notion that essential verities may well appear in confused ideas (Augustinian reaction against Cartesian spirit.)

2462 *Lasswitz, Kurd:* Geschichte de Atomistik vom Mittelalter bis Newton. 2. Band: Höhepunkt und Verfall der Korpuskulartheorie des 17. Jahrhunderts. Hamburg & Leipzig, Voss, 1890, 55–126. See 380.

2463 —: "Zur Genesis der cartesischen Corpuscularphysik." Vierteljahrschrift für wissenschaftliche Philosophie 10: 1886, 166–89. See 380.

2464 *Latham, Marcia L.* (transl., editor).: The Geometry of René Descartes. 1925. See 88.

2465 *Launay, Louis de:* Descartes. Payot, 1923. 126 p. (Les grands hommes de France).

Nicely written introduction.

2466 *Lavalée-Poussin, Ch. de:* Les œuvres inédites de Descartes et de Leibniz. Bruxelles, Decq, 1861. 69 p. (Reprint from: Revue belge et étrangère, formerly: La Belgique).

Discusses the Foucher de Careil edition (see 75).

2467 *Lavelle, Louis:* La philosophie française entre les deux guerres. Paris, Aubier (Éditions Montaigne), 1942. 279 p. (Les chroniques philosophiques

v. 2). – Italian tr. by Pia Sartori Treves: La filosofia francese tra le due guerre, 1918–1940. Brescia, Morcelliana, 1949. 150 p. See 11.

2468 —: Introduction à l'ontologie. Paris, PUF, 1947. See 293.

2469 —: "De Descartes à Fontenelle." Temps, 4 July 1932. Also in no. 11 (2467), 55–62.

2470 —: "L'esprit cartésien." Temps, 26 January 1936. (On Laberthonnière). Also in no. 11 (2467), 33–40.

2471 —: "Sagesse cartésienne." Temps, 29 November 1936. Also in no. 11 (2467), 45–53.

2472 —: "Grundsätzliches zum Descartes-Kongress 1937, Paris." Die Tatwelt (Berlin) 14: 1938, 74–90.

2473 —: "Le Congrès Descartes." Temps 77/27811: 31 October 1937. Also in no. 11 (2467), 239–50.

2474 —: "Centenaire de Descartes." Temps 77/27658: 1937. (BP 1938/2).

2475 *Lawler, D.:* "Influence of Descartes on modern science." Thought 12: 1937. (Baldensperger)

2476 *Lazzeroni, Virgilio* (i.e. Virgilio Lazzeroni Albani): La formazione del pensiero cartesiano e la scolastica. Padova, CEDAM, 1940. 265 p. (Problemi d'oggi). See 214a.

2477 —: "Il medievalismo di Cartesio." CD 3: 25–31. 1937. See 214a.

2478 *Leander, Pehr Johan Herman:* Om substanzbegreppet hos Cartesius, Spinoza och Leibnitz. Dissertation Lund, 1862. (BM)

2478a *Lesbesgue, Henri:* Leçons sur les constructions géométriques. Gauthier-Villars, 1950. [Discussed by Vuillemin, no. 398].

Le Blond: see Blond.

2479 *Lecky, William Edward Hartpole:* History of the rise and influence of the spirit of rationalism in Europe. 2 vols. (1865). London, Longmans, Green & Co., 1910. Vol. 1, p. 336–44.

Descartes' purely spiritual conception of the soul helped destroy the notions of hell fire, visible demons, and inner body.

2480 *Lecointre, Léon:* Analyse de Descartes appliquée aux lignes des deux premiers ordres. Bruxelles, 1865. 4to. [BN]

2481 *Leder, Hermann:* Untersuchungen über Augustin's Erkenntnistheorie in ihren Beziehungen zur antiken Skepsis, zu Plotin und Descartes. Dissertation Marburg, 1901. ()

2482 *Lee, Rensselaer W.:* "Ut pictura poesis: The humanist theory of painting." Art Bulletin 22: 1940, 197–269. See 415.

2483 *Leenhardt, Henry:* "Cartesianisme et pensée chrétienne." ETR 12: 1937, 266–281.

2484 *Lefebvre, Henri:* Descartes. Paris, Éd., Hier et aujourd'hui, 1947. (Grandes figures). Polish tr.: Kartezjusz. Warsaw, Książka i wiedza, 1950. 192 p. See 179.

2485 — and N. Guterman: "Le problème de la conscience." Eur 15: 1937, 384–405. See 2164.

2486 —: "De la morale provisoire à la génerosité". Royaumont 237–55; discussion 256–72. 1957. See 295.

2487 *Lefèvre, Roger:* La vocation de Descartes. Paris, PUF, 1956. 228 p. BPC. Thèse Paris. See 179a, d.

2488 —: L'humanisme de Descartes. Paris, PUF 1957. viii, 284 p. BPC. See 179 b, d.

2489 —: Le criticisme de Descartes. Paris, PUF, 1958. 340 p. BPC. See 179c–d.

2489a —: La bataille du cogito. Paris, PUF, 1960. 231 p. BPC. See 179d.

2489b —: La métaphysique de Descartes. Paris, PUF, 1959. (Initiation philosophique.) See 179d.

2489c —: "Le procès Biran-Descartes." RScH no. 101: 1961, 13–22.

Maine de Biran's critique of the cogito jumps the gap between soul and body, is brought before the court of Judge Lefèvre, and dismissed after a fair trial.

2490 —: "Le doute cartésien, épreuve des objets de pensée." RHPh 5: 1931, 1–23. [Boorsch]

2491 —: "Le cogito, activité irréducible du sujet." RHPh 5: 1931, 236–51.

2492 *Legendre, M.* "Descartes et Cervantes." Les lettres, June 1924.

2493 *Legrand, Georges:* "Maine de Biran et Descartes." RNS 21: 1914, 71–78.

2494 *Leisegang, Gertrud:* Descartes' Dioptrik. Meisenheim a.G., Westkultur-Verlag Hain, 1943. 168 p. (Monographien zur Naturphilosophie, v. 2). See 87.

2495 *Leisegang, Hans:* "Dem Gedenken des Philosophen René Descartes, 1596–1650." Berlin, 1950. In: Gedenkfeier (see 543), p. 7–32.

2496 *Lekovič, Dragutin:* "René Dekart. Povodom 300 godiśnjice smrti." Borba (Beograd) 15, no. 51: March 1950, 2–3.

Le Lionnais: see Lionnais.

2497 *Lemaire, Paul:* Le cartésianisme chez les Bénédictins. Dom Robert Desgabets: son système, son influence et son école, d'après plusieurs manuscrits et des documents rares. Paris, Alcan, 1901. 424 p. Thèse Grenoble. See 457a.

2498 *Lémeray, E.-M.:* L'éther actuel et ses précurseurs (simple récit). Préface de L. Lecornu. Paris, Gauthier-Villars, 1922. ix, 142 p. (Asci).

2498a *Le Moine, Augustin:* Des vérités éternelles selon Malebranche. Paris, Vrin (Marseille, Ged), 1936. 292 p. Thèse-lettres, Aix-Marseille. See 457b.

2499 *Lemos, Miguel* (tr.): Descartes. Discourso sôbre o método, tr. Miguel Lemos. Rio de Janeiro, Apostolado positivista do Brazil, ... Mars 1896 .... 86 p. See 146.

2500 *Lenoble, Le P. Robert:* Mersenne ou la naissance du mécanisme. Paris, Vrin, 1943. lxiii, 633 p. (BHP). Thèse Paris. See 215.

2501 —: "Le Père Mersenne." Gmet 3: 1948, 311–29. See 215.

2502 —: "La psychologie cartésienne." RIP 4: 1950, 160–89. See 381.

2503 —: "La représentation du monde physique à l'époque classique." DSS no. 30: 1956, 5–24.

Stresses the importance to the development of the modern scientific world view of the new concept of the indefinite universe as represented in Descartes' vortex model, more influential perhaps than the Copernican revolution and the repercussions of Galilei's condemnation.

2504 —: "Liberté cartésienne ou liberté sartrienne?" Royaumont, 302–24; discussion 325–35. 1957. See 192.

2504a —: "La vocation et l'humanisme de Descartes." RMM 63: 1958, 349–357. [Review article of no. 2487–88.] See 179d.

2505 *Léon, Albert:* Les élements cartésiens de la doctrine spinoziste sur les rapports de la pensée à son objet. Alcan, 1907. 294 p. Thèse Paris.

On the dialectic development of Cartesian thought in Spinoza's doctrine of the relation between thought and object. A study not of the psychological and historical genesis of Spinoza's theses but of the Cartesian foundations he was able to give them afterwards. *Reviews:* RMM 1909, no. 3; MF Oct. 1909; Études religieuses 20: 1909, no. 9; PhdG 1: 1908–09, no. 950.

2506 *Lerminier, E.:* "Du cartésianisme et de l'eclecticisme." RDM 1843. 15 December 1843.

Discussion of Bordas-Demoulin and F. Bouillier.

Le Roy, Georges: see Roy.

2507 *Leroy, Maxime:* Descartes, le philosophe au masque. Paris, Rieder, 1929. 2 vols. 201 p.; 191 p. See 124.

2508 —: Descartes social. Avec un portrait inédit de Descartes, dessiné par Jean Liévens aux environs de 1643. Paris, Vrin, 1931. xxxix, 73 p. See 298.

2509 —: "L'humain Descartes." Eur 15, no. 175: July 15, 1937, 289–96. Also in: Descartes (37, 527.)

2510 —: See 515 (Causeries, 1938).

2511 —: "Descartes précurseur du social moderne." Rsyn 63: 1948, 9–67; discussion 68–72. See 298.

2512 *Lesage, H.:* "La morale de Descartes." RCO no. 44: 1937, 675–85. Also: Hommages, Poitiers, 1937 (see 531), 35–41.

2513 *Lespire, Roger:* "Descartes." Flambeau 33/2: 1950, 121–39.

2514 *Levett, M. J.:* "Note on the alleged Cartesian circle." Mind 46: 1937, 206–13.

2515 *Levi, Adolfo:* Il pensiero di Francesco Bacone considerato in relazione con le filosofie della natura, del Rinascimento e col razionalismo cartesiano. Torino, Paravia, 1925, p. 89–144. See 299.

2516 — (editor). Renato Descartes. Discorso sul metodo. Introduzione e commento. Napoli, Loffredo, 1937. liii, 109 p. (Text edition).

2517 — (editor). Renato Descartes. Principi di filosofia. Libro primo. Introduzione e commento. Napoli, Loffredo, 1937. lix, 74 p. (Text edition).

2518 —: "Il pensiero di Descartes nelle Regulae ad directionem ingenii e nella metodologia del Discours de la méthode." LogosN 20: 1937, 465–98.

On the disagreement between Descartes' earlier and later conception of methodology.

2519 —: "Il problema dell'errore nella filosofia di D." LogosN 11, no. 2: 1928, 93–108. Also: Napoli, Perella, 1928. 17 p.

See 299, and Bontadini's careful analysis of Levi's critique of Descartes (Cartesio 100–104; also in no. 1277, 64–69).

2520 —: "Sul concetto di luce naturale e su altri concetti fondamentali della gnoseologia del Descartes." RF 28: 1937, 14–31.

2521 *Levi, Anna:* La filosofia di Aristotele e quella di Cartesio. Venezia, Ferrari, 1900. 58 p.

2522 *Levi, Alessandro:* "L'influence de l'esprit cartésien dans le droit. Ses avantages et ses limites." CD 3: 49–54. 1937. See 466d.

2523 *Lévy-Bruhl, Lucien:* History of modern philosophy in France. Chicago, Open Court, 1899. x, 498 p. Reprinted 1924. Also in: Descartes. Meditations, and selections from the Principles of philosophy, transl. John Veitch. Chicago, Open Court. See 180.

2524 —: "The Cartesian spirit and history." In: Cassirer Festschrift (Philosophy and history, ed. R. Klibansky and H. J. Paton. Oxford, Clarendon Press, 1935, 191–96). See 180.

2524a —. See: Gilson, "Le Descartes de Lévy-Bruhl." RPFE 147: 1957, 432–51. See 180.

2524b *Lewin, Bertram D.:* Dreams and the uses of regression. New York, International Universities Press, 1958. 64 p. (New York Psychoanalytical Institute, Freud anniversary series.) See 104a.

2525 *Lewis, Geneviève* [Mme Geneviève Rodis-Lewis]: L'individualité selon Descartes. Paris, Vrin, 1950. 254 p. BHP. Thèse Paris. See 215a.

2526 —: Le problème de l'inconscient et le cartésianisme. Paris, PUF, 1950. 302 p. (BPC). Thèse complémentaire, Paris. See 215b.

2527 —: René Descartes, français, philosophe. Par Geneviève Rodis-Lewis. Tours & Paris, Maison Mame, 1953. 160 p. (Collection Service de la France, v. 6). Illustr. See 145.

2528 —: La morale de Descartes. Par Geneviève Rodis-Lewis. Paris, PUF, 1957. 132 p. (Initiation philosophique.) See 215c.

2529 — (editor). Descartes. Meditationes de prima philosophia. Texte latin et traduction du Duc de Luynes. Introduction et notes par Geneviève Lewis. 2nd ed. Paris, Vrin, 1946. xiv, 174 p. BTP Reprinted 1960. See 89.

2530 — (editor): Descartes. Correspondance avec Arnauld et Morus. Texte latin et traduction. Introduction et notes par Geneviève Lewis. Paris, Vrin, 1953, 187 p. BTP. See 84.

2531 — (editor): Descartes. Les passions de l'âme. Introduction et notes par Geneviève Rodis-Lewis. Paris, Vrin, 1955. 240 p. BTP. See 91.

2532 —: "La critique leibnizienne du dualisme cartésien." RPFE 136: 1946, 473–85. See 317.

2533 —: "Le problème de l'inconscient chez Descartes." Proceedings of the Tenth Intern. Cong. of Philos. Amsterdam 1948, 1125–27.

2534 —: "Une source inexplorée du Traité des passions." RPFE 138: 1948, 330–34.

Vives, De anima et vita.

2534a —: "La personne chez Descartes." Recherches et débats, suppl. philosophique no. 8, Jan.-Feb. 1950.

2535 —: "L'âme et la durée, après une controverse cartésienne." RIP 4: 1950, 190–209. See 347a, 457a.

2535a —: "Sagesse et unité des sciences selon Descartes." Actes du Ve Congrès des sociétés de phil. de langue française, Bordeaux 1950 (Paris, PUF, 1950).

2535b —: "Augustinisme et cartésianisme à Port-Royal." In: Descartes et le cartésianisme hollandais, 1950 [see 38], 131–182.

2536 —: "Âme et conscience chez Descartes." BSPF 45: 1951, 133–54. Discussion (E. Bréhier, H. Gouhier, L. Prenant, E. Wolff, lettre de R. Lenoir) 154–64. See 215b.

2537 —: "Bilan de cinquante ans d'études cartésiennes." RPFE 141: 1951, 249–67. See 12.

2538 —: "L'innéité cartésienne et sa critique par Lelarge de Lignac." RScH no. 61: 1951, 30–41.

In 1752, Lignac (Éléments de métaphysique tirés de l'expérience) develops a solution between inneism and empiricism through appeal to the "sens intime." [BAn 1954, 4165.]

2539 —: "Augustinisme et cartésianisme." In: Augustinus magister; Congrès international Augustinien. Études Augustiniennes, 1954, v. 2, p. 1087–1104. See 302.

2540 —: "Descartes et Poussin." DSS 3, no. 23; 1954, 521–49. See 415.

2541 —: "Le principe de vie chez Platon et Descartes." In: La vie, la pensée. Actes du VII Congr. des SPLF. Grenoble. PUF, 1954. ()

2542 —: "Machineries et perspectives curieuses dans leurs rapports avec le cartésianisme." Par G. Rodis-Lewis. DSS no. 32: 1956, 461–74. See 236.

2543 —: "Maîtrise des passions et sagesse chez Descartes." Par G. Rodis-Lewis. Royaumont, 208–27; discussion, 228–36. 1957. See 220.

2543a —: "Le paradoxe cartésien." In: L'âme et le corps. Recherches et débats du Centre catholique des intellectuels français, cahier no. 35, Paris, Fayard, 1961, p. 149–62 [par Geneviève Rodis-Lewis.]

2544 *Lewkowitz, J.:* Spinozas Cogitata metaphysica und ihr Verhältnis zu Descartes und zur Scholastik. Breslau, Schatzky, 1902. Dissertation Breslau.

Discipline of Freudenthal who complements and rectifies F.'s findings. See 1937.

2545 *Leyden, W. von:* "Descartes and Hobbes on waking and dreaming." RIP 10: 1956, 95–101. See 306.

2546 *Liard, Louis:* Descartes. Paris, Baillière, 1882. 230 p. 2nd ed. 1903. 3rd ed. Paris, Alcan, 1911. BPC. See 181.

2547 —: "Du rôle de l'expérience dans la physique de Descartes." Annales de la faculté des lettres de Bordeaux no. 3, 1879. 19 p. [Schrecker]

2548 —: "La méthode et la mathématique universelle de Descartes." RPFE 10: 1880, 569–600.

2549 *Libertini, Crescenzo:* Problemi di Cartesio. Napoli, Conte, 1951. 16 p.

2550 *Liebmann, Curt:* Die Logik von Port-Royal im Verhältnis zu Descartes. Dissertation Leipzig, 1902. 47 p.

2551 *Liedtke, Heinrich:* Die Beweise für das Dasein Gottes bei Anselm von Canterbury und Renatus Descartes. Heidelberg, Horning, 1893. 37 p. Dissertation Heidelberg.

2552 *Lindner, Ernst Otto:* De relatione quae inter Spinozae cogitata metaphysica et Cartesii doctrinam intercedit. Vratislavae, Fritz, (?1844). 31 p. Dissertation Breslau. [NN]

2552a *Lindroth, Sten:* "Harvey, Descartes, and young Olaus Rudbeck." J. History of Medicine 12: 1957, 209–19.

Rudbeck, discoverer of the lymphathic vessels, published his De circulatione sanguinis in May 1652, showing his Cartesian indebtedness by rejecting spiritus naturalis and spiritus vitalis, but retaining spiritus animalis. His teacher Olaus Stenius seems to have been the first Cartesian in Upsala; Queen Christina's personal physician, Grégoire François Durietz, friend of Descartes and Chanut, was also Rudbeck's friend.

2552b *Lindner, H.:* "Die Klassengrundlage des Zweifels in der Philosophie Descartes'." DZP 8: 1960, 720–29.

D.'s doubt is denial of authority, a bourgeois reaction: denial of God in MM, denial of feudal authority in DM. But the alienation stops short of breaking the bonds: the cogito reaffirms what has been doubted.

2553 *Lindsay, Julian:* "Coleridge marginalia in a volume of Descartes." PMLA 49: 1934, 184–95.

Notes in Coleridge's copy of D.'s Opera omnia (1685) indicate that he read D. in 1800–03 and again and more philosophically around 1815, which left traces in his discussion of relation between thoughts and things in his Biographia litteraria.

2554 *Liñera, Antonio A. de:* "Las relaciones entre el alma y el cuerpo en Descartes y Santo Tómas." RevF 6: 1947, 113–23.

On Manuel Barbado's Études de psychologie expérimentale (BP 1947/1).

2555 *Lins, Ivan* [i.e. Monteiro de Barros Lins]: Descartes; época, vida e obra. Preface by Roquette Pinto. Rio de Janeiro, Emiel, 1940. 595 p. Bibliography, 575–85. See 146.

2556 *Lion, Ferdinand:* Lebensquellen französischer Metaphysik: Descartes, Rousseau, Bergson. Tr. from the French by Ruth Gillischewski. Hamburg, Claussen und Goverts (Zürich, Europa-Verlag), 1949. 128 p. Italian translation by L. Anceschi: Cartesio, Rousseau e Bergson. Saggio di storia vitalista della filosofia. Milano, Bompiani, 1949. 183 p. (Portico, v. 21). See 216.

2556a —: Les rêves de Racine. Paris, Laffont, 1948. 282 p.

Finds the philosophical roots of Racine's drama in two concepts of D.: sovereignty of thought, and passions. See 414.

2557 *Lionnais, F. Le:* "Descartes et Einstein." RHSA 5: 1952, 139–54. See 383.

2558 *Lippmann, Edmund Oskar von:* "Gedächtnisrede zum dreihundertjährigen Geburtstage R. Descartes'." Naturforschende Gesellschaft zu Halle. Abhandlungen 22: 1901, 1–35. Also in his: Abhandlungen und Vorträge zur Geschichte der Naturwissenschaften, Leipzig, 1906, 488–526.

2559 *Lipps, Theodor:* "Worte." Psychologische Untersuchungen, ed. Th. Lipps, 2, no. 1: 1912, 30–61.

The noted German psychologist discusses "meaning" in terms of semantic theory, using Descartes' alleged confusion in spiriting "soul" into "self," and his "mythological" use of the term "causality," as examples.

2559a —: "Das cogito ergo sum." Psychologische Untersuchungen, ed. Th. Lipps, 2, no. 1: 1912, 62–80.

Applies the psychological viewpoint to the epistemological problem, with interesting and original results.

2560 "*La littérature cartésienne au XXe siècle.*" Rsyn 14/1: 67–114, 1937. See 15.

2561 *Little, Arthur:* "René Descartes. The tercentenary of his Discours de la méthode." Studies (Dublin) 26: 1937, 581–94.

2561a *Ljubimov, N. A.:* Filosofija Dekarta. St. Petersburg, 1886.

2561b *Llanos, Alfredo:* El problema del voluntarismo en Descartes. Cuadernos del Sur, Bahía Blanca, Universidad nacional del Sur, 1960. 40 p.

2562 *Locke, Arthur W.:* "Descartes and seventeenth-century music." Musical Quarterly 21: 1935, 423–31.

A rather general discussion.

2563 *Loewe, Johannes Hermann:* "Das spekulative System des R. Descartes, seine Vorzüge und Mängel." AcWien, Sitzungsb., Philos.-histor. Klasse, 14: 1855, 238–98.

2564 *Löwit, Alexandre:* "L'époché de Husserl et le doute de Descartes." RMM 62: 1957, 399–415.

Husserl's radicalization of Cartesian doubt destroys rather than heightens its radical character; epoché is definitive and universal, Cartesian doubt provisional and only as an attempt universal. At the root of these differences is the identification of thinking self and âme in D., their differentiation in Husserl; D. questions the certainty of knowledge while Husserl questions "avant tout son sens." See 174.

2565 *Löwith, Karl:* "Descartes' vernünftiger Zweifel und Kierkegaards Leidenschaft der Verzweiflung." CD 1: 74–79. 1937. See 304.

2566 *Longer, abbé:* "Descartes, sieur du Perron." Le glaneur châtelleraudais 4: no. 14, May 1937.

2567 *Lopatin, Lev Mikhailovič:* "Dekart kak osnovatel' novago filosofskago i naučnago mirosozerčanija." VFP 1896, 608–49.

D. as founder of the modern philosophical and scientific world view. [In Russian.]

2568 *Lopes de Mattos, Carlos:* "Spinoza, intérprete de Descartes." RbrasF 5: 1955, 409–15.

2569 —: "A moral provisória de Descartes e o método." Rbras F 7: 1957, 326–30.

Lopez, J. García: see García Lopez.

2570 *Lorenzo, A. di:* "L'obiezione detta del circolo cartesiano." Bolletino filosofico 2: 1936, 225–32.

2571 *Loria, Gino:* Storia delle matematiche dell'alba della civiltà al secolo XIX. 2. ed. riv. e aggiornata. Milano, Hoepli, 1950. 974 p. See 382.

2572 —: "Pour une histoire de la géométrie analytique." Verhandlungen des 3. Intern. Mathematiker-Kongresses zu Heidelberg 1904. Leipzig, 1905, 562–74.

2573 —: "Descartes e la teoria dei numeri." Bolletino di matematica 1923. [Schrecker]

2574 —: "Da Descartes e Fermat a Monge e Lagrange. Contributo alla storia della geometria analitica." AcLincei. Atti. Memorie della classe di scienze fisiche 14: 1923, 777–845.

2575 —: "Un periodo di storia delle scienze: da Galileo a Newton." Scientia (Bologna) 1926. [Bontadini]

2576 —: "Descartes géomètre." RMM 44: 1937, 199–220.

2576a —: See also: Faggi, A., and G. Loria.

2577 *Lortie, Léon:* "Le message scientifique de Descartes." Action universitaire (Montréal), December 1937 [Brie: Jan.-Feb. 1938], 66–68.

2578 *Losacco, Michele:* Il problema della creazione in Cartesio. Appendix: Per la storia del cartesianismo in Italia. Napoli, 1913, 34 p. Reprinted from: Società Reale di Napoli, R. Acc. di scienze morali e politiche. Atti 42/2: 1912–13, 285–318.

On conflicts and contradictions in the doctrine. See Bontadini, no. 1277.

2579 *Lotze, Hermann:* "Philosophy in the last forty years. I." Contemporary Review 15: 1880, 134–155. Also in his: Kleine Schriften. Leipzig, Hirtzel, v. 3, 1891, 451–79.

On D.'s influence upon the early thought of Leibniz (K. Schr., 455ff.)

2580 —: "Pensées d'un idiot sur Descartes, Spinoza et Leibniz." In his: Kleine Schriften, v. 3, Leipzig, Hirtzel, 1891, 551–66.

Youthful attempt at philosophical discussion written between 1840 and 1844 as an exercise in French, which the distinguished philosopher found worthy of rescue.

2581 —: [Review of Bordas-Demoulin, Le cartésianisme.] Gött 1846, no. 89–91, 881–93. Reprinted in his: Kleine Schriften, v. 1, 1885, 388–97. See 437.

2582 —: [Review of Bouillier's Histoire du cartésianisme.] Gött 1844, no. 170–72, p. 1675–1710. Reprinted in his: Kleine Schriften, v. 1, 1885, 257–67. See 438.

2583 *Lovejoy, Arthur Oncken:* The revolt against dualism. An inquiry concerning the existence of ideas. New York, Open Court (New York, Norton), 1930. xii, 325 p. (Paul Carus Foundation Lectures, no. 2). See 182.

2584 —: The great chain of being. A study of the history of an idea. The William James Lectures, 1933. Harvard UP, 1936, 123–25 (Ch. 4: Plenitude and the new cosmography).

Descartes, no cosmological innovator, illustrates the affinity between the new cosmologies, particularly of G. Bruno, and the old religious temper (otherworldiness). Cartesianism deserves and received credit for the rapid spread of the theories of the plurality and infinity of worlds, though Descartes' own role was small.

2585 *Lowndes, Richard:* Descartes, his life and Meditations. A new translation of the Meditations, with introduction, memoir, and commentary. London, F. Norgate, 1878. 16mo. viii, 297 p.

2586 *Lubnicki, Narzyz:* "Construction de la science par l'application de la méthode cartésienne." CD 8: 195–202. 1937.

Rejects the Cartesian "saltus in concludendo" from act to substance but accepts hyperbolic doubt as a method for constructing a non-dualist science, with postulates rooted in "the reality of the immediate."

2587 —: "Les travaux polonais sur Descartes depuis 1900 environ." Rsyn 14: 1937, 103–08. See 15.

2587a —: "Descartes et le matérialisme moderne" [in Polish]. Annales de l'université M. Curie-Sklodovska 8: 1953, 1–37 (published in 1957).

Brings D. close to modern materialism, both in his physics and his psychology; also in his naturalist and democratic doctrines (le bon sens), his attitude towards Scholasticism, his notions of the utility of science, and his method of negative dialectics. [Bsig 1958, 13968].

2588 *Luc, Jean:* "Tombeau de René Descartes. Poème à la mémoire du philosophe." Eur 15: 15 July 1937, 312–14. Also in no. 37.

2589 *Lucas, Peter G.:* "Descartes and the wax. Rejoinder" (to J. J. C. Smart, q.v.). PhQ 1: July 1951, 348–52. See 235c.

2590 *Lucas de Pesloüan, C.:* "La théorie d'Einstein, système cartésien." RdePh 29: 1922, 225–58. See 383.

2591 —: "Le dernier projet littéraire de Barrès. Descartes et la princesse Elisabeth." Figaro, 16 June, 23 June 1928.

2592 — et G. Cohen: Le dernier projet littéraire de Maurice Barrès. Paris, "Les amis d'Édouard, 143." 1929. 85 p. 16mo.

2593 *Ludewig, Carl (S.J.):* "Die Substanztheorie bei Cartesius in Zusammenhang mit der scholastischen und neueren Philosophie." PJGG 5: 1892, 157–71, 433–49; 6: 1893, 61–84, 273–84.

Inherent contradictions in D.'s substance concept. What is tenable in his doctrine was unconsciously borrowed from Scholasticism.

Review: C. M. Schneider, JST 9: 1894, 498–99.

2594 *Ludwig, H.:* Marin Mersenne und seine Musiklehre. Halle, Waisenhaus, 1935. 120 p. (Beiträge zur Musikforschung, v. 4).

2595 *Lüdtke, H.:* "Materialien über die Beziehungen zwischen Jungius und Descartes." Sudhoff's Archiv f. Geschichte d. Medizin u. d. Naturwissenschaften 29: 1937, 409–22.

Joachim Jungius of Lübeck (1587–1657) annotated his copy of Descartes' DM and PP and discussed his Descartes reading with correspondents.

2596 *Luguet, Henri:* Étude sur la notion d'espace d'après Descartes, Leibnitz et Kant. Durand & Lauriel, 1875, iv, 250 p. Thèse Paris.

".... difficile, abstrus et d'une obscurité qui tient à la nature du problème" (Renouvier's review in CrPh 12: 1877, 134–39.)

2597 *Lukasiewicz, J.:* "Kartezjusz." KF 15: 1938, 123–28.

2598 *Lumbreras, Pedro (O.P.):* De dubio methodico Cartesii. Dissertatio historico-critica. Friburgi Helv., ex typis consoc. St. Pauli, 1919. xxiii, 166.

Review: É. Gilson in RPFE 1919, 324–25.

2599 —: Estudios filosóficos: la duda metódica de Descartes; Fray Tomás Campanella y la duda metódica del renascimiento; el tomismo, filosofía católica oficial. Madrid, & Valencia, Tip. moderna, 1930. viii. 116 p. (Biblioteca de Tomistas españoles, ser. 3, v. 1).

2600 *Lusczewska-Romahnowa, Seweryna:* "Kartezjański ideal wiedzy." KF 19: 1950, 25–38. French summary, 162–64.

On Descartes' ideal of knowledge: Distinguishes the methodological and the utilitarian concept of science. Descartes' connection between science and certainty led later thinkers into error, e.g. the 19th century intuitionists and J. S. Mill, who thought that absolute general laws could be found by induction. Obligatory reference to Friedrich Engels' polemic against intuitionists. Progress of science viewed as the principal cause of the decline of Descartes' scientific ideal.

2601 *Lutosławski, W.:* "Descartes jako filozof." Wielka Encyklopedia Powszechna Ilustrowana, Warszawa, 1895, v. 15, 412–17. Also in his: Z dziedziny myśli. Warszawa, 1900, 312–29. [Bar]

2602 *Luzzatto, Guido Lodovico:* "La prosa di Descartes:" Riforma letteraria 1938, no. 13–15. [Not located.]

2603 *Lyon, Georges:* L'idéalisme en Angleterre au XVIIIe siècle. Paris, Alcan, 1888. See 460.

Descartes (17–46). Le cartésianisme en Angleterre (47ff.)

2604 *McCormick, J. F.:* "A Jesuit contemporary of Descartes." ModSch 14: 1937, 79–82.

On Thomas Compton Carleton (1591–1666), with reference to the teachings of Descartes.

2605 *McCracken, David J.:* Thinking and valuing; an introduction, partly historical, to the study of the philosophy of value. London, Macmillan, 1950. ix, 238 p. See 217.

2606 *Macdonald, Margaret:* "Sleeping and waking." Mind 62: 1953, 202–15. See 306.

2607 *McHugh, Joseph:* "Enemy of doubt." Blackfriars 10: 1929, 1369–74.

2608 *MacIver, A. M.:* "A note on the ontological proof." Analysis (Oxford) 8, no. 3: Jan. 1948, p. 48.

2608a *MacLean, J.:* "De historische ontwikkeling der stootwetten van Aristoteles tot Huygens. Amsterdam, Vrye Universiteit, 1959. 59 p. (Dissertation)

Beeckman was first in deriving a rule of impact (algebraic sum of moments). Descartes uses Beeckman's rule but substitutes the arithmetic sum. The role of Huygens and Mersenne in the final establishment of the laws of impact is analyzed in detail. See D. J. Struick in Isis 51: 1960, 390.

2608b *Macmurray, John:* "The rejection of dualism." In his: The self as agent. The Gifford Lectures 1953. London, Faber & Faber, 1957, ch. 3, 62–83. See 307.

2609 *McRae, Robert:* "Descartes: the project of a universal science." In his: The problem of the unity of the sciences, Bacon to Kant. University of Toronto Press, 1961, 46–68.

D.'s concepts of universal wisdom, unity of method according to Regulae and DM, the logical ordering of the sciences; mathesis universalis as related to physics, mathematics. Based on the texts. Good brief comments on "bona mens" and on hypothesis, induction and deduction in physics.

2609a —: "The unity of the sciences: Bacon, Descartes and Leibniz." JHI 18: 1957, 27–48. See 2609.

2610 *McWilliams, James:* "Aristotelian and Cartesian motion." NSch 17: 1943, 307–321.

M

2611 *M., B.:* "Dy fjali mbi filosofine morale te Descartes-it." Perp 2: 1937, 175–79.

"Two words on Descartes' moral philosophy." [In Albanian.]

2612 *Maar, Vilhelm:* Lidt om Descartes og Danmark. København, Thiele, 1931. 81 p.

Traces the relations between Descartes and Denmark: Tycho Brahe, Danish students at Leiden; remarks on Schooten's portrait of Descartes. Documented.

Mabire, P. H.: see Ombres de Descartes.

Mac ....: see 2604–2610.

2613 *Mach, Ernst:* Die Mechanik in ihrer Entwicklung historisch-kritisch dargestellt. 6. verb. und verm. Aufl. Leipzig, Brockhaus, 1908. (Internationale wissenschaftliche Bibliothek, v. 59).

Passing criticism of Descartes' mechanics. Fundamental epistemological opposition.

2614 *Mager, Alois (O.S.B.):* "Die anthropologische Bedeutung der Affektenlehre Descartes'." Cartesio 567–75. 1937.

Descartes' belief to be the first in solving the problem of passions is explained by the fact that he knew only "die Entartungen der Spätscholastik" (575). St. Thomas saw the anthropological problem better (the psychic as mediary between the physical and the intellectual), though certain problems remained unresolved by either thinker.

2615 *Magnaghi, Alberto:* Il problema dell'origine delle sorgenti, da Cartesio (1639) a Vallisneri (1725). Rocca S. Casciano, Capelli, 1911. 68 p.

2616 *Mahaffy, J. P.:* (i.e. Sir John Pentland Mahaffy): Descartes. Edinburgh & London, Blackwood 1880 (Philadelphia, Lippincott, 1881). vi, 211 p. (Philosophic classics for English readers).

A delightfully Victorian life of Descartes – all the facts that subsequently proved to be fiction.

2617 —: "Descartes and theology." Princeton Review 14 [?] (So cited by Keeling, Rsyn 1937).

2618 *Mahieu, abbé Léon:* François Suarez, sa philosophie et les rapports qu'elle a avec la théologie. Paris, Desclée de Brouwers, 1921. xvii, 532 p.

Discusses the influence of Suárez on Descartes. See also Mahieu's "L'ecclecticisme suarezien", Rthom 33:1925, 250.

2619 *Mahler, Karl:* Die Entstehung des Irrtums bei Descartes und bei Spinoza. Leipzig, Heller, 1910. 41 p. Dissertation Leipzig.

Exposition and critique of their doctrines of mind and will, developing from it their doctrines of the origin of error (PhdG 2: 1910, no. 568).

2620 *Mahoney, Michael Joseph (S.J.):* Cartesianism. New York, Fordham UP, 1925. 151 p.

"Descartes' error, according to the Roman faithful." [Morgan.]

Main, A.: see S. H. Hodgson et al.

2621 *Maire, Gilbert:* "L'actualité de Descartes." Revue critique (?) Paris, 22: 1913, 299–315. [NN]

2622 *Maisonneuve, Jean:* "La religion chez Descartes et chez Pascal." DSS no. 19, 1953, 173–76.

Cartesian philosophy does not pose the problem of "destinée," and this is why Pascal considers it "useless and uncertain," not without a certain amount of incomprehension.

2623 *Malcolm, Norman:* "Dreaming and scepticism." PhR 65: 1956, 14–37. See 306.

2623a —: Dreaming. London, Rutlege and Kegan Paul, 1959. 128 p. (Studies in Philosophy and Psychology 124–25.) See 306.

2624 *Mamiani della Rovere, Terenzio conte di:* Le meditazioni cartesiane rinovate nel secolo XIX. Firenze, Le Monnier, 1869. xix, 387 p.

2625 *Manuel M., Fr.:* "No centenário de Descartes." Pax et bonum (Lisboa) 22: 1950, 109–14.

2626 *Marc-Wogau, Konrad:* "Der Zweifel Descartes' und das cogito ergo sum." Theoria 20: 1954, 128–52.

The indubitable character of the cogito rests on this presupposition: the truth of a proposition supposes that it is thought by me. This kind of idealistic presupposition does not convert all knowledge into "conscience de soi," and plays no further role in the system once the methodical doubt is overcome.
(Bsig 10: 1956, no. 89).

2627 *Marcel, Victor:* Étendue et conscience. Essai de réfutation du dualisme cartésien. Préface de M. Souriau. Paris, Vrin, 1933. viii, 130 p. Thèse complémentaire (Nancy, G. Thomas, 1932). See 216a.

2628 *Marck, Siegfried:* "Le moi de Descartes et la 'psychologie' de la connaissance." CD 1: 173–80, 1937.

Richard Hönigswald's neocritical "Denkpsychologie" evades the ambiguities of Descartes' cogito.

2629 *Maréchal, Christian:* "La Mennais, Descartes et saint Thomas." RPFE 137: 1947, 443–51.

2630 *Maréchal, Joseph (S.J.):* Le point de départ de la métaphysique. Leçons sur le développement historique et théorique du problème de la connaissance. Cahier II: Le conflit du rationalisme et de l'empirisme dans la philosophie moderne avant Kant. (1923). 3rd ed. Paris, Desclée de Brouwers (Bruxelles, Éd. Universelle), 1944. (Museum Lessianum, Section philosophique v.4).

See Book 2 (p. 43ff.) on Descartes, Malebranche, and the monism of causality; Spinoza and the monism of substance; the "Scholastic Cartesianism" of Leibniz and Wolff; and on Cartesian mathematicism.

2631 *Margerie, A. de:* "Notes sur les rapports de l'âme et du corps chez Descartes." RdePh 5: 1904, 115–20.

2632 *Marías, Julián:* "Los dos cartesianismos, 1650–1950." RPGA 5: 1950, 505–15.

What is reality? The fact that this problem had no meaning for D. distinguishes his Cartesianism from its modified modern version. Another stumbling block: D.'s "Adamism," i.e. lack of sense of history.

Review: A. Roldán in PenM 8: 1942, 263–64.

2633 *Marichalar, A.:* "Cordura y conocimiento en el tricentenario del Discurso del método." Sur (Buenos Aires) 7: 1937, no. 36, 39–52.

2634 —: "Gomez Pereira, un ancêtre espagnol de Descartes." Transl. Robert de Ribon. Rheb 46: December 1937, 391–403.

2635 *Maritain, Jacques:* "Descartes ou l'incarnation de l'ange." In his: Trois réformateurs: Luther, Descartes, Rousseau [1925]. Nouvelle éd. revue et augmentée. Paris, Plon, 1937, p. 73–128; notes, p. 293–306. Italian tr. by G. G. Montini: I tre reformatori. Brescia, La Scuola, 1928. English tr. by

Mabelle L. Andison: Three reformers. London, Sheed and Ward, 1929, 1947; New York, Philosophical Library, 1945; New York, 1948, 1950. 234 p. Spanish tr. by Angel Alvarez de Miranda: Tres reformadores. Madrid, E.P.E.S.A., 1948. Polish transl.: Trzej reformatorzy. Preface by K. Michalski. Warszawa, 1939. See 184.

2636 —: Le songe de Descartes, suivi de quelques essais. Paris, Corrêa, 1932. xii, 345 p. English tr. by Mabelle L. Andison: The Dream of Descartes. New York, Philosophical Library, 1945, and London, Editions Poetry, 1946. Spanish tr. by A. Svanascini: El sueño de Descartes. Buenos Aires, Biblioteca nueva, 1947. 206 p. See 183.

2637 —: "L'esprit de la philosophie moderne: La réforme cartésienne." RdePh 26: 1914/1, 601–25; 27: 1914/2, 53–82.

2637a —: "A propos de la révolution cartésienne: Philosophie scolastique et philosophie mathématique." RThom 1918, 159ff.

2638 —: "Le songe de Descartes." RU Dec. 1, 1920, 593–607. Also in his: Le songe (see 183), Ch. 1.

2639 —: "L'esprit de Descartes." Les lettres, Feb.-March 1922, 175–204, 371–448. Also in his: Le songe, no. 183, Ch. 2, 3.

2640 —: "Réponse à Jacques Chevalier" [regarding 2639 above]. Les lettres, 1 March, 1922. [Giraud I].

2641 —: "Descartes ou l'incarnation de l'ange." RU 15 December 1924. See 184.

2642 —: "La pensée religieuse de Descartes." RdePh Jan.-Feb. 1925. [Discussion of Gouhier's book; see 168].

2643 —: Réflexions sur l'intelligence et sa vie propre. Nouvelle Librairie française, 1924. 2e éd. 1926. 3e éd. Paris, Desclée de Brouwer, 1931. (Bibliothèque française de philosophie.) See 184a.

Ch. 6: "La physique de la quantité et la révolution cartésienne." See also p. 27–142, 288ff. of the third edition.

2644 — et Boris Vycheslavzeff: Descartes: Textes suivis de débats au Studio franco-russe, 27 janvier 1931. Cahiers de la quinzaine, ser. 21, no. 5. 1931. 109 p. See. 184a.

2645 —: "Le conflit de l'essence et de l'existence dans la philosophie cartésienne." CD 1: 38–45. 1937. Also in: Homenaje 1: 11–20. 1937. Reprinted in his: De Bergson à Thomas d'Aquin. Essais de métaphysique et de morale. New York, Maison française, 1944 (Paris, Hartmann, 1947), Ch. 6, app., 253–65. See 184.

2646 —: "Descartes et la religion." Christus, Sept.-Oct. 1937, 244–53.

2647 —: See 525 (L'esprit cartésien, 1938).

2648 —: "Descartes and religion." Blackfriars 23: 1942, 298–304. See 2646.

2649 *Markus, R. I.:* "Method and metaphysics. The origins of some Cartesian pre-suppositions in the philosophy of the Renaissance." DomSt 2: 1949, 356–84.

Claims that the work of Renaissance thinkers (Cusanus, Bovillus, Zabarella, Marsilio Ficino, Galileo) made D.'s achievement in establishing mathematical intelligibility as the knowledge criterion "possible if not inevitable." Leans heavily on Cassirer and Burtt, without making its point.

2650 *Maron, Stanley:* "A critical examination of Descartes." PhQ (Amalner, India) 26: 1953, 61–70.

2651 *Maros dell'Oro, Angiolo:* "L'évidence cartésienne et la science contemporaine." CD 3: 88–93. 1937.

Descartes' treatment of evidence from the viewpoint of aprioristic certitude is today impossible: ideas are merely working tools. Interesting application to the theory of light.

2652 *Marque, Paul:* "Descartes et la Montagne Sainte-Geneviève." Reprinted from Montagne Sainte-Geneviève, October 1950. 12 p. [A lecture.]

2652a *Marsak, Leonard M.:* "Cartesianism in Fontenelle and French science, 1686–1752." Isis 50: 1959, 51–60. See 457c.

2653 *Martegani, G. (S.J.):* "Studi sul Cartesio e sullo Hume." CivC 3: 1937, 53–60. [Book review.]

2654 *Martin, Francelin:* De illa quam Cartesius sibi ad tempum effinxit ethica. Douai, Delattre & Goulois, 1894. 92 p. Thèse Paris.

Mentioned with approval by H. Gouhier.

2655 *Martin, J. (abbé):* Descartes. Première Méditation, avec une notice biographique et une étude sur la philosophie de Descartes. Paris, Poussielgue, 1882. xviii, 29 p. [BN]

2656 *Martin, Robert Charles Gontran:* Descartes médecin. Paris, Legrand, 1924. 72 p. Illustr. (Thèse Paris, Faculté de médecine de Paris, année 1924). See 365.

2657 *Martin, W. A. P.:* "The Cartesian philosophy before Descartes." Jl of the Peking Oriental Society 2: 1888, 121–41. Also: Peking, Pei T'ang Press, 1888. 21 p. See 310.

2658 *Martineau, James:* Types of ethical theory. Vol. 1 (1885). 3rd ed., revised, Oxford, Clarendon Press, 1891, 122–58.

2659 *Martínez, A. M.:* "Fundamentos de la moral en Descartes." RFChile 1: 1950, 419–35.

2660 *Martínez Gómez, Luis:* "La luz natural, superviviente de la duda cartesiana." PenM 6: 1950, 173–205.

2661 *Martínez Paz, Enrique:* "La influencia de Descartes en el pensamiento filosófico de la Colonia." Homenaje 3: 15–33. 1937. See 448.

2662 *Martins, Diamantino:* "Descartes ou Balmes? A volta do problema crítico fundamental." RPFil 1: 1945, 251–69.

2663 *Marx, Karl:* "Kritische Schlacht gegen den französischen Materialismus." In: K. Marx und F. Engels, Die heilige Familie, oder Kritik der kritischen Kritik. Frankfurt a.M., 1845, Ch. 6, § 3c, p. 195–211. (Marx-Engels Gesamtausgabe, Abt. 1, v. 3, p. 301–07). French transl.: "Descartes et les sources du matérialisme français," Pensée no. 28, 1950, 3–7. Serbian transl.: "Dekart i izvori francuskog materijalizm," Knjizvnost (Beograd) 5 Sept. 1950, 197–202. See 150.

2664 *Maseres, Francis:* "Ferrarius redivivus: or a Comparison Between the Methods invented by Lewis Ferrari for resolving certain biquadratick equations by the mediation of cubick equations, and the method afterwards given by Des Cartes .... for the same purpose. Intended to show the superiority of the former...." In his: Tracts of the Resolution of Cubick and Biquadratick Equations. London, 1803, 91–356. "Additional Observations on Lewis Ferrari's Method ...." p. 357–468.

Claims that Descartes' Geometry goes back to Ferrari (ca. 1543), perhaps via Bombelli (1579).

2665 *Masi, R.:* "Dio e il mondo nel pensiero di Cartesio." DTP 43: 1941, 293–314.

2666 *Masnovo, Amato:* "L'ascesa a Dio in R. Cartesio ed E. Kant." CD 1: 111–17. 1937.

On divine nature and divine free-will in Descartes and St. Thomas, using Gilson (see 164) as a starting point.

2667 —: "L'uomo di San Tommaso e l'uomo di R. Cartesio." Cartesio, 577–80. 1937.

"Autocoscienza" the deciding issue between Thomism and Averroism, as well as between Thomism and Cartesianism.

2668 *Massolo, Arturo:* "Husserl e il Cartesianismo." GCFI 20: 1939, 434–52.

2669 *Masson-Oursel, P.:* "Commémoration de Descartes 1937: tricentenaire du Discours de la méthode." MF 277: 1937, 581–85.

List of RMM and RPFE articles.

2670 *Mateu, F.* [i.e. Felipe Mateu y Llopis]: Descartes. Barcelona, Editorial Seix Barral, 1945. 115 p. (Grandes filósofos).

Factual introduction (45 p.), and selected texts.

2671 *Mathieu, Félix:* "Pascal et l'expérience du Puy-de-Dôme." RPar 2: 1906, 568–89, 772–94.

Accuses Pascal of lack of honesty in his priority claims for the achievements of others, including Descartes. Article caused much controversy; see the Pascal chapter in Cabeen, v. 3.

2671a *Mathrani, G. N.:* "A positivist analysis of Descartes' ontological arguments for God." PhQ (India) 30: 1957, 183–87.

The arguments do not withstand critique by logical positivism. Whatever meaning one may give to the truth criterium of the cogito for clear and distinct ideas, it is inapplicable to the idea of God. Equally dubious is the representative theory of ideas as copies which entails a petitio principii and a contradiction, illegitimately considering existence an attribute. [Bsig 1958, 8625].

2672 *Mattei, André:* L'homme de Descartes. Paris, Aubier, 1940. 262 p. (PhE). See 218.

2672a *Mattos, L. de:* "A moral provisória de Descartes e o método." RbrasF 7: 1957, 326–30.

2673 *Mauchaussat, Gaston:* "La signification du cartésianisme: de la liberté au cogito." RHPh ns 5: 1937, 145–60. ("Causerie au radio").

2674 *Maugain, Gabriel:* Étude sur l'évolution intellectuelle de l'Italie de 1657 à 1750 environ. Paris, Hachette, 1909. See 461.

2675 *Maulnier, Th.:* "Marx et Descartes." RU 67: 1936, 496–99.

2676 *Maumus, Elisée Vincent (O.P.):* Saint Thomas d'Aquine et la philosophie cartésienne. Études de doctrines comparées. 2 vols. Paris, Lecoffre, 1890. xliv, 506 p.; 455 p.

Enthusiastic exposition of Thomism by way of attacking later doctrines from Descartes to German Idealists. Unlike Cartesian science, Thomist science is never a priori, though often deducted from "incontestable principles" (p. 401). Early work of Neothomist revival, most interesting in its polemical treatment of "ontologism" (Malebranche, and 19th century "ontologists").

2677 *Maurício Gomes dos Santos, Domingos:* "A primeira alusão a Descartes em Portugal." Bro 25: 1937, 177–87. See 430.

2678 —: Para a história do cartesianismo entre os Jesuítas do século XVIII." RPFil 1: 1945, 27–44. See 430.

2679 *May, L.-Ph.:* "Descartes et les physiocrates." Rsyn 68: 1950, 7–38.

2680 *Maydieu, J.-J.:* "Rationalisme ou fidéisme? Notes sur Descartes et Pascal." France Franciscaine 17: 1934, 207–15.

2681 *Maymone, A.:* "Della conoscenza del mondo fisico nella filosofia cartesiana." Annuario del R. Liceo Meli, 1934. Also: Palermo, Fratelli Vena, 1934. 10p.

2682 *Mazarelli* [i.e. Claire Marie La Vieuville de Saint Chamond, marquis de Mazarelli]: Éloge de René Descartes, par l'auteur de Camédris. Paris, La veuve Duchesne, 1765. 82 p. See 126.

2683 *Mazin, Paul:* "René Descartes au Collège de La Flèche, 1604–1612". La province d'Anjou 12: August 1937, 145–52.

2684 *Mazure, Adolphe:* Études du cartésianisme, ou principes de la philosophie de René Descartes. Hachette, 1828. xiii, 208 p.

A small text of philosophy.

2685 *Mazzarella, Pasquale:* "Considerazioni intorno alla polemica Caterus-Cartesio." S 20: 1952, 310–21.

Critique of Olgiati (see 14) who sees in this controversy proof of Descartes' "phenomenalism": For Descartes, ideas have thought-immanent ontological reality, which is what Caterus, in the name of all Thomism, attacks as incomprehensible from the viewpoint of pure gnosiological reality. [BAn 1954, no. 126].

2686 *Mboria, Perikli:* "Descartes-i si skëncëtár." Perpj 2: 1937, 171–74.
Descartes as scientist. [In Albanian.]

Mc . . . .: see 2604–2610.

2687 *Medicus, Fritz:* "Descartes' cogito und der deutsche Idealismus." CD 3: 55–62. 1937. [Quotations and source references. See 171a.]

2688 *Meier, Friedrich O.T.:* Die Lehre vom Wahren und Falschen bei Descartes und bei Spinoza. Dissertation Leipzig, 1897. viii, 54 p.

2689 *Meier, Matthias:* Descartes und die Renaissance. Münster i.W. (München, Haber), 1914. x, 68 p. Bibliography, p. vii–x. See 311.

2690 —: "Descartes' Stellung zu den Alten in seinem Traktat Les passions de l'âme." In: Abhandlungen aus dem Gebiet der Philosophie und ihrer Geschichte; eine Festgabe zum 70. Geburtstag Georg Freiherr von Hertlings. Freiburg i.B., Herder, 1913, 183–209.

2691 —: "Der Begriff der Methode bei Descartes." Jahresbericht der Görresgesellschaft 1926–27, p. 48. [Schrecker]

2692 *Meijer, W.:* "Het leven na den dood van René Descartes." De Tijdspiegel (Hague) 1911/3, 372–84; 1916/2, 226–39. See 110.

2693 —: "Wat er met het vermeende stoffelijke overschot van Descartes is geschied." De Tijdspiegel [Hague] 74: 1917/2, 135–37. See 110.

Transfer to France of the supposed remains of Descartes, and the sequel.

2694 *Meincke, Rudolf-A.:* Descartes' Beweise vom Dasein Gottes. Heidelberg, J. Hörning, 1883. 46 p. Dissertation Heidelberg.

2695 *Mellone, Sidney Herbert:* "Descartes." In his: The dawn of modern thought: Descartes, Spinoza and Leibniz. With an introductory note by W. D. Ross. Oxford UP, 1930, 9–46.

2696 *Melzer, Ernestus:* Augustini atque Cartesii placita de mentis humanae sui cognitione, quomodo inter se congruant a seseque differant, queritur. Dissertation Bonn, 1860.

2697 *Menasci, Roberto:* Le prove dell'esistenza di Dio in Cartesio. Saggio filosofico. Livorno, Belforte, 1911. iv, 109 p. [PhdG 3: 1911, 2693].

2698 —: "Infinito e indefinito in Cartesio." RF 3: 1911, 420–27.

Finds it hard to separate the two concepts. Positivist approach, and a weak one [Bontidini I].

2699 *Mendoza de Montero, Angélica:* "Ensayo acerca de los valores en el Cartesianismo. Descartes y Espinosa." Escritos 127–39. 1938. Also: La Universidad (México) 1938, no. 23, 4–11.

On Descartes' ethics and Spinoza's Ethics.

2700 *Menéndez y Pelayo, M:* Historia de las ideas estéticas en España. 2nd ed. Madrid, 1901, and in his: Obras completas, 1946–47, esp. vol. 2, 3, 5.

"On the Cartesian influence in general" [Robertson, no. 420.]

2701 *Mentré, François:* "La théorie physique d'après Descartes. Lettre ouverte à M. Duhem." RdePh 5: 1904/II, 217–25. See 368.

2702 *Mercadier, E.:* "Les théories musicales de Descartes." Revue d'histoire et de critique musicales, 1901. [Pirro]

2703 *Mercier, Désiré-Joseph* (Cardinal): "Pourquoi le doute méthodique ne peut être universel." RNS 4: 1897, 182–98. See 312.

2704 —: "La psychologie de Descartes et l'anthropologie scolastique." RNS 3: 1896, 183–99, 229–41; 4: 1897, 386–407; 5: 1898, 193–99. Also in his: Les origines (see 385 and 2705).

2705 —: Les origines de la psychologie contemporaine. 2nd ed. Louvain, Institut supérieur de philosophie (Paris, Alcan), 1908. xvi, 493 p. See 385.

2706 *Mercier, Jeanne:* "Expérience humaine et philosophie cartésienne." Cartesio 581–98. 1937.

In Descartes' dualism, "toute l'expérience cartésienne se résume . . . ., toute la philosophie s'y suspend, toute la sagesse y commence" (p. 591). But his "philosophie de la suffisance de l'âme" (p. 596) fails to integrate human experience as a whole.

2707 —: "Descartes et Pascal." Cahiers de Neilly 5: 1946, 24–37.

Not "Descartes or Pascal" but "Descartes and Pascal." [BAn 1947, 1490.]

2708 *Mercier, Louis Sébastien:* Éloge de Descartes. Genève et Paris, La veuve Pierre, 1765. 83 p. See 126.

2708a —: Discours prononcé le 18 Floréal, sur René Descartes. Corps Législatif, Conseil des Cinq-Cents, an IV (1796). 16 p. Reprinted from: Moniteur universel, 15 pluviôse an IV (4 février 1796), 539, 936–37. See 112.

2709 *Merleau-Ponty, Maurice:* La structure du comportement. Paris, PUF, 1952. viii, 314 p. (BPC). Nouvelle éd., 1949, préface d'A. de Waelhens: "Une philosophie de l'ambiguïté." See 311a.

2710 —: "Le cogito." In his: Phénoménologie de la perception. Paris, Gallimard, 1945, 423–68. See 311a.

2711 *Merrylees, W. A.:* Descartes; an examination of some features of his metaphysics and method. Melbourne UP (Oxford UP), 1943. xxviii, 330 p. See 219.

2712 —: "Descartes' theory of knowledge." AJPP 5: 1927, 202–15.

2713 *Mersenne, Marin:* Correspondance du P. Marin Mersenne, religieux minime. Publiée par Mme Paul Tannery, éditée et annotée par Cornelis de Waard avec la collaboration de René Pintard. v. 1: 1517–1627. Paris, Beauchesne 1932 (PUF, 1945). v. 2: 1628–1630. Beauchesne, 1936 (PUF 1945). v. 3: 1631–1633, commencée par Mme Paul Tannery, éditée et annotée par Cornelis de Waard, PUF, 1946. v. 4: 1634. PUF, 1955. v. 5: 1635. Paris, Éditions du Centre national de la recherche scientifique, 1959. v. 6: 1636–1637, ibid., 1960. v. 7: Jan-Jul 1638, ibid., 1962. [In progress.] See 82.

2714 *Merxhani, Branko:* "Kush është Descartes-i?" Perpj 2: 1937, 141–50.

"Who is Descartes?" Main article in this Albanian commemorative issue.

2715 *Mesnard, Pierre:* Essai sur la morale de Descartes. Paris, Boivin, 1936. 234 p. Thèse supplémentaire, Paris. See 220.

2716 — (editor): Descartes. Les passions de l'âme. Paris, Poivin, 1937. xxix, 167 p. See 91.

2717 —: "L'esprit de la physiologie cartésienne." Aph 13, no. 2: 1937, 181–220. See 386.

2718 —: "Méditations sur Descartes en la compagnie de Péguy." Et 230: February 20, 1937, 450–68. See 186.

2719 —: "Les preuves cartésiennes de l'existence de Dieu dans les Méditations métaphysiques." Cartesio 599–614. 1937.

Descartes tried to satisfy the "exigences techniques d'une exposition scolastique," presenting his proofs "sous l'aspect le plus voisin du langage traditionnel," his "mentalité scolastique" showing in the uniquely causal character of his dialectics, though the spirit is very different indeed.

2720 —: "Qu'est-ce qu'une 'méditation'?" RCO no. 44: 1937, 663–74. Also: Hommages à Descartes, Poitiers, 1937 (see 531), 23–34.

2721 —: "L'union de l'âme et du corps." CD 1: 152–59. 1937.

How the question is posed in MM.

2722 —: "Le rationalisme de Descartes." Eph 5: 1950, 174–84.

Critical discussion of the controversy over D.'s alleged rationalism: J. Laporte, J. Maritain, M. de Corte. See 244a.

Review: C. Dollo in S 19: 1951, 139.

2723 —: "L'esprit cartésien est-il compatible avec le sens de l'histoire?" In: L'homme et l'histoire. Société Strasbourgeoise de philosophie. Actes du VIe Congrès des SPLF. Paris, PUF 1952, p. 273–80. See 313.

2724 —: "L'arbre de la sagesse." Royaumont, 336–49; discussion 350–59. 1957. See 220.

On the Cartesian Tree of Wisdom as a Baroque-type emblem, image, and symbol, and on its link with Descartes' concept of man. The discussion speakers consider Cartesian meditation and the 'exercitium spirituale' of St. Ignatius of Loyola.

2725 —: "Les débuts du cartésianisme et la fin de la renaissance." Eph 13: 1958, 191–95.

Review article, discussing Gouhier's Les premières pensées.

2726 *Metzger, Hélène:* Les doctrines chimiques en France, du début du XVIIe siècle. Vol. 1, Paris, PUF, 1923. 496 p. See 387.

Meurthe: see Boulay de la Meurthe.

2727 *Meyer, François:* "Gassendi et Descartes." In: Tricentennaire de Pierre Gassendi, 1655–1955. Actes du Congrès (4–7 août 1957). Paris, PUF, 1957, 217–26.

2728 *Meyer, Franz:* Zur systematischen Stellung der Descartes'schen Irrtumstheorie. Breslau, Schatzky, 1920. 45 p. Diss. Breslau.

2729 *Meyer, J. G.:* "Vlefta filosofike dhe vlefta morale e Kartesianizmit." Perpj 2: 1937, 163–68.

The philosophical and ethical value of Cartesianism. [In Albanian.]

2730 *Meyer, Rudolf:* "Descartes, Valéry, Husserl." Hamburgische Akademische Rundschau 3: 1950, 194–221.

Meyer, W.: see Meijer.

2731 *Meyer, Wilhelm Anton Josef:* Descartes' Entwicklung in der Erklärung der tierischen Lebenserscheinungen. Giessen, Münchow, 1907. 92 p.

2732 *Meyer-Abich, Adolf:* "Joachim Jungius und sein Werk, mit besonderer Berücksichtigung seiner Beziehungen zu Leibniz." In: Gottfried Wilhelm Leibniz. Vorträge .... aus Anlass seines 300. Geburtstages .... Hamburg, Hansischer Gildenverlag, 1946, 79–96.

2733 *Meyerson, Émile:* De l'explication dans les sciences. 2 vols. in 1. Paris, Payot, 1921 (reprinted 1927). Ch. 14 et passim.

2734 *Michéa, R.:* "Les variations de la raison au XVIIe siècle. Essai sur la valeur du langage employé en histoire littéraire." RPFE 126: 1938, 183–201. See 417.

2735 *Michel-Béchet, Henri:* "Le masque de Descartes." In his: En marge. Avignon, Rullière, 1947. (Collection des Cahiers venaissins).

2736 *M(ieli) A.:* "Descartes, le centenaire du Discours de la méthode et l'histoire des sciences." Archeion 21: 1938, 180–81.

2737 *Miéville, H. L.:* "Le cogito dan la phénoménologie de Husserl et le cogito de Descartes." JSPG 1: 1941, 1–19. See 174.

2738 *Mighiorini, B.:* "Una lettera di Cartesio e il problema della lingua internazionale." La cultura, ns 8: 1929, 670–73.

To Mersenne, Amsterdam, 20 novembre 1629.

2739 *Miles, T. R.:* "On the difference between men and machines." BJPS 7: 1956–57, 277–92.

Critique of R. O. Kapp: "Men can relate their perceptions to a body-scheme, but in the case of machines there is no body-scheme to which perceptions can be related." See T. S. Szasz (no. 3380) for an attempted refutation.

2740 *Milhaud, Gaston:* Num Cartesii methodus tantum valeat in suo opere illustrando quantum ipse senserit. Montpellier, Coulet, 1894. 72 p. Thèse Paris.

2741 —: Descartes savant. Paris, Alcan, 1921. 249 p. BPC. See 388.

For content of this posthumous collection of papers see 2742–54.

2742 —: Nouvelles études sur l'histoire de la pensée scientifique. Alcan, 1911. 237 p.

Contains: "Descartes et la géométrie analytique"; "Descartes et la loi des sinus"; "Descartes et Newton"; evaluation of the vortex theory.

2743 —: "Descartes et la loi des sinus." RGPSA 1907. Also in his: Descartes savant, Ch. 5.

2744 —: "Les premiers essais scientifiques de Descartes." RGSPA 27: 1916, 502–10. Also in his: Descartes savant, Ch. 1.

2745 —: "Une crise mystique chez Descartes en 1619." RMM 23: 1916, 607–21. Also in his; Descartes savant, Ch. 2.

2746 —: "Le double aspect de l'œuvre philosophique de Descartes." Scientia (Bologna) 19: 1916, 348–67. Also in his: Descartes savant, Ch. 11.

2747 —: "La querelle de Descartes et de Fermat au sujet des tangentes." RGSPA 28: 1917, 332–37. Also in his: Descartes savant, Ch. 7, pt. 1.

2748 —: "Descartes et Bacon." Scientia 21: 1917, 185–98. Also in his: Descartes savant, Ch. 10.

2749 —: "Descartes et l'analyse infinitésimale." RGSPA 28: 1917, 464–69. Also in his: Descartes savant, Ch. 7, pt. 2.

2750 —: "Note sur Descartes: La notion du travail." RPFE 85: 1918, 497–508. Also in his: Descartes savant, Ch. 8.

2751 —: "L'œuvre de Descartes pendant l'hiver 1619–20. I. La méthode et la mathesis. II. Les premières travaux d'analyse et de géométrie." Scientia (Bologna) 23: 1918, 1–8, 77–90. Also in his: Descartes savant, Ch. 3.

2752 —: "Descartes expérimentateur." RPFE 86: 1918, 221–40. Also in his: Descartes savant, Ch. 9.

2753 —: "Note sur Descartes. Ce que rappelait à Descartes la date du 11 novembre 1620." RMM 25: 1918, 163–75. Also in his: Descartes savant, Ch. 4.

2754 —: "La question de la sincérité de Descartes." RMM 26: 1919, 277–311. Also as Introduction to his: Descartes savant.

2755 *Milhaud, Gérard* (editor): Adam & Milhaud, Correspondance de Descartes. 1936ff. See 79.

2756 —: "Trois lettres de Descartes." Eur 1937, 406–14. Also in: Descartes.... (see 37). See also 74.

1. To Mersenne, Deventer, end November 1633. 2. To Mersenne, Leiden, 28 January 1641. 3. To C. Huygens, Endegeest, 13 October 1642.

2757 —: "Descartes vu par la génération française contemporaine." Rsyn 14: 1937, 67–86. See 15.

2758 —: "Sur les obscurités de la Géométrie de Descartes." CD 2: 21–26. 1937.

Holds the obscurities in the work not to be intentional but the result of a defense mechanism. Comment on Florimond De Beaune's Notes on the Géométrie of Descartes.

2758a —: "Descartes est-il rationaliste?" Les cahiers rationalistes no. 169, February 1958, 44–68.

2759 *Millán Puelles, Antonio:* "El segundo argumento cartesiano de la existencia de Dios." RevF 7: 1948, 49–90.

2759a *Miller, Conrad:* "Descartes' Géométrie und die Begründung der höheren Analysis." Südhoff's Archiv 40: 1956, 240–58.

2760 *Miller, Dickinson S.:* "Descartes' Myth and Professor Ryle's Fallacy." JP 48: 1951, 270–80. See 190.

2761 *Miller, James Wilkinson:* "Descartes's conceptualism." Rmet 4: 1950, 239–46.

Regarding universals, Descartes was neither realist nor nominalist but "conceptualist"; his view still prevails in spite of Whitehead, Russell, Santayana, Husserl, Neoscholasticism.

2762 *Miller, Leonard G.:* "Descartes, mathematics, and God." PhR 66: 1957, 451–65. See 314.

2763 *Miller, Robert G.:* "The ontological argument in St. Anselm and Descartes." ModSch 32: 1955, 341–49; 33: 1955–56, 31–38.

Concludes that Kant's critique of the proof is unjustified.

2764 *Millet, Joseph:* Descartes, sa vie, ses travaux, ses découvertes avant 1637. Paris, Didier, 1867. xxxii, 492 p.

First work to attempt an explanation of the puzzling early fragments first published by Foucher de Careil, and to give a documented picture of Descartes' formative years. See the interesting anonymous critique (by Renouvier?) in: Grand Dictionnair Universel Larousse, t. 6, 532–33: "L'ouvrage de M. Millet est l'un des signes de la décomposition de l'école" (viz. the Scottish school and Cousin's eclecticism) "en France .... Le cartésianisme est pour lui un positivisme vrai."

2765 —: Descartes, son histoire depuis 1637, sa philosophie, son rôle dans le mouvement général de l'esprit humain. Paris-Clermont, Dumoulin, 1870. 372 p.

Disappointing sequel to author's "Descartes .... avant 1637," being a "historical analysis and critique" of Descartes' main work, no longer of any interest. According to Varet (p. 393), Millet here defends the value of cartesian metaphysics in D.'s scientific work against the positivist interpretation; but see note to no. 2764.

2766 *Millet, Louis.* "Descartes et le symbolisme algébrique." Eph 11: 263–86, 1956.

Places D. in relation to Simon Stevin and François Viète whose algebraic symbolism remained confined to particular operations, while D.'s new symbolism expresses intellectual operations in general, transcending any special operations. But see J. Klein (no. 378) and P. Boutroux (no. 353).

2767 *Minich, Serafino Raffael:* Sopra un teorema della geometria dei solidi osservato dal Cartesio e sopra altri teoremi concernenti i poliedri. Venezia, Antonelli, 1866. 29 p.

2768 *Mino-Bezzi:* La vita considerata secondo il sistema cartesiano. Milano, Rubini, 1905; v. 1: xxviii, 192 p. [No more published].

2769 *Miranda, C.:* "Tercer Centenario del Discurso sobre el método." CT 56: 1937, 263–67.

2770 *Miró, Quesada, F.:* "Descartes y su obra científica." R Perú 5: 1937, 568–600.

2770a *Mitin, M.:* "Rene Dekart i ego Rassuždenie o metode." Pod znamenem Marksizma, no. 8, 1937.

On the Discours de la méthode. [In Russian.]

2771 *Mitrovich, Radicha:* La théorie des sciences chez Descartes d'après sa Géométrie. Paris, Croville, 1932. 64 p. Thèse Paris, 1931.

On the relationship between Cartesian Method and mathesis universalis.

2772 *Miyake, Gōiti:* "Descartes ni okeru Entȳo." Tetugaku-Kenkyū (Kyoto) 23/1: 1938, 1–51.

Descartes' concept of extension. [In Japanese.]

2773 *Mönch, Walter:* "Renatus Cartesius, Magister Galliae." Geist der Zeit (Berlin) 15: 1937, 582–91.

Descartes, Richelieu and Corneille are the political, pedagogical, and spiritual heroes who made France a solidly united great power. Appreciation of Descartes' role from the viewpoint of cultural history and "Kulturpolitik." A remarkably sympathetic appraisal in the journal of the National Socialist German Student Exchange Service.

Moffey, F.: see Agoglia, R.

2774 *Moigno, François Napoléon Marie:* Note sur la détermination du nombre des racines réelles ou imaginaires d'une équation numérique, comprises entre des limites données. Théorèmes de Rolle, de Budanou, de Fourier, de Descartes, de Sturm et de Cauchy. Paris, 1840. 4to. [BM]

2775 *Molina, S.:* "Renato Descartes y su obra: El discurso sobre el método." Heraldo (Caracas) 15, no. 4573, 1–3.

2776 *Molinari, José Luis:* "Descartes y la medicina." E 57: 1937, 515–30.

Descartes in the development of 16th and 17th century medicine and as creator of psycho-physiology.

2777 *Molitor, Emil:* Über die Realitätstheorie Descartes'. Mayen, Schreder, 1935. 49 p. Dissertation Bonn.

2778 *Monchamp, Georges* (abbé, later Mgr.): Histoire du cartésianisme en Belgique. Bruxelles, Hayez, 1886. 643 p. (AcBelg. Mémoires couronnés. Collection in-8°, v. 39). See 458.

2779 —: Notes sur Descartes. Préface de Jacques Laminne. Liège, Société industrielle d'arts et métiers, 1913. xxiv, 125 p. See 97.

2779a —: Le Flamand et Descartes, d'après des documents nouveaux. Saint-Trond, impr. J. Leenen, (1880). 48 p.

2780 —: "Un correspondant belge de Descartes: le P. François Fournet, S.J." Bruxelles, 1893. [Balz]

2781 —: Isaac Beeckman et Descartes, à propos d'une lettre inédite de Descartes à Colvius. Bruxelles, 1895. Reprinted from: AcBelg ser. 3, v. 19/1: January 1895, 117–48.

Descartes' letter to Colvius is a frigid letter of sympathy on the occasion of Beeckman's death. In this documented study of the estrangement between Descartes and Beeckman, Monchamp leans towards Descartes' side – "Beeckman, tout en se montrant homme de talent, n'arrive pas guère à la hauteur de Descartes" (p. 123).

2782 —: "Descartes et Bossuet." AcBelg Bulletins 1896, no. 5. ()

2783 —: "Une lettre 'perdue' de Descartes. À propos de la nouvelle édition de ses œuvres." AcBelg ser. 3, v. 37, p. 2: 1899, 632–44.

2784 *Mondadon, Louis de (S.J.):* "Descartes en Hollande. Pascal." Et 177: 1923, 145–48. [Review of G. Cohen, Écrivains.]

2785 *Mondolfo, Rodolfo:* Memoria e associazione nella scuola cartesiana (Cartesio, Malebranche, Spinoza), con appendice per la storia dell'inconscio. Firenze, Ricci, 1900. 35 p.

2786 —: Il dubbio metodico e la storia della filosofia: prolusione. Padova, Drucker, 1905. 188 p.

2786a *Montagne:* "Le doute méthodique selon S. Thomas d'Aquin." RThom 1910, 433ff.

Monteiro de Barros Lins: see: Lins, Ivan.

Montero: see Mendoza de Montero.

2787 *Montorgueil, G.:* "Où sont les restes de Descartes?" Temps, 17 December 1927.

Montoya, Celia Ortiz: see Ortiz de Montoya.

2788 [*Montpellier, Gervaise de*]: Histoire de la conjuration faite à Stockolm contre M. Descartes. 1695. See 2004a.

2789 *Monzel, A.:* Die historischen Voraussetzungen und die Entwicklung der Kantischen Lehre vom inneren Sinn. Bonn, 1912. 135 p. Diss. Bonn.

Ch. 1 discusses the doctrine of the "sens intérieur" in Descartes and his successors, with emphasis on those elements that became important in the Kantian treatment of the problem.

2790 *Moorman, Richard Herbert:* Some educational implications of Descartes' synthesis of mathematics and physics. Nashville, Tenn., Peabody College for Teachers, 1940. 8 p. (Ph. D. thesis, Abstract. Contributions to Education no. 278).

2791 *Morand, H.:* "La maison de Descartes à Châtellerault." Jdeb, 8 March 1925.

2792 *More, Louis T.:* "The occult obsessions of science – with Descartes as an object lesson." HJ 10: 1912, 626–41.

2793 *Moreau, Joseph:* "Le cercle cartésien." RCO no. 44: 1937, 651–661. Also Hommages à Descartes, Poitiers, 1937 (see 531), 11–21.

2794 —: "La réalité de l'étendue chez Descartes." Eph 5: 1950, 185–200. See 315.

2795 —: "Le réalisme de Malebranche et la fonction de l'idée." RMM 51: 1946, 97–141. See 315.

2796 *Moreno, Julio del C.:* "Descartes desde el punto de vista didáctico." Homenaje 2: 113–28. 1937.

A mélange, by a professor of education. On the application of Descartes' four rules of method to education, especially language teaching. No plums in this pudding, but a few pedagogical raisins.

2797 *Morgan, Douglas N.:* Cartesiana: an informal, inconsistent, incomplete and inaccurate list of works by and about René Descartes. September 1955. Northwestern University. 29 pp. (Hectographed.) See 13.

2797a *da Motta Capitão, M. Amélia:* "R. Descartes e o problema do método." Filosofia (Lisboa) 6: 1959, 110–25.

2798 *Mouchet, Enrique:* "Descartes fundador de la psicología fisiológica." Homenaje 1: 67–74, 1937.

2799 *Mouchot, A.:* La réforme cartésienne étendue aux diverses branches des mathématiques pures. Gauthier-Villars, 1876, viii, 179 p.

Part I and II attempt a new interpretation of Cartesian method in mathematics (application of the four rules of method): study the significance of each element in an equation; combine these elements, rising from simple to increasingly complex equations (T.V. Charpentier in his review, RPFE 5: 1878, 220–26). Note the contrast between Mouchot's and Brunschvicg's approach.

2800 *Mougin, Henri:* "L'esprit encyclopédique et la tradition philosophique française." Pensée no. 5: 1945, 8–18; no. 6: 1945, 24–38; no. 7: 1946, 65–74. See 459.

2801 *Mourant, John A.:* "Cartesian man and Thomistic man." JP 44: 1957, 373–83. Rejoinder by A. G. A. Balz, ibid, 383–90. See 431.

2802 *Mourgue, Raoul:* "Méthode cartésienne et conception biologique de la personalité humaine." Atti del 5. Cong. intern. di filosofia, 1924. Also: Napoli, Perella, 1925. 7 p.

2803 *Mouy, Paul:* Le développement de la physique cartésienne, 1646–1712. Paris, Vrin, 1934. x, 343, p. BHP. See 390.

2804 —: "L'influence de Descartes sur le développement de la physique." Scientia 48: 1930, 227–36.

2805 —: "L'exposition Descartes à la Bibliothèque Nationale." Runiv 2: 1937, 326–31. See 1.

2806 —: "La théorie cartésienne de l'arc-en-ciel, ses origines, son développement." CD 2: 47–53. 1937. See 356.

2807 —: "La pensée scientifique cartésienne et la physique de notre temps." Archeion 21: 1938, 313–24.

2808 *Müler, Władysław:* "Teoria uzsuć Descartesa." Sprawozdanie dyrekcij gimnazjum w Sanoku za r. 1904–05, p. 1–10. [Bar]

On Descartes' theory of sensation.

2809 *Mueller, Gustav:* "Cogito ergo sum." Pers 11: 1930. [Balz]

2810 *Müller, Hermann:* J. Clauberg und seine Stellung im Cartesianismus, mit besonderer Berücksichtigung seiner Stellung zur occasionalistischen Theorie. Dissertation Jena, 1891.

Reviewed by B. Erdmann in AGP 7: 1893–94, 524–25.

2811 *Müller, Johannes:* Der Begriff der sittlichen Unvollkommenheit bei Descartes und Spinoza. Leipzig, Akad. Buchhandlung W. Faber, 1890. 61 p. Diss. Leipzig.

2812 *Muirhead, John H.:* The Platonic tradition in Anglo-Saxon philosophical studies and the history of idealism in England and America. New York, Macmillan, 1931. (Muirhead's Library of philosophy).

Some comment on the relationship of the English Neoplatonists to Descartes and Malebranche. Ch. Peirce and his relation to Descartes, Berkeley and Kant (328–31).

2813 *Muller, Maurice:* De Descartes à Marcel Proust. Essais sur la théorie des essences, le positivisme et les méthodes dialectique et réflexive. Neuchâtel, Baconnière, 1943 and 1947. 161 p. (Être et pensée, v. 2). See 316.

2814 *Munhoz (Muñoz) da Rocha, Gabriel:* "Os antecedentes psicológicos da dúvida cartesiana." RBrasF 1: 1951, 62–85. Spanish tr.: "Los antecedentes psicológicos de la duda cartesiana." RFChile 1: 1950, 469–90.

"Psychological antecedents" refers to Descartes' formative years (DM, pt. I).

2815 *Muñoz, Jesús:* "La esencia de la mente humana, según Descartes." PenM 6: 1950, 173–205.

2816 *Munoz, S. V.:* "El cogito cartesiano." RFChile 1: 1950, 532–34.

2817 *Mursell, James Lockhardt:* Descartes' theory of space. Harvard thesis, 1918. 202 p. [Unpublished]

2818 —: "The function of intuition in Descartes' philosophy of science." PhR 28: 1919, 391–409.

2819 *Mury, Gilbert:* Descartes: introduction et choix de textes. Paris, À l'enfant poète, 1947. 322 p. (Les jeunes humanistes).

Interesting introduction ("La poésie de la raison," 9–38) on D.'s rationalism (see Bouvier, no. 1328, p. 90–92); perceptive appraisal of D.'s attitude to religion as compared to Pascal's: "Ce qu'un croyant ne peut pardonner à D., c'est d'être un homme heureux et tranquille, dans l'univers fermé de la raison" (24). Frontispiece: anonymous Kiev portrait of D. (first publication.)

2820 *Muscato, Orazio:* Cartesio e la filosofia moderna. Palermo, Corselli, 1913. 83 p.

N

2821 *Napoli, Giovanni di:* "Fenomenismo e .... fenomenismo." RFNS 33: 1941, 59–70. See 1277 (Bontadini).

2822 *Nadler, Käthe:* "Der Begriff des Selbstbewusstseins bei Descartes und die gegenwärtige Problemsituation." CD 8: 153–60. 1937.

Compares Descartes with Heidegger, Jaspers, Ludwig Klages.

2823 *Nardi, Bruno:* Soggetto e oggetto del conoscere nella filosofia antica e medievale. 2a ed. riv. ed accr. di una appendice su Giovanni Rodington e il dubbio iperbolico di Cartesio. Roma, Ateneo, 1952. 92 p. (Centro Romano di studi.)

2824 —: Il dualismo cartesiano. Ed. Tullio Gregory. Roma, La B oliardica 1953. 48 p. (Università degli studi di Roma. Facoltà di lettere e filos. Anno accad. 1952–53).

2825 *Nardi, Pietro de:* La teorica rosminiana della forma dell'umana intelligenza ne suoi rapporti colle teoriche di Kant, Cartesio etc. Voghera, Gatti 1891. 67 p.

2826 —: Fonti, cause e critica del sistema filosofico di Cartesio. Saggio. Forli, Mariani, 1896. 39 p.

2827 —: Della matematica e della fisica nella logica e nella metafisica di Cartesio, Spinoza, Leibnizio e Kant: esposizione critica. Forli, tip. Sociale, 1905. 68 p.

2828 *Nason, John W.:* "Leibniz' attack on the Cartesian doctrine of extension." JHI 7: 1946, 447–83. See 317.

2829 *Nass:* "Descartes' Staats- und Verwaltungslehre." Reichsverwaltungsblatt (Berlin) 58: 1938, 196–201.

On Descartes' influence upon the development of administrative law, by a German Regierungsrat.

2830 *Natorp, Paul:* Descartes' Erkenntnisstheorie. Eine Studie zur Vorgeschichte des Kriticismus. Marburg, Elwert, 1882. viii, 190 p. See 221.

2831 —: "Die Entwickelung Descartes' von den Regeln bis zu den Meditationen." AGP 10: 10–28, 1897. French translation: "Le développement de la pensée de Descartes depuis les 'Regulae' jusqu'aux 'Méditations'." RMM 4: 1896, 416–32. See 221.

2831a *Nantucci, A.:* "Il concetto di lavoro meccanico in Galileo e Cartesio." In: Actes du symposium international des sciences .... dans la première moitié du XVIIe siècle (see 1005a).

2832 *Navarrete, S.:* "Bajo el signo de Descartes." La Universidad (San Salvador) 1938, no. 2, 7–38. [Brie 11891]

2832a *Navratil, Karl:* "Wie ist Metaphysik nach Kant möglich?" K 50: 1958–59, 163–177.

Searching for a fundamental metaphysical total experience, which he finds in the experience of "Ich bin," author discusses the cogito and especially Kant's comment on thinking and existing.

2833 *Navratil, Michel:* Introduction critique à une découverte de la pensée. PUF, 1954. 112 p. BPC.

On the cogito ergo sum.

2834 *Néel, Marguerite:* Descartes et la princesse Élisabeth. Préface de Jean Laporte. Paris, Éditions Elzevir, 1946. 143 p. (Les jeunes études philosophiques, v. 1). See 119.

2835 *Neill, Thomas Patrick:* "Descartes: Pure reason's failure." In his: Makers of the modern mind. Milwaukee, Bruce, 1949, 70–101.

Catholic critique.

2836 *Nelson, Robert J.:* "Descartes and Pascal, a study of likenesses." PMLA 69: 1954, 542–65. See 318.

2837 *Netter, Abraham:* La Fontaine et Descartes, ou Les deux rats, le renard et l'œuf. Paris, Berger-Levrault, 1886. iii, 92 p.

2838 —: "Notes sur la vie de Descartes et sur le Discours de la méthode." Mém. de l'Acad. de Stanislas, ser. 5, 13: 1896, 101–29. Also: Nancy, Berger-Levrault, 1896. 31 p.

2839 *Neunheuser, Karlheinz:* Der Zweifelsbeweis des Descartes. Darstellung und methodologische Interpretation. Bochum-Langendreer, Pöppinghaus, 1935. iv, 42 p. Dissertation Köln.

2840 *Neurath, Otto:* "Die Verirrten des Cartesius und das Auxiliarmotiv. Zur Psychologie des Entschlusses." Philosophische Gesellschaft an der Univ. zu Wien. Jahresbericht 26: 1913, Wissensch. Beilage 43–59.

Interesting discussion of Descartes' "morale provisoire" by a leading member of the Schlick-Kreis in Vienna.

2841 *Neuschlosz, Simón M.:* "El problema epistemológico en la filosofía de Descartes." Escritos 141–44. 1937.

2842 *Neyron, G.:* "Cartésianisme et religion. Simple coup d'œil historique." Revue apologétique (Paris) 61: 1935, 5–23.

2843 *Nicol, E.:* "L'opération cartésienne et la présence dialogique de l'être." [Transl. from the Spanish]. RMM 61: 1956, 303–27.

Descartes, Husserl and Heidegger. Critique of the phenomenological method.

2844 *Nicolson, Marjorie:* "The early stages of Cartesianism in England." SP 26: 1929, 356–74. See 460.

Nieuwenhuis: see Domela Nieuwenhuis.

2845 *Noce, Augusto del:* "Nota sull'anticartesianismo di Malebranche." RFNS 26: 1934, 53–73. See 435b.

2846 —: "La gnoseologia cartesiana nell'interpretazione di Arnauld." Cartesio 259–84, 1937.

Critical survey of the literature of the Malebranche-Arnauld controversy, and statement of the points at issue regarding the doctrine of ideas.

2847 —: "Spiritualità cartesiana e machiavellismo." In: Enrico Castelli (ed.), Umanesimo e scienza politica. Atti del I congresso internazionale di studi umanistici. Roma, Firenze, 1949, p. 105–27. (Centro internazionale di studi umanistici). See 320.

2848 —: "Cartesio e la politica." RF 41: 1950, 3–30. See 320.

2849 —: "La crisi libertina e la ragion di stato." In: Cristianesimo e ragion di stato. Atti del II Cong. intern. di studi umanistici. Milano, Bocca, 1953, 35–47.

2850 —: "La crisi del molinismo in Descartes." In: Metafisica ed esperienza religiosa (Afil 1956), 39–77. See 319.

2851 *Noda, Matao:* Descartes. Kyoto, Kobundo, 1937. 324 p. [In Japanese.] Vol. 7 of a collection of classics of philosophy.

2852 *Noica, Constantin:* Viața și filosofia lui René Descartes. București, Bibl. p. toti, 1937. 157 p. (In Rumanian). ()

2852a *Noodt, G.:* Die Prinzipien der Descartes'schen Naturphilosophie kritisch beleuchtet. Dissertation Rostock. 1893. [Balz]

2854 *Noordmans, O.:* "René Descartes." Stemmen des tijds (Zeist) 26: 1937, 22–50.

2855 *Norburn, R. G.:* "The Cartesian faux-pas and the malignant demon." CQR 272: Jan.-March 1946, 127–54. See 193a.

2856 *Nordlindh, Arvid:* Descartes' lära om känslan. Upsala, Almqvist & Wicksell, 1897. 129 p. Dissertation Upsala.

Descartes' theory of sensation.

2857 *Nordstrøm, Johan* (editor): "Un ballet de Descartes." RGenève 1920. See 78.

2858 —: "Cartesius och drottning Christinas omvändelse." Lychnos 1941, 248–90. See 243.

2858a —: "Till Descartes' ikonografi." Lychnos 1957–58, 194–250. See 1.

2859 *Nourisson, Jean Félix:* "Descartes." In his: Portraits et études: histoire et philosophie (1860). Nouvelle éd. considérablement augmentée, Paris, Didier, 1863, 403–30.

Discussion of Saisset's "Précurseurs et disciples de D.", expanded into a valuable study of the attacks upon Descartes from 1650–1700 and of the Descartes revival in the 19th century (Emery, Maine de Biran, Cousin etc.).

2860 —: "Descartes." In his: Tableau des progrès de la pensée humaine depuis Thalès jusqu'à Hegel (1858). Paris, Didier, 1867; reprinted 1886, 347–86.

2861 —: "De l'idée du plein et de l'idée du vide chez Descartes et Pascal." AMP 116: 1881, 58ff. [Schrecker]

2861a —: La philosophie de Saint Augustin. Paris, Didier, 1865. 2nd ed. 1866, v. 2.

On Bérulle's influence upon D.; Augustinian and Cartesian cogito. Unduly neglected, according to Koyré (no. 214).

2862 *Nutting, Willis Dwight:* How firm a foundation? New York, London, Sheed & Ward, 1939. vii, 174.

On the Discours de la méthode.

O

2862a *Obersteiner, Jakob:* "Der Ausgang vom Selbstbewusstsein bei Augustinus und bei Descartes." Theolog.-praktische Quartalsschrift 102: 1954, 277–88.

2863 *Odhner, H. L.:* "Swedenborg and the Cartesians. Some paradoxes as to influx." New Philosophy 62: 1959, 33–43.

Swedenborg attributed to D. his concept of spiritual influx, which he identified with occasional causality.

2863a *Oedingen, Karlo:* "Der genius malignus et summe potens et callidus bei Descartes." K 50: 1958–59, 178–87. See 321.

2863x *Oegema van der Wal, Th.:* De mens Descartcs. Amsterdam, Querido, 1960. ()

2863b *Oeing-Hanhoff, Ludger:* "Descartes und das Problem der Metaphysik. Zu F. Alquié's Descartes-Interpretation." K 51: 1959–60, 196–217.

Basing his perceptive analysis upon Alquié's "metaphysics without ontology" in his La nostalgie de l'être, author finds the weakness of Alquié's D. interpretation in his failure to understand historicity. See 149.

2864 *Oggioni, E.:* "La conoscenza umana e la veracità divina nel sistema cartesiano." In: Scienza e filosofia. Milano, Bocca, 1942, 105–34. (R. Istituto di studi filos., Sezione di Bologna.)

2864a —: Cartesio filosofo della contrariforma; saggio sulle Meditazioni. Bologna, Patron, 1959. 242 p. ()

2865 *Ojardias, Albert:* "Port-Royal et Descartes en fonction de Chanut et du type auvergnat." Repr. from: "Un diplomate riomois au XVIIe siècle: Pierre Chanut." Bull. hist. et scient. de l'Auvergne (1906). 16 p. [BN]

2866 *Olgiati, Francesco:* Cartesio. Milano, Vita e pensiero, 1934. UCSC, v. 20. See 14.

2867 —: La filosofia di Descartes. Milano, Vita e pensiero, 1937. xvi, 588 p. (UCSC, Scienze filosofiche, v. 26). See 185.

2868 —: "Le phénoménisme de Descartes." CD 1: 105–10, 1937. Also in Cartesio, 615–21. 1937. See 185.

2869 —: "Il concetto di 'realismo' e di 'fenomenismo.' " RFNS 32: 1940, 289ff. [See Bontadini's critique, no. 1277, 219–34].

2870 —: "La genesi e la natura del fenomenismo." RFNS 34: 1942, 253–75. [See Bontadini, no. 1277, 219–34].

2871 *Les ombres* de Descartes, Kant et Jouffroy à M. Cousin, par un professeur de philosophie [P. H. Mabire?]. Lyon, Pélagaud, 1844. 249 p. See 114.

2872 *Oprescu, Georg:* Descartes' Erkenntnislehre. Studie zur Vorgeschichte des Kritizismus. Göttingen, Dieterich, 1889. 55 p. Dissertation Leipzig.

2873 *Opzoomer, Cornelis Willem:* Cartesius. Een redevoering te Utrecht uitgesproken. Amsterdam, Gerhardt, 1861. (vi), 46 p. [Academic address.]

2874 *Orcibal, Jean:* "Descartes et la philosophie jugés à l'Hôtel Liancourt, 1669–1674." In: Descartes et le cartésianisme hollandais, 87–108. See 38.

2875 —: "Descartes et les Provinces-Unis." In: Descartes et le cartésianisme hollandais (see 38), 109–12.

Two unpublished letters of Descartes to Mersenne (Amsterdam, 7 may 1641) and to Math. Passor, professor of philosophy at Groningen (26 mai 1645).

2876 *Orrilard:* "Ascendance de Descartes." Le glaneur châtelleraudais 4, no. 14: May 1937.

2877 —: "Les pérégrinations posthumes de René Descartes." Le glaneur châtelleraudais 4, no. 14: May 1937.

2878 —: "Descartes et la musique." Le glaneur châtelleraudais 4, no. 14: May 1937.

2878a *d'Orsi, Domenico:* "Il tramonto della filosofia moderna, ossia verso la 'quarta età.' Prima puntata: Renato Cartesio." Sophia 28: 1960, 167–85.

With Descartes, source of all errors and immanentist illusions created by Idealism, philosophy moves into its fourth, the modern stage. For Descartes the real world disappears, preparing the ground for Berkeley, the greatest immanentist of them all. A lively survey of the problems of Idealism vs. Realism, knowing vs. being in D., with rich references, especially Italian.

2879 *Ortiz de Montoya, Celia Arigós:* "Descartes en la historia de la educación y de la cultura." Homenaje 2: 209–33. 1937. See 265.

2880 —: "Pascal y Voltaire contra Descartes." Escritos 145–64. 1937.

2881 *Ottaviano, Carmelo:* L'unità del pensiero cartesiano, e Il cartesianesimo in Italia. Padua, CEDAM, 1943. 221 p. (Problemi d'oggi, ser. 2, v. 3). See 222 and 461.

2882 —: Metafisica dell'essere parziale. 2nd ed., rev., augm. Padova, CEDAM, 1947. xlii, 625 p. See 252.

Contains Ottaviano's cogito critique.

Review: J. de Finance in Aph 18, no. 2: 1949, 161–63.

2883 *Otten, Alois:* Der Grundgedanke der cartesischen Philosophie aus den Quellen dargestellt. Zum 300-jährigen Geburtstag Descartes'. Freiburg i.B., Herder, 1896. 142 p.

2883a *d'Ouakil, Basil G.:* Les grands moralistes laïques au XVIIe siècle: Descartes, Pascal, La Rochefoucauld, La Bruyère. Harissa, The Paulist Fathers, 1957. 63 p.

2883b *Ouy, A.:* "Descartes le mortel." MF 1957, 352–54.

2884 *Ovink, Berent Jan:* "Descartes." In his: De zekerheid der menschelijke kennis. Zutphen, 1928, 323–60.

2885 *Owen, Roberts B.:* "Truth and error in Descartes." In: SHI, v. 1, 1918, 149–71.

Descartes' effort to bring his physical and psychological theories within the scope of his postulates regarding thought and reality.

2886 *Ozorio de Almeida, Miguel:* "Descartes physiologiste." CD 2: 54–59, 1937.

His reduction of physiology to physics, and anticipation of the biochemist attitude of many modern physiologists.

P

2887 *P., B.:* "Dvije značanje godišnjice." Stvaranje (Cetinje) 5, no. 3–5: 1950, 171–75.

Two significant anniversaries: Giordano Bruno and Descartes.

2888 *Pabst, Heinrich:* Der Mensch und seine Geschichte. Wien, 1830.

Collaborator of Anton Günther develops Descartes' epistemological distinction of res cogitans and res extensa into "Dualismus der Substantialität selbst." Cited by Dempf (Cartesio, p. 287–88).

2889 *Padovani, Umberto A.:* "Cartesio e Machiavelli. Osservazioni sui rapporti tra politica e morale." Cartesio 623–634. 1937. See 320.

2890 *Paeschke, Hans:* René Descartes: Die Geburt des Friedens. [Transl. from the prose of Aragon.] Neuwied a. Rh., Lancelot-Verlag, 1949. 38 p. See 78.

2891 *Pagel, Walter:* "The reaction to Aristotle in 17th century biological thought: Campanella, van Helmont, Glanvill, Carleton, Harvey, Glisson, Descartes." In: Science, medicine and history. Essays .... in honor of Charles Singer, ed. W. A. Underwood. Oxford UP, 1953, v. 1: 489–509.

2892 *Pait, J. A.:* The influence of Descartes on 17th century English philosophy. Dissertation. University of Virginia, 1941. [Unpublished]

2893 *Palacios, Alfredo L.:* "El retorno a Descartes." Homenaje 1: 29–32. 1937.

2894 *Palau, Joaquin Xirau:* see Xirau Palau.

2895 *Palcos, Alberto:* "Descartes psicológico de la afectividad." Homenaje 3: 105–15. 1937.

Contains a brief comparison of Descartes' psychology of emotions with modern somatic theories, especially that of Revault d'Allonnes.

2896 *Paliard, Jacques:* "Le cogito cartésien et le cogito biranien." Cartesio 635–54. 1937.

2897 —: "Le cogito biranien et la notion d'existence personnelle." Eph: 1940, 6–10. Discussion: Marcel Blondel, 10–11.

2898 *Palmes, Fernando M. (S.J.):* Las doctrinas cartesianas en un manuscrito anónimo Placentino de fines del Setecientos. Cartesio 655–84. 1937.

Text dictated by a professor at Piacenza, 1797, partly defending and partly attacking Cartesianism. The discussion of the authorship leads to an interesting discussion of the Neothomist revival in the 1790's at Italian universities despite the suppression of the Jesuit order. Manuscript summarized with key quotations, p. 662–84. Complements the Appendix in Gilson's Études (see 165).

2899 *Papakostas, Alkis:* Ντεκάρτ. Ὁ Αἰώνας μας 5: May 1, 1950, 149–50. [Commemorative article].

2900 *Papanastassiou, Charles E.:* Les théories sur la nature de la lumière de Descartes à nos jours et l'évolution de la théorie physique. Paris, Jouve, 1935. 162 p. Thèse Paris.

Examines early theories of light and their role in the development of modern physical theory.

Reviews: RPFE 125: 1938, 449; L. Brunet in Thalès 3: 1936, 186–87.

2901 *Papillon, Fernand* [i.e. J.-Henri Fernand]: "De la rivalité de l'esprit cartésien au XVIIIe siècle, suivi d'une notice sur Guéneau de Montbeillard. Mémoires lus à l'Académie des sciences morales . . ., séance du 18 mai, 24 et 31 août 1872." Orléans, impr. de E. Colas, 1872. 32 p. From: AMPS 98:1872, 689–720.

2903 —: "Newton considéré comme disciple de Descartes." AMPS 99: 1873, 537ff. (?)

2904 *Papini, G.:* "Le poète René Descartes." NL, 24 July 1937.

2904a *Parain-Vial, J.:* "Remarques sur le doute et sur la purification de l'amour." Eph 13: 1958, 172–86.

The dubito-cogito is the discovery of an "ego sum," a consciousness aware of its own insufficiency and that of the world. From the movement of purification of the doubt, the author tries to derive an evaluation of different types of awareness that become evident in the dubito, without a priori metaphysical presuppositions and without accepting D.'s dualism. [Bsig 1959, 6260.]

2905 *Parenty, Henri:* Les tourbillons de Descartes et la science moderne. Paris, Champion, 1903. viii, 220 p. (Acad. de Clermont-Ferrand. Mémoires, ser. 2, v. 16). See 392.

2906 *Parks de Gallagher, Mercedes:* "En defensa del maestro Descartes." RPerú 9: 1941, 283–90.

2907 *Parmentier, Georges:* Éloge de Descartes. Macon, 1937. 16 p. (Académie de Macon. Tricentennaire de Descartes.)

2908 *Parodi, D.:* "Le cartésianisme avant Descartes." RFrance 3: 1921, 428–34.

2909 —: See 515 (Causeries, 1938).

2910 *Parrot, A.:* "Erreur de Sprengel relative à l'éducation de René Descartes." L'Investigateur (Journal de l'Institut historique) 9, ser. 4, 1869, 157–59.

2911 *Passmore, John Arthur:* "Descartes, the British empiricists, and formal logic." PhR 62: 1953, 545–53. See 335.

2912 *Pastor, Julio Rey:* "Descartes y la filosofía natural." Homenaje 2: 43–66. 1937.

From the viewpoint of the philosophy of science, "la famosa revolución cartesiana es una frase, pero no una realidad" (p. 57); Descartes' struggle against Scholasticism was a Quixotic battle with windmills, his pyramidal edifice has crumbled – but his "espíritu unificador, su ensueño fáustico" is triumphant – in his anniversary year, at any rate.

2913 *Pastore, Annibale:* "Novità sulla logica di Descartes." AFil 4: 1934, 337–49. See 321a.

2914 —: "Approfondimento del pensiero di Descartes." Filosofia (Torino) 1: 1950, 229–37. See 321a.

2914a —: "Presentazione degli 'Studi cartesiani' di Gallo Galli." AcTorino v. 79, t. 2, 1943–44. See no. 209.

2915 *Patri, Aimé:* "Descartes, Sartre und Maritain." Merkur 1: 1947, 615–24. See See 183, 184, 192.

2916 —: "Sur les notions d'essence et d'existence humaine." In: L'homme, le monde, l'histoire. Grenoble, B. Arthaud, 1948 (Cahiers du Collège philosophique), 110–38.

Logical interpretation of the cogito [Alquié.]

2917 —: "Sur l'interprétation de Descartes par Ferdinand Alquié." RMM 56: 1951, 208–22. See 149.

2918 *Patroni, Giuseppe:* Cartesio e il dubbio metodico. Riflessioni filosofiche. Roma, 1870.

Review: Anon. in La filosofia delle scuole ital. 1: 1870, 277–78: Descartes was neither sceptic nor atheist; book written with clarity and order.

2919 *Patru, Guillaume-Anne:* De la méthode de Descartes. Grenoble, Impr. Maisonville, 1851. vi, 117 p. [BN]

2920 —: Du cartésianisme. Lecture faite à l'Académie delphinale, 19 janvier 1855. Grenoble, Impr. de Prudhomme, 1863. 14 p. [BN]

2921 *Paulus, S.:* Über Bedeutung, Wesen und Umfang des cartesischen Zweifels. Dissertation Jena, 1875. [Überweg.]

Paz: see Martínez Paz.

2922 *Peghaire, J.:* "Un thomiste devant Descartes." Revue de l'Université d'Ottawa 8: 1938, 29*–59*. ()

2923 *Péguy, Charles:* Note sur M. Bergson et la philosophie bergsonienne. Note conjointe sur M. Descartes et la philosophie cartésienne. 5e éd. Paris, Gallimard, 1935. 322 p. Also in his: Œuvres complètes. Paris, Gallimard, v. 9, 1924, p. 57–331. Spanish transl. by M. Brugnoli: Nota conjunta sobre Descartes y la filosofía cartesiana. Buenos Aires, 1946. See 186.

2924 *Peine, Paul:* Descartes als Pädagoge. Erfurt, Luther. 1901. 36 p. Diss. Rostock.

2925 *Peirce, Charles Sanders:* "Questions concerning certain faculties claimed for man." "Some consequences of four incapacities." "Grounds of validity of the laws of logic: further consequences of four incapacities." JSPh 2: 1868–69, 103–114, 140–57, 193–208. Also in: Collected papers of Charles Sanders Peirce, ed. Charles Hartshorne and Paul Weiss. Cambridge, Mass., Harvard UP, v. 5, 1934, p. 135–222 (5: 213–5: 357), with revisions of 1893. "Some consequences" reprinted in: The philosophy of Peirce: Selected writings, ed. Justus Buchler. London, Routledge & Kegan Paul, reprinted as: Philosophical writings of Peirce. New York, Dover, 1955, p. 228–250. See 187.

2926 —: "Descartes and his works." Nation 59: 27 December 1894, 476–77.

Review of an article in RIE (November 15, 1894) on the proposed edition of Descartes' works; draws attention to the lost item "C" of the Stockholm Inventory (Olympica, Parnassus, etc.)

Pelayo: see Menéndez y Pelayo.

2927 *Pelikán, Ferdinand:* "La méthode de Condillac et de Descartes." CD 3: 43–48. 1937.

All modern "fictionalism" comes from Condillac. Comparison of his organic theory of the self and D.'s cogito.

2928 *Pelloux, Luigi:* "Centenario cartesiano. La metafisica dell'essere e Cartesio." Stud 33, no. 10: 1937, 357–61.

2929 —: "Descartes e Laberthonnière." Cartesio 685–93. 1937. See 177.

2930 —: "L'interpretazione data a Cartesio da Maine de Biran." RFNS 27: 1935, 259–67.

Concerns Maine de Biran more than Descartes [Bontadini.]

2931 *Pelseneer, Jean:* "Gilbert, Bacon, Galilée, Kepler, Harvey et Descartes; leur relations." Isis 17: 1932, 171–208. See 120.

2932 —: "Descartes et le théorème de Poincaré. A propos de la question des précurseurs." Isis 28: 1938, 24–28.

Henri Poincaré's theorem (if a phenomenon admits one complete mechanical explanation, it admits an infinity of others) anticipated by D. in PP IV, § 204 (God has an infinity of ways of producing a phenomenon; mind cannot determine which way He chose.)

2933 *Pemartín, José:* " 'Epígonos' de la era cartesiana: La fisicomatemática post-cartesiana." RevF 3: 1944, 435–68.

On the foundation problem in modern physics, with survey of its development since Descartes.

2933a [*Pepys*]: The diary of Samuel Pepys. [See entries of August 5 and 8, 1663; April 3 and 18, 1668, December 25, 1668.]

"So home and to dinner alone with my wife, who, poor wretch! sat undressed all day till ten at night, altering and lacing of a noble petticoat: while I by her, making the boy read to me the Life of Julius Caesar, and Des Cartes book of Musick – the latter of which I understand not, nor think that he did well that writ it, though a most learned man. Then after supper I made the boy play upon his lute – and so, my mind in mighty content, we to bed." Christmas-day, December 25, 1668.

2934 *Peradotto, Lydia:* "Descartes y Galilei." Homenaje 1: 141–93. 1937.

Contrasts Descartes the philosopher with Galilei the scientist.

2934a *Perkins, Merle L.:* "Descartes and the Abbé de Saint-Pierre." MLQ 19: 1958, 294–302.

Claims that the Abbé's "Projet de paix perpétuelle" adopts Cartesian method, advocating unity of science and geometric method and rejecting syllogism as means of discovery. The project is deduced from a first principle, adopted from Hobbes rather than D. ("fear is reason"), with external union among men, an invention imposed by a sovereign. Descartes would have approved the method and rejected the principle. The reader may ask: What, on such terms, is not Cartesianism?

2935 "*Perkujtimi Kartezian ne Balkan.*" Perpj 2: 1937, 193–95.

2936 *Persiani, Vincenzo:* Considerazioni sopra le dottrine filosofiche di Cartesio. Napoli, Morano, 1879. 112 p.

2937 *Persigout, Gabriel:* "L'illumination de René Descartes rosi-crucien. Contribution à l'étude de l'imagination créatrice." CD 2: 123–30, 1937. See 105.

2938 —: Rosicrucisme et cartésianisme. Extrait. X Novembris 1619. Paris, Editions de la paix, 4, rue César Franck, 1938. 48 p. 8vo.

2939 *Pescador, Augusto:* "Descartes y el hombre moderno." Kollasuyo (La Paz, Bolivia) 10: 1951, no. 67, 21–24.

2940 *Petit, Henri:* Images: Descartes et Pascal. Paris, Rieder, 1930. 3e éd., 1937. 287 p. (Prosateurs français contemporains.)

Protracted meditation, verging on litany, on Pascal the Christian vs. D. the Cartesian. "Descartes incapable de se fondre en Jésus" (252) receives honors but no credit. Mystical tone without the peculiar clarity of the genuine mystic.

2941 *Petit, Léon:* "L'affaire Galilée vue par Descartes et Pascal." DSS no. 28: 1955, 231–39.

Where Descartes concealed his bitterness beneath serene words, Pascal, 25 years later and in a wholly different political climate, lashes out in the Provinciales. Two different reactions to pressure.

2942 *Pétrement, Simone:* "La liberté selon Descartes et Sartre." Crit 1: 1946, 612–20. See 192.

2943 —: Le dualisme dans l'histoire de la philosophie et des religions. Paris, Gallimard, 1946. 131 p.

2944 *Petrovici, Ion:* "Privire asupra operei și personalitatii lui Descartes." Academia Romāna (Lit.), ser. 3, v. 8, Memor. 4 (Sedenta festiva de la 5 Noemvrie 1937).

A glance at Descartes' work and personality. Commemorative address. [In Rumanian.]

2944a *Peursen, Cornelis van:* "Some remarks on the Ego in the phenomenology of Husserl." In: For Roman Ingarden [Festschrift], The Hague, Nijhoff, 1959, 29–41.

2945 *Pfaff, Rudolf Franz:* Die Unterschiede zwischen der Naturphilosophie Descartes' und derjenigen Gassendis und der Gegensatz der beiden Philosophen überhaupt. Borna-Leipzig, Noske, 1905. 65 p. Diss. Leipzig.

2946 *Pfeffer, W.:* "Die Entstehung der Philosophie Descartes' nach seiner Korrespondenz." AGP 16 (ns 9): 1903, 1–26.

Appendix (p. 24–26) raises the question how long (in 1629) Descartes was occupied with metaphysical problems. Paul Tannery answered (ibid.).

2947 *Pflugbeil, R.:* Der Begriff der ewigen Wahrheiten bei Leibniz, mit einer einleitenden Übersicht der Geschichte dieses Begriffs in der christlichen Philosophie bei Descartes und Spinoza. Diss. Leipzig. 1903 or 1904. ()

2948 *Philippe, Marie-Dominique (O.P.):* "Réflexions sur la nature et l'importance de la liberté dans la philosophie de Descartes." Rthom 52: 1952, 586–607.

Affirming the primacy of the knowing subject, Descartes is led to affirm the superiority of will over mind. (BAn 1954, no. 4170).

2949 *Picard, Émile:* "Sur le développement de l'analyse mathématique et ses rapports avec quelques autres sciences." Bull. des sciences mathématiques ser. 2, 28: 1904, 267–96.

2950 —: "Sur le Discours de la méthode." RFrance 14: 1934, 55–66.

2951 —: Une édition nouvelle du Discours de la méthode de Descartes. Paris, Gauthier-Villars, 1934. (4), 10 p.

Preface for an "édition de grand luxe que publie un groupe d'anciens élèves bibliophiles de l'École Centrale des Arts et Manufactures."

2951a *Picard, Gabriel (S.J.):* Le problème critique fondamental. Beauchesne, 1930. – Réflexions sur le problème critique fondamental. Beauchesne, 1937.

Attempts to found realism on the cogito. Neoscholastic attitude "very close to D.'s" (Gilson, no. 2041, p. 747.)

2952 *Picavet, François:* "Les origines de l'idéologie du XVIIe au XVIIIe siècle." In his: Les idéologues. Essai sur l'histoire des idées et des théories scientifiques, philosophiques, religieuses, etc. en France depuis 1789. Paris, Alcan, 1891, p. 1–19.

Rapid survey of Cartesianism, condensed from a 200 page study setting forth "des affirmations fort opposées à tout ce qu'on lit dans la plupart des Histoires des philosophies" (p. 10, n.3).

2953 —: "Descartes et les philosophes médiévales." In his: Essais sur l'histoire générale et comparée des philosophies et des théologies médiévales. (Editio ultima). Paris, Alcan, 1913, 328–45.

2954 *Pichler, Hans:* "Zur Entwicklung des Rationalismus von Descartes bis Kant." K 18: 1913, 383–419.

2955 *Pierini, Aldo:* "Il Descartes del Laberthonnière e i suoi critici." GCFI 21: 1940, 350–68. See 177.

2956 *Piérola, Raúl A.:* "Elementos éticos en la filosofía de Descartes." Escritos 165–74. 1937.

2957 *Piéron, H.:* "De l'influence sociale des principes cartésiens" [on Poullain de la Barre]. Revue de synthèse historique 1902, 153–85; 270–82.

2958 *Pillon, François:* "L'évolution de l'idéalisme au XVIIe siècle." AnPh 1883–1904. See 462.

For titles of the 12 articles forming this series see Varet, 1: 383, note 1.

2959 —: "La première preuve cartésienne de l'existence de Dieu et la critique de l'infini." AnPh 2: 1891, 43–190.

2960 *Pimienta, R.:* "Une résurrection de Descartes." Temps, 20 August 1937. [The BN exhibition. See 1].

2961 *Piñera Llera, Humberto:* "Descartes, el sentido común y la filosofía." RcubF 1/6: 1950, 7–16.

2962 *Pinsky, L.:* "Do machines think about machines thinking?" Mind 60: 1951, 397–98. See 350.

2963 *Pintard, René* (co-editor): Correspondance du P. Marin Mersenne. 1932ff. See 82.

2964 —: Le libertinage érudit dans la première moitié du XVIIe siècle. Paris, Boivin, 1947. 2 vols.

Important background material, exceptionally rich in biographical and historical detail.

2965 —: "Descartes et Gassendi." CD 2: 115–22. 1937. See 325.

2966 *Pinto Ferreira, J. A.:* "O problema da experiência em Descartes." RPF 11: 1955, no. 3–4, 256–61. (Actas do I Congresso nacional de filosofia).

Dioptrique and Météores deductively utilize experience, i.e. move from causes to effects.

2967 *Piobetta, Jean-Baptiste:* Pierre Chanet; une psychologie de l'instinct et des functions de l'esprit au temps de Descartes. Paris, Hartmann, 1937. xx, 115 p. Thèse compl. Paris.

2968 —: "Au temps de Descartes. Une polémique ignorée sur la connaissance des animaux (Pierre Chanet et Marin Cureau de la Chambre)." CD 2: 60–66. 1937.

The Chanet de la Chambre controversy (1643–48) shows that Descartes' theory had its adherents and opponents even before the publication of the Discours de la méthode (Chanet wrote in 1636 but did not publish until 1643).

2969 *Piper, R. F.:* "From defect to Deity. A restatement of Descartes' Second argument for the existence of God." CD 1: 118–24. 1937.

2970 *Pirro, André:* Descartes et la musique. Paris, Fischbacher, 1907. vii, 127 p. See 418.

2971 *Pita, Enrique B.* (S.J.): "Descartes y su estructura mental." E 57: 1937, 369–72.

2972 —: "Descartes, padre de la filosofía moderna." E 66: 1941, 141–58. Also in: Tribuna Católica (Montevideo) 141, 179–89. Also in his and J. I. Cifuente's: El punto de partida de la filosofía. Buenos Aires-México, Espasa-Calpe, Argentina, 1941 (Bibl. ibero-americana de filosofía, sec. D, v. 2), p. 7–40.

2973 —: "La metodología filosófica de Descartes y su repercusión en la filosofía moderna." CyF 8: 1952, no. 31–32, 15–27.

Descartes reaches the conclusions of St. Thomas by a different method. Modern philosophy, following him, develops metaphysical categories without reference to experience; but, more consequent than he, it rejects his traditional conclusions. [BAn 1954, 10033.]

2974 *La Plata.* Universidad Nacional. Escritos en honor de Descartes (1938). See 39.

2975 *Plessner, Paul:* Die Lehre von den Leidenschaften bei Descartes. Ein Beitrag zur Beurteilung seiner praktischen Philosophie. Leipzig, Hesse, 1888. 63 p. Diss. Leipzig.

2976 *Poggendorf, Johann Christian:* "Descartes." In his: Geschichte der Physik. Leipzig, Barth, 1879, p. 305–18. See 393.

2977 *Poincaré, Henri:* "Note sur les principes de la mécanique dans Descartes et dans Leibniz." In: G. W. Leibniz. La monadologie, publié par Émile Boutroux, suivie d'une note ... par H. Poincaré. 5th ed., Paris, Delagrave, 1900, 225–31.

2978 —: Leçons sur les hypothèses cosmogoniques professées à la Sorbonne, rédigées par Henri Vergne. Paris, Hermann, 1911. 294 p. (Cours de la faculté des sciences à Paris.) 2nd ed. 1913.

2979 *Poirier, René:* Art. "Descartes" in: Dictionnaire des lettres françaises, publié sur la direction du Cardinal Georges Grente et al.: Le Dix-septième Siècle. Paris, Fayard, 1954. 15 p.

2980 *Polak, Leo:* "De betekenis van Descartes voor de wijsbegeerte." ANTWP 31: 1937, 17–22.

2981 *Pollnow, Hans:* "La psychologie infantile chez Descartes." CD 1: 160–66. 1937. See 268.

2982 *Popkin, Richard H.:* "Charron and Descartes: the fruits of systematic doubt." JP 51: 1954, 831–37. See 322.

2982a —: "Éloge: Robert Lenoble, 1900–1959." Isis 51: 1960, 200–202. See 215.

2982b —: The history of scepticism from Erasmus to Descartes. Assen, van Gorkum – Prakke & Prakke, 1960. xvii, 236 p. (Wijsgerige texten en studies, v. 1.) See 322a.

2983 *Pos, H. J.:* "René Descartes voor onze tijd." Groot Nederland 36, I. 6: 1937, 521–27.

2984 —: "Descartes en Husserl." ANTWP 31: 1937, 23–38.

2985 —: "L'origine de la méthode." CD 4: 31–36. 1937.

2986 — et C.-A. Steenbergen: "Les ouvrages sur Descartes publiés dans les Pays-Bas de 1910 à 1937." Rsyn 14: 1937, 112–14. See 15.

2987 —: "Descartes, Pascal, Spinoza." In: H. van Oyen (ed.), Philosophia. Beknopt handboek tot de geschiedenis van het wijsgeerig denken, v. 2 (Utrecht, de Haan, 1949), 1–28.

2988 —: "Descartes' geestelijke erfenis." ANTWP 42: 1950, 113–26.

2989 —: "La complexité de la pensée de Descartes." In: Descartes et le cartésianisme hollandais (see 38), 1–20.

General appraisal; revised translation of 2988.

2990 *Poulain, abbé:* "La vérité du système cartésien mise à la portée de tout le monde." Dieppe, 1882. [BN 8°. R. pièce 2321.]

2991 *Poulet, Georges:* "Descartes." In his: Études sur le temps humain. Edinburgh UP, 1949, v. 1, ch. 2, 60–88. Reprinted: Paris, Plon, 1950. English transl. by Elliott Coleman: Studies in human time. Johns Hopkins Press and Oxford UP, 1956. Reprinted: Harpers Torchbooks, 1959. See 106.

2992 *Pouliot, M.:* "Les relations de Descartes avec Poitiers." BSA Ouest 12: 1939–41, 350–64.

2993 *Prabhu Dutt Shastri:* "Descartes' method in the light of Hindu metaphysics." CD 3: 99–104. 1937. See 310.

2994 *Pratt, James B.:* "Descartes and the psychophysical problem." CD 1: 167–72. 1937.

Descartes has three theories: Mechanism, Interaction, Occasionalism; as his thought matures, he leans more and more towards Interaction.

2995 *Prenant, Lucie:* "Les moments du développement de la raison chez Descartes." Europe (Paris), July 15, 1937, 315–63. Also in: Descartes (see 37).

Notable contribution, trying to determine the meaning of Descartes' rationalism.

2996 —: "Esthétique et sagesse cartésiennes." RHPh ns. 10: 1942, 3–13, 99–114. See 419.

2997 —: "Le sentiment de l'évidence." RPFE 141: 1951, 168–98.

Study, written 1922–25, on the affective aspect of the evidence problem.

2998 —: "Rôle et limite de la psychologie dans la méthode et la philosophie de Descartes." Royaumont, 413–37. 1957. See 323.

2999 *Prévost, Jean:* "La sagesse de Descartes." Le navire d'argent 1, no. 5: Oct. 1, 1925, 44–57.

3000 *Prévost, René:* "L'humanisme économique de Descartes." RHES 29: 1951, 130–46. See 324.

3000a *Pring-Mill, R. D. F.:* "Grundzüge von Lulls Ars inveniendi veritatem." AGP 43: 1961, 239–66. [Contains reproductions of schemata and pictures from various early editions. See 328].

3001 *Prost, Joseph:* Essai sur l'atomisme et l'occasionalisme dans la philosophie cartésienne. Paris, Paulin, 1907. 275 p. Thèse Lyon. See 463.

3002 —: "Le cartésianisme à Saumur: Louis de la Forge." Revue de l'Anjou, 1904. ()

3003 —: La philosophie à l'Académie protestante de Saumur, 1606–1685. Paris, Paulin, 1907. 180 p. See 464.

3004 *Prost-Biraben, J. H.:* "Lull et Descartes." CDS August-October 1942, 215–23. [Special issue: "Le génie d'Oc et l'homme méditerranéen."]

3005 *Prouhet, E.:* "Notice sur la partie mathématique des œuvres inédites de Descartes, deuxième partie, publiée par le comte Foucher de Careil." Revue d'instruction publique Nov. 1, 1860, 484–87.

See AT X, 257–63 on Prouhet's and C. Mallet's publications regarding the De solidorum elementis of Descartes, to which this notice refers.

3006 *Prudhomme, Sully:* "Descartes" [a poem]. BSA Touraine 11: 1er trim. 1897, 16–18.

3007 *Prussen, Jules:* "Science et philosophie chez Descartes." Société des naturalistes luxembourg. Bulletin 1950, 3–30. [BP 1951].

3009 *Pucciarelli, Eugenio:* "La causalidad en Descartes." Escritos 193–206. 1937.

D.'s failure to distinguish adequately between the principle of sufficient reason and principle of causality.

Review: W. S. Weedon in PPR 1: 1940, 248.

3010 —: "Las ideas innatas en Descartes." Boletín de la Univ. Nacional de La Plata 19: 1937, 9–23. Also in: Escritos 175–93, 1937.

".... scholarly treatise .... an admirable demonstration of the way in which this complex doctrine is basic to the whole of Cartesian thought" [W. S. Weedon in PPR 1: 1940, 248].

3011 —: "La psicología de Descartes." Escritos 207–26. 1937. Also in: Boletín de la Univ. Nacional de La Plata 19: 1937, 24–36.

D. develops the notion of a psychology of awareness, and elaborates the elements of an empirical psychology.

Reviews: C. Lialine in Irenicon (Belgique) 16: 1939, 500; W. S. Weedon in PPR 1: 1940, 248.

3012 *Pucelle, Jean:* "La théorie de la perception extérieure chez Descartes." RHPh ns 3: 1935, 297–339.

3013 —: "Descartes et l'idéalisme." RCO no. 44: 1937, 701–11.

3014 *Puchelle, P.:* La vie tourmentée de René Descartes. Vannes, impr. A. Commelin fils, 1937. 15 p.

3015 *Puglisi, Filippo:* "L'ontologismo critico di Cartesio." S 17: 1949, 258–60.

Puig: see Font Puig, P.

3016 *Puigrefagut, R. (S.J.):* "El mecanicismo en la obra científica de Descartes." Cartesio 695–709. 1937.

3017 *Pujiula, Jaime (S.J.):* "¿Qué influjo ha ejercido el mecanicismo fisiológico de Descartes en el mecanicismo biológico moderno?" Cartesio 711–18. 1937.

Descartes' mechanistic approach had no influence upon the development of modern biological theory; even the newer biomechanistic theories arose independently.

Q

3018 *Quattrocchi, L.:* "Descartes." GCFI 4: 1950, 475–80.

3019 *Quercy, Pierre:* "Remarques sur le Traité des passions de Descartes." JPNP 1924, 670–93.

3020 *Quintero, Vicente:* "El cogito cartesiano en la Crítica de la razón pura de Kant." Homenaje 2: 335–39. 1937.

Kant did not understand "la naturaleza del cogito," interpreting it as a mere empirical consciousness.

3021 *Quiring, Heinrich:* "Der Traum des Descartes. Eine Verschlüsselung seiner Ätherwirbeltheorie." Universitas (Stuttgart) 8: 1953, 955–61. See 107.

3022 —: "Der Traum des Descartes. Eine Verschlüsselung seiner Kosmologie, seiner Methodik und der Grundlage seiner Philosophie." K 46: 1954–55, 135–56. See 107.

3023 *Quiroga, Blanca H.:* "El problema de las causas del conocimiento en Descartes y Malebranche." Philosophia 12: 1955, 65–85.

3024 *Quiroga, G., Luis A.:* "Crítica de la estructura gnoseológica cartesiana." La nueva democracia 32: 1932, no. 3. [Rép. 1954, 541].

R

3025 *Raček, Jan:* "Contribution au problème de l'esthétique musicale chez Descartes." Revue musicale 11, no. 109: 1930, 288–95.

Merit of the Compendium musicae lies in its exclusively scientific and analytic character, yet it had an indirect influence on "les idées esthétiques ultérieures."

3026 *Radetti, Giorgio:* "Cartesianismo e spinozismo nel pensiero del Tschirnhaus." CD 3: 32–36. See 3027.

3027 —: "Cartesianismo e Spinozismo nel pensiero di E. W. von Tschirnhaus." AcLincei, Classe de scienze morali. Rendiconti, ser. 6, 15: 1938, 566–601. Bibliography.

Tschirnhaus tries to translate Spinoza's thought into terms accessible to Cartesian thinking; hence he expresses Spinoza's rationalism in essentially realistic terms.

3028 *Raeymaker, Louis de:* "Cogito ouvert et cogito fermé." Educ 1: 1950, 129–32.

3029 *Raggio, Amalia H.:* "Desarrollo de algunos problemas gnoseológicos. De las Reglas .... de Descartes al sistema de Spinoza." Homenaje 3: 333–48. 1937.

From the realism of Regulae to the idealism of MM with their view of "el juicio como acto voluntario"; the unresolved "dualidad de motivos" in D.'s theory of substance (conocimiento nouménico y fenoménico) is resolved by Spinoza; there is in Descartes an "afirmación resuelta y victoriosa de la persona," while Spinoza "rompe los límites de la persona" as he dissolves it in God.

3030 —: "El papel de Dios en la filosofía cartesiana." Escritos 223–36. 1937.

God's role in cartesian philosophy: certitude of cognition.

Ramírez, José Artigas: see Artigas Ramirez.

3031 *Ramos de Carvalho, Laerte:* "Descartes e os ideais de uma pedagogia moderna." Revista de história (S. Paulo) 5: 1952, 449–53. Reprinted from O Estado de S. Paulo, Nov. 29, 1946.

La Flèche confronted Descartes with the tradition and style of medieval understanding embodied in the pedagogy of memory of the trivium-quadrivium. The "physiognomy" of this pedagogy reflects the technical limitations of the preprinting era. Rising against this, Descartes gave posterity the notion of a pedagogy of reasoning, capable of supplanting the older tradition.

3032 *Rapp, A.:* "Les rapports de la pensée et de la vie chez Descartes." In: La vie, la pensée; Actes du 7e Congrès des SPLF (Grenoble), PUF, 1954.

Raulica: see Ventura da Raulica.

3033 *Rava, Adolfo:* Descartes, Spinoza et la pensée italienne. Paris, Colin, 1928. 19 p.

Commemorative address.

3034 *Read, Sir Herbert:* "Descartes." In his: The sense of glory; essays in criticism. Cambridge University Press, 1929, ch. 3, p. 57–77. See 324a.

3035 *Redanò, U.:* "Da Galileo a Descartes." Afil 7: 1937, 97–111.

3036 *Regueiro, Manuel Núñez:* "El problema de la razón en la filosofía cartesiana." Homenaje 3: 171–201. 1937.

Descartes, Scholasticism, and Catholic tradition.

3037 *Reichardt, Konstantin:* "Ernst Cassirer's contribution to literary criticism." In: Paul Schilpp (ed.), The philosophy of E. Cassirer. Evanston, Ill., 1949, 663–88 (Library of living philosophers, v. 6). See 243.

Analysis and critical discussion of Cassirer's views of Descartes, Christina and Corneille (p. 672–76).

3038 *Reid, Thomas:* Essays on the power of the mind, v.1. Edinburgh, Bell & Bradfoote. s.d. Also in: The works of Thomas Reid, edited by Sir William Hamilton. Sixth edition. Edinburgh, 1862, v. 1. See 223.

Essay II (Of the power we have by means of our external senses): Ch. 7 (Of the theory of Father Malebranche, 175–88); ch. 8 (Of the common theory of perception, and of the sentiments of the Peripatetics, and of Descartes, 188–216); ch. 13 (Of the sentiments of Anthony Arnauld, 285–94.) Also Reid's Inquiry into the human mind, ch. 1 (v. 1, 99–101, 262–67) on Malebranche, and Sir Wm. Hamilton's "Note P" in v. 2, 966–68. Abridged edition: Essays on the power of intellectual man, ed. A. D. Woozley. London, Macmillan, 1941, ch. 8, 91–100. Cf. Revouvier's harsh critique of the Scottish School in his: Manuel de philos. moderne, 1842, 556–58.

3039 —: Œuvres complètes de Thomas Reid, chef de l'école écossaise, publiées par M. Th. Jouffroy, avec des fragments de M. (Pierre-Paul) Royer-Collard et une introduction de l'éditeur. 6 vols. Santelet (v. 1: Masson), 1828–36. See 223.

3040 *Reinhold:* Über Locke's Widerlegung der von Descartes aufgestellten Lehre von den angeborenen Ideen. Zeulenroda, Programm, 1910. 16 p. [PhdG 2: 1910, 1517.]

3041 *Rème, E.:* "Quelques théorèmes de géométrie élémentaire. Le limaçon de Pascal et les ovales de Descartes." Revue des mathématiques spéciales 38: 1927, 265–68, 289–91.

3042 *Rémusat, Charles comte de:* "Descartes." "De la possibilité d'une conciliation entre Descartes, Reid et Kant." In his: Essais de philosophie. Ladrange, 1842, vol. 1, Ch. 2, 5; p. 94–171, 431–77. See 224.

3043 *Renouvier, Charles:* Manuel de philosophie moderne. Paris, Paulin, 1842. 446 p. Spanish tr. of Book 2: Descartes. Buenos Aires, Espasa Calpe, 1950. 146 p. See 188.

3044 —: "La physique de Descartes." CrPh 3/1 (v. 5): Feb. 5, 1874, 1–16; March 5, 1874, 65–76; March 19, 1874, 101–12. See 188.

3045 —: "Descartes fondateur de la philosophie de la physique, d'après Huxley." CrPh 6/2 (12): Nov. 1, 1877: 209–19. See 188.

3046 —: "La physique de Descartes et la physique de Newton." CrPh 11/1 (21): March 11, 1882, 81–95. [Review of Liard's Descartes]: ibid., April 10 and 29, 1882: 145–56, 195–204. See 188.

3047 —: "Les labyrinthes de la métaphysique." CrPh 6–8 (v. 11–16): 1877–79. Contains: "L'infini et le continu" (on Bordas-Demoulin), 6/1 (11): Apr. 19, 1877, 177–83. "Une évolution personelle," 6/2 (12): Nov. 29, Dec. 13, 1877; Jan 19, 1878: 273–79, 304–13, 377–85. "Le déterminisme socratique de Descartes" 8/2 (16): Oct 23, 1879, 177–87; "Spinoza et Malebranche," 8/2 (16): Nov. 27, 1879, 257–67; "Le déterminisme et le libre arbitre: Malebranche," 8/2 (16): Dec. 25, 1879, 321–33. See 188.

3048 "*A representative philosopher.*" Edinburgh Review 204: 1906, 157–78.

Rough biographical sketch drawn from Haldane, Mahaffy, Fouillée etc.

3048a *Rescher, Nicholas:* "The legitimacy of doubt." Rmet 13: 1959–60, 226–234.

All doubt needs justification. D.'s "generically warranted doubt" is justifiable only when no ad hoc information about the statement at issue is available. But sensory perception offers a guarantee of certainty; hence D.'s "contention that sensory perceptions are necessarily dubious lacks adequate logical warrant."

3049 *Restrepo, J. B.:* "Renato Descartes." UC Bolivariana (Medellin) 11: 1945–46, no. 39. [Brie 11539.]

Reulet, A. S.: see Sanchez Reulet, A.

3050 *Revault d'Allonnes, O.:* "L'esthétique de Descartes." RScH no. 61: 1951, 50–55. See 419.

3051 *Revue générale du Centre-Ouest de France.* Descartes number 1937 (RCO no. 44, August 1937). Also, with separate pagination, as: Hommages à Descartes. Poitiers, 1937. See 531.

3052 *Rey, Abel:* "De Viète à Descartes." CD 2: 27–32. 1937.

Transition from ancient to modern algebra well summarized under 10 headings.

3053 *Reyes, Alfonso:* "En torno a la estética de Descartes." Escritos 237–40. 1937.

3054 —: "Breve apunto sobre los sueños de Descartes." Homenaje 3: 11–14. 1937.

3055 *Reymond, Arnold:* "Le cogito, vérification d'une hypothèse métaphysique." RMM 30: 1923, 539–62.

Defense of the cogito as verification of a metaphysical hypothesis. See the related view of R. N. Beck.

3056 —: "De la méthode dans la recherche métaphysique." Université de Lausanne. Recueil des travaux, June 1937, 9–43.

"L'idée serait de découvrir un fait qui .... soit perçu immédiatement par la pensée" and recognized as indubitable, i.e. the Cartesian cogito. [BP 1937/2.]

3057 —: "Le cogito: rapport du 'je' pensant avec l'être." CD 8: 161–67. 1937.

3058 —: "A propos du cogito de Descartes." JSPG 2: 1942, 78–83.

3059 —: "Le problème cartésien des vérités éternelles et la situation présente." Eph 8: 1953, 155–70.

Reyna: see Wagner de Reyna.

3060 *Reynier, G.*· "La science des dames au temps de Molière." RDM 15 May 1929, 436–64.

"Diffusion des idées scientifiques de Descartes" [Giraud I].

3061 *Reynolds, Paul A.:* "Implication of circularity in Descartes." PhR 48: 1939, 423–27.

On A. Boyce Gibson's Descartes (see 210).

3062 *Rhodes, E. H.:* "A view of the philosophy of Descartes." JSPh 18: 1884, 225–46.

3063 *Ribes, A.:* Enseignement sur la méthode positive, suivi de réflexions sur la méthode catholique, la méthode de Descartes et l'analyse de Condillac. Ladrange, 1857. 124 p.

On the cogito of Descartes: p. 105–122.

3064 *Ricci, Clemente:* "Descartes y el problema religioso." Homenaje 2: 79–112. 1937.

Sweeping, loosely constructed exercise in the history of intellectual movements from the Renaissance to Descartes and somewhat beyond, rather than an analytical study of the title problem.

Richard, R. Weibel: see Weibel Richard.

3065 *Richard, Vedastus* (i.e. Antoine-François Gaston Michel): De psychologico apud Cartesium mechanismo. Neocastri, Gontier-Kienné, 1891. 85 p. Thèse Paris.

3066 *Richet, Ch.:* Art. "Descartes." Dictionnaire de physiologie, v. 4, Paris, Alcan, 1900.

3067 *Richter, Liselotte C.:* René Descartes. Dialoge mit deutschen Denkern. Hamburg, Hoffmann und Campe, 1942 (reprinted 1946). 96 p. (Geistiges Europa.) See 225.

3068 *Richer, Paul:* [Notice on the skull claimed to be that of Descartes.] Aesculape (Paris), 1913. See 1707.

3069 *Rideau, Émile (S.J.):* "Descartes." In his: Descartes, Pascal, Bergson. Paris, Boivin, 1937, p. 11–110. See 225a.

3070 *Rimaud, Jean:* Thomisme et méthode. Que devrait être un Discours de la méthode pour avoir le droit de se dire Thomiste? Beauchesne, 1925. 276, xxxv p. (Bibl. des Archives de philosophie).

See especially Pt. IV: De la pensée philosophique – méthode cartésienne et méthode thomiste.

3071 —: "Les malheurs de Descartes. Petite préface aux solennités d'un tricentenaire." Et 229: 1936, 743–52.

Against misunderstandings of Descartes as "parrain des philosophies sans problèmes, parrain du plus naïf et du plus paresseux empirisme" (p. 746); calls for a just appreciation without exaggerations.

Ríos, F. Gonzáles: see Gonzáles Ríos.

3072 *Ripault, Louis:* "La naissance de René Descartes." Le glaneur châtelleraudais 4: no. 14, May 1937.

3073 *Ritarossi, Carlo:* "Pasquale Galluppi e la sua interpretazione del pensiero cartesiano." S 19: 1951, 222–27.

Galluppi, a Calabrese philosopher (Lezioni di logica e metafisica, 2nd e., 1845), criticized Cartesian doctrine for neglecting the role of experience. Orientation: French Idéologues.

3074 *Ritter, Heinrich:* Welchen Einfluss hat die Philosophie des Cartesius auf die Ausbildung der des Spinoza gehabt, und welche Berührungspunkte haben beide Philosophen gemein? Leipzig, Brockhaus, 1817. vii, 120 p.

3075 —: Geschichte der Philosophie. 12 vols. Hamburg, Justus Perthes, 1829–53. Vol. 9–12: Geschichte der neueren Philosophie.

Comparing Ritter's judgment of Descartes with Hegel's, Paul Janet remarks: "Il est difficile de porter sur un grand homme un jugement plus acerbe et plus superficiel" (no. 142, p. 31.)

3076 *Rivaud, Albert:* "Descartes." In his: Histoire de la philosophie. v. 3. Paris, PUF, 1950, 92–610.

Based on author's own Descartes research, with good bibliography. See also p. 161–85 on Cartesianism and its influence. Vol. 2, Ch. 24, p. 420–33, surveys the state of science which Descartes encountered, and notes what he retained.

3077 —: "Descartes." MF 277: July-Aug. 1937, 5–29.

Careful explanation of what Cartesian reason and reasonableness is, against the distortions of Schoolmen, pedants, faux-semblants, social reformers with their inhuman theories, et hoc genus omne.

3078 —: "Quelques remarques sur la notion d'essence dans les doctrines de Descartes et de Spinoza." Septimana Spinozana (Hagae Com.) 1933, 208–25.

3079 —: "Quelques réflexions sur la méthode cartésienne." RMM 44: 1937, 35–62.

Cartesian method not an orthodoxy but a discipline of the mind, independent of the dogmatic assertions to which Descartes linked it. This theme is developed through a vigorous exploration of DM and PP.

3080 —: "Remarques sur le mécanisme cartésien." RPFE 123: 1937, 290–306.

The connection between distinct ideas is different in the orders of extension and of thought. There are two juxtaposed mechanisms, "celui des machines corporelles, dominé par les lois cinématiques, et celui de l'esprit, dominé par les liaisons internes des notions."

3081 —: "Pierre Chanut." BHSA 64: 1944, 243–53.

3083 *Robbers, H.:* "Descartes en de metaphysiek." ANTWP 42: 1950, 127–34.

3084 *Robert, André:* "Descartes et l'analyse des anciens." Aph 13, no. 2: 1937, 221–245. See 378.

3085 *Robert-Pimienta:* "La résurrection de Descartes." Temps no. 27748, 1937, p. 3.

3086 *Robertson, John George:* Studies in the genesis of romantic theory in the eighteenth century. Cambridge UP, 1923. See 420.

3087 *Robertson, T. Brailsford:* "Historical continuity of science." Scientific Monthly, October 1916, 389–98.

Sketch of the period "which awaited Descartes." [Balz]

3088 *Robin:* "Le système de Descartes." APC February 1912.

3088a *Robin, Léon:* See 525 (L'esprit cartésien, 1937).

3089 *Robinet, André:* "Variations sur le nom de Descartes." Crit 14: 1958, no. 135–36, 774–91. See 42.

3089a —: "La pensée et le temps." RIP 12: 1958, 196–201.

Review of Gouhier's Premières Pensées, no. 96.

3090 *Robinson, Daniel Sommer:* "The Cartesian Studies of the Ninth International Congress of Philosophy." JP 1938, 180–83.

Review article.

3090a —: "Precursors of Descartes' cogito argument." In his: Crucial issues in philosophy. Boston, Christopher, 1955, ch. 6, 255–66.

Campanella, St. Thomas and Aristotle as possible precursors, with references to the literature.

3091 *Robinson, Lewis:* "Le cogito cartésien et l'origine de l'idéalisme moderne." RPFE 123: 1937, 307–35.

Tracks modern idealism in its immaterialist form back from Kant through the English idealists to 17th century France, claiming its French (i.e. Cartesian) origin.

3092 —: "Les débuts philosophiques de Descartes." RMM 38: 1931, 237–57.

Study of Descartes' formative period, Cogitationes privatae, Dream. Doubts, despite DM, that Descartes discovered his method as early as 1619–20 in the poêle.

Rocha: see Munhoz da Rocha.

3093 *Rochedieu, E.:* "Cartésianisme et néo-scolastique." RTP 41: 1938, 226–37. On Olgiati (see 14 and 185).

3094 *Rochemonteix, Camille de (S.J.):* Un collège des Jésuites aux XVIIe & XVIIIe siècles: le Collège Henri IV de La Flèche. Le Mans, Leguicheux, 1899. 4 vols. See 98.

3095 *Rochot, Bernard:* "La vie, le caractère et la formation intellectuelle." "Le philosophe." In: Pierre Gassendi, 1592–1656. Paris, A. Michel, 1955, p. 9–58, 71–115. (Centre international de synthèse). See 325.

3096 —: "La querelle entre Descartes et Gassendi, d'après la Disquisitio metaphysica" (of 1644). Proceedings of the 10th Int. Congr. of Philosophy. Amsterdam. 1949, v. 2, 1119–21.

3097 —: "Gassendi et le Syntagma philosophicum." Rsyn 67: 1950, 67–79. See 326.

3098 —: "Les vérités éternelles dans la querelle entre Descartes et Gassendi." RPFE 141: 1951, 280–98. See 326.

3099 —: "Descartes retrouvé" (by Gueroult and G. Lewis). Rsyn 74: 1953, 139–48.

3100 —: "L'infini cartésien." Rsyn 75: 1954, 35–53. (XVIIIe Semaine de synthèse: L'infini et le réel).

3101 —: "Gassendi et la 'Logique' de Descartes." RPFE 145: 1945, 300–08. See 326.

3102 —: "Sur la preuve cartésienne de l'existence de Dieu." Rsyn 77: 1956, 79–87.

On the Gueroult-Gouhier controversy concerning the ontological proof. See Louis Cognet's review in DSS no. 32: 1956, 568–70.

3103 —: "A propos des Rose-Croix, de Descartes et des rêves de 1619." Rsyn 77: 1956, 351–61.

Review of P. Arnold and A. Georges-Berthier (see 102 and 104), with useful details.

3104 —: "Actualité de Descartes." Rsyn 78: 1957, 143–57.

Review article, discussing Alquié: Descartes, l'homme et l'œuvre.

3104a —: "Sur quelques-unes des Premières Pensées de Descartes." Rsyn 79: 1958, 309–320. [Review of no. 96.]

3104b —: "Sagesse chez Descartes." Rsyn 79: 1958, 123–30.

Review of de Sacy, no. 146a and 3173a; Rodis-Lewis, no. 215c; Royaumont, no. 42; Lefèvre, no. 179b.

3104c —: "La preuve ontologique interprétée par M. Gueroult: Réponse aux 'Objections' de M. Jacques Brunschwig." RPFE 151: 1961, 125–30. See 270, 270a, 1406a.

3104d —: "L'abbé de Catelan." RHSc 11: 1958, 289–301 and 13: 1960, 135–38.

3105 *Rodhe, Sven Edvard:* Zweifel und Erkenntnis. Über das Problem des Skeptizismus und den Begriff des Absoluten. Lund, Gleerup (Leipzig, Harrassowitz), 1946. 250 p. (Lunds universitets arsskrift. ns. avd. 1, vol. 39/4).

The fundamental problem of epistemology in Descartes, Spinoza, Kant, Fichte, Schleiermacher.

Rodis-Lewis: see Lewis, Geneviève.

3106 *Rodocanachi:* "Descartes et le Panthéon." Jdéb 25 March 1925.

3107 *Rodriguez, Gustave:* L'existence du monde extérieur d'après Descartes. Paris, Société nouv. de librairie et d'édition, 1904. 65 p. (Paris thèse: Quid de mundi externi existentia senserit Cartesius. 1903. 67 p.)

3107a *Röd, Wolfgang:* "Zum Problem des premier principe in Descartes' Metaphysik." K 51: 1959–60, 176–95. See 326a.

3107b —: "Zur Problematik der Gotteserkenntnis bei Descartes. (Le cercle cartésien)." AGP 43: 1961, 128–52.

"Wie jedes Beziehungssystem mit Objektanspruch stösst auch der Cartesianismus auf jene Grenze der Deduzierbarkeit, die durch das unaufhebbare Wissen von der Wirklichkeit gezogen ist." See 270a and 179c–d.

3108 *Rogers, Henry:* "The genius and writings of Descartes." In his: Essays selected from contributions to the Edinburgh Review. 2nd ed. London, 1855, v. 1, 332–408 (From the E.R., January 1852).]Not in the first edition of the Essays[.

3109 *Rohmer, Jean:* "La substitution cartésienne de l'intentionalité intellectuelle à l'intentionalité sensible." RScR 26: 1952, 109–31.

The problem of intellectual intentionality in Descartes from the Dioptrics (visual impressions and the ideas they generate) to MM (no difference between actual and imagined sensation) to the consequences in the Cartesian school and to Condillac. Cartesian perception and matter.

3110 *Roig Gironella, Juan:* "El vinculum substantiale de Leibniz, peldaño entre Descartes y Kant." Pensamiento 11: 1947, 301–27.

If substance is gradually reduced to an invisible, inoperative, immovable bond foreign to reality, the end result are the a priori forms of Kant. Solipsism cannot be avoided. [BAn 1948, 6169.] See Blondel, Une énigme historique: le vinculum substantiale (no. 1255).

3111 —: "Reflexiones metafísicas a propósito del racionalismo cartesiano." Educ 1: 1950, 211–17.

3112 *Rojas, Nerio:* "Descartes y Claudio Bernard." In: Homenaje 3: 97–104. 1937. See 394.

3113 *Roland-Gosselin, M.-D.:* "Un texte de la correspondance de Descartes sur la 'distinction de la raison'." RSPT 4: 1910, 306–07.

3113a —: "La révolution cartésienne." RSPT 4: 1910, 678–93.

Cartesian and Aristotelian intellectualism. The individualistic realism of the "idée claire." The nominalism of the "idée générale." The autonomy of thought.

3114 *Roland-Manuel:* "Descartes et le problème de l'expression musicale." In: Royaumont, 438–42. 1957. See 421.

3115 *Rome, Beatrice K.:* "Created truth and 'causa sui' in Descartes." PPR 17: 1956, 66–78. See 327.

3116 *Romefort, Thomas de:* "Descartes et l'aliénation de l'homme." Témoignages 1951, no. 29, 140–46. [Rép. 3: 2467.]

3117 *Romero, Francisco:* "Descartes y Husserl." Escritos 241–62. 1937.

Descartes' influence (through MM) is most evident in Husserl's "Ideen," though Husserl's purpose is epistemological, Descartes' metaphysical. Distinguishing effective from methodological doubt, Romero suggests a simple link between effective doubt and "epoché." The differences chiefly regard the function of reason. *Review:* W. S. Weedon in PPR 1: 1940, 249–50.

3118 —: "Sobre la oportunidad histórica del cartesianismo." RcubF 1: 1950, 4–6.

3119 —: "El Congreso Descartes." Sur (Buenos Aires) 7: 1938, 66–73.

3119a —: Filosofía de la persona (1938). Sobre la historia de la filosofía (1943). Papeles para una filosofía (1945). Filosofía de ayer y de hoy (1947).

These books contain texts on Descartes, cited by M. Harris in no. 2188, 2188a.

3120 *Romero, J. N.:* "La intuición del cogito." RcubF 1/6: 1950, 46–54.

3121 *Rondeau, J.:* "Les origines de Descartes ...." Illustration (Paris) 196: 1937, April 3, 1937, 342–44. For Grandmaison's reply (Aug. 21, 1937, 531–32) and Rondeau's rejoinder, ibid., see 2114.

3122 *Ropartz, Sigismond:* La famille de Descartes en Bretagne, 1586–1762. Rennes, Verdier, 1877. 238 p. (Mémoires de l'Association bretonne, 1876). See 99.

3122a *Rosa, A.:* "El problema del ser en la filosofía de Descartes." RFChile 1: 1950, 525–31.

3123 *Rose, Fritz Otto:* Die Lehre von den eingeborenen Ideen bei Descartes und Locke. Ein Beitrag zur Geschichte des a priori. Bern, Sturzenegger, 1901. 34 p. (Berner Studien zur Philos. u. ihrer Geschichte, v. 31). Dissertation Zürich.

3124 *Rosell, Anton:* Betraktelse af Lockes och Cartesii sätt att besvera frägan om kunskapens objektivitet. Dissertation Upsala. 1857. [BM].

D.'s and Locke's position regarding the objectivity of knowledge.

3125 *Rosenfield, Leonora Cohen* [Leonora Davidson Cohen]: From beast-machine to man-machine; animal soul in French letters from Descartes to La Mettrie. Preface by Paul Hazard. New York, Oxford UP, 1941. xxviii, 353 p. Bibl. 303–40. Columbia diss.: Oxford UP, 1940 [.... the theme of animal soul ....] See 16 and 226.

3126 —: "Descartes and Henry More on the beast-machine. A translation of their correspondence pertaining to animal automatism." By Leonora D. Cohen. AnSci 1: 1936, 48–61. See 84 and 226.

3127 —: "Un chapitre de l'histoire de l'animal-machine, 1645–1749." RLC 17: 1937, 461–81. See 226.

3128 —: "Essai bibliographique sur les principaux ouvrages concernant la controverse de l'animal-machine en Angleterre (1649–1733)." RLC 17: 1937, 482–87. See 226.

3128a —: Aristotelian and Scholastic tradition." In: A critical bibliography of French literature, v. 3 (see no. 3a), 1961, 486–90. See 465.

3129 —: "Pardies and the Cartesian beast-machine." PMLA 52: 1937, 763–72. See 226.

3130 —: "Peripatetic adversaries of Cartesianism in 17th century France." RevR 22: 1957, 14–40. See 17.

3131 *Ross, G. R. T.* (translator): The philosophical works of Descartes. 1931. See 77.

3132 *Rossi, Amedeo:* "Realismo cartesiano. La 'essenza oggetiva della idea chiara e distinta' e 'l'ente di ragione'. " Studia Anselmiana (Roma) 7/88: 1938, 51–71. (Miscellanea philosophica R. P. Josepho Gredt). Also in: DTP 42: 1939, 495–512.

3133 *Rossi, Paolo*: "Il mecanismo di Descartes e le teorie fisiche moderne." Cartesio 719–27. 1937.

3133a —: "Studi sul Lullismo e sull'arte della memoria nel Rinascimento. La memoria artificiale come sezione della logica: Ramo, Bacone, Cartesio." RCSF 15:1960, 22–62. See 328.

3134 *Rostand, Jean:* "Descartes et la biologie." RHSc 3: 1950, 265–69.

3135 *Roth, Leon:* Spinoza, Descartes and Maimonides. Oxford, Clarendon Press (London, Humphrey-Milford), 1924. 148 p. See 329.

3136 — (editor): Correspondence of Descartes and Constantijn Huygens, 1635–1647, ed. from mss. now in the Bibliothèque Nationale, formerly in the possession of the late Harry Wilmot Buxton, by Leon Roth. Preface by Charles Adam. Oxford, Clarendon Press, 1926. lxxv, 351 p. 4to. See 81.

3137 —: Descartes' Discours on method. Oxford, Clarendon Press, 1937. vi, 142 p. See 189.

3138 —: "Correspondance de Descartes et Huygens." AMP 201: 1924, 411–36.

3139 —: "Spinoza and Cartesianism." Mind 32: 1923, 12–37, 160–78. See 329.

3140 —: "Falsa Cartesiana." RPFE 106: 1928, 148–51. See 74.

3141 —: "Note on the relationship between Locke and Descartes." Mind 44: 1935, 414–16. See 456.

3142 —: "The Discourse on Method, 1637–1937." Mind 46:1937, 32–43. See 189.

3143 —: "The Descartes-Huygens Correspondence." CD 2:101–38. 1937. See 81.

3143a —: "Cartesian studies." Cambridge Jl 7:1953–54, 466–75.

Review of N. K. Smith, no. 192b and 193.

3144 *Rotta, Paolo:* "Le Platonisme de Descartes." Cartesio 729–33. 1937. Also in: CD 3: 3–8. 1937.

3145 *Rouchon, U.:* "Un Auvergnat, ami de Descartes: Pierre Chanut." Jdéb 19 April 1944.

3146 *Rouges, Alberto:* "La refutación Kantiana del idealismo problemático. El realismo empírico." Homenaje 3: 161–70. 1937.

3147 *Rougier, Louis:* "La révolution cartésienne et l'empirisme logique." CD 4: 92–98. 1937.

Both the Scholastic and the Cartesian concepts of truth (vérité-copie, vérité-code) are superseded by the modern "vérité cohérente (réussite)," in Lalande's language.

3148 *Roustan, Désiré:* "Une nouvelle biographie de Descartes" [i.e. G. Cohen, Écrivains.] RFrance 2: 1921, 392–401.

3149 —: "Descartes au Panthéon." RPLL, 14 January 1928.

3150 —: Art. "Descartes" (revised by René Pintard) in: J. Bédier et Paul Hazard, Littérature française. Nouv. éd., Larousse, 1948, v. 1, 367–76.

Lively, thoughtful introduction for the general reader. Too much stress on DM, less than justice towards Galilei and Pascal, but sustaining a high level of insight and interest.

3151 —: See 515 (Causeries, 1938).

3152 *Roy, Georges Le* (editor): Descartes. Regulae ad directionem ingenii. Texte présenté, revu et traduit par G. Le Roy. Paris, Boivin, 1933. xxi, 217 p. Bph. See 92.

3153 —: "Le dualisme cartésien et la notion biranienne d'effort." CD 9: 115–20. 1937.

"Devant le mystère humain, il faut invoquer l'expérience biranienne et non la métaphysique cartésienne...."

3154 *Roy, Jean H.:* L'imagination selon Descartes. Paris, Gallimard, 1944. 2037 p. (La jeune philosophie). See 227.

3155 [*ROYAUMONT*]: Descartes. Cahiers de Royaumont, Philosophie no. II. Paris, Éditions de minuit, 1957. 493 p. See 42.

3155a [*ROYAUMONT*]: Husserl. 1959. See 2254b.

3155b *Rožanski, V. Ja.:* "Dekart' i ego filosofija." Kazan Universitet. Učennja zapiski 1865, t. 1, 341–84. [In Russian.]

3155c *Rozaven, Jean Louis de Leisségues de:* Examen d'un ouvrage intitulé: Des doctrines philosophiques sur la certitude dans leurs rapports avec les fondements de la théologie, par l'abbé Gerbet. Avignon, Seguin ainé, 1831. lxiii, 400 p.

3156 *Rubczyński, Witold:* "Kryterium prawdy w teorii poznania pierwszych stoików i u Kartezjusza." Prz 9: 1906, 358 ff.

Ably chosen quotations attempt to prove that Cartesian key concepts are taken from the early stoics: "bête-machine" and "malin génie" (from Chrysippos); inneism; clear and distinct ideas – "mais il manque l'examen historique prouvant l'influence réelle des textes stoïciens sur D." [Lubnicki's review; see 15, p. 104.]

3157 *Rubin, S.:* Die Erkenntnistheorie Maimons in ihrem Verhältnis zu Cartesius, Leibniz, Hume und Kant. Bern, Steiger, 1897. (Berner Studien zur Philos. u. ihrer Geschichte, v. 7).

3158 *Rubinstein, M.:* "K' voprosu o metodologii i gnoseologii Dekarta." VFP 1909, no. 8, 143–170.

The problem of D.'s methodology and epistemology. [In Russian.]

3159 *Rudi, Zwi:* "Chenath Descartes." Moznayim (Tel Aviv) 6: 1937, 548–52. [In Hebrew].

The Descartes year: notes on Descartes' influence on Nietzsche and Kierkegaard. [BP 1938/2.]

3160 *Rüsche, Franz:* "Zur Lehre Descartes' von den Lebensgeistern." PJ 60: 1950, 450–56.

A note on the history of the animal spirits concept.

3161 —: "Das kartesianische Menschenbild in der Neuzeit. Urbild, Wandlung und Wende." AGP 97: 1936, 73–81.

3162 *Russell, Bertrand:* A history of Western philosophy and its connection with political and social circumstances .... London, Allen & Unwin, 1946, Book 3, ch. 9, 580–91.

"Consistency might have made him merely the founder of a new Scholasticism, whereas inconsistency made him the source of two important but divergent schools of philosophy, namely empiricism and rationalism." A shrewd, tongue-in-cheek appraisal. See C. Ferro in RFNS 42: 1950, 198–99.

3163 —: "Philosophy's ulterior motives." In his: Unpopular essays. New York, Simon & Schuster, 1950 (p. 46–48).

Descartes' "system, psychologically, was as follows: No God, no geometry; but geometry is delicious; therefore God exists." (p. 48).

3164 *Russier, Jeanne:* Sagesse cartésienne et religion. Essai sur la connaissance de l'immortalité de l'âme selon Descartes. Paris, PUF, 1958. 156 p. BPC. See 228.

3165 *Ruvo, Vicenzo de:* "Descartes et le problème de la certitude." Acta Secundi Cong. Thom. Intern. (see 41), 515–17.

3166 *Ruyssen, T.:* "Prudence, sagesse, générosité; ou, les trois morales de Descartes." In: Les sciences et la sagesse; Actes du 5e Congrès des SPLF (Bordeaux). Paris, PUF, 1950. 235–38.

3167 *Ryan, J. K.:* "Anthony Legrand, 1629–99: Franciscan and Cartesian." NSch 9: 1935, 226–50; 10: 1936, 39–55.

3168 *Rychlicki, St.:* "Das Folium von Descartes." Programm des Seminars in Wagrowitz, 1884. [Bar]

3169 *Ryle, Gilbert:* The concept of mind. London, Hutchinson's University Library, 1949 (New York, Barnes & Noble, 1950), 334 p. Italian transl. by F. Rossi-Landi: Lo spirito come comportamento. Torino, Einaudi, 1955. 372 p. See 190.

S

3170 *Saboia de Medeiros, Roberto (S.J.):* "El hombre Descartes." E 57: 1937, 373–440.

Interesting biographical sketch with broad emphasis on Descartes' formative period.

3171 —: "Primeros lineamientos de la sabiduría cartesiana." Homenaje 3: 342–59. 1937.

Good study of the Regulae, with scholarly consideration of the literature.

3172 —: "De sabiduría griega en Descartes." Escritos 263–74. 1937.

On the ethical aspects of knowledge.

3173 *de Sacy, Samuel:* Descartes par lui-même. Paris, Écrivains de toujours – Éditions du seuil, 1956. 192 p. See 146a.

3173a —: Sagesse de Descartes. Choix des textes, intr. et notes par Samuel S. de Sacy. Paris, Club des libraires de France, 1956. 369 p. Index.

A very well received selection of texts, interestingly introduced and annotated; its theme answers what appears to be a current trend. B. Rochot in Rsyn 79: 1958, 123–26 has some reservations.

3174 —: "Des Regulae aux Cogitationes en remontant." MerF 329, no. 1124, 1957, 734–48.

10-year phases in Descartes' thought: 1618–1628–1637–1649; parallels between Regulae and Cogitationes (Olympica), and some fresh light on DM.

3175 *Sacy, Sylvestre de:* Procès-verbal de la remise à MM. les Commissaires de M. le Préfet de la Seine, Mabillon et Montfaulcon, des restes de Descartes, qui étaient déposés dans le Jardin des Petits-Augustins à Paris. Discours prononcé dans cette Cérémonie par M. Sylvestre de Sacy, Président de l'Académie des Inscriptions et belles-lettres. Paris, 1819. 8vo. 4 p. (Extrait du Moniteur).

3176 —: "Bacon et Descartes (5 décembre 1834)." In his: Variétés littéraires, morales et historiques. 2nd ed. Paris, Didier, 1859, v. 1, 414–24.

"Le point de départ de Descartes comme son but ce n'est pas la doute, c'est la foi au spiritualisme" (p. 418). Pure Victor Cousin.

Saint-Germain: see Bertrand de Saint-Germain.

3177 *Saint-Jacques, A.:* "Le cogito est-il un premier principe?" LTP 11: 1955, 100–25.

A refutation ad hominem of Descartes' opinion concerning the cogito as a first principle. Discussion of the value of universal doubt which Descartes justly thought capable of use for this purpose. [Bsig 10: 1956, no. 89.]

3178 *Saint-René Taillandier, Henri:* "La philosophie spiritualiste depuis Descartes." RDM année 31, ser. 2, v. 35, Sept.-Oct. 1861, 62–94.

Review of Saisset (Essai de philosophie religieuse, and his book on Spinoza). Patriotic, devout, and long.

3179 *Sainte-Beuve, C.-A.:* "Descartes." In his: Les grands écrivains français. Études des Lundis et des Portraits, classés selon un ordre nouveau et annotés par Maurice Allem. XVIIe siècle: Philosophes et moralistes. Descartes, Saint-Evremont, La Rochefoucauld, Pascal, La Bruyère, Bayle. Garnier, 1928. viii, 391 p.

See also Sainte-Beuve's Port-Royal on the relations between Jansenism, Cartesianism Jesuits (good introduction for readers not too familiar with philosophical terminology – H. Gouhier in RIP 1938, p. 169).

3180 *Sainton, P., et J. Dagnan-Bouvret:* "Descartes et la psychophysiologie de la glande pinéale." Nouvelle iconographie de la Salpêtrière 1912, 172–92. [Schrecker]

3181 *Saisset, Émile-Edmond:* "Le Dieu de Descartes." In his: Essai de philosophie religieuse. Paris, Charpentier, 1859, 3–39.

Aims to give "un nouvel éclat et une force nouvelle aux grandes vérités du spiritualisme" (p. xxv). See 3178.

3182 —: "Descartes, sa vie et son œuvre." "Spinoza et Descartes." In his: Précurseurs et disciples de Descartes. Paris, Didier, 1862, 81–184, 330–52.

3183 *Sáiz Barberá, Juan:* De Descartes a Heidegger. Madrid, Ediciones Hispano-Americanas, 1951. xiii, 493 p.

Review: A. G. Fuente in EsFil 2: 1953, 494–95.

3184 *Šajkovič, R.:* "Pod izgovorom proslavljanja nacionalšovinističko umanjivanje Descartesa." Universzitetski vesnik (Beograd) 4: Jan. 1951.

"Chauvinistic belittling of Descartes behind the cover of an anniversary": a view from behind the Iron Curtain.

3185 — and *M. Markovič:* "René Dekart. Povodom tristogodnišnjice smrti." Knijzevne novine (Beograd) 3: 1950, 3–4.

3186 *Sajón, Raquel:* "El amor y la expresión en Descartes y en algunas teorías estéticas del siglo XVII." In: Homenaje 2: 261–87. 1937. See 422.

3187 *Salmon, Elizabeth G.:* "The Cartesian circle." NSch 12: 1938, 378–91.

Survey of proposed solutions.

3188 *Saltykow, N.:* "La Géométrie de Descartes. 300e anniversaire de la géométrie analytique." Bull. des sciences mathématiques (Paris) 62: 1938, 83–96, 110–23.

3189 *Salvatierra, Sofonías:* Sobre la formación de una cultura propia en América, a la luz de Descartes. Tema desarrollado en el paraninfo de la Universidad nacional de El Salvador, durante el ciclo de conferencias verificadas en celebración del tricentenario .... del Discurso del método de Descartes. s.l., tipogr. Progreso, 1937. 34 p.

3190 *Salzy, Pierre:* "Descartes et Marx, ou la thèse et l'antithèse." PsyP no. 40: Feb. 5, 1950, 178–82.

3191 *Sanchez Reulet, Anibál:* "Descartes, hombre moderno." Escritos 275–86. 1937.

3192 *Sánchez Vega, Miguel:* "Estudio comparativo de la concepción mecánica del animal y sus fundamentos en Gómez Pereyra y Renato Descartes." Selección de textos de la Antoniana Margarita. RevF 13: 1954, 359–508. [Rép 7: 1955, 2954].

3193 *Sander, Franz:* Die Entwicklung der Raumtheorien in der zweiten Hälfte des 17. Jahrhunderts. Halle a.S., John, 1931. 383 p.

3194 *Santayana, George:* Scepticism and animal faith; introduction to a system of philosophy. New York, Scribner's, 1923. xii, 314 p. See 191.

3195 *Santinello, Giovanni:* "Il circolo vizioso cartesiano." Gmet 6: 1951, 381–93.

3196 *Santos, Délio Nobre:* Descartes e a speciosa generalis. Dissertation. Lisboa 1940. ()

3197 *Sarailieff, Ivan V.:* "Devetiat mejdounaroden filosofski Kongres." Godchnik na sofiiski Universitet, Istorico-filos. fac., 24: 1938, 1–22.

Report on the Congrès Descartes. [In Bulgarian.]

3198 *Sarano, R.:* "De la liberté chez Descartes, plus particulièrement de la liberté humaine." Eph 5: 1950, 202–22. See 331.

3199 *Sardemann, Franz:* Ursprung und Entwicklung der Lehre von einem lumen rationis aeternae, lumen divinum, lumen naturale, rationes seminales, veritates aeternae bei Descartes. Kassel, Röttger, 1902, 76 p. Dissertation Leipzig.

Useful references to Greek, Patristic, Scholastic texts in which author seeks the roots of the concepts under discussion.

3200 *Sarias, Alejandro C.:* "Descartes." In his: Estudios literarios y filosóficos. Montevideo, C. García, 1941, 204–32.

3201 *Sartre, Jean-Paul:* "La liberté cartésienne." In his: Descartes. Paris, Trois collines, 1946, p. 9–52. (Les classiques de la liberté). Also in his: Situations. Gallimard, v. 1, 1947, p. 314–35. German tr.: Descartes und die Freiheit. Preface by Karl Jaspers. Mainz, Internationaler Universum-Verlag, 1948 (reprinted in: Descartes. Discours de la méthode, ed. K. Fischer. Ibid., 1948). See 192.

3202 —: L'imagination. Alcan, 1936. 262 p. (Nouvelle encyclopédie philosophique).

On Descartes' notion of imagination (7ff.) and that of Spinoza, Leibniz, Hume.

3203 —: "La transcendence de l'Ego. Esquisse d'une déscription phénoménologique." RechPh 6: 1936–37 (1938), 85–123.

"Le cogito comme conscience réflective; Le Je et la conscience dans le cogito" etc. Cf. the Introduction to Sartre's L'être et le néant (Paris, Gallimard, 1943).

3204 *Sassen, Ferdinand:* "Descartes." In his: Geschiedenis van de nieuwere wijsbegeerte tot Kant. Nijmegen 1933, 124–42.

3205 —: Henricus Renerius, de eerste "cartesiaanische" hoogleraar te Utrecht. Amsterdam, Noord-Hollandsche Uitgevers Maatschappie. 1941. 50 p. (Mededeelingen der Nederl. Akad. van Wetenschappen, Afd. Letterkunde, ns. Pt. 4, no. 20).

Cf. P. Dibon (see 6, 289–97) on Reneri.

3206 —: "Adriaan Heerebord, 1614–1661. De opkomst van het Cartesianisme te Leiden." ANTWP 36: 1942, 12–22.

3207 *Sasso, Antonio Dal:* "La influenza di Cartesio sulla formazione dell'Illuminismo francese." Cartesio 227–38. 1937.

Useful collection of pertinent and impertinent passages from Voltaire.

3208 *Saulnier, Robert:* "François-Joachim Descartes et ses deux mariages (1690–1729)." BSA d'Ille-et-Vilaine 14: 1880, 245ff.

3209 *Saultchevreuil, Guillaume de:* "Le hardi cavalier de l'absurde." Bulletin du Cercle Thomiste Saint-Nicolas de Caen, 1956, no. 5, 28–40.

3210 *Saumagne, Ch.:* "Notes sur l'Imam Abou al-Ghazali et le doute méthodique de Descartes." Con July-August 1921, 541–49. See 344.

3210a *Saveson, J. E.:* "Descartes' influence on John Smith, Cambridge Platonist." JHI 20: 1959, 258–63. See 465.

3210b —: "Differing reactions to Descartes among the Cambridge Platonists." JHI 21: 1960, 560–567. See 465.

3210c *Sawada, Nobushige:* [Descartes and existence; a consideration of the history and nature of existential thought. In Japanese]. Philosophy (Tokyo) 1951, no. 27. English summary 4–6. (To be continued.)

3210d *Saxl, Fritz:* "Veritas filia temporis." In: Philosophy and history, essays presented to Ernst Cassirer. Ed. R. Klibansky and H. J. Paton. Oxford, Clarendon Press, 1936, 197ff. See 465a.

3211 *Sayre, Charles A.:* Moral implications in the philosophy of Descartes in the light of the philosophy of Pascal. Dissertation Drew University, 1951-1252. [Unpublished].

3212 *Scerbo, Giuseppe:* Vico e il cartesianismo a Napoli. Roma, Signorelli, 1933. See 461.

3213 —: "Il metodo cartesiano e la riduzione vichiana della filologia a scienza in Vico." LogosN 17: 1934, 19–25.

3214 *Schaarschmidt, Carl Max W. von:* Des Cartes und Spinoza. Urkundliche Darstellung der Philosophie beider. Bonn, Marcus, 1850. 204 p.

By a disciple of H. Lotze, influenced by Ritter.

3215 *Schaerer, René:* "La dialectique platonicienne dans ses rapports avec le syllogisme et la méthode cartésienne." RTP 36 (146): 1948, 24–40.

3216 *Schedin, Gustaf Theodor:* Är occasionalismen en konsequent utveckling af Cartesianismen? Dissertation Upsala, 1864. [Is occasionalism a logical consequence of Cartesianism?]

3217 *Schelling, Friedrich Wilhelm Joseph von:* "Cartesius." In his: Zur Geschichte der neueren Philosophie. Münchener Vorlesungen (Sämtliche Werke, Cotta, 1. Abt., v. 10, 4–32). Reprinted: Stuttgart, Kohlhammer, s.d. See 192a.

3218 *Scherchen, Hermann:* Das Wesen der Musik. Winterthur, Mondial Verlag, 1948. Engl. tr.: The nature of music. Chicago, Regnery, 1950. Ch. 1: The foundations of modern music.

Scherchen, conductor and musicologist, finds some of Descartes' observations on acoustics and esthetics "so surprisingly novel that Hugo Riemann's enthusiastic support of the work .... seems almost restrained" (p. 16).

3218a *Schier, Donald S.:* Louis Bertrand Castel, Anti-Newtonian Scientist. Cedar Rapids, Iowa, 1941.

Père Castel, scientific correspondent of Montesquieu, was the author of Le vrai système de physique de M. Isaac Newton exposé et analysé en parallèle avec celui de Descartes (1743).

3219 *Schinz, Albert:* "Le songe de Descartes et l'exposition de 1937." MerF 281: Jan-Feb 1937, 468–84.

Descartes' Dream as "l'indice d'une profonde angoisse morale" which often forced him to sacrifice his luminous intelligence. Critique of M. Leroy (no. 124).

3220 *Schlatter, Adolf:* Die philosophische Arbeit seit Cartesius nach ihrem ethischen und religiösen Ertrag. Gütersloh, C. Berthelsmann, 1906. 255 p. (Beiträge zur Förderung christlicher Theologie 10: 1906, no. 4–5). 2nd ed., revised: 1910. 267 p. 3rd ed., rev., 1923.

3221 *Schmid (aus Schwarzenberg), Franz Xaver:* René Descartes und seine Reform der Philosophie. Nördlingen, Beck, 1859. viii, 178 p.

3222 *Schmid, Paul Johannes:* Die Prinzipien der menschlichen Erkenntniss nach Descartes. Dissertation Leipzig. s.d. 47 p. [Harvard]

3223 *Schmitt, Carl:* "Der Staat als Mechanismus bei Hobbes und Descartes." Emge 158–68. 1937.

Hobbes transferred the Cartesian notion of man to the state, making it a mechanism whose soul is the person of the sovereign. This, though, is not a true concept of the state of totalitarianism because a mechanism is incapable of totality, scil. the "organic" totality of the latter-day Leviathan's Tausendjähriges Reich. By a brilliant, controversial German political theoretician.

3224 *Schneider, Hermann:* Die Stellung Gassendis zu Descartes. Halle a.S., 1904. 67 p. Dissertation Halle.

3224a *Schoeck, Helmut:* "Naturphilosophie und Naturwissenschaft bei Descartes. Zum 300. Todestage des Philosophen." Naturwiss. Rundsch. 1950, H. 2, 59–64.

In Descartes, the struggle between science and philosophy took place within one person, with the result that neither physics nor the philosophy of nature benefitted. Jaspers' evaluation of his historical influence appears to be the most satisfactory one.

3225 *Schönberger, Stephan:* "A dream of Descartes; reflections on the unconscious determinants of the sciences." Intern. Jl. of Psychoanalysis 20: 1939, 43–57. See 108.

3226 *Schönfeld, K. D.:* Cartesius als wiskundige. Groningen, 1869. (Stedelijk Gymnasium Groningen, Progr.)

3227 *Schött, (Friedrich) Wilhelm:* Das Kausalprinzip bei den Cartesianern. Neuwied, Häuser, 1899. iv, 64 p. Dissertation Bonn.

3228 *Scholz, Heinrich, Adolf Kratzer und Joseph Hofmann:* Descartes. Drei Vorträge. Münster, Aschaffendorff, 1951. 80 p. (Abhandlungen der Gesellschaft zur Förderung der westfälischen Landes-Universität, v. 2). See 229.

3229 *Scholz, Heinrich:* "Über das cogito, ergo sum." K 36: 1931, 126–47. See 333.

3230 —: "Augustinus und Descartes." BDtPh 5: 1931–32, 405–23. See 334.

3231 —: "Descartes' Bedeutung für die Umgestaltung des abendländischen Geistes." In: H. Scholz et al., Descartes (see 3228), 3–37. See 229.

3232 *Schrecker, Paul:* "Bibliographie de Descartes savant." Thalès 3: 1936, 145–54. See 18.

3233 —: "La méthode cartésienne et la logique." RPFE 123: 1937, 336–37. See 335.

3234 —: "La République, fille de Descartes." In: La République Française v.1., no. 2, New York, 1944. [Schrecker]

3235 —: "Descartes and Leibniz in 1946 on their 300th and 350th birthday." Phil 21: 1946, 205–33.

The Cartesian revolution assessed as a philosophical revolution during a period in which a revolutionary political ideal was beginning to take shape. On the inspiration which Spinoza, Locke, Rousseau, Montesquieu, Voltaire drew from Descartes and Leibniz in developing the new political ideas.

3236 *Schütz, Antal:* "Descartes és Szent Tamás." Bölcseleti közlemények (Budapest) 1937, no. 3, 1–8. [Descartes and St. Thomas. In Hungarian[.

3237 *Schütz, Ludwig Harald:* Die Lehre von den Leidenschaften bei Hobbes und bei Descartes. Dissertation Göttingen. 1901. 121 p.

3238 *Schuhl, Pierre-Maxime:* "Un souvenir cartésien dans les 'Pensées' de la reine Christine." RPFE 123: 1937, 368–69.

The reference is to Christine's 'Sentiments,' no. 261: "Tibère" [i.e. Descartes] "avait raison de dire .... que tout homme qui a passé les trente années de sa vie, doit être son propre médecin." (Did Tibère consider the Swedish climate?)

3239 —: "Y-a-t-il une source aristotélicienne du cogito?" RPFE 138: 1948, 191–94. See 200.

3240 *Schultz, P.:* "Descartes als Naturforscher." Deutsche Rundschau 81: June 1897, 345–65.

Descartes' physiology sympathetically appraised in the light of turn-of-the-century physiological thought.

3241 *Schumann, Rudolf:* Die Stellung des Dualismus in der Lehre des Descartes. Dresden, 1910. 32 p. Dissertation Leipzig.

3242 *Schwarz, Balduin:* "Descartes und das geistesgeschichtliche Problem der neueren Philosophie." Cartesio 735–43. 1937.

The philosophia perennis acknowledges the liberating deed of Cartesianism, recognizes its tragic character, but sees hope: "Die Wege des Menschen sind geheimnisvoll." And so they are.

3243 *Schwarz, Hermann:* Die Lehre von den Sinnesqualitäten bei Descartes und Hobbes. Halle a.S., Geibel, 1894. vii, 68 p. Habilitationsschrift Wittenberg-Halle.

3244 —: "Les recherches de Descartes sur la connaissance du monde extérieur." RMM 4: 1896, 459–77. German: "Descartes' Untersuchungen über die Erkenntnis der Aussenwelt." ZPPK ns 110: 1897, 105–24.

Descartes' doctrine has two roots; idealism developed one of them ("connaissance imaginative,") while the other ("connaissance non-imaginative") still awaits the development of a realist psychology of knowledge. Cf. author's book: Die Umwälzung der Wahrnehmungshypothesen durch die mechanistische Methode. Leipzig, Duncker & Humblot, 1895.

3245 *Schwarz, Josef:* "Die cartesianische Reflexion und die Methode der Denker des deutschen Idealismus (Fichte, Schelling, Hegel)." CD 3: 63–69, 1937.

The cogito seen as a "Denkbewegung", a development of thought, rather than as a simple position. The German idealists determine the possibilities of Being, latent in the "Denksetzung" of the cogito, not only as substance but as "Aktivität, Potenz, Negation, schöpferische Verwirklichung."

3246 —: "Die Bedeutung der Philosophie Descartes' für das mechanistische Denken." ZFSL 62: 1938, 342–63.

3247 *Sciaky, Isallo:* "Prolegomena a Cartesio. Saggio storico sul problema della certezza." StU 12: 1938, 27–93.

3248 *Scimè, Salvatore:* "Tommaso d'Aquino e Descartes di fronte all'assoluto." Educ 1: 1950, 156–66.

3249 —: "Valore della filosofia di Descartes. Nel III centenario della morte, 1650–1950." CivC 101, no. 2397: 1950, 274–87.

Survey of Catholic evaluations: Was Descartes the first idealist or the last realist? Consequences of the cogito; Cartesian method and Thomism.

3250 *Scott, Joseph F.:* The scientific work of René Descartes (1596–1650). Foreword by H. W. Turnbull. London, Taylor & Francis, 1952. vii, 211 p. See 396.

3251 *Séailles, G.:* Quid de ethica Cartesius senserit. Paris, Baillière, 1883. 77 p. Thèse Paris.

3252 *Sebba, Gregor:* Nicolas Malebranche, 1638–1715; a preliminary bibliography. Athens, Ga., The University of Georgia, January 1959. 90 p. (Mimeographed). See 19.

3252a —: Descartes and his philosophy; a bibliographical guide to the literature, 1800–1958. v. 1, Athens, Ga., University of Georgia, Bureau of Business Research, 1959. xv, XVI, 393p. See 18a.

3253 —: "René Descartes." "Nicolas Malebranche." In: D. C. Cabeen (ed.), A critical bibliography of French literature, v. 3, ed. by Nathan Edelman. Syracuse UP, 1960, 490–556. See 19a.

3253a —: "Some open questions in Descartes Research." MLN 75: 1960, 222–229. See 30.

Sédail, Charles: see Chaigne et Sédail.

3254 *Segond, J.:* "La sagesse cartésienne et la doctrine de la science. Paris, Vrin, 1932. 321 p. See 230.

3255 —: "La sagesse cartésienne et la sagesse antique." CD 1: 46–51. 1937. Also in Eph 1: 1940, 11–12.

3256 —: "Les études cartésiennes du Père Laberthonnière." Eph 1: 1940, 27–33. See 177.

3257 —: "La liberté divine et la liberté humaine. Prélude cartésien à l'existentialisme." Eph 5: 1950, 223–32. See 331.

3258 *Seiffert, August:* "Das Ich und die Welt. Zum 300. Todestage Descartes'." ZPF 4: 1950, 584–87.

3259 *Seligkowitz, B.:* "Causa sui, causa prima et causa essendi." AGP 5: 1892, 322–36. [Varet]

3260 *Senn, G.:* "Descartes und Theophrastos von Eresos." Gesnerus 2: 1945, 16–22.

Comparison of their starting points [BAn 1947, 1486.]

3260a *Sentroul:* "Doute 'méthodique' et doute 'fictif'." RSTP 1909, 433ff.

3261 *Sepich, Juan R.:* "La Teología de la Fe en la crítica cartesiana." Homenaje 1: 243–328. 1937.

Thomistic exposition of the structure of theology. Comparison with the Cartesian position leads to the conclusion that the two are incompatible. "Todo ensayo de conciliación es estéril si no se sacrifica un punto esencial a ellas." Descartes tried to make theology as a science impossible, but in vain: "Qui scrutator est Majestatis, opprimetur a gloria" (328).

3262 *Sergescu, Pierre:* "Un soldat oublié de la mécanique cartésienne au début du XVIIIe siècle: Antoine Parent (1666–1726)." Sphinx (Bruxelles) 8: 1938, 196–97.

3263 —: "Descartes mathématicien." RHSc 3: 1950, 262–65.

3264 *Sérgio, António:* Cartesianismo ideal e real. Lisboa, Seara nova, 1937. 45 p. (Cuadernos de Seara nova; estudos filosóficos.)

3265 *Serrurier, Cornelia:* "Saint-François de Sales, Descartes, Corneille." Neo 3: 1918, 89–99. See 423.

3266 —: Descartes. Leer en leven. s'Gravenhage, Nijhoff, 1930. xii, 295 p. See 125 and 3267.

3267 —: Descartes, l'homme et le penseur. Préface de Henri Gouhier. Paris, PUF – Éditions françaises d'Amsterdam, 1951. 362 p. [French translation of 3266]. See 125.

3268 —: "Descartes' levenskunst (briefwisseling met Prinses Elisabeth)." De Gids 1929/2, 77–101.

"Rapporte la morale de Descartes à son tempérament, et en analyse les éléments chrétiens et stoiciens." [Pos-Steenbergen, Rsyn 1937, 113.]

3269 —: "Descartes' Discours de la méthode. Doel en karakter van dit geschrift." De Gids 101/2: 1937, 270–84.

3270 —: "Descartes' moraal en persoonlijkheid." ANTWP 31: 1937, 8–16. [A commemorative lecture.]

3271 —: "Descartes, l'homme et le croyant." In: Descartes et le cartésianisme hollandais (see 38), 45–70. 1951.

3272 *Serrus, Charles:* La méthode de Descartes et son application à la métaphysique. Alcan, 1933. 125 p. (BPC). Thèse Paris. See 231.

3273 —: "Au Congrès Descartes: Les problèmes de la méthode des sciences et de la transcendance." Runiv 47, no. 6: 1938, 19–29.

3274 *Sertillanges, le P. Antonin-Gilbert* [i.e. Antonin-Dalmace], *S.J.:* Le christianisme et les philosophes. Vol. 2: Les temps modernes. L'âge moderne. Paris, Aubier, 1941, 592 p. Vol. 2, Ch. 8: La révolution cartésienne. Ch. 9: La postérité de Descartes (Pascal, Malebranche, Leibniz, Spinoza).

Though Cartesianism secularized philosophy, "Descartes est un philosophe chrétien de tradition, de volonté et pour une large part de doctrine" (p. 68).

3275 *Seyfarth, Heinrich:* Louis de la Forge und seine Stellung im Occasionalismus. Ein Beitrag zur Geschichte der Philosophie. Gotha, Behrend, 1887. ii, 59 p. Dissertation Göttingen.

3276 *Seyring, F.:* "Über Descartes' Urteilslehre." AGP 6: 1893, 43–59.

"Willensdeterminierung und Urteil; das falsche und das wahre Urteil."

3277 *Sganzini, Carlo:* "Le fonti del principio gnoseologico vichiano e il significato della opposizione di Vico al cartesianismo." Sophia 1937. [Barié, see 129.]

See also author's "Vico gegen Descartes" in: Der kleine Bund (Literarische Beilage des Bund, Bern), October 1937.

Shestov (Shestoff): see Chestov.

3278 *Sichirollo, Livio:* "Problematica cartesiana e storiografia idealistica. Note sull'aforisma e sulla genesi dell'interpretazione dell' idealismo." StU 26: 1952, 152–80.

3279 *Sidgwick, H.:* "On the fundamental doctrines of Descartes." Mind 7: 1882, 435–40.

3280 *Sierra, M. J.:* "Las pasiones y Descartes." UC Bolivariana (Medellin) 1: 1937, 265–90.

3281 *Signoret, E.:* "Cartésianisme et aristotélisme." RMM 44: 1937, 287–304.

Letting Descartes speak for himself most of the way, author deftly leads up to the point that "le thomisme est bien l'air que respire le cartésianisme naissant" and that the Cartesian return to the "inspiration de Platon" must be judged relatively to Aristotelianism (p. 299): in the end, the revolutionary method of Descartes is "orientée vers l'application, dans tous les sens du mot. L'intelligence, pour lui, ressemble, plus qu'au discours, à l'habitude elle-même," and the elliptic treatment of the title topic culminates in the equally elliptic but transparent statement that: "La vérité ressemble plus à la coutume qu'à l'instabilité" (p. 304).

3282 *Sigwart, H. C. W.:* Über den Zusammenhang des Spinozismus mit der Cartesischen Philosophie. Ein philosophischer Versuch. Tübingen, 1816.

3283 *Silva Carvalho, Augusto da:* "O cartesianismo e a medicina em Portugal." AcLisboa. Classe de ciências. Memórias. 2: 1939, 71–107. See 430.

3284 *Simon, Daniel:* "Nietzsche et le rationalisme français." CDS 25/205: 1938, 357–61.

Descartes and Voltaire.

3285 *Simon, H.:* "Deux attitudes de philosophes chrétiens: Pascal contre Descartes." Nouvelle revue des jeunes, 25 July 1929.

3286 *Simoncini, Helda:* Le prime polemiche sulle meditazioni di Descartes. Palermo, Trimarchi, 1930. 131 p.

3287 *Simone, Ludovico de:* "La morale provvisoria nel Discurso del metodo di Cartesio." Cartesio, 299–303. 1937.

3289 *Sirven, J. (abbé):* Les années d'apprentissage de Descartes (1596–1628). Albi, Impr. coopérative du sud-ouest, 1928. Thèse Paris. Also: Paris, Vrin, 1930. 498 p. See 100.

3290 —: Bibliographie des Années d'apprentissage de Descartes. Albi, Imprimerie coopérative du Sud-Ouest, 1928. 34 p. (Thèse complementaire, Paris.) Also in his: Années d'apprentissage de Descartes (Vrin, 1930), p. 471–98. See 20.

3291 — (editor): Descartes. Règles pour la direction de l'esprit. Paris, Vrin, 1945. Reprinted 1959. B.T.P. See 92.

3292 —: "La déduction cartésienne dans les recherches mathématiques et physiques." Cartesio 745–51. 1937.

Cartesian "deduction" designates both mathematical and experimental (inductive) reasoning.

3293 —: "Le Discours de la méthode et l'évolution de la pensée cartésienne." BLET 38: 1937, 145–66, 193–212.

Review of Descartes' formative period (to 1628), with discussion of the historical value of the autobiographical part of DM.

3294 —: "L'idéalisme cartésien." Acta Secundi Cong. Thom. Int. (no. 41), 518–22. 1937.

Descartes' methodological idealism (nosse ad esse valet consequentia) is neither a metaphysical nor a critical idealism.

3295 *Sirwy, Alain:* "Clef des songes." MerF 308: Feb. 1950, 262–78.

Contributes nothing new on Descartes' dreams.

3296 *Sitkovskij, E.:* "Dekart i francuzkij materializm." Pod znamenem Marksizma, no. 8, 1937.

D. and French materialism. [In Russian.]

3297 *Siwek, Paul (S.J.):* "La théorie cartésienne du vide implique-t-elle le panthéisme?" Cartesio 753–59. 1937.

Only by equivocation can pantheism be derived from Descartes' concept of the external world. His theory of creation "se rapproche singulièrement de la thèse de S. Thomas" in his De aeternitate mundi contra murmurantes.

3298 —: "Problema valoris in philosophia S. Thomae et Cartesii." Greg 18: 1937, 518–33. Cf. Bull. thomiste 6: 1940–42, 196–97.

3299 *Six, Karl (S.J.):* "Descartes im Jesuitenkolleg von La Flèche. Zur Chronologie im Leben Descartes'." ZKT 38: 1914, 494–508. See 101.

3300 —: "Die 'Objectiones septimae' zu Descartes' 'Meditationes'. Zur Charakteristik der Beziehungen zwischen Descartes und den Jesuiten." ZKT 38: 1914, 161–182. See 338.

3301 —: "Die Gottesbeweise Descartes' in der Kritik seiner Zeitgenossen. Ein Beitrag zur Geschichte des Rationalismus." ZKT 38: 1914, 705–722.

A study of the controversy over Descartes' proofs in the Objections and Responses to MM.

3302 *Slebodziński, Wladimir:* "Rola Descartesa w rozwuju novożytnej matematiki." KF 19: 1950, 67–70.

Descartes' role in the development of mathematics. [In Polish.]

3303 *Slök, Johannes:* Den filosofiske rationalisme. Descartes-Spinoza-Leibniz. Bidrag til filosofiens historie. Copenhagen, Gad, 1952. 76 p.

3304 *Smart, H. J. C.:* "Descartes and the wax." PhQ 1: October 1950, 50–57. See 235c.

3305 *Smart, Harold Robert:* The philosophic presuppositions of mathematical logic. New York, Longmans Green, 1925.

On the Cartesian roots of modern logic.

3306 *Smith, David Eugene* (transl., editor): The Geometry of René Descartes. 1925. See 88.

3307 *Smith, Norman Kemp:* Studies in the Cartesian philosophy. London, Macmillan, 1902. xiv, 276 p. Reprinted: New York, Russell & Russell, 1962. See 192b.

3308 —: New studies in the philosophy of Descartes; Descartes as pioneer. London, Macmillan (New York, St. Martin's Press), 1952. xii, 370 p. See 193.

3309 *Snow, A. J.:* "Descartes' method and the revival of interest in mathematics." Monist 33: 1923, 611–17.

Stresses the inductive part in Descartes' Method which is too often misinterpreted as Euclidean deductiveness.

3310 —: "Newton's objections to Descartes' astronomy." Monist 34: 1924, 543–57.

3311 *Soddy, Frederick:* Cartesian economics. The bearing of physical science upon state stewardship. London, Henderson's, 1922, 22 p.

Neither Cartesian nor economics.

3312 *Sodnik, Alma:* "Descartes. Ob tristoletnici njegovega dela." Sodobnost (Ljubliana) 5: 1937–38, 392–401.

Commemorative article. [In Slovene.]

3313 —: "Der Begriff des Wollens in der Theorie der Erkenntnis bei Descartes und Spinoza." CD 1: 141–46. 1937.

3314 *Sokolov, V. V.:* "Filosofija Dekarta i ideologičeskaja bor'ba v sovremennoj Francii." VF 2: 1950, 104–27. Transl.: La philosophie actuelle et la lutte idéologique en France à l'heure actuelle. Paris, Comité Central du Parti Communiste Français. Études et documents théoriques no. 1, Sept. 1951.

Official Stalinist view: D., falsified by Blondel, Gilson, Laporte, Sarte, was materialist and anticlerical.

Reviewed by M. Soriano in Pensée 1952, no. 40, 113–14 ("admirable study.")

3315 —: Art. "Dekart." In: Bolšaja Soveckaja Enciklopedija, 2nd ed., 13: 596–600 (1952). German tr. by Else Jandera: d'Alembert, Demokrit, Descartes, Diderot. Grosse Sowjet-Enzyklopädie, Reihe Geschichte und Philosophie, v. 27, 17–33. Berlin, Aufbau-Verlag, 1954. See 150.

3316 *Soleri, G.:* "Realismo e fenomenismo." Segni dei tempi (Firenze) 9: 1942, 49–68. See 1277 (Bontadini).

3317 —: "Il realismo e alcune sue implicanze." RFNS 35: 1943, 125–29. See 1277 (Bontadini).

3318 *Sommer, Robert:* Locke's Verhältnis zu Descartes. Preisschrift der Berliner Universität. Berlin, Mayer und Müller, 1887, 63 p. [BM]

3319 *Sommer, R.:* Die Entstehung der mechanistischen Schule in der Heilkunde am Ausgang des 17. Jahrhunderts. Ein Vortrag. Leipzig, F. C. W. Vogel, 1889. 23 p.

3320 *Soriano, Marc:* "Ouvrages récents sur Descartes." Pensée 40: Jan-Feb 1952, 107–14. See 31.

3321 *Sortais, Gaston (S.J.):* La philosophie moderne depuis Bacon jusqu'à Leibniz. Études historiques. P. Lethielleux, 1920–22. Vol. 1: Francis Bacon. Vol. 2: Gassendi et Hobbes.

Richly documented work. A third volume on Descartes was planned but not published (references to v. 3, 1929 are erroneous).

3322 —: Le cartésianisme chez les Jésuites français au XVIIe et au XVIIIe siècle. Aph 6, no. 3, 1929. 109 p. See 466.

3323 —: "Descartes et la Compagnie de Jésus; ménaces et advances, 1640–46." E 57: 1937, 441–68. See 466.

3324 *Soto, Luis Emilio:* "Discurso sin método sobre Descartes." Escritos 287–94. 1937.

3325 *S(ouday), P.:* "Descartes et Constantin Huygens." Temps, 7 December 1925.

3326 —: "De Ronsard à Descartes." Temps, 25 June 1928.

3327 *Souilhé, Joseph:* La philosophie chrétienne de Descartes à nos jours. Vol. 1: De Descartes à Châteaubriand. Paris, Bloud & Gay, 1934. (Bibl. catholique des sciences religieuses, v. 51).

3328 *Sousa, J. Fernando de:* "Descartes e o seu Discurso do Método." AcLisboa, Classe de ciências. Memórias 2: 1939, 109–24.

Commemorative lecture stresses Descartes' conflict with Scholastics, notes his alleged errors and triumphs.

3329 *Sousa-Ribeiro, Ilídio de (Fr.):* Francisco de Santo Agostino de Macedo. Um filósofo escotista português e um paladino da Restauração. Coimbra, Acta Univ. Coimbrigensis, 1952. 177 p. See also 1504.

3330 *Spann, Othmar:* Philosophenspiegel. Die Hauptlehren der Philosophie begrifflich und lehrgeschichtlich dargestellt. Leipzig, Quelle & Meyer, 1934. (Wissenschaft und Bildung).

Cartesianism is one of the "Fehl- und Mischsysteme des Idealismus" (226–30): "Nicht mit dem Zweifel soll der Mensch beginnen, sondern mit dem Glauben."

3331 *Spaventa, Bertrando:* La filosofia italiana nelle sue relazioni con la filosofia europea. Bari, Laterza, 1909.

See p. 203–11, 256–65 et passim on Descartes (important, according to Ottaviani).

3332 *Spectorsky, Eugene:* "Descartesov utjecaj na društvene nauke." Arhiv za pravne i drustvene nauke 5: 1937, 401–08.

Descartes' influence on the social sciences. [In Croatian.]

3333 *Spiegelberg, Herbert:* "Indubitables in ethics: a Cartesian meditation." Ethics 58: 1947–48, 35–50.

Descartes failed to extend hyperbolic doubt to ethics; not until Husserl was this step taken. Spiegelberg tries to carry the Cartesian principle into the field of ethics.

3333a —: "The new 'cogito': Being-within-the-world (Être-au-monde)." In his: The phenomenological movement, v. 2, The Hague, Nijhoff, 1960, 549–552. See 311a.

3334 *Spink, J. S.:* French thought from Gassendi to Voltaire. University of London, Athlone Press, 1960. ix, 345 p. See 466a.

3335 *Spir, African:* "Réflexions sur Descartes." RPFE 141: 1951, 312–13.

3336 *Spitzer, Leo:* "Le poêle de Descartes." MLN 56: 1941, 110–13.

A linguistic note on the word "poêle," and a welcome one.

3337 *Spoerri, Theodor:* "La puissance métaphorique de Descartes." Royaumont 273–87; discussion, 288–301. See 403.

3338 *Springmeyer, Heinrich:* "Zur Lehre des Descartes von den res simplices." Actes du XIe Cong. Int. de philos. 13: 18–24. 1953.

Nikolai Hartmann objected to the notion of res simplices because it leads to an aprioristic-deductive ontology. Author points out that Descartes dealt with things not "prout revera existent" but "in ordine ad cognitionem nostram": his doctrine may yet prove useful.

3339 *Spruzzola, Ciribini:* "Francisco Sánchez alla luce delle ultime ricerche." RFNS 28: 1936, 372–91. See 277.

3340 *Streenivasa Iyengar, K. R.:* "The nature of Descartes' method." CD 2: 15–20. 1937.

Descartes' méthode is not deductive but presuppositional.

Stabeck, Bernhard: see Grubbe et al.

3341 *Starcke, Carl Nicolai:* René Descartes, 31te marts 1596 - 11te februar 1650; mindefortrag holdt paa universitetet den 10. november 1919. Copenhagen 1919 (p. 148–160). [Harvard.]

Note the date of this memorial lecture: the tercentenary of Descartes' Dream.

3342 *Starobinsky, J.:* "Descartes et la médicine." SynB 7: 1953, 333–38.

Descartes method was not based on experience, which explains the difficulties of Cartesian medicine. Our knowledge has since widened, but the unity of man is lost. What remains of Descartes' work is the idea of quantitative research [BAn 1954, 12997.]

3343 *Staubach, Charles Neff:* "Feijóo on Cartesianism; a chapter on French influence in Spain." Michigan Academy of science, arts and letters 24, no. 4: 79–87, 1938. Michigan thesis abstract. See 449.

3344 —: "Feijóo and Malebranche." HR 1941, 287–96. See 449.

3345 *Stein, Karl Heinrich von:* "Über den Zusammenhang Boileau's mit Descartes." ZPPK 86: 1885, 199–275. See 424.

3346 *Steinbüchel, Theodor:* "Franz von Baaders Descartes-Kritik im Rahmen ihrer Zeit und in ihrer grundsätzlichen Bedeutung." WW 10: 1943, 41-60, 103–26; 11: 1944, 24–42. See 466b.

3347 *Steinitzer, M.:* Die menschlichen und tierischen Gemütsbewegungen als Gegenstand der Wissenschaft. Ein Beitrag zur Geschichte des neueren Geisteslebens. München, Literarisch-artistische Anstalt, 1889. vi, 256 p.

3348 *Sterkman, P.:* "De betekenis van Descartes als methodisch denker." Annalen d. crit. philosophie (ANTWP, suppl.) 5: 1934, 81–97.

3349 —: De betekenis van Descartes' wijsgeerige methode. Assen, van Gorcum, (1937). 40 p. [See the summary of this lecture in: Haagsch Maandblad 2: 1937, 162–69.]

3350 *Stewart, Dugald:* The collected works of Dugald Stewart, ed. Sir William Hamilton. Edinburgh, Constable, 1854–58. 10 vols. See 223.

Vol. 1: Dissertation, exhibiting the metaphysical, ethical and political philosophy, since the revival of letters in Europe, p. 112–141. See also vol. 2, p. 90ff., 473ff. on Thomas Reid and Descartes, and the Index (v. 10 s.v. Descartes) for summaries of the arguments.

3351 *Stewart, H. L.:* "The Cartesian tercentenary. Descartes and his age." Transactions of the Royal Society of Canada, Section 2, 31: 1937, 1–11. [Presidential address.]

3352 *Stewart, W. F. M.:* "A survey of work on 17th century rationalism, 1945–51. Part I: Descartes, Geulincx, Leibniz." PhQ 2: 1952, 359–68. See 32.

3353 *Stewart, William McC:* "Descartes and poetry." RR 29: 1938, 212–42. See 425.

3354 —: "Racine et Descartes." RCC 39, pt. 2: 1937–38, 385–94, 499–511. Also: Boivin, 1938, 23 p. See 414.

3355 *Stieler, Georg:* "Descartes." Literarische Berichte aus dem Gebiete der Philosophie 5: 1925, 25–28. (Forschungsberichte, Heft 5). [A review of four books].

3356 *Stock, Hyman:* The method of Descartes in the natural sciences. Jamaica, Marion Press, 1931. 95 p. Columbia dissertation.

3357 *Stock, Otto:* Descartes' Grundlegung der Philosophie. Dissertation Greifswald, 1888. 64 p.

3358 *Stöcker, Ferdinand:* Das Problem der Methode bei Descartes. Bonn, Georgi, 1911. 64 p. Dissertation Bonn.

The method of the Regulae, of Descartes' metaphysics and physics. Cf. PhdG 3: 1911, no. 1189, and RMM v.20: 1912, suppl.

3359 *Stölzle, Remigius:* "Descartes und die Scholastik." Historisch-politische Blätter für das katholische Deutschland 124: 1899, 29–35.

3360 *Stout, A. K.:* "The basis of knowledge in Descartes." Mind 38: 1929, 330–42, 458–72.

Obscurities left by Descartes and his interpreters regarding the cogito, distinct and clear ideas, veracity of God, in their systematic relationship. See 3362.

3361 —: "Descartes' proof of the existence of matter." Mind 41: 1932, 191–207. See 340.

3362 —: "The alleged petitio principii in Descartes' appeal to the veracity of God." CD 1: 125–31. 1937.

Author rejects his earlier view (see 3360) that Descartes did commit a circle. Careful analysis of the problem yields a valid reply to the charge of circularity, which author believes to represent Descartes' own view, however ambiguously he expressed himself. Important contribution.

3363 *Straus, Erwin (W.):* "Descartes' Bedeutung für die moderne Psychologie." CD 9: 52–59, 1937.

Only the mechanistic part of Descartes' psychology of error was influential, until modern psychology developed its anthropological part.

3364 —: "Some remarks about awakeness." TP 18: Sept. 1956. 20 p.

A psychiatrist's comment on Descartes' difficulties in finding a reality criterion to decide between sleeping and waking: "The choice is not between two predicates, real-unreal or true-false"; "the one who awakens is not a 'mind' making judgments, not a 'consciousness' attending to an outside world but a human being experiencing the world in its corporeality" (15–16). See also author's: Vom Sinn der Sinne. Berlin-Göttingen-Heidelberg, Springer, 1956, ch. 2.

3365 *Stroh, Alfred H.:* "Relics of Descartes' visit to Sweden, especially a newly discovered portrait by David Beck." Bericht über den III. Int. Kongr. f. Philos. Heidelberg, 1908, p. 241.

3366 —: "The Cartesian controversy at Upsala, 1663–1689, its connections with Swedenborg's nebular hypothesis." In: Bericht über den III. Internationalen Kongress für Philosophie zu Heidelberg, 1908, p. 248–55. See 466c.

3367 *Strong, Edward William:* Procedures and metaphysics. A study in the philosophy of mathematical-physical sciences in the 16th and 17th centuries. Berkeley, University of California Press (London UP) 1936. vii, 301 p. Columbia dissertation.

3368 *Strowski, Félix:* Pascal et son temps. Paris, Plon, 1907–8. Vol. 1: De Montaigne à Pascal.

3369 —: "Descartes et la science." In his: La sagesse française: Montaigne, saint François de Sales, Descartes, La Rochefoucauld, Pascal. Paris, Plon, 1925, ch. 6, 137–69.

3370 *Struve, Wolfgang:* "Das 'ergo' in Descartes' 'ego cogito, ergo sum' und 'sum, ergo Deus est'." Lexis 2, no. 2: 1950–51, 239–61. See 342.

3371 *Studnička, F. J.:* Article in: Jednota československých matematikú a fysikú v Praze. Slavnost pořadaná na pamět 300-letých zenin R. Descartesa v Praze dne 6. Prosince 1896. Náklada Jednoty českých matematikú, 1897. 36 p. See 501.

3372 *Suárez, Sofía:* "En torno a Descartes, filósofo." Escritos 295–300. 1937.

3373 —: "Descartes y Pascal. La 'gnosis'." Homenaje 2: 173–97. 1937.

Collection of quotations; no new findings.

3374 *Susini, E.:* Franz von Baader et le romantisme mystique. Paris, Vrin, 1942 v. 3, 185–94. See 466b.

3375 *Suter, Rufus:* "Science without experiment. A study of Descartes." Scientific Monthly 1944, 265–68.

3376 *Swarte, Victor de:* Descartes directeur spirituel. Correspondance avec la princesse Palatine et la reine Christine de Suède. Paris, Alcan, 1904. iii, 292 p.

3377 *Świeżawski, Stefan:* "Tomistyczna a kartezjańska koncepcja człowieka." Prz 43: 1947, 87–104.

The Thomist and the Cartesian concept of man.

3378 *Sykes, Leslie Clifford:* A philosophy for the modern university. An inaugural lecture. Leicester (England), University College, 1951 (published 1952). 24 p.

3379 *Szasz, Thomas S.:* "The definition of psychosomatic disorder." BJPS 7: 1956–57, 231–34. See 3530.

3380 —: "Men and machines." BJPS 8: 1957–58, 310–17.

Szasz finds no difference between men and machines, from the psychological standpoint. See 2332.

3381 *Szczurat, W.:* "Zur Frage nach den nominalistischen Äusserungen bei Descartes." Lemberg, 1908. Programm. 6 p. [PhdG 1. no. 1732. Not listed in Bar.]

3382 *Szumowski, Wladyslaw:* "Kartezjusz i Malebranche jako poprzednicy teorii uczuć Karola Langego." Prz 8: 1905, 1–17.

Descartes and Malebranche, "forerunners of the affective theory of Karl Lange" (mechanistic theory of passions).

T

3383 *Tabbah, Bichare* [i.e. Bishāra Tabbākh]: "Le cartésianisme et l'École du droit de la nature des gens." In his: Du heurt à l'harmonie des droits; essai doctrinal sur les fondements du droit, suivi d'exemples tirés des systèmes juridiques du Levant. Paris, Desclé de Brouwers, 1936, p. 67–102. (Bibl. internatl. de philosophie du droit, v. 3). Thèse Paris. See 466d.

3384 *Taborda, Saúl A.:* "Descartes y el ideal pedagógico francés." Escritos 301–27. 1937. See 265.

3385 *Tannery, Paul* and Ch. Adam (ed.): Œuvres de Descartes. 1897–1913. See 74.

3386 —: Mémoires scientifiques publiés par J. L. Heiberg et H. G. Zeuthen. Vol. 6, edited by Gino Loria. Paris, Gauthier-Villars, 1926. 608 p. See 397.

3387 —: La correspondance de Descartes dans les inédits du Fonds Libri, étudiée pour l'histoire des mathématiques. Gauthiers-Villars, 1893. vii, 94 p. Reprinted: See 3386, v. 6, 149–268.

3388 —: "Descartes physicien." RMM 4: 1896, 479–88. Reprinted: See 3386, v. 6, 305–19.

Attempts to determine the rank of Galilei and Descartes as physicists: neither of them was an experimental physicist in the modern sense; Galilei a mathematician leaning towards applied physics, Descartes a system-builder without the desire (though not without the ability) to make exact experiments. Thesis corroborated by brief, precise survey of the concrete physical problems which Descartes tackled.

3389 —: "Un mot sur Descartes." AGP 16: 1903, 301–06.

Rejoinder to Pfeffer (ibid., 1–26) concerning Descartes' work during the critical years 1629–30.

3390 —: "Sur une erreur mathématique de Descartes." AGP 17 (ns 10): 1904, 334–40.

Answers J. Chazottes (ibid., 171–75): Descartes did indeed err regarding the law of free fall, while Beeckman was right. See 1519.

3390a —: Art. "Géométrie de Descartes." In: La Grande Encyclopédie 14: 219–20. Reprinted: See 3386, v. 6, p. 530–36.

3390b —: "Pour l'histoire du problème inverse des tangentes." See 3386, v. 6, p. 457–77.

3390c —: "Les Excerpta ex mss. R. Descartes." (1899). See 3386, v. 6, 323–55.

3390d —: "Une lettre inédite de Descartes" [to Mersenne, Endegeest, 20 oct. 1642]. RPFE 22: 1886, 293–96.,

3391 *Tannery, Mme Paul* (publisher): Correspondance du P. Marin Mersenne. 1932ff. See 82.

3392 *Taton, René:* "La vie et l'œuvre scientifique de Descartes." Nature (Paris) April 1950, 121–24.

3393 *Taylor, A. E.:* "Back to Descartes." Phil 16: 1941, 126–37. See 155.

3394 *Taylor, William:* The relationship between psychology and science. New York, Grune & Stratton, 1953. 243 p.

Rejecting the "ghost-in-the-machine" model (see Ryle), Taylor attempts to retain Descartes' epistemological dualism while abandoning Cartesian psycho-physical dualism.

3395 *Teicher, Jacob:* "Spunti cartesiani nella filosofia arabo-giudaica." GCFI 16: 1935, 101–30, 235–49. See 344.

3396 *Teixeira, F.-G.:* "Sobre o folium de Descartes." Annaes científicos da Academia polytécnica do Porto (Coimbra) 1913, 186. [Schrecker]

3397 *Teixeira, Lívio:* "A religião de Descartes; notas à margem de alguns livros." Revista de história (São Paulo), 6 (v. 10): 1955, 171–208. See 345.

3398 —: Ensaio sôbre a moral de Descartes. São Paulo, Boletim da faculdade de filosofia, ciências y letras, 1955. 224 p. See 231.a.

3399 *Tellier, Auguste:* Descartes et la médicine ou les relations de Descartes avec les médecins de son temps, suivi d'un exposé des idées médicales de Descartes. Paris, Vigné, 1928. 72 p. (Thèses médicales, Paris, no. 491). See 365.

3400 *Temple, William* (Archbishop of York, later of Canterbury). "The Cartesian Faux-Pas." "Mathematics and Logic." In his: Nature, man and God. The Gifford Lectures 1932–33, 1933–34. London, Macmillan, 1934, Lecture III and IV, p. 57–108. See 193a.

3401 *Tennemann, Wilhelm Gottlieb:* "Geschichte der Philosophie des René Descartes." In his: Geschichte der Philosophie, v. 10, Leipzig, Ambrosius Barth, 1817, 198–317. "Malebranche," ibid., 317–74.

The Descartes chapter also treats followers and adversaries. Cf. Hagmann (see 10), 77–78.

3402 *Tennenbaum, Anne:* "Descartes i jego bête-machine." Prz 32: 1929, 169–81.

Notes the relaxation in Descartes' formulation of the beastmachine theory around

1646–49 (letters to Newcastle and Henry More), admitting that animals have consciouness. Cf. Lubnicki (see 15), p. 105.

3403 [*Tercentenary* of the death of R. Descartes]. Vestnik Akad. Nauk SSSR, May 1950.

Report on the commemorative session of the Soviet Academy of Science, history of philosophy section. [In Russian.]

3404 *Terraillon, Eugène:* La morale de Geulincx dans ses rapports avec la philosophie de Descartes. Paris, Alcan, 1912. ii, 226 p. Thèse complémentaire, Paris. [Cf. PhdG 4: 1912, 1751.]

3405 *Teucher, A.:* Die geophysikalischen Anschauungen Descartes'. Dresden, Adam, 1908. 85 p. Dissertation Leipzig.

3406 *Tex, Jan den:* "Descartes et les Hollandais." BAFH 10, no. 10: 1929.

3407 *Thamin, Raymond:* "Les idées morales au XVIIe siècle." RCC 1896. ()

3408 *Thévenaz, Pierre:* "La conscience de soi dans le cogito cartésien." In: L'homme, métaphysique et conscience de soi. Neuchâtel, Baconnière, 1948, 17–35. (Être et pensée, v. 27).

3409 —: "La question du point de départ radical chez Descartes et chez Husserl." In: Problèmes actuels de la phénoménologie (Actes du colloque international de phénoménologie, 1951). Bruxelles, Desclée de Brouwer, 1952, 9–30. See 174.

3410 *Thibaudet, A.* (editor): "Un ballet de Descartes." RGenève 1: 1920, 163–85. See 78.

3411 *Thijssen-Schoute, C. Louise:* Nederlands cartesianisme. Amsterdam, N.V. Noord-Hollandsche Uitgevers, 1954, 744 p. (Verhandelingen der K. Nederlandse Akademie van Wetenschappen, Afd. Letterkunde, ns. v. 60). See 467.

3412 —: "Le cartésianisme néerlandais." Proceedings of the Tenth intern. Cong. of Philos., Amsterdam, 1948, 1128–29.

3413 —: "Descartes en het Nederlands cartesianisme." ANTWP 42: 1950, 152–59.

3414 —: "Le cartésianisme aux Pays-Bas." In: Descartes et le cartésianisme hollandais (see 38), 183–260. 1950.

3415 —: "Een correspondent van Descartes: Andreas Colvius." NAK 38: 1952, 224–45.

3417 —: Lodewijk Meyer en diens verhouding tot Descartes en Spinoza. Leiden, Brill, 1954. 28 p. (Mededelingen vanwege het Spinozahuis).

Reviewed by L. in NAK 40: 1954, 256.

3418 *Thilly, Frank:* "Locke's relation to Descartes." PhR 9: 1900, 597–612.

3419 *Thilo, Christfried Albert:* "Die Religionsphilosophie des Descartes." Zeitschrift für exakte Philosophie 3: 1862, 121–82. Reprinted in his: Die Religionsphilosophie des Descartes und Malebranche. Langensalza, Beyer, 1906, 76 p. (Religionsphilosophie in Einzeldarstellungen, ed. D. Flügel, v. 6).

Protestant analysis. Finds the seeds of Spinozian monism and Leibnizian pluralism in Descartes.

3420 *Thomas, Antoine Léonard:* Éloge de René Descartes. Discours qui a remporté le prix de l'Académie Française en 1765. Paris, Regnard, 1765. 126 p. Also in his: Œuvres diverses, Amsterdam, Moutard, 1773, v. 4, p. 3–172. Reprinted by Victor Cousin in v. 1 of his edition of Descartes' works (1824). See 126.

3421 *Thomas, F.:* "Descartes et Gassendi." APC 118 (ns 20): September 1889, 548–85.

Careful study of Gassendi's Objections regarding cogito and proofs of God. Gassendi finds Descartes' weak spots; instead of using the controversy to advance his own views, he forces Descartes to be more precise in his statements. Gassendi's Objections therefore do not always reflect his own viewpoint.

3422 *Thomas, Jacques-François:* "Le rationalisme de Descartes." Rsyn 63: 1948, 73–83 [Review article].

3422a —: "Pascal et Descartes. Compatibilités et incompatibilités." Rsyn 80: 1959, 113–19.

Despite Pascal's anticartesianism, Thomas sees a certain compatibility between Pascal's analytical spirit and Descartes' rationalism.

3423 *Thomas, L. E.:* "Waking and dreaming." Analysis 13: 1953, 121–37. See 306.

3424 *Thomist Congress 1936:* See 41.

3425 *Thorndike, Lynn:* "The cursus philosophicus before Descartes." AIHS 4: 1950, 16–24.

Uses four early 17th century courses (2 unpublished) to illustrate, with concrete examples, pre-Cartesian scientific instruction in France.

3426 —: "The attitude of Francis Bacon and Descartes toward magic and occult science." In: E. A. Underwood (ed.), Science, medicine and history; essays .... in honor of Charles Singer. Oxford UP, 1953, v. 1, p. 451–54.

Thorndyke's collection of superstitious notions in Bacon's works is intriguing, amusing, and rich, but although he introduces D. with Gilson's comment that Cartesian philosophy was largely a clear explanation of facts which do not exist, his search for such facts yields almost nothing (p. 453–54). Gilson had a different kind of fact in mind.

3427 *Thouverez, Émile:* "La famille Descartes d'après les documents publiés par les Sociétés savantes de Poitou, de Touraine et de la Bretagne." AGP 12 (ns 5): 1899, 505–28; 13 (ns 6): 1900, 550–77. Bibliography.

Valuable compte-rendu of the many scattered studies on the subject.

3428 —: "La vie de Descartes d'après Baillet." APC 117 (ns 19): March 1899, 646–67; APC 118 (ns 20): April 1899, 58–78; May, 160–76; July, 440–52; August, 523–42; February 1900, 515–34, March, 618–30.

3429 —: "Troisième centenaire du Discours de la méthode." AcToulouse. Mémoires sér. 12, 16: 1938, 2–32.

3430 *Tiger, J.:* "De la méthode cartésienne: Aristote et Descartes. APC 1897, 74–84.

3431 *Tilman-Timon, Alexandru:* Etica lui Descartes. Bucureşti, Vacarescu, 1946. 67 p. Reprinted 1947. See 231a.

3432 *Tissi, Silvio:* L'ironia creatrice. Il Dio di Cartesio e il nulla di Leopardi. Da un problema critico a un dramma religioso. Milano, Colgiati, 1922. 99 p.

3433 —: Cartesio. Milano, Athena, 1926. 89 p. (I maestri del pensiero.)

"Lyrical but evocative" [Bontadini I]

3434 *Tocco, F.:* "Descartes jugé par Vico." RMM 4: 1896, 568–72. See 461.

3435 *Todhunter, Isaac:* A history of the theory of elasticity and of the strength of materials, from Galilei to the present time. [Posthumous]. Edited by Karl Pearson, v. 1: Galilei to Saint-Venant (1639–1850), Cambridge UP, 1886.

3436 *Toffanin, G.:* "Cartesio e il classicismo aristotelico." In his: La fine del umanesimo. Torino, 1920, 247ff. [Cited by Robertson; see 420, p. 7].

3437 *Tokoro, T.:* [The God of Descartes; an analysis of its to determinations, perfectissimum and infinitum.] Tetsugaku zasshi 1952, no. 1, 60–81. [In Japanese. Rép. 7: 1955, 454].

3438 *Toohey, John (S.J.):* "The mythical doubter." Thought 8: 1934, 606–14.

3439 *Torciani, L.:* "L'argomento ontologico di Sant'Anselmo nella storia della filosofia." RRFC: 1911, 7: 1912.

Pt. 3: Descartes and Gassendi. Pt. 4: Bossuet, Malebranche, Fénelon (6: 1911, 82–89, 119–29, 231–39, 333–48). Survey carried forward to Rosmini, Gioberti, Mamiani, and other 19th century Italian philosophers. Cf. PhdG 4: 1912, 2628.

3440 *Tornau, Hartwig:* Syntaktische und stilistische Studien über Descartes. Leipzig, Hoffmann, 1900. 91 p. Dissertation Leipzig. See 403.

3441 *Touchard, Georges:* La morale de Descartes. Paris, Leroux, 1898. 152 p. Thèse Dijon.

Review: F. Pillon in AnPh 9: 1898, 312–13 (superficial treatment of the relationship between Descartes' ethics and the general movement of ideas of the time).

3441a *Travaux* du IXe Congrès Intern. de Philosophie (Congrès Descartes). See 36.

3442 *Trendelenburg, A.:* "Ist Leibniz in seiner Entwickelung einmal Spinozist oder Cartesianer gewesen?" AcBerlin, Monatsberichte, 1857. [Varet]

3443 "*Tricentenario* de la muerte de Descartes." Comercio (Lima, Peru) May 17, 1950, evening edition.

3444 "*Le tricentennaire* du Discours de la méthode. Descartes à la Bibliothèque Nationale." Illustration 197: 1937, 21 August, p. 531. See 1.

3444a *Tricentennaire* du Discours de la méthode, 1637–1937. Le glâneur châtelleraudais, 1937. See 518.

3445 *Trognitz, B.*: Die mathematische Methode in Descartes' philosophischem Systeme. Saalfeld, Wiedemann, 1887. 16 p. [Col.]

3445a *Troisième centenaire* de Descartes. Tours, 1897. See 504.

3446 *Tropfke, J.*: "Das 'x' als Symbol der Unbekannten bei Descartes und seinen Nachfolgern." Archeion, 13: 1931. [Schrecker]

3447 *Trostler, Josef*: "Les cartésiens hongrois." Revue des études hongrois 12: 1934, 100–25. See 469.

3448 *Trouillard, J.*: "Sagesse platonique et sagesse cartésienne." In: La science et la sagesse; Actes du 5e Congrès des SPLF (Bordeaux). Paris, PUF 1950, 227–29.

3449 *Truc, Gonzague*: "La vraie figure de Descartes." Opinion, 5 March 1927.

3450 —: "Descartes et la raison." Grande revue 153: 1937, 107–09.

Tuduri de Coya: see García Tuduri de Coya.

3450a *Tulloch, John*: Rational theology and Christian philosophy in England in the seventeenth century. 2nd ed., Edinburgh and London, 1874. Vol. 2: The Cambridge Platonists. See 465.

Still useful for its treatment of John Smith, Ralph Cudworth and Henry More.

Turbiano: see Castro Turbiano.

3451 *Turbiglio, Sebastiano*: Storia della filosofia di Cartesio. Torino, Tipogr. Italiana, 1866. xxii, 83 p.

3452 —: Le antitesi tra il medio evo e l'età moderna nella storia della filosofia, in ispecie nella dottrina morale di Malebranche. Roma, 1877.

"Mediocrissimo lavoro italiano" (Del Noce) shows Descartes, Malebranche and Spinoza captives of "Scholastic aprioristic ontology." See Turbiglio's Preface for his other relevant works.

Turienzo, Alvarez: see Alvarez Turienzo.

3453 *Turrière, E.:* "La notion de transcendance géométrique chez Descartes et Leibnitz." Isis 2: 1914, 106–24.

3454 *Tvrdý, J.:* "Descartes et la pensée tchécoslovaque." CD 3: 140–45. 1937. See 15.

Descartes in Prague (p. 140–42).

3455 *Twardowski, Kasimir:* Idee und Perception. Erkenntnistheoretische Untersuchungen aus Descartes. Wien, Konegen, 1892. 46 p.

U

3456 *Umov, N. A.:* "Značenie Dekarta v istorii fisičesknikh nauk'." VFP 1896, 489–520.

D.'s importance in the history of the physical sciences. [In Russian.]

3457 *Urbain, Ch.:* Sur un opuscule du P. Daniel Huet. Paris, Le Clerc, 1911. 15 p. (Reprinted from: Bull. du bibliophile, 1911).

On a manuscript draft of Huet's Nouvelles mémoires (see 2249) and Huet's corrections.

3458 *Uriburu, C. P., and B. Blank:* "El problema de la causa en Descartes." Sustancia (Tucumán) 4: 1934, no. 14. [Brie 11667.]

3459 *Urmeneta, Fermín de:* "La psicología educativa de las pasiones según Luis Vives y Renato Descartes." In: Congreso Intern. de Pedagogía, Santander-San Sebastián, 1949, v. 2, Madrid, 1950.

3460 —: "Luis Vives y el tercer centenario del tratado cartesiano sobre 'Las pasiones'." RPGA 4/12: 1949, 681–92.

3461 *Useničnik, Alexius (Aleš):* "De methodo cartesiana." Cartesio 761–66. 1937.

Critique of Descartes' methodical doubt as "positive," hence as precluding any a priori road to certainty. His proofs of God are inconclusive.

3462 —: "René Descartes, oce moderne filozofije." Čas (Ljubliana) 30/10: 1937, 357–65.

Descartes as father of modern philosophy. [In Slovene.]

V

3463 *Valdez, A. M.:* "Descartes y el pensamiento moderno." RUC Perú April 1942. [Brie 11914.]

3464 *Valensin, Auguste (S.J.):* "Descartes." In his: Regards, v. 1, Aubier, 1955, 179–202.

Urbane popular essay on Descartes, a true believer because he was able to separate (rather than reconcile) faith and science.

3465 *Valéry, Paul:* Le retour de Hollande. Descartes et Rembrandt. Maastricht, A. A. M. Stols, 1926. 22 p. [Printed in 300 copies.] Also: Paris, Impr. M. Darantière. Figures de P. Guastalla. 41 p. Reprinted in his: Variété II, 21–38. Dutch transl.: De terugreis uit Holland. Bussum, A. M. Stols, 1926. See 194.

3466 —: "Fragment d'un Descartes." NRF 1 April 1925, 825–40. (Preface to: R. Descartes, Discours de la méthode, suivi de six lettres, de pensées et de fragments. Avant-propos de P. Valéry. Illustrations de G. Gorvel et J.-L. Perrichon. Paris, Helleu & Sergent, 1925. x, 207 p.) Reprinted in his: Variété II, 7–18. See 194.

3467 —: "Descartes." RMM 44: 1937, 693–710. See 194.

Review: Anon. in Mind 3: 1939, p. 118.

3468 —: "Une vue de Descartes." In: Les pages immortelles de Descartes, choisies et expliquées par Paul Valéry .... Paris, Éditions Corrêa, 1941, 7–66. Reprinted in his: Variété V, 209–53. English transl. by H. L. Binsse: The living thoughts of Descartes, presented by Paul Valéry. Philadelphia, McKay, 1947. See 194.

3469 —: "Seconde vue de Descartes." In his: Variété V, 254–59. See 194.

3470 *Valson, C.-A.:* "Descartes." In his: Les savants illustres du XVIe et du XVIIe siècle. Genève, 1880, 85–189.

3471 *Vanni-Rovighi, Sofia:* "Il cogito di Cartesio e il cogito di Husserl." Cartesio 767–80. 1937.

Descartes' cogito leads to an empirical self, Husserl's to a transcendental one; Husserl is preoccupied with staying within the cogito, Descartes with finding realities beyond it. Husserl's "Formale und transzendentale Logik" and "Logische Untersuchungen" provide the main texts.

3471a —: "L'ontologia spinoziana nei Cogitata metaphysica." RFNS 52: 1960, 399–412. [Question of its Cartesian character.]

3472 *Varet, Gilbert:* Manuel de bibliographie philosophique. Vol. 1: Les philosophes classiques. Paris, PUF, 1956. (Coll. Logos). See 21.

3473 *Vartanian, Aram:* Diderot and Descartes; the role of Cartesian ideas in the growth of scientific naturalism in 18th century France. Ann Arbor, University Microfilms, 1951. Columbia dissertation. See 3473a.

3473a —: Diderot and Descartes. A study of scientific naturalism in enlightenment. Princeton, Princeton UP, 1953. 336 p. (History of ideas series, v. 6). Italian translation by G. Garritano: Diderot e Descartes. Milano, Feltrinelli, 1956. 301 p. (Columbia dissertation). See 468.

3474 —: La Mettrie's L'Homme machine; a study in the origins of an idea. Critical edition with an introductory monograph and notes. Princeton UP, 1960. 264 p.

Text of the 1751 edition with apparatus. The introductory monograph relates La Mettrie's man-machine concept to D.'s beast-machine theory. Critical comment by Leonora Cohen Rosenfield in RR 52: 1961, 233–34.

3474a —: "Scientific literature. Medicine." In: A critical bibliography of French literature, v. 3 (see no. 3a), 1961, 462–76. See 397a.

3475 *Vasallo, Angel:* "Regreso intencionado al punto de partida de Descartes: conciencia y finitud." Escritos 230–35. 1937.

3476 *Vasquez, M. C.:* "La certeza cartesiana y el problematismo contemporáneo." RFChile 1: 1950, 397–418.

3477 *Vassails, Gérard:* "Descartes pionnier de la science moderne." Pensée 1950, (ns) no. 29, 10–22; no. 30, 69–72.

Forward-looking, progressive Descartes! – had not Engels recognized in him the prophet of machine age and mass production?

3477a *Vasil'ev, S. F.:* "Ěvoljucjonnye idei v filosofii Dekarta." In his: Iz istorii naučnykh mirovozzrenij. Moskva-Leningrad, 1935. [Evolutionary ideas in D.'s philosophy. In Russian.]

3478 *Vattier, G.:* "La doctrine cartésienne de l'Eucharistie chez Pierre Cally." APC 12, no. 163: 1911–12, 274–96, 380ff.

Vega: see Sanchez Vega.

3478a *Veitch, John:* The Discourse on Method, Meditations, and selection of the Principles of Philosophy of Descartes. Translated from the original texts. Sixth edition, with a new introduction by John Veitch. Edinburgh and London, Blackwood, 1879. clxxxi. 292 p. Latest reprint: Chicago, Open Court, 1960; Appendix: see no. 2523.

The most widely used English translation, first published in 1850 (DM) and 1853, with a lengthy introductory study by Veitch, chiefly of Descartes' metaphysics and epistemology, from an idealistic point of view.

3479 *Velásquez Jiménez, Juan:* El Discurso del método y la obra científica de Descartes. Lima (Peru), 1937. 42 p. Reprinted from: Boletín de minas, industrias y construcciones. [Col.]

3480 *Veloso, Agostinho (S.I.):* Nas encruzilhadas do pensamento. Vol. 1: Sob o signo de Descartes. Porto, Livraria Apostolado da Imprensa, 1956. 300 p.

3481 *Ventura da Raulica, Gioacchino:* Essai sur l'origine des idées et sur le fondement de la certitude, suivi de nouvelles observations sur le cartésianisme à l'occasion d'un nouvel écrit de M. le vicomte de Bonald. Paris, Vaton, 1853. 262 p.

À propos Bonald's "La défense des principes philosophiques de M. de Bonald: de la philosophie nouvelle et ses erreurs." Sharp Catholic critique of Descartes and Bonald.

3481a *Ventura, J.:* De methodo philosophandi. Romae, 1828. ()

Vergara: see Zahar Vergara.

3482 *Verme, Maria Eugenia dal:* "Intorno all'influenza esercita da Cartesio su Hume a proposito del problema dell'anima umana e della sua unione col corpo." Cartesio 239–47. 1937.

Finds Hume using Cartesian concepts, though the dualism problem is more complex than Descartes, Locke and Hume thought: St. Thomas had already furnished what it takes to set aside the positions of Descartes and Hume.

3483 —: "Il IX Congresso internazionale di filosofia." RFNS 29: 1937, 422–40.

3484 *Verneau:* [On the authenticity of the skull of Descartes.] Aesculape (Paris), 1912. ()

3485 *Verneaux, Roger:* Les sources cartésiennes et kantiennes de l'idéalisme français. Paris, Beauchesne, 1936. 526 p. (Bibl. des Archives de philosophie). See 232.

3486 —: "La sincérité critique chez Descartes." Aph 13, no. 2: 1937, 15–100. See 346.

3487 —: "L'idée critique dans les Regulae cartésiennes." MSR 3: 1946, 109–24, 269–86.

3488 —: "La notion de problème dans le Regulae de Descartes." RPhL February 1951, 51–67.

The elements of the concept of problem are already in the Regulae: the unknown, the indication of the unknown, the data, etc.

3489 *Versfeld, Marthinus:* An essay on the metaphysics of Descartes. London, Methuen, 1940. 192 p. See 233.

3489a —: "Larvatus prodeo, or the masque in the mirror." In his: The mirror of philosophers. London and New York, Sheed & Ward, 1960, 195–99.

A bit of philosophical fooling, with clever comment on the malin génie as "a declaration of the will to power which enables us to get beyond the domain of rationality" (198).

3490 *Vertés, Augusta O.:* "Descartes chez les Lapons." RLC 17: 1937, 488–98.

Compte-rendu of Huet's Nouvelles mémoires .... (1692), and not a study of Descartes' "influence upon the Laplanders," as one bibliographer has it. See 2249 and 110.

3491 *Vial Larrain, J. de Dois:* "Descartes, su metafísica esencial." RFChile 1: 1950, 525–31.

3492 *Viallet, C. Paul:* Je pense, donc je suis. Introduction à la méthode cartésienne. Paris, Alcan, 1897. 138 p.

3493 *Victoria, Marcos:* "Descartes y la música." Homenaje 1: 354–67. 1937.

Loose biographical sketch of Descartes' early years, barely touching the subject.

3494 *Vidari, Giovanni:* "L'educazione cartesiana in Italia e le idee pedagogiche di G. B. Vico." AcTorino. Atti 1926, 585–602. See 461.

3495 *Vigier, J.:* "Les idées de temps, de durée et d'éternité chez Descartes." RPFE 89: 1920, 196–233, 321–48. See 347a.

3496 *Vigny, Alfred de:* "Le compas ou la prière de Descartes." Journal d'un poête (1829). In his: Œuvres complètes. Pléïade, 1948, v.1, p. 901–02. See 426.

3497 *Vigorelli, Giancarlo:* "Circonstanze cartesiane della letteratura francesa contemporanea." Cartesio 781–91. 1937. See 427.

3498 *Virasoro, Miguel A.:* "Nuevas meditaciones metafísicas." Homenaje 3: 203–42. 1937.

The first "new meditation" (220–30) deals with the structure of the self, the second with the antinomies of freedom (230–42). A reconsideration of the classical concept of reason in the light of Kant, Hegel, phenomenology, and existential analysis.

3499 *Vleeschauwer, Herman Jean de:* René Descartes. Levensweg en wereldbeschouwing. Nijmeegen-Utrecht, Decker (Antwerpen-Brussel, Standaard Boekhandel), 1937. 281 p. (Philos. Bibl.)

3500 — (editor): Jacobus Acontius, Tractaat de metodo. Antwerp, Univ. Gent, Fac. d. Wijsbegeerte, v. 67, 11–135. See 278.

3501 —: "Descartes et Comenius." CD 2: 109–14, 1937.

Undocumented summary of a promised but apparently still unpublished extensive study. On the subject cf. Thijssen-Schoute (see 467), 613–22, with ample source references.

3502 —: "Bij het eeuwfeest van Descartes." Streven (Brugge) 4: 1937, 369–75.

3503 —: "Balthasar Bekker, avocat de Descartes." Revue belge de philosophie et d'histoire 18: 1939, 63–84.

3504 —: "Arnold Geulincx, der Vertreter des germanischen Geistes in der flämischen Philosophie." Tatwelt 18: 1942, 63–76. See also his: "De orationes van Arnold Geulincx." Mededelingen van de koninklijke vlaamsche academie voor wetenschappen .... 4/3: 1942, 24–25.

Cf. the sharp critique by C. L. Thijssen-Schoute in her: Nederlands Cartesianisme, no. 467, § 60, 156–62 ("How Prof. Dr. H. J. de Vleeschauwer in 1942 modified his Geulincx interpretation to please the Nazis.")

3505 *Vloemans, Ant.:* "Beginselen der cartesiaansche philosophie." In his: Spinoza. De mensch, het leven en het werk. s'Gravenhage, 1931, 261–83.

3506 *Volkmer, Franz:* Das Verhältnis von Geist und Körper im Menschen (Seele und Leib) nach Cartesius. Historisch-philosophische Abhandlung. Breslau, Aderholz, 1870. 73 p.

3507 *Vooys, C. J.:* "Renatus Descartes over Seneca." Hermeneus (Holland) 22: no. 4, 15 December 1950, 66–68.

3508 *Vree, Paul de:* "Descartes en wij." Westland (Antwerpen) 2: Oct. 1943, 49–51.

3509 *Vries, H. L. de:* "De Géométrie van Descartes en de Isagoge van Fermat." NTW 4: 1916–17, 145–68. See 355.

3510 *Vries, Joseph de (S.J.):* "Von den 'Ewigen Wahrheiten' Descartes' zu den analytischen Urteilen der Scholastik." Cartesio 305–24. 1937.

Turns the customary approach upside down, showing that late Scholasticism was influenced by Descartes' "eternal verities" concept. Valuable discussion of pertinent Catholic philosophical doctrine since the early 18th century.

3511 *Vrijer, M. J. A. de:* Henricus Regius. Een "cartesiaanscher" hoogleeraar aan de utrechtsche hoogeschool. s'Gravenhage, Nijhoff, 1917.

Cf. P. Dibon's detailed discussion of this rehabilitation of Regius in: Descartes et le cartésianisme hollandais (see 6), p. 281–87.

3512 *Vuillemin, Jules:* "Note sur l'évidence cartésienne et le préjugé qu'elle implique." RScH no. 61: 1951, 42–49.

Descartes' cogito, critique of all prejudice, rests itself upon the fundamental prejudice of evidence confounded with apodictic certitude. Phenomenology, on the contrary, considers truth a return to the innocence of the pre-reflective state, avoiding the real circulus vitiosus of Descartes (from an apodictic theory of knowledge to a theory of consciousness and vice versa).

3512a —: Mathématiques et métaphysique chez Descartes. Paris, PUF, 1960. 188 p. (Coll. Epiméthée: Essais philosophiques.) See 398.

3512b —: "Sur la différence et l'identité des méthodes de la métaphysique et des mathématiques chez D. et Leibniz, et sur la conception classique des principes de causalité et de correspondance." AGP 43: 1961, 267–302.

3513 *Vvedenski, Aleksandr Ivanovich:* Dekart i okkasionalism. Berlin, Grshtchebina, 1922. 80 p. [In Russian.]

3514 *Vycheslavzeff, Boris:* "Descartes et la philosophie moderne." In: J. Maritain et B. Vycheslavzeff, Descartes, 1931 (Cahiers de la quinzaine), 37–54. With discussion. See 184a.

W

3515 *de Waard, Cornelis (Cornelius)* (editor): Correspondance du P. Marin Mersenne, religieux minime. Publiée par Mme Paul Tannery. Editée et annotée par Cornelis de Waard avec la collaboration de René Pintard. Paris, 1932– . See 82.

3516 — (editor): Journal tenu par Isaac Beeckman de 1604 à 1634, publié avec une introduction et des notes par Cornelis de Waard. 4 vols. La Haye, Nijhoff, 1939–1953. See 80.

3517 —: "Les objections de P. Petit contre le 'Discours' et les 'Essais' de Descartes." RMM 32: 1925, 53–89. See 400.

3518 —: "Le manuscrit perdu de Snellius sur la réfraction." Janus 39: 1935, 51–73. See 399.

3519 —: L'expérience barométrique, ses antecédents et ses explications. Thouars, 1936. viii, 198 p.

3520 —: "Isaac Beeckman." In: Twee Nederlandsche figuren uit de zestiende en zeventiende eeuw: Simon Stevin [by E. J. Dijksterhuis], Isaac Beeckman. The Hague, Nijhoff, 1941.

3521 —: "Descartes et Regius: à propos d'une lettre ouverte peu connue adressée à Descartes." RPFE 137: 1947, 344–56.

The Regius side of the controversy, with documents.

3522 —: "Un entretien avec Descartes en 1634 ou 1635 (John Dury)." AIHS 6: 1953, 14–16.

3523 *Waddington, Charles:* Descartes et le spiritualisme. Paris, 1868. (Reprinted from Revue de l'instruction, December 3, 1868).

3524 *Waelhens, Alphonse de:* "Descartes et la pensée phénoménologique." RNS 41: 1938, 571–89. See 347.

3524a *Wagner, Hans:* "Kritische Betrachtungen zu Husserls Nachlass." PhRu 1: 1953–54, 93ff. See 174.

3525 *Wagner de Reyna, Alberto:* "La certeza en Descartes." RFChile 1: 1950, 459–68. Also in Mar del Sur (Lima, Peru) 3, v. 5/13: Sept.-Oct. 1950, 21–24; also in RevF 10: 1951, 156–73.

3525a —: "La certeza en Descartes." In: Miscelânea de estudos a Joaquim de Carvalho, t.l. Figueira da Foz (Portugal), Biblioteca-Museu Joaquim de Carvalho, 1959. ()

3526 *Wahl, Jean:* Du rôle de l'ideé de l'instant dans la philosophie de Descartes. Paris, Alcan, 1920. 48 p. Reprinted: Paris, Vrin, 1953 (BHP). See 347a.

3527 —: "Notes sur Descartes." RPFE 123: 1937, 370–72.

On the concept of idea in Descartes.

3528 —: "Exemple d'une règle inconnue: le verbe 'être' chez Descartes (deuxième, troisième et quatrième Méditation.)" Royaumont, 360–66; discussion, 367–75. 1937.

Distinguishes several meanings in Descartes' use of "esse," e.g.: epistemological, essential, referring to origin; the "unknown rule": Descartes uses "esse" for "l'être mathématique," "existere" for the self, God, things.

3528a —: "Au sujet des jugements de Husserl sur Descartes et sur Locke." In: Royaumont: Husserl, 1959 [see 2254b], 119–31. Discussion: Gadamer, Strasser, Breton, Boehm, van Breda, de Gandillac, Löwit, van Peursen, Levinas; réponses de J. Wahl, 132–42. See 174.

Discusses four charges of Husserl against D.'s treatment of doubt and cogito (the doubt is not universal, D. should have bracketed the world out instead of denying it, he confuses cogito and cogitatum, he conceives the idea as an image.) Husserl's critique of Locke's alleged naturalism or objectivism turns out to be a continuation and sharpening of his D. criticism; Husserl found in English empiricism the means for formulating his D. critique.

3529 *Walker, Gordon Patrick Chrestien:* A restatement of liberty. London, Hutchinson, 195. 429 p.

Former Oxford don, former junior member of British Labor government, repudiates the "Cartesian view" of man and society. Cartesianism-Calvinism bred capitalism, Cartesian science-worship bred Marxism. Walker's "hankering after a conservative philosophy to buttress his socialist faith in planning .... does much to enliven his polemics against thinkers of the 'Cartesian' school" (Arnold's review).

Revieuws: G. L. Arnold ("The New Commonwealth") in 20th Century 151, no.899: Jan.1952,55–71; J.P.de C. Day in Mind 62:1959,386–96.

3530 *Walker, Nigel:* "The definition of psychosomatic disorder." BJPS 6: 1955–56, 265–99.

Critique of the "Cartesian" (dualistic) definition of psychosomatic disorder as somatic symptoms with psychic causes. Attempts to develop an operational definition satisfying both dualists and "functional materialists." For the ensuing controversy see Szasz, W. P. D. Wightman, and Walker's rejoinder (BJPS 7: 1956–57, 235–36).

3531 *Wallace, William:* Art. "Descartes." Encycl. Britannica, 11th ed.

3531a *Wallace, William A. (O.P.):* The scientific methodology of Theodoric of Freiberg. A case study of the relationship between science and philosophy. Fribourg (Suisse), Editions univers., 1959. xvii, 395 p.

In assessing Theodoric's contribution to the theory of the rainbow, Descartes comes in for harsh criticism (p. 261ff.) Cf. Boyer's review in Isis 51: 1960, 594–96, and no. 1335b.

3532 *Wallach, E.:* "Descartes und Harvey." Archiv für die Geschichte der Medizin 20: 1928, 301–06.

3533 *Waller, Zeper S. A.:* "Descartes et Franeker." BAFH 10, no. 10: 1929.

3534 *Wallon, Henri:* "Descartes et nous." In: Cercle Descartes (see 516), 34–40. 1937.

3535 —: "La psychologie de Descartes." Pensée ns no. 32: 1950, 11–20.

Descartes' psychology is "évidemment progressiviste," modern, ambiguous because it is ahead of his time-bound metaphysics. Friendly appraisal by way of carefully picked quotations.

3536 *Walsh, F. A. (O.S.B.):* "The decline of Cartesianism." [Critique of A. O. Lovejoy.] Cartesio 793–801. 1937. See 182.

3537 *Walter, O. M., Jr.:* "Descartes on reasoning." Speech monographs (USA) 18: 1951, 47–53.

3538 *Ware, Charlotte S.:* "The influence of Descartes on John Locke." RIP 4: 1950, 210–39. See 456.

3539 *Wasik, W.:* "Kartezjusz w Polsce." Prz 40: 1937, 199–240, 414–63. See 470.

3540 *Wasilewski, M.:* "Kartezjusz i Malebranche." Prz 40: 1937, 172–84.

3541 *Watson, John:* "The Cartesian cogito ergo sum and Kant's criticism of rational psychology." K 2: 1898, 22–49.

3542 *Wavre, Rolin:* "Note sur l'influence de Descartes en philosophie mathématique." RTP 26: 1938, 50–57.

Fecundity and weakness of Cartesian thinking stem from the search for simple natures which often proves fruitless.

3543 *Weber:* "Descartes et la glande pinéale." La médecine scolaire 1933, 212–16. [Schrecker]

3544 *Weber, Jean-Paul:* "Les Méditations' de Descartes considerées en tant qu'œuvre d'art." Revue d'esthétique 9: 1956, 249–81.

After a desultory paragraph on the structure of MM, author treats D.'s greatest work as rationalization of a childhood event, loss of the mother at age two. Impertinent, misleading title.

3544a —: "Sur une certaine 'méthode officieuse' chez Descartes." RMM 63: 1958, 246–50.

Maintains against Dąmbska, no. 247a, that the two methodologies she distinguishes are only two different manners of exposition, one popular, the other detailed and scholarly. Purely logical hypotheses appear already in Regulae, which Dąmbska denies.

3545 *Weelen, J.-E.:* "Un admirateur tourangeau de Descartes: Pierre de Perrien, marquis de Crenan." Rbleue 75: 1936, 141–42.

3546 —: "A propos du IIIe centennaire .... : Descartes est-il né en Touraine?" Rbleue 75: 1937, 381–83.

3547 *Weibel, Richard Roberto:* "Notas sobre el clasicismo francés y el pensamiento cartesiano." Homenaje 3: 261–93. 1937. See 429.

3548 *Weiler, G.:* "Yahaso shel Husserl le Descartes." Iyyun (Israel) 4: 1953, no. 3, 149–61.

Husserl's relation to Descartes. [In Hebrew.]

3549 *Wein, Hermann:* "Von Descartes zur heutigen Anthropologie." ZPF 2: 1947–48, 296–314. See 347b.

3550 —: "Der wahre cartesische Dualismus." ZPF 10: 1956, 1–28. See 347b.

3550a *Weizsäcker, Carl Friedrich von:* Descartes und die neuzeitliche Naturwissenschaft. Hamburg, Universität, 1958. 29 p. (Hamburger Universitätsreden, 23.) See 146b.

3551 *Wentscher, Else:* Geschichte des Kausalproblems in der neueren Philosophie. Leipzig, Felix Meiner, 1921. viii, 389 p.

3552 *Werner, Ch.:* "Un grand anniversaire: le tricentennaire du Discours de la méthode." Journal de Genève, 18 May 1937.

3553 *Werner K.:* Geschichte der katholischen Theologie Deutschlands seit dem Trienter Konzil. München, 1866. xii, 658 p. (K. Bayerische Akademie der Wissenschaften. Historische Commission, Geschichte der Wissenschaften, v. 6).

3554 *Werner, Karl:* "Die cartesisch-malebranchische Philosophie in Italien." AcWien. Philos.-historische Klasse. Sitzungsberichte 102: 1883, 75–141, 679–794. See 433.

3555 *Whitehead, A. N.:* Process and reality. An essay in cosmology. Cambridge UP (New York, Macmillan), 1929. Reprinted: N.Y., Harper Torchbooks 1960. See 194a.

3555a —: Science and the modern world. Lowell lectures, 1925. New York, Macmillan, 1925. Reprinted: Mentor Books MD 162. See 194a.

3556 —: Adventures of ideas. 1933. See 182.

3557 *Whittaker, Sir Edmund* [Edmund Taylor Whittaker]. The modern approach to Descartes' problem: the relation of the mathematical and physical sciences to philosophy. Herbert Spencer Lecture, Oxford. London, Nelson, 1948. 30 p. See 401.

3558 —: A history of the theories of aether and electricity from the age of Descartes to the close of the 19th century. London and New York, Longmans Green, 1910, v.1, ch. 1, 1–11. 2nd ed., rev. London, Nelson, 1951. See 359.

3559 —: Space and spirit. Theories of the universe and the arguments for the existence of God. London, Nelson, 1946 (Chicago, Regnery, 1948), 71–75.

3560 *Wieleitner, Heinrich Karl:* Die Geburt der modernen Mathematik. Historisches und Grundsätzliches. Vol. 1: Die analytische Geometrie. Karlsruhe, Braun, 1924. (Wissen und Wirken, v. 12).

Ch. 6 and 7 (p. 43ff.) on Descartes and Fermat: neither of them recognized the true power of analytical geometry or went beyond the scope of Greek thought. Euler (1748) took the next step: everything needed is in the equation itself, and no recourse beyond it is needed.

3561 —: "Über zwei algebraische Einleitungen zu Descartes' Geometrie." Blätter für Gymnasialschulwesen 49: 1913, 299–313.

3562 —: "Das Gesetz vom freien Falle in der Scholastik, bei Descartes und Galilei." ZmnU 45: 1914, 216–23.

3563 —: "Die Anfänge der analytischen Raumgeometrie." ZmnU 47: 1916, 73–79.

3564 —: "Zur Erfindung der analytischen Geometrie." ZmnU 47: 1916, 414–26.

3565 *Wielenga, Bastiaan:* Spinozas Cogitata metaphysica als Anhang zu seiner Darstellung der cartesianischen Prinzipienlehre. Heidelberg, Winter, 1899. vii, 59 p. Dissertation Heidelberg.

3566 —: Spinozas Cogitata metaphysica und ihr Verhältnis zu Descartes und zur Scholastik. Breslau 1902. [So quoted by Lachièze-Rey, no. 2413, p. 288. Not located.]

3567 *Wiener, Norbert:* Cybernetics. 1948. See 350.

3568 *Wightman, William P. D.:* "Note on Descartes and psychosomatic medicine." BJPS 7: 1956–57, 234–35.

Arguing against Nigel Walker (see 3530) and Ryle, Wightman makes the important observation that Descartes did not conceive mind as a "ghost in the machine" or a "pilot in the cockpit," as the texts show. He was neither an "official" nor a "Cartesian" dualist. See 3379, 3530, and Walker's rejoinder (BJPS 7: 1956–57, 235–36).

3569 *Wild, John:* "The Cartesian deformation of the structure of change and its influence on modern thought." PhR 50: 1941, 36–59. See 348.

3569a *Willey, Basil:* The seventeenth-century background. London, Chatto & Windus, 1934. Reprinted: New York, Doubleday Anchor, 1953. See 429a.

3570 *Wisdom, J. O.:* "Three dreams of Descartes." International Journal of Psycho-Analysis 28: 1947, 11–18.

Detailed account of the Dreams, quoting much of Baillet's text in translation. Notably restrained psychoanalytical evaluation: the dreams reveal Descartes' fear of impotence, desire for "life," his use of philosophy as a retreat from poetry and life, and as an escape from fundamental inner conflict.

3571 *Witzenmann, Walter:* "Giambattista Vico und René Descartes. Die geschichtliche Kritik des cartesischen Realismus." Emge 97–115. 1937. See 461.

3572 *Wize, Kasimierz* [Casimir]: "Descartova analytickà geometria a filosofický empirism." Ruch filosofický (Praha) 1939, no. 1–2. French tr.: "La géométrie analytique de Descartes et l'empirisme philosophique." CD 6: 144–46. 1937.

Temperamental paper urging the "non-Eulerian" vs. the non-Euclidean viewpoint in modern geometry.

3573 *Wohlwill, Emil:* "Die Entstehung des Beharrungsgesetzes." ZVS 15: 1884, 70–135, 337–87.

Gives Galilei priority in discovering the law of inertia, but defends D. against the charge of plagiarism.

3574 *Wolf, Abraham:* Art. "Descartes." Encycl. Britannica, 14th ed.

3575 *Wolff, E.:* De La Forge's Psychologie und ihre Abwendung von Descartes. Dissertation Jena, 1891.

3575a *Wolff, Edgar:* "Conscience et liberté chez Descartes et chez M. Sartre." RPFE 145: 1955, 341–48. See 192.

In both thinkers, human freedom is linked to the negativity of human consciousness: in Descartes at the expense of man devalued before God, in Sartre to man's sole profit. Is it not possible, despite Sartre, to find a place for the freedom of man in the face of the existence of a "hidden God"? [Bsig 10: 1956, 7728.]

3576 *Wolfson, H. A.:* "Causality and freedom in Descartes, Leibniz, and Hume." In: Freedom and experience, essays presented to Horace M. Kallen. Ed. by Sidney Hook and Milton R. Konvitz. Ithaca & New York, Cornell UP, 1947, 97–114. See 349.

3577 *Wolz, Henry G.:* "The function of the will in Descartes' proofs for the existence of God." NSch 20: 1946, 295–322.

3578 —: "The will as a factor in Descartes' proof for the existence of material things." NSch 22: 1948, 209–26.

3579 —: "The double guarantee of Descartes' ideas." Rmet 3: 1950, 471–89.

Study of the Cartesian circle: The clear and distinct idea is true only as long as that perception is actually present to the mind. Restatement of the thesis that God's veracity guarantees the memory of the cogito.

3580 —: "The universal doubt in the light of Descartes' conception of truth." ModSch 27: 1950, 253–79.

Critical discussion of the literature (following Olgiati's scheme), especially of Hamelin, Mercier, Lantrùa, Gouhier. [BAn 1951, 1505.]

3581 *Wood, Ledger:* "Descartes' philosophy of mind." PhR 41: 1932, 466–77.

Self in D. "a philosophical superfluidity" (473): unity and self-identity of mind remain unexplained. Sees a parallel between D.'s doctrine that mind is more easily known than body, and Kant's substance as a category of understanding.

3582 —: "Descartes on the structure of knowledge." S 1/14: 1946, 6–20; Italian tr. p. 122–30.

Subjective and objective aspects of Descartes' epistemology in the Regulae.

3583 *Woodbridge, Benjamin M.:* "The Discours de la méthode and the spirit of the Renaissance." RR 25: 1933, 136–42.

Descartes claims no borrowings, but took his property where he could find it, without acknowledging his debt. The "destructive" part of his philosophy is already found in Montaigne.

3584 *Wootton, F.:* "The physical work of Descartes." Science progress 21, no. 83: Jan. 1927. ()

3585 *Wright, Georg Henrik von:* "Descartes och den vetenskapliga idéutvecklingen." Aj 16: 1950, 103–71. See 402.

3586 *Wright, J. N.:* "Descartes and the wax. Rejoinder" [to J. J. C. Smart, q.v.] PhQ 1: July 1951, 348–55. See 235c.

3587 —: "The method of Descartes." PhQ 5: 1955, 78–82. Review of L. J. Beck's book of the same title.

3588 —: "Kemp Smith's Descartes." PhQ 5: 1955, 365–72. See 193.

3589 *Wundt, Max:* "Cogito ergo sum." ZdtK 10: 1944, 81–100.

3590 —: "Wandlungen des Descartes-Bildes." ZPF 7: 1953, 315–25. See 33.

3591 —: "Der Traum des Descartes." K 46: 1954–55, 367. [Answer to Quiring, see 107.]

3592 *Wust, Peter:* "Das Rätsel des Philosophen Descartes." Hochland (München) 1929–30, 323–28.

X - Z

3593 *Xirau Palau, Joaquín:* Descartes y el idealismo subjetivista moderno. Barcelona, Universidad de Barcelona, Facultad de filosofía y letras, 1927. 122 p.

3593a *Xirau, Ramón:* "Lo que no se lee en Descartes." RcubF 1: 1950, 17–22.

Yanosvskaia: see Janovskaja.

3594 *Yastreboff-Ragozine, Nadine:* "Descartes moraliste." In her: Conception et analyse de l'homme en France au XVIIe siècle; idées morales et répercussions littéraires. Praha, Russki svobodnyi universitet, Brochures v. 25. 1936, 65 p. (Bull. de l'Association russe pour les recherches scientifiques à Prague, v. 4 (IX), Section des sciences philosophiques .... no. 25; Descartes: p. 240–48.)

3595 *Yost, R. M. Jr., and Donald Kalisch:* "Miss Macdonald on sleeping and waking." PhQ 5: 1955, 109–24. See 306.

3596 *Yost, R. M., Jr.:* "Professor Malcolm on Dreaming and Scepticism. I. Sleep and consciousness." PhQ 9: 1959, 142–51.

Author attempts "to play the same language-game that Malcolm does," to prove that Malcolm's criteria for distinguishing sleeping consciousness and dreaming do not hold as stated and do not refute Descartes' scepticism of the senses. See 306.

3597 *Young, J. Z.:* Doubt and certainty in science; a biologist's reflections on the brain. The B.B.C. Reith Lectures 1950. Oxford, Clarendon Press, 1951. viii, 167 p. See 350.

3598 *Zahar Vergara, Alfonso:* "Dos actitudes escépticas: San Agustín y Descartes." FyL 23, no. 45–46: 1952, 327–32.

St.Augustine a sceptic who humbly recognizes his ontological deficiency, while Descartes' doubt arises from pride (the self as central part of reality.) [BAn 1954.]

Żeleński, T.: see Boy.

3599 *Zgórski, Alfred:* "Goethe i Descartes." Świt (Lwów) 1872, no. 1–5. [Bar]

3600 *Zijderveld, A.:* "De Calvinist Constantijn Huygens en de Roomskatholieke wijsgeer Descartes." Neo 22: 1937, 241–56. French summary.

Reprints Huygens' poem "In Cartesium."

3601 *Zolnai, B. Miklos:* Eszmenyei. Budapest, Minerva Konyntar, 1937. ["Influence du cartésianisme et du jansénisme." Giraud II]

3602 *Żółtowski, Adam:* Descartes. Poznań, 1937. xii, 256 p. (Poznańskie towarzystwo przyjaciół nauk. Prace komisji filoz., v. 5).

Major Polish work. Descartes' philosophy as a forerunner of modern intuitionism, while its critical spirit makes Cartesian "imagination" an indubitable prototype of Kantian "transcendental imagination." [Lubnicki's review: see 15, 107–08.]

3603 —: "Descartes polemistą." Prz 45: 1937, 152–71.

On Descartes' controversies, particularly the Responses to the Objections.

3604 —: "Théorie cartésienne et théorie idéaliste de la connaissance." CD 3: 75–80. 1937.

Specifies "toute une série d'assertions" of Descartes which, apart from the principle of Regula VIII, will become "les idées directrices des grands systèmes idéalistes," viz., unity of knowledge, interdependence of concepts and their necessary and progressive development "à travers leurs contradictions," the insufficiency of finite knowledge.

3605 —: "Teoria poznania kartezjańska a idealistyczna." Prz 41/1: 1938, 3–8.

The Cartesian and the idealistic theory of knowledge. [Same as 3604].

3606 *Zoppi, G. B.:* "La Fontaine e Descartes." RRFC 1920–22, 345–60, 472–82. (?)

3607 *van der Zwan, A.:* "Descartes en de geneeskunde." Bijdragen tot de geschiedenis der geneeskunde 38: 1960 (1958): 37–41.

3608 *Zwierzynski, Chiel:* Descartes, Malebranche et Spinoza. Genève, rue Micheli Du Crest 16, 1950. 16 p.

ALLOTRIA

3609 [*Conférence Descartes*]. CrPh 12: 1877–78, p. 351.

Announcement of the organization in 1876 of a group ("Conférence Descartes") devoted to the free discussion of philosophy and related scientific questions.

3610 *Richter, Mischa:* Cartoon in: The New Yorker, November 1, 1958, p. 38.

One mathematician to the other, looking at the tape delivered by a giant electronic computer: "I'll be damned. It says, 'Cogito ergo sum'."

3611 *Steinberg, Saul:* Cartoon in: The New Yorker, December 22, 1962.

Reproduced below, by permission of The New Yorker.

3612 *Visages de Descartes:* Ed. J. Conilh. Paris, Hachette, s.d. (Collection Visages de l'homme.)

A 10-inch long-playing phonograph record, containing readings from Descartes and his contemporaries: "Le démolisseur, le constructeur, le sage."

Drawing by Steinberg

PART THREE

INDICES

SYSTEMATIC INDEX

Selected headings from the Analytical Index, conveniently grouped. The most comprehensive headings are *italicized.*

BASIC & COMPREHENSIVE ENTRIES

GEOGRAPHIC INDEX

ANTHROPOLOGY (CARTESIAN MAN)

BIOGRAPHY OF DESCARTES
[see also: COGITATIONES, DESCARTES, RELIGION]

biography (general)
birth, birthplace
Bohemia
burials of Descartes
celebrations, commemorative events
Chanut
childhood of Descartes
Christina Queen of Sweden
condemnation
correspondence
death of Descartes
Descartes family
development of Descartes' thought & work (chronology)
Dream of Descartes
education of Descartes
Elisabeth von der Pfalz
Éloges
exile
formative period
Francine Descartes
Franeker
Huygens, Constantijn
iconography
La Flèche
La Haye-Descartes
La Rochelle, siege
larvatus prodeo
legend of Descartes
longevity
Loretto, Descartes' pilgrimage
Mersenne
orthography of Descartes
Panthéonisation
Perron
personal relations
polemics & controversies
Puy-de-Dôme
reception of Descartes' works
skull (crâne) of Descartes
Stockholm inventory
Tours
transfers (actual & proposed) of Descartes' remains
travels
vocation
White Mountain, battle

BIOLOGY, MEDICINE, PHYSIOLOGY

anatomy
animal spirits
beast-machine
biology, biomechanism
brain
circulation of the blood, Harvey
death
embryology
genetics
humors
life
longevity
medicine
memory
organism
pineal gland
reflex action
sleep
therapeutics
vision & perception
vitalism

CARTESIAN ERA, ENLIGHTENMENT
(17TH & 18th CENTURY)

anticartesianism
anti-Renaissance
Aristotle, Aristotelianism
art
Baroque
beast-machine
Cartesian discussion groups
Cartesian era
Cartesian Scholasticism
Cartesianism
classicism
Counterreformation
cursus philosophicus
eclecticism
Enlightenment
heroic ideal
honnête homme
Jansenism
Leibniz
literature
man-machine
Malebranche

mechanism
Mersenne
Molinism
"moralistes"
Newton
ontotheology
Orders & Congregations
painting
persecution of Cartesianism
perspectives curieuses, anamorphoses, automata
philosophia & theologia novantiqua
querelle des anciens et des modernes
Scholasticism
seventeenth century
theater
universities

COGITATIONES PRIVATAE & DREAM OF DESCARTES

automata
catena scientiarum
Cogitationes privatae
Corpus poetarum
Dream of Descartes
Enthusiasm
Est et non
inventum mirabile
larvatus prodeo
Loretto
Lullus
mathesis universalis
Olympica
"poêle" (word)
poetry (poetic cognition)
Quod vitae sectabor iter?
Rosicrucians
scientia mirabilis
scientia universalis
semina scientiae
symbol
Una est in rebus vis activa

COSMOGONY, COSMOLOGY
[see also: PHYSICS]

chaos
cosmogony
cosmology
Genesis (Old Testament)
indefinite
plurality (of worlds)
universe
world

DESCARTES, THE MAN & THE WORK
[see also: BIOGRAPHY, RELIGION]

angelism
apologetics
bene vixit qui bene latuit
"cavalier français"
Christianity, Catholicism
Columbus, the new
conformism of Descartes
contradictions, paradoxes, obscurities
Descartes' role in science
Descartes' role in Western philosophy
development of Descartes' thought (chronology)
dogmaticism
"encore un qui va se tromper"
God (of Descartes)
heritage of Descartes
humanism of Descartes
image of Descartes in scholarship & popular mind
intellectualism
larvatus prodeo
legend of Descartes
mask & enigma of Descartes
mathematicism
metaphors
philosophy of Descartes (general, chief orientation, basic characteristics)
polemics & controversies
priority, plagiarism charges, originality of Descartes
"prudence" of Descartes
religiosity
sagesse
science, scientism

sincerity of Descartes
style of Descartes
unity of Descartes' system
vocation of Descartes

ESTHETICS, ART, LITERATURE

art
Classicism
Compendium musicae
Corneille
dance
esthetics
expression
irony
literature, influence of Descartes
metaphors
Molière
music
Naissance de la paix
painting
poetry
poems
Poussin
querelle des anciens et des modernes
Racine
style of Descartes
Symbolists, French
theater

FUNDAMENTAL CONCEPTS

âme
Being, esse, être
body
causa sui
causality
certitude
circle, Cartesian
clear & distinct
cogito
cognition
"conscience"
doubt
dualism
error, falsity
eternal verities
extension
external world
evidence
God
idea
idealism
innate ideas, inneism
intuition
liberté, libre-arbitre
mathesis universalis
méthode
ontological argument
order
pensée
proofs of God
protophilosophy (axioms, presuppositions) of Descartes
rationalism
realism
scepticism
scientia universalis
sense, senses
substance
time
truth
union (âme-corps)
unity of Descartes system
unity of science
veracity of God
volonté, voluntarism
understanding, intellectio

INTERPRETATIONS OF DESCARTES' PHILOSOPHY

anthroposophic
Bergson
"Cartesius" vs. "Descartes"
Catholic
existentialist
histories of philosophy
interpretations of Descartes' philosophy (general)
logical positivism
Marxist
Neoscholastic, Neothomist
phenomenology
pseudocartesianism
psychoanalytical
spiritualistic

LOGIC & EPISTEMOLOGY
[see also: FUNDAMENTAL CONCEPTS]

abstraction
accident
analogy
analysis & synthesis
apriorism
ars combinatoria
ars inveniendi
attention & judgment
attribute
axioms
bien juger
bon sens
catena scientiarum
certitude
circle, Cartesian
clear & distinct
cognition
concept
conceptualism & realism
confusion
connaissance d'autrui
contradiction, principle of
contradictions, paradoxes, obscurities
criticist philosophy
deduction
definition
development of Descartes' thought (chronology)
dialectics of Descartes
Discours de la méthode
distinction
doubt
dualism
dreaming & waking
empiricism of Descartes
enumeration
epistemology
epoché
error, falsity
evidence
existential statements
experiment, experimentalism
hypothesis
idea
identity
image, theory of
imaginary
imagination, phantasia
induction
inference
ingenium
instrumentalism of Descartes
intelligence
intuition
judgment
Kant
liaison nécessaire
logic of Descartes
logical positivism
Lullus
lumen naturale
mastery of nature
mathesis universalis, pura, vulgaris
memory
méthode
model
negation
nominalism
objectivity of knowledge
operationalism
Peirce
perception
petites perceptions
phenomenology
Positivism
pragmatism
principle
probability, probabilism
problem
proof (logical demonstration)
propositions
protophilosophy (axioms, presuppositions) of Descartes
quantity
questions parfaitemant comprises
Regulae
rules of method, four (DM)
sensation
sense, senses
sensory qualities
sign
simple natures
sleeping, dreaming
species
sufficient reason
syllogism
symbol
syntactic rules
systematization
truth
understanding, intellectio
wax (morceau de cire)

MATHEMATICS

MECHANISM

METAPHYSICS

[see also: FUNDAMENTAL CONCEPTS]

immanence, immanentism of Descartes
immortality
indefinite
individuality, individuation
infinite, infinity
innate ideas
intentionality
intuition
laws of nature
liaison nécessaire
liberté, libre-arbitre
life
lumen naturale
malin génie
materialism
matter
medievalism
"meditation" (word)
Méditations métaphysiques
memory
mens corporea
metaphysics
monism
natural belief
necessity
negation
Nihilism
nothingness
nominalism
ontological proof, argument
ontologism
ontology
pensée, mens, res cogitans
phenomenalism
phenomenology
pluralism
plurality
possibility
probability, probabilism
proofs of God
protophilosophy (axioms, presuppositions) of Descartes
qualities
quantity
rationalism of Descartes
realism
reality
reason
scepticism
self, ego, moi
sense, senses
solipsism
space
species
spiritualism of Descartes
subjectivism
substance
substantial form
time
transcendence
truth
union (âme-corps)
unity
veracity of God
vinculum substantiale
volonté, voluntarism

MORALE, PASSIONS DE L'ÂME

amour
arbre de la philosophie (sagesse)
beatitude
bien juger pour bien faire
Cartesian "ethics"
"cœur"
dualism
ethics
expression & emotion
générosité
immortality
Lettres sur la morale
metamorale
morale
morale provisoire
"moralistes"
passions
pedagogy
sagesse
Traité des passions de l'âme
union (âme-corps)
value

NATURE

laws of nature
mastery of nature ("maîtres de la nature")
mechanisms
Molinism

PHILOSOPHERS & PHILOSOPHIES

PHYSICS

atom, atomism
capillarity
dynamics
elements
ether
extension
external world
force
free fall
Galileo
geology, geophysics
gravity
hydraulics, hydrodynamics
impact (choc)
impetus
kinematics
laws of nature
light
magnet
mechanics
movement, motion
Newton
optics
pendulum problem (centre des oscillations)
physics
planetary system
plurality (of worlds)
refraction
space
springs (fontaines)
statics
thermodynamics
tides (marées)
vacuum
velocity
vortex theory
work (travail mécanique)

POLITICAL AND SOCIAL PHILOSOPHY

absolutism
authority & reason
bourgeoisie
capitalism
"citoyen"
communism
  Fascism, National Socialism
law, jurisprudence
liberalism
Machiavelli
Marx
Marxist interpretations
Montesquieu
  natural law
physiocrats
political philosophy
Poulain de la Barre
progress
progressivism of Descartes
Rousseau
social philosophy
totalitarian state
Vico

PSYCHOLOGY

association of ideas
behavior
child psychology
dreaming & waking
dualism
emotions
expression
individuality, individuation
passions
prenatal experiences
psychoanalytic interpretations
psychology
psychophysiology
sensations
sense, senses
sensory qualities
species
synaesthesis
vision & perception

RATIONALISM, REASON

authority & reason
beast-machine
faith & reason
fenomenismo razionalistico

intelligence
irrationalism
lumen naturale
rationalism of Descartes
rationes seminales
superstition
unconscious mind
understanding

RELIGION, THEOLOGY; RELIGIOUSNESS OF DESCARTES

agnosticism
angels
angelism
apologetics
atheism
Augustine, Saint
Augustinianism
Calvin
Catholic collectanea etc.
Catholic interpretations
Christianity, Catholicism of Descartes
Conformism of Descartes
dogmaticism of Descartes
faith & reason
Genesis (Old Testament)
God
  ontological proof
  proofs of God's existence
  veracity of God
grace
Jansenism
Jesuits
laicism of Descartes
Libertins, Libertinism
Loretto, Descartes' pilgrimage
Luther
miracles
Molinism
mystery, mysteries
mysticism
natural religion, natural theology
Neoscholastic interpretations
occultism
ontologism
ontotheology
original sin
Orders & Congregations
Pantheism
Pelagianism of Descartes
Port-Royal
Protestantism
"Protestant principle" in philosophy
Providence
"prudence" of Descartes
raison & foi: see faith & reason
religion
religiosity of Descartes
Revelation
sagesse
Scholasticism
sincerity of Descartes
supernatural
superstition
theism
theodicy
theology
theologia novantiqua: s.v. philosophia novantiqua
Thomas Aquinas, Thomism
Transsubstantiation

SCIENCE

biology
catena scientiarum
chemistry
cosmology
cosmogony
Dioptrique
empiricism
experience
experiment, experimentalism
Galileo
genetics
geology, geophysics
Huygens, Christian
laws of nature
mastery of nature ("maitres de la nature")
mathematicism
mechanics
Mersenne
Météores, meteorology
nature
Newton
physics
Principia philosophiae
probability, probabilism
science, scientism
scientia mirabilis
scientia universalis
statics

SPACE

TIME

WORKS OF DESCARTES

ANALYTICAL INDEX

CROSS REFERENCES

above, below refer to the same entry. Example: [Cartesianism ...... causality: see under occasionalism below] refers to the word "occasionalism" under the *same* heading [Cartesianism].

q.v., s.v. (*quod vide, sub voce*) refer to headings *elsewhere* in the Analytical Index.

NUMBERS

The Analytical Index refers to the serial numbers in Part I & II, not to page numbers.

italicized numbers after the name of an author refer to his publications on Descartes, ordinary numbers to discussions of his work.

numbers in [ ] indicate years ,not serial numbers. For example, Opuscula [1619–21] means: Opuscula of the years 1619–21.

ABBREVIATIONS

b., d. (after names): born, died.

AM refers to the "Table des noms propres" in Adam-Milhaud's edition of the correspondence of Descartes (no. 79) where the user will find a complete summary of factual information on the person referred to.

Cabeen refers to: A Critical Bibliography of French Literature, vols. 3 & 4 (see no. 3a).

CP, DM, MM, O&R, PP, TP refer to works of Descartes. See p.502.

A

Abra de Raconis, Charles François d', S.J. [AM, v. 4]: 165, 263.

absolutism: D.'s social ideal 1579–80; his ambiguous attitude 320; absolute monarchy: the Cartesian God in politics 1410; & s.v. political philosophy.

abstraction: texts 7; 178, 193; Thomist & Cartesian 281; from D. to Leibniz & modern mathematics 316; the simple & the merely abstract 193.

Académie française: Le Brun's Cartesian "esthetic legislation" 415; D. & Pascal [1933] 2004; prize essays [1765]: see Éloges.

Académie [Royale] des sciences, 17th c.: 390, 466a.

Académie des sciences morales et politiques: [1839] prize essays 126, 188, 437, 451.

accident: texts 7; 83, 178; St. Augustine & Descartes 302; substance 1414; Thomistic and Cartesian 282.

Aconzio (Acontius), Giacomo [b. 1520]: Opusculum de metodo, & DM:influence? 278.

action: texts 7; divine action: instantaneous or continuous? 457a; dualism: thought-action 307, 1292; morale provisoire as philosophy of action 163; & passion: problem of grace 215b; & s.v. God, morale, passion, Traité des passions.

actual occasions (Whitehead): & Cartesian substance 194a.

Adam, Charles Ernest: *1006–22;* editor *74, 79, 86;* biography *121, 1022;* Abra de Raconis 263; biography 123; English correspondents of D. *1020;* Foucher de Careil criticized 75; Liard's influence 181; religiosity, sincerity of D. 1075; science D.'s chief concern 14, 181; & s.v. Adam-Tannery.

Adam-Tannery (AT) edition of Descartes' works: *74;* Tannery's studies 397; new edition desirable 30.

aesthetics: s.v. esthetics.

agnosticism of Descartes: critical discussion 168; "Christian agnosticism" 152; disguised 124; enlightened, tolerant, scientific 230; accepts the incomprehensible, infinite 152, 320,; & s.v. atheism, religiosity.

Alain [i.e. Emile Chartier]: *147, 148, 1029–35;* 24.

Albania: commemorative items 508, 1750, 2395, 2611, 2686, 2714, 2729, 2935.

Alembert, Jean Lerond d' [1717–1783]: 150, 468, 1374 & s.v. Enlightenment.

Algazali (al-Ghazzālī), Abu-Hamed: doubt, cogito 344; 1662.

algebra: 83, 1323; history from D. to modern algebra 3052; imagination limited to simple images 353; & s.v. analytical geometry, analysis (math.), Descartes' rule of signs, equations, algebraic notation.

algebraic notation (mathematical symbolism): 74, 83; Stevin, Vieta, D. 378, 2766; "x" for the unknown 3446.

alienation of man: 179, 432a, 3116, 3161; & s.v. anthropology, modern man, modern mind.

Allotria: 1272, 1449, 1751, 2112, 3311, 3609–12.

Alquié, Ferdinand: *1045–56a;* Découverte *149;* Descartes *127;* expérience ontologique *1056;* immédiat *1049;* Marxisme *150;* Nostalgie *1046a;* ordre *1051a, 1055;* Royaumont *42;* discussed 22, 26, 31, 42, 2863b, 2916–17, 3104.

ambiguities: s.v. contradictions.

âme, anima, soul: texts 7; 83, 149, 165, 170, 171, 179c, 185, 193, 215a–b, 226, 1259, 2168, 2351; anima rationalis, sensitiva, vegetativa, naturalis, âme locomotrice 7, 83, 165, 431, 466a (Maignan), âme materielle (Gassendi, Epicureans) 466a, âme pensante (history of vitalism) 1305; animal soul (q.v.) 226; Cartesians 431, Cartesian theology 215b; cognition: âme less known than God, better known than body 165, 170, 208, 1259, connaissance d'autrui 215a; "conscience": âme is not uninterrupted consciousness 215b; distinction between soul & body, their union (q.v.) 165; duration 347a, 457a; finality, corporeity 170; freedom & individuality 215a; God 170; immortality 215a, 228; individuality required by cogito 215a; passivity 178; âme-pensée 179c; soul & self: semantic confusion 190, 2559; vitalism 1305; & s.v. pensée, distinction, union, metaphysics, morale.

âme des bêtes: s.v. beast-machine.

America: s.v. Latin-America, United States.

amour: Cartesianism a "philosophie de l'amour" 218; Renaissance, D., Chapelin, Pascal, Testelin 422; amour de soi: D. & La Rochefoucauld 215b; amour intellectuel-passion: texts 7; purification 2904a; D. & Elisabeth 93, 119 & s.v. morale, passions, Traité des passions.

Ampère, André-Marie: concept of physics 370.

Amsterdam: Cartesianism 452, 467; Maison Descartes, D. in Amsterdam 38, 123, 1348, 1570; portrait of D. 1; & s.v. biography, Holland, universities.

anaclastic curves: 83; model of D.'s mathematical reasoning 321a.

analogy: 83; as epistemological tool 268a; & s.v. metaphors.

analysis (mathematics; infinitesimal calculus): 83, 178, 388 & 2749, 2759a, 2949; D.'s tangent method (q.v.) as substitute 355, 398, Vieta 378; Cartesians: difficulties of transition to analysis 372.

analysis and synthesis (method, ratio demonstrandi): texts 7 ("méthode"); 83, 165, 170, 198, 231, 1402; analytical cognition is self-sufficient 161; ordre des raisons 170; & syllogism (q.v.) 231; & circle 2005; & s.v. order.

analytical geometry: 388, 1088, 1222, 1448, 1517, 2268a, 2478a, 2572, 2574, 2576, 3188, 3390a; D.'s first attempts [1619–20] 388 & 2751; from CP to Géométrie 388 & 2742; from D. to Euler 3560–61, 3563–64; did the Greeks have it? 2334; D.'s historical role 355, 355a, 382, 1469; ars inveniendi 355; & empiricism 3572; a logical transform 321a; metaphysical interpretation 131, 156–159; & modern non-Euclidean g. 1309; substitute for unattainable mathesis universalis 353; as theory of proportions 321a; geometric transcendence (Leibniz & D.) 3453; & s.v. anaclastic, analysis, curves, Dream of D., folium Cartesii, Fermat, Géométrie, mathesis universalis, ovals, spirals, tangents.

analytical judgments: s.v. judgment.

anamorphoses: CP & Baroque art 236.

anatomy: 365, 2139; & s.v. biography, experiments of D., medicine, physiology, pineal gland.

André, Yves-Marie, S.J. ["le P. André," 1675–1764]: 438, 450, 466; & see Malebranche.

Andreae, Johann-Valentin [1587–1654]: Noces chymiques 102.

Andreae, Tobias [1604–1676; AM, v. 6]: 451, 452, 467.

angels (anges): texts 7; 178, 184; D.'s malicious comments neither bold nor original 267.

angelism of Descartes: angelic cognition ascribed to man 184, disputed 149; 225a, 1723, 1749.

"animal faith" & scepticism (Santayana): 191.

animal soul: s.v. beast-machine.

animal spirits (esprits animaux, Lebensgeister): texts 7; 83, 165, 178; history of concept 313, 3160; root of beast-machine doctrine 386; 17th century Epicureanism 466a; Cartesians 431; & s.v. medicine, physiology.

Anjou: Cartesianism & Oratoire 1817.

Anselm, Saint: cogito 1790; ontological argument 83, 149, 159 & 1396, 165, 214, 2280, 2551, 2763, 3439; Anselm, D., Kant 1114a; D. found Anselm's argument refuted in St. Thomas 83, 214; his proof different from Anselm's 211a (Henrich), 1893a, identical with Anselm's third proof 211a (Hartshorne), free of objections to Anselm's argument 1257.

anthropology, philosophical (D.'s concept of man): 151, 196, 206, 218, 1043, 2089; alienated, lost modern man anticipated 179, 3116; asociality of Cartesian man 153, 196; atomistic concept of man, & the state 3223; biology & individuation 215a, 1443, & méthode 2802; degeneration of man: concept rejected but not replaced by D. 1418; dualism 1026; DM & Montaigne 404; DM should have led not to dualism but to dialectic existential anthropology 347b; "l'homme concret" 169, difficulty 149; "l'homme total" unreconciled with mechanism 149; idealism of freedom, & passions 206a; D.'s metaphysical discovery of man 149; "whole man" opposed to morbidly terrestrian Cartesian man 196; TP as anthropology 176; & s.v. existentialist interpretations, générosité, humanism of D., liberté (humaine), modern man, modern, mind, morale, sagesse.

anthropology, philosophical: *doctrinal comparisons:* Augustinian & Cartesian man 1210, 1336 & s.v. Augustine; Diderot, Helvetius, Locke 468; Montaigne (q.v.) 404; modern liberalism against Cartesian man 3529, critique 1080; modern man 179, 432a, 3116, 3161 & s.v. modern mind; Scholastic and Cartesian 165, 2667, 3377; dualism of Thomist man disputed 431, 1130, 1132, 2801.

anthroposophic interpretation: 1288.

anthropotheism of Descartes: 183–184a.

anticartesianism: *17th & 18th century* 200a, 438 (v. 1, 2), 441a, 454, 466a, 467, 2859; persecution of Cartesianism 390, 435a, 436, 438, 450, 458, 466a, 467, 1918; Belgium 458; England 406, 409; France 442, 450, 3179, Jesuits 466; Germany 436; Holland 109, 435a, 436, 452, 467; Italy 433, 461; Poland 1541; Spain 449; *modern:* Catholic 166–67, 184–84a, 1449, 2676, 3536, & s.v. Neoscholastic interpretations; existentialist 347; German 153, 225, 466b, 304, 1267, 2229, 2888; liberal 3529; Protestant 193a, 1149, 1667; science 359; & s.v. Malebranche, Pascal, Vico, Voltaire, Huygens (Christiaan), Newton; also Aristotelianism, beast-machine, condemnation of Descartes, Jesuits.
anti-Renaissance: 96, 319.
apodictic evidence: assertive & apodictic evidence 212a; certitude confused with evidence 3512; innate ideas 212a; from apodictic evidence to theory of "conscience" 3512; & s.v. certitude, evidence.
apologetics: Descartes as Catholic apologist 163, 179a–b, 446, 1896a, 1905, discussed 168, defends science against Church 164, saves Church from science 179a,d, his apologetics produce non-religious philosophy 168, Catholic apologetics in his time 163, 179b; Descartes as defender of bourgeoisie against feudalism & Church 150, 154, & s.v. Marxist interpretations, Libertinism, religiosity.
apprentissage, années d': s.v. formative period, Dream.
apriorism of Descartes: epistemological 212a, limited apriorism of Regulae, DM, MM 247, disputed 3544a.
Arabic philosophy: influence, parallels 260a, 344, 1662, 1947; & s.v. Algazali, Averroes, Avicenna.
arbre de la philosophie (sagesse): 220, 230, 2724; & s.v. morale.
archetype: Dream 103; Deus instar archetypi 170.
Archimedes: 379.
Argentina: commemorative publications 512, 524, 537.
Arianism & Western thought: Wolzogen vs. D. 1541.
Aristotle, Aristotelianism (fortunes), Peripatetic adversaries of Descartes: bibliography 16, 17, 464a; 7, 83, 165, 226, 402, 431, 438, 441a, 446–47, 449–51, 452, 454, 458, 461, 466–66a, 467, 1839, 2521, 3281; Aristotelianism foreign to D. & St. Augustine alike 235; Aristotelianism, Platonism, Cartesianism 165, 2272, D.'s implied Aristotelianism vs. his "Platonic inspiration" 3281; beast-machine 226, 431; biology 2891; causality, concept of change 262, 348, 3551; certitude of existence 1978; cogito 200, 1246, 3090a; esthetics 3436; logic 211b, 231; motion 2610; physics 165, 177, 379, 402, Maignan's Aristotle critique 449; psychology 165, 1363; science: Aristotelian & Cartesian spirit 165, 175, 402, 1250; substance 282, & accident 1414; substantial forms 7, 83, 165, 431; time 1359; & s.v. Cartesian era, Cartesianism (fortunes), Scholasticism, St. Thomas, classicism, esthetics, universities.
Arnauld, Antoine, "le grand Arnauld" [1612–1694; AM, v. 4; Cabeen, v. 3]: correspondence with D. 84; animal soul 226; Cartesianism 438, 441; "conscience" 212a; grace 215b; Holland 467; libre-arbitre 243, 248; mediary between D. & Boileau 424; O&R (q.v.) 204, 204a, 233; pensées imperceptibles 215b; Scholasticism, D.'s knowledge of it 263; Scottish realists 3038–39; theory of ideas 161, 212a, 451a, 1713a, 2846.
Arnold, Matthew: *1081.*
ars analytica (Vieta): 378.
ars combinatoria: 328; Lullus (q.v.), D., Leibniz 2146.
ars inveniendi: 83, 198, 321a; Ars inveniendi veritatem (Lullus) 328 & 1217, 3000a; analytical geometry as problem-solving 355, before D. 378; formal logic vs. ars inveniendi (Bacon to Mill) 335; D.'s méthode not an ars inveniendi (Jaspers) 175.
art: not metaphysical truth but mere personal delectation 419; influence of TP upon painting 415; Cartesian shift from things to méthode, & painting 1438a; Cartesian art ideal & theory of genres 419 (Revault); Enlightenment 443.
association of ideas: 381, 2785.
assumptions of Descartes: s.v. protophilosophy.
Astorini, Pietro Elia [1651–1702]: Cartesian controversy at Padua 1824a.
astronomy: s.v. cosmogony, cosmology, Newton & Newtonianism, planetary motions, vortex theory.

AT: s.v. Adam-Tannery.
atheism: 466a; among D.'s friends 124, 179a, b; concealed atheism of D. 435b; destroyed by Cartesianism (Gerdil) 431; "querelle de l'athéisme" (Brunschvicg et al.) 24; anticartesianism is atheistic 235b (Daly); & s.v. agnosticism, libertinism, religiosity, scepticism.
âtman-brahma & cogito: 310.
atom, atomism: texts 7; history 380; D. & Cartesianism 463, 2134.
attention: & judgment 149, 178 & 2453; attention à la vie (Bergson) 1677.
attribute: texts 7; 178, 193, 455a & s.v. God.
Aubry, Jean d': early 17th century physician & magician, anticipates catenam scientiarum 328.
Augustine, Saint: 214, 235, 1488, 2273; D. closer to St. Augustine than to St. Thomas 214, 215b, "Platonic family likeness" 235; D.'s formal borrowings 163; accident 302; anthropology 1210, 1336; beast-machine 302, 1210; certitude 1867; cogito & doubt: four texts 149, discussion 163, 165, 200, 235, 334, 1336, 1337, 1790; "conscience" 2696, 2862; connaissance d'autrui 244; epistemology 192b, 2481; illuminism, innate ideas, lumen naturale 214; scepticism 3598; self 2349; voluntarism 2327.
Augustinianism: influence upon D. 163, 165, 168; 17th century Augustinianism, & Cartesianism 302; Augustinian reaction against D. (Malebranche, Bossuet, Fenelon) 2461; Augustinian tradition protects D.'s & Malebranche's unorthodoxy 235; D.'s & Pascal's incompatible Augustinianisms 165, 431a, united in Malebranche 1157 who achieves alliance between Cartesianism & anticartesian Augustinian tradition 302; Port-Royal 38; Augustinianism & D.'s epistemology 161, voluntarism 1043.
Ausonius: 103, 2349a, & s.v. Dream, Est et non, Quod vitae sectabor iter.
authentic freedom (Sartre): 192.
authority & reason: D.'s ambiguity 175.
autographs of Descartes: 1909, 2374.
automata: 149; & doubt 236; & s.v. Cogitationes privatae.
automatism vs. organism: 276; & s.v. beast-machine, man-machine, mechanism.
Averroes, Averroism: doubt, cogito 344; & Thomism, Cartesianism 2667.
Avicenna: cogito & homme volant 260a; 1947.
axioms: texts 7; six fundamental assumptions of D. 238; Scholastic axioms defended by D. against contemporaries 231; axiomatic systems & méthode 2350; & s.v. protophilosophy.

B

Baader, Franz Xaver von [1765–1841]: 409, 466b.
Bachelard, Gaston: *235c, 1106–07*, 1402.
Bacon, Francis: 120, 451, 1079, 1168; Bacon & D. as students at Poitiers 1172; his scientific vs. D.'s metaphysical concern 256; parallel texts 2425; spiritualist interpretation 3176; doubt 1903; logic: Bacon & English empiricists accept, D. rejects formal logic 335; Lullus rejected 328; lumen naturale 299; methodology & méthode 189, 211, 388 & 2748; rationalism 299; superstitious notions 3426.
Baillet, Adrien, Abbé [1649–1706]: *122, 1111;* sollicits assistance for his biography 450, 467; his D. biography assessed, used 121–124, 3428, criticized 124, defended 142; asserts D.'s religiosity 14, slights Beeckman, Mersenne 215.
Baldi, Bernardino [1553–1617]: 369.
Ballet of Descartes: s.v. Naissance de la paix.
Balmes, Jaime Luciano [1810–1848]: admires D.'s Catholicism despite philosophical opposition 1905, 2662; time, space, plurality of worlds 1826, 1981.
Balz, Albert Georg Adam: *1116–32; 23, 151, 431;* 463; Thomistic, Cartesian man *431, 1130, 1132*, 2801; Whitehead *226*, 194a; 1114.
Balzac, Jean-Louis Guez sieur de [1597–1654; AM, v. 1]: gives D. form & style of Essay 404; D.'s letters to him 419; student at Leiden, with Théophile de Viau 123; & s.v. biography.
Bannan, J.: *22*, 96, 179d.
barometer: s.v. Pascal; Puy de Dôme; vacuum.
Baroque: bibliography 3a; anamorphoses, perspectives, & CP 236; D. as philosopher of Baroque & Counterreformation 10, 319, 2864a; his universe a Baroque clockwork 1671; "arbre de la sagesse" a Baroque symbol 2724; his epistemology, & Baroque painting 415, 1438a; nonrhetorical philosophy 2098; & s.v. Molinism.

Barrès, Maurice: 1566, 1568.
Barrow, Isaac [1630–1677]: history of mechanics 367.
Barth, Karl: attack on Cartesianism 193a, 1149, 1667.
Bartholinus, Erasmus [1625–1698]: commentary to Géométrie 358; judges three portraits of D. 1.
Basch, Victor: *419*.
Baudelaire, Charles: his Cartesian classicism 429.
Baudin, Émile: *1156*, 1437.
Bayle, Pierre [1647–1706; Cabeen, v. 3, 4]: 157, 438, 441a, 451, 454, 467, 468; beast-machine 226, 466a; Chinese influence? 310; epistemology 161; idealism: Bayle & Malebranche 462; infinite: antinomies 161.
beast-machine: 147, 226, 276, 386, 466a, 467, 1846, 2731, 3347; texts 7, 83, 84; bio-bibliography 16, 226; animal spirits as root of doctrine 386; apologetic purpose: keystone of D.'s defense of Church against science 163, 179b,d; "conscience" 276; D. denies to animals only reason 1202, 3402, thus preparing 18th century materialism 468; human sensation made unquantifiable 398; individuation 170, 1443; metaphysics (âme-corps) 170; organism vs. mechanism 276; *doctrinal history:* 226, 1260; St. Augustine 302, 1210; Bayle 438, 1576; Boullier 244; Campailla 41, 1439; Chanet & Cureau de la Chambre 1260, 2967–68; Cartesians 431, 467, 1764; Chrysippos 3156; the happy beast 1260 & English theriophily 2256; Macy vs. Boullier 244; man-machine: La Mettrie 226, 468, 3474; Pardies 3129; Pereyra as D.'s forerunner? 3192; John Smith, Cambridge Neoplatonist 465; modern controversy 2332, 2739, 3380 & social problem 1576; poem "D. & the animals" 426; & s.v. machines, man-machine, mechanism.
beatitude: 178, 228; sagesse 230.
Beaune: s.v.: De Beaune.
Beck, David: portrait of D. 3365, 467, & s.v. iconography.
Beck, Leslie J.: *1174–76;* Regulae *198;* Royaumont *42;* 3587.
Beckmann, Nikolaus: comments on D.'s philosophy 2133.
Beckett, Samuel: D., Geulincx & the absurd 402a.
becoming: D.'s concept of matter incompatible with it 2188–88a; "becomingness" (Whitehead) 155.
Beeckman, Isaac [1588–1637; AM, v. 1]: Journal *80*, 379, 2373; correspondence with Mersenne *82;* biography, assessment 121–123, 467, 3520 & s.v. biography; his death: D.'s cold letter of condolence 2781; initiates, anticipates scientific achievements 215 (p. 427), 367; anticipates Galilei 363 & 1768 on free fall, correcting D. 371, 379, 3390; laws of impact 2608a.
behavior: the unconscious, & revealing behaviour 215b; mistaken for substance 190; see also habitus.
Being, esse, être, Sein: texts 7; D.'s different uses of the term 3528; causa essendi 3259, & s.v. causa sui, God; cogito 208, & existence, Being 466b, 2916, cogito misses Being 172; D.'s discovery of Being, "déréalisation de l'objet" (Alquié) 149, 1056; epoché: dialectic presence of Being 2843; esse & nosse 165, 170, 179d, 182, 466b, 1643, 1987, 2148, 2928, step from nosse to esse is valid 165, does not constitute idealism 3294, relation made central in philosophy by D. (Schelling) 192a; esse est percipi 1710; esse & existere 466b, 2916, 3528; ideas 165, 170; objective Being 212a, objective vs. formal Being 1643, 2843, Cajetan 1685; Thomistic & Cartesian concepts 208, 1723; unknowability of Being, & liberté 149; "Verlust des Seins" 172, 175; & s.v. ens, cogito, dualism, existence, ontology, Heidegger, Husserl.
Bekker, Balthasar [1634–1698]: 438, 441, 454, 467, 3503.
Belgium: Cartesianism 458, 1781, & s.v. Holland.
Belin, Jacques, & D.'s Stockholm burial: 124 (v. 2, app.).
Belot, Emile: vortex hypothesis *351*, *1189–90*, 359.
Belot, Jean: his "tourbillons de la matière" [1603], source of D.'s theory? 328.
bene vixit qui bene latuit: 121, 1967a, & s.v. biography.
Benedetti, Giambattista [1530–1590]: 379.
Benedictine Order: 438, 457a; teaching of Cartesian philosophy 450, 466a.
Bentley, Richard [1662–1742]: time, space, God 379a; beast-machine 3127–28.
Berdyaeff, Nikolai Alexandrovič: *184a*.
Bergson, Henri: 186; durée & cogito 203; intellectual intuition 281; intuition &

attention: parallels with D. 1677; time 347a; Bergsonizing interpretations of D. 216, 1672, 1677.

Berkeley, George: attacks pensée-substance concept 259; cosmology 379a; esse et percipi 1710; latent Cartesianism in English philosophy 1944 via Malebranche 1943; D., Malebranche, Berkeley 2156.

Berlin, University: Tercentenary address [1950] 543.

Bernard, Claude: D. his precursor? 394.

Bérulle, Pierre de, Cardinal [1575–1629]: anti-libertinism, influence upon D. 14, 124 (v. 2, app.), 149, 163, 267; child psychology and theological symbolism 268a; mysticism 267; Chandoux episode at Papal Nuncio, & D. 2, 100, 124, 149, 163, 189; & s.v. biography, Oratoire.

bibliography, reference, research tools: section 1–33; 1231, 2441; encyclopedias, dictionaries 1091a, 1320, 1433, 1548, 1861, 2130, 2348, 2601, 2979, 3150, 3315, 3531, 3574; animal soul 16, 226; biography 79, 458, 467, 1241; Cartesian era (q.v.) 3a 16–21, 397a, 454, 464a, 466a, 467; commemorative items 501–560, 2669; definitions, terminology, texts 7, 83, 165; doubt 1548; Enlightenment 454, 466a; histories of philosophy 10; manuscripts 466a; mathematics, science 18, 396, 397a; medicine 397a; medieval sources, influences 7, 214, 263; physiology 3066; theology 1379, 1548; Transsubstantiation 2288; works of Descartes 3, 149, 1091a.

Bibliothèque Nationale: 1, 3, 3444.

bien juger pour bien faire (DM): 215a, 347b.

bifurcation: s.v. dualism, Whitehead.

biography, general: basic works 79, 121–123; section 93–126; 1, 2, 14, 36, 83, 129, 131, 132, 138–40, 145, 146, 146a, 150, 163, 1777, 1808, 1935a, 2131a, 2616, 3014, 3048, 3428, 3499; documents 1, 121–124, 528, 538, 1022.

biology, biomechanism: 170, 386, 1443, 1691, 2167, 3134; anti-Aristotelianism of 17th c. biology 2891; Cartesian & modern 2281; D.'s biomechanism 1815a & Enlightenment 468; no Cartesian influence upon modern biomechanics 3017; evolutionary outlook of D.'s genetics 2369a; final causes 149, 170, 179c, 1443; individuation 215a, 1443; méthode 2802; Sweden: French influence 2237; utility of instinctive beliefs, & epistemology 340; & s.v. evolution, individuation, medicine, psychology.

birth & birthplace of Descartes: 1095, 1141, 1142, 1534, 2113–14, 3072, 3121, 3546; commemorations [1696–1896] 501–04, 2567; [1696–1946] 541; & s.v. biography, family.

Blanchet, Léon: *200; 165*, 215.

Blondel, Maurice: 1255–57, 152, 435b, 27, 181, 1824c; falsifies D. 3314.

blood: s.v. circulation.

Boas, George: *1260–64, 200a, 238;* 226.

body, bodies, corps: texts 7; 170, 179c, 193, 215a; body less known than âme & God 165, 170, 208, 1259; essence 170; hygiene of body, & morale 220; individuality 215a; plurality of bodies & unicity of extension 170, 215a, 290, 463; proof of existence: s.v. external world; see also extension, matter, physics, âme, dualism, substance, union.

Bohatec, Josef: *436;* 6, 38, 452, 467.

Bohemia, Descartes in: 37 & 1193, 1022, 3454; also s.v. biography, Czechoslovakia.

Boileau-Despréaux, Nicolas [1636–1711; Cabeen, v. 3]: D.'s influence 412, indirect 424, denied 411 (Abercrombie).

Bolzano, Bernhard: 1824.

Bombelli, Raffaele [ca. 1530 - after 1572]: source of Géométrie? 2664.

bon sens: 83, 170, 1721a, 2609, 2961; bon sens ruins cogito (Husserl) 174; equality of bon sens, not intellect 215a, a democratic doctrine 2587a; individuality 170; Vico's senso commune 1506; & s.v. Studium bonae mentis.

bona mens: s.v. bon sens, Studium bonae mentis.

Bonald, Louis Gabriel vicomte de: *1273–76;* attacked 3481.

Bonaventura, Saint: influence on D.'s concept & proofs of God, infinitum 214.

Bontadini, Gustavo: *1277–86,* Studi *239,* ed. DM *1280;* 2519.

Bordas-Demoulin, Jean-Baptiste: *437;* 126, 451, 2506, 3047.

Borkenau, Franz: *154;* 179.

Born, Max: "minimalist" in physics 375.

Borrichius, Olaus [Borch, Oluf; 1626–1690]: 1 & 2858a (Nordström).

Boschet, Antoine, S.J. ["Académicien"; 1642–1699]: 122.

Bossuet, Jacques Bénigne, Bishop of Méaux: 438, 441a, 446–47, 451, 454, 2782; Augustinian reaction against Cartesianism 2461; beast-machine controversy 226, 466a; history

313; literary influence of D. 412; psychology 215a; truth even in confused ideas 2461.
Bouillier, Francisque Cyrille: *1304–06*, Histoire *438*; Brunetière & Fouillée *442*; 6, 126, 223, 451, 1929, 2506.
Boullier, David Renaud [1699–1759]: beast-machine 226, 244, 431, 467.
Bourdin, Pierre, S.J. [1595–1653; AM v. 4]: 438, 441a; O & R VIII: metaphors 403; D.'s scepticist dilemma 322a; threatens to denounce D. in Rome 338; & s.v. Jesuits, Objectiones.
bourgeoisie: D. as representative of rising bourgeoisie 37, 150, 154, 295; contemporary bourgeois scholarship belittles D. 3184 as philosopher of resignation 1726; & s.v. Marxist interpretations.
Boursier, Laurent François, S.J. [1679–1749]: 438, 441a, 451.
Bovillus (Bouillé, de Bouelles), Carolus [1475–1553?]: 2649.
Bowman, Archibald: *155*, 191.
Boyle, Robert [1627–1691]: light, ether 3558; mechanics 367; & Dutch Cartesians 467.
Brahe, Tycho [1546–1601]: 2612.
brain: patterns 193, 2242; modern epistemology & brain physiology 350; & s.v. pineal gland, memory.
Bréhier, Emile: *1349–59*, *200*, *241*; 215b, 2536.
Brentano, Franz: *1361*; 10, 288; classes of "conscience" 212a.
Bretagne: Descartes family 99.
Bridgman, Percy Williams: 247.
Brucker, Jakob: *441a*; 10.
Brunetière, Ferdinand: *1381–83*, *442*; appraisal 14, 429; date of RV 242 & 1485; D.'s literary influence 411, 429; Port-Royal: corrected on anticartesianism 38.
Bruno, Giordano [1548–1680]: 2584.
Brunschvicg, Léon: *1387–1406*, Descartes *131*, Écrits *159*, Pascal *158*, 1393, philosophie mathématique *358*, *1396*, Progrès de la conscience *157*, Spinoza *156*; 14, 28, 184; Montaigne 158, 1155; "religion cartésienne" 24; Brunschvicg's & Maritain's D. interpretation 184.
Brunschwicg, Jacques: *270a*, *3104c*.
Bulgaria: Descartes items 1973, 3184–85, 3197.
burials of Descartes: Stockholm burial & rumors about it 110, 124 (v. 2, app.) & s.v. biography, Panthéonisation, transfers.
Buridan, Jean: 1074.
Burman, Francis, the Elder: see: *Entretiens avec Burman.*
Burthogge, Richard [1638–1701?]; 161, 441.
Burtt, Edwin Arthur: *444*, *1417*; 2649.

C

Caen: Cartesian meeting 438 (v. 1).
Cajetan, Tommaso de Vio [1470–1534]: source of D.'s être objectif? 1685.
Calcul de Monsieur Descartes: ed. 74, 79 (*Introduction à la géométrie.*)
Cally, Pierre [1630–1709]: Transubstantiation 3478.
Caloprese, Gregorio [1650–1714], Neapolitan Cartesian: 433, 438, 1648.
Calvin, Jean [1509–1564]: Institutions & TP 1970; Calvinist interpretation 1845.
Cambridge Platonists: 211a, 429a, 456, 465, 1482, 2228a, 2812, 3450a.
Campailla, Tommaso [1668–1740]: Cartesian poem, scientific writings 41 & 1439.
Campanella, Tommaso [1568–1639]: Augustinianism 302; cogito 165, 200, 3090a; CP 163; doubt 2599; space 377.
Cantecor, Georges: *93*, *1445–47*; RV *242*, 1485; discussion & critique 83, 100, 119, 179d.
capillarity: 390.
capitalism: D.'s metaphysics expresses capitalistic spirit 154; DM its manifesto 179; fruit of Cartesianism 3529; & s.v. Marxist interpretations.
Carabellese, Pantaleo: *204*, *204a*, *1452–1456*; 4, 129.
Caramuel de Lobkowitz, Juan, O.S.B. [1606–1682]: early Spanish Cartesianism 449.
Carbonara, Cleto: *205*, *1458–60*; 4, 1966.
Carleton, Thomas Compton, S.J. [1591–1666]: 2604.
Carlini, Armando: *4*, *1461–63*; Galli's study 1961.
Carneades: probabilism 1651; & s.v. scepticism.
Cartesian discussion groups (conférences cartésiennes): 390, 438 (v. 1, 2), 450, 466a; modern 516, 3609.
Cartesian era: bibliography 3a, 16–21, 397a, 454, 461, 464a; documents, sources 450, 466a; section 430–470; history of ideas, political, social background 429a, 446, 447, 450, 454, 457, 466a, 468, 2859; science 352, 357–59, 367, 377–79, 380, 382, 387, 390, 434, 467, 1005a; &

s.v. seventeenth century, Cartesianism, Enlightenment.
"Cartesian ethics": modern deductive ethics (Hare) 2183a, 1023; 3333.
Cartesian man: see: anthropology (philosophical.)
Cartesian Research Society of Philadelphia: 2242.
Cartesian Scholasticism: s.v. philosophia & theologia novantiqua; Holland; "scholastic" tendency of modern D. scholarship 172a, 179d (Lenoble).
Cartesian tensors: 2297.
Cartesianism, *doctrinal development:* "Cartesianism before Descartes" 2908; *after Descartes:* 138, 157, 161, 171a, 177, 192a, 200a, 202, 431, 438, 441, 441a, 451, 467, 1320, 1350, 3076, 3274, 3401; atomism 380, 463, 2134; Augustinianism 38, 161, 235, 302, 1157; beast-machine (q.v.) 16, 226, 467; chemistry 165, 352, 387, 390, 466a, 467; causality: see occasionalism below; cosmogony, cosmology 351, 359, 374, 379a, 402, 457c, 466a,c, 1825, 2503, 2584; Enlightenment 112, 434, 454, 455, 459, 468, 2901; esthetics, art, literature: section 403–429a, 2700; individuality, individuation 215a; mathematics: bibliography 18, 397a, history 355, 355a, 372, 378, 382, 390, 466a, 467, 1448; mechanics 361, 367–69, 377a, 390; medicine 433; ontological argument (q.v.) 211a; occasionalism (q.v.) 138, 431, 438, 441a, 451, 463, 2338, 2810, 3216, 3227, 3275, 3513; physics 356, 357, 371, 377, 377a, 380, 390, 444, 449, 466a, 468, 1005a, 1099, 2575; physiology 360, 373, 468, 1916; political & social philosophy 2934a, 2957, 3235, jurisprudence & law 253, 264, 412, 435, 445, 466d, 1065a, 2829, 3235; religion & theology 215b, 431, 435a–b, 436, 446–47, 454, 457, 2228a; scepticism 322a; unconscious & subconscious mind 215b; & see Cartesian era, Malebranche, Spinoza, Leibniz, occasional causes.
Cartesianism, *fortunes:* 434, 438, 441a, 466a, 467, 468; America (North & South) 40, 448, 1099, 1345, 1473, 3189; Belgium 458, 1781; France 138, 357, 438, 450, 451, 453, 454, 466, 466a, 1817, 1876, 3218a, 3425, documents 450, religion 446–47, persecution 450, 466a; Germany 436, 438, 1824b; Holland 6, 38, 109, 138, 435a, 436, 438, 458, 467, 1763–64, 3205–06, 3411–14, universities 452, persecution 1918; Hungary 469, 1151, 3601; Italy 222, 420, 433, 438, 443, 461, 1265, 1648, 1824a, 2003, 2578, 2898, 3331; Poland 15, 470, 1137, 1541, 1544, 1676, 1678; Portugal & Spain 430, 449, 1553; Sweden 466c, 2237, 2552a; Switzerland 436, 438; & s.v. Cartesian era, Cartesianism (doctrinal development), persecution of Cartesianism.
"Cartesius" vs. "Descartes" (Balz): 151.
Cassirer, Ernst: *1475–86; 5, 160, 161, 242, 243, 465;* 14, 2649.
Castel, Louis-Bertrand [1688–1757]: 3218a.
Catelan, Abbé de: 390, 2147, 3104d.
Catelet, Abbé de: 2147; tides 1027a.
catena scientiarum: 83, 2609; in magic literature before D. 328; concatenation of sciences through sagesse: common notion before D. 220; & philosophes 455; & s.v. Cogitationes privatae, unity of science, arbre de la sagesse, Dream.
Caterus (Kater), Johannes [d. 1656; AM, v. 4]: relations with D. 458; ens objectivum 212a; O & R (q.v.) 165, 2685.
Catholic collectanea, commemorative publications: 35, 41, 520, 526.
Catholic interpretations & viewpoints: survey 14; Collectanea & commemorative contributions 35, 41, 520, 526; general 132, 152, 166–69, 177, 179a–d, 183–184a, 185, 186, 206, 1239, 1813, 2138, 2229, 3249; German Romantic revival 466b; Cartesianism & modern science 1914; D. & Bonald 3481; pure reason's failure 2835; Socratic, Cartesian, Catholic inquiry 1798; traditional charges of irreligiosity 14; & s.v. Neoscholastic interpretations, religion, religiosity.
Cauchy, Augustin-Louis: vortices 392.
Caus, Salomon de [ca. 1576–1626]: automata, perspectives 236.
causa sui, & created truth: 83, 165, 204, 327, 455a, 3259; Cartesians 431; causa sui, causa prima, causa essendi 3259; & s.v. causality, God, proofs of God.
causality, causes: definitions, texts (Cartesian & Scholastic) 7, 83, 165; general 83, 150, 161, 170, 178, 185, 193, 1874, 3458; change: D.'s anti-Aristotelian limitation to efficient causation, consequences 348; Christian concept identical with D.'s 291a; divine & natural causality not connected: root of occasionalism 463; external & internal 291a; & freedom 349; & idea (q.v.) 204; mythological abuse by D. 2559; ontological & logical: causality as constructive world principle 262; physical causality & human

experience 1394; proof of God by causality 165 & s.v. proofs of God; similarity of cause & effect: Cartesian axiom 238; sufficient reason not distinguished from causality 3009; substance 160, 193; time 160, 347a; unites inner certitude with stability of physical order 1545; & s.v. causa sui, finality, occasional causes.

causality, *doctrinal history:* 213, 262, 349, 453a, 2366, 3551 (monograph); Cartesians 3227; Hume 262, 348, 349, 453a, stays within Cartesian notion of change 348; Kant 2366; Leibniz 213, 262, 349, 453a; Locke 453a, & cognition 1061; Malebranche 213, 262, 453a; John Norris 453a; occasionalism (q.v.); Spinoza 213, 262, 455a, & monism 2630.

cavalier: D. as cavalier français (Goethe) 2057 "qui partit d'un si bon pas" (Péguy) 186; as "hardi cavalier de l'absurde" 3209.

Cavalieri, Bonaventura-Francesco [1598–1647; AM, v. 2]: gravity 379; mathematics 378.

Cavendish, Sir Charles [1591–1654; AM, v. 4]: 118, 1020.

Cavendish, William, Duke of Newcastle [1592–1676; AM, v. 4]: 118, 1020.

celebrations, commemorations, exhibitions: Amsterdam 1788; Châtellerault 518, 1748; Franeker 505, 1752; La Haye-Descartes [an II] 114, 124 (app.), [1937] 528; Moscow 3403; Paris 1; Poitiers 553; Prague 501, 1823; Rumania 2944; Tours 504, 538.

cendres de Descartes: s.v. burials, Panthéonisation, skull, transfers.

Cercle Descartes (19th century): 516; other Cartesian circles: s.v. Cartesian discussion groups.

certitude: texts 7; 83, 165, 170, 171, 175, 178, 179c, 185, 204, 204a, 3165, 3247, 3476, 3525; autonomy & heteronomy 177; Cartesian & Scholastic 177, 208; circle 185; confounded with evidence 3512; mathematical & experimental certitude unreconciled 181; not attainable by méthode 1377a or through 'conscience' 187; not guaranteed by cogito 208; opposed to probability (q.v.); sapientia universalis 1575; science: God & causa sui 327, less useful than probabilism 231, impossible 2651, obsolescent in modern science 2600; terminal 175; theology 3155e; theoretical & religious: Aristotle to Heidegger 1978, D. & St. Augustine 1867, Thomist & Cartesian 208; & s.v. probability.

Cervantes, Miguel de: 2492.

Chandoux, Sieur de: & D.'s introduction to Bérulle 2, 100, 124, 149, 163, 189, & s.v. biography.

Chanet, Pierre [ca. 1603–after 1649]: beast-machine controversy 226, 1260, 2967–68; scepticism 322a.

change: consequences of D.'s abandonment of Aristotelian concept 262, 348; substance & relative change 160, 1068; epistemology 160, 161.

Chanut, Hector-Pierre [1601–1662; AM, v. 5] his family 1011; 2865, 3081, 3145; Lettres sur la morale 90, 215c; role in D.'s life 121–123; reproduction of Chanut's inscriptions on D.'s tomb 122.

chaos: 359, & s.v. cosmogony.

Chapelain, Jean [1595–1674]: "amour" 422.

Charron, Pierre [1546–1603]: sagesse (q.v.) 220; mystic-fideistic scepticism **246**; doubt: leap into Revelation 322, 322a.

Châtellerault: 99 & 1140, 2791; D.'s family 99 & its possessions 1699; celebrations [1937] 518, 1748; & s.v. biography.

Chauveau, François, S.J., of Melun ,[1598–1647; AM, v. 4]: 97, & s.v. biography.

chemistry: Cartesian & Scholastic 165; D.'s disciples, influence 352, 387, 390, 466a; iatrochemists 467; Rohault 390.

Chevalier, Jacques: *1523–33; 132* & *1532;* ed. *90;* 27, 209a, 2640.

Cherbury: s.v. Herbert, Edward.

childhood of Descartes: 93, 95, 108, 121–123, 3544; lutte contre l'enfance 14; & s.v. biography.

child psychology (psychologie infantile): 268, 381; clear, distinct ideas 268; symbolism 268a; unconscious mind 215b; Wordsworth & D. 429a.

Chinese & Cartesian philosophy: 310.

chiquenaude: Pascal misunderstands D.'s God 318; Malebranche & origin of motion 373a.

Chouet, Jean-Robert [1642–1731]: Swiss Cartesian at Saumur 464; introduces Cartesianism in Geneva 438 (v. 2).

Christianity, Catholicism of Descartes: s.v. faith & reason, God, religion, religiosity, theology.

Christiansen, Broder: D.'s theory of judgment *1550*, disputed 212a.

Christina Queen of Sweden [1626–1689; AM, v.7]: Lettres sur la morale 90, 215c, 1186,

1922, 3376; role in D.'s life 121–123, 1011, 1186, & s.v. biography; Cassirer's studies 243, 1477–79, 3037; D. not disappointed in her 81; his medical advice to her 3238; his role in her religious development & conversion to Catholicism 243; her physician Durietz a friend of D. 2552a; Christina & heroic ideal 243; RV written for her? 242 & 1485.

chronology of D.'s thought, works: s.v. development.

Chrysippos: beast-machine & malin génie 3156.

chûte des corps: s.v. free fall.

cire, morceau de (MM): s.v. wax.

Ciermans, Jean (Joâo Parcásio Cosmander) S.J., [1602–1648; AM, v. 1]: controversy with D. 458; first Cartesian in Portugal 430.

Cinq-cents, Conseil des: 112 & 2077 & s.v. Panthéonisation.

circle (the Cartesian circle): 83, 149, 170, 171, 178, 185, 204, 204a, 210, 214, 2414, 2793; also 2369a, 2446, 2570, 3061, 3195; survey of proposed solutions 3187; circularity of argument denied 215 (p. 292), 1226a, 1784, 1824d, 1910, 2005, 2514, 3362; circularity eliminated 1144; circularity legitimate, inevitable in any epistemology 214, 233; circle or nexus rationum? 170; existence & doubt 2092; from apodictic epistemology to theory of "conscience" 3512; reality as limit of the deducible 3107b; transcendental philosophy anticipated 2197.

circulation of the blood, Harvey & Descartes: 120, 386, 402, 467, 2552a, 3532; Scholasticism, Harvey, Descartes 165; D.'s role in winning acceptance for Harvey's discovery 165, 386, 2552a; his influence on Rudbeck's work 2552a.

citoyen: Cartesian pedagogical ideal 265 (Taborda).

clarté: D., Spinoza, Leibniz 2261; "fausses clartés" of D. 183, of his méthode 1251–52; "trompe-l'œil clarté" of DM 1951; & s.v. clear & distinct; contradictions.

Classicism: bibliography 3a, survey 14; section 403–429a passim; background 429a, 446, 447, 454, 457, 1930; Aristotelian classicism & D. 3436; art 415 & s.v. painting; D.'s "pensée classique" 134; England 406, 409, 429a, 460; Enlightenment 443; France: controversies over D.'s role 14, 243 (Reichardt), 411, 412, 417, 422, 429 & s.v. literature; French "pseudoclassicism" [1680–1750]: no Cartesian influence 429, modern French "classics" & Cartesian spirit 429; Holland 467; Italy 420; & s.v. art, esthetics, literature, querelle des anciens et des modernes.

Clauberg, Johann [1625–1665]: 441, 451, 452, 467; animal soul 226; occasionalism 431 & 1123, 2810.

Claudel, Paul: 408 & 1556.

clear & distinct ideas, notions, perceptions: 83, 178, 211, 212a, 221, 232; texts 7; Brentano 1361; Cartesians 161; child psychology (q.v.) 268; circle 2446; & "conscience": contradictions 453b; confused ideas may contain truth: Bossuet 2461; idea & perception: distinction difficult 2007; law: influence 264, 466d, 2829; logical status 231; Malebranche: his destruction of clear, distinct philosophy, replaced by mystical intuition 453c; objective essence, Cartesian realism 3132; obscurities 3360, Géométrie 2758; poetry: detrimental influence 409; positivist critique 2671a; realism 3113a, 3132; Romero 2188–82a; scepticism the inevitable consequence of the doctrine, & Spinoza 329; subjectivist view of conscious perception 1414a; union (âme-corps), pensée distincte 178; & s.v. clarté, confusion, idea.

Clerselier, Claude [1614–1684; AM, v. 6]: 431; his family 1011; editor, translator of D. 79, 84, biased 81, suppresses letters on Transsubstantiation 452a; D.'s Catholicism affirmed 14, 431; dualism 431; physics 390.

Cocceius (Koch), Johannes [1603–1669]: 109, 435a, 436, 467; controversy with Voetius 435a, 436.

Code Napoléon: Cartesian spirit? 466d.

"cœur": "fond du cœur" vs. "surface de la pensée" 215b.

Cogitationes privatae: text & editorial problems 74, 75; basic studies, reconstructions 96, 100, 2764; sources 96, 102, 220, 328; interpretations 149, 1526, 3092; anamorphoses, automata 236; moral concerns 220; "physicist without physics" 96; poetic dialectics & epistemology 244a; reflect D.'s ideological difficulties 179; science & mathematics: first efforts 388 & 2744; beginnings of 10-years cycle of development 3174; stoicism 220; symbolism (q.v.) 163, 268a; & s.v. biography, Dream, formative period, Opuscula & their individual titles, larvatus prodeo.

cogito ergo sum: 83, 129, 170, 171, 178, 179d, 185, 210, 219, 221, 233; also 206, 1062, 1153, 1284, 1538, 2230, 2364, 2491, 2809, 2816, 2833, 3063, 3492, 3589; *individual terms: ego* 169, 288, 342; different meanings 1114; different types of awareness, & unity of soul 215b, 2009; personal self, not phenomenologically pure ego (Husserl) 174; ego & res 2536; *cogito* 170 & 2148; mere description, unsatisfactory 1175; merely poetic 235b (Daly); confused with cogitatum 3528a; *ergo* 342, 1281; intuitus & deductio 321a; non-inferential 2337b; "*sum*": merely demonstrative 235b, not an existential qualifier 2337b; misses Sein & Zeit under Scholastic influence 172; existential "sum" (not poetic "cogito") first term 235b; *ego sum* 2904a, 2832a; "ego sum" = sum 276; *variants:* aliquid cogitans sum 1663; cogito ergo non sum 307; Deus cogitatur, ergo Deus est 214; dubito ergo sum 333, 334; ego cogito et cogito me (etc.) 1114; ego sum cogitans (Spinoza) 272; ego volo (Nietzsche) 172b; sedeo ergo sum 2370; somnio ergo sum 104a; sum, ergo Deus est 342; sum res cogitans 333; there is a thought now 235a, b; also 2041, 3610, 3612.

cogito, *special points:* ambiguity 149; Being 171, 172, 175, 204, 204a, 208, 466b, 3057, and s.v. Being; biological epistemology 350; bourgeois cogito & antibourgeois doubt 2552b; certitude (formal, material) 335, 3512; circularity denied 1226a, 1824d, eliminated 1144, cogito neither circular nor plausible 1226a; cognition made absolute 466b; condition humaine: problem unsolved 347b; "conscience" 2352, 2626, 2904a, 3408; defensible as metaphysical hypothesis 3055; different meanings distinguished 1114; DM & MM concepts distinguished & opposed 149; divine guarantee not needed 165; doubt (q.v.) 209, 2092, 2626; genesis: cogito earlier than physics 177, first concept [1628] "docte ignorance Socratique" 269; "engagé" 311a; "enjoyment of conscious experiences" (Whitehead) 194a; epoché (q.v.) 174, 184a; essential & substantial 179d; essence: Scholastic 192b, & existence 1037, D. disregards difference 466b; eternal verities 201; être & penser 170, 2148; evidence confused with certitude 3512; existence & thought 2232, existence merely identified 307, & doubt 307, 2092, & essence 1037, 2916, of objects as well as of self: direct emergence 1377a; existential interpretation 235b (Daly); fact, axiom, principle 326a; form & content 466b; fundamental ontology 1498; générosité 2158; greatest discovery since Plato: D. unaware of this 194a; individuation 215a; innate relation or necessary articulation? 252; "Innerlichkeit des Denkens" 171a; insufficiency of scientific order 1056, of self & world 2904a; idealism intended, not quite attained 192a; intuition 2232, 3120; intuitive & deductive 179d; knowledge of God (q.v.) 214; liberté (q.v.) 2673; literature: search for cogito of poetry 420; logic: formal analysis 2337b, cogito syllogistically provable 333, principle of contradiction: 17th c. controversy 436, language analysis 235a, b, logical interpretation 2916, cogito non-inferential 2337b; man-machine 350; memory (q.v.); metaphysical realism 281; méthode (q.v.) 231; morale (q.v.) 230; cogito not a first principle 3177, not meaningless but peculiar & degenerate 235b, not "first truth" but "truth form of Cartesian science" 230; obscurities 3360; ontological critique 208; open & closed 3028; pour penser il faut être 170, 252; "plaisir étrange d'être soi, même vis-à-vis du vrai" 1407; proofs of God 447a, the ontological argument (q.v.) 270a is higher than cogito 293, is its equivalent 171a; psychological 2559a; "purification de l'âme" 206, 2904a; realism 1677, 2009, realist concepts, idealistic method 1722; sagesse 206; scepticism not refuted 192, 322a; Stoic aspects 208; systematic role 170, denied: only passing epistemological function 2626; theatrical, dramatic: mask, not self 1509a; thinking machine 350; time missed 172, & eternity 1506a; transition: act to substance-saltus in concludendo 2586, cogito to sum 208, ego to sum 3057, pensée-conscience to pensée-substance 259; unconscious mind 215b; validity upheld 1178; value appraised 1450, cogito still true 2316, dangerous 1552; "Verlust des Seins" 175.

cogito, *precursors, antecedents, parallels:* 83, 200, 215 (ch. 8); Anselm 1790; Aristotle 200, 1246, 3090a; St. Augustine & Augustinian tradition: four texts 149, discussion 200, 163, 165, 1790, cogito & doubt (q.v.) 1336–37, metaphysical similarity 334, D.'s independence despite Platonic rseemblance 235, St. Augustine's cogito preferred: leaves man real, creator-oriented 1336, 1337, Pascal's view of St. Augustine 165; Al-Ghazali, Averroes, Maimonides 344; âtma-brahma 310; Avicenna 260a, 1947; Campanella 200 & 165, 3090a; Eusebius 149, 1909; medieval Augustinian currents 165; Protagoras 172b; St. Thomas 208, 1663, 2196, 2232a, 3090a; Thomists 1987; *successors & critics:* survey of interpretations 27, 252, 333, 1117, 1178, 1677; Ayer 235a,b; Baader: Ich-Verbundenheit vs. Ich-Einsamkeit 466b; Blondel 27, 1256; Casanova 1472; Catholic view of its consequences 3249; Chevalier 27; Condillac: theory of self 2927; Deutinger 466b, 1754–55; Dilthey 1828; Gassendi (q.v.) 2121a, 3421, & s.v. O&R; Gilson, Gouhier, Hamelin 252; Heidegger 172b, 333, 1472a, 1498; Hegel 171a, 333; Husserl (q.v.) 173 & 3528a, 174, 184a, 1472a, 1828, 2737, 2944a, 3409; Huxley 1177–78, 2255; Idealism 232, 1677, 2687, 3091, 3245; Jaspers 175; Jolivet 252; Kant 10, 333, 455a & 2412, 1177–78, 1237, 1413, 1472a, 1910, 2412, 2832a, 3020, 3541; Koyré 1777–78; Laporte, Lavelle 27; Liard 1910; Locke 192b, 1711; Maine de Biran 1828, 1910, 2489c, 2896–97; Malebranche (q.v.) & vision des choses en Dieu 435c; Marxist man 150 (Alquié), Marxist view 150, 2552b; Merleau-Ponty 311a; Molière (abuse of speculation?) 407; Neocriticism (evades its ambiguities) 2628; Nietzsche 172b; Olgiati 252; Ottaviano 27, 252 & 2882; Phenomenalists, Realists 1677; Positivists 235a, 235b, 2671a; reality (Husserl, Maine de Biran, Dilthey, Scheler) 1828; Reymond 3055–58; Rodis-Lewis 27; Sartre 192, 3203; Scheler 1828; Schopenhauer (cogito equivalent to Welt als Wille etc.) 10, 333, 1923; Spinoza (q.v.) 272, 333, 455a; Spiritualists (19th c.) 1862; Thomists 1987, 2041; Veitch 1177–78, 3478a; Vico's remarks 438 (v. 2); Whitehead 194a.

cognition, knowledge, connaissance: texts 7, 178; analytical cognition is selfsufficient 161; âme (knowability) 170, 208, 1259; "angelic cognition", D.'s model 184, 1723; causality: Locke, anticartesians 1061; D.'s critique of mathematical & scientific cognition 160; dualism: understanding & senses 178, 204; error 190; God 2091, knowledge of God & self 269, 1148; imaginative knowledge 3244; of immortality 228; Leibniz & D. 211; limits of rational knowledge 178, absolute limits (Peirce) 187; Malebranche (q.v.) & D. 3023;méthode (q.v.) 198; object, origin, faculties of cognition 178; objectivity of knowledge: Malebranche & Arnauld 451a, D. & Locke 3124; obscurities of D.'s concept of knowledge 3360; philosophical cognition as poetic activity 244a; rational knowledge & union âme-corps 178; Regulae (q.v.) 198, 3582; scientific & human knowledge 210; self & body, & Kant's substance category 3581; the unknowable 178, 187; unknowability of Being, & freedom 149; & s.v. epistemology, imagination, intuition, understanding, connaissance d'autrui, poetic cognition, error, Being (esse & nosse), God.

Cohen, Gustave: *123, 1565-74;* 3148.

Coleridge, S. T.: his Biographia litteraria & reading of D. 2553.

Collectanea cartesiana: sections 35–42, 501–562.

Columbus (Descartes the new philosophical C.): lands on rock of vulgar belief 191, misses America 194a.

Colvius, Andreas [1594–1676; AM, v. 1]: 3415; D.'s letter on Beeckman's death 2781 & s.v. biography; asks D. about "si fallor"-cogito parallel 467.

Comenius: s.v. Komenský.

Communism: 432a; Communist view: see Marxist interpretations, Russia.

Compendium musicae: edition 74; 2562, 2702, 2878, 3218; esthetics 418, 419, 421, 3025; scientific, mathematical aspects 1044, 3025; Pepys does not understand it 2933a; & s.v. Beeckman, biography, esthetics, music.

Comte, Auguste: his D. interpretation 298; affinities with D. 1800; D. his precursor? 146; D.'s psychology 385, physics 188; D. & Comte: history of ideas 316; & s.v. Positivism.

concept: texts 7; & existence: Geulincx 161; source of knowledge, product of perception 212a; Leibniz's critique of conceptual explanation 317.

conceptualism & realism of D.'s epistemology: 2344–45.

condemnation: of Descartes 1276 & s.v. biography, Jesuits; of Galileo (q.v.).

Condillac, Étienne Bonnot de [1715–1780]: abstraction 316; Cartesian intentionality 3109; Enlightenment 455, 1374; self, cogito 2927.

Condorcet, Antoine-Nicolas, Marquis de [1743–1794]: 1374.

Condren, Charles de, Oratorian [1588–1641; AM, v. 1]: 267, 438; & s.v. biography, Oratoire.

Conférence Descartes: 3609.

conformism of Descartes: philosophical 150, 164, 173, 174, 179, 3535; political, social 150–154, 169, 179–9a; religious 150, 152, 164, 169 179, 192; concessions to Church to protect science 164, with damage to his epistemology 231; his God: impotent hybrid of faith & reason 167; spiritual timidity balanced by excessive materialism 1146; scientific ideas theologically disguised 2329; theologizing existential compromise surrenders free creative act to God 192.

confusion: texts 7; 170, 2461; & s.v. clear & distinct.

Congrès Descartes, Paris 1937: Travaux *36;* 29, 1198, 1225, 1261, 1303, 1405, 1563, 2082, 2198, 2472–73, 3090, 3119, 3197, 3273, 3483.

Conimbricenses: texts 7; 208, 263, 430; mechanistic tendencies 1839.

connaissance: s.v. cognition, connaissance d'autrui.

connaissance d'autrui (knowledge of the other self): 190, 215a, 243, 244.

"conscience": classification 212a, 2904a: "engagée & perceptive" 311a; immediate & reflective 215b; âme & unconscious, subconscious mind 215b; "conscience" a category mistake 190; clear & distinct ideas: contradiction 453b; cogito (q.v.) 2904a, 3408; cogito does not convert all knowledge into self-awareness 2626; failure to include animals' awareness 276; finitude 3475; implies presence of God 158; originality of D.'s philosophy 323; psychological determination: Regulae, MM, PP, Notae 2352; its reality 221; rejected as certitude criterion 187; & signs 1056a; types of "conscience" present in cogito 2904a; & s.v. âme, cogito, dreaming, dualism, pensée.

"conscience," *doctrinal history:* surveys 157, 161; St. Augustine 2696, 2861a; St. Thomas *208,* 2196, 2667; decisive issue between Thomism Averroism, Cartesianism 2667; D. to Kant 161, 2789; Cartesian rationalism 204a; Cartesians, Port-Royal, Spinoza, Leibniz 215b; D., Hegel, Nietzsche, Marx, Lenin 2164; D., Heidegger, Jaspers, Klages 2822; origin of all modern metaphysics 176; & s.v. cogito (doctrinal history), Heidegger, Husserl.

consciousness, (self) awareness: s.v. "conscience."

Conti, Abbé de: 2147.

Conti, Antonio [1677–1749]: Cartesian influence in his poetry 420, 433.

contradiction, principle of: 178; & doubt 2444; & s.v. logic.

contradictions, paradoxes, obscurities in D.'s philosophy: 150, 151, 170, 173, 174, 175, 179; fundamental 204, 204a, unreconciled, flagrant contradictions 2307, paradoxes 459, neuralgies of system 1536; D.'s own statements misleading 210; philosophical contradictions resolved by structural analysis, but impasses remain 170; profitable results (Bertrand Russell) 3162; iron rigorousness of D.'s system asserted 170, 398; *special points:* âme-corps (real distinction, substantial union) 165, 170, 2543a; clear, distinct ideas 329, 453b, 2758, 3360; cogito (q.v.) 1910, 3360, 1722 (insoluble conflict between idealism & realism); created truths, causa sui 327; creation 2578; DM (q.v.) 149, disparate texts in DM 260; epistemology 3360; extension & plurality of bodies 290; God's indifference & physics metaphysics 214; intuition: MM opposed to DM 159 & 1401–2; mathematics: proof of necessary truth 314; mathematicist Procrustes bed 166 ruins experimentalism 112; metaphysics 183, 1251–52; pure thought & ideological difficulties 179; religion: 124, 152, 166, 167, 183, 184, 319, contradictions denied 168, 169, 179a–d; D.'s philosophy of religion leads Spinoza to monism, Leibniz to pluralism 3419; compromises with Scholasticism contradict radicalism of D.'s thought 124, 150, 154, 175, 1967a; simple natures (q.v.) vs. méthode 1251–52; substance 1068, 2593; veracity of God 3360; & s.v. personality of Descartes, conformism.

controversies of Descartes: s.v. polemics.

Convention nationale: 112 & 2077, & s.v. Panthéonisation.

Cordeiro (Cordeyro), Antonio, S.J. [1640–

1722]: mechanistic tendencies in Coimbra Scholasticism 1839.
Cordemoy, Géraud de [1600–1684]: 431 & 1121, 451, 463; animal soul 226; physics 390; & s.v. occasionalism.
Córdoba (Argentina): 448.
Corneille, Pierre [1606–1684]: psychological & moral affinities with D. 243 & 1477–78, 3037; D., Corneille, Richelieu as French symbols 2773; héro & générosité: TP as Corneille's source 413, disputed 1509b, 2024a; François de Sales as common source for TP & Corneille 423; générosité 295; Corneille ridicules D. as miles gloriosus elegans? 405.
Cornelio, Tommaso: 1824a.
corps: s.v. body, external world, matter, plurality.
Corpus poetarum: 96, 168, 220, 244a, 346, 1639, & s.v. Dream.
correspondence of Descartes: editions 74, 76, 79, 1040, 1734; inedita 38, 124, 2783, 2875, 3390d; dating, identification of correspondents 74, 1017; Fonds Libri 3387; Arnauld, More 84; Huygens 81; Mersenne 82, 215; & s.v. Lettres sur la morale.
cosmogony: 149, 1091c, 1201, 1871, 2323, 2369a, 2387; texts, Russian translation, commentaries 1739a; chaos 359; Timaeus-type cosmogony of PP 4; precursors, contribution, influence of D. 359, 374, 1825; & theory of knowledge 359; Belot 351 & 1188–90; Poincaré 2978; Swedenborg 466c; & s.v. cosmology, vortex theory.
cosmology: 178, 370, 402, 1091c, 1692; texts, Russian translation & commentary 1739a; D. not an innovator, Cartesians more influential than he 2584; D.'s "indefinite universe": 2503, theologization of space 379a; scientific & magical 268a; Cambridge Neoplatonists 465; Chinese and Cartesian cosmology 310; Ferrier 1882–82a; Fontenelle 457c; & s.v. cosmogony, Newton, plurality (of worlds), space, vortex theory.
Counterreformation: Spanish Scholasticism & Cartesianism as its two forms 319; D. its philosopher 2864a; & s.v. Baroque.
Cournot, Antoine Augustin [1801–1877]: probabilism & evidence 274, 1374, 2306.
Cousin, Victor: *1653–55, 450;* his D. edition & teachings launch 19th c. D. revival 438 (v. 2), 450, 1655; his D. image is influential 126, 180, 223, 224, 249, 365, 2764, 2859, 3176, but not unopposed 114, 188, 453, 462; & s.v. spiritualist interpretations.
CP: s.v. Cogitationes privatae.
crâne de Descartes: s.v. skull.
Crashaw, Richard [1613–1649]: 2225.
creation: texts 7; 83, 171, 178; actual & possible worlds (Malebranche) 453a; conflicts in D.'s doctrine 2578; D. has no theory of creation & art 1441; his doctrine singularly like St. Thomas' 3297; & eternal verities (q.v.) 241; final causes, immutability of God 327; matter 241; influence on chemistry 387; *continuous creation:* texts 7; 83, 241; force 373a; self 455a; time 170, 347a.
criticist philosophy: Descartes its forerunner, his critique of reason & cognition 160, 161, 179c, 221, 398, 1194, 1911, 2241, 2872, 3486, 3602; & s.v. idealism.
Croce, Benedetto: D.'s influence 14.
Cudworth, Ralph [1617–1688]: 438, 456, 2121, 3450a; charges D. with atheism 468; theology 465; & s.v. Cambridge Platonists.
cum plenus forem Enthusiasmo: s.v. Dream, Enthusiasm.
Cureau de La Chambre, Marin [1594?–1669; AM, v. 1]: 226, 1260, 2967–68.
cursus philosophicus: before D. 3425; 17th, 18th century manuscript courses 165, 430, 452, Peru 433, Piacenza 2898, Pisa 433; & s.v. universities.
curves: classification 398, 2480; anaclastic 83, 321a; folium Cartesii 2228, 3168, 3396; ovals 1158; 3041; transcendental curves, spirals 398, 1876; & s.v. Géométrie.
Cusanus (Nikolaus von Kues), Cardinal [1401–1464; AM, v. 7]: 1503, 2649.
cybernetics: 350, 1412.
Czechoslovakia: 15, 37, 3454; commemorative items 501, 1823, 3371; & s.v. Bohemia.

D

Dalen, Cornelis van: portrait of D. 1.
Dąmbska, Izydora: *246, 247;* 3544a.
Damiron, Jean Philibert: *451,* 188.
Damodos, Vikentios [1679–1752]: 1689a.
dance: Compendium musicae 418.
Daniel, Gabriel, S.J. [1649–1728]: *110;* 17, 466, 468, 3536; accepts mechanism, abandons substantial forms 390; animal soul 226; D.'s méthode 189; scepticism 322a.
Darwinism: s.v. evolution.

death: 83, 178, 467, & s.v. immortality, longevity, medicine.
death of Descartes: 121–123, 467, 1760; Alquié's existentialist view 149; Baillet 76, 122; truth & legend 110, 124; commemoration [1650–1950] 542–560, 2625; & s.v. biography; longevity; medicine.
De Beaune, Florimond [1601–1652; AM, v. 1]: *79;* 358, 2758.
deception: why D. feared it 149.
deduction: 83, 171, 175, 178, 193, 198; Cartesian & Kantian 1226; D.'s definition includes mathematical & experimental 3292, i.e. deductive & inductive inference 1243; deduction-induction dualism breaks unity of system 1070; intuition 171, 198, 353; deducibility limited by knowledge of reality 3107b; méthode presuppositional, not deductive 3340; D.'s physics positive, not deductive 1721a; syllogism 198; systematic deduction vs. ontological experience 1056; & s.v. hypothesis, induction.
definition: nominal & real, pensée & idée 170; D.'s mathematicism alters the concept 1251–52.
degeneration of man: concept rejected by D. 1418.
Democritica: 74, 96, 100, 2764, & s.v. Cogitationes privatae, Opuscula.
Democritus: source of Dream? 100, 244a.
demonstration: s.v. analysis & synthesis, proof.
Denmark: D.'s personal relations 2612.
Derham, William [1657–1735]: 2228a.
Descartes family, genealogy of René Descartes: 99 & 1140, 121–124, 179a, 1011, 1076, 1142, 1298, 2113, 3121, 3208, 3427; financial situation, estate, D.'s patrimonial share 94, 1699; the Phélippes Beaulieux manuscripts 1854; Brittany 1864; Sucé 1863; & s.v. biography, Descartes.
"Descartes": origin of name 1076.
Descartes, Cathérine [1635–1706]: beast-machine controversy 226.
Descartes, François-Joachim: two marriages [1690–1729] 3208.
"Descartes, R.," author of astrological work 1107
Descartes, René [1596–1650]: see the Systematic Index s.v. biography, Descartes; for dates, events, names see AM, v. 1.
Descartes' law of sines: s.v. refraction.
Descartes' role in science: revolutionary pioneer of mathematization 131, 156–161, 188, 1427; failure of his Platonized, geometricized physics 189, 379, 398, Cartesian mathematization ruinous 126, 166, 183–84, 2643; archaic attitude in science & concept of certitude 175, 231, 235c, 1901, 2600; defender of new science against guardians of the past 150, 154, 164, 179, 179a–d; revolutionary subjectivist & dualist, establishes new nature concept leading to mastery of nature 171a–172b, 177, 192a; he made no difference to development of modern science 355a, 356, 358, 369; & s.v. influence, mathematicism, physics, science.
Descartes' role in Western philosophy: Brucker's ranking 441a; founder of modern idealism 450; founder of modern philosophy: 2152, 2284, 3462, Balz: modern spirit of inquiry 151, Catholic view 2972, Hegel, Erdmann 171a, Heidegger: D.'s interpretation of Being 172–172b, Husserl: "der urstiftende Genius" 174, Renouvier: climax from Plato to Kant 188, Schelling: second childhood of philosophy 192a; Bacon more fundamental 171a; only méthode was effective 2271; initiator of modern anti-Christian revolt 176, 1950; revolutionary in spirit, not in results 444; founder of French materialism, encyclopedic realist 150, 459.
Descartes' rule of signs (algebra): 1666, 2311.
Desgabets, Robert, O.S.B. [1620–1678]: 450, 457a, 2357; critique of occasionalism 463.
Deshoulières, Mme [Antoinette du Ligier de la Garde, 1638–1694]: 226, 466a.
Desmarets (Maresius), Samuel [1599–1673; AM, v. 5]: 121, 125, 435a, 436, 467.
De solidorum elementis: 74, 100, 388, 2312–13, 3005, & s.v. Opuscula.
determinism: 185, 188 & 3047, & s.v. libre-arbitre.
development of Descartes' thought & work: systematic vs. developmental interpretation 149, 151, 170, 193 & s.v. interpretations; from mechanistic hopes to discovery of Being & man 149; four stages of development 4; ten-year phases [1618–1628–1637–1649] 1540, 1542, 3174; early optimism, mature disillusionment 124; méthode to sagesse 199, 206; from realism (Regulae) to idealism (MM), & Spinoza's resolution of dualism 3029; Regulae to MM: phenomenological viewpoint 1643;

chronology 2, 149, 168, 179a,d (doubt), 189, 199, 2764–65, & s.v. biography; [*1596–1628*] 97, 100, 2764 & s.v. formative period, Regulae, rules of method; [*1606–1618*] "l'enquête" 179a; [*1618–20*] 96, 100, 168; "maturité du doute" 179a; metaphysics: first project 83, 165; méthode, DM rules not yet found 169, 3092; science & mathematics 388, 2744–75, 2751, 2753, 3092; [*1619*] "the vision" 189, 3092, & s.v. Dream; [*1620*] 388, 2753, & s.v. inventum mirabile; [*1620–1637*] "la doctrine" 179a; [*1620–1628*] 168; [*1628*] "the mission" 189; origin of MM 269, D. has metaphysics 121, 189, does not have it yet 149; [*1629–30*] 3389, first thoughts of metaphysics 193; [*1629–1635*] PP conceived 189; [*1630*] "discovery of Being, metaphysics" 149; [*1631–1637*] scientific preoccupations 149; [*1637*] s.v. DM; [1637–1650] 179a–d, & s.v. Discours (DM), Méditations (MM), Principia (PP), morale, sagesse.

dialectics of Descartes: texts 7; critique 206; causal in form, not spirit 2719; of certainty 1575; of cogito & proofs of God 149; negative 2587a, poetic 244a; Cartesian & Marxist 179, 1091b, & s.v. Marxist interpretations; Platonic dialectics & méthode 3215; D. in the dialectic history of philosophy 138.

Diaz de Gamarra, Don Juan Benito, [1745–1783]: Mexican Cartesianism 1473.

Diderot, Denis [1713–1784]: 468; 126, 459.

Dietrich (Theodoric) von Freiberg [died ca. 1310]: rainbow theory 356.

Dieu-trompeur argument: 165, 169, 2086; deflects cogito from straight idealism (Schelling) 192a; lumen naturale 321; "petit doute naturel" striking memory of evidence 270, 270a; 17th century scepticism 322a; & s.v. veracity, malin génie, certitude, circle.

Digby, Sir Kenelm [1603–1665]: 467, 1020; beast-machine 226.

Dilthey, Wilhelm: *206a;* 424, 1828.

Dioptrique: editions 74, 76; translations & commentaries: German 87, Russian 1737a; scientific results 396; méthode 198, 402, 2966; methodology: instrumentalist 247; Petit's objections, & Mersenne 400; visual impression & idea 3109; & s.v. refraction, Essais, priority.

diplomacy: D. and French as international diplomatic language 1557.

Discours de la méthode [DM]: *editions* 74 (grande édition), 76, 77, bibliophile 1773, 2951; *commentaries:* Gilson 83, 2038; Alain 1031; Gadoffre 1951; Italian (Bontadini, de Feo, Levi) 1280, 1875, 2516; English (Veitch) 3478a; Portuguese 146; Russian 1737a; *genesis & chronology* 81, 124, 179a; DM a composite of texts from different periods 189, 260, 292, 1951, disputed 149; title borrowed from Aconzio? 278; conceived later than MM & PP 189; DM & MM 269; 10–years cycles in D.'s thought 1540, 1542, 3174; & s.v. development of D.'s work; *historicity* (autobiographical reliability) 83, 93, 96, 142, 163, 165, 169, 179a, 3293; *reception & reputation* 404; D.'s contemporaries preferred MM, PP 326; DM as D.'s masterpiece 142; Positivists introduce it to Brazil 146.

Discours de la méthode [DM]: *general* 149, 189, 1104, 1181, 1782, 2330a, 2838, 2862, 2950, 3269; *special topics:* bien juger, bien faire 215a, 347b; conflict with Scholastics 3328; contradictions (q.v.) 149; D. as miles gloriosus (Corneille) 405; La Flèche (q.v.):education 98; eternal verities 241; existential interpretation 347b; four rules of method older than Regulae 100; Deus-Pater-Creator, not Christ its center 1526; Genesis (q.v.); Jacobi's lecture [1846] 2277; Jungius's annotations 2595; leads to idealism as well as materialism 2255; manifesto of rising bourgeoisie 179; Marxist interpretation (q.v.) 2770a; méthode (q.v.) 210, aprioristic 247, discipline of mind 3079; MM & DM: opposition 149, 159 & 1401 & s.v. Méditations, morale (q.v.) 220; Petit's objections 400; Regulae (q.v.) 83, 198, 2518; scientific work 3479; Spinoza's De intellectus emendatione 1490; spirit of Renaissance (Montaigne) 3583; style 408, 1890; Thomist view 3070.

Discours de la méthode, Tercentenary [*1637–1937*]*:* section 506–540; 1165, 1404, 2231, 2561, 2633, 2854, 3071 ("Les malheurs de D."), 3328, 3351, 3429.

dissociation of sensibility: T. S. Eliot & Cartesian spirit 429a.

distinct: s.v. clear.

distinction: texts 7; formal, real, distinctio rationis 178, 2212, 3113; Spinoza 455a; & s.v. âme-corps, dualism.

dix-septième (XVIIe) siècle: s.v. seventeenth century, Cartesian era; dix-huitième (XVIIIe): s.v. Enlightenment.

DM: s.v. Discours de la méthode.
dogma: s.v. theology.
dogmaticism of Descartes: 175, 1779.
Domat, Jean [1625–1696]: 466a, d.
Dominis, Marco Antonio de [1564–1624]: rainbow theory 356.
doubt (doute méthodique, hyperbolique): texts 7, 83; critical literature survey 3580; different forms 169; *general* 83, 147, 169–171, 179a,d, 185, 204, 204a, 219, 221, 1038–39, 1548 (bibliography), 1866a, 1903, 2068, 2490, 2552b, 2598, 2823, 2921; *special topics:* D. attempts doubt without critical-phenomenological basis 1377a; automata 236; bourgeois reaction against divine & feudal authority 2552b; doubt carried to methodic negation 268; cogito (q.v.) 209, 2092, 2626; condition humaine not encompassed 347b; doubt controls everything except principles inherent in existence itself (Gouhier) 2092; D.'s critical sincerity incomplete, not radical 191, 346; dangerous enterprise 83, 165, 184 (n. 47); DM doubt selective, MM doubt ontological (Alquié) 149; effective vs. methodological doubt 3117; epoché (q.v.) 173, 3117; eternal verities 201; evidence & spirituality: cleavage 2417; existentialist view 2104–05; first principle 3177; four stages (empirical, methodical, metaphysical, didactic: Lefèvre) 179a, 179d; fundamentally, secretly anti-Christian 176; histrionic, insincere 191; hyperbolic doubt ineffective against extrarational knowledge 228; idealistic & realistic 1722; inapplicable to problem of dreaming-waking 306; limitations 179d; lumen naturale 321, 2065; méthode 2839; methodical & ficticious 3260a; modern biology: epistemological consequences 350; modern ethics 1023, 2183a, 3333; morale (q.v.) 230; the mythical doubter 3438; origin of naturalism 1097; neither sceptical nor atheistic 2918; positive & precluding a-priori certitude 3461; principle of contradiction & idea of Being not affected 2444; psychological origins: D.'s formative years 179a, 2814; "purification de l'amour" 2904a; resolves D.'s ideological difficulties, not his dualism 179; sensory perception: doubt unwarranted 3048a; solipsism 1828; time 106, 1506a; universal doubt impossible 312; & s.v. certitude, evidence, méthode, morale.
doubt, *doctrinal, history:* survey 2786; D., Campanella, Renaissance, Thomism 2599; from D. to Spinoza, Kant, Fichte, Schleiermacher 3105; Arabo-Judaic precursors 344, 3210, St. Augustine 1337; Bacon & D. 1903; Clauberg et al.: Socratic & Cartesian doubt identical 436; Husserl's objections 173, 3528a; Kierkegaard: passionate despair vs. rational doubt 304, 2355a; Peirce 187; Sanchez 277; Schelling 192a; St. Thomas 2786a.
Dream of Descartes: section 102–108; 2, 75, 83, 96 & 2099, 100, 168, 169, 195, 220, 3054, 3092, 3103, 3295, 3570; classical sources 244a; La Flèche as its setting 98; recurrences of the date 123, 3341; *its meaning:* survey of interpretations 100; analytical geometry applied to lenses 100; angelism 183; appetites vs. super-ego 108; attack of tuberculosis, liberation from Jesuitism 1993; D.'s divine mission 210; creative vision of the future system 1672; dream world vs. reality, imagination vs. doubt 227, 1879; dualism 104a; ideological difficulties (class-situation) 179; Jungian archetypes & symbols 103; mental anguish 3219; méthode 171, 181; mystical crisis? 388 & 2745; night of ecstasy 195; only third Dream has philosophical significance 104a; pagan quest for tranquillity, Pythagorean Idyllia of Ausonius 2349a; poetic cognition 244a, 3092, poetic dialectics 244a; psychoanalytical interpretations 108, 124, 3570; Rosicrucianism (initiation scenario 105, pastiche of dream parables 102); saving Transsubstantiation with new theory of matter & beast-machine 163; scientia mirabilis: innate ideas 144; secret code for heretical vortex theory 107; "temps humain," Cartesian version 106; turn from mysticism to rational relativism 1879; unity of science 83, 123, 183; unity of system (morale & physics) 220; "vision of 1619" 189. See also: Corpus poetarum, Est et non, Loretto, Quod vitae sectabor iter, scientia mirabilis.
dreaming & waking: D.'s psychology of the unconscious 215b; imagination 227; reality criterion 306, 1112, 3364, 3595–96; root of Cartesian doubt 227.
dualism: 83, 170, 171, 177 & 2407, 185, 204, 204a, 216a, 347b, 437, 1717, 1838a, 2187, 2824, 2888; types, multiplicity of dualisms 182

(Murphy), D. fails to systematize 1114; *âme-corps* 182, 2543, central to D.'s morale, 220, & s.v. union; "conscience perceptive" (Merleau-Ponty) 311a; defended against modern monists 155; dependent on epistemological dualism 1281; mind a "ghost-in-the-machine," dualism is non-sense 190; proof of real distinction (Gueroult) 170; *epistemological (esse-nosse):* cogito (q.v.) 170, 1987, 2148; defended against Russell, Whitehead 182; evidence 179d; substance 178 & 2455; *subject-object:* "conscience" 215b; decisive for Western thought 192a; idealistic interpretations surveyed, rejected 1206; transcendent reason 1206; *substance dualism* 155, 170, 178 & 2455, 347b, 2888; logical status 231; Thomist critique 216a; *other dualisms:* absolute-relative: certainty vs. morale provisoire 347b; action vs. thought 307, 1292; anthropological (Thomist-Cartesian) 431; "becomingness" vs. permanence 155; cosmogonic (vortex & collision, Belot) 351; deduction-induction dualism: breaks unity of system 321a, 1070; logical & mystical 321a; real vs. ideal 321a; science vs. sagesse 1070; thought vs. senses 192b; *special topics:* beast-machine 226; "conscience" & Dream 104a; does not integrate all human experience 2706; D. not a Cartesian dualist 3568; D.'s epistemological dualism may yield non-dualistic modern science 2586; immortality 228; modern monistic revolt 155, 182; philosophy of religion 1341; position in D.'s system 3241; psychology 381, 1118; truth 1096; unity of system 201; & s.v. union (âme-corps), monism.

dualism, *doctrinal history:* survey 2943; D., Malebranche, Spinoza, & "conscience" 215b; D., Locke, Hume, vs. St. Thomas 3482; Cartesians & anticartesians 226; Descartes & Kant vs. new concept of self 307; Günther 2888; Hegel: secondary feature of D.'s system 171a; Hume 3482; Husserl 174, 3333; Kant 307, 1206; Klages 2227; Leibniz (q.v.) 317, 2269; Locke (q.v.) 3482; Maine de Biran 3153; Malebranche (q.v.) 215b, 453c, 1206, 2150–51; Merleau-Ponty 311a; Renaissance 1481; Rohault, La Forge 431; Bertrand Russell 182; Ryle 190; Santayana 155; Schelling: secularization of Christian discord between God, World 192a; John Smith 465; Spinoza (q.v.) 215b, 1284, 1789; St. Thomas (q.v.) 431, 2554, 3482; Whitehead 155, 182, 194a, 226, 1124.

Duncan, Daniel: his Cartesian Chimie naturelle [1682] 387, 466a.

Duns Scotus, Scotism: D.'s reading, Scotist influence 214, 1503; liberté 164; ens objectivum 1685; individuation 215a; voluntarism of D. 2327.

duration: 149, 347a, 457a; Cartesian & Bergsonian 203; & s.v. time.

Durietz, Grégoire François, Queen Christina's physician: 2552a.

Du Roure, Jacques: 17, 233.

Dury, John: conversation with D. 3522.

Dutch, Flemish language: D.'s knowledge 458, 2779a.

Du Vaucel's D. criticism: 38 & 2535b.

dynamics: 354, 361, 373a, 1810; & metaphysics 2145; D.'s historical position 354; Cartesian physicists 390; D. & Leibniz 2145; & s.v. mechanics.

E

eclecticism: D.'s eclecticism asserted by Sturmius 436; beast-machine controversy 226; Italy 433; Jesuits 466, 2287; Spain 449; Villemandy 464; & s.v. philosophia novantiqua.

economics: s.v. political & social theory.

editions of Descartes' works: sections 74–92b, 1727–1747; & under individual titles.

education (principles, philosophy): s.v. pedagogy.

education of Descartes: 83, 97, 98, 100, 101, & s.v. biography, La Flèche, Discours (historicity).

ego, moi: s.v. cogito (individual terms), "conscience," pensée, self.

eighteenth century: s.v. Enlightenment, Cartesian era.

Einstein, Albert: 370, 375, 383, 1001a, 1427.

elasticity: 3435.

Eleatic philosophy: 205.

elements: texts 7; 83.

Eliot, T. S.: "dissociation of sensibility," & Cartesianism 429a.

Elisabeth von der Pfalz, Abbess of Herford [1618–1680; AM, v. 5]: relation with D. 93, 119, 121–123, 125, 1011, 1218, 1920–22, 2295, 3268, 3376; biography 117; William Penn her

last directeur spirituel 1802; influences D.'s medical interests 365; Molinist viewpoints in her correspondence with D. 1060; & s.v. Lettres sur la morale, Traité des passions.
Éloges of Descartes: 126 & 3420, 438 (v. 1), 1649, 1821, 1856, 1956, 2109, 2682, 2708, 2907.
embryology: 193, 365 & s.v. genetics.
Emery, Jacques André, Abbé: *1836;* 19th century Descartes revival 14, 2859.
emotions: D.'s definition 1859; animal & human 3347; music 419, 421; D., Malebranche, & Lange's affective theory 3382; D. & modern theories 2895; & William James 2267; & s.v. morale, Traité des passions.
empiricism of Descartes: beast-machine doctrine, Empiricists in opposition 226, its inherent empiricism accepted & developed by philosophes 468; Cartesian geometry 3572; English Empiricists are in the Cartesian succession 174; logical empiricism against D.'s truth concept 3147; Malebranche's physical empiricism vs. D's mathematicism 366; medicine: difficulties resulting from non-empiricist méthode 3342; psychology 394, 2259, 3011; radical, integral pluralistic empiricism of D. (Laporte) 178; science: effects of dualism 192a; theory of "conscience" 215b; utilitarian, reformist empiricism of D. 178, 459; & s.v. Enlightenment, experience, experiment, science, Marxist interpretations.
"*encore un qui va se tromper*" (Alain): 148.
Engels, Friedrich: texts 150, 1091a; against intuitionists 2600; D. & machine age 3477; & s.v. Marxist interpretations.
England: D.'s English correspondents 84, 120, 121, 1020; modern D. scholarship 193, 198, 210, 217; *influence of D. & Cartesianism:* 438, 2892, latent Cartesianism 1944; literature & esthetic theory: early Cartesianism 460, Cartesianism acclaimed, attacked, then rejected [1637–1700] 406, Cartesianism elevates prose, lowers poetry 429a, Cartesian denudation of nature vs. Shakespearean nature feeling 409; logic: English Empiricists reject formal logic, accept D.'s ars inveniendi 335; Royal Society 1078; science 456, 1508; D.'s physics preferred to his metaphysics 367.
enigma of Descartes: s.v. mask, larvatus prodeo.
enjoyment of conscious experiences (Whitehead): & cogito 194a.
Enlightenment, Encyclopédistes, philosophes, eighteenth century: bibliography 5, 8–10, 21, & Cabeen, v. 4; general: 434, 438, 441a, 443, 453–455, 457, 459–462, 466a, 468, 1374, 1451, 1507, 1931; background: philosophy, theology, literature related to 17th c. 457; Cartesianism (q.v.; rise & fall 454, Cartesian spirit 2901 discounted 434); D.'s science, méthode more influential than English sensationalism 468; no direct influence in France beyond Voltaire 453; Encyclopédistes (critique of D. 112, D.'s true heirs 459, 468, antihistoricism, science, epistemology 455); historians of philosophy 10; materialism (crude materialism, Neo-Epicureanism derived from D. 2139b; Marxist view 3296, 3314 & s.v. Marxist interpretations); modern revolt against Christianity, initiated by D. 176; "pre-Enlightenment" in D. 319; Poland 470; Portugal 430; rationalism (1507, radical difference between D.'s & philosophes' rationalism 434, their antichristian rationalism is Cartesian 1640); utilitarian, technological direction influenced by D. 1935; Voltaire (q.v.): texts 3207.
ens: texts 7; ens infinitum 3437 & s.v. infinite, God; ens necessarium: foundation of modern metaphysics 211a, antinomy (Schelling) 192a, & s.v. ontological proof; ens objectivum 83, 212a, 1685; ens perfectissimum: 170, 214, 3437, Anselm's concept historically ineffective 211a, possibility of contradiction in perfect Being: Leibniz 273, & s.v. ontological proof; ens rationis & essentia objectiva 3132; entia iam nota 198, & s.v. Regulae.
enseignement: s.v. pedagogy.
entendement: s.v. understanding.
Enthusiasm ("cum plenus forem Enthusiasmo"): 83, 96, 100, 123, & s.v. Dream.
Entretien avec Burman: editions 74, 76, 86.
enumeration: 83, 161, 198; concreteness & representationalism 2246; Lullism & Regulae 328.
Epictetus & D.'s stoicism (q.v.): 283.
Epicureanism, 17th & 18th c.: 434, 461, 466a, 468; âme, beast-machine 226; Bayle's critique 462; "Neo-Epicurean revival" derived from D. 2139b; free-will tradition 349; merges with "Cartesian" mechanism

434; & s.v. Enlightenment, Gassendi, Cartesianism.
epistemology of Descartes: 127, 156–161, 193, 202, 212a, 219, 221, 232, 1242, 1495, 1904, 2010, 2066, 3222, 3478a; apriorism 212a, 247; Augustinian & Cartesian 161; dualism 1118; epistemology vs. mechanism: méthode is reductive rather than inductive 1402; earlier and later stage of D.'s epistemology 193; epistemology by Socratic paradigm: Regulae 266; medicine: anarchic isolation of an idea, vitalism 365; structure (170, critique 3024); Cartesians 431; D. as forerunner of criticist epistemology 2872; Malebranche 453b; modern science non-Cartesian 235c; modern biology 350. See also s.v. cognition, ideas.
epoché: & cogito 173, 174, 184a, 3528a; dialogic presence of Being 2843; doubt of Husserl more radical than D.'s 2564, different functions of reason 3117; epoché & doubt of Carneades 1651; & s.v. Husserl, phenomenology.
equations: D.'s theory 398; as analytical experiment 321a; real & imaginary roots 2774; biquadratic: Ferrari's & Bombelli's earlier solution were better 2664; & s.v. algebra, analytical geometry.
Erdmann, Johann Eduard [1805–1892]: *171a;* 10.
error, falsity: texts 7; general 83, 170, 204, 204a, 209, 214, 1161, 2048, 2519, 2728, 3276; error & human freedom 164; imagination-passion 227; innate ideas: Lelarge de Lignac 2538; morale 230; origin 268, 268a; physics, psychology, & truth postulates 2885; region of sensation 170; theism & error unreconciled in D. 299; Carneades 1651; Plato to Kant 2339; Spinoza 1368, 2619, 2688; & s.v. truth, certitude.
Essais: 37, 168, 2404; examples of méthode 1770, 1774; relation to DM, MM 260, 269; & s.v. Discours, Dioptrique, Météores, Géométrie.
Espinas, Alfred: *163, 1848–52;* D.'s religiosity 14, 345; appraisals, critiques 14, 28, 149, 164, 165, 168; influence 179a, d.
esprit: "esprit cartésien" concept vague, misleading, pseudocartesian 25, 434; "esprit de finesse" & the unconscious mind 215b; "esprit de géométrie" identified with Cartesian mathematicism 443; esprits animaux: s.v. animal spirits.
esse: s.v. Being, ens.
essence: texts 7; 170, 178, 193, 316; essence & existence 184; cogito 192b, 1037; ens rationis 3132; God 165; essence & idea: distinction 170, objective essence of clear, distinct ideas 3132; relational & emotive 316; Spinoza 455a, 3078; & s.v. eternal verities, simple natures.
Est et non (Ausonius): 83, 100, 244a; & Scholastic Sic et non 83; & s.v. Dream.
esthetics: section 402a–429a; 42, 171, 185, 1950a, 2427, 3053; D. has an esthetics 411, 419; has no esthetics: esthetic judgment impossible 419, no theory of creation, hence no esthetics 1441, "le beau se confond dans le vrai" 412; Compendium musicae: 3025, precise link between music & emotion asserted in Compendium, later denied 419, 421; perennial Cartesian esthetics alive in modern French "classicists" 429; sagesse 419; & s.v. art; Classicism literature.
eternal verities: 178, 201, 214, 1060, 1554; & analytical judgment 3510; created truths 241, 327; genesis of D.'s doctrine 149, 241, 269; God's will 2021, verities depend on being known by God: D. vs. Suarez 1661c; insufficiency of finite essence: religion & science 1056; separation of knowledge & Being 149; theory of a priori conditions of science 149; values & eternal verities 419; *doctrinal history:* Greek, Patristic, Scholastic roots 3199; D. & Cartesians 161; D.'s influence upon late Scholasticism 3510; Gassendi 241, 326; D., Spinoza, Leibniz 161 (v. 2), 1578, 2947; Grotius, Pufendorf: eternal verities in law & ethics 253; Malebranche (q.v.) 161, 457b; John Norris 161 (v. 2); Poiret sees mystical element in them 2318; Régis 161; Thomistic & Cartesian 209a; Vazquez: parallel or source? 183; contemporary philosophy 3059.
ether: 375, 2498; & materia subtilis 258.
ethics: "Cartesian" ethics 2183a, 1023; Husserl & D. 3333; ethics of Descartes: s.v. morale.
être: s.v. Being, ens.
Eucharist: s.v. Transsubstantiation.
Euclid: 3572; D.'s mathesis & Euclidean space 378; Euclidean analogy, & syllogistics 321a; D.'s Géometrie as theory of proportions 321a, 398.
Euler, Leonhard [1707–1783]: 3560, 3572.
Eusebius: source of cogito? 149, 1909.
Eustachius de Sancto Paulo [d. 1640; AM, v. 4]: texts 7; studied by D. 263.

F

Fabri, Honoré, S.J. [1607–1688; AM, v. 6; Cabeen, v. 3]: 17, 390, 466; mechanics 368.

faith and reason: 168, 178, 210, 2220; Augustinian tradition 168; St. Thomas & D. 165, 183, 184; D.'s formulation is Molinist rather than Thomist 319; like the Scholastics he refuses to admit possible conflict 168; succeeds in separating faith & reason 3464, robs faith of reason's service (Blondel) 152; immortality doctrine 228; "Cartesian mission" 321a; & s.v. religion, religiosity, theology.

Falckenberg, Richard: Geschichte der neueren Philosophie [1886] 10.

Faraday, Michael [1791–1867]: Cartesian spirit 370.

Fascism, National Socialism: Fascists acclaim Vico's anticartesianism against D.'s social atomism 461 (Witzenmann); Cartesianism against "Blut & Boden" 153 & 1266–67; also 225, 2773, 3233, 3504.

Faust: Descartes a 17th century Faust 295, 2135a, 2391, 2912.

Faustus, Saint, Bishop of Riez [fl. 5th c.]: connaissance d'autrui 244.

Fechner, Gustav Theodor [1801–1887]: measurement of sensation, & D.'s spirals 398.

Feijóo y Montenegro, Benito Jerónimo [1676–1764]: 449, 1715.

Fénelon, François de Salignac de La Mothe [1651–1715]: 438, 451; grace, psychology 215b; Christianity & Cartesianism 2461; & see Malebranche.

"fenomenismo razionalistico" of Descartes: 14, 185, 239, 256, 1277–86, 1344, 1440, 2015, 2821, 2866–70, 3316–17; different concepts 1883–84; Objections of Caterus (O&R) 2685.

Fermat, Pierre de [1601–1665; AM, v. 1]: analytical geometry, differences from D., historical position 355a, 382, 1323, 1448, 3560, 3564; tangents controversy 1808a, 2117, 388 & 2747.

Ferrari, Ludovico [1522–1565]: source of D.'s Géométrie? 2664.

Ferro, Carmelo: *14, 25, 256, 1883–87;* 1286.

Fetscher, Irving: *26,* 176.

Fichte, Johann Gottlieb [1762–1814]: his "creative activity" noncartesian 1710; D., Fichte, Kant 2362, 3105; res cogitans, "Ich" 10, 1413; resumes Cartesian criticist tradition 398.

Ficino, Marsilio [1433–1499]: 2649.

field theories: D.'s paternity 375, & s.v. physics.

finality, final causes: 170, 178, 185; creation of final causes, immutability of God 327; final causes vs. nature (external vs. internal finality) 291a; the infinite 164; biological finality 149, 179c; organic bodies, âme, senses 170; individuation 1443; D. rejects final causes only in science as unperceivable 262, destroys them to establish physics 164; Cartesianism eliminates final causes from chemistry 352 & physiology 386; & s.v. causality.

finitude: & "conscience" 3475; of the world 379a; & s.v. infinite, indefinite.

Fischer, Kuno: *138, 1894–95;* Russian translation 150; his D. view 10.

Flèche: s.v. La Flèche.

Flemish: s.v. Dutch-Flemish, Belgium.

Fludd, Robert [1547–1637]: controversy with Gassendi 2121a.

foi: s.v. Christianity, faith & reason, religion, religiosity, theology.

folium Cartesii: 2228, 3168, 3396.

Fonds Libri: 397, 3387.

Fonseca, Pedro de [1528–1599]: influence upon D. 430; & s.v. Scholasticism.

Fontenelle, Bernard Le Bouvier de, André [1657–1757]: 457c, 468, 2469; & D.'s concept of history 313; a Cartesian positivist (Brunschvicg) 157, not Cartesian except in daring 457c; physics, cosmology 390, 457c, 1906; influence upon Montesquieu 435; vortex theory 438 (v. 2).

force: 178, 373a, 402; monograph 377a; constant force & acceleration 1810; continuous divine creation & force 373a; concept of work (travail) 388 & 2750; mechanics: D. & his contemporaries 361, 390; Malebranche 161, metaphysics & physics 373a; Leibniz: vis viva vs. quantity of motion 373a, 377a, 432, 1338; & s.v. mechanics.

forma substantialis: s.v. substantial form.

formative period (années d'apprentissage) of Descartes: section 93–101; 2, 20, 121–124, 163, 168, 169, 179a, 215c, 242, 1112a, 2764, 3092, 3170, 3293; Augustinian influence 163; doubt 179a, 179d, 2814; fear of deception, search for Being 149; psychological studies 93, 95, 108; symbolism 268a; & s.v. Cogitationes privatae, Dream, Rosicrucians.

Forge: s.v. La Forge.
Foucher de Careil, Louis Alexandre, comte: *75, 1917–22;* criticized as editor 75, 2466.
Fouillée, Alfred: *1923–5,* Russian transl. *150;* Schopenhauer & D., controversy 442, 1306, 1924; evaluation of his book 1518.
Fournet, François, S.J. [1581–1638; AM, v.1]: 2780.
France: Cartesian era: bibliography 3a, 464a, history 138, 446–447, 450, 451, 453–55, 466, 466a. 468, documents 450, scientific, philosophical instruction 466a, 1876, 3425 & s.v. universities; D. & French materialism 3296, 3314 & s.v. Marxist interpretations; literary influence of D. 243, 411, 457 & s.v. Corneille, Racine, Molière; French national character: Cartesian spirit 453, "la République, fille de D." 3234, D. as French super-ego 1547; 19th century D. revival: s.v. spiritualistic interpretations; modern D. scholarship 14, 15, 22, 26, 138, 169, 179d, 180, 193, 459, 1726, 1765, 1824c, 2342, 3184 & s.v. interpretations; see also French language, Enlightenment.
Francine, daughter of René Descartes [1635–1640]: 121–123, 1011, 2217; & see biography.
François de Sales, Saint, Bishop of Geneva [1567–1622]: mystical theology 267; his Traité de l'amour de Dieu: common source of TP, Corneille? 125, 423, 3265.
Franeker: 123, 436, 452, 3533; D.'s matriculation 467, commemoration 505, 1235, 1569, 1752.
free fall: survey 363; Galileo, Beeckman, Descartes 371, 379, 388 & 2744, 402, 1519, 1767–8, 3390; Scholastics, Galileo, Descartes 3562.
freedom: s.v. liberté, libre-arbitre.
freethinkers, free thought: s.v. Libertines.
freewill: s.v. liberté (libre-arbitre), volonté.
Freinsheim (Frenshemius), Johann [1608–1660; AM, v. 7]: translates Naissance de la Paix 1072; & see biography.
French language: D. the first scientific user of French: disputed 410; DM & international diplomatic language 1557; D. & Voltaire: philosophical French 1358; Gassendi 410.
Freud, Sigmund: analyzes Dream of Descartes *124 & 1936.*
Freudenthal, Jakob: *1937;* 311, 436, 2544.
Froidmont (Fromondus), Libert [1587–1653; AM, v. 1]: controversy with D. 458, & see biography.

G

Gadoffre, Gilbert: *260, 404, 405;* 292.
Gadrois, Claude: physics 390.
Galilei, Galileo [1564–1642; AM, v. 1]: 14, 42, 120, 161, 375, 379, 461, 1135, 1661, 1841, 1885, 2050, 2649, 3035; his and D.'s scientific temperament & aim contrasted: 175, 256, 379, 379a, scientist vs. philosopher 2934, experimentalist vs. system-builder 3388, Archimedean vs. Platonic physics 379, both Platonists, apriorists, inneists 2380a; Galileo's condemnation: effect upon Descartes 2, 121–123, 144, 168, 214, 215, D. accepts & Pascal defies Church action 2941; Galileo & 17th c. scientific revolution 2383; cogito & epoché 174; D.'s critique 161; innate ideas 2380a; methodology 211, 2214, D.'s instrumentalism goes beyond Galileo 247; free fall 363, 371, 379, 3562, Beeckman 363, 1768; inertia 3573; mechanics 367, 369, 379, 2831a; D., Mersenne, Niceron 82, 1868; Galileo more influential in Italy than D. 461; marginal notes in his Systema mundi not in D.'s hand 74.
Galli, Gallo: *1959–67a; 209;* 2914a.
Galluppi, Pasquale [1770–1846]: charges D. with neglect of experience 3073.
Garasse, François, S.J. [1585–1631]: scepticism 322a.
Garin, Pierre: *209a;* 28, 263.
Gassendi (Gassend), Pierre [1592–1655; AM, v. 1]: 154, 161 (v. 2), 200a, 451, 467, 2727, 3095–98, 3101, 3224, 3321; relations with D. 116, 325; Disquisitio metaphysica 3096; Syntagma philosophicum & non-metaphysical science 326, 465a, 2121a, 3097; animal soul 226; critique of Descartes [O&R] 204, 204a, 212a, 325, 1669, D.'s difficulties and Spinoza's critique 156 & 1391, cogito, doubt, dualism 2121a, ens objectivum 212a, O&R reflect Gassendi's therapeutic purpose 3421, revive D.'s eternal verities doctrine 241, ontological proof (q.v.) 211a, 3439; extension 291 & 2452; gravity 379; logic of D. 326; philosophy of nature 2945; physics 379; scepticism 322a, 466a; space 377; Gassendi's scientific French 410; Mersenne 82; Sorbière 431; Italy: Gassendi's atomism, not Cartesianism, follows Galileo's anti-Aristotelianism 461; Netherlands: relations, influence 467; 18th century influence 468.

genealogy of Descartes: s.v. Descartes family.
general Descartes literature not cited in Part I: *books* 1112a, 1150, 1269, 1301, 1340–41, 1505, 1540, 1564, 1659, 1700, 1776–77, 1808, 1819–20, 1847, 1866, 1923, 1935a, 1972–73, 2011, 2049, 2070, 2274, 2322, 2431, 2465, 2620, 2670, 2764–65, 2819, 2826, 2852, 2863x, 2883, 3014, 3173a, 3221, 3264, 3433, 3451–52, 3480, 3499, 3602; *chapters & essays* 1001, 1024, 1035, 1042, 1071, 1077, 1094, 1234, 1333, 1367, 1395, 1509, 1652, 1660, 1803, 1862, 1897, 1919, 1941, 1977, 2066, 2123, 2289, 2359, 2430, 2695, 2859–60, 2884, 3075, 3076, 3179, 3181–83, 3200, 3204, 3271, 3274, 3303, 3327, 3372, 3470, 3505; *articles* 1223, 1295, 1870, 1932, 2001, 2055, 2112, 2333, 2390, 2513, 2549, 2621, 2650, 2832, 2972, 2983, 2990, 3048–49, 3062, 3108, 3170, 3534, 3592; *lectures:* Bierens de Haan 1235, Carr 1464, Gibson 2017, Jacobi [1846] 2277, Keeling 2347, Leisegang 2495, v. Lippmann [1896] 2558, Opzoomer [1861] 2873, Patru [1863] 2920, Starcke 3341.
générosité: 147, 176, 206, 215a, 220, 231a, 1365, 3166; cogito: parallels 2158; Corneille (q.v.) 295, 413; highest expression of individuality 215a; sagesse (q.v.) 1292; technology 324; & s.v. morale, passions, Traité des passions.
Genesis (Old Testament): 83, 100, 149, 178, 195; Journal des savants 466a.
genetics: 193, 365, 386, 2369a, 2433; & s.v. physiology.
Geneva: Cartesianism, followed by empiricism 438 (v. 2); portrait collection 1492.
geology, geophysics: 1692, 3405; origin of springs 2615.
Géométrie: editions 74, 76–78, Russian translation & commentary 1737a; 42, 157, 355, 358, 378, 388, 398, 1551, 1737a, 2283a, 2759a, 3188, 3560–64; survey in modern notation 396; commentaries by Erasmus Bartholinus, De Beaune 79, 358, 2758; Bombelli as source? 2664; from formal proof to certainty & ars inveniendi 355; & Fermat's Isagogé: s.v. Fermat; mathematical work beyond & outside Géométrie 398; metaphysics 366, 398; méthode 355 & 2019, 358, 398, 402; obscurities 2758; Regulae & Géométrie 355, 358, 2019; theory of science 366, 2771; historical significance 14, 157; position in D.'s work 355; & s.v. analytical geometry, mathematics.
Gerbet, Olympe-Philippe, Abbé [1798–1864]: 3155c.
Gerdil, Giacomo Sigismondo, Cardinal [1718–1802]: 438; Malebranche's influence 433; animal soul, critique of Spinoza 431.
Germany: Cartesian era 438, universities 436; Cartesian influence, Leibniz to Neokantians 1208; Romantic Revival 466b; D. interpretations, Kant to Heidegger, & histories of philosophy 10; modern anticartesianism, antirationalism 153, 225, 304, 1267; D. & French national image 453, 2773; D. invoked against 20th century ideologies 432a; D., scholarship 14, 128, 138, 142, 175, 176, 393; commemorations 523, 543 & s.v. idealism (role of D.)
Gervaise de Montpellier: 110, 2004a; summary 243.
Gestalttheorie: & D.'s substance theory of self 259.
Geulincx, Arnold [1624 1669]: 32, 438, 441, 451, 458, 467; critique of D. 453b; critique of reason, epistemology 160, 161; Ethica 217, 467; ideas 212a; moral philosophy 217, 3404; philosophy of nature 2128; rational concepts & absolute existence, metaphor & allegory 161; subject-object 1206; Germanic spirit 3504, 467; S. Beckett 402a.
"ghost-in-the-machine": 190; no evidence in the texts 3568; interpretation rejected 3394.
Giacon, Carlo: *262, 2012–15;* 1286.
Gibieuf, Guillaume [ca. 1591–1650; AM, v. 1]: 438; relation to D. 267; libre-arbitre 164, 209a, 248; refers D. to Duns Scotus 214.
Gide, André: Cartesian spirit 427, 429.
Gilbert, William [1540–1603]: 120; vortex theory 2240.
Gillot, Jean [born ca. 1614; AM, v. 1]: 123; in Portugal 430.
Gilson, Etienne: *2025–43*, editor DM *83;* Index scolastico-cartésien 7, Liberté *164*, *Etudes 165*, English works *166*, *167*, Lévy-Bruhl *180*, Malebranche *453a*, Spinoza *272;* discussion & critique of his work 14, 24, 28, 33, 93, 179d, 311, 2666; his anticartesianism *166*, *167*, 2041, 3426; causality 291a, 2450; cogito 252; DM commentary *83*, 1396, 2038; Duns Scotus 214; existence of matter 340; être objectif 1685; falsifies D. 3314; Liberté & théologie *164*, 214, 248, 291, 2453; Koyré's critique 214; morale provisoire 245; Scholastic roots of D. 7, *165*, 235, 288, 1147a; union âme-corps 170 (v. 2).
Gioberti, Vincenzo [1801–1851]: *2043a;* critique

Groningen: University 125, 452.
Grotius (de Groot), Hugo [1583–1645]: D.'s true opposite 253.
Guéneau de Montbéliard, Philibert [1720–1785]: 2901.
Günther, Anton [1783–1863]: his anticartesianism 466b, 2229, 2888.
Gueroult, Martial: *2140–57, 29, 36, 42,* ordre des raisons *170,* ontological proof *270a,* Spinoza & cogito *272,* Leibniz *317,* Malebranche *373a, 453c;* discussion & critique of his work 22, 26, 42, 184, 193, 1765; cogito 252; logic *1226;* ontological argument: s.v. Gouhier-Gueroult; biological individuation 1443; his methodology 42, 149, 193, 1051a, 1055–56, 1376a; physiology of passions 220, time 347a.
Guez de Balzac: s.v. Balzac.
Gutschoven, Gerard van [1615–1668]: relations with D. 458.

H

habitus: texts 7; 178, 183, 214; individuation 215a; unconscious mind 215b.
Hague, The: Descartes monument 1990.
Hals, Frans [1584–1666]: his portraits of D. 169, 1707, products of his imagination? 1 (Nordström); Alain's comment 148; & see biography, iconography.
Hamelin, Octave: *171, 2177–79;* discussion, critique of his work 14, 316, 1068, 1765, 2159; cogito 252; doubt 3580.
Hamilton, Sir William [1730–1803]: *2179a;* 223, 3038.
Hamlet: 295.
Hartley, David [1704–1759]: 2256, 3127–28.
Hartmann, Nikolai: critique of D. 2191; res simplices, ontology 3338; also 1206.
Hartshorne, Charles: 211a.
Harvey, William [1578–1675]: s.v. circulation of the blood.
Heereboord, Adrien [1614–1661? AM, v. 5]: 452, 3206.
Hegel, Georg Wilhelm Friedrich [1770–1831]: *171a;* his view of D. 10, 14, 33, 453, 459, 3075; cogito 171a, 333, 1144; "conscience" 2164; German antirationalism 304; revival of ontotheology 211a; "Zeitgeist" & D. 162; Erdmann, Feuerbach 171a; Kuno Fischer 138; Ritter 3075; Schelling 192a.
Heidanus (Heydanus, van der Heyden), Abraham [1597–1678; AM, v. 5]: 6, 125, 452, 467, 1658.
Heidegger, Martin: *172, 172a, 172b;* discussed 10, 28, 342, 1192, 2843; certitude of existence independent of God 1978; cogito 333, 1472a; "conscience" 2822; existential opposition to D.'s rationalism 347; immanentism 1977–78, 2878a; Schelling 192a.
Heisenberg, Werner: 1427.
Helmholtz, Hermann von: physics 370; vortices 392.
Helmont, Johann Baptist van [1577–1644]: medicine 365.
Helvétius, Claude Adrien [1715–1771]: 468.
Herbert, Edward [Lord Herbert of Cherbury, 1583–1648; AM, v. 3]: correspondence with D. 1020; Gassendi 2121a; scepticism 322a.
Herder, Johann Gottfried von: 225.
heritage of Descartes: 179c, 183, 468, 1204, 1220, 1384, 1925, 1938, 2983, 2988–89; concept criticized 434.
Hermes, Georg [1775–1831]: 466b.
heroic ideal of the 17th century: Baillet offends it 122; Corneille 413, 1509b, 2094; Christina (q.v.) 243 & 1479; & s.v. générosité, passions; TP.
Hertling, Georg Freiherr von: *2221;* 311, 436.
Hertz, Heinrich Rudolf: 392.
Hindu thought, & cogito: 310.
Hippocrates: theory of humors, & D.'s medicine 365.
historicity: s.v. Discours de la méthode.
histories of philosophy, treatment of Descartes: survey 10, 33; works: 171a, 188, 192a, 441a, 1001, 1024, 1094, 1157, 1234, 1316, 1349–51, 1660, 1844a, 1889, 1894, 1941, 2289, 2310, 2630, 3075–76, 3162, 3204, 3274, 3327, 3401, 3480.
historiography: D. & its origin 10.
history: 83, 175, 178, 185, 347a, 443, 2632; history negated by D.: existential ambiguity (Alquié) 149, Alquié misunderstands both history and D. 2863b; Cartesian spirit 180; deformation of D.'s doctrine by Bossuet, Malebranche 313; Encyclopedists' antihistoricism: D.'s influence 455.
Hobbes, Thomas [1588–1679; AM, v. 4]: 154, 451, 1020, 3321; relations with D. 118; D.'s influence 456; & Cartesianism 444; dreaming & waking 306; ens objectivum 212a; Jansenists 466a; liberté 206a; mechanics 367, & Leibniz (dynamics) 2145; mechanistic philosophy of nature 221; O & R (q.v.) 204, 204a, 212a; passions 3237;

sensation 3243; transfers Cartesian concept of man to state 3223.
öffding, Harold: his D. view 10.
Holland: bibliography 6, 15; Holland in D.'s time 122, 123, 2612; *Descartes in Holland* 38, 110, 121–123, 125, 165 & 2035, 467, 1270, 1571–72, 2102, 3406, 3465; his "exile" 1113, 1516; & s.v. biography, Amsterdam, Franeker, Leiden; *fortunes of Cartesianism:* 38, 109, 110, 138, 435a, 436, 438, 441a, 452, 458, 467, 1658, 3205–06, 3411–14; beast-machine (q.v.) 226, 1764; earliest Cartesians 1763–64; Cartesian physicists 390; Cartesian Scholastics, theologia novantiqua, theological controversies 215, 435a, 436, 452, 1379, 2228a; persecution of Cartesianism 1918; *commemorative items* 38, 505, 507, 513, 542, 549; & s.v. Belgium, Dutch & Flemish language, Amsterdam, Franeker, Groningen, The Hague, Leiden, Utrecht.
"homme volant" (Avicenna) & cogito: 260a.
honnête homme: 83; classicism 1930; RV: scientific naturalism 468.
Hügel, Friedrich Freiherr von [1852–1925]: 193a.
Huet, Pierre-Daniel, Bishop of Avranches [1630–1721]: 17, 200a, 438, 441a, 451, 3457, 3490; Censura: eclipse of D.'s méthode 189; Nouvelles mémoires *110, 2249*, 3490, Huet's corrections 3457; Huet vs. Régis: immediate or reflexive consciousness 215b; ontological argument 211a; scepticism 246 322a.
humanism of Descartes: 2509; D. & humanistic disciplines 1346; Cartesianism is humanism 179b; D.'s anthropology of limitations ("der reduzierte Mensch") 432a; his new humanism, & politics 2094; his economic humanism: technology liberates labor 324; inhumanity of his science ideal 184; Montaigne's "humanisme de la sagesse" made dominant by D. 157; non-symbolic, non-rhetoric humanism 268a; TP 149; Christian humanists and D. 283.
Hume, David [1711–1776]: 1237, 2046; critique of D. 192b; D.'s influence 3482; causality 262, 348, 349, 453a; libre-arbitre 349; ontological argument 211a; self as bundle of perceptions 259; Whitehead 194a.
humors, theory (medicine): 365.
Hungary: Cartesianism 469 & 2171–72, 1151, & Jansenism 3601.
Husserl, Edmund: *173, 174, 2251–54a;* discussed 4, 10, 347, 1726, 1828, 1891, 2163, 2254b, 2668, 2843, 2944a, 2984, 3548; D., Husserl: same attitude, different doctrines 1756; four objections to cogito & doubt 173 & 3528a; cogito & epoché 1203, 1472a, 2737, 2944a, 3471; doubt, epoché, pensée, âme 2564, 3117, 3333; posthumous works 3524a; Locke 3528a; D., Valéry, Husserl 2730; & s.v. cogito, epoché, phenomenology.
Huxley, Thomas Henry [1825–1895]: *2252–56;* D. & modern physics 188 & 3045; cogito 1178; "extra-Christian" D. 1081.
Huygens, Christian [1629–1695; AM, v. 7]: 367, 375, 390, 467, 1806–07; Huygens in Paris 1378; his Cartesianism asserted, disputed 367, 390, 1807; eclipse of D.'s méthode 189; dynamics: influence upon Leibniz 2145; laws of impact 2608a; pendulum problem 369; pensées imperceptibles 215b; refraction: asserts Snell's priority 399; vortex theory, centrifugal forces, gravity 377, 377a; Rohault 390.
Huygens, Constantijn, de Zuylichem [1596–1687; AM, v. 1]: correspondence with D. *81*, 1294, 3138; new documents 1567; his family 1011; relation with D. 2371; 123, 125, 405, 3325, 3600, & s.v. biography.
hydraulics, hydrodynamics: 388 & 2744; Newton's critique of vortex theory 377a, 390.
hypothesis: 231, 247, 321a, 2609; aprioristic in Regulae, DM, MM, instrumentalist in Essais, PP 247, denied 3544a; D. admits even false hypotheses if consequences are verified 247; his hypotheses are positive-experimental, not abstract-deductive 1721a; physics: méthode is suppositional, not deductive 1721a.

I

Ich-Einsamkeit (Baader) & cogito: 466b.
Iconography: 1, 74, 121, 123, 131, 139, 145, 146a, 504, 505, 528, 538, 1296, 1492, 1707, 2353, 2858a; *portraits:* Amsterdam 1; Beck 3365; Jacquet & Tours 1, 2213; Kiev 2819; Leeuwarden 505; Liévens 298; Schooten 1, 2612; Weenix 1054; D. & Newton 465a; Geneva collection 1492.
idea: texts 7; 83, 160, 161, 165, 170, 171, 178, 192a, 193, 198, 204, 212a, 214, 219, 3527; types of ideas distinguished 83; ideae adventitiae

170, 193, 212a, 214, ideae sensibiles 170, idée-tableau 183, 184 (n. 50), innate ideas (q.v.), simple ideas: s.v. simple natures; *special topics:* ambiguity of D.'s concept 149; association of ideas, & memory (q.v.) 381, 2785; causality 165, 204; clear, general ideas 3113a; clear & distinct ideas (q.v.); dualism of ideas 182; geometric ideas 170 & s.v. Regulae; Caterus & Thomists vs. D. 2685; pensée & idée: definitions 170; & perception 2007, 3455; & reality 149, formal, material, objective reality 178; representative theory 210 & below (doctrinal history, Arnauld-Malebranche); separability of ideas 2397, no transition from one distinct idea to another: collapse of méthode 329; visual impression & idea 3109; *doctrinal history:* 161, D. to Locke 437; Arnauld-Malebranche controversy 161, 212a, 451a, 1713a, 2846; D., Malebranche, Berkeley 2156; Malebranche cartesianizes Descartes 435b (Fagnola); Geulincx 212a; Whitehead 194a; & s.v. clear & distinct ideas, eternal verities, idealism, innate ideas.

idealism of Descartes: surveys 4, 14; general: 131, 159–161, 170, 171–72b, 192a, 207, 211, 221, 232, 451a, 1194, 1420, 1911, 2362, 2872, 2878a, 3013, 3091, 3593, 3604–05; idealism in D. questioned or denied 166 ("idealistic failure"), 221, 2445, 3330; cogito 232, 1677, 2687, 3091, 3245; conclusion from "conscience" to existence, reversed by Spinoza 272; concrete, objective, immanentist idealism 209; "fenomenismo razionalistico" (q.v.) 185, 2015; "idealism of freedom," & passions (Dilthey) 206a; "imaginative knowledge" 3244; "logocratic" idealism 1993; mathesis pura vs. mathesis universalis 159 & 1396; methodological (not: metaphysical or critical) idealism 3294; provisional, paradoxical idealism 156 & 1391; realism & idealism in D. 129, 222, 2015, "réalisme de l'idée" 132, "inferential realism" between idealism & realism 222, weakness of D.'s realism opens road to idealism 2398; Regulae 281, 3487; representational (not: absolute) idealism 2344; D.'s semi-idealism, completed by Kant 221; space: realism (Regulae) & idealism (Geometrie) 159 & 1396; spiritualistic idealism 1677; truth concept of D.: pre-idealistic 214a; & s.v. idealistic interpretations, realism.

idealism, *role & influence of Descartes:* surveys 4, 10, 14, 3278; D. as father of modern idealism 157, 161, 171a, 172–72a, 173–74, 192a, 3091, & s.v. criticist philosophy; D.'s Géometrie the decisive advance beyond Plato 157; Arnauld's concept of idea points towards Kantianism 451a; Malebranche (q.v.) 161, his Catholic philosophy (not D.'s metaphysics) at origin of modern idealism 462; Spinoza reverses D.'s step from "conscience" to existence 272; Bayle & evolution of 18th century idealism 462; Berkeley 1710; French idealism: Cartesian & Kantian roots 232, exclusive French (Cartesian) origin of modern immaterialistic idealism 3091; German idealism: 4, 10, 14, 171a, 1208, Kant (q.v.) 170, 398, 451a, 1710, 2241, 2362, 3091, Fichte 1710, 2362, cogito & German Idealism 171a, 192a, 1413, 2362, 2687, 3245; Italy 14; & s.v. criticist philosophy, idealistic interpretations.

idealistic interpretations of Descartes: surveys 4, 10, 14, 1677; 138, 156–61, 171, 171a, 174, 192a, 200, 202, 211, 221, 230, 273, 358, 1068, 2049, 3478a; rejected 459, 1710; of cogito 200, 1677, 2628; of D.'s metaphysics, morale 230; & s.v. criticist philosophy, idealism.

"idée": word used for "pensée" 50 years before D. 1244.

identity: numerical identity (texts) 7; identity as axiom 238.

Idéologues: 3073; Cartesianism & origin of Idéologie 2952.

Ignatius de Loyola, Saint [1491–1556] & his Exercitium spirituale: meditation and MM 1112a, 2724.

image, theory of: image an analogy, not a sign 268a; image & dream, reality 227; Regulae (q.v.), mathesis universalis (q.v.) 353; & s.v. idea, memory, simple natures.

image of Descartes (das Descartesbild) in scholarship & popular mind: concept introduced by Lévy-Bruhl, survey [1650–1900] 180; legendary & popular image 109–15; Baillet & Clerselier 81, 122, 126; difference between image & interpretation 180; modern 10, 14, 22, 26, 33, 82, 180, & s.v. Catholic, existential, idealistic, Marxist, Neoscholastic, psychoanalytical, spiritualistic interpretations; personality & character of D.; philosophy of D. (chief orientation).

imaginary: malin génie as threat to the imaginary 227.
imagination, phantasia: texts 7; 83, 147, 170, 178, 185, 227; creative imagination & Italian esthetic theory 420; dream & reality 1879; imagination part of ghost-in-the machine 190; "imagination-passion" 227; mathematics & Regulae (q.v.) 83, 198, 353; material bodies, proof of their existence 170; perception 198; Greek phantasia & Stoic imaginatio 378; phantasmata: s.v. species intentionales; Rosicrucians 105; time: imagination is in time, understanding outside time 353; Sartre on D., Spinoza, Leibniz, Hume 3202; Sorbière, Louis de La Chambre 431.
immanence, immanentism of Descartes: 209, 2685; interiorization of the Numinous, "Fehl Gottes" 192a; Plato, D., Berkeley, Husserl, Heidegger 1977–78, 2878a; Romero's critique 2188–88a; sagesse as pure immanence 206; spiritualist immanence 157.
immediate: for D., factual experience only is immediate 1049.
immortality: texts 7; 83, 185, 187, 215a, 228; immortality & self, D. to Kant 1342.
impact, laws (lois du choc): Beeckman (q.v.) & D. 1796, 2608a; Huygens, Malebranche, Mariotte 373a, 390, 1645; Mersenne 2608a; & s.v. force, Galileo, mechanics.
impetus: 377a, 379, 2145, & s.v. force.
incapacities of mind (Peirce): 187.
indefinite: 83, 214, 379a, 1275, 2698; D.'s influence upon the English concept of infinity 460; his "indefinite universe" 379a, 2584, more influential than Copernican revolution? 2503; Bonaventura 214; & s.v. infinite.
indifference: s.v. liberté.
individualism: 2224; D. & Rousseau 2053; law 466d.
individuality, individuation: 215a; affirmation by D., dissolution in God by Spinoza 3029; biological (man & animal) 1443; equality of understanding (bon sens) 170; extension: Leibniz 317; immortality 228; méthode 2802; unity & unicity 215a, 2534a.
induction: texts 7; 161, 175, 178, 193, 231, 321a, 1097; D.'s "deduction" includes experimental induction 1243, 3292; imagination 353; & intuition: same type of cognition, different object 2103; méthode (q.v.) 3309; physics of D.: positive, not deductive 1721a; & s.v. deduction, empiricism, experiment, Regulae.
inertia: 375; Galileo 379, 3573; Malebranche & Leibniz 373a, 390; Einstein 1001a; & s.v. force, mechanics, motion.
infantile: s.v. childhood.
inference: 178 & s.v. deduction, empiricism, experiment, hypothesis, logic.
infinite, infinity: texts 7; 83, 160, 161, 178, 193, 204, 3100; its absolute transcendence accepted by D. 152, 320, leads him to religious agnosticism 2847; D.'s critique & first proof of God 2959; epistemology 161; exceeds rational knowledge 178; final causes 164; God 149, 214; metaphysical & ontological 293; cosmology: the closed, indefinite, infinite universe 379a, Cartesians spread D.'s doctrine 2584; infinity & continuum 188 & 3047; Bayle's antinomies 161; Bonaventura 214; Leibniz 188; Spinoza 455a; Scholastic predecessors of D. 7, 214; & s.v. indefinite.
infinitesimal calculus: s.v. analysis (mathematical).
influence of Descartes: art 415, 422, 1438a; causality, change 262, 348; chemistry 352, 387; cosmogony, cosmology 351, 359, 374, 379a, 392; economics, political philosophy 324; Enlightenment 434–35, 443, 445, 453–55, 457c, 459, 462, 466a, 468; literature & poetry 243, 316, 402a–29a passim, 442, 457, 1648; logic 335; mathematics 355, 355a, 358, 378, 382, 388, 397; modern intellectualism 1024; phenomenology (q.v., & s.v. Husserl); physics 357, 367–72, 373a, 375, 376, 379, 383, 388, 390, 393, 401, 1004, 2399a, 2807, 3133; physiology 360, 373, 394; Protestantism 193a, 435a, 436, 438, 452, 467, 1149, 1667, 2228a; psychology 381, 385, 386, 1363, 1487, 2282, 3363; religion (q.v.) 168, 183–184a, 443, 446, 447, 452a; science 144, 146b, 468, 1998, 2475, 2586; Scholasticism 3510; *countries:* the Americas 440, 448, 1099, 3189; England 406, 456, 460, 465–65a, 1508, 1944, 2892; France 3a, 138, 446, 447, 450, 451, 453–55, 466, 466a, 468; Germany 138, 436, 438, 466b, 1208; Greece 1689a; Holland & Belgium 38, 109, 110, 138, 435a, 436, 438, 441a, 452, 458, 467, 1658, 1918, 2228a, 3205–06, 3411–14; Hungary 469 & 2171–72, 1151, 3601; Italy 222, 433, 438, 443, 461, 1648, 1824a, 2003, 3331; Poland 470, 1137, 1541, 1544, 1678; Portugal 430, 1553; Spain 449, 2700; Sweden 465, 2237; Switzerland 1945.

"influx, spiritual": Swedenborg & D. 2863.
Ingarden, Roman: *375;* Husserl 173; physics 370.
ingenium: 83, 178, 193, & s.v. pensée.
innate ideas: texts 7, two meanings distinguished 161; 178, 204, 204a, 210, 212a, 214, 232, 1281, 2124, 2369; basis of D.'s system 3010; in the child 84; conscious and unconscious: D., Leibniz, Locke 215b; epistemological presuppositions 161; God (q.v.) 165, 167, 1105; natural law 466d; poetic cognition 244a; Regulae: inneism claimed 1401, disputed 149, simple natures 2190; sensation 170, 212a; *doctrinal history:* theological origins 165; Augustine's illuminism 214; Galileo 2380a; Kant: a priori forms 2166, pure reason 2422; Lelarge de Lignac 2538; Leibniz 192b, 215b, 1496; Locke 215b, 1496, 3040, 3123; Malebranche (q.v.); Scholasticism 165; & s.v. idea, God.
"Innerlichkeit": D. establishes modern metaphysical Innerlichkeit (Hegel) 171a; lacks Christian Innerlichkeit 176; "Natur ohne Innerlichkeit" 276.
instant, moment: central role in D.'s philosophy 347a; physics: only the instant is real 371; continuous creation, instant, continuous time (Laporte, Gueroult) 170, 188, 347a; D. & Spinoza 455a.
instrumentalism: 2008; in the Essais & PP 247.
intellectualism: Aristotelian & Cartesian 3113a; atomistic & Cartesian 159 & 1396: modern: D.'s influence 1024.
intellectus: s.v. intelligence, pensée.
intelligence: essence of substance, mode 170; individuality 215a; psychology 171.
intentionality: intellectual or Cartesian, & sensible 3109; & s.v. phenomenology.
interpretations of Descartes' philosophy: critical surveys 2, 4, 5, 10–12, 14, 22–33, 1231, 1540, 1543, 1577, 1765; methodological controversies 23, 25, 42, 149, 170, 171, 179, 193, 198, 447a, 1055, 1726, 3278; image & interpretation distinguished 180; & s.v. anthroposophic, Catholic, existential, idealistic, Marxist, Neoscholastic, psychoanalytical, spiritualistic interpretations; also s.v. Bergson, phenomenology.
Introduction à la Géométrie (formerly: *Calcul de Monsieur Descartes):* 74, 79.
intuition, intuitus, intuitionism: 83, 159, 171, 178, 193, 198, 353; "anticartesian intuition" in MM, PP, morale, primacy of intuition in DM, Géométrie 159, 1401; attention 1677; cogito (q.v.) 3120; "conscience & intuition divinatrice" 215b; creative intuition guarantees unity of system 1672; deduction & intuition 198, 2103; D. not an intuitionist 149; forms of intuition distinguished 447a; intellectual intuition 281; logic: intuitive proof permissible if not based on innate ideas 1226, 1226a; mathematics 353; ontological proof & total intuition 159 & 1396; intuition of the perfect: same cognitive type as induction of the imperfect 2103; poetic cognition 324a; primacy of the eye, philosophy of domination 342; Regulae: Lullism 328; scepticism 2394; science 2818, rejected 2600; *doctrinal history:* 281, 1259, 2789; Bergson 281, 1677, D. as precursor of modern intuitionism 3602; Kant 281, 2789; Leibniz & D. (formalism vs. intuitionism) 432; Malebranche (q.v.) 1401; Peirce: concept rejected 187; Spinoza 1259, 1401; St. Thomas 281; & s.v. deduction, Regulae.
"inventum mirabile" (10 November 1620): 2, 121; identified as astronomical lenses 388 & 2753, as méthode 123, 3092.
irony: DM 176; creative (D. & Leopardi) 3432; Socratic & Cartesian 346.
irrationalism: 170, 1155a; "trompe-l'oeil clarté" 1951; D.'s "anticartesian intuition" (MM and later) 159 & 1401.
Isnardi, Teófilo: *376;* 356.
Italy: bibliography, D. scholarship & interpretations 14, 15, 35, 433, 461, 1278–79, 1286, 1539, 1984, 2674, 3554; modern D. revival 2011; Italian philosophy before D. 1265, D. & Italian philosophy 3033; fortunes of Cartesianism 222, 420, 433, 438, 443, 461, 1648, 1824a, 2003, 2578, 2898, 3331; Galileo & Gassendi's atomism, not Cartesianism, destroy Aristotelian rule 461; Cartesianism & early Neothomism 2898; "Cartesian reform" 1265; eclecticism 433; philosophical centers: Pisa, Naples 433, 438, 1648, Padua 433, 1824a, 2111, Piacenza 2898; Cartesianism & literature 420; Cartesian pedagogy, & Vico 461; & s.v. Galileo, Vico.

J

James, William: compared with D. 194a, 2267 (theory of emotions), anticipated by D. 1681.

K

Koyré, Alexandre: *144, 214, 379, 379a;* 154, 377a, 1178.
Krantz, Emile: *411,* Russian transl. *150;* influence, controversy 419, 420, 424, 429, 1347.

L

Laberthonnière, Lucien: *177, 2406–10;* discussed 28, 181, 1352, 1426, 1824c, 2929, 3256.
La Bruyère, Jean de [1645–1696]: Cartesian spirit 411, influence 412.
Labyrinths of metaphysics (Leibniz): 188.
La Chaise, François d'Aix de, S.J. [1624–1709]: 17, 466.
La Chambre, Louis de [1594–1669]: 431, 451.
La Chilliolière, property of D.'s family: 94.
La Flèche, & Descartes' education: 2, 83, 97, 98, 100, 101, 169, 179a, 220, 402, 2317, 2683, 2910; antilibertinist influence 163; chronology, teachers, courses 100; date of D.'s entry 96, 100, of his leaving 2, 97, 100, 101, 121; history of La Flèche 98, 1559; ratio studiorum 1684; D. rejects its pedagogy 3031; Scholastic authors & doctrines taught 83, 164, 208, 209a, 215a, 286, 1827; sonnet written by D.? 425.
La Fontaine, Jean de [1621–1695]: beast-machine, Les deux rats 226, 2837; 3606.
La Forge, Louis de: 431, 451, 3002, 3275; animal soul 216; critique of substantial forms 431 & 1122; occasionalism 463; physics 390.
Lagrange, Joseph Louis [1736–1813]: oscillations problem 369.
La Haye-Descartes: celebrations [1795]: 114, 124 (v. 2, app.); [1937] 528.
Laicism: D. its precursor 319.
Lammenais, Hugues Félicité Robert de [1782–1854]: 2629.
La Mesnardière, Hippolyte Jules Pilet de [1610?–1663]: theory of literature 424.
La Mettrie, Julien Offray de [1709–1751]: beast-machine, man-machine 226, 468, 2255, 3474.
La Mothe le Vayer, François de [1588–1672]: rational scepticism 246, 466a.
Lamy, Bernard, Oratorian [1640–1715]: 438, indirect Cartesian influence upon Rousseau 1356.
Lamy, François, O.S.B. [1636–1711]: 438, 451; animal soul 226; pensées imperceptibles, & grace 215b; Spinoza critique 431.
Lange, Karl: affective theory of passions 3382.
language: D.'s philosophy of language 185; D. & Voltaire: philosophical language 1358; D. proposes universal language 121, 2738; & s.v. Dutch-Flemish, French language, logical positivism.
Lanion, G. de, Abbé: "connaissance d'autrui" 244.
Lanson, Gustave: *412, 413, 457, 2437–41;* D.'s influence on literature, Corneille's heroic ideal 295, 411, 429, & s.v. Corneille.
Lantrùa, A.: *41, 2442–46;* 14, 3580.
Laplace, Pierre Simon, marquis de [1749–1827]: cosmogony 359, 466c; drops God hypothesis 379a.
Laporte, Jean: Rationalisme *178;* Etudes *291, 291a; 2248–55;* discussed 4, 26, 27, 1765, 2369a, 3314; creation: Gueroult's comment 170; rationalism 2384, disputed 1533; his school 215a; D.'s time concept & Gueroult's comment 347a.
La Rochefoucauld, François VI duc de [1613–1680]: "amour de soi" 215b.
La Rochelle, siege: 121, 1022 & s.v. biography.
"larvatus prodeo": 96, 100, 183, 1967a, 3489a; God too is masked 195; hermeneutic commonplace before D. 328; "Mona Lisa of philosophy" 1988; "philosophe au masque (Leroy) 124; "philosophe sans masque" (Gouhier) 169; theatralic-dramatic metaphysics 1509a; written after Dream? 183, 184; & s.v. Cogitationes privatae, mask & enigma of Descartes.
Laski, Harold: 140.
Latin America: Cartesian influence & philosophical instruction: colonial era 40, 448, 1473; D. & rise of Latin-American civilization 3189; Positivism & D. 146; Descartes studies & commemorative items 39, 40, 146, 231a, 526, 537, 544, 545, 555.
Lavelle, Louis: *11, 293, 2467–74;* 27.
La Ville, Louis: s.v. Valois.
law, jurisprudence: D.'s legal studies 83; attitude & influence 185, 264, 466d; administrative law 2829; eternal verities & justice: Grotius, Pufendorf, Leibniz vs. D. 253; Montesquieu (q.v.) 412, 435, 445, 1065a, 3235.
law of sines: s.v. refraction.
laws of nature: 83, & s.v. nature, physics.
Le Brun, Charles [1619–1690]: applies D.'s principles to painting 415; physiognomics & TP 467.
Lefèvre, Roger: *179a–d, 2487–91;* 22, 163.

legend of Descartes: section 109–115; 467.
Legrand, Antoine (Anthony), [1629–1699]: 438, 451, 3167; beast-machine 226, 467; John Sergeant's attack 1339.
Leibniz, Gottfried Wilhelm [1646–1716]: 177, 192b, 211, 239, 390, 432, 1285, 1317, 2430; meets Huygens, Malebranche 390, copies manuscript texts of D. 74, 75, 92; his early thought influenced by D. 2579; Cartesian or Spinozist phase? 3442; depends on D. in method, psychology, science? 1416; his "Scholastic Cartesianism" 2630; attacks D. as chef-de-secte 286 & as plagiarist 399, comments 2298; French reaction to Leibniz 317; *special topics:* abstraction 316; beast-machine & soul 466a; causality (q.v.) 213, 262, 349; Chinese influence? 310; dynamics: Galileo, D., Hobbes, Huygens 2145; epistemology 211; eternal verities 161 (v. 2), 1578; extension, Transsubstantiation, dualism 317, 2269; force 373a, 377a, 1338; innate ideas 192b, 215b, 1496; Labyrinths of metaphysics 188; law & theology 253; liberté 206a, 1949; libre-arbitre 349; logic 198; Lull's ars combinatoria 2146; mathematics & philosophy 2238, geometric transcendence 3453; mechanics 367, 373a, 377a, 390, 1338; D.'s metaphysics indecisively transformed by Leibniz 172a; méthode 1012; occasionalism 463; ontological argument 211a, 273, 1657; optics 399; petites perceptions, idées innées: against Locke 215b; physics 188, 373a & 1102, 390; philosophical revolution & political ideal 3235; pluralism rooted in D.'s philosophy of religion 3419; his "prudence" vs. D.'s personal courage 124; Sanchez 277; Scholasticism: knows it less well than D. 286; space 377, 379a, 390; his modern scientific spirit compared with D.'s archaic attitude 175; substance 2478; Transsubstantiation 317; understanding 1535; vinculum substantiale 3110.
Leiden, University: 123, 125, 436, 452, 1658; Danish students in D.'s time, 2612; French students 123.
Lelarge de Lignac, Joseph-Adrien, Abbé [ca. 1710–1762]: 438; critique of innate ideas 2538.
Lémery, Nicolas de [1645–1715]: chemistry 387, 467.
L'Encre, Richard: used word "idée" for "pensée" before D. 1244.
Lenin, Vladimir Ulyanov: 2164.
Lenoble, Robert, Abbé: Mersenne *82; 192, 215, 381, 2500–04a;* cited 179d; Eloge 2982a.
lenses, optical: s.v. optics.
Leonardo da Vinci [1452–1519]: from empiricism to method 211; pendulum problem 369.
Leopardi, Giacomo [1798–1837]: his & D.'s creative irony 3432.
Le Roy, Edouard: 28.
Leroy, Maxime: Philosophe au masque *124,* Descartes social *37, 298; 2507–11;* influence, discussion, critiques 28, 169, 176, 179d, 324, 345, 3219.
Le Senne, René: 28.
Lettres sur la morale (correspondence with Elisabeth, Chanut, Christine): editions 74, 90; 215c, 1920–22, 3376; & s.v. morale.
Le Valois: s.v. Valois.
Lévy-Bruhl, Lucien: *180, 2523–24a;* 181, 298, critique 245.
Lewis, Geneviève: s.v. Rodis-Lewis.
Leydekker, Melchior [1642–1721]: anticartesianism 435a, 467.
L'Hospital, Guillaume François de, marquis de Sainte-Mesme [1661–1704]: 372.
liaison nécessaire: 198; idea & reality 178 & 2451; refers to substance, not cause 2451.
Liancourt, Hôtel: critique of D. 38.
Liard, Louis: *181, 2546–48;* influence, discussion, critique 121, 171, 188, 223, 412; cogito & circle 1910.
Liberalism (political): & origin of DM 179; liberal repudiation of Cartesian man & society 3529 & 1080.
liberté & libre-arbitre: texts 7; 178, 185, 214, 248, 1028, 1562, 1703, 2135b; *liberté:* antinomies 3498; causality 349; conflicting views, difficulties regarding free-will 331; existentialism 192, 331; faith 1004a; D. has genuine freedom concept despite primacy of physics 291; God 206, divine indifference 164, 327 & physics, metaphysics 214; divine arbitrariness, human voluntarism yield negative theology 1060, God absorbs man's own freedom 192, God's immutability 327; D.'s idealism of freedom (Dilthey) 206a; reason 2070; root of individuality 215a; theology 164; unknowability of Being 149; "Verlust des Seins, Befreiung ins Leere" (Jaspers) 175; *libre-arbitre:* difficulties 331; divine 2666, creation & guarantee of scientific certainty 327; Elisabeth's objections 119;

eternal verities 201; human experience (Alquié) 149; moral life 210; society 2290; why D.'s doctrine is not ethical & theological 248; *doctrinal history:* Jansenism & Cartesianism 164; causality: D., Leibniz, Hume 349; Malebranche 291, 3047; D., Mersenne, Sartre 3575a; Oratorian theology 164; Philonic vs. Epicurean freedom 349; D., Spinoza, Leibniz, Kant 1949; & s.v. voluntarism.

Libertins, Libertinism: bibliography 464a; 163, 466a, 2964; in D.'s time 163, mortal danger to Catholicism in France 179b; faith & reason 168; D. a free-thinker 1340; Epicureanism & "Cartesian" mechanism merge [after 1660] 434; raison d'état 2849.

life: according to D.'s system 2768; "pensée & vie" 2115, 3032; philosophy & life incompatible? 149; life principle: Plato & D. 2541; & s.v. vitalism.

light: texts 7: historical survey 2900, 3558; anthroposophic interpretation 1288; Cartesian & modern epistemology 2651; D., Malebranche, Huygens, Roemer, speed of light 87, 390, 1783; & s.v. Dioptrique, optics, refraction.

literature, influence of Descartes: bibliography 3a, survey 14, section 402a–429a; 1973; Aristotelian theory & D. 3436; literary genres 419; Enlightenment 420, 433, 443; *England* 406, 409, 429a, influence on prose style 460, Crashaw 2225; *France:* Renaissance influence stronger than D.'s 422, beast-machine controversy in French literature 226, 466a, D. creator of French classicism (Krantz) 411, Cartesian analytical spirit a universal influence 417, D.'s influence: controversies 14, 411, D. only indirectly & posthumously effective (Lanson, Bray) 412, classical principles operative before D. (Abercrombie) 411, his influence denied 442, 1347; D.'s "reflexive analysis" & attitude of Racine and moralistes are two permanent influences 316, French influence on Italian esthetic theory & Cartesianism 420, pseudo-classicism 1680–1750: no influence of D. 429, "Cartesian spirit" in modern French classical literature 429; *Holland* 467; *Italy* 420, 433; *Spain* 2700; & s.v. classicism, esthetics, querelle des anciens et des modernes; Boileau, Corneille, La Fontaine, Racine; Gide, Valéry.

Locke, John [1632–1704]: 3318, 3418; D.'s influence on Locke: 456, dualism 2187, Cartesian principles 192b, Locke in the Cartesian succession 174 but rejects D.'s physics & metaphysics 189, dependent on D. 1994; Italy: Locke continues Galilean, not Cartesian influence 461; anthropology (D., Diderot, Helvétius) 468; ars inveniendi 335; attacks pensée-substance 259; causality 453a & cognition 1061; cogito 192b, 1711; Enlightenment 468, his influence greater than D.'s 455; epistemology 2022; Husserl on Locke & D. 3528a; ideas 437, innate ideas 215b, 1496, 3040, 3123; lumen naturale 1994; Malebranche & Norris 456; objective knowledge 3124; political philosophy 3235; substance 1940; understanding 1535; Whitehead on Locke 194a.

logarithmic curve, spiral: excluded from Géométrie, applications 398.

logic of Descartes: 36, 83, 198, 321a, 1250; analytical geometry as logical transform 321a; Aristotelian logic & méthode 211b, 231; "Cartesian systems": their postulates 1376; causality & sufficient reason 3009; cogito merges logic & metaphysics (Deutinger) 466b; "imagination-passion" & error 227; intuitive proof: condition of its acceptability 1226a; "logique naturelle" of Meyssonnier, & D.'s mathesis universalis 328 in which logic & mathematics are fused 160–61; modern, symbolic logic 231, anticipated but not conceived by D. 1226, its Cartesian roots 3305, & cogito 335; méthode & Aristotelian logic 211b, & modern logic 335; D.'s mathematicism modifies logic 1252; principles of identity & contradiction 178; proof 165, 231, 353; syllogism treated by D. as Euclidean analogy 321a; systematic & genetic orders, & their unity in man 1051a; voluntaristic interpretation 1550, criticized 212a; Clauberg, du Roure, philosophia novantiqua 436; Deutinger 466b; Gassendi 326; Peirce 187, his view of logic of 17th c. science 1833a; Logic of Port-Royal 2550, in America 440; Régis 390; Spinoza's logic diametrically opposed to D.'s 329; & s.v. analysis & synthesis, judgment, order, syllogism.

logical positivism, language analysis, applied to Descartes: cogito 235a, b; doubt 1330; dreaming & waking 306, 1112, 3364, 3595–96; malin génie 1331; mind 190; ontological

argument 2608, 2671a; scepticism of the senses 1330, 3596.
longevity: 83, 110, 121, 124, 166, 365, 1022, 1760.
Lorentz, Hendrik Anton [1853–1929]: concept of physics 370, 375.
Loretto, Descartes' pilgrimage: 96, 100, 121, 122, 124, 163, 169; & s.v. Dream.
Lotze, Hermann: *2579–82;* 3214.
Louvain, University: Cartesianism, struggle, condemnation of D. 458, 467; Neoscholasticism & D. 1238.
Lovejoy, Arthur Oncken: *182, 2583–84;* 194a, 3536.
Lullus (Lull), Raimundus [ca. 1232–1316; AM, v. 1]: 96, 328, 2146, 3000a, 3004; Lullian influences on D. 326 & 1217; D. rejects Lullism but CP & Regulae use it 328.
lumen naturale: texts 7; 83, 178, 193, 214, 243, 2241, 2363, 2420, 2520; as axiom 238; D.'s "Baconian belief" 299 is non-rational 321; doubt 321, 2065, 2660; mathematical truth 314; morale 230; truth 243 & 1483; *doctrinal history:* Greek, Patristic, Scholastic texts 3199; St. Augustine, St. Thomas, D. 214; Bacon 299; Locke 1994.
Lumières, les: s.v. Enlightenment.
Luther, Martin: his & D.'s heterodoxy linked by Gioberti 14, by Maritain 184; German antirationalism 304.

M

Macdonald, Margaret: dreaming & waking *306,* 3595.
Macedo, Francisco de Santo Agostino [1594–1681]: 3329, & early Jansenism 1504.
Mach, Ernst: *2613:* his D. critique 375; ether 258; optics 399.
Machiavelli, Niccolo [1460–1527; AM, v. 7]: D.'s critique 119, 169, 179b, 2847–49; D.'s Machiavellism denied 220; Machiavellism & Cartesian spirituality 320.
machines: can they think? 350, 1412, 2739; no psychological difference between machine & man 3380, disputed 2332; & s.v. technology.
Macy, Abbé: connaissance d'autrui 244; animal soul. critique of Valois (Louis de la Ville) 226.
magic: s.v. occultism.
magnet: Gilbert & D.'s vortex theory 2240; magnet & matter 1508.
Maignan, Emmanuel [1601–1676]: 449; between Aristotle & Epicurus 466a; his unpublished theory of Transsubstantiation 2110.
Maimon, Moses ben (Maimonides), [1135–1204]: 329; doubt & cogito 344; epistemology: Maimonides, D., Leibniz, Hume, Kant 3157; Maimonides' Guide for the Perplexed serves Spinoza as anticartesian arsenal of arguments 329.
Maine de Biran (Marie-François-Pierre Gonthier de Biran), [1766–1824]: 377a, 1828, 2493, 2930; Biranian experience, Cartesian metaphysics, mystery of man 3153; cogito 1828, 1910, 2489c, 2896–97; D. revival 2859.
"maîtres de la nature" (DM): s.v. mastery of nature.
Malaval (Malleval) & Descartes: 2125.
Malcolm, Norman: dreaming *306, 2623–23a;* 3596.
Malebranche, Nicolas [1638–1715]: bibliography 19, 19a, 21 & his Œuvres, ed. Robinet, v. 20; literature survey 5, documents 450; 157, 161, 170, 177, 202, 223, 435b, 438, 441, 441a, 450, 451, 453a-c, 1376a, 1640, 2676, 3401, 3540, 3608; D.'s Traité de l'homme converts him to Cartesianism 390, 435b & 2078; his anticartesianism debated 435b, 457b; absolute time & space, God 379a; actual & possible worlds 453a; his Augustinian unorthodoxy 235 combines Augustinianism of D. & Pascal 1157, Christian alliance between St. Augustine & D. 302; beast-machine 226; Cambridge Neoplatonists 2812; causality & occasionalism (q.v.) 213, 262, 453b,c, 463; cosmogony 359; critique of D. 192b; Desgabets (q.v.) 457a; determinism & free-will (Spinoza & Malebranche) 188 & 3047; dualism 215b, 453c, 1206, 2150–51; epistemology 161, 453b-c, 3023; eternal verities 161, a theocentric, anticartesian doctrine 457b; extension 161, 241, 291 & 2451, & psychology 2152; "fenomenismo razionalistico" 1282; Fontenelle attacks Malebranche's theocentric scientism 457c; force 161, 373a, 390; God 379a, 447, 2360, Christian God cartesianized by Malebranche 453a; gravity 390; history depreciated 313; idealism begins with Malebranche's Catholic philosophy, not with D. 462; ideas 315, controversy with Arnauld 161, 212a, 451a, 1713a, 2846, innate ideas 215b; influence 438 upon Balmes 1826,

Feijóo 449, Montesquieu (q.v.) 435, in Italy 433; intuitus 1259, 1401; laws of impact 1645a; liberté, libre-arbitre 291; Locke controversy 456; mathematics 358; matter, inertia 390; memory 2785; motion, its origin 373a; mysticism 453c & 2142, Malebranche not a Cartesian mystic 2318; ontology: aprioristic, Scholastic 3452; ontological argument 211a; passions 1466, 1857, 3382; physics 366, 390; proofs of God 211a, 447a; "pur amour" 215b; religion 447; opposes pluralistic scepticism derived from D. 329; realism & theory of ideas 315; Scottish Realists 3038–39; subject-object dualism 215b, 1206.

Malherbe, François de [1555–1628]: has already the esthetic principles ascribed to D. 411 (Abercrombie).

"malin génie": 169 & 2087, 170, 3489a; beast-machine, Chrysippos 3156; creation of eternal verities 241; defeated by non-rational belief in lumen naturale 321; D.'s unconquered irrationalism is the true malin génie 193a; disappears under Oxford exorcism 1331; discloses ethical rift between pensée & irrational action 1155a; & dreaming: threat of the imaginary 227; "grand doute" striking evidence itself 270, 270a; scepticism 322a; & s.v. certitude, Dieu-trompeur, veracity of God.

Mallemans de Messanges: "curieux adversaire de Descartes" 1695.

Mamert, Claudien (Claudianus Mamertus), [d. 476 A.D.]: connaissance d'autrui 244.

Mamiani della Rovere, Terenzio (1799–1885]: *2624;* ontological proof 3439.

man, concept of: s.v. anthropology.

man-machine: 147, 149, 226, 3474, 3530; from beast-machine to cybernetics 350; D.'s mechanistic biology, & philosophes 468; new sciences of man need no metaphysics or ontology 350; no psychological difference between man & machine 3380, denied 2332; & s.v. beast-machine, La Mettrie, mechanism.

Marburg School: 14, 160, 161, 211, 221.

Mariotte, Edme, Abbé [1620?–1684]: 390; laws of impact 1645a.

Maritain, Jacques: *183–184a; 2635–48;* discussed 23, 28, 324, 324a, 466d, 1252, 2915; angelism thesis disputed (Alquié) 149.

Marlowe, Christopher [1564–1693]: 295.

Marx, Karl [1818–1883]: *150, 2663,* texts 1091a; "conscience" 2164; D. & Marx 2675 are like anthropotheism & theandrism 184a, thesis & antithesis 3190; Marxism & D.'s anthropology, scientism 150 (Alquié) 3529: D. & Marx: Russian philosophy [before 1917] 184a; & s.v. Marxist interpretations.

Marxist interpretations: Descartes as bourgeois apologist, anticlerical materialist, empiricist, pre-encyclopedist, his metaphysical paradoxes, compromises with Scholasticism: 150, 154, 179, 459, 1091a, 3315; also 37, 295, 3184, 3314, 3477, 3534; interpretation principles defended 42; editions, commentary 1091a, 1737a, 1739a; certitude 2600; "conscience" 2614; cosmology, cosmogony 1091c, 1739a; critique of contemporary D. scholarship 31, 3314, 3184; dialectics of D. 1091b; DM & Essais 1737a, 2283a, 2770a; doubt 2552b; esthetics 1950a; evolution 3477a; French materialism 150, 459, 3296; générosité 295; Géométrie 1737a, 2283a; metaphysics 1426c; méthode 1265b, 1426d; physics today 2399a; psychology 3535; Regulae 2337a; reflex 1067a, 1941a; religion 1426a; science 2404–05, 2600; commemorative items: Albania 2887, France 552, Poland 550, Russia (q.v.); & s.v. Marx, Russia.

Masaryk, Tomas Garrigue [1850–1937]: 1193.

mask & enigma of Descartes: 124 (le philosophe au masque), 125, 175, 1652, 2735, 3489a, 3592; "Mona Lisa of philosophy" 1988; le philosophe sans masque 169; & s.v. larvatus prodeo.

mastery of nature ("maîtres de la nature," DM): text 83; angelism, hybris (Maritain) 183; Bacon, D., Enlightenment 1670; cybernetics, man-machine 350; conquest of material world D.'s goal (Laberthonnière) 177; D.'s dualism leads to scientific, empiricist subjection of nature (Schelling) 192a; mastery of nature, not introspection, D.'s ultimate purpose 1726, denied 1527, 1533; méthode does not achieve control of nature 189; "morale de puissance" (DM) 220, 230; object-subject split is decisive (Heidegger) 172b; Proudhon, Cournot, Nietzsche in pessimistic revolt against D. 2306; & s.v. nature.

Mastricht, Peter van [1630–1706]: orthodox Dutch anticartesianism 435a, 467.

Mateo de Zapata, Diego: Sevilla School 449.
material things, existence, proof of: s.v. body, external world.
materialism: D.'s affinities with modern materialism 2587a; conflict between D.'s basic materialism & Scholastic heritage, origin of French materialism 150, 459, 3296, 3314, & s.v. Marxist interpretations; D. & Enlightenment (q.v.) 468; his mechanistic vs. Marxian dialectic materialism 150; D. true father of materialism (Lange) 2434; from mechanism to evolutionary materialism 468.
mathematicism of Descartes: 156–59, 165, 166, 183–84a, 231, 321a, 353–55, 358, 371, 378, 398, 1083, 2061, 2630; cogito: St. Augustine & D. 334; D. & Malebranche 366; medicine 3342, metaphysical derivation 170 & metaphysical conflicts 326a; physics mathematized 1001a but not quantified by D. 398, quantified 1427, 2643; transition from mathematics to physics difficult 361, he recognizes uselessness of geometric ideal in physics (Roth) 189; modern mathematical physics & D.'s mathematicism 146b, 371; psychological roots of his mathematicism: Dream 104a; ruthless mathematization of all types of knowledge (Gilson) 166; & s.v. mathematics, mathesis universalis, physics, Regulae.
mathematics: bibliography 18, 229; texts 7, 74, 1720; 36, 185, 229, 378, 388, 396, 397, 1005a, 1769, 2169, 2330, 2335, 3226, 3263, 3386–87, 3390a–c; axiomatic systems 2350; Cartesian mathematics: "l'usine succedant au métier" 1323; extension: Euclidization of space 378; external world 1103; imagination 353; D.'s historical role & influence 3302, 3542; Jesuit teachings at La Flèche 83; logic 2827; Mersenne 215; metaphysics 159, 1396, requires understanding of D.'s mathematical concepts 398, mathematical method as model & limitation of D.'s metaphysics 398; méthode 198; memory 353; modern science: its hypothetic-deductive character not seen by D. 231, disputed 321a; mathematics & philosophy: D., Spinoza, Leibniz 432, 2238, 2266; physics 1911; position in D.'s system 1468; reality 178; rules of method 2799; time, space, mathematics 1162; truth 314; & s.v. algebra, analysis (math.), analytical geometry, Géométrie, mathematicism, mathesis universalis, physics, Regulae; curves, Descartes' rule of signs, equations, folium Cartesii, ovals, polyhedra, spirals, tensors.
mathesis universalis, pura, vulgaris: 83, 100, 161, 175, 181, 232, 2609; analytical geometry substituted for unattainable mathesis 353; asceticism & purification 206; before D. 378; in early 17th c. magical literature 328; existentialist view 175; guaranteed to correspond to reality 157, 378; influence on science 175; logic & mathematics fused 160, 161; mathematical method as matrix of D.'s philosophy 398; a mechanics of universe, not an algebra 1323; D.'s metaphysics is its metamathematics 321a; méthode 2548, 2771, [in 1619–20] 388 & 2751; from mathesis pura & abstracta to mathesis universalis: analysis to physics 159 & 1396; order & measure vs. number & figure (m. universalis vs. m. vulgaris) 198, 243 & 1484; philosophy of nature 1224; pure non-real quantities independent of imagination 353; pure theory of proportions & relations 161; realism of m. universalis, idealism of m. pura 159 & 1396.
matter: texts 7; 178; St. Augustine vs. D. 302; & creation 241; & extension: Henry More's critique 379a; Galileo's certainty of universal world of bodies, & Husserl's epoché 174; magnet 1508; proof of existence of matter 170, 290, 340; reduction to extension: an apologetic stratagem 163; subtle matter: doctrinal history 258, 431; & s.v. bodies, extension, external world.
Maurice of Nassau [1567–1625]: 378 & s.v. biography.
Maurolico, Francesco, O.S.B. [1494–1575]: rainbow theory 356.
Maxwell, James Clerk [1831–1879]: Cartesian-type concept of physics? 375; ether 258; vortices 392.
Mayow, John [1645–1679]: Cartesianism in chemistry 352, 467.
mechanics: 354, 361, 363, 367–69, 373a, 388, 390, 402; kinematics 1001a; Leibniz (q.v.) 2977; Mach's criticism 2613; mechanical labor: Galileo & D. 2831a; Poincaré's mechanical systems theorem anticipated by D. 2932; rest & motion 467; Spinoza 1759; statics 161, 368, 373a, difficult transition to dynamics 361, 372; work (travail mécanique) 373a, 388 & 2750; & s.v. force, free fall, impetus, movement.

mechanism: 149, 185, 215, 1818, 2341, 3246; biology (q.v.) 1815a, 3017; before D. 221; Cambridge Platonists 465; corporeal & mental mechanism 3080; early experimental mechanists oppose D.'s "Aristotelian" physics of abstract principles 215; D.'s mechanistic failure to account for the organic 171a; "homme total" & mechanism unreconciled 149; medicine 3319, 3342; Mersenne's empirical pragmatism vs. D.'s speculation 215; mechanism only a passing stage of D.'s thought 149; mechanism & modern physics 3133; physiology 373; positivistic "Cartesian" mechanism [after 1660] not in D.'s spirit 434; precursors of D. & Hobbes 221; psychology 3065, 3363; science 3016; mechanism a secondary feature of D.'s philosophy (Hegel) 171a; mechanistic physics, not metaphysics, expresses D.'s true intention (Schelling) 192a; social foundations 154; totalitarianism 3223; & s.v. beast-machine, Enlightenment, machines technology.

medicine: bibliography 397a; 83, 467, 1167, 1183, 1191, 1305, 1428, 1443, 1865, 2244, 2776, 3238, 3607; D.'s studies & experiments 83, 277; Cartesianism 430, 1824b; D.'s concept of medicine 365; is medicine a science? 170; anticipates modern discoveries 365; his growing disappointment 83, 124 & s.v. longevity; consequences of D.'s metaphysics for his medicine 170; creation of psychophysiology 2776; difficulties of deductive method, success of quantification 3342; mechanism 3319, 3342; methode 1969; moral philosophy 170; psychosomatic disorders 3379, 3530; & s.v. biology, longevity, physiology.

medievalism: attitude towards science 210 (ch. 1); Eleatic-Platonic tradition: influence on D. 205; D.'s "medievalism" & archaic attitude 175, 214a; D. & medieval metaphysics, science, tradition 7, 165, 214, 214a, 1912, 2953; psychology: D.'s "medieval" psychology lacks unity, his anti-Aristotelian revolt harmful? 1363; his scientism has medieval roots 214a, is incompatible with medieval concepts 210; his technique & exposition are traditional, Scholastic 2719; his truth concept rooted in medieval gnosiology 214a; & s.v. Aristotelianism, Scholasticism, Thomism.

"meditation" (word & meaning): 149, 2720, 2724; D.'s reasons for chosing it 165; & s.v. Ignatius de Loyola.

Meditations cartésiennes, Cartesianische Meditationen (Husserl): 173.

Méditations métaphysiques, Meditationes de prima philosophia (MM): editions 74, 76, 77, 89; text & commentaries 2585, 2655, 3478a; *general:* 149, 151, 168, 169, 170 (basic), 204, 233, 2624; *genesis:* 149, 164, 165, 193; chronology, early stages 269; first thoughts [1619–20] 83, 165 & s.v. formative period; first draft under Oratorian influence 163, MM originated in [1628–39] 121 & are therefore "older" than DM (Roth) 189; D.'s attempt to win Jesuit approbation 466, obstacles 101; publication 168; French Preface of 1647 & editorial practices 1831a; MM better received than DM 326; *special topics:* "conscience" 2332; control problem: dreaming & threat of the imaginary 227; DM & MM 149, 159 & 1401, 189, 247; eternal verities 241; Husserl's interpretation 173; méthode 198, 199 is aprioristic 247, metaphysical 210; ontological proof: Gouhier-Gueroult controversy 270, 270a; philosophy of Counterreformation 2864a; MM as rationalization of D.'s loss of his mother 3544; Regulae 221, 2207; scepticism 246, "super-Pyrrhonism" 322a; support for physics 199; transcendental spiritualism 4; veracity of God 169 & 2100; & s.v. Objectiones (O&R).

Méditations métaphysiques (by G. Wander, recte G. de Lanion): 244.

Meinong, Alexius, Ritter von Handschuchsheim [1853–1920]: objective reality 212a.

memory: texts 7; 83, 185, 2432; ars memorativa, mnemotechnics, Lullism, & méthode 328; association of ideas & the unconscious 2785; deception & doubt 268, 270, 270a; guarantee of the memory of the cogito (q.v.) 3579; mathematical notions 353; mémoire intellectuelle, corporelle 227, 2432 & individuation 215a; méthode 198.

mens corporea: solves D.'s metaphysical paradoxes 459.

Mercier, Désiré Joseph, Cardinal: *312, 385, 2703–05;* discussed 14; doubt 3580.

Mercier, Louis Sebastien [1740–1814]: *112, 2708–08a;* Thomas' Eloge 126.

Merleau-Ponty, Maurice: *311a, 2709–10;* 149.

Mersenne, Marin [1588–1648; AM, v. 1]: *82, 2713;* Lenoble's monograph 215; 163, 368, 438,

441a; his antilibertinism 163; Augustinianism 302; Dioptrique: Mersenne suggests verification 400; French correspondents 1016; liberté 3575a, divine freedom (Mersenne, D., Sartre) 164, 192; mechanics 368, 2608a; music 2594; ontological proof 214; scepticism epistemologically refuted 246, 322a; & s.v. biography.

Mesland, Denis, S.J. [1616–1672? AM v. 6]: personal relations with D. 466; D.'s letters on Transsubstantiation (q.v.) 164, 2nd & 4th letter first published by Emery 452a, reprinted by Bouillier 438.

Mesnard, Pierre: *2715–25, 42, 186, 220, 244a, 313, 386;* editor *91;* discussed 28, 373.

metamathematics: D.'s metaphysics as metamathematics of mathesis universalis 321a.

métamorale: 220.

metaphors: Descartes' metaphors (architect-certainty, traveler-méthode) 403, (solidity, lucidity, linearity) 408, analogy as epistemological tool 268a, metaphors as protophilosophy 238; Geulincx: allegory & metaphysics 161, 402a.

metaphysics: texts 7; general 127, 170, 171, 177, 179c, d, 185, 193, 202, 204, 219, 233, 323, 1426c, 1830, 2056, 2563, 3083, 3478a; genesis & chronology 96 (CP: physicist without metaphysics), 193, 3389 & 2946; animal soul 226; anthropomorphic since D. (Heidegger) 172b; aristocratic 168; Augustinianism (q.v.) 235; fundamental concepts (pensée, étendue, union) 1021; Gassendi: metaphysics as science is impossible 2121a; hidden insecurity of D.'s & modern metaphysics 176; méthode 210, 231, 398, 3056; not fundamental in D.'s system (Liard) 181; "ordre des raisons" 170; physics 83; philosophia novantiqua 436; purpose: defense of Catholic Church 163, 179b, to prove union of real self & real God 210; "réalisme de l'idée" 132; ruins D.'s system 112; Scholastic, not Kantian 256; Scholasticism plus inappropriate scientism 231; science & metaphysics unconnected in D. 375; spirit of D.'s metaphysics (Gouhier) 2085; D.'s system not metaphysical but projective 1074; time 347a; two-substance dualism tends to negate metaphysics 216a; D. & Heidegger's "Überwindung der Metaphysik" 172a; unifies system 185; & s.v. Méditations [MM], philosophy of Descartes, & under individual problems.

metaphysics, *histories:* survey (Hagmann) 10; Abbagnano 1101, Bierens de Haan 1234, Boas 200a, Bréhier 1351, Brunschvicg 157, 1399, 1400, Bullón y Fernandez 1411, Cousin 1654, Delbos 134, Deutinger 1755, Dilthey 206, 1775, Erdmann 171a, Feuerbach 171a, Kuno Fischer 1894, Frischeisen-Köhler 1941, Gilson 166, 167, Hegel 171a, Heidegger 172b, Husserl 174, 2254a, W. Jansen 2289, Maréchal 2630, Renouvier 188, Ritter 3074, 3075, Rivaud 3076, B. Russell 3162, Sáiz Barberá 3183, Schelling 192a, Sertillanges 3274, Souilhé 3327, Tennemann 3401, Whitehead 3555a.

Météores & meteorology: editions 74, 76, Russian transl. & commentary 1737a; texts 7; 396, 2419, 2966; methodology: 402, deductive 2966, instrumentalist 247; Scholastic & Cartesian meteorology 165; & s.v. rainbow.

méthode: texts 7; general 83, 160, 161, 171, 177, 178, 181, 185, 189, 192b, 193, 198, 199, 209, 211b, 219, 221, 231, 273, 1265b, 1403, 1426d, 1510, 2119, 2136, 2358, 2691, 2740, 2797a, 2919, 2985, 3158, 3348–49, 3481a, 3492; *genesis & chronology* 149, 179a–c, 2064, first concept [1619–20] 100, disputed 3092; *special topics:* axiomatic systems 2350; dialectics 3215; dualism: aprioristic in Regulae, DM, MM & instrumentalist in Essais, PP 247, disputed 3544a; characteristic feature: proof 149, doubt 179a, 2839; Dream 195; Essais as example 1770, 1774, Géométrie 355 & 2019, 358, 398, 402; Four rules of method (DM) anterior to Regulae? 100; induction, not Euclidean deductiveness 3309; literature of magic 328; mathematics 321a, 1227, 1323, 2799, 3445, mathematics & metaphysics 1396, mathematico-scientific method of Regulae, DM vs. metaphysical method of MM 210; mathesis universalis 2548, 2771, as model for D.'s metaphysics 398; MM 198, 199, 247; metaphysics & méthode 231, 3056; modern usefulness 2008; neither orthodoxy nor dogma but discipline of mind 3079; nonempirical character claimed & disputed 189; only outwardly mathematical: méthode means experience of freedom (Laporte) 2454; physics: mapping concepts upon concepts without time parameter 371; Positivist & Cartesian 1800; postulates 1680; presuppositional, not deductive 3340; rainbow as example 356; psychology 323; Regulae 100, 189, 193, 198, 210, 231, 247, Regulae & DM 4 & 1463, discrepancies 2518, dehumanization & object-orientation 149, metaphysics & physics 3358; rules, definition 198; in science 468, 1300, 3356, barren formalism (Jaspers) 175, thought experiment vs. causal research 402; syllogism 3215; theory of relations 231; unity of method 159 & 1396; weakness 189; "Wissenschaftsgesinnung" 175; & s.v. Discours [DM], epistemology, rules of method.

méthode, *doctrinal history:* Aristotelian & Cartesian method 1421, 3430; Bacon 211, 388 & 2747, his rules & Regulae, DM 189; 17th century 1973; eclipse of D.'s méthode [1650–1700] 189; Enlightenment 468; Leibniz 211, 1012; survival in Locke 189; Spinoza 455a, 1012; Platonic dialectics, syllogism 3215.

Mexico: Cartesian disciple 1473.

Meyer, Lodevijk (Ludwig) [1629–1681]: Cartesian Spinozist 467, 3417, his Preface to Spinoza's Ethica 329; & Dutch Protestant anticartesians 435a.

Meyssonnier, Lazare, Royal astrologer & physician [1602–1672]: his & D.'s philosophical concepts 328.

Mickiewicz, Adam [1798–1855]: nationalism & philosophy 1676.

Mill, John Stuart [1806–1873]: formalization of logic 335; his Cartesian error 2600.

Millet, Joseph: *2764–65;* 96.

mind: s.v. cognition, pensée, understanding.

miracles: 178, 349.

MM: s.v. Méditations métaphysiques.

model: 83; anaclastic as model of mathematical reasoning 321a; beast-machine: confusion of thought models 276; mathematics as model for metaphysics 398; D.'s thought model method vs. causal research 402; & s.v. wax.

modern man: anticipated by D. 179, 3116; alienation 179, 196, 432a, 3116, 3161; & s.v. anthropology.

modern mind: D. & its formation 151, 153, 162, 166, 171a–172b, 175, 176, 179, 183–84a, 189, 192a, 193a, 196, 200a, 216, 225, 262, 307, 347b, 348, 350, 432a, 459, 1087, 1932, 2195, 3161, 3508; D. & modern rootlessness 1840; self-destruction of metaphysics 1996; D. to the rescue! 432a, 1938, 3393.

modern philosophy & Descartes: 1052, 1192, 1491, 2820, 3463, 3476, & s.v. modern mind.

Molière, Jean-Baptiste Poquelin [1622–1673]: attitude towards D. 466a; cogito: Amphitryon 407; Femmes savantes 438.

Molin, Agostino, O.C. [d. 1840]: Cartesianism in Padua 2111.

Molinism: 14, 154, 164, 319, 1060.

moment: s.v. instant.

Monde, Le: editions 74, 92b; 2, 83, 193, 467; inertia & gravity 379; Enlightenment 468; methodology: instrumentalist? 247; RV a first sketch of it? 242, 2321; Le Monde: D.'s universal physics 193.

monism: opposed by St. Thomas & D. 1130; D.'s ethical monism 1822; modern monistic revolt against Cartesian dualism 155, & s.v. Russell, Santayana, Whitehead; Cartesianism as value monism 1822.

Montaigne, Michel de [1533–1592]: 158, 404; Montaigne & D. as critics of culture 217; D. absorbs Montaigne, asserts what he rejected 158; brings Montaigne's humanism & sagesse to domination 157; Montaigne & DM 404, has already the destructive part of DM 3583; D. & Pascal: relation to Montaigne 158, 1436a; scepticism 246, 322a; Montaigne, not Aristotle or St. Thomas, is D.'s true opponent 144.

Montesquieu, Charles Louis de Secondat, Baron de [1689–1755]: his Cartesianism 1065a; indirect influence of D. through Fontenelle & Malebranche 435; Esprit des lois: direct influence 412; Lettres persanes are Cartesian, later works Malebranchean in inspiration 445; law & political theory 412, 435, 445, 466d, 1065a, 3235, D. & Leibniz 3235.

morale: texts 7; editions: s.v. Lettres sur la morale; 83, 129, 132, 163, 168, 169, 171, 176, 177, 179a–d, 185, 206, 210, 215c, 218, 220, 230, 231a, 1240, 1273, 1869, 2070, 2512, 2654, 2658–59, 2956, 3251, 3441, 3594; 17th c. moral philosophy 3407; *special topics:* ambiguity: two orders, three notions of morale in D. 267; Cartesianism defined as deductive ethics 1023, as classical value monism vs. modern pluralism 1822, as ethico-religious humanism 179a–d; certitude: only "certitude vulgaire" applies to moral conduct 228; D.'s critique of Thomist & Molinist attitudes towards life 154; early ethical preoccupations 96, 100, 163; Elisabeth's objections 119; ethical consequences of D.'s metaphysics 170 (v. 2); ethics needs hyperbolic doubt, supplied by Husserl & Spiegelberg 3333; evidence 2060; genesis & principles 1493; "l'homme concret" 149; "itinéraire morale" 169 & 2084; D. as lay moralist 2883a; limits of Cartesian rationalism in ethics 1386; medicine 83; méthode 2569; "morale de béatitude": s.v. sagesse; "morale de puissance" (DM) 220, 230; morale provisoire (q.v.); morale & ideal society 1579; moralism & perfect theoricity reconciled 1070; D.'s morale is neither Stoic nor Epicurean 149, has Stoic, Christian elements 3268; D.'s personality, & morale 3270; physio-psychological basis of morale 215c; its principles, experience, progress, ideal 179b; three ethics of D.: prudence, sagesse, générosité 3166; roots, purpose, system 163; suffering not its root 321a; systematic position 1948; technique: naturalistic, "quasi athée," eudaimonistic 170; worthless 126 though respectable 2210; *doctrinal history:* religion & ethics in D. & after 3220; Cartesian & Thomist ethics 154, 1913; Molinism 154; Geulincx 217, 467, 3404; D. & Pascal 3211; Spinoza 2699, moral imperfection according to D. & Spinoza 2811; modern "Cartesian" ethics 2183a & 1023, & s.v. ethics, générosité, sagesse, morale provisoire.

morale provisoire: 163, 245, 1318–19, 2840, 3287; decision theory 2840; générosité 295; méthode 2672a; morale provisoire, morale de puissance, métamorale 220, 230; morale provisoire vs. search for certainty: D.'s existential failure 347b; root of operationalist attitude 196; rules of method 245; & s.v. morale.

"moralistes" (France): their Cartesian spirit 453; their un-Cartesian spirit 316.

"morceau de cire": s.v. wax.

Morcillo, Sebastián Fox [1526?–1560]: 449.

More, Henry [1614–1687]: correspondence with D. *74, 84;* 121, 161 (v. 2), 438, 441a, 456, 1020, 1482, 3450a; beast-machine 226; mechanics 367; motion 2435; reaction to Cartesianism 444, 456; Regius 467; religion & science 465, 1063; space: 377, critique of D.'s concept of extension 315, 379a, spiritualizes extension 241, finite world in infinite space 379a; & s.v. Cambridge Platonists.

Morfouace de Beaumont, Gilles: beast-machine poetry 226.

Mouy, Paul: *356, 390, 2803–07;* 367.

movement, motion: texts 7; doctrinal history 161 (v. 1, 2), 377a, 390; Aristotelian & Cartesian motion 2610; Huygens, Newton 390; individuation 215a; involuntary movement: s.v. reflex action; kinematics 1001a; Henry More 2435; movement of the earth 2, 83, 149, 178; origin of movement, force: D. & Malebranche 373a, 390; physiological movement 179c; planetary motion 390, 1027c; quantity of motion (work) vs. vis viva: D. & Leibniz (q.v.) 377a, 375, 390, 1338, 2145; relativity of motion: D. & Bruno 161; rest & motion 1001a, D. & Malebranche (force at rest) 373a; time 347a.

Muratori, Lodovico Antonio [1672–1750]: poetic verisimilitude & Cartesian canon 420.

music: 2878; D.'s contribution & historical position 418; Mersenne 2594; musical expression: correspondence with emotion 419, 421; musical scale: Pythagoras & D. 1971; & s.v. Compendium musicae; esthetics.

Mydorge, Claude [1585–1647; AM, v. 1]: use of French in scientific writing (but not publishing) 410.

mystery, mysteries: Christian mysteries & religion 178; D. abandons the absolute Christian mystery attainable by will through Grace 152; his youthful interest in mystification (*Cogitationes privatae*), not mystery 236.

mysticism: Bérulle 267; Cartesian circle is close to mystic view of God 214; Christian mysticism 152, 178, as countervailing force against Cartesian pedagogy 196: Cogitationes privatae not mysticist 236; D. banishes mysticism from philosophy 152, 162; his mystical drive 175 & mysticism 1816; England acclaims Cartesianism for its mystical, poetic appeal 406; logical & mystical dualism in D. 321a; Malebranche's mystical intuition, & Cartesian clarity 453c; Poiret: 438, Cartesian mysticism 2318, the unconscious 215b; rationalist mysticism of D. 345, 1362; scepticism: mystic-fideistic (Charron, Pascal, Huet) 246, 322a; D.'s sense of interiority, & medieval

mysticism 1147a; 17th c. theology 267; mysticism & voluntarism in Regulae 1638.
myth: D.'s philosophy is antimythical 153; "Myth of Descartes": as dualistic mind concept (Ryle) 190 & as French national image 453.

N

Naissance de la paix: editions 78, 1072; 28, 425.
Naples (Napoli): Cartesians & anticartesians 433, 438, 1648.
nativism: s.v. innate ideas.
Natorp, Paul: *221, 2830–31*; 14, 1162.
natural belief: 193; "inclination" 170; "teachings of nature" 340.
natural law: 154, 443, 466d; & eternal verities 253.
natural religion, natural theology: s.v. religion, theology.
naturalism of Descartes: close to modern materialism 2587a; its origin: doubt 1097; Renaissance naturalism: D.'s theoretical adversary 319; D. & Enlightenment 466a, 468; modern naturalism fails to bypass Cartesian dualism 155; Spinoza's transformation of D.'s naturalism 1656.
nature: texts 7; 83, 165; Cartesian "denudation of nature" vs. English, German, Romantic nature ideal 276, 409, 466a, 466b; D.'s dualism: impact on Western nature attitude (Schelling) 192a; experience: méthode, Regulae 2120; "inclination," its veracity 170, 340; internal finality vs. mechanism 170, 178, & 2450, 291a; laws of nature 83; loss of reality 149; natural & supernatural: Scholasticism & D. 177; order of nature as protophilosophy 238, "philosophy" of nature rejected by D. 149, natural vs. metaphysical order (Gouhier-Gueroult controversy) 170, 270, 270a, 1051a, 2155, 3102, 3104c; natural (mechanistic) vs. spiritual order of justice (Montesquieu) 435; pure nature: D. & Molinism 319; scientific vs. magical cosmology 268a; separation of self & ideas from nature: subjectivism 1414a; "teachings of nature" & error, union, 340; *doctrinal history:* mechanistic view 221; Cartesians 431; Cambridge Platonists 465 & 1482 (Cassirer); D., Malebranche, Berkeley 2156; French rationalism & scepticism 466a; Molinism 319; Montesquieu 435; philosophes 468; & s.v. "maîtres de la nature," mechanism, "roman de la nature," simple natures.
nebular hypothesis: Swedenborg influenced by D. 466c.
necessary connection: s.v. liaison nécessaire.
necessity: 161, 178, & s.v. liaison nécessaire.
negation: D. carries doubt to methodical negation 268; D. & Spinoza 455a; negative theology: s.v. theology.
Neocartesianism: Husserl 1756 & s.v. phenomenology; Whittaker's proposed Neocartesian science 401.
Neoidealism: s.v. idealistic interpretations.
Neokantianism: Cartesian influence 1208; Marburg School (q.v.); Neokantian interpretations: s.v. idealistic interpretations.
Neoplatonism: mystic soul vs. beast-machine theory 226; ontological proof 214; Oratoire 163; also Cambridge Platonists.
Neoscholastic, Neothomist interpretations: survey 14; Collectanea 35, 41; general 132, 183–84a, 211b, 244a, 312, 385, 1503, 1776–77, 1858, 1866, 2598–99, 2620, 2676, 2922, 2951a, 3093, 3113a, 3209, 3249; Cartesianism incompatible with theology 3261, a bundle of contradictions acceptable only to Descartes himself 2307, a liberating but tragic philosophy 3242; methodology: D. confirms St. Thomas, his conclusions are now rejected 2973; "cartesianizing Scholasticism" 2041, 2951a; psychology 385; Cartesian self, defended against Neoscholastic critique 1238; Laberthonnière's "horreur du ghetto scolastique" 177; & s.v. Catholic interpretations.
Neothomism: s.v. Neoscholastic.
Newcastle, Duke of: s.v. Cavendish, William.
Newton, Isaac [1642–1727]: 188, 357, 359, 367, 371, 375, 377, 379a, 380, 390, 432, 444, 468, 1860, 2575, 3046, 3218a; D. prepares ground for Newton, influences him 375, 378, 456, 1435, 2903; popular view & iconographic symbolization of D.'s defeat 113, 465a; Cartesianism vs. Newtonianism 357, 367, fortunes, fluctuations of Newtonianism 1027b, 2139a, Campailla's anti-Newtonianism 1439; Newton's influence upon Huygens (q.v.) 367, Einstein closer to D. than to Newton? 383; *special topics:* astronomy 359, 379a, 3310, Kepler's law:

Newton's errors 375; dynamics 354; mathematicism 371; metaphysical concepts 357, 379a, 444; mechanics 354, 367; physics 188, 390, "minimalist" 375; space & time 378, 379a, 444.
Nicéron, Jean-François [1613–1646]: mechanical curiosa 236.
Nicole, Pierre [1625–1695]: 438, 441a; grace & imperceptible thoughts 215a.
Nietzsche, Friedrich [1844–1900]: 172, 172a, b, 225, 304, 1192, 2164, 2306, 3159; Nietzsche & D., Voltaire, French rationalism 3284.
Nihilism: D. & Nietzsche (Heidegger) 172, 172a, b; Schelling 192a.
nominalism: 3113a, 3381; French scepticism 246; & individual differences 215a.
Norris, John [1657–1711]: 192b, 3127–28; beast-machine 226; causality 453a; eternal verities 161 (v. 2); Locke's critique 456.
Notae in programma: editions 74, 77, 92a; "conscience" & cognition 2352.
Nothingness: 195.
"nullum problema non solvere": & méthode 198; before D. 378.
numbers: 178, 2573; genesis of numbers & unity of sciences 243 & 1484; number concept: Stevin, D., Wallis 378; number, time, space 178; number & figure: mathesis vulgaris 198, 243 & 1484.

O

O & R: s.v. Objectiones.
object-subject: irremediable Cartesian split deplored by Feuerbach 171a & 1889 & by Schelling 192a; & s.v. dualism.
Objectiones cum responsionibus authoris (O & R): editions 74, 76, 77; general 179d, 204, 204a, 3286, 3603; arguments continued in correspondence 84; ideas 212a; metaphors 403; proofs of God 165, 3301; rationalism 3301; substance 156 & 1391; Bourdin & the Jesuits 338; Caterus 165, 2685; Gassendi (q.v.) 211a, 241, 325, 2121a, 3421, 3439; Spinoza 156 & 1391; & s.v. Méditations (MM).
objectivity of knowledge: D. & Stoics 2208; Malebranche & Arnauld (q.v.) 451a.
obscurity: s.v. confusion, clear & distinct.
occasional causes, occasionalism: Descartes 178, 212a, leaves divine & natural causality unconnected: root of occasionalism 463; occasionalism: 138, 431, 438, 441a, 451, 463, 2338, 2810, 3227, 3513; Bayle 438; La Forge (q.v.) 3275; Swedenborg's misunderstanding 2863; psychophysical parallelism 431; relation to Cartesianism 3216; theory of consciousness 215b.
occultism: texts ("magie") 7; Dream purges D. of occult concepts 179; occult sciences 163; magic & astrological literature anticipates early concepts of D. 102, 103, 328; magical cosmological symbolism vs. scientific nature concept 268a; superstitious notions in Bacon & D. 3426.
Olgiati, Francesco: *14, 185, 2866–70;* 23, 252, 239, 411, 1282, 1286, 2442–43, 3093; & s.v. fenomenismo razionalistico.
Olympica: 96, 100, 121, 2764, 3092; hermeneutic literature before D. 328; "pensée de jeunesse abandonnée" 96; & D.'s rationalism 2349a; & Regulae, DM 3174; symbolism 268a; & s.v. Cogitationes privatae, Dream, Opuscula.
ontological principle (Whitehead): 194a.
ontological proof, argument: 83, 165, 170, 171, 183, 193, 204, 210, 211a, 219, 233, 270 & 2101, 270a, 1284, 1673, 1705, 2071, 2608 & s.v. proofs of God; cogito & ontological proof are equivalent (Hegel) 171a; cogito doubly subordinated to ontological proof (Lavelle) 293; controversies ignore differences between types of ideas in D. 149; does not prove God's existence but establishes concept of ens necessarium (Schelling) 192a; "logic of perfection" 183 (Maritain), 211a (Hartshorne); not in D.'s metaphysical project [of 1628] 269; order & rank of proofs: Gouhier-Gueroult controversy 170, 270, 270a, 1406a, 2155, 3102, 3104c; proof rehabilitated by Third Meditation 1131; total intuition 159 & 1396; untenable against positivist critique 2608, 2671a & s.v. proofs of God.
ontological proof, argument, *doctrinal history:* sources 83, history 211a, 2389, 3439; St. Anselm (q.v.) 83, 149, 159 & 1396, 165, 211a, 214, 1114a, 2280, 2551, 2763, 3439, D.'s proof avoids objections to Anselm's 1257; D. & Suarez, Mersenne, Silhon 214; D. is in the Neoplatonic-Christian tradition 214; 18th century critique 211a, 467; Hegel 171a; Kant's critique 211a, 1114a, 1657, rejected 2155, 2763; Kant on D. & Leibniz 1657; proof defended against Leibniz's critique 273; Male-

branche's proof by excellence 447a; Schelling 192a; & s.v. proofs of God.
ontologism: D.'s "critical ontologism" 3015; Gioberti 205; Malebranche (q.v.): Neo-thomistic critique 2676; & D.'s psychology 385.
ontology: cogito 171a, 172, 204, 204a, 208, 293, 1498; D. & the ontological tradition 205, transfers medieval ontology to res cogitans (Heidegger) 172, reaches a "metaphysics beyond ontology" (Alquié) 149, 2863b; D.'s "negative ontology" 1050; fundamental ontology 1498 & s.v. Heidegger; "itinéraire ontologique" of his metaphysics 169 & 2081; Lavelle 293; ontological experience vs. systematic deduction (Alquié) 1056; Spinoza 455a, 3471a; & s.v. Being.
ontotheology: history of the ontological argument 211a.
operationalism: contrasted with méthode 235c; D. missed it because of his quest for certitude 231; morale provisoire 196; psychosomatic medicine controversy 3379, 3530, 3568.
optics: 83, 100, 388, 390, 396; color: D., Malebranche, Huygens, Newton, 390; lenses 87, 388, 399; Mach 399; & s.v. Dioptrique, light,refraction.
Opuscula: editions 74, 75; 96, 100, 121, 220, 2764, 2926; Renaissance influences 163; scientific beginnings 388 & 2744; & s.v. Cogitationes privatae, & individual titles.
Oratoire: influence upon D. 149, 163; & Cartesianism 438, 1817; suppresses teaching of D.'s philosophy 466a; Jesuit pressures 450; Augustinian influence upon D. 163; D.'s doctrine of divine freedom & Oratorian philosophy 164; innate ideas 165; mystical theology 267; Oratorian theologians & first concept of MM 163; Poisson 1558; modern Oratorians 177, 215; & s.v. Bérulle, Condren.
order: 83, 178, types 170; of axioms: D. & Spinoza 272; Cartesian genetic-systematic order not a uniquely logical system (Alquié vs. Gueroult) 1051a; Cartesianism: denunciation of disorder (Péguy) 186; Encyclopedists & epistemological order 455; hierarchic order of reality: D. & Spinoza 455a; D.'s mathematical order concept obviates measurability 398; mathesis vulgaris & universalis 198; metaphysical & scientific ideas: different orders 1056; order of nature & metaphysical order (Gouhier-Gueroult controversy) 170, 270, 270a, 1046a, 2155, 3102, 3104c; order of nature 170, in D., Malebranche, Berkeley 2156; natural vs. spiritual order of justice (Montesquieu) 435; order of philosophical exposition 171, 447a; "ordre des raisons" (Gueroult) 170, 270a, 1055, methodology distinguished from metaphysical argument 2005, Spinoza & D. 272, & Gouhier-Gueroult controversy above; order & probability (Cournot) 274; order of proofs of God: most exact in PP 1646, & Gouhier-Gueroult controversy above; social order & freedom 2290; structural order vs. ratio demonstrandi 270a; & s.v. analysis & synthesis.
Orders & Congregations (religious): 438, 450, 458, 466a, & s.v. Benedictines, Jesuits, Oratoire.
organism: & beast-machine concept 276; D.'s failure to account for organism (Hegel) 171a; individuality of organic bodies 215a; organic growth & D.'s transcendental curves 398; Whitehead's philosophy of organism & D. 194a; & s.v. vitalism.
original sin: 437.
originality of Descartes: s.v. priority.
orthography of Descartes: 74, 75.
oscillations: s.v. pendulum problem.
Ostwald, Wilhelm: "minimalist" in physics 375.
Ottaviano, Carmelo: *222, 252, 461, 2881–82;* 27.
ovals of Descartes: 1158, 3041.
Oxford analysis: s.v. logical positivism.

P

Padua: Cartesians & anticartesians 433, 1824a, anti-Scholastic "Cartesians" 2111.
painting: D.'s influence 415, 422, 1438a.
Pantheism: & D.'s denial of vacuum 3297.
Panthéonisation of Descartes: 112, 121 (documents), popular reaction [against the decree of 1796] 114; also 1501, 1520–21, 2326, 3106, 3149, & s.v. transfers.
Pappus, problem of: 388, 398, 1227, 3386.
paradoxes of Descartes: s.v. contradictions.
Pardies, Ignace Gaston, S.J. [1636–1673]: 17, 466; beast-machine 226, 1576; proof of God by asymptotic areas 1147b.

Parent, Antoine [1666–1716]: Cartesian physics 3262.

Paris: 17th c. Cartesian meetings 450; Montagne Saint-Geneviève 2652; Aristotelianism & Cartesianism at the University 390, 450, 466a, 1876; the Prades affair 438 (v. 2).

Parnassus: 96, 100, 2764, & s.v. Cogitationes privatae, Opuscula.

Pascal, Blaise [1623–1662; AM, v. 4]: 154, 157–159, 161, 189, 431a, 2940, 3368-9; *general comparison with Descartes:* affinities (cœur, esprit, chair) 318; anticartesianism 431a; believes in science as D. believes in God (Brunschvicg) 1393; no borrowings from D. 431a; condemnation of Galileo: his vs. D.'s reaction 2941; Calvinist view 1845; Pascal the Christian vs. Descartes the Cartesian 2940; Pascal's experimentalist "sagesse" vs. D.'s faith in reason 1682; Pascal's Jansenism root of his anticartesianism 2303, sombre Jansenist vs. happy anthropocentrist 2819; opposition in physics & metaphysics 1326, "opposition intégrale" with science & religion linking them 159 & 1393; "revanche du réalisme sur le spiritualisme" 158; some compatibility 3422a; two Christian philosophers 3285; D. and (not: or) Pascal 2707; *special points:* Augustinianism 235, Pascal's & D.'s Augustinianisms diverge, reconciled in Malebranche 1157; "amour" 422; critique of D. 189; epistemology 161; fideism 2680; "gnosis" 3373; history accepted by Pascal, negated by D. 149; D.'s literary influence 412; mechanics 367, 368; Molinism 319; Montaigne, Descartes, Pascal 158, 1436a; morale 3211; physics of D. 188, 1326; religious attitude of D. & Pascal 1393, 1526, 2303, 2622, 2819, 2940, 3285; scepticism 246; scientific method 1431; scientific work of D. & Pascal 1236; vacuum & Puy de Dôme experiment 121, 402, 1013, 1772, 2861, 3519, Pascal's honesty impugned 2671; Voltaire & Pascal against D. 466a, 2880; French 20th century Pascal revival, & D. scholarship 1824c.

Pascal, Etienne [d. 1651]: Pascal's limaçons & D.'s ovals 1158, 3041.

passions: texts 7; 147, 168, 171, 178, 193, 206a, 215c, 220, 243, 402, 1290, 2975, 3019, 3280; anthropological significance 2614; classification, control & education of passions 220; educational psychology: Vives & D. 3459–60; emotions 1859; influence of D.'s theory upon jurisprudence 264; medicine, psychology, morale 365; remedies for passions 147; theory of passions, & metaphysics 1147; D.'s theory of expression merely clarifies Renaissance concepts 422; *doctrinal history* 243 & 1479; Greek philosophy 2690; Hobbes 3237; Malebranche, Spinoza 1466, 1857, 2072; John Smith 465; Vives 3459–60; & s.v. Traité des passions; morale; emotions; amour, générosité, sagesse.

Patristic & Cartesian concepts: 3199.

Pavlov, Ivan Petrovič [1849–1936]: D. precursor of conditioned reflex theory 150, 421, 1067a, 1941a.

pedagogy of Descartes: 185, 196, 265, 1474, 2790, 2924, 3031, 3378; D.'s precepts are pedagody for adults, not children 265; D., Durckheim, modern French educational reforms 265 (Taborda); education of body & soul: sagesse 220; intermediate education: Cartesian méthode 1415; Italy: D. & Vico 461 (Vidari); modern Americanized education 265; passions: Vives & D. 3459; Port-Royal 441; Thomism & mysticism as antidote against Cartesian spirit in pedagogy 196.

Peirce, Charles Sanders [1839–1914]: *187, 2925–26;* 1833a.

Peiresc, Nicolas-Claude Fabri de [1580–1637; AM, v. 3]: correspondence with Mersenne 82.

Pelagianism of Descartes: 178.

Pell, Dr. John [1611–1685; AM, v. 4]: meets D. 118, correspondence 1020.

pendulum problem: 369.

Penn, William [1644–1718]: last spiritual director of Princess Elisabeth 1802.

pensée, mens, res cogitans, mind: texts 7, 83; general 127, 129, 131, 132, 147, 149, 151, 160–61, 170, 171, 173–74, 178, 179c, d, 181, 183–185, 190, 192a, 193, 202, 204, 209, 210, 219, 221, 233, 259, 455a; action & pensée 1292; âme & pensée: identified by D., separated by Husserl 2564; cogitatio: D.'s description unsatisfactory 1175; cogito as "mouvement de la pensée" 2232; denaturalization of mind, from Aristotle to D. 2291; D. makes pensée center of all modern metaphysics (Schelling) 192a; essence of mind 2815; evidence 1413, 2490; finitude of pensée & infinite power of affirmation (Lavelle) 293; first verity 129; "ghost-in-the-machine" 190;

idée & pensée: definition 170; incapacities of mind 187; limits, lacunae 179c; méthode & pensée, their unity 198; D.'s monstrous perversion of cognition (Maritain) 184; multiplicity of thinking substances 215a; "pensée distincte & union âme-corps" 178; pensée intuitive 1401, & s.v. intuition; "pensée sensible & pensée pure": D.'s critique 179c; pensées imperceptibles & theory of grace (Nicole, Leibniz, Huygens) 215b, 438; object of thought 2505; ontological status 208; pensée-substance: Berkeley's critique 259; "pour penser il faut être" 170, 252; res cogitans & medieval ontology (Heidegger) 172, & the Cartesian observer, mathematicism 104a; Sanchez 208; substance 83, 208, 259; substantial existence, individuality, immortality 228; "surface de la pensée" vs. "fond du cœur" 215b; Thomistic intellect, & Being 208; unity, interiority, sufficiency, substantiality, ontological status 208; unity of pensée guarantees unity of sciences 243 & 1484; "vie & pensée" 2115; volonté dominates pensée 2948; doctrine from D. to Hume 259; Spinoza 455a, 1401, 2505, 2619; psychologistic transformation in England 460; & s.v. âme, cogito, "conscience," intelligence, metaphysics, understanding.

Pepys, Samuel [1633–1703]: reads D.'s Compendium musicae, & so to bed 2933a.

perception: 170, 185, 192b, 193, 210, 3012, 3038–39, 3243; conception & perception 212a; D.'s doubt of sensory perceptions is logically unwarranted 3048a; dualism difficulties 192b; idea & perception 2007, 3455; imagination 198; judgments of perception: logical status 231; matter & Cartesian perception 3109; memory vs. perception: mathematics 353; qualities 185; sense perception & problem of metaphysics 1642; thinking-machines 2739; vision, & perception of material objects 1785; Berkeley, Malebranche, D. 2156; & s.v. idea, sensation.

Peripatetics: s.v. Aristotelianism.

Perricone, Filiberto (O.S.B.): Padua Cartesianism 2111.

Perrien, Pierre de, Marquis de Crenan: 3545.

Perron: Descartes sieur du Perron 121, 2566 [& AM, v. 1, s.v. Perron].

persecution of Cartesianism: 390, 438, 450, 466a; Belgium 458; France 450, 466a; Holland 435a, 436, 467, 1918; Naples 438 (v. 2).

persona: in the cogito 1509a; & s.v. larvatus prodeo, mask.

personal relations of Descartes: section 116–120; 79; Belgian philosophers & theologians 458, 467, 1781; Denmark 2612; Holland, France 467; Jesuits 466; medical men 365 (Tellier); Picot, Villebressieu et al. 1 & 2858a, 121, 124; Sweden 2552a; theologians 124, 163, 267, 467; & s.v. biography, & individual names.

personality & character of René Descartes: 93, 95, 116, 121–126, 142, 146a, 147, 148, 163, 168, 169, 175, 176, 179a–d, 183, 184, 186, 194, 1531; archaic in his scientism 175; attitude towards royalty: reverence or adulation? 93, 119, 169, 215c; blind pride, contempt for work of others 368 & s.v. priority; brutal in controversy 116; capricious young amateur 93; so Catholic, so reasonable! 454; cavalier français 186, 2057; courageous, physically fearless 124; enigmatic, passionate, driven by will to power & mystical urge 175; frank, good-humored 86; happy, radiant, content 169, 245, 2819, perfect equilibrium 381; heroic thinker 179, "incoerciblement fier" 168, a compromiser 179a, d, "non fu un eròe, Cartesio" 1967a; insecure, latent homosexuality 95; intellectual hybris 183–84; magnificent virility of thought 225a; mysterious & enigmatic: "larvatus prodeo" (q.v.), secretive, curious, restless, loves travel 124, 142; oisiveté 93; originality 214 & s.v. priority; outsider, "sorcier maudit" 179; "penseur de granit" 170; baffled, uncertain pioneer 193; practical, utilitarian, reform-minded 124, 177, 298, & s.v. Marxist interpretations; prudence (q.v.) 164, 168, 179a, 215c, 231, 3166; psychoanalyzed 108, by Freud 124; reckless theorizer 166; réformateur malgré lui 418, sceptique malgré lui 322a, hérétique malgré lui 183–84; sardonic, agnostic, wise 124; scientist: brilliant, persevering, proud, overestimating his results, hasty through arbitrary impatience 356; superb mathematical elegance, utter confusion in physics 379; sincerity (q.v.) 14, 132, 168, 388 & 2754, 1527, insincerity 214; style of DM reflects personality of writer 1890; uneasiness, anxiety revealed in his metaphors 403; & s.v. apologetics, biography, contradictions,

mask, prudence, rationalism, religiosity, sincerity.
personality, theory of: 215a, 2534a; biological concept, & méthode 2802; in the cogito 1509a; & individuum 215a; & s.v. individuality.
perspectives curieuses, anamorphoses, automata: 236.
Peru: 18th c. Peruvian ms. on D.'s physics 1099; commemorative item 3443.
Petau, Denis, S.J. [1583–1652, AM, v. 6]: his Dogmata theologica, & D. 164.
Petit, Pierre [1598–1667; AM, v. 2]: "le petit chien" objects to Dioptrique & DM 400; D.'s sceptical dilemma 322a.
petites perceptions (Leibniz): 215b.
phantasia (Greek) & imaginatio: 378; & s.v. imagination.
phenomenalism of Descartes: passing phase, viewed in historical context 1503; cogito: phenomenalist interpretation 1677; & s.v. fenomenismo razionalistico.
phenomenology: influence of D. 311a, 3333a; is phenomenology Neocartesianism? 174 (under reviews), 1926, 1946; Brentano & Reid 288; Cartesian operation, & presence of Being 2843; Cartesian evidence 3512; D.'s 17th c. rationalism & phenomenology 347; D. & epoché 170; Heidegger's phenomenological destruction of the cogito 172; Merleau-Ponty's noncartesian phenomenology 311a; point of separation between Husserl & D. 173, 174; phenomenological reading of D. 1643; & s.v. epoché, Husserl.
Philo Judaeus: Philonic tradition of free-will modified by D. 349.
philosophes: s.v. Enlightenment.
philosophia & theologia novantiqua: 436, 467, 1658; Gabriel Daniel's compromise, Du Hamel et al. 390; Holland & Germany 436, 452; logic 436; & s.v. ecleticism.
philosophical anthropology: s.v. anthropology.
philosophical instruction, 17th & 18th century: s.v. cursus philosophicus, universities.
philosophy: D.'s definition, his & Scholastic texts 7, 83, 165; definitions (Plato to Balmes) 1878.
philosophy of Descartes: *introductions:* section 127–146b; 2, 441, 1112a, 1923, 1941, 2396, 2415, 2431, 2465, 2616, 2670, 3150, 3162, 3179, 3433; *systematic analyses:* section 147–194a; 121, 198, 199, 202, 204, 209, 210, 213, 219, 221, 233, 441a, 1973, 2049, 2322, 2620, 2851, 2852, 3076, 3155b, 3499; & s.v. biography, general D. literature.
philosophy of Descartes, *chief orientation & basic character:* survey of viewpoints 10, 12, 14, 25; concise summary 222; anthropology: metaphysical discovery of man 149; agnosticism 124, 152; angelism, hybris, "grand péché français" 183–84; apologetic: defense of Catholic Church against agnostics & new science 163, 172a, b, of bourgeoisie & capitalism against Catholic Church & feudalims 150, 154, 179; a Baroque philosophy 10, 319, 1671, 2864a; Christian 125, 132, 3274, non-Christian 166, 177, 195, 225a, 2940, anti-Christian 176, 193a, 1640; contradictory 2307, intentional unity, actual disunity 131, 159, 3162, rigorously unified, monolithic 170; discovery-oriented, pioneering 22, 149, 151, 193; dynamic 22; epistemological: primacy of méthode 131, 156–161, 187, 210, of méthode & physics 181, ordered, systematic knowledge 200a, metaphysical-epistemological primacy 173–74; experimental philosophy of mind 223, 224; God-directed, moralistic: sagesse 132, 163, 179a–d, 206; idealism 138, 171–74, 192, 221, Platonism 156, 157; fusion of disparate elements 25; joyous spirituality, humanism, religious moralism 179a–d, 206, 432a; mastery of self, not mastery of nature 132; materialism diluted by metaphysics 150, 179; mathematicism (q.v.) 157, 2637a, recklessmathematizationofallknowledge 166, 167, control of evidence surrendered to mathematicians 334; metaphysics, not physics, its primary concern 129, 149, 151, 168–171a, 185, 192, 192a, 221, also 173, 174; poetic, nonrigorous 231; pluralistic 178; positivistic 146, 152; practical, utilitarian, technological, optimistic 177; "Protestant principle" in philosophy 171a, 192a; quantification of physics 144, 2643; Quixotic, Faustian dream 2912; rationalism 14, 153, 185, denied 178; realism 1710, 2344–45, "réalisme de l'idée" 132; scientism: primacy of physics over metaphysics 121, 128, 146b, 150, 152, 164, 177, 180, 181, 188, 189, 199, 211b, 214a, 230; scientism hampered by idealism 150, 205; spiritualism 129, 223–24, 1653–55; unity of intuition 131, of system 170, 171; & s.v. interpretations; science (place).

phyllotaxy & logarithmic spiral: 398.
physics: texts 7; section 351–402 passim; also 83, 146b, 150, 165, 171, 175, 177, 183, 185, 193, 215, 229, 388, 393, 432, 1004, 1426c, 2054, 2399a, 3044–45; *physics of Descartes:* surveys 185, 376, 390, 396, 402, 1973; Aristotelian & Cartesian physics 165, 177, 402; the Cartesian model simpler, unnecessarily metaphysical 1901; collapse of D.'s physics (Gilson) 166; Dioptrique & Météores the main contribution 402; epistemology & méthode 161, 178, 179, 198, 199, 235c, 371; experimentalism: role of experiment 2547, D.'s physics experimental-practical rather than deductive 1721a; D.'s fundamental achievement: quantification 1427; geometric spirit 371 (Gagnebin), "géométrisation à l'outrance" 379, empiricism vs. geometricism (Malebranche & D.) 366, transition difficulties from mathematics to physics 361, geometric ideal useless in physics 189; Greek character of D.'s physics 371; D.'s historical significance 3456; metaphysics & physics: literature survey 14, relation 165, 166 & s.v. metaphysics; metaphysical foundations from Kepler to Newton 444, physics metaphysically conceived by D. & Leibniz 432; motion & matter 171; philosophical foundation: Marxist view 1426c; D.'s physics is nonpredictive 371 (Gagnebin), nonontological (Alquié) 149; physics is D.'s main concern, metaphysics is auxiliary 121, 128, 146b, 150, 152, 164, 177, 180, 181, 188, 189, 199, 211b, 214a, 230, opposite view s.v. philosophy of Descartes; Regulae & méthode 198; religious-apologetic intention of D.'s physics 163, 179b; "rudimentary" & "mathematical" physics of D. distinguished 1720; time 347a, no time parameter in D.'s physics 371, 379; unity, viability 1795; universal physics: Le Monde 193; & s.v. cosmology, Dioptrique, dynamics, Enlightenment, force, hypothesis, mechanics, méthode, Météores, optics, priority, space.
physics, *history:* 17th & 18th century background 215, 466a, 468, 1005a; survey, Galileo to Newton 390, 2575, metaphysical foundations 444; "Amperian" vs. "Cartesian" physics 370; Aristotle (q.v.) 165, 177, 402, Maignan's critique 449; Cartesians 390; Cartesian corpuscular physics transformed under influence of dynamics 380; Cartesian epistemology & 17th c. physics 371; 18th century Cartesian physics (Peru) 1099; Galileo (q.v.) 161, 175, 379, 1841, 1885, 2380a, 2934, 3035, 3388, Galileo's Archimedean vs. D.'s Platonic physics 379, 2380a; Leibniz (q.v.) 175, 188, 317, 432, dynamics, concept of force 373a, 377a, 1338, 2145, optics 399; Malebranche (q.v.): concept of physics 366, 390, cosmogony 359, force 161, 373a, 390, impact 373a, 1645a; "maximalist" physics (D. to Einstein) vs. "minimalists" (Newton to Planck) 375; Mersenne: mechanism, subtle matter, vacuum 215; Newton (q.v.); modern physics & Descartes: 370, 375, 1004, 2399a, 2807, epistemology 235c, mechanism 3133, D.'s physico-mathematics & the modern foundation problem 2933, revolt against dualism 182, Whittaker's "Neo-cartesian" philosophy of science 401; & s.v. Cournot, Pascal.
physico-mathematics: s.v. Beeckman, Cogitationes privatae, formative years.
Physiocrats & Descartes: 2679.
physiology: 193, 365, 386, 1067a, 1799, 2244; survey 402, 1973, 3066; history 1916; appraisal of D.'s contribution 386, 3240; D. anticipates biochemistry 2886; beast-machine (q.v.) 226; D. & 19th c. physiology 2255; gap between D.'s physiology & morale 365; he anticipates Hartley's neurophysiology 2256; méthode 1661a; mechanism 373; philosophical spirit 360; Enlightenment 468.
Piacenza: manuscript [1797] on Cartesianism 2898.
Picart, Bernart [1673–1733]: Cartesian engraving & its Newtonian copy 465a.
Picavet, François: *2952–53;* 311.
Picot, Claude, Abbé [ca. 1601–1668; AM, v.4]: biography 121, 124 (app.), 1 & 2858a.
Pillon, François: *462, 2958–59;* reaction against Reid & Cousin 223.
pineal gland: 178, 193, 402, 1725, 2296, 3180, 3543; various theories 1310.
Pisa: Cartesianism & anticartesianism 433.
plagiarism: s.v. priority.
planetary system: modern vortex theory 351; planetary motion: s.v. movement; & s.v. cosmogony, cosmology.
Plato, Platonism: 156–57, 159, 205, 3144; Timaeus 4, 163; D.'s formal borrowings 163; no direct filiation: Plato the hope, D. the

triumph of mathematicist idealism 1398; D. adds to Platonism the evidence of first verities 156, 157; Aristotelianism, Platonism, Cartesianism 165, 2272, D.'s implied Aristotelianism vs. his Platonic inspiration 3281; Augustinus & D.: Platonic family likeness 235; dialectics, méthode, syllogism 3215; Leibniz & D. 2270; life principle in Plato & D. 2541; D.'s physics: "revanche de Platon" vs. Galileo's Archimedean physics 379, 2380a; Regulae 221; & Platonic paradigm 266; Renaissance influences upon D. 311; sagese 3448; scepticism: 17th c. anti-Platonic sceptics become anticartesian 322a; see also s.v. Cambridge Platonists, Socrates.

Plempius (Plemp), Vopiscus-Fortunatus [1601–1661; AM, v. 1]: controversy with D. 458, & s.v. biography.

plenum: s.v. vacuum.

Plotinus: epistemology of St. Augustine, & D. 2481; D.'s proofs of God 214; & s.v. Neoplatonism.

pluralism: D.'s philosophy is pluralistic 178; his social pluralism 320.

plurality: of bodies 215a, 463, & extension 290; plurality of thinking substances 215a; plurality of worlds: actual & possible worlds 161, 453a, Balmes 1826, 1981, Fontenelle, Huygens 390, Cartesians spread the doctrine 2584.

poêle (word): explained 83, 123 (texts p. 718f.), 3336; & s.v. Dream.

poetry: D.'s view in DM 83; his Dream: Corpus poetarum & cognition 96, 168, 220, 244a, 346, also s.v. Dream; poetic cognition 244a, & imagination 3092, in literature 429; poetic dialectics of D. 244a; his philosophy is non-poetic 324a, is "poésie de la raison" 2819 & accepted in England because of its poetic appeal 406, "le poète D." (Papini) 2904; literature: Cartesianism is not order & clarity but belief in power of poetic cognition 429; poetic verisimilitude (Muratori) & Cartesian canons 420; poetic strain in D., repressed in Cartesianism & Enlightenment 189.

poems: by Descartes (La Flèche sonnet?) 425 & s.v. Naissance de la paix; poems about Descartes 426, 1549, 2588, 3006, 3600; animal soul poetry 226, 426 (Bergonzoni).

Poggendorf, Johann Christian [1796–1877]: *393;* his attack upon D.'s originality rejected 356, 375, & s.v. priority.

Poincaré, Henri [1854–1912]: *2977–78;* Poincaré's mechanical systems theorem anticipated by D.? 2932; Poincaré's principle in logic 335; noncartesian physics 370.

Poiret, Pierre [1646–1719]: 438; Cartesian mysticism & the unconscious 215b; recognizes mystical element in eternal verities 2318; influence upon Protestant theology 2228a.

Poisson, Nicolas-Joseph, Oratorian [1637–1710]: 1558, & s.v. biography.

Poitiers, Poitou: D.'s family 99, his relations with Poitiers 2992, he & Bacon at the University of Poitiers 1172; commemorative items 531, 553, 1467.

Poland: bibliography 15, 1137; Cartesianism 470, 1137, 1541, 1544, 1678; D. scholarship 1541, 1676, 1678, 2601, 3602–05, commemorative issues 532, 550.

polemics & controversies of Descartes: editions 74, 77, 92a; 2, 121, 125, 207, 298, 458, 467, 3603; with Fermat (q.v.) 355a, 382, 1448, 3564, tangents (Fermat & Roberval) 369, 388 & 2747, 1808a, 2117; oscillations (pendulum, Roberval) 368; Plempius 458; Voetius (q.v.) 1814, 1815; & s.v. Gassendi, Notae in programma, Objectiones, Petit, Regius, Stampioen-Waessenaer.

Polignac, Melchior de, Cardinal [1661–1742]: 226.

political philosophy of Descartes: 163 (v. 2), 169, 179b, 185, 215c, 220, 264, 298, 320, 443, 1346, 1489, 2829, 2847–49; the absolute monarch: a Cartesian God 1410; absolutism & authority: D.'s ambiguous attitude 175, 320, his social ideal 1579–80; Cartesianism destroys the foundations of government 1993; D.'s "economic humanism" 324, "new humanism" 2094, religious-moral humanism 179b; D. a metaphysical absolutist, social pluralist 320; Machiavelli: D.'s critique 119, 169, 179b, 2847–49, his own moral Prince 179b, his Machiavellism denied 220, Machiavellian & Cartesian spirituality 320; morale: its political consequences 220; political orders are purely historical, without rational or religious necessity 320; D.'s political indifference 2847; he has no political philosophy 154, denied 169, 172b; his reformism 124, 177, 298; social attitude 264,

298; totalitarian state & Cartesian man 3223; influence of D. (Spinoza to Rousseau) 3235, on Abbé Saint-Pierre 2934a; & s.v. jurisprudence, law, Machiavelli, Montesquieu, social philosophy.
polyhedra: D. & Euler 1133, 2767.
Porta, Giovanni Battista della [1541–1615]: Magia naturalis, influence 236.
Port-Royal: 215b, 438, 2865; Sainte-Beuve's Descartes 3179; Arnauld (q.v.) as mediary between D. & Boileau? 424; Augustinianism & Cartesians 38; Logic of Port-Royal 440, 2550; pedagogy 441; theology 267; & s.v. Arnauld, Nicole.
Portugal: Cartesian influences 430, literature 1553.
positivism: Comtean 146, 188, 298, 316, 385, D. Comte's precursor? 146, 181, 2765, contradictions between Comte & D. minimized 1800; D.'s méthode does not know verification principle 1968; D.'s consequent positivism, & attitude towards Christianity (Blondel) 152; his rational positivism (Gueroult) 170; his morale provisoire 2840; his physics (bon sens) is positive & experimental 1721a; therapeutic posit. 350 (Pinsky); positivism [after 1660] gains control of Cartesianism 434; Brazil: positivism & D. 146; logical positivism supersedes Scholastic & Cartesian concepts of truth 3147; & s.v. logical positivism (language analysis).
possibility: texts 7; 2002; region of understanding, existence of material things (Gueroult) 170.
Poulain (Poullain) de la Barre, François [1647–1723]: D.'s influence on society 2957.
"pour" (word): "pur" & "pauvre" 1494.
"pour penser il faut être": 170, 252.
Poussin, Nicolas [1563?–1665]: 415.
PP: s.v. Principia philosophiae.
Praeambula: 96, 100, 2764; & s.v. Cogitationes privatae, Opuscula.
pragmatism: idealistic pragmatism of Peirce 187.
Prague (Praha): D. in Prague 3454 & s.v. Bohemia; Tercentenary of D.'s birth 501, 1823.
prenatal experiences: psychological consequences 381.
Prenant, Lucie: *37, 323, 419, 2995–98;* âme & conscience 2536.
preuve: s.v. ontological proof, proof (logical), proofs of God, external world.
Priestley, Joseph [1733–1804]: 2255.
Principia philosophiae (PP): editions 74, 76, 2517, commentaries 1047, 3478a; 168, 2352; Dedication [of 1644] 119; Preface 168; work goes back to [1628–29], is therefore "earlier" than DM (Roth) 189; attracts the "lecteur honnête homme" more than DM does 326, 404; inertia, gravity 379; methodology 247; Jungius reads & annotates PP 2595; PP as last "roman de la nature" 388; mathematics 198, no mathematics 358; méthode 3079; science 402; Timaeus-type cosmogony 4; Spinoza's commentary 165, 258, 272, 2356, 2568; his Cogitata metaphysica 2544, 2552, 3471a, 3565–66.
principle: texts 7; & s.v. axiom, protophilosophy.
priority & plagiarism controversies, originality of Descartes: did D. conceal his reading and deny knowledge of precursors? 83, 100, 163, 168, 175, 214, 368, 388, accused of insincerity & dissimulation 214, by Leibniz (charge rejected) 286; Poggendorf's accusation of plagiarism in physics 383, discussed 1766, D.'s originality asserted 375, 1071; analytical geometry: D. or Fermat? 355a, 382, 1323, 1448, 3560, 3564; animal soul: Gómez Pereyra? 3192 Dream of D.: pastiche of Rosicrucian literature? 102, discussed 96; inertia: Galileo's priority, D.'s independence 379, 3573; mechanics: D. found nothing, belittled others 368, 369; oscillations (pendulum problem) 369; Puy-de-Dôme experiment (D. & Pascal) 2, 121, 402, 1013, 1772, 2671, 2861, 3519; rainbow 356, 3531a, 1071; reflex action: D. or Willis? 360; refraction: documents 399, Snell's priority asserted 1108, by Huygens 399, D.'s originality defended 388 & 2742–43, 1071; tangents (Fermat, Roberval) 382, 388 & 2747, 1808a, 2117.
Prix de l'Académie Française [1765]: s.v. Eloges; Académie des sciences morales et politiques [1839] q.v.
probability, probabilism: 83, 178; Carneades: his epoché leads to probabilism, D.'s doubt to certainty 1651; Cournot & D. 274; D. & Enlightenment 1374; metaphysics: region of imagination (Gueroult) 170; D. underestimates power of probabilism 231; & s.v. physics.

problem: concept in Regulae (q.v.) 3488; problem-solving, problema problematum 198, before Descartes 378; & s.v. ars inveniendi.
progress (concept of): 1716; D. & Enlightenment 1931; moral progress 179b; Cartesianism knows neither progress nor degeneration of man 1418.
progressivism of D.: 3535 & s.v. Marxist interpretations.
proof (logical): texts 7; 165, 231, 353; méthode & proof (Regulae) 198, méthode makes proof meaningless (DM) 329; & s.v. analysis & synthesis, logic, syllogism.
proofs of God's existence: 83, 165, 170, 171, 183, 193, 204, 209, 210, 211a, 219, 233, 270, 270a, 1284, 1409, 1673, 1705, 1835, 1979, 2071, 2097, 2127, 2205, 2245, 2389, 2608, 2694, 2697; historical survey 3559; proofs a priori & a posteriori: their rank & metaphysical status (Gouhier-Gueroult controversy) 170, 270, 270a, 1406a, 2155, 3102, 3104c; D.'s proofs are inconclusive 3461; their logical status 231; their order 83, more exact in PP than in DM 1646; relationship between proofs of God & cogito 447a; role of will 3577; technique & exposition is Scholastic, traditional 2719; their unity 24, asserted by Alquié 149, denied by Gueroult 170, 270a; they have no "valeur apostolique" 225a; *individual proofs, except ontological proof (q.v.):* first proof 2959, Thomist critique 2069; by causality 165; from continuity of creation 214; by effects 1674, two proofs by effects distinguished 170; mathematical proofs (17th c.) 1147b; perfectissimum & infinitum 3437; the second argument 2759 reformulated 2969; *doctrinal history:* Plotinus, St. Augustine, Bonaventura 214; D., Leibniz, Wolff, Kant 1647; Malebranche's proof by excellence & D.'s ontological proof 447a, opposition between them 453c; O & R (q.v.) 3301, Gassendi's objections 3421; Spinoza 156 & 1391, indirect filiation with D. 455a; & s.v. ontological proof.
proportions: D.'s geometry as theory of proportions, Greek model, metaphysical analogies 321a, 398.
propositions: & simple natures (q.v.) 198; in Descartes' theory of judgment 1550; & s.v. logic.
Protagoras: Heidegger's analysis of cogito (Protagoras, D., Nietzsche) 172b.
Protestantism: Cartesian impact 435a & 2228a; Protestant Orthodoxy & Cartesianism 435a, Reformist & Lutheran theologians 436, Dutch Protestantism 452, 467, 3179; modern Protestant views 193a; Calvinist view of D. & Pascal 1845; & s.v. Holland, influence, theology.
"Protestant principle" in philosophy: D. & "autonomous inwardness," Hegel 171a & Schelling 192a.
protophilosophy, axioms, presuppositions of D.: 231, 238, 2421; four necessary & sufficient axioms of Cartesian doctrine 229; list of Scholastic axioms which D. defended 231; lumen naturale 299 & knowability of God 321; similarity of cause & effect 238; & s.v. axioms, metaphors.
Providence: 119; & finality 178.
Proudhon, Pierre Joseph [1809–1865]: 2306.
Proust, Marcel [1871–1922]: search for the absolute in the self 316.
"prudence" of Descartes: 164, 168, 179a, 215c, 231, 3166; his religious faith, & prudence 168; scientific prudence prevents D. from recognizing deductiveness of mathematics, probabilism of physics 231; D. not prudent but naive, sincere 132, hence doubly destructive to religion 183–84; & s.v. personality, sincerity.
pseudocartesianism: modern 25; vulgarized rationalism [1680–1750] 429.
psychoanalytical interpretations: 95, 104a, 108, 124, 3544, 3570; D. not a forerunner of Freud 2325.
psychology of Descartes: 36, 171, 177, 323, 381, 385, 1363, 2365, 3535; survey 402, 1973; D.'s achievements anticipate modern findings 381, his seven legacies to modern psychology 1363; he has no psychology proper 1487; dualism: 1118, spiritual-mechanistic, metaphysical-physiological 385, physio-psychological dualism untenable 3394; empiricism in D.'s psychology 2259, 3011, anticipation of Claude Bernard's psychology 394; mechanism 3065, 3363; D.'s modern psychology marred by metaphysics 3535, his mechanism influenced old, his anthropology effective in modern psychology 3363; his personality & his psychology 381; his "psychological sincerity" 346; psychophysiology: D. its founder 394, 2798, its dualism untenable 3394, psychophysics, psychophysiology, mathe-

matics 398; no unity in his "medieval" psychology, his revolt against Aristotle probably harmful 1363; Scholastic & Cartesian psychology 2704; Pierre Chanet & D. 2967–68; D. & Malebranche 2150–51; Italian critics 207; & s.v. child psychology, emotions, passions, Traité des passions.
psychophysiology, psychophysics: 170, 2776, 2798, 3394; & mathematics 398; psychophysical parallelism: Cartesians 431; psychosomatic disorders: modern controversy 3530, 3379, 3568.
Pufendorf, Samuel [1632–1694]: law & theology 253; is his aprioristic method Cartesian? 466d.
Puy-de-Dôme experiment: 2, 121, 125, 402, 1013, 1772, 2861, 3515, 3519, Pascal's honesty impugned 2671.
Pyrrhonism: from Renaissance to D.'s "super-Pyrrhonism" 322a; & s.v. scepticism.
Pythagoras: CP 96; Dream (q.v.) & D.'s Stoic quest for tranquility 2349a; musical scale 1971; & s.v. Ausonius.

Q

quadrature: 398.
qualities, modi: texts 7; 165, 170 (v. 2), 178, 185, 1312; primary & secondary qualities 170, 193; D. & Hobbes 3243; & s.v. sensation, sensory qualities, perception.
quantity: texts 7; quantification of physics: s.v. mathematicism, physics.
querelle des anciens et des modernes: texts 74 (v. 10); 417, 466a; 1716; Cartesians on both sides 420; England 460; l'honnête homme, & classicism 1930; Italy 420, 461, 1824a; the winner: not D. but positivist scientism 434; & s.v. classicism, esthetics, literature.
questions: "questions parfaitement & imparfaitement comprises" 100, 237, & s.v. Regulae.
"Quod vitae sectabor iter?" (CP): 83, 96, 163, 183, 2349a; & s.v. Dream.

R

Racine, Jean [1639–1699]: & D.'s "reflexive analysis" 316; concept of passion related to TP 414; TP & Phèdre 2042; Cartesian roots of Racine's drama 2556a; see also Krantz, Lanson.
Racine, Louis [1692–1763]: beast-machine poetry 226.
Raconis: s.v. Abra de Raconis.
rainbow, explanation of: history, D.'s contribution & priority 356; Dietrich von Freiburg 3531a; D.'s originality defended 1071; méthode exemplified 402.
raison & foi: s.v. faith & reason.
Raphson, Joseph [d. ca. 1715]: divinization of space 379a.
Rapin, René, S.J. [1621–1687]: 17, 466.
rationalism of Descartes: 151, 170, 178, 216, 1694, 2384, 2395, 2758a, 3111, 3162, 3450; its meaning 37, 178, 2995; controversy surveyed 2722; anthropocentrism 183–84a, 2819; autonomous yet insecure, Christian doubt in reason's power assailed but not overcome by D. 176; causality 262; Cartesianism not pure rationalism but merely ordered, systematic knowledge 200a; Cartesian reason & its distorters 3077; God-centered, seeks mastery of self 1533; "infinite expansion of reason": D. against Montaigne 158; irrationalism not defeated by D. 193a; Laporte: D. not a rationalist 178, Chevalier's critique 1533; limits of D.'s rationalism 170, moral limits 1386; metaphysical rationalism 1166, turns into positivist mechanism after D.'s death 434; méthode: rational purpose, irrational tendencies 314; O & R 3301; phenomenalism of D.: s.v. fenomenismo razionalistico; rationalism & poetic cognition 244a; realism 1723–24; religion 177 & 2410; Romero's critique 2188–88a; superstition destroyed by D. 2479; veracity of God is foundation of D.'s rationalism 149; & s.v. faith & reason, irrationalism, reason.
rationalism, *doctrinal history:* D. & St. Thomas (realism vs. metaphysics) 1723–24; Bacon & D. 299; Gassendi & D. co-founders of 17th century rationalism 326; Enlightenment 466a, 468, 1507; D.'s true rationalism & its Cartesian vulgarization [1680–1750] 429, his metaphysical rationalism superseded by Cartesian positivist mechanism 434; D., Spinoza, Leibniz 299, 3303; from D. to Kant 2954; Cournot's probabilism 274; modern reconsideration 3498; existential 20th century rationalism derived from D.

432a; Cartesian rationalism no longer an historical power (Heidegger) 172a.
rationes seminales: Greek, Patristic, Scholastic precursors of D. 3199.
realism in Descartes: 221, 232, 249, 311a, 3317; clear & distinct ideas 3113a, 3132; cogito 1677, 2009; idealism & realism 129, "réalisme de l'idée" 132, idée claire 3113a, "realismo illazionistico" between idealism & realism 222, weakness of D.'s realism opens road to idealism 2398; indirect realism 232; "instinct réaliste" 249; D. neither nominalist nor realist but conceptualist 2761, his realistic conceptualism 2344–45; "réalisme méthodique" 2041; realism & scepticism reconciled 375; phenomenalistic realism 1284, 2015, 2869; D.'s substance realism ruins his idealistic intuition 156 & 1391; Scholasticism 1139, 2041, 2951a; D. & Reid (q.v.) 249, Scottish School 223, 3038.
reality: D.'s theory 2777, his new concept: rational phenomenalism 185 & s.v. fenomenismo razionalistico; reality has no meaning for D. 2632; Cartesian & Thomist concept 2685; cogito (modern philosophers) 1828; correspondence between theory & reality: D. & modern logic 335; "déréalisation de l'objet par l'être" (Alquié) 1056; error problem 2885; hierarchic order of reality: D. & Spinoza 455a; ideas: formal, material, objective reality 178; knowledge of reality limits deducibility 3107b; mathesis universalis guaranteed to correspond with reality 157, 378; objective reality 212a, 3455; scientific reality concept, Copernicus to Newton 1465; D.'s influence upon modern thought 212a; reality criterion (distinction between waking, sleeping, dreaming) 227, 306, 1879, 3595–96, psychiatric comment 3364.
reason: texts 7; 178, 179c, 3132; absolute & finite: God & man 161; independent of things 184; Cartesian reason & its distorters 3077; liberté 2070; divine design & government of the world transcends reason 178 & 2450; D., Scholasticism, Catholic tradition 3036; & s.v. faith & reason, lumen naturale, pensée, rationalism.
reception of D.'s works: MM, PP preferred to DM 326; PP & TP, not DM, attract the "lecteur honnête homme" 404; rainbow theory (Dioptrique) received with indifference 356; England prefers D.'s physics to his metaphysics 367; & s.v. influence.
Recherche de la vérité, La: editions 74, 76, 77; 100, 121, 168, 243, 1485–86; date of writing 242–43, 1446, 1485–86, 2080, 2321; first sketch of Le Monde? 242 & 2321; RV & Regulae: D.'s new method 220; RV anticipates Enlightenment 468.
reduction, phenomenological: the Cartesian way to transcendental reduction 174.
reference works: s.v. bibliography.
reflex action: 360, 381, 402, 1872, 1941a; priority: D. or Willis? 360; conditioned reflex: D. anticipates Pavlov? 150, 1067a, 1941a, reflex reaction to musical expression (Compendium musicae) as conditioned reflex 421.
refraction: 87, 121, 356, 388 & 2742–43, 396, 399, 2385; difference between Snell's law & D.'s law of sines 87, 356, 399; D.'s originality, priority asserted 375, 388 & 2742–43, 1071, denied 393, 399, 1108.
Régis, Pierre-Sylvain [1632–1707]: 233, 451; beast-machine 226; eternal verities 161; theory of ideas 212a; logic, physics, physiology 390; immediate vs. reflexive consciousness (Huet controversy) 215b; Cartesian meetings 468 (v. 1).
Regius (de Roy), Henricus [1598–1679; AM, v. 3]: D.'s letters, Notae in programma 74, 77, 92a; controversy: documents, studies, defense of Regius 6, 121, 123, 125, 390, 467, 3511, 3521; beast-machine 226; his Philosophia naturalis 92a, 390; physics, medicine 390; Regius & Henry More 467; see also biography.
Regulae ad directionem ingenii: editions 74, 76, 77, 92; 2, 100, 121, 198, 210, 212, 221, 355 & 2020, 2276, 2337a, 3171; aprioristic methodology 247; CP 3174, Dream reminiscences 244a; Compendium musicae 419; "conscience" 2352; criticist position 3487; date of writing 83, 100, 121, 189; DM: disagreement 2518; enumeration (q.v.) 2246; epistemology 161, 221, subjective & objective 3582; experience: analysis 2120, logic of experience 161; Regulae are first stage of D.'s philosophy 4, superseded by later works 1163, later than rules of method (DM) 100; Géométrie & Regulae 355, 358; imaginatio: correspondence between mathematicism & reality 378; inneism 1401, disputed 149; mathematics 353; MM & Regulae 2207,

epistemology 221; méthode 189, 193, 231, 247, four rules of method (DM) 100; mnemotechnics, intuitus, deduction, magical literature, Lullism 328; mysticism & voluntarism 1638; Platonic paradigm 266; problem concept 3487; road to idealism 281; see also deduction, enumeration, epistemology, mathematics, méthode, simple natures.

Reid, Thomas [1710–1796]: *223, 3038–39;* 224, 249; influence on French D. interpretation 223, reaction against it 462; Brentano, phenomenology 288; D.'s theory of perception 1785; Renouvier's critique 223, 3038; see also Scottish School.

religion: surveys 14, 185, 345, philosophy of religion: history 446–47, 1973, 3220, 3327; general 2, 83, 96, 121–193a passim (especially 121, 122, 149, 152, 165, 167, 168, 175, 176, 178, 179b, 183–84, 193a), 196, 206, 214, 218, 228, 230, 446–47, 452a, 454, 457, 1081, 1341, 1426a, 2036a, 2070, 2106, 2483, 2646, 2648, 2842; D. reconciles science & religion through eternal verities & cogito 1056; his "religious metaphysics" 22, 26; his theory of faith 168, 177 & 2408–09 & s.v. faith & reason; his philosophy is Christian 3274, is non-religious yet paradoxically helps Catholicism 168; divine government & reason: identity of D.'s & the Christian concept 178 & 2450; metaphysics & physics, actions & ideas 179b; D.'s Molinist loyalties in conflict with his antinaturalistic concept 319; "un mystique de l'univers" 195, 218, 225a; natural religion & theism 243, 443: D. & Pascal (q.v.) 2622; religion & reason, physics, ethics 178; "religion cartésienne de l'esprit" controversy 24; revealed religion 178; sagesse 206, Cartesian & Christian 177, & immortality 228; influence of D. & early Cartesians 447; upon 18th century natural religion 443, Cartesianism first religiously ineffective, then [after 1660] destructive 446; Cartesian roots of Spinozist monism, Leibnizian pluralism 3419; see also religiosity, God, agnosticism, apologetics, atheism, faith & reason, libertinism, scepticism, theology.

religiosity, religious sincerity of Descartes: three problems distinguished (religious sincerity, belief in Christian doctrines, Christian spirit) 168 & 2083; literature surveys 14, 345; general 121, 122, 124, 125, 152, 163, 164, 165, 168–69, 176, 177, 178, 179a, b, 183, 193a & s.v. religion; D.'s "abstención de lo divino" 196; pervaded by the divine he perverts God's initial work 195, believes in his divine mission, loses faith in reason 210; does not love God, God embarrasses him 177; his agnosticism: critical discussion 168, asserted 320, agnostic in disguise 124, positivistic "agnosticisme Chrétien" 152, enlightened, tolerant, scientific agnosticism 230, a religious agnostic who accepts the transcendent infinite 152 (Epelbaum); D. a Christian believer 3271, but not a Christian philosopher (despite good intentions) 1866; too happy & tranquil for somber Jansenist religiosity 2819; "extra-Christian" 2255, denied 1081; "incapable de se fondre en Jésus" 2940, anti-Christian 1640, anticlerical 3314; a Catholic apologist 163, 179a, b, 446, 1896a, 1905, apologetic success of his non-apologetic, non-religious philosophy 168, not an apologist 164, neither believer nor apologist 176; irreligiosity, impiety asserted & denied: survey 14, a true Catholic, faithful to Church 1075 who succeeds in separating faith & science 3464 with catastrophic consequences for religion 183, 184; his Catholic orthodoxy affirmed 2229; Protestant charges & denial of his irreligiosity 193a; concealed atheism 435a, neither an atheist nor a sceptic 2918, God-oriented, God-centered 132, 179a, b, 1526–27, denied 176, 177; humanizes God into a "bon diable" 159 & 1401, does not know God of love & suffering 196, 321a, postpones the God problem ad calendas Graecas 196; his humanism upheld against antihumanist eschatological Christian ideology 432a; his Christian God-centered humanism 179b; his metaphysics is Christian, his ethics semi-Stoic 1862; D. "un mystique de l'univers" 195, 218, but with little religiosity 225a; see also faith & reason, God, religion.

Renaissance: 83, 210, 311; D.'s precursors: mathematical intelligibility as knowledge criterion 161, 2649; Renaissance influences upon D. 210, Platonism & Stoicism 311; D.'s concept of "amour" derived from Renaissance 422; DM & Renaissance spirit 3583; doubt 2599; humanism, Molinism 319;

applicability 193; Bacon, Regulae, DM 189; fourth rule, & méthode 398; morale provisoire & rules 245; rules are a reformulation of Regulae 198, conceived in [1619–20] & therefore older than Regulae 100, denied 169; mathematics: new application proposed 2799; & s.v. méthode enumeration, Discours, Regulae.

Rumania: D. studies 231a & 3431, 2852; DM tercentenary, commemorative session 2944.

Russell, Bertrand: *3162–63;* formal logic 335; monistic revolt 182.

Russia: D. studies & commemorative items, Czarist Russia 503, 1265a, 2131a, 2135, 2135a, b, 2561a, 2567, 3155b, 3158, 3456, 3594; did pre-1917 Russian philosophy reject D. & Marx? 184a; U.S.S.R. contributions & commemorative items 150, 539–40, 560, 1067a, 1091a–c, 1265b, 1426a–d, 1737a, 1739a, 1941a, 1950a, 2283a, 2337a, 2770a, 3296, 3314, 3403, 3477a.

Ruvio: s.v. Rubio.

Ryle, Gilbert: *190, 3169;* 340, 3394, 3568.

S

sagesse: texts 7 & commentary 3173a; 83, 169, 170, 177, 179b, 183, 206, 215c, 218, 220, 230, 2471, 2999, 3166; aim of D.: sagesse, not mastery of nature 1527; sagesse dethroned by D. 183; defined as "morale de béatitude" 230, naturalistic, intellectualistic, anthropocentric 183, practical, terrestrian, irreligious 196; esthetics & sagesse 419; méthode: a come-on for sagesse 1511, culminates in sagesse 199; religion & sagesse 228; science & sagesse 230, 2309, sagesse is purified rationalistic ethics for the conquest of science 230, satisfies both physics & metaphysics & unifies system 220, moral dissociation despite metaphysical union 170, indecision between science & sagesse leads D. to metaphysical dualism 1070, sagesse & unity of the sciences 2535a, sagesse triumphs over D.'s epistemology & science 206; sagesse universelle 2609, & certitude 1575; Graeco-Roman & Cartesian 3254, Platonic & Cartesian 3448; Christian vs. Cartesian 177; Montaigne's humanistic wisdom brought to domination by D. 157; Pascal & D. 1682; Spinoza & D. 177; sagesse: a Baroque concept 2724; see also morale.

Saint-Cyran, Jean du Vergier de Hauranne, Abbé de [1581–1643]: mystical theology 267.

Sainte-Beuve, Charles-Augustin: *3179;* D.'s literary influence 411.

Sainte-Geneviève, Montagne de (Paris): 2652.

Saint-Pierre, Charles Irénée Castel, Abbé de: his Projet de paix perpetuelle, & Cartesian method 3218a.

Saisset, Emile Edmond: *3181–82;* his D. interpretation & the 19th c. French D. revival 223, 2859, 3178; & s.v. spiritualistic interpretations.

Sanchez, Francisco [1552?–1632]: Quod nihil scitur, & Cartesian doubt 277; res cogitans 208; rationalistic-nominalistic scepticism 246.

Santayana, George: *191;* 2761; revolt against dualism 155.

Sartre, Jean-Paul: *192, 3201–03;* 2915; his D. interpretation 10, falsifies D. 3314; existential freedom & the hidden God 3575a; the imaginary 227.

satires, anticartesian: 110.

Saumur, Académie Protestante: Cartesianism, La Forge, Chouet 438, 464, 3002–03.

scepticism: 322, 322a, 329; 17th century scepticism 466a, two types, three refutations 246; D.'s "histrionic" vs. true scepticism (Santayana) 191; clear & distinct ideas doctrine: scepticism the inevitable consequence 329; intuition 2394; scepticism a consequence of D.'s premises (Spinoza) 329; D.'s scepticism & realism metaphysically reconciled 375; D. a "sceptique malgré lui," his sceptical dilemma 322, 322a; his scepticism of the senses 306, subjected to Oxford language analysis 1330, 3596; scepticism from D. to Schleiermacher 3105; Socrates & D. 1205; St. Augustine & D. 2481, 3598; Bayle 462; & s.v. doubt, error.

Scheler, Max: 1828.

Schelling, Friedrich Wilhelm Joseph von [1775–1854]: *192a;* his D. critique 10, 453, 1192, 1992.

Schook (Schockius), Martin [1614–1665]: 452, 467; & D.'s sceptical dilemma 322a; see also biography.

"Scholastic Cartesianism"; of Leibniz, Wolff 2630; "Cartesian Scholasticism": 2041, 2951a, & s.v. philosophia novantiqua.

Scholasticism: texts of D. & Scholastics

confronted 7; bibliography of 17th century Peripateticism 464a; general 83, 165, 177, 208, 209a, 214, 214a, 1425, 2953, 3036, 3359 & s.v. St. Thomas; rediscovery of D.'s Scholastic roots by Freudenthal 1937, 2544, Hertling 2221, Gilson 7, 164, 165, 2037, Koyré 214; D.'s knowledge of Scholasticism: teachings at La Flèche (q.v.) 83, 164, 208, 209a, 215a, 286, 1827, D. knows Scholastic doctrine better than his critic Leibniz 286, knows late, eclectic, degenerated Jesuit Scholasticism, not genuine Thomism 209a, 263, 2614 (theory of passions); Scholastic influence on D. minimized, excepting his Jesuit teachers (Alquié) 149, Augustinian rather than Thomist influence 214, 235, medieval tradition rather than late Scholasticism 214, 1912, 2953, Toledo's influence 1827, unconscious borrowings 2593; Scholasticism alive in D. despite his scientism 214a; Brentano recognizes D.'s Scholastic affinities 288; D.'s compromise with Scholasticism detrimental to his scientism & materialism 150 & s.v. Marxist interpretations; his revolutionary break with Scholasticism, & foundation of modern philosophy ab ovo (Hegel) 171a; *doctrinal comparisons:* metaphysics, epistemology, physics, physiology 7, 165; common points, differences between D. & Scholastics 1832; Scholastic axioms accepted by D. 231; anthropology 165, 385, 2129, 2667, 3377; eternal verities 3199, 3510; free fall 3562; individuation by matter 215a; lumen naturale 3199; mechanistic tendencies in Coimbra Scholasticism 1839; objective Being 1685; ontology: Scholastic concept transferred to res cogitans, loss of Being (Heidegger) 172; proofs of God: Scholastic technique & mentality 2719; "psychologie du lecteur scolastique" 165; Spanish Scholasticism & Cartesianism the two forms of Counterreformation philosophy 319; theology (q.v.) 168, 177, 267; substance: D.'s unconscious Scholasticism 2593, Spinoza's view 2544, he objects to D.'s Scholastic superstitions 156 & 1391; the supernatural 177; Scholastic theory of faith & Cartesian certitude 177; truth, Scholastic & Cartesian (copy vs. code) 3147; D.'s voluntarism & Augustinian, Scotist Scholasticism 1043, 2327; & s.v. Augustinus, Duns Scotus, Neoscholastic interpretations, philosophia novantiqua, Thomas, cursus philosophicus.

Schooten, Frans van, de Jonge [1615–1661; AM, v. 1]: 74, 121, 123, 467; his portrait of D. 1 & 2858a, 74, 123, 2612.

Schopenhauer, Arthur [1788–1860]: his D. view 10; "Wille als Vorstellung" & cogito 333, 1923; his alleged Cartesian spirit debated 442, 1306, 1923–24.

science, scientism of Descartes: texts 7; section 351–402; bibliography 18, 397a; surveys & appraisals of D.'s scientific work 185, 396, 402, 1820, 2770, 2852a; what he found, what he retained 3076, D.'s work compared with Scholastic-Peripatetic science 7, 165, with Mersenne & other contemporaries 215, judged by modern standards 146b; *place & role of science in D.'s system of thought:* controversies surveyed 14; primacy of science over metaphysical substructure asserted 121, 128, 146b, 150, 152, 164, 177, 180, 181, 188–189, 199, 211b, 214a, 230; primacy of metaphysics & epistemology, secondary role of science asserted 129, 149, 151, 168–171a, 173, 174, 185, 192, 192a, 221; *D.'s scientific spirit & scientism:* archaic compared to Galileo, Leibniz, modern science 175, 235c; revolutionary, modern: D. protects new physics from Church & Aristotelianism 164, 179a, d, anticipates modern advances & approaches Marxist conception of scientist 150, 2404–05, provides far more than science needs 231, 1901, which made his ideal of scientific certi tude a victim of scientific progress 2600; his scientism inappropriate to science as well as metaphysics 231; his "myth of science": divinization of scientific understanding 183–84; medieval roots of his scientism 214a, medieval science & Cartesian scientism incompatible 210 (ch. 1); "occult obsessions of science" exemplified in D. 2792; his utilitarian, reformist scientism 177; its "unconscious psychoanalytical determinants" 108; Cartesian scientism & mathematicism the ruin of philosophy 166, 167, 183–84, 1819; *special topics:* Cartesian spirit vs. obscurantism: D.'s influence on chemistry 352; certitude as scientific ideal 231, 1901, 2600; experiments, experimentalism (q.v.); final causes 164, 262; mathesis universalis (q.v.) & science 1224; metaphysics & science 129, 149, 170, 171,

402, 1053, D.'s science unconnected with his metaphysical speculation 375; nonmetaphysical science (Gassendi) 326, 2121a, 3097; methode (q.v.) & science 175, 402, 468, 1300, 2771, 3356, méthode & modern philosophy of science 231; morale (q.v.) & science 230, 1319; D.'s panlogistic science concept 230; philosophy & science 134 & 1709, 170, 3007 & above (see: place & role of science); religion (q.v.) & science 168, 178, metaphysically reconciled 1056; sagesse 230, 3369, science & philosophy both symbolize sagesse, not logos 2418a; & s.v. unity of science.

science of Descartes, *historical contexts:* science before D. 3087, concept of science from Copernicus to Newton 1465, Aristotelianism & Cartesianism 164, 165, 402, 1250; metaphysics & science in the 16th, 17th century 3367, Cartesians 431; Geulincx 2128; Fontenelle's scientific Cartesianism 457c; Enlightenment (q.v.) 466a, secularization of science, influence of D.'s Monde, méthode 468; D. & modern science: influence 1998, 2475, Cartesian spirit alive though its body be dead 144, biology & biomechanics 2281, 3017, physics (q.v.) 146b, 370, 375, physiology (q.v.) 386, psychology (q.v.) 1363; Mach's epistemology 2613; modern nondualistic science can be derived from D.'s dualistic epistemology 2586.

scientia mirabilis ("X novembris 1619, cum .... mirabilis scientiae fundamenta reperirem"): 96, 100, 121, 123, 124, 388, & s.v. Dream; basic study 96; interpreted as correspondence between mathematicism & reality, per imaginationem 378; opposed to "science curieuse" 96; Psalm CXXXVIII a possible source 1574, denied 96; "scientia mirabilis" means "semina scientiarum," i.e. innate ideas 144, universal science through méthode 100, unity of science as core of D.'s philosophy 183.

scientia universalis: 2241, & s.v. scientia mirabilis, unity of science.

Scottish School: works of Reid, Hamilton, Stewart 3038–39, 3350; D. interpretation 223, 224, 249, 2179a, 2764; & s.v. spiritualist interpretations.

Scudéry, Madeleine de [1607–1701]: 226.

Segond, J.: *230, 331, 3254–57;* 14.

self (ego, moi): 129, 179d, 193, 233, 259, 307, 1238, 3498; its meaning in D. 175; angelism 184; St. Augustine & D. 2349; Condillac's organic theory of self, & cogito 2927; "conscience" implies presence of God in the self 158; continued creation 455a; the embodied self (TP) 193; Gestalt vs. substance theory 259; "Ich-Gefühl," mental & bodily, in D.'s Dream 104a; immortality (D. to Kant) 1342; le "je" éternel 169; D.'s & Kant's dualism of self rejected 307; D.'s "magnifique & mémorable moi" (Valéry) 194; man-machine challenges cogito-self 350; problem of other selves: s.v. connaissance d'autrui; D.'s self philosophically superfluous, its unity & self-identity unexplained 3581; self in Regulae, Traité de l'homme, TP 193; D. rejects absolute evidence yet avoids transcendental self 1413; semantic confusion between self & soul 2559; D.'s substance-self attacked, Locke to Hume 259; world & self 3258; & s.v. "conscience," connaissance d'autrui, pensée.

Seine: "D. et le conseil général de la Seine" 2176.

semina scientiae: 108, 468; interpreted as innate ideas 144; & s.v. Dream.

Seneca: Stoicism 283, 3507; source of beast-machine concept 163.

sensation: texts 7; 179c, 1313, 2300, 2808, 2856; actual & imagined sensation not differentiated 3109; bodily affectation & sensation 340; Cartesians 431; Gassendi 466a; innate character 170; Maignan 466a; quantification & measurement of human sensation impossible under beast-machine doctrine 398; rejection of dualistic theory of sensation 190; D.'s opposition to sensualism 1232; sensation & the innate ideas model 212a; & s.v. perception, sense, sensory qualities.

sense, senses: texts (sens, sens commun) 7; 83, 170, 179c; bon sens: q.v.; "critique de la pensée sensible" 179c; distinction between sense perception & thought, & epoché 174; imagination & sense: mathematics 198; error: "région du sens" 170; D.'s scepticism of the senses 306; internal sense (sens intérieur), D. to Kant 2789; sensus communis 83, 2416; understanding 204; & s.v. doubt, error, scepticism.

sensory qualities (qualités sensibles): texts 7; proof of practical value 209; proof of

external world (q.v.) 209 & 1967.
Sergeant, John: his attack [1698] on D. & Legrand 1339.
Serrus, Charles: *231, 3272–73;* critique 321a.
seventeenth century (XVIIe siècle): bibliography 3a, 397a, 464a; background studies 429a, 446, 447, 450, 453, 457, 466a, 3179; Augustinianism & Cartesianism 302; Cartesian or renascent century? 2090 & 96; French scientific instruction 3425; Libertinism 2964; moral philosophies 3407; scepticism 322a; science 1005a, 3367; social foundations related to philosophy 154; & s.v. Baroque, Counterreformation, Cartesian era.
Sevilla: Cartesianism 449.
Sévigné, Marie de Rabutin-Chantal, Marquise de [1626–1696]: 1701.
Shakespeare, William: his nature concept opposed to D.'s 409.
"si enim fallor, sum" (St. Augustine): 165, 200; D.'s cogito independent of it 235, 302; overwhelming similarity between cogito & Augustinian argument 333, 334; & s.v. Augustine, cogito.
Sic et non: see Est et non (Ausonius).
sign: "conscience" & signs (Alquié) 1056a; no thinking without signs (Peirce) 187; D. replaces sign by signal (Gouhier) 268a; & s.v. symbol; in algebra: s.v. algebraic notation, Descartes' rule of signs.
Silhon, Jean de [1596–1667]: ontological proof 214.
simple natures, ideas, images (natures simples, res simplices): simple ideas & intellectual intuition 281; simple images in algebra 353; simple natures 192b, 198, 1251–52, fecundity & weakness of concept 3542; fundament of méthode 1251–52; Nikolai Hartmann's objections 3338; incompletely enumerated, hence a stumbling block for D. 193; mathematical truth 314; origin of innate ideas concept 2190; & D.'s representational idealism 2344; synthesis of realism & conceptualism, & abstractness of physics 2345.
sincerity of Descartes: 168, 175, 178, 346, 388; critical sincerity (true doubt) distinguished from moral, psychological, intellectual sincerity 346; D.'s sincerity asserted 14, 132, 168, 388 & 2754, 1527, denied 214; his "critical sincerity" (doubt) incomplete & not radical 346, histrionic & insincere 191; his religious & moral sincerity appraised 168, 345; his Christianity is sincere, agnostic, religiously disastrous 152, 183–84; & s.v. prudence.
sines, Descartes' law of: s.v. refraction.
skull (crâne) of Descartes in Paris, Musée de l'Homme: question of authenticity 3068, 3484; measurements correspond to Louvre portrait by Frans Hals 1707, which is called unauthentic 1 & 2858a; & s.v. transfers, biography.
sleep: texts 7; 83; distinction between sleeping & waking 227, 306, 1879, 3364, 3595–96; & s.v. dreaming.
Smith, Adam [1723–1790]: 223; natural religion, & economics 310.
Smith, John (the Cambridge Platonist): 3450a; his Select Discourses [1668] 465; theology 429a.
Smith, Norman Kemp: *192b, 193, 3307–08;* 3143a, 3588; D.'s theory of perception 1785.
Snellius (Snel[l] van Rojen), Willebrord [1580?–1626]: Snell's law of refraction & D.'s law of sines 121, 388 & 2742–43, 399, 2385; priority question 375, 393, 1071, 1108, & s.v. refraction.
social philosophy of Descartes: 169, 441; its sources, doctrine, practice 179b; lack of a social philosophy in D. noted 154, deplored 112; D.'s social ideal: philosopher-king, intellectual aristocracy on democratic basis 1579–80, his democratic doctrine of bon sens 2587a, D. & social optimism 177, 298, his social pluralism 320 & economic humanism 324; his social atomism opposed by Fascism 461 (Witzenmann); Cartesian self an unsocial conception 153, 196, 307, 3223; Cartesian man unfit for any society with historical mission 196; Cartesian principles of social science 2957, order & freedom 2290; "Cartesian view" of modern society 3529, critique 1080; "citoyen" ideal 265 (Taborda); D.'s influence on 18th c. society (Poulain de Barre) 2957; his influence on the social sciences 3332; sociology: Cartesian method of anarchic tabula rasa rejected 2458; Socialism is D.-inspired 298; & s.v. political philosophy.
Socrates: common source of Aristotle & D. (cogito) 200 (Schuhl), Socratic "docte ignorance" & D.'s cogito concept [of 1628] 269; D. continues Socrates 346; his "Socratic determinism" 188 & 3047; scepticism

1205; Socratic vs. Cartesian inquiry 1798, & method of Regulae 266.
solipsism & D.'s substance concept: 3110.
Sorbière, Samuel [1615–1670; AM, v. 4]: 431, 1120.
soul: s.v. âme.
space: texts 7, 83; 178, 185, 1162, 2817; history of space concept 377, 379a, 1436a, 1995, 2596, 3193; distance & contiguity (Balmes & D.) 1981; dream space is neither âme nor étendue 227; epistemological foundation of D.'s physics: space identified as extension 161, geometrization of space 378, 379a, & limits of D.'s mathematics 398; God & space: D.'s difficulties 149; theologization (H. More) & divinization (Raphson) of space 379a; modern mathematical physics & Cartesian space 370; & s.v. extension.
Spain: Cartesianism 449, influence on literature 2700; Spanish precursors of D. 1411; Spanish Scholasticism & Cartesianism: two forms of Counterreformation philosophy 319; commemorative item 551; & see the Systematic Index.
Spanheim, Friedrich [1600–1649; AM, v. 5]: 109, 467.
Spann, Othmar: *3330;* 466b.
Spaventa, Bertrando: *3331;* D.'s influence 14.
species: texts 7; 165; D. avoids the term 100; species intentionales, sensibiles, intelligibiles 165, 175; La Forge 431.
Spink, J. S.: *466a;* 113.
Spinoza, Baruch de [1632–1677]: 138, 156, 157, 159, 161, 162, 165, 202, 329, 441a, 451, 455a, 467, 1079, 1675, 1937, 2165, 2505, 2544, 3214, 3505, 3608; *relation to Descartes:* Spinoza as D. interpreter 2568, & see Principia philosophiae cartesianae below; doctrinal relation: basic study 455a, Spinoza's Cartesian principles 192b, D. his starting point 156, D.'s influence 3074, thought & object: Cartesian foundations 2505, Spinoza the Cartesian antithesis to Renaissance 217, divergences from D. 1987a, transforms D.'s doctrine 1656, objects to D.'s "Scholastic superstition" 156 & 1391, fundamental opposition 329, 3139; Tschirnhaus tries to translate Spinoza's thought into Cartesian terms 3026–27; *Principia philosophiae cartesianae* 258, 455a, 2356, 2568, transforms D.'s order of axioms (Gueroult) 272, proof of existence of material things (Gilson) 165 & 2036; *Cogitata metaphysica* 3565–66, are they Cartesian? 3471a, & Cartesian doctrine 2552, D. & Scholasticism 2544; *De intellectus emendatione* & DM 1490; *Ethica:* seminal idea from D.'s TP (Brochard) 1371, Ethica & D.'s philosophy 2180, & D.'s morale 2699; *special points:* comparative doctrinal study 455a; causality 213, 262, 455a, 2630; cogito 272, 333, 455a; consciousness: limits, subject-object problem 215b; dualism 215b, 1284, 1789; error 1368, 2619, 2688; essence 455a, 3078; extension 241; freedom 206a, 1949; intuition 156, 1259, 1401; liberté 1949; mathematics 358; mechanics 1759; memory 2785; méthode 1012; monism in metaphysics, dualism in epistemology 1284, Spinoza's monism rooted in D.'s philosophy of religion 3419, substance monism 2630; O&R studied by Spinoza 156 & 1391; ontological argument 211a; opposition to D.'s pluralistic scepticism 329; origins of Spinozism 2178; passions 1466, 1857, 2072; political theory 3235; sagesse 177, substance 196 & 1391, 455a, 2275, 2478, 2630; *Spinozism & Cartesianism:* D., Spinoza, Maimonides 329; from Cartesianism to Spinozism 1908, relation between them 3282, Cartesians misrepresent Spinozism 466a, Gerdil & Lamy: Cartesian refutations of Spinoza 431; Spinoza & Malebranche 188 & 3047, 1079, 3608, intuition 1259, passions 1466; Tschirnhaus as mediator between Spinozism & Cartesianism 3026–27.
spiritualism of Descartes: 24, his tendency towards spiritualistic immanence 157, spiritualistic idealism 1677; Cartesian spiritualism vs. Pascal's realism 158; D.'s rationalistic "ontocoscienzialismo" 204, 204a; spiritualism: the Cartesian failure (Gilson) 166; spiritualistic faith, not doubt, is D.'s starting point 3176; D.'s transcendental spiritualism in MM 4; Bayle's critique 462; D. & Gassendi 431; D. spiritualistically falsified by 17th century Cartesians & 20th century bourgeois Descartisants 459.
spiritualistic interpretations of Descartes: Cousin & spiritualistes universitaires (Bouillier, Jouffroy, Royer-Collard, Saisset et al.) discussed 180, 438 (v. 2), 2859, 3523; influence of Scottish Realists 223, 3038–39, 3350; Cousin & his influence 126, 180, 223, 224, 249, 365, 1655, 2764, 2859, 3176; Sylvestre de

Sacy 3176; Saisset 223, 2859, 3178; reaction against Cousin & spiritualistes universitaires 114, 188, 453, 462, who falsify D. by overstressing cogito 1862; spiritualistic falsification of D. initiated by 17th century Cartesians 459; Bonald's critique 1274.
spirals of Descartes: 398, 1786.
spiral nebulae: & vortex theory 359 & 3558.
springs (formation of springs & rivers): texts (fontaines) 7; theory from D. to Vallisneri 2615.
Stabeck, Bernhard: 2133.
Stampioen, Jan Jansz. de Jonge [b. 1610; AM, v. 3]: Stampioen-Waessenaer affair 74, 81, 121–123, 125, 1233, 1294.
statics: 368, 373a; D.'s difficult transition to dynamics 361, 372; he discovered nothing (Duhem) 368; epistemology 161, & s.v. dynamics, force, mechanics.
statistics: style & composition of DM statistically analyzed 292.
"Staurophorus, Rhodophilus" (pseud.): Raptus philosophicus [1619] imitated by D.? 102, critique 96.
Stenius, Olaus: first Cartesian in Upsala 2552a.
Stensen, Nicolaus [1638–1686]: his judgment of D.'s physiology 1916.
Stevin, Simon [1548–1620; AM, v. 1]: 1771, 2766, 3520; algebraic notation 2766; his number concept profounder than D.'s 378; see also biography.
Stewart, Dugald [1753–1828]: *223, 3350;* 224; & s.v. Scottish School, spiritualistic interpretations.
Stockholm: burial of D. 74, 110, 121, 123, 124, Baillet's account, picture of monument with inscriptions by Chanut 122; Histoire de la coniuration faite à Stokolm (by Gervaise de Montpellier) 2004a, 110, 243; & s.v. biography, Christina of Sweden.
Stockholm Inventory of Descartes' papers [1650]: "un petit registre en parchemin" 74, 96, 100, 121–123; & s.v. Cogitationes privatae, Opuscula.
Stoicism of Descartes: 178, 243 & 1479, 283, 322a; Stoicism in France in D.'s time 466a; literature survey 283; D.'s debt to Stoics (Brochard) 1370, Stoic sources: beast-machine, malin génie, clear & distinct ideas, inneism 163, 3156; influences: Renaissance 311, La Flèche 220; D. & the 17th c. Stoic revival 119, 243; D. uses & refutes Stoicism rationally, not theologically 283; *special points:* cogito 208, générosité (q.v.) 176; Stoic imaginatio & phantasia 378; morale 83, its Stoic & Christian elements 3268, its second-hand Stoicism 2210, Stoicism subordinated to Epicureanism 170, Stoicism in morale denied 149; D.'s rationalistic & Christian humanistic Stoicism 283; objectivity 2208; Stoicism in TP 2690.
Studium bonae mentis: edition 74; 83, 100, 121–123, 220; bona mens, bon sens 83; morale 220.
Sturmius (Sturm), Johann Christoph [1635–1703]: 436.
style of Descartes: 121, 403, 408, 2439, 2602; "Begriffssprache" 2314; style of DM 260, derived from Guez de Balzac 404, reveals D.'s personality 1890, he uses "je" [583 times] in DM 1147a; style of D.'s thinking 1293; & s.v. metaphors.
Suarez, Francisco [1548–1617]: parallel texts 7; studied by D. 263; influence upon D. 2618; eternal verities 1661c; ontological proof 214.
subconscious mind: D.'s treatment of it, relation to "conscience" 215b.
subject: 172b, 192a, 215b, 1206.
subjectivism: critique of D.'s subjectivism 1414a; D. the father of modern subjectivism 171–172b, 192, 207.
substance: texts 7; definitions, distinctions 83; 131, 149, 160, 161, 170, 178, 233, 1068, 2126, 2369a, 2593; accident 83, 178, 282, 1414; attribute: distinctio rationis 2212, Spinoza & D. 455a; causality 160, 193, 213; change & substance, motion & rest: contradictions 160, 373a, 1068; dualism (q.v.) 155, 170, 178 & 2455, 204, 204a, 216a, 231, 347b, 2888; forma substantialis: s.v. substantial forms; Kantian-type substance concept of D. 221; liaison nécessaire (q.v.) 2451; O&R 156 & 1391; Scholastic borrowings, & contradictions 2593; spirituality of substance 129, 204, 204a; thinking substance: a ghost 190; *doctrinal history* 282; Cartesians: substance & causality 213; D. & Spinoza 156 & 1391, 455a, 2275, 2478, 2630; D. & Leibniz 2478; Malebranche: motion & rest, dilemma 373a; Locke 1940; vinculum substantiale, D., Leibniz, Kant 1255, 3110; Whitehead's "actual occasions" 194a; s.v. extension, pensée.
substantial form: texts 7; 83, 165; beast-

machine controversy 226; from critique of substantial forms to methodical doubt (Gilson) 165; Cartesians (Clauberg, La Forge) 431.

sufficient reason: & causality 3009; & s.v. logic.

supernatural: 96, 178, 2329; Scholasticism & Cartesianism 177; & s.v. Olympica.

superstition: 2479.

Suyderhoef, Jonas: his engraving of D. 1 & 2858a.

Sweden: D. in Sweden 121–123, relics of his visit 3365; Stabeck's & Beckmann's comments on his philosophy 2133; Cartesian influence: Stenius 2552a, biology 2237, Cartesian controversy in Upsala 466c; & s.v. biography, Christina, death of D., Stockholm.

Swedenborg, Emmanuel von [1688–1772]: Cartesianism in Sweden, his nebular hypothesis & D. 466c; attributes his "spiritual influx" concept to D. 2863.

Switzerland: Cartesianism 436, 438; D. & Swiss science 1945.

syllogism: texts 7; 83, 161, 178, 193, 198, 231; analysis & synthesis (q.v.), vs. syllogistics 161, 231, 1402; D.'s aversion against syllogistics prevents him from developing a universal logic 1226; Clauberg & D. 436; deduction & syllogistics 198; Euclidean analogy & syllogism 321a; méthode 231, & Platonic dialectics 3215, barren syllogism opposed to méthode 231; & s.v. analysis & synthesis, logic.

symbol: arbre de la sagesse 220, 230, 2724; childhood psychology: Bérulle vs. D. 268a; "conscience" & signs 1056a; CP & Regulae: symbolism of magical literature 328; symbolism of CP 96, 100, 163, 268a, 328; D.'s theory of image an extreme theory of symbol 227; Olympica: from mathematicism to sagesse 96, language of man, not things 268a, code to conceal scientific discovery? 107; symbolism is error: D. rejects it 268a in his mature years 96 & 2101a; D.'s scientific symbolism & religious agnosticism 230; symbols common to St. Augustine & D. 163; 17th century: Christian theology vs. magical, symbolic cosmology 268a; mathematical symbolism: s.v. algebraic notation; & see Dream, Olympica.

Symbolists (French literature): D. influence 453.

synaesthesis: 215b.

syntactic rules: 238.

synthesis: s.v. analysis & synthesis.

synthetic judgments: Ottaviano's theory, & cogito 252.

Syntagma philosophicum (Gassendi): 326, 466a, 2121a, 3097.

systematization: D.'s rules 238.

T

tangents, Descartes' method of: 355, 397, 398, 3390b; controversy with Fermat 388 & 2747, 1808a, 2117, with Roberval 369; method of Géométrie distinguished from extrageometrical method 398, both substitutes for infinetesimal calculus 355, 398; D.'s tangent treatment contains roots of all modern algebra 355.

Tannery, Paul [1843–1904]: *74, 397, 3385–90d;* free fall 1519; chronology of D.'s metaphysics 2946; obituary 1812.

technology (technique, Technik): 179, 179b; theory & technology (Canguilhem) 1441; morale as technique 169; science, metaphysics, technology 149; D. as prophet of modern technology 3477; D. & the survival of humanism 432a.

Teilhard de Chardin, Pierre, S.J.: 1155a.

telescope: D.'s improvements 193.

Tennemann, Wilhelm Gottlieb: *3401;* his pre-Hegelian view of D. 10, 33.

tensors, Cartesian: 2297.

Testelin, Henri ["le jeune," 1616–1695]: TP applied to visual art 422.

theater: D. as figure in stage plays 113, 114; D. & 17th century French theater 466a, & s.v. Corneille, Molière, Racine.

theism: 17th century natural religion and universal theism 243 & 1479; theism & error problem 299; Bayle's critique of theism 462.

theocentrism: Malebranche (q.v.) 435b, 453c, 457b.

theodicy: & psychophysical problem in D. 170.

Theodoric (Dietrich) von Freiberg [died ca. 1310]: rainbow theory 356.

theology: 83, 164, 165, 168, 178, 179a, b, 185, 211a, 267, 435a, 436, 1060, 2091, 2095, 2228a; history: post-

tourbillons: s.v. vortex theory.
totalitarian state: & Cartesian mechanism 3223; & s.v. Fascism.
Tours, Touraine: D.'s origins 1534; Tours portraits of D. 1 & 2858a, 2213; celebrations & exhibitions 504, 538.
TP: s.v. Traité des passions de l'âme.
tragedy: s.v. Corneille, Racine.
Traité de février 1620: 75, 83, 96, 100, 121, 122, 2764.
Traité de la lumière: s.v. Monde.
Traité de l'homme: editions 74, 76; the embodied self 193; Malebranche's first reading in Descartes? 435b, 2078; & s.v. physiology.
Traité des passions de l'âme (TP): editions 74, 76, 77, 91; general 125, 147, 168, 1290, 3019; attracted the "lecteur honnête homme" more than DM did 404; Calvin's Institutions 1970, Corneille's hero 413, 423, 1509b, 2024a; embodied self 193; influence of Greek philosophy 2690, of François de Sales 423; morale, medicine, physiology 220, 365; Racine 414, 2556a, his Phèdre 2042; Spinoza: TP contains seminal idea of his Ethics 1371; theory of expression, & Renaissance concepts 422; Vives (De anima & vita) & TP 2534, 3459–60; & s.v. passions, morale, physiology, art.
transcendence: 205 & 1460; transcendentalism & Cartesian circle 2197; from cogito to transcendental self 1144, & s.v. idealism; geometrical transcendence: D. & Leibniz (q.v.) 3453, & s.v. curves.
transfers (actual & proposed) of Descartes' remains: 110, 124, 1308, 1501, 2877, 3175; where are D.'s remains? 2787; see also burial, Panthéonisation, skull of Descartes.
Transsubstantiation: texts (Cartesian & Scholastic) 7; survey & bibliography 279, 2288; 163, 164, 168, 178, 179b, 185, 2324; history of D.'s texts, letters to Mesland 189, 452a; two 17th century manuscripts on D.'s view 450; D.'s difficulties: Letters to Mesland vs. MM 164; Pierre Cally & Cartesian doctrine 3478; & individuation 215a; Leibniz's critique 317; Maignan 1500, 2110; D.'s physics a device to save Transsubstantiation from new science 163, 179b.
travels of Descartes: 83, 121–123, 146a, 179a, & s.v. bibliography, Bohemia, Holland, Sweden.
tree of philosophy, wisdom (PP): s.v. arbre.
Trevisan, Bernardo: Malebranche's influence 433.
trisection of the angle: 388 & 2744.
truth: texts 7; 83, 125, 161, 170, 178, 243 & 1483, 1027; definition 83, truth is avoidance of error (D.), Will to Power makes truth (Nietzsche) 172b, Being & truth: synonyms for D. 161; D.'s truth concept 248, wavering between moralism & theoreticity 1070, is rooted in medieval gnosiology, not idealism 214a, dominates modern metaphysics to Nietzsche 172a; certitude 178; created truths: difficulty 327; dualistic conception 1096; eternal verities (q.v.); existentialist humanism 192; guarantee of truth 208 & s.v. Dieu-trompeur, malin génie, veracity of God; habit & instability 3281; lumen naturale 243 & 1483; proofs of necessary truth in mathematics 314; Scholastic & Cartesian truth (copy vs. code) 3147; sense, sensation 170; truth criterion: D. moves towards a material criterion, modern logic has none 335, D.'s truth not verifiable: modern scientific vs. Cartesian epistemology 350; Veritas filia temporis 465a; veritas rationum, veritas rei 170; & s.v. certitude, Dieu-trompeur, epistemology, error, eternal verities, malin génie, veracity of God.
Tschirnhaus, Ehrenfried Walter Freiherr von [1651–1708]: Cartesianism & Spinozism 3026–27; motion & rest 467.
Twardowski, Kasimir: *3455*; 1844; objective reality 212a.
Tycho Brahe: s.v. Brahe.

U

Umgreifende, das (Jaspers): not grasped by D. 175.
"Una est in rebus vis activa" (CP): hermeneutic commonplace before D. 328.
unconscious mind: 203, 215b & 2533; association of ideas, memory 2785.
understanding, intellectio, entendement: texts 7; 131, 147, 170, 178, 204, 1904; imagination vs. understanding 227; incorporeal understanding is outside time 353; & perception, sense 192b; theory of possibility, sensation, judgment, volonté 170; D., Locke, Leibniz, Kant 1535, 3581; & s.v. cognition, epistemology, pensée.

union (âme & corps): texts 7; 83, 119, 147, 149, 165, 170, 171, 178, 185, 193, 215c, 1704, 2179, 2367, 2369a, 2631, 3506; conflicts & difficulties: union substantielle &distinction réelle 165, distinction & eternal verities 201; "enseignements de la nature" 340; logical status 231; in MM 170, 2721; morale 230, moral consequences & demands 220; proof 170, not provable per imaginationem 227; rational knowledge 178; steps towards parallelism (Cartesians) 1126; three theories: mechanism, interaction, occasionalism 2994; St. Thomas vs. D., Locke, Hume 3482; Cartesians 431, 1126; & s.v. âme, dualism, psychophysiology.
unity: of méthode (DM) 159 & 1396, 2609; of knowledge (interdependence of concepts) 3604–05, denied (no link between distinct ideas) 329; of modern physics, & methode 370; of self & nature, & idea of time 347a; systematic & genetic orders unified in man (Alquié) 1051a; of thought & science, & method 198.
unity of Descartes' system & thought: asserted (on differing grounds) 131, 132, 157, 159, 170, 171, 222, 1396, 1402, 1527–28, questioned or denied 25, 149, 193, 1540; intentional unity, methodological dualism 1070; unity of creative intuition guarantees unity of system 1672; hidden, intended unity of intuition vs. "dimorphism" of system as it is (Brunschvicg) 131, 159 & 1402; metaphysical unity of system 170, 185; unity of morale & physics 220; & s.v. interpretations.
unity of science: 83, 243 & 1484, 2609–09a; in D.'s Dream 96, 100, 123, 183; unity of science guaranteed by unity of pensée (prototype: genesis of numbers) 243 & 1484; & méthode 83; physics 1795; sagesse 220, 230, 2535a; Peripatetics, Cartesians, Eclectics 436; Encyclopedists 455; & s.v. scientia universalis, unity of Descartes' system.
universals: D. a "conceptualist" 2761.
universe: from closed to infinite universe 379; & s.v. cosmogony, cosmology, world.
Upsala: Olaus Stenius, earliest Cartesian 2552a; Cartesian controversy 466c.
United States of America: first Cartesian work in North America 440; three D. interpretations 151, 187, 191.
universities: philosophical & theological teaching, Aristotelianism & Cartesianism 121–5, 168, 436, 438, 450, 452, 466a, 467, science instruction before D. 3425; *Belgium:* Louvain 458, 467, Neoscholasticism &1238; *France* 450, 466a, 1876, 3425; Anjou 390, Paris 390, 450, 466a, 1876, suppression of Cartesianism 390, 450, Pardes affair 438 (v. 2); Poitiers (q.v.) 1172; *Germany:* Altdorf, Leipzig, Herborn, etc. 436, 438, Berlin [1950] 543; *Holland* 123, 436, 452, 466a, 467; Amsterdam (Athenaeum & University) 452, 467; Franeker (q.v.) 3533, philosophical instruction 452 & 1957, French students, D.'s matriculation 123, 467; Groningen 125, 452; Leiden 123, 452, 1658, Danish students 2612, French students, Cartesian controversies 121–23, 125; Utrecht (q.v.) 121–23, 125, 436, 452, 1933, physicists, 390; *Italy* 433, Cartesianism & Neothomist revival 2898; *Latin America*, Córdoba (Argentina) 448; *Portugal* 430; *Switzerland* 436; & s.v. cursus philosophicus.
utilitarianism of Descartes: 177, 2508, 2511, 3281; utilitarianism in D.'s time 1375.
Utrecht: D.'s stay in Utrecht, relation with University 21–123, 125, 436, 452, 1933; Carsian physicists 390; Utrecht controversies: s.v. Voetius (Gisbert), Regius, Desmarets.

V

vacuum & plenum: texts 7; 121, 125, 390; D.'s plenum doctrine does not necessarily lead to pantheism 3297; subtle matter 258; Henry More & empty space 315; Newton vs. Cartesian plenum 390; Pascal & Puy-de-Dôme 2, 121, 402, 1013, 1772, 2671, 2861, 3519; Rohault 390; & s.v. extension, physics.
Vaihinger, Hans [1852–1933]: D.'s "inofficial" methodology anticipates "Als Ob" 247.
Valencia: fortunes of Cartesianism 449.
Valéry, Paul: *194, 3465–69;* 2730; his Cartesian spirit 427; le Retour de Hollande 467; his "poetry of Dreams" & D. 453.
Vallisneri, Antonio [1661–1730]: theory of the origin of springs 2615.
Valois, Louis Le, S.J. (recte: Louis La Ville): 438; physics 390.
value: D.'s theory of values unifies his ethics & metaphysics 217; eternal verities & values 419; St. Thomas & D. 3298; & s.v. morale.
Varignon, Pierre [1654–1722]: Cartesian mathematics in transition 372; vortex theory, force 377a.

Vries, Gerard de [1648–1705]: 109, 436, 452, 467.
voyages imaginaires: 467.
"vulgaire": D.'s Christian "foi banale & commune" (Blondel) 152; his "vulgar belief in the inner life of the body" (Santayana) 191; "Vulgarkartesianismus" 109, 110, 113–115, supplants genuine Cartesianism 453.
Vyčeslavzev (Vycheslavzeff), Boris: 14, 184a.

W–Z

Waessenaer (Wassenaer), Johann Jakob van [AM, v. 3]: Stampioen-Waessenaer controversy 74, 81, 121–123, 125, 1233, 1294.
waking: s.v. sleeping, dreaming.
Waldschmidt, Johann Jakob [1644–1687]: diffusion of Cartesian medicine 1824b.
Wallis, John [1616–1703]: number concept 378.
Wander, Guillaume (pseud.): s.v. Lanion.
wax: "morceau de cire" (D.'s example) 147, 149, 170, 235c; already used by St. Augustine 163.
Weenix, J. B.: his portrait of D. 1054, & s.v. iconography.
Weisse, Christian Hermann [1801–1866]: revival of ontotheology 211a.
White, Thomas [1593–1676; AM, v. 5]: D.'s correspondent 121, 1020.
White Mountain, Battle: 121, 1022.
Whitehead, Alfred North: *182, 194a, 3555–56;* 324a, 2761; dualism 155, & "union of opposites" 182, bifurcation of nature 226 & 1124, his monism leads to new dualisms 155, dualism & beast-machine 226; St. Thomas, D., Whitehead on matter & scientific efficiency 431 & 1129.
Whittaker, Sir Edmund (Edmund Taylor): *401, 3557–59;* 359.
will: s.v. liberté & libre-arbitre, volonté & voluntarism.
Will to Power, Wille zur Macht: Nietzsche & cogito 172b; malin génie 3489a.
Willis, Thomas [1621–1675]: nvoluntary reflexes: priority? 360.
Windelband, Wilhelm: his D. interpretation 10.
Wittgenstein, Ludwig: 190, 198, 1330–31.
Wittich, Christoph [1625–1687]: anticartesian controversies 435a, 467, 2228a.
Wolff, Christian Freiherr von [1679–1754]: proofs of God 211a, 1647; "Scholastic Cartesianism" 2630.
Wolzogen, Ludwig [1633–1690]: anticartesian controversies 435a, 467; Arianism & Western thought combined against D. 1541.
women: D.'s "amitiés féminines" 121, 298, 1011, 1019, 2116; his influence on French society women 466a, 1920; Mme de Sévigné 1701; diffusion of scientific ideas 3060; & s.v. Christina, Elisabeth.
Wordsworth, William [1770–1750]: childhood experience & psychology 429a.
work, travail mécanique, Leistung: 373a, 388 & 2750; eliminates from concept of force all nongeometric elements 2145; & s.v. force.
works of Descartes: sections 74–92b, 1727–1747; chronology (origin, publication) 149; & under individual titles.
world: texts 7; cogito fails to bracket out world (Husserl's critique) 174; real world disappears in D.'s idealism 2878a; existentialist view of world unnecessarily abandoned by D. (Sartre) 192; failure to identify world phenomenologically, misconstruction of world as extension (Heidegger) 172, Husserl 174; God & world 171, 214a, 2665; real & possible worlds 161, 453a, plurality of worlds 390, 1826, 1981, 2584; & s.v. cosmogony, cosmology, external world, finite, universe.
Yugoslavia: commemorative articles 1136, 1689, 1892, 1907, 2418, 2496, 3184–85, 3312, 3463.
Zabarella, Giacomo [1533–1589]: 161, 452, 2649.
Zanotti, Francesco Maria [1692–1777]: Malebranche's influence 433.

ABBREVIATIONS

()	incomplete information
app.	appendix
ms	manuscript
ns	new series, nouvelle série, neue Reihe
sb	supplément bibliographique
ser	series, série, Serie, Reihe
v.	volume

WORKS OF DESCARTES

AM	Correspondence, ed. Adam-Milhaud (no. 79)
AT	Œuvres, ed. Adam-Tannery (no. 74)
CP	Cogitationes privatae
DM	Discours de la méthode
MM	Méditations métaphysiques
O & R	Objectiones cum responsionibus authoris
PP	Principia philosophiae
Regulae	Regulae ad directionem ingenii
RV	Recherche de la vérité
TP	Traité des passions de l'âme

GENERAL

AcAngers	Académie des sciences et belles-lettres d'Angers
AcBelg	Académie Royale des sciences, des lettres et des beaux-arts de Belgique, Bulletin de la classe des lettres
AcBerl	Akademie der Wissenschaften, Berlin, Historisch-philosophische Klasse
ACFM	Académie des beaux-lettres et arts de Clermont-Ferrand, Mémoires
AcLincei	Reale accademia nazionale dei Lincei (Roma), Classe di scienze morali, storiche e filosofici, Rendiconti
AcLisboa	Academia das ciëncias de Lisboa, Clase de ciëncias, Memorias
AcPadova	Atti e memorie dell'Accademia di scienze, lettere e belle arti di Padova
AcTorino	Atti della Regia Accademia delle scienze di Torino
AcToulouse	Académie des sciences, inscriptions et belles-lettres de Toulouse.
AcWien	Kaiserliche Akademie der Wissenschaften in Wien
AESC	Annales: économies, sociétés, civilisations [see: AHES]
Afil	Archivio di filosofia (Roma)

AGP	Archiv für Geschichte der Philosophie
AGPs	Archiv für die gesamte Psychologie
AHES	Annales d'histoire économique et sociale [later: AESC]
AHR	American Historical Review
AIHS	Archives internationales d'histoire des sciences
Aj[atus]	Ajatus; filosofisen yhdistyksen vuosikirja
AJP	American Journal of Philology
AJPP	Australasian Journal of Psychology and Philosophy
AM	*Descartes. Correspondance*, ed. Adam-Milhaud [no. 79].
AHR	American Historical Review
AMP	Académie des sciences morales et politiques, Paris, Comptes-rendus
AMPM	(idem), Mémoires
AMPS	(idem), Séances et travaux
AmSocR	American Sociological Review
Analysis	Analysis (Oxford)
AnCagl	Annali della facoltà di lettere e filosofia della R. Università di Cagliari
AnBr	Annales de Bretagne (Faculté des lettres de Rennes)
AnP[h]	Année philosophique [formerly: CrPh]
AnSci	Annals of Science (London)
Ant	Antonianum (Roma)
ANTWP	Algemeen Nederlands Tijdschrift voor Wijsbegeerte en Psychologie
APC	Annales de philosophie chrétienne
Aph	Archives de philosophie (Paris)
Archeion	Archeion, archivio di storia delle scienze [see AIHS]
ArSocPr, ASP	Aristotelian Society, Proceedings
Asci	Actualités scientifiques et industrielles (Paris, Hermann)
ASFI	Archivio di storia della filosofia italiana [later: Archivio della cultura italiana]
ASR	American Sociological Review
AT	*Oeuvres de Descartes*, ed. Adam-Tannery [no. 74]
ATA	Année théologique augustinienne
AUP	Annales de l'Université de Paris
BA	Books abroad (University of Oklahoma)
BAFH	Bulletin de l'Alliance Française en Hollande
Baldensperger	F. Baldensperger & W. P. Friedrich, Bibliography of comparative literature, Chapel Hill, 1950
Balz	A.G.A. Balz (unpublished bibliographical checklist)
BAn	Bulletin analytique: Philosophie. France, Centre national de la recherche scientifique, Ministère de l'éducation nationale [now: Bsig]
Bar	Bar, "Kartezjusz w Polsce." KF 19: 1950, 151–60 [no. 1137]
BCLF	Bulletin critique du livre français
BCM	Biblioteca di cultura moderna
BdtPh, BDP	Blätter für deutsche Philosophie [formerly: Beiträge zur Geschichte des deutschen Idealismus]
BFL	Bulletin de la faculté des lettres de....
BHP	Bibliothèque d'histoire de la philosophie
BHR	Bibliothèque d'humanisme et renaissance
BICP	Bulletin de l'Institut Catholique de Paris
Bij[dragen]	Bijdragen, tijdschrift voor philosophie en theologie (Maastricht-Leuven)
BJPS	British Journal for the Philosophy of Science
BLET	Bulletin de littérature ecclésiastique de l'Institut Catholique de Toulouse
BM	British Museum
BN	Bibliothèque Nationale (Paris)

Bontadini I	G. Bontadini, "Les ouvrages italiens sur Descartes...." Rsyn 14: 1937, 87–97 [no. 1278]
Bontadini II	G. Bontadini, "Annotazioni ad alcune scritti italiani su Cartesio." Cartesio 85–104 [no. 1279]
BP	Bibliographie de la philosophie (Institut international de collaboration philosophique), 1937–1953
BPC	Bibliothèque de philosophie contemporaine
Bph, Bphil	Bibliographie de la philosophie. Bibliography of philosophy. Institut international de philosophie – UNESCO, 1954ff.
Brie	G. A. de Brie, Bibliographia philosophica 1934–1945, v. 1. (Utrecht-Bruxelles, 1950)
Bro	Brotéria, Revista de sciências naturaes do Collégio de S. Fiel.
BSA Ouest	Bulletin de la société des antiquaires de l'Ouest
BSA Tours	Bulletin de la société archéologique de Tourraine
BSFP	Bulletin de la société française de philosophie
RSHP	Bulletin de la société de l'histoire de Paris et de l'Île de France
Bsig	Bulletin signalétique: Philosophie [formerly BAn]
Bthom	Bulletin thomiste (Paris)
BTP	Bibliothèque des textes philosophiques
Cabeen	Cabeen (ed.), Critical Bibliography of French Literature, v. 3, 1961 [no. 3a]
Cartesio	Cartesio nel terzo centenario del Discorso del metodo. Milano 1937 [no. 35]
CD	Congrès Descartes. Travaux du IXe Congrès International de Philosophie, Paris 1937 [no. 36]
CDS	Cahiers du Sud
Cfil	Cultura filosofica (Firenze)
Christus	Christus. Revue d'information et de culture catholique (Lyon)
CG	Collationes Gandavenses
CHR	Catholic Historical Review
CivC	La civiltà cattolica (Roma)
CleR	Clergy Review (London)
CLF	Chronique des lettres françaises
Col	Columbia University Library (New York)
Con	La connaissance; revue de lettres et d'idées
Conv	Convivium (Barcelona)
Cordié	C. Cordié, Avviamente allo studio della lingua e della letteratura francese (Milano, 1955)
Corr	Le Correspondant (Paris)
CP	*Descartes. Cogitationes privatae*
Cph	Les classiques de la philosophie
CQR	Church Quarterly Review (London)
Crisis	Crisis (Madrid)
Crit	Critique, revue générale des publications françaises et étrangères
CrPh	La critique philosophique
CT	La ciencia tomista
Cth	Cahiers thomistes (Paris)
Cuad	Cuadernos de filosofía (Instituto de filosofía, Facultad de filosofía. Universidad de Buenos Aires)
CUN	Les cours de l'université nouvelle
CUP	Cambridge University Press
CyF	Ciencia y fé (San Miguel, Argentina)
Dcom	Doctor communis (Roma)
Dlit	Deutsche Literaturzeitung

DM	*Descartes, Discours de la méthode*
DomSt	Dominican Studies (Oxford)
DR	The Downside Review (Bath)
DSS	Le dix-septième siècle
DTF	Divus Thomas, Freiburg [formerly: Jahrbuch für Philosophie und spekulative Theologie]
DTP	Divus Thomas (Piacenza)
DZP	Deutsche Zeitschrift für Philosophie
E	Estudios (Academia literaria del Plata, Buenos Aires)
EAPG	(Erdmann's) Abhandlungen zur Philosophie und ihrer Geschichte
Edu, Educ	Educare; rivista di pedagogia e cultura generale
EHR	The English Historical Review
Emge	Archiv für Rechts- und Sozialphilosophie 30: 1937, Heft 4: "Dem Gedächtnis an R. Descartes," ed. Emge [no. 523]
Eph	Les études philosophiques
EPM	Études de philosophie médiévale
Er	Erasmus (Basel)
Escritos	Escritos en honor de Descartes .... La Plata, 1938 [no. 39]
EsFil	Estúdios filosóficos (Las Caldas de Besaya, Santander)
Et	Études, Paris [formerly: Études de théologie, de philosophie, d'histoire]
Eth[ics]	Ethics, an international journal of social, political and legal philosophy
ETL	Ephemerides theologicae Lovanienses
ETR	Études théologiques et religieuses (Montpellier)
Eur	Europe (Paris)
F	Filosofia (Torino)
FAPG	(Falckenberg's) Abhandlungen zur Philosophie und ihrer Geschichte
Figaro	Le Figaro (Paris)
FigLit	Le Figaro, Supplément littéraire
FC Lille	Mémoires et travaux des facultés catholiques de Lille
Flam[beau]	Le Flambeau, revue belge des questions politiques et littéraires
FR	The French Review (New York)
FS	French Studies (Oxford)
FyL	Filosofía y letras, revista de la Faculdad de filosofía y letras, Universidad nacional de Mexico
FyL Oviedo	Filosofía y letras, revista de la Universidad de Oviedo
GCFI	Giornale critico della filosofia italiana
Genava	Genava. Genève, Musée d'art et d'histoire
Giraud I, II	J. Giraud, Manuel de bibliographie littéraire, v. 1, 2 [no. 8, 9]
Gmet	Giornale di metafisica
Gött	Göttinger gelehrte Anzeigen
Greg	Gregorianum
Harvard	Widener Library, Harvard University
HJ	Hibbert Journal
Hochland	Hochland (München)
Homenaje	Descartes; homenaje en el tercer centenario, Buenos Aires, 3 vols. [no. 40]
HR	The Hispanic Review
Humanitas	Humanitas (Brescia)
ILPP	International Library of Philosophy and Psychology
Isis	Isis, revue consacrée à l'histoire de la science. Isis, international review
Janus	Janus, archive pour l'histoire de la médecine
Jdeb	Journal des débats (Paris)
JHI	Journal for the History of Ideas

JP	Journal of Philosophy
JPNP	Journal de psychologie normale et pathologique
JRel	Journal of Religion
JSPG	Jahrbuch der schweizerischen philosophischen Gesellschaft
JSPh	Journal of Speculative Philosophy
K	Kantstudien
KCTS	Katholiek Cultureel Tijdschrift Streven [later: Streven]
KF	Kwartalnik filosoficzny (Kraków)
Lanson	G. Lanson, Manuel bibliographique de la littérature française moderne, 1910 (no. 2441)
LBGP	Literarische Berichte aus dem Gebiete der Philosophie
LC	Library of Congress, Washington, D.C.
LilleM	Mémoires et travaux, Facultés catholiques de Lille
LogosN	Logos, rivista internazionale di filosofia (Napoli)
LogosT	Logos, internationale Zeitschrift für Philosophie der Kultur (Tübingen)
LTP	Laval théologique et philosophique (Quebec)
MAS	Mémoires, Académie des sciences (Paris)
MerF	Mercure de France
Merkur	Merkur, deutsche Zeitschrift für europäisches Denken
Meth[odos]	Methodos; rivista trimestrale di metodologia
MF	Mercure de France
Mind	Mind, a quarterly review of psychology and philosophy
MLF	Modern Language Forum (Los Angeles)
MLJ	The Modern Language Journal
MLN	Modern Language Notes
MLQ	Modern Language Quarterly
MLR	Modern Language Review
MM	*Descartes. Méditations métaphysiques*
ModSch	The Modern Schoolman (St. Louis University)
Morgan	D. N. Morgan, Cartesiana, 1955 [no. 13]
MPF	Les maîtres de la pensée française
MSA	Mémoires de la société archéologique de ....
MSAS	Mémoires de la société des arts et des sciences de ....
MScR, MSR	Mélanges de science religieuse (Lille)
Mus	Museum (Leiden)
NAK	Nederlandsch archief voor kerkgeschiedenis
Nature	La nature, revue des sciences (Paris)
NAW	Nieuw archief voor wiskunde (Amsterdam)
Neo	Neophilologus
NL	Nouvelles littéraires (Paris)
NN	New York Public Library
NRF	Nouvelle revue française
NRJ	Nouvelle revue des jeunes
NRT	Nouvelle revue théologique (Tournai)
Nsch	The New Scholasticism (Baltimore)
O	Opinion (Paris)
O & R	*Descartes. Objectiones cum responsionibus authoris*
OrleansM	Mémoires de la société d'agriculture, sciences, belles-lettres et arts d'Orléans
Osiris	Osiris; studies in the history and philosophy of science
OUP	Oxford University Press
PA, PhAb	Philosophical Abstracts (New York)
PAS	Proceedings of the Aristotelian Society

PenM	El Pensamiento (Madrid)
Pensée	La pensée, revue du rationalisme moderne (Paris)
Perpj	Perpjekja Shqiptare (Albania)
Pers	The Personalist (Los Angeles)
PhAb	Philosophical Abstracts (New York)
PhdG	Die Philosophie der Gegenwart, eine internationale bibliographische Jahresübersicht, ed. Arnold Runge (Heidelberg, 1910–1915)
PhE	La philosophie de l'esprit
Phil	Philosophy (London)
Philosophia	Philosophia (Mendoza)
PhJ, PJ	Philosophisches Jahrbuch
PhLit	Philosophischer Literaturanzeiger
PhQ	Philosophical Quarterly
PhR	Philosophical Review
PhRu	Philosophische Rundschau
PhS, PhSt	Philosophical Studies
PJ, PhJ	Philosophisches Jahrbuch
PJGG	Philosophisches Jahrbuch der Görres-Gesellschaft
PMLA	PMLA, Publications of the Modern Language Association of America
Pos-Steenbergen	Pos & Steenbergen, "Les ouvrages sur Descartes publiés dans les Pays-Bas," Rsyn 14: 1937, 112–14 [no. 15 & 2986]
PP	*Descartes. Principia philosophiae*
PPR	Philosophy and Phenomenological Research
PRRM	La pensée, revue du rationalisme moderne
Prz	Przeglad filosoficzny (Warszawa)
Pscience	Philosophy of Science (Baltimore)
PsychB	Psychological Bulletin
PsyH	Psyche, Zeitschrift für Tiefenpsychologie und Menschenkunde (Heidelberg)
PsyP	Psyché, revue internationale des sciences de l'homme et de psychoanalyse (Paris)
PUF	Presses universitaires françaises
RAF	Revue de l'Alliance Française
RANL	Rendiconti, Accademia Nazionale dei Lincei
RassF	Rassegna di filosofia (Roma)
Rbén, RB	Revue bénédictine
Rbleue	Revue bleue
RbrasF	Revista brasileira de filosofia (Instituto brasileiro de filosofia, Sao Paulo)
RCC	Revue des cours et des conférences
RCO	Revue générale du Centre-Ouest de la France
Rcr	Revue critique
RCSF	Rivista critica di storia della filosofia (Milano)
RcubF	Revista cubana de filosofía
RdePh	Revue de philosophie (Paris)
RDM	Revue des deux mondes
Rdom	Revue dominicaine
REA	Revue des études augustiniennes (Paris)
RechPh	Recherches philosophiques (Paris)
Regulae	*Descartes. Regulae ad directionem mentis*
Ren	Rencontres
Rép	Répertoire bibliographique de la philosophie (Louvain)
RevF	Revista de filosofía (Madrid)
RevPF	Revista Portuguesa de filosofia

RevR	The Review of Religion
RevSR	Revue des sciences religieuses (Strasbourg)
RF	Rivista di filosofia (Modena)
RFChile	Revista de filosofía (Santiago de Chile)
RFNS	Rivista di filosofia neo-scolastica
RFrance	Revue de France
Rgén	Revue générale (Bruxelles)
RGenève	Revue de Genève
RGS[PA]	Revue générale des sciences [pures et appliqués]
RH	Revue historique
Rheb	Revue hebdomadaire
RHE	Revue d'histoire ecclésiastique (Louvain)
RHEF	Revue d'histoire de l'Église de France
RHES	Revue d'histoire économique et sociale
RHist	Revue historique
RHL[F]	Revue d'histoire littéraire de la France
RHPh	Revue d'histoire de la philosophie et d'histoire générale de la civilisation [now: RScH]
RHPR	Revue d'histoire et de philosophie religieuses (Strasbourg)
RHR	Revue de l'histoire des religions
RHSA, RHSc	Revue d'histoire des sciences et de leurs applications
RicF	Ricerche filosofiche
RIE	Revue internationale de l'enseignement
RIF	Rivista italiana di filosofia
RIFD	Rivista internazionale di filosofia del diritto
RIHS	Revue internationale d'histoire des sciences
Rint, RInt	Revue internationale
RIP	Revue internationale de philosophie
RLC	Revue de littérature comparée
Rmet	Review of Metaphysics
RMM	Revue de métaphysique et de morale
RN	La revue nouvelle (Tournai)
RNS	Revue néoscolastique de philosophie
RomF	Romanische Forschungen
Royaumont	Cahiers de Royaumont, Philosophie no. II: Descartes [no. 42].
RPar	Revue de Paris
RPerú	Revista de la Universidad Católica de Perú
RPF, RPFil	Revista portuguesa de filosofia
RPFE	Revue philosophique de la France et de l'étranger
RPGA	Revista de psicología general y aplicada (Madrid)
RPhL	Revue philosophique de Louvain [formerly: RNS]
RPLL	Renaissance politique, littéraire, artistique
RQH	Revue des questions historiques
RQS	Revue des questions scientifiques
RR	Romanic Review
RRFC	Rivista Rosminiana di filosofia e di cultura
RScH, RSH	Revue des sciences humaines [formerly: RHPh]
RSA	Revue des sciences et de leurs applications
RSG, RSGA	Revue des sciences générales et appliquées
RScR, RSR	Recherches de science religieuse
RSF[I]	Rivista di storia della filosofia [italiana]
RSPPA	Revue Suisse de psychologie pure et appliquée
RSPT	Revue des sciences philosophiques et théologiques

RSR	Recherches de science religieuse
Rsyn	Revue de synthèse (Paris)
RT, Rthom	Revue thomiste
RTP	Revue de théologie et de philosophie
RTPL	Revue de théologie et de philosophie (Lausanne)
RU	Revue universelle
RUB	Revue de l'Université de Bruxelles
RUC Perú	Revista de la Universidad Católica de Perú
Runiv	Revue universitaire
RV	*Descartes. La Recherche de la vérité.*
RV	Revue des vivants
RyF	Razón y fé (Madrid)
S, Sophia	Sophia (Napoli)
SAg	Société d'agriculture, science, etc....
Sal	Salesianum (Torino)
SAQ	South Atlantic Quarterly
Sch	Scholastik (Eupen, Freiburg i.B.)
Schrecker	Schrecker, "Bibliographie de Descartes savant," Thalès 3: 1936, 145–54 [no. 18]
Scientia	Scientia (Bologna)
SHI	Studies in the history of ideas, 3 vols. (New York, Columbia University Press, 1925)
SJInst	Studien aus dem C.- G. Jung-Institute (Zürich)
SLSA	Société des lettres, sciences et arts de ....
SP	Studies in Philology
SPhS	Schweizerische philosophische Studien
SPLF	Sociétés de philosophie de langue française
SRL	Saturday Review of Literature
StP	Studia Patavina
Streven	Streven, Brugge [formerly: KCTS]
Stu[d]	Studium (Roma)
StU	Studi Urbinati (Urbino)
Studiën	Studiën (s'Hertogenbosch)
SyB	Syntese (Bussum)
SynB	Synthèses (Belgique)
Szellem	Szellem és Elet (Szeged)
Temps	Le Temps (Paris)
Thalès	Thalès (Université de Paris)
Theoria	Theoria, tidschrift för filosofi och psykologi (Göteborg)
Thom	The Thomist (Washington)
Thought	Thought (New York)
TLS	The Times Literary Supplement (London)
TM, Tmod	Les temps modernes
TP	*Descartes. Traité des passions de l'âme*
Tph, TP	Tijdschrift voor philosophie (Gent, Leuven)
TW	Tijdschrift voor wijsbegeerte
U	Universitas (Stuttgart)
UC	Universidad católica, Università cattolica
UCSC	Università cattolica del Sacro Cuore (Milano)
Univ	Universitas (Stuttgart)
UP	University Press
UPA	Université de Paris, Annales
UPL	Université de Paris, Bibliothèque de la faculté des lettres

Utrecht	Utrecht University Library
Varet	G. Varet, Manuel de bibliographie philosophique, v. 1 [no. 21]
VInt	La vie intellectuelle
VFP	Voprosy filosofii [i psychologii] (Moskwa)
VP	La vie des peuples
VWPh	Vierteljahrsschrift für wissenschaftliche Philosophie
WW	Wissenschaft und Weisheit (Freiburg i.B.)
WZP	Wiener Zeitschrift für Philosophie, Psychologie, Pädagogik
Yale	Sterling Library, Yale University
ZDK, ZdtK	Zeitschrift für deutsche Kulturphilosophie (Tübingen)
ZFSL	Zeitschrift für französische Sprache und Literatur (Jena)
ZKT	Zeitschrift für katholische Theologie (Innsbruck)
ZmnU	Zeitschrift für den mathematischen und naturwissenschaftlichen Unterricht
ZPF	Zeitschrift für philosophische Forschung
ZPPK	Zeitschrift für Philosophie und philosophische Kritik (Fichte's Zeitschrift)
ZSoz	Zeitschrift für Sozialforschung (Frankfurt a.M., Paris)
ZTK	Zeitschrift für Theologie und Kirche
ZVS	Zeitschrift für Völkerpsychologie und Sprachwissenschaft